In accordance with the latest syllabus presc...
Indian Certificate of Secondary Education Examination, New Delhi.

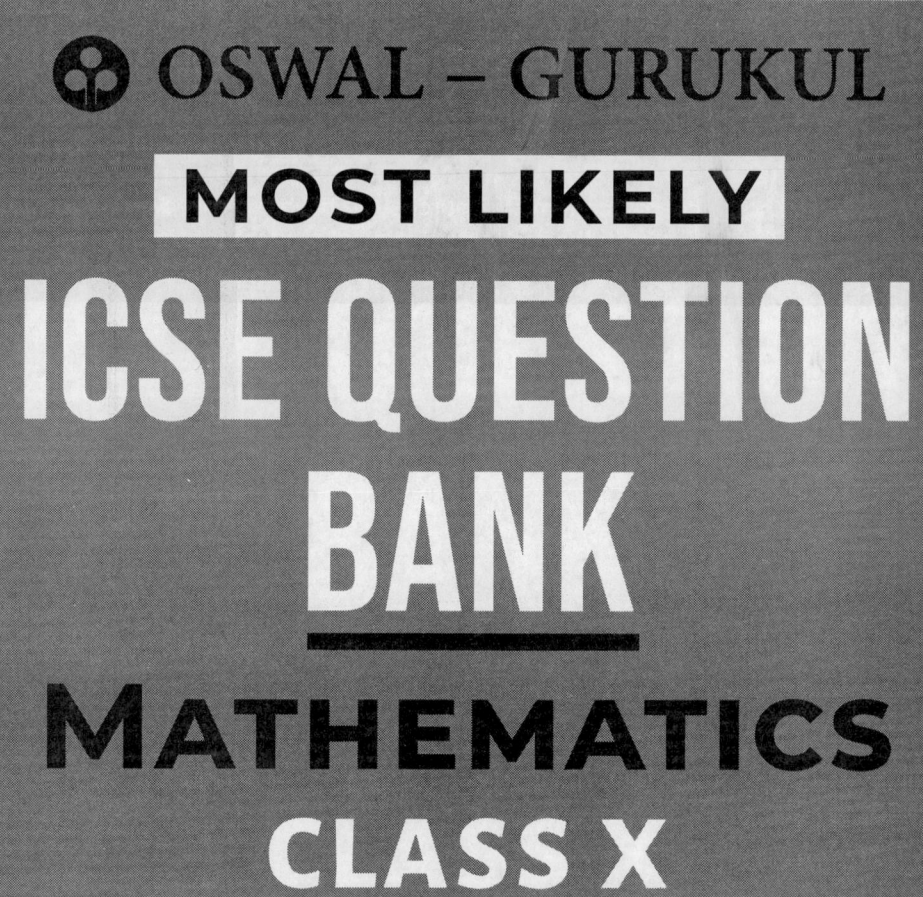

⚙ OSWAL – GURUKUL

MOST LIKELY

ICSE QUESTION BANK

MATHEMATICS

CLASS X

By

PANEL OF AUTHORS

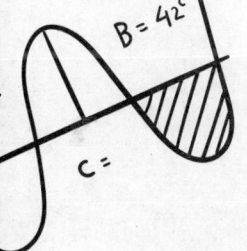

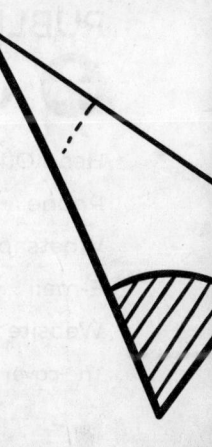

DISCLAIMER

With the ambition of providing standard academic resources, we have exercised extreme care in publishing the content. In case of any discrepancies in the matter, we request readers to excuse the unintentional lapse and not hold us liable for the same. Suggestions are always welcome.

EDITION : 2022

ISBN : 978-93-92563-79-9

PRICE : ₹ 350.00

PRINTED AT : Upkar Printing Unit, Agra

PUBLISHED BY

 **OSWAL PUBLISHERS**

Head Office : 1/12, Sahitya Kunj, M.G. Road, Agra – 282 002

Phone   : (0562) 2527771-4

Whatsapp   : +91 74550 77222

E-mail   : info@oswalpublishers.in

Website   : www.oswalpublishers.com

The cover of this book has been designed using resources from Freepik.com

PREFACE

It is a matter of immense pride for us to present our 'MOST LIKELY ICSE QUESTION BANK' series, especially prepared for students appearing for Board examinations in the oncoming year.

This book is a perfect capsule for building self-confidence during exam preparation. Based on chunking strategy, the 'Categorywise–Chapterwise' format with its exhaustive set of questions allow the students to cover every category in a chapterwise manner.

Covering easy categories first boosts student's self-esteem and the ascending score braces them to take up challenging categories without fear. This prepares the student to see the exam paper as achievable at all times.

With its simple language and style, it is a one-stop solution for smart study. We are confident that the book will enable the candidates to develop a better understanding of the curriculum and help them organize their learning process. This book shall definitely prove to be a fruitful tool for the students and encourage them towards scholastic excellence.

Constructive suggestions for further improvement of the book are always welcome.

Note: Questions marked with '*' are frequently asked in previous years board examinations.

—**Publisher**

LET'S GO ORGANIC

 Growing microgreens can be a good, easy and economical way for a student to start practicing plantation at home.

 You can spread a mixture of coco-peat and fertile topsoil or a stack of moist tissue papers over it. Remember to keep the tissue paper moist till the seeds start germinating.

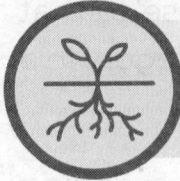 Microgreens are highly nutritious plants that are harvested after the sprout-stage and just before the maturity phase.

 Cover the box with newspaper and keep it in a place where there is no direct sunlight.

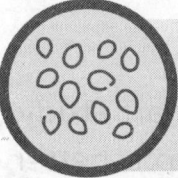 Microgreens may include mustard, coriander, basil seeds, dried peas, beans, broccoli, radish, spinach, beetroot, cauliflower and others.

 Spray water twice a day atleast.

 It is more convenient to start growing microgreens that require low maintenance like mustard, coriander, peas, basil and others.

 On third and fourth day, once the leaves start to appear, start exposing the germinating microgreens to indirect sunlight.

 Start with finding a flat tray or a shoe-box or any tetra-pack carton.

 You can try to expose them to direct sunlight for not more than 4 hours.

 Make holes in the box for easy drainage of water.

 By ninth or tenth day, your microgreens will be ready, harvest them!

 Spread two inches of soil in the box. You can get ready-made soil from the garden or nursery. Sprinkle your desired seeds over the soil.

 Microgreens can be eaten with sandwiches, wraps, salads, smoothies, juices or as garnishers on pizza, soup and curries.

SUGGESTIONS FOR STUDENTS

1. Read all questions carefully.

2. Utilise reading time judiciously to make the right choice of questions.

3. Show all steps of working. All rough work should be done alongside the solution, on the answer script only.

4. Give specific and logical reasons in geometry.

5. Round off the answers correct to the required number of decimal places.

6. Convert units from one system of unit to another system of unit carefully.

7. Use logarithm table book to find square root or to cross check the value of a square root or other powers/roots.

8. Plotting on graphs and selection and use of a suitable scale should be done carefully.

9. Follow the given instructions carefully, especially in reflection sums and construction-based problems.

10. Revise all calculations to avoid calculation errors. Practice simple methods of calculation.

11. Practice number line with due importance to arrows at both the ends.

12. Join all the points in the given order, especially in problems of reflection.

13. While finding cumulative frequency, verify that the last cumulative frequency tallies with the sum of all frequencies.

14. Plot Ogive with respect to upper boundaries and corresponding cumulative frequency.

15. Practice basic constructions, such as, construction of standard angles, side bisectors and angle bisectors regularly.

16. Prove trigonometrical identities by starting from left hand side and then proving it equal to right hand side or vice a versa.

17. Write reasons while solving Geometry problems.

18. Use mathematical tables to find square root, cube root of a number etc. to save time.

19. Show clearly all traces of construction while working with Geometrical Constructions.

20. Practise thoroughly all formulae related to Coordinate geometry, mensuration etc.

CONTENTS

Word of Advice   7 - 14

1. Chapter at a Glance   15 - 25

2. Formulae Based Questions   26 - 51

3. Data Based Questions   52 - 61

4. Determine the Following   62 - 129

5. Prove the Following   130 - 174

6. Figure Based Questions   175 - 236

7. Graphical Depiction   237 - 263

8. Concept Based Questions   264 - 297

9. Practice Exercises   298 - 318

   Answers of Practice Exercises   319 - 324

   ICSE Solved Paper 2020 (With Comments of Examiners)   325 - 342

Note: Questions marked with '*' are frequently asked in previous years board examinations.

Word of Advice

Chapter 1. Goods and Services Tax

1. The concept of finding GST as simple percentage was not clear to some candidates.
2. Several candidates missed out the discount given in question and directly calculated the tax. Hence, they got incorrect value of GST.
3. Many candidates calculated the total amount of tax and total bill amount correctly, but the answer was not expressed correctly to two places of decimal. Some candidates made errors in calculation.
4. Many candidates were not clear about the concept of successive discount.
5. Some candidates found the amount paid by the customer correctly but GST paid by shopkeeper was incorrect. Similarly, some candidates found the discounted price but were unable to find the GST paid by dealer.

Chapter 2. Banking (Recurring Deposit Account)

Topics Found difficult By Students
  ➤ Rate of interest in Banking
  ➤ Maturity value and interest in banking sums.

1. Mistakes were made in applying the formula for interest. Candidates were unable to find rate of interest, r.
2. Some candidates considered maturity value as monthly instalment.
3. A number of candidates made errors in determining the qualifying principal to find the interest and in finding the maturity value. For finding matured value, some candidates added monthly instalment and the interest.
4. Some candidates missed out the word 'successive' and found the amount directly for two years and subtracted the repayment amount.
5. Candidates made mistakes in finding minimum balance of various months. Students got confused with information: *balance is zero in a particular month when the account is opened or closed.*

Chapter 3. Shares and dividend

Topics Found difficult By Students
  ➤ Shares and Dividend

1. Common errors made by many candidates were in finding annual income and the market value of each share. Some candidates found the dividend on only one share instead of finding the total amount of dividend paid by the company. Annual income was also calculated incorrectly due to error in finding the number of shares.
2. The concept of *return percent* was not clear to most students.
3. Common errors made by many candidates were in considering Market Value (MV) *i.e.*, instead of taking discounted MV. Thus, made mistake in finding the number of shares purchased and annual dividend calculated was also incorrect. Many candidates could not find the correct answer for number of shares due to error in calculating the sale proceeds.

Chapter 4. Linear Inequation

Topics Found difficult By Students
- Linear inequation.
- In equation solving and representing solution on number line
- Linear inequation and representation
- Inequation solving and representing solution on number line.
- Inequation solving and representing solution.
- Representing solutions on number line.
- Inequation: writing solution and representation on number line

1. Many candidates made errors in transposing like terms on the same side. Some candidates made various types of errors in simplification.

2. A large number of candidates made errors in representation of solution set on the number line. e.g., Real number solution was represented incorrectly by using dots or $x \in N$ was considered as $x \in R$ or $x \in R$ instead of $x \in Z$. Some candidates failed to put extra numbers on each side of the solution for indicating the continuity of the number line; others drew the number line without arrows..

3. Some candidates made mistakes in solving the inequation. Most of the errors were pertaining to positive and negative signs.

4. A number of candidates did not write down the solution set after solving the given inequation.

5. The solution set was not represented in set builder form. Some did not use set notation method with curly brackets, and some represented as real number solution stating $x \in R$.

Chapter 5. Quadratic Equations

Topics Found difficult By Students
- Forming correct equation in Quadratic word problem
- Quadratic equation problem
- Reasons must be provided for all geometry problems.

1. Most students used incorrect formula for finding roots of the quadratic equation. Some students Used correct formula but substituted the values incorrectly. Number of candidates used division method instead of using mathematical tables and thereby made calculation errors; some did not go up to the required number of decimal places. Hence, the final answer was incorrect.

2. Candidates made mistakes in arranging the equation in standard quadratic equation form.

3. Majority of candidates found the discriminant correctly but did not equate it to 0 as per the condition of equal roots. Some candidates took x along with coefficient to find discriminant.

Chapter 6. Ratio proportion

Topics Found difficult By Students
- Properties of Ratio and Proportion
- Properties of proportion.

1. Some candidates were not aware of the basic concepts of ratio and proportion, hence were unable to write mean proportion.

2. Some candidates cross multiplied the equations and did not use componendo and dividendo to work out the sum.

3. While applying Componendo and Dividendo, many candidates made errors in signs and especially in the denominator. Mistakes were made while squaring both the sides. Calculation errors were also common. The final expression was not worked out following all the steps of correct working. Being a proof, some candidates wrote the correct answer from incorrect working.

4. Some candidates did not use the property of proportion correctly. Some candidates applied properties of proportion only on one side.

5. Many candidates used arithmetic progression to solve the sum instead of ratio and proportion. A number of candidates used componendo and dividendo but their working was incorrect.

6. Several candidates made mistake in squaring the expressions.

7. Some made mistakes by taking LCM and working with both RHS and LHS simultaneously.

Chapter 7. Factorization

Topics Found difficult By Students
  ➢ Remainder and Factor Theorem
  ➢ Remainder-Factor theorem
  ➢ Factorization in various problems.
  ➢ Use of Remainder and Factor Theorem.
  ➢ Properties of Ratio and Proportion.

1. Many candidates did not use factor theorem to identify the first factor. Some made mistakes in finding out the quotient while dividing the given polynomial by the factor found. Many candidates did not write the answer in the product form, e.g. $(x + 2)(3x - 2)(2x + 3)$.

2. Some made mistakes in finding out the quotient by dividing the given polynomial by the factor found using factor theorem.

3. Some candidates were unable to factorize the quotient obtained by dividing the polynomial.

4. Some students did not use the brackets in the equations, leading to incorrect answers.

5. A large number of candidates did not use Remainder-Factor Theorem to show the factor of the given polynomial. Few of them did not conclude the remainder to be equal to 0.

6. Many candidates expressed the answer by separating the factors by comma instead of expressing them in the product form.

7. Many candidates could not apply the Remainder theorem correctly. Due to incorrect substitution or incorrect working some candidates found the incorrect remainder. Several candidates instead of adding the two remainders, equated each remainder to zero.

8. A few candidates substituted the factors of the given polynomial correctly but failed to equate them to zero at the time of calculation.

Chapter 8. Matrices

Topics Found difficult By Students
  ➢ Matrix multiplication
  ➢ Matrix- scalar multiplication and multiplication of 2 Matrices

1. Matrix multiplication was a very common area of error, *e.g.* for finding square of 'A' and square of 'B', candidates found the square of each corresponding element instead of finding A × A and B × B. Many candidates found the product A × B by multiplying the corresponding elements of each matrix. Many were not aware that the matrix multiplication is not commutative and changed matrix from right side as given in question to left side.

2. Some candidates were unable to find the order of the matrix.

3. Some candidates made mistake in framing the simultaneous equations and some could not find the values of the unknowns. A few got the values of the unknowns but did not arrange them in a matrix form.

4. Some candidates made mistakes in scalar multiplication of the matrix e.g., $2(y - 5)$ was written as $2y - 5$ instead of $2y - 10$.

5. Some made mistakes in addition and equating corresponding elements of two matrices.

6. A few candidates skipped major steps of working, while solving the equations.

7. Most candidates failed to differentiate between a constant term and a matrix.

Chapter 9. Arithmetic Progression

Topics Found difficult By Students
➢ Arithmetic Progression

1. Some candidates did not know the basic concepts of Arithmetic Progression (A.P.). Many candidates tried to solve the sum by trial & error method and got the six terms, but the necessary working was incorrect. Few candidates without framing equations like $a + 3d = 8$ and $a + 5d = 14$, wrote $d = 3$. Some candidates either used incorrect formulae or made errors in calculation. Therefore, they failed to get the value of the first term, common difference and sum of the first n terms correctly.

2. Many candidates were unable to identify the common difference 'd', hence failed to equate the difference between two pairs of consecutive terms to evaluate 'k'.

3. Some candidates, without using given conditions, guessed the series and identified the values of 'a' and 'd'. A few candidates did not know the formula for summation.

Chapter 10. Geometric Progression

Topics Found difficult By Students
➢ Geometric Progression

1. Some candidates took the terms as of A. P. instead of G. P. The values of 'a' and 'r' were correctly found by many candidates, but they could not find the value of 'n' correctly.

2. Due to conceptual errors related to Geometrical Progression, many candidates were unable to find the value of n. Some tried to find n by trial and error method.

3. Some candidates used incorrect formula for finding the sum of n terms.

Chapter 11. Co-ordinate Geometry

Topics Found difficult By Students
➢ Graphs: axis and reading the results from the graph.
➢ Applying Section formula and points on x and y axes
➢ Graphs – Axes and choice of scale
➢ Problems based on graph. Choosing correct axis and scale.

1. Several candidates did not take the point on y - axis as $(0, y)$. Some candidates could not apply the section formula correctly. Many applied mid-point formula to get the coordinates of the required point. Others found the ratio correctly but did not write it in ratio form.. Multiplication of $(m + n)$ by 0 was taken as $(m + n)$ instead of '0'. Simple calculation errors were common.

2. As some candidates obtained incorrect coordinates, they made error in finding the slope of the line. Some candidates were not conversant with the formula to find the slope of a line.

3. Some candidates found the slopes correctly but made mistakes in applying the condition that for two lines to be perpendicular, the product of slopes is -1.

4. Common errors were observed in taking the scale and plotting the points. A few candidates plotted the points incorrectly. Some candidates made mistakes in marking the X-axis and the Y-axis. Positive and negative points of the two axes were incorrectly marked. A few candidates did not name the figure as 'octagon' or 'trapezium', etc, wherever required.

5. Several candidates made errors in identifying coordinates of points on x-axis and y-axis, e,g., $(x, 0)$ and $(0, y)$ was taken as $(0, x)$, $(y, 0)$ or as (x_1, y_1) and (x_1, y_1).

6. Some candidates used section formula but made mistakes in substitution. Some candidates obtained the coordinates but did not write them within the brackets.

Word of Advice

Chapter 12. Reflection

1. Few students chose incorrect scale in graph-based question. Some marked axes incorrectly or plotted the coordinates incorrectly. Few plotted the points correctly but did not label them while some neither join the points nor completed the figure.

2. Students were confused in trapezium and isosceles trapezium.

3. Most candidates made mistakes in identifying the line of symmetry or writing down its equation.

4. Some candidates committed errors in plotting points which led to an incorrect figure. Candidates who did not complete the figure were unable to name it. Figure being irregular some candidates were unable to name the figure correctly and some could not name the line of symmetry.

Chapter 13. Similarity

Topics Found difficult By Students
  ➢ Size Transformation
  ➢ Solving Geometry problems on circles and similar triangles using the appropriate property
  ➢ Size Transformation
  ➢ Solving Geometry
  ➢ Geometry based problems using properties of circle and similar triangles.
  ➢ Maps and models.
  ➢ Geometry: Constructions and solving problems using properties of circle and similar triangles.
  ➢ Similarity
  ➢ Coordinate geometry, Section formula and identifying points on x or y axis.
  ➢ Conditions of collinear.

1. Many candidates were not clear about the *scale factor*.

2. Many candidates made mistakes in applying the scale factor to find the height of the actual building.

3. Some candidates made mistakes in applying the scale factor to find the ratio of area as square of the scale factor.

4. Many candidates were not clear about the phrase *map drawn to a scale*....

5. Some candidates were not clear about proportionality condition and corresponding scale factor k, k^2, k^3 for length, area and volume respectively. Most could find the length but some were unable to find area and volume.

6. Several candidates made errors in calculation and conversion of units

Chapter 14. Loci

Topics Found difficult By Students
  ➢ Geometrical Constructions and locus

1. Concept of Locus was not clear to some candidates.

2. Concepts of locus theorems were not clear to some candidates.

3. Many candidates did not show the necessary traces of construction. Midpoint of BC was not located by construction instead used ruler. Some were unable to identify the point A as the intersection of perpendicular bisector and semi-circle.

4. Some candidates bisected two sides instead of two angles for locating the in-centre. A number of candidates identified the centre correctly but did not drop a perpendicular from the centre to any one side of the triangle so as to find the length of radius of required in-circle.

5. Many candidates could not identify the correct pairs of equal angles. A few could not write the corresponding ratio of sides of similar triangles.

Chapter 15. Circles

Topics Found difficult By Students
- Circle Theorems and their application in solving problems
- Solving Geometry problems on circles and similar triangles using the appropriate property
- Circle theorems
- Solving Geometry
- Geometry based problems using properties of circle and similar triangles.
- Geometrical Constructions.
- Geometry: Constructions and solving problems using properties of circle and similar triangles.
- Application of Circle Theorems.
- Geometry solving problems using properties of circle and similar triangles
- Rounding off final result e.g. significant figures.
- Theorems on properties of circle.

1. In figure based questions, many candidates were unable to find angles correctly. A few candidates could not use the properties of isosceles triangle and congruency of triangles correctly. Appropriate reasons supporting the answers were also missing in many scripts.

2. Properties of circles like, angle in a semicircle, equal arc subtends equal angle at circumference, angle at the centre is double the angle at the circumference, radius tangent perpendicular relation, angle sum property of quadrilateral, tangent secant relation, etc. were not applied correctly.

3. A few candidates solved the question without giving proper reasoning.

4. Some candidates could not apply the appropriate property of circle theorem to find out the unknown angles.

5. Some failed to locate angles in the same segment while some did not apply the Properties of cyclic quadrilateral correctly.

6. Most candidates calculated the distance between the two chords correctly. Some wrote the equation using Pythagoras theorem incorrectly.

Chapter 16. Constructions

Topics Found difficult By Students
- Geometry constructions
- Geometrical Constructions.
- Constructing a circle about a constructed Hexagon.
- Quadratic equation problem
- Construction of incircle.

1. The most common error was that for perpendicular bisector, candidates drew arcs only on one side of the line to be bisected. Many others did not measure and record the radius of the circle.

2. Some candidates bisected the *angles* instead of *sides* to draw the circumcircle. Quite a few candidates constructed circumcircle without bisecting two sides of the triangle so as to locate the circumcentre.

3. Some students did not construct the arcs for side bisectors and angle bisectors.

4. Some candidates followed some other incorrect methods for construction. A number of candidates measured the length of the tangent incorrectly.

5. Some candidates wasted time in writing the steps of construction which was not asked in the question.

6. Candidates lost marks in the question for not constructing a hexagon using a ruler and compass. To construct the lines of symmetry candidates failed to use the steps of construction of perpendicular bisector of side and bisector of an angle.

Chapter 17. Measurements

Topics Found difficult By Students
➢ Mensuration formulae of volumes of solids
➢ Mensuration formula

1. A number of candidates used incorrect formulae to calculate volume of a sphere e.g. $4/3\ \pi r^2$ or $2/3\ \pi r^3$.

2. To find r, several candidates simplified and came to the result r^3 but could not find the value of r by taking cube root.

3. Some candidates used incorrect formulae for volume of cone and cylinder. Some made minor error in putting the values of diameter and radius in the respective equations.

4. Some candidates did not use the value of π given in the question paper, hence, got incorrect answer.

5. Many candidates used incorrect formula for finding curved surface area of the cylinder, e.g., used $2\pi r^2$ h instead of $2\pi rh$.

6. Some candidates applied incorrect formulas for finding out the radius of the cylinder, *i.e.*, the circumference of the base of the cylinder was taken as πr^2 or $2\pi rh$ instead of $2\pi r$.

7. Some candidates were unable to identify the length or breadth of the rectangle using the radius of the given circle and semi circles.

Chapter 18. Trigonometry

Topics Found difficult By Students
➢ Trigonometry
➢ Trigonometrical Identities and Heights and Distances.
➢ Properties of Ratio and Proportion.
➢ Trigonometry, complementary angles and Heights and Distances.

1. Some candidates failed to express tan A and cot A in terms of sin A and cos A correctly. Errors were also made in writing the numerator and denominator of resulting trigonometric expressions. Some took the LCM correctly but went wrong in simplifying the expression.

2. Many candidates made mistakes in substituting the reciprocal relations for the trigonometric ratios for example, cosec θ was taken as $1/\cos \theta$ instead of $1/\sin \theta$ etc. while some candidates made mistakes in simplification of the expressions on the Left-Hand Side of the question.

3. Some expanded the whole expression and made mistakes in simplification using standard identities.

4. In solving identities, some candidates squared the identity either on one side or both sides before proceeding for proving the identity. Many candidates were unable to use identities like $\sec^2 \theta = 1^+ \tan^2 \theta$ etc. Some solved the two sides of the identity simultaneously or interchanged terms from one side to the other.

5. A number of candidates made mistakes while multiplying the two expressions on the Left-Hand Side of the question.

6. Some were unable to simplify by applying algebraic identity $(a + b)\ (a - a) = a^2 - b^2$, hence, could not get the correct answer.

7. Many candidates could not draw the diagram on heights and distance as per the given conditions. Their concept of angle of depression was not clear. Some took both ships on the same side of the light house.

8. Some candidates interchanged the values of tan 60° and tan 30° in the solution of the problem i.e., substituted the opposite of the correct values. A few candidates did not round off the height of the tower to the nearest metre as per the requirement of the question.

9. Errors in application of complementary angles was very common among candidates. Some candidates wrote sin 28° = sin (90° − 28°) instead of cos (90° − 28°) or sin (90° − 62°) etc. A few candidates applied complementary angles directly without showing any working or giving any reasons.

10. Candidates substituted incorrect values for sec 30°.

Chapter 19. Statistics

Topics Found difficult By Students
  ➤ Statistics- Calculation of Central tendency of non-grouped frequency distribution, drawing an ogive.
  ➤ Calculation of Mean by Short-cut Method
  ➤ Statistics: finding mean by using step-deviation Method.
  ➤ Calculation of mean
  ➤ Short cut method of calculation of mean

1. Many candidates did not show the kink while plotting the histogram. The three guidelines to locate mode were not drawn correctly. A few candidates did not join the end points of highest bar with corresponding end points of preceding and succeeding bars to locate mode. The chosen scale was not used correctly. Some calculated cumulative frequency and then plotted the bars of increasing heights.

2. Students made mistakes in the calculation of mean of ungrouped frequency distribution. Some candidates converted it to grouped frequency distribution which did not tally with the given data and hence went wrong with the sum. Many candidates wrote incorrect Class mark of the given distribution which led to incorrect value of Σfx.

3. Some made mistakes in applying the formula for mean and solving the equation to find 'f'.

4. Some candidates made mistakes in finding the cumulative frequency. In many cases, the last cumulative frequency did not tally with the total of the given distribution.

5. A number of candidates did not follow the scale given in the question.

6. Some plotted the ogive with respect to the lower boundaries instead of upper boundaries. In a few cases, perpendicular lines were not dropped to find the values from the ogive.

7. A few candidates used a ruler to draw the graph instead of a freehand curve.

8. Some candidates made mistakes in finding median marks, upper quartile marks and number of students. The values of median, upper quartiles were read incorrectly from the graph, by a number of candidates.

9. A large number of the candidates were unable to understand that the given data is a non-grouped frequency distribution. To identify the median, instead of finding the cumulative frequency, they tried to find it directly. Some tried to find the median by plotting the points directly on a graph paper.

10. Bars drawn by a few candidates were not of equal width.

11. In the question, the given data was arranged in ascending order but some candidates could not identify the middle term.

12. Some candidates did not use step deviation method to find mean as specified in the question.

13. Some candidates went on to draw the histogram to find the modal class instead of using the table formed by using the given graph.

Chapter 20. Probability

Topics Found difficult By Students
  ➤ Probability.

1. A few candidates used incorrect form for finding probability (total outcomes / number of favourable outcomes).

2. Some students calculated the Total outcomes or favourable outcomes incorrect.

3. Answers were not expressed in the simplest form.

4. Some candidates did not consider '2' as a prime number.

5. 0/10 was not expressed as 0.

Chapter 1. Goods and Services Tax (GST)

1. GST is an indirect tax that will be levied on manufacture sale and consumption of goods and services.
2. The importance of GST is that when applicable it will abolish all indirect taxes. Hence, the entire system of taxation will be simpler.
3. The GST is paidly consumers, but it is remitted to the government by the business setting the goods and services. In effect, GST provides revnue for the government.
4. It is tax on the value added to each transfer of goods, from the original manufacture to the retailer. (example)

GST Supply Chain (assuming GST @ 8%)				
Supply of Goods	GST Flow	Input Cost	Sale Price	GST Collected
A weaver sells a fabric to a tailor for ₹ 108/m	The weaver pays GST of ₹ 8	0	₹ 100	₹ 8
The tailor sells a ready made completed shirt to a tailor for ₹ 270	Tailor pays GST of ₹ 12 (after input tax claim weaver claims tax credit for ₹ 8)	₹ 100	₹ 250	₹ 12
The retailer sells the readymade shirt in this showroom for ₹ 540	Retailer pays GST of ₹ 20 (after in-put claim. Tailor claims tax credit for ₹ 12)	₹ 250	₹ 500	₹ 20
You purchase the shirt for ₹ 540	No tax credit claim. You pay entire GST ₹ 40 @ 8%	NA	NA	Total ₹ 40

5. The difference of tax recovered on the sale value and paid on the pruchase value is deposited with the government as GST.

Chapter 2. Banking (Recurring Deposit Account)

1. Banking is a business of receiving, safe-guarding and lending of money.
2. Recurring deposit Account : In this account a depositor chooses to deposit a specified amount (in multiples of ₹ 5) every month for a specified number of months. This period may vary from 3 months to 10 years. At the expiry of this period the depositor gets the amount deposited by him together with an interest compounded quarterly at a fixed rate. The rate of interest is revised from time to time.
3. Calculation of maturity amount on recurring deposit :

The interest on the recurring deposit account can be calculated by using the formula :

$$\text{S.I.} = P \times \frac{n(n+1)}{2 \times 12} \times \frac{r}{100}$$

where S.I. is the simple interest, P is the money deposited per month, n is the number of months for which the money has been deposited and r is the simple interest rate percent per annum.

Chapter 3. Shares and Dividends

1. The nominal value (N.V.) of a share is also called the Register value, printed value, Face value (F.V.), etc.
2. The price of a share at any particular time is called its Market value (M.V.).
3. The market value of a share can be the same, more or less than the nominal value of the share depending upon the performance and profits of the company.

(i)   If the market value of a share is the same as its nominal value, the share is said to be at par.

(ii) If the market value of a share is more than its nominal value, the share is said to be above par or at a premium.

(iii) If the market value of a share is less than its nominal value, the share is said to be below par or at a discount.

4. The profit, which a share-holder gets (out of the profits of the company) from his investment in the company, is called dividend.

The dividend is always expressed as a percentage of the nominal value of the share.

5.   Sum invested = No. of shares bought
          × M.V. of 1 share

If the share is at par, market value
          = nominal value

i.e.,   M.V. = N.V.

6. No. of shares bought

$$= \frac{\text{Sum invested}}{\text{M.V. of 1 Share}}$$

Also, no. of shares bought

$$= \frac{\text{Total dividend}}{\text{Dividend on 1 Share}}$$

$$= \frac{\text{Total income (profit)}}{\text{Income (profit) on 1 Share}}$$

7. Income (return or profit)
          = No. of shares × rate of dividend
                    × F. V. of a share

F.V. = Face value = Nominal value = N.V.

8.   Return % = Income (profit)%

$$= \frac{\text{Income}}{\text{Investment}} \times 100\%$$

Chapter 4. Linear Inequations

Two permissible rules :

1. Addition – Subtraction Rule :

If the same number or expression is added to or subtracted from both sides of an inequation, the resulting inequation has the same solution (or solutions) as the original.

2. Multiplication – Division Rule.

   (i) If both sides of an inequation are multiplied or divided by the same positive number, the resulting inequation has the same solution (or solutions) as the original.

   (ii) If both sides of an inequation are multiplied or divided by the same negative number, the resulting inequation has the same solution (or solutions) as the original if the symbol of the inequality is reversed.

Thus, the only difference between solving a linear equation and solving an inequation concerns multiplying or dividing both sides by a negative number. Therefore, always reverse the symbol of an inequation when multiplying or dividing by a negative number.

3. Properties of absolute values :

   (i) $|-x| = |x| \ \forall \ x \in R$

   (ii) $|xy| = |x| |y| \ \forall \ x, y \in R$

   (iii) $\left|\dfrac{x}{y}\right| = \dfrac{|x|}{|y|} = \forall \ x, y \in R \ \& \ y \neq 0$

   (iv) $|x| = \sqrt{x^2} \ \forall \ x \in R$

   (v)   If $a > 0$,
         then $|x| \leq a \Leftrightarrow -a \leq x \leq a$
         $|x| \geq a \Leftrightarrow x \geq a$ or $x \leq -a$.

Chapter 5. Quadratic Equations

1. The standard form of a quadratic equation is $ax^2 + bx + c = 0$, where a, b and c are all real numbers and $a \neq 0$.

   e.g., equation $4x^2 + 5x - 6 = 0$ is a quadratic equation in standard form.

2. Every quadratic equation gives two values of the unknown variable and these values are called roots of the equation.

3. Zero Product Rule : Whenever the product of two expressions is zero; at least one of the expressions is zero.

If $(x + 3)(x - 2) = 0$
⇒ $x + 3 = 0$, or $x - 2 = 0$
⇒ $x = -3$, or $x = 2$

4. Solving quadratic equations using the formula :
The roots of the quadratic equation $ax^2 + bx + c = 0$; where $a \neq 0$ can be obtained by using the formula :

$$x = \frac{-b \pm \sqrt{b^2 - 4ac}}{2a}$$

5. To examine the nature of the roots :
Examining the roots of a quadratic equation means to see the type of its roots *i.e.,* whether

they are real or imaginary, rational or irrational, equal or unequal.

The nature of the roots of a quadratic equation depends entirely on the value of its discriminant $b^2 - 4ac$.

Case I : If a, b and c are real numbers and $a \neq 0$, then discriminant :

(i) $b^2 - 4ac = 0 \Rightarrow$ the roots are real and equal.

(ii) $b^2 - 4ac > 0 \Rightarrow$ the roots are real and unequal.

(iii) $b^2 - 4ac < 0 \Rightarrow$ the roots are imaginary (not real).

Case II : If a, b and c are rational numbers and $a \neq 0$, then discriminant.

(i) $b^2 - 4ac = 0 \Rightarrow$ the roots are rational and equal.

(ii) $b^2 - 4ac > 0$ and $b^2 - 4ac$ is a perfect square, $\Rightarrow$ the roots are rational and unequal.

(iii) $b^2 - 4ac > 0$ and $b^2 - 4ac$ is not a perfect square $\Rightarrow$ the roots are irrational and unequal.

(iv) $b^2 - 4ac < 0 \Rightarrow$ the roots are imaginary.

6. **Sum and product of the roots :** If α and β are the roots of quadratic equation $ax^2 + bx + c = 0$ then

$$\alpha = \frac{-b + \sqrt{b^2 - 4ac}}{2a}$$

and

$$\beta = \frac{-b - \sqrt{b^2 - 4ac}}{2a}$$

then $\alpha + \beta = \dfrac{-b + \sqrt{b^2 - 4ax} - b - \sqrt{b^2 - 4ac}}{2a}$

$\Rightarrow \quad \alpha + \beta = \dfrac{-2b}{2a} \Rightarrow \alpha + \beta = \dfrac{-b}{a}$

Product of the roots

$\alpha\beta = \left(\dfrac{-b + \sqrt{b^2 - 4ac}}{2a} \right)\left(\dfrac{-b - \sqrt{b^2 - 4ac}}{2a} \right)$

$= \dfrac{(-b)^2 - \sqrt{\left(b^2 - 4ac\right)^2}}{4a^2}$

$= \dfrac{b^2 - b^2 + 4ac}{4a^2}$

$\alpha\beta = \dfrac{4ac}{4a^2} \Rightarrow \alpha\beta = \dfrac{c}{a}$

7. To form a quadratic equation with given roots : Let α, β be the roots of the required quadratic equation, then
$x^2 - (\alpha + \beta)x + \alpha\beta = 0$
$x^2 - $ (sum of the roots)x + product of roots = 0
will be the required quadratic equation.

8. To find the roots of the quadratic equation we use quadratic equation formula which is

$$x = \frac{-b \pm \sqrt{b^2 - 4ac}}{2a}$$

Chapter 6. Ratio and Proportion

1. Ratio of two quantities of the same kind and in the same units is a comparison which is obtained by dividing the first quantity by the other.

2. Ratio between a and b written as $a : b$ has no unit.

3. In ratio $a : b$, the first quantity a is called the first term or the antecedent and second quantity b is called the second term or the consequent of $a : b$.

4. The second term of a ratio can not be zero.

5. A ratio must be expressed in its lowest terms *i.e.*, the H.C.F. of its both the terms is unity.

6. When two or more ratios are multiplied together, they are said to be compounded.

   Thus, if $\dfrac{a}{b}$ and $\dfrac{c}{d}$ are any two ratios, then $\dfrac{ac}{bd}$

   is their compounded ratio.

   $\therefore$ Compounded ratio of $a : b$ and $c : d$ is $ac : bd$.

7. A ratio compounded with itself is called duplicate ratio of the given ratio.

   $\therefore$ duplicate ratio of $a : b$ is $a^2 : b^2$.

   Similarly, triplicate ratio of $a : b$ is $a^3 : b^3$.

   Sub-duplicate ratio of $a : b$ is $\sqrt{a} : \sqrt{b}$.

   Sub-triplicate ratio of $a : b$ is $\sqrt[3]{a} : \sqrt[3]{b}$.

8. The reciprocal ratio of $a : b$ is $b : a$.

9. **Proportion :** An equality of two ratios is called a proportion.

   Four (non-zero) quantities a, b, c, d are said to be in proportion if $a : b = c : d$ *i.e.*, if $= \dfrac{a}{b} = \dfrac{c}{d}$.

   We write it as $a : b :: c : d$.

   The quantities a, b, c and d are called the terms of the proportion; a, b, c and d are the first, second, third and fourth terms respectively.

First and fourth terms are called extremes (or extreme terms). Second and third terms are called means (or middle terms).

If the quantities a, b, c and d are in proportion then $\dfrac{a}{b} = \dfrac{c}{a} \Rightarrow ad = bc$.

⇒ Product of extreme terms
= Product of middle terms.

10. If the four quantities are in proportion then the product of extreme terms = product of middle terms. This is called cross product rule.

11. **Fourth proportional :** If a, b, c and d are in proportion then d is called the fourth proportional.

12. The (non-zero) quantities of the same kind, a, b, c, d, e, f, ..., are said to be in continued proportion if $\dfrac{a}{b} = \dfrac{b}{c} = \dfrac{c}{d} = \dfrac{d}{e} = \dfrac{e}{f} = \cdots$

13. In particular, three (non-zero) quantities of the same kind, a, b and c are said to be in continued proportion if the ratio of a to b is equal to the ratio of b to c i.e., if $\dfrac{a}{b} = \dfrac{b}{c}$.

For example :
2, 4 and 8 are in continued proportion, since $\dfrac{2}{4} = \dfrac{4}{8}$.

14. **First proportional :** If a, b are c are in continued proportion, then a is called the first proportional.

15. **Third proportional :** If a, b and c are in continued proportion, then c is called the third proportional.

16. **Mean proportional :** If a, b and c are in continued proportion, then b is called the mean proportional of a and c.

Thus, if b is the mean proportional of a and c, then

$$\dfrac{a}{b} = \dfrac{b}{c} \Rightarrow b^2 = ac \Rightarrow b = \sqrt{ac}.$$

Hence, the mean proportion between two numbers is the positive square root of their product.

17. **Properties of Ratio & Proportion :**

If $\dfrac{a}{b} = \dfrac{c}{d} \Rightarrow$

(i) $\dfrac{b}{a} = \dfrac{d}{c}$ By Invertendo

(ii) $\dfrac{a}{c} = \dfrac{b}{d}$ By Alternendo

(iii) $\dfrac{a+b}{b} = \dfrac{c+d}{d}$ By Componendo

(iv) $\dfrac{a-b}{b} = \dfrac{c-d}{d}$ By Dividendo

(v) $\dfrac{a+b}{a-b} = \dfrac{c+d}{c-d}$

         By Componendo and Dividendo

(vi) $\dfrac{a}{a-b} = \dfrac{c}{c-d}$ By Convertendo

(vii) If $\dfrac{a}{b} = \dfrac{c}{d} = \dfrac{e}{f}$, then each ratio.

$$= \dfrac{a+c+e}{b+d+f}$$

$$= \dfrac{\text{sum of antecedents}}{\text{sum of consequents}}$$

Chapter 7. Factorization

1. **Factor Theorem :** If $f(x)$ is a polynomial and α is a real number, then $(x - \alpha)$ is a factor of $f(x)$ if $f(\alpha) = 0$.

2. **Remainder Theorem :** If a polynomial $f(x)$ is divided by $(x - \alpha)$, then remainder $= f(\alpha)$.

Chapter 8. Matrices

1. An $m \times n$ matrix usually written as :

$$\begin{bmatrix} a_{11} & a_{12} & \dots a_{1j} & \dots a_{1n} \\ a_{21} & a_{22} & \dots a_{2j} & \dots a_{2n} \\ a_{i1} & a_{i2} & \dots a_{ij} & \dots a_{in} \\ a_{m1} & a_{m2} & \dots a_{mj} & \dots a_{mn} \end{bmatrix} \begin{matrix} \rightarrow 1^{st} \text{ row} \\ \rightarrow 2^{nd} \text{ row} \\ \\ \rightarrow m^{th} \text{ row} \end{matrix}$$

$\downarrow$ $\downarrow$ $\downarrow$
1st   2nd n^{th}
column   column   column

Generally the matrix is represented by

$A = [a_{ij}]_{m \times n}$ or $A = [a_{ij}]$.

The numbers a_{11}, a_{12}, ..., a_{mn} are called the elements of matrix A.

2. Order of Matrix = Numbers of Row
× Numbers of Column

3. **Equality of matrices :** Two matrices $A = [a_{ij}]_{p \times q}$, $B = [b_{ij}]_{r \times s}$ are equal i.e., A = B if and only if

Chapter at a Glance

(i) A and B are of same order *i.e.*, $p = r$ and $q = s$

(ii) Each element of A is equal to corresponding element of B *i.e.*, $a_{ij} = b_{ij}$.

4. A matrix which has only one row is called row matrix.

5. A matrix which has only one column is called column matrix.

6. A matrix which has an equal number of rows and columns is called square matrix.

7. A matrix in which number of rows are not equal to the number of columns is called a rectangular matrix.

8. If each element of a matrix is zero it is called zero or a null matrix.

9. A square matrix which has all its elements zero each except on the principal diagonal is called a diagonal matrix.

10. Transpose of a matrix is the matrix obtained by interchanging its rows and columns. If A is a matrix, then its transpose is denoted by A'.

11. Addition of matrices : Let A and B be two matrices each of order $m \times n$. Then their sum A + B is a matrix of order $m \times n$ and is obtained by adding the corresponding elements of A and B.

   Example : Let

$$A = \begin{bmatrix} 1 & 2 \\ 3 & 4 \end{bmatrix} \text{ and } B = \begin{bmatrix} 0 & 5 \\ 1 & 2 \end{bmatrix}$$

   then $A + B = \begin{bmatrix} 1+0 & 2+5 \\ 3+1 & 4+2 \end{bmatrix} = \begin{bmatrix} 1 & 7 \\ 4 & 6 \end{bmatrix}$

12. Properties of matrix addition :

   (i) Matrix addition is commutative

      i.e., $A + B = B + A$

   (ii) Matrix addition is associative for any three matrices A, B and C.

      $A + (B + C) = (A + B) + C.$

   (iii) Existence of identity.

      A null matrix is identity element for addition

      i.e., $A + 0 = A = 0 + A.$

   (iv) Cancellation laws hold good in case of matrices

      $A + B = A + C \Rightarrow B = C.$

(v) If O is the null (zero) matrix of the same order as matrix A, then $A + O = O + A = A$ and $A + (-A) = (-A) + A = 0$ where $-A$ is the additive inverse.

13. Subtraction of Matrices :

   For two matrices A and B of the same order, we define

$$A - B = A + (-B).$$

   Example : If $A = \begin{bmatrix} 2 & 9 \\ 6 & -7 \end{bmatrix}$ and $B = \begin{bmatrix} 0 & -2 \\ 3 & 4 \end{bmatrix}$.

   then $A - B = \begin{bmatrix} 2-0 & 9-(-2) \\ 6-3 & -7-4 \end{bmatrix}$

   $= \begin{bmatrix} 2 & 11 \\ 3 & -11 \end{bmatrix}$

14. Two matrices can be added or subtracted together if they are of the same order.

15. To multiply a matrix by a scalar, we need to multiply each of its elements by this scalar.

16. Multiplication of Matrices : Two matrices A and B can be multiplied together if and only if the number of columns of A is equal to number of rows of B.

17. Properties of Matrix Multiplication :

   (i) Matrix multiplication is not commutative in general for any two matrices $AB \neq BA$.

   (ii) Matrix multiplication is associative *i.e.*, $(AB) C = A (BC)$ when both sides are defined.

   (iii) Matrix multiplication is distributed over matrix addition *i.e.*,

      (i) $A (B + C) = AB + AC$
         $(A + B) C = AC + BC.$

   (iv) If A is an $n \times n$ matrix then
      $I_n A = A = A I_n$

   (v) The product of two matrices can be the null matrix while neither of them is the null matrix.

18. Product of two matrices A and B = AB

$= \begin{bmatrix} \text{1st row of A} \times \text{1st column of B} & \text{1st row of A} \times \text{2nd column of B} \\ \text{2nd row of A} \times \text{1st column of B} & \text{2nd row of A} \times \text{2nd column of B} \end{bmatrix}$

19. If A is a matrix of order $m \times n$ and B is a matrix of order $n \times p$ then
   $A_{m \times n} \times B_{n \times p} = C_{m \times p}$
   where C is the matrix of order $m \times p$.

Chapter 9. Arithmetic Progression

1. A group of numbers, which are arranged in a definite order following a certain rule is called a sequence.

2. If in a sequence of numbers in which each term can be obtained by adding a certain quantity to its preceding term is called arithmetic progression.

3. In an A.P. the difference between two consecutive terms is called common difference and is denoted by d.

4. (i) If $d > 0$, the A.P. is increasing.

   (ii) If $d < 0$, the A.P. is decreasing and

   (iii) If $d = 1$, all the terms of the A.P. are same.

5. For an A.P. the nth term is given by

   $$a_n = a + (n-1)\, d$$

   where a_n is the nth term and a is the first term of the given A.P.

6. If a sequence has n terms, its r th term from the end = $(n - r + 1)$th term from the beginning.

7. Sum of n terms of an A.P. is

   $$S_n = \frac{n}{2}[2a + (n-1)\, d]$$

If a, n, l are known

$$S_n = \frac{n}{2}(a + l)$$

8. Arithmetic mean between a and b = $\dfrac{a+b}{2}$

9. Properties of A.P. :

   (i) If a fixed non-zero number is added or subtracted from each term of a given A.P., then the resulting sequence, is also an A.P.

   (ii) If a fixed non-zero term is multiplied or divided by each term of given A.P. the resulting sequence is also an A.P.

Chapter 10. Geometric Progression

1. A sequence in which each of its terms can be obtained by multiplying or dividing its preceeding term by a fixed quantity is called a geometric progression and the fixed quantity is called common ratio r.

2. In a G.P., common ratio is obtained by dividing any term of it by its preceeding term.

3. The nth term of a G.P. is given by $a_n = ar^{n-1}$.

   where r is common ratio, a_n is nth and a is first term of given A.P.

4. nth term from end of G.P. is given by $\dfrac{1}{r^{n-1}}$

   where l is last term of the given G.P.

5. If a, b and c are in G.P.

   $\Rightarrow \qquad \dfrac{b}{a} = \dfrac{c}{b}$

   $\Rightarrow \qquad b^2 = ac$

6. The sum of n terms of a G.P. is given by

   Case-I. When $r = 1$

   $$S_n = na$$

   Case-II. When $r < 1$

   $$S_n = \frac{a(1-r^n)}{1-r}$$

   Case-III. When $r > 1$

   $$S_n = \frac{a(r^n - 1)}{r-1}$$

7. If there are infinite terms in given G.P. and $|r| < 1$ then sum of infinite terms in G.P.

   $$= \frac{a}{1-r} \text{ , if } |r| < 1$$

8. If a, b are two positive numbers then G = $\sqrt{ab}$

   where G is the geometric mean between a and b.

Chapter 11. Co-ordinate Geometry

1. Section Formula : The co-ordinates of the point which divides the line segment joining the points P (x_1, y_1) and Q (x_2, y_2) in the ratio $m_1 : m_2$ are

   $$\left(\frac{m_1 x_2 + m_2 x_1}{m_1 + m_2}, \frac{m_1 y_2 + m_2 y_1}{m_1 + m_2} \right)$$

2. Mid-point Formula : The co-ordinates of the mid-point of the line segment joining the points P (x_1, y_1) and Q (x_2, y_2) are

   $$\left(\frac{x_1 + x_2}{2}, \frac{y_1 + y_2}{2} \right)$$

3. Centroid Formula : The co-ordinates of the centroid of a triangle whose vertices are A (x_1, y_1), B (x_2, y_2) and C (x_3, y_3) are

   $$\left(\frac{x_1 + x_2 + x_3}{3}, \frac{y_1 + y_2 + y_3}{3} \right)$$

4. Slope of a straight line :

   (i) If the inclination of a line is θ ($\neq 90°$), its slope, $m = \tan \theta$.

(ii) Slope of a line through (x_1, y_1) and (x_2, y_2) is given by $m = \dfrac{y_2 - y_1}{x_2 - x_1}$.

5. Equation of a straight line :

(i) Equation of a line parallel to *x*-axis is $y = b$.

(ii) Equation of a line parallel to *y*-axis is $x = a$.

(iii) Equation of a line with slope *m* and *y*-intercept *c* is $y = mx + c$.

(iv) Equation of a line through (x_1, y_1) and with slope *m* is $y - y_1 = m(x - x_1)$.

6. Conditions of Parallelism and Perpendicularity : Two lines with slopes m_1 and m_2 are :

(i) parallel if and only if $m_1 = m_2$.

(ii) perpendicular if and only if $m_1 m_2 = -1$.

7. The slope of a straight line is the tangent of its inclination and is denoted by *m*

$$m = \tan \theta$$

where θ is the inclination of a line.

8. Two lines are parallel if their slopes are equal.

9. Two lines are perpendicular to each other if product of their slopes is -1.

Chapter 12. Reflection

1. Rule to find the reflection of a point in the *x*-axis :

(i) Retain the abscissa *i.e.* *x*-co-ordinate.

(ii) Change the sign of ordinate *i.e.* *y*-coordinate.

2. Rule to find the reflection of a point in the *y*-axis :

(i) Change the sign of abscissa *i.e.*, *x*-coordinate.

(ii) Retain the ordinate *i.e.*, *y*-co-ordinate.

3. Reflection of a point in a line parallel to *x*-axis : The reflection of the point P (x, y) in the line $y = a$ is the point P $(x, -y + 2a)$.

4. Reflection of a point in a line parallel to *y*-axis : The reflection of the point P (x, y) in the line $x = a$ is the point P' $(-x + 2a, y)$.

5. Reflection of a point in the origin :

(i) Change the sign of abscissa *i.e.*, *x*-co-ordinate.

(ii) Change the sign of ordinate *i.e.*, *y*-co-ordinate.

6. A point is called an invariant point with respect to a given line if and only if it lies on the line after reflection in the same line.

Chapter 13. Similarity

1. Similarities of triangles : When two triangles are similar, their corresponding angles are equal and corresponding sides are proportional.

For example :

If $\triangle$ ABC is similar to $\triangle$ DEF,

i.e., $\triangle$ ABC ~ $\triangle$ DEF;

$$\angle A = \angle D, \angle B = \angle E, \angle C = \angle F,$$

and $\quad \dfrac{AB}{DE} = \dfrac{BC}{EF} = \dfrac{AC}{DF}$.

The sign '~' is read as, 'is similar to'.

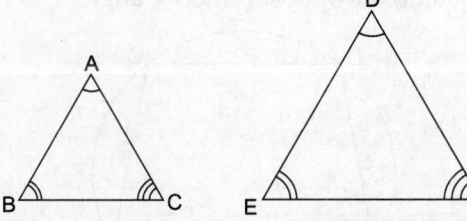

2. Axioms of similarity of triangles : (*i.e.*, three similarity postulates for triangles)

(i) If two triangles have a pair of correspond-

ing angles equal and the sides including them are proportional, then the triangles are similar (SAS postulate).

(ii) If two triangles have two pairs of corresponding angles equal; the triangles are similar (AA or AAA postulate).

(iii) If two triangles have their three pairs of corresponding sides proportional, the triangles are similar (SSS postulate).

3. Basic Theorem of Proportionality :

A line drawn parallel to any side of a triangle, divides the other two sides proportionally.

In the given figure, DE $\parallel$ BC

$$\Rightarrow \qquad \dfrac{AD}{BD} = \dfrac{AE}{CE}$$

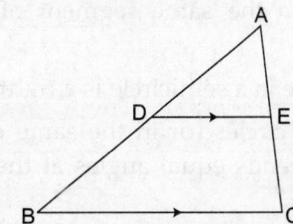

Conversely : If a line divides two sides of a triangle proportionally, the line is parallel to the third side.

i.e., if $\dfrac{AD}{BD} = \dfrac{AE}{CE} \Rightarrow DE \parallel BC$.

4. Relation between the areas of two triangles : The areas of two similar triangles are proportional to the squares of their corresponding sides.

If $\triangle ABC \sim \triangle DEF$
such that $\angle BAC = \angle EDF$,
$\angle B = \angle E$ and $\angle C = \angle F$.

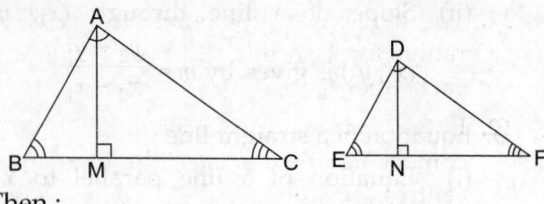

Then :

$$\dfrac{\text{Area of } \triangle ABC}{\text{Area of } \triangle DEF} = \dfrac{AB^2}{DE^2} = \dfrac{BC^2}{EF^2} = \dfrac{AC^2}{DF^2}$$

5. Similar figures and congruent figures both have the same shape. The difference between similar figures and congruent figures is that congruent figures also have the same shape and size, while in case of similar figures (like triangles) there sides are proportional having same shape.

Chapter 14. Loci

Theorems on Locus :

(a) The locus of a point equidistant from a fixed point is a circle with the fixed point as centre.

(b) The locus of a point equidistant from two intersecting lines is the bisector of the angles between the lines.

(c) The locus of a point equidistant from two given points is the perpendicular bisector of the line joining the points.

Chapter 15. Circles

1. A straight line drawn from the centre of the circle to bisect a chord, which is not a diameter, is at right angles to the chord.

   Conversely, the perpendicular to a chord, from the centre of the circle, bisects the chord.

2. There is one circle, and only one, which passes through three given points not in a straight line.

3. Equal chords of a circle are equidistant from the centre.

   Conversely, chords of a circle, equidistant from the centre of the circle, are equal.

4. The angle which an arc of a circle subtends at the centre is double, that which it subtends at any point on the remaining part of the circumference.

5. Angles in the same segment of a circle are equal.

6. The angle in a semicircle is a right angle.

7. In equal circles (or in the same circle), if two arcs subtends equal angles at the centre, they are equal.

Conversely, in equal circles (or in the same circle), if two arcs are equal, they subtend equal angles at the centre.

8. In equal circles (or in the same circle), if two chord are equal, they cut off equal arcs.

   Conversely, in equal circle (or in the same circle, if two arcs are equal the chords of the arcs are also equal.

9. The opposite angles of a cyclic quadrilateral (quadrilateral inscribed in a circle) are supplementary.

10. The exterior angle of a cyclic quadrilateral is equal to the opposite interior angle.

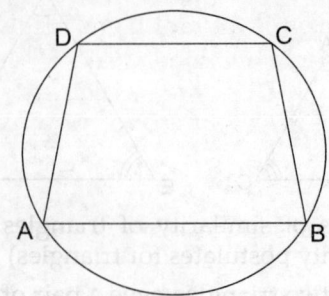

11. The tangent at any point of a circle and the radius through this point are perpendicular to each other.

12. If two circles touch each other, the point of contact lies on the straight line through the centres.

13. From any point outside a circle two tangents can be drawn and they are equal in length.

14. If a chord and a tangent intersect externally, then the product of the lengths of segments of the chord is equal to the square of the length of the tangent from the point of contact to the point of intersection.

15. If a line touches a circle and from the point of contact, a chord is drawn, the angles between the tangent and the chord are respectively equal to the angles in the corresponding alternate segments.

16. If two chords intersect internally or externally then the product of the lengths of the segments are equal.

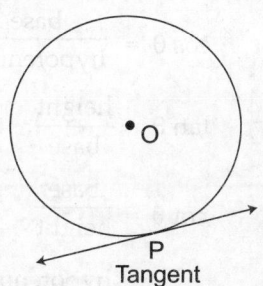

Chapter 17. Mensuration

1. **Perimeter :**

   Perimeter of a plane figure = sum of lengths of its sides.

2. Surface area and volume of solids :

   Solid Cylinder :

   Let r and h be the radius and height of a solid cylinder, then

   (i)   Curved (lateral) surface area = $2\pi rh$.

   (ii) Total surface area = $2\pi r\,(h + r)$.

   (iii) Volume = $\pi r^2 h$.

   Hollow Cylinder :

   Let R and r be the external and internal radii, and h be the height of a hollow cylinder, then

   (i)   External curved surface area = $2\pi Rh$.

   (ii) Internal curved surface area = $2\pi rh$.

   (iii) Total surface area

   $$= 2\pi\,(Rh + rh + R^2 - r^2).$$

   (iv) Volume of material = $\pi\,(R^2 - r^2)\,h$.

   Cone :

   Let r and h be the radius and height, and l be the slant height of a cone, then

   (i)   Slant height = $l = \sqrt{r^2 + h^2}$.

   (ii) Curved (lateral) surface area = πrl.

   (iii) Total surface area = $\pi r\,(l + r)$.

   (iv) Volume = $\dfrac{1}{3}\,\pi r^2 h$.

Solid Sphere :

Let r be the radius of a solid sphere, then

(i)   Surface area = $4\pi r^2$.

(ii) Volume = $\dfrac{4}{3}\,\pi r^3$.

Spherical Shell :

Let R and r be the radii of the outer and inner spheres, then

(i)   Thickness of the shell = R – r.

(ii) Volume of material = $\dfrac{4}{3}\,\pi\,(R^3 - r^3)$.

Solid Hemisphere :

Let r be the radius of a hemisphere, then

(i)   Curved (lateral) surface area = $2\pi r^2$.

(ii) Total surface area = $3\pi r^2$.

(iii) Volume = $\dfrac{2}{3}\,\pi r^3$.

Hemispherical Shell :

Let R and r be the radii of the outer and inner hemispheres, then

(i)   Thickness of the shell = R – r.

(ii) Area of base = $\pi\,(R^2 - r^2)$.

(iii) External curved surface area = $2\pi R^2$.

(iv) Internal curved surface area = $2\pi r^2$.

(v)   Total surface area = $\pi\,(3R^2 + r^2)$.

(vi) Volume of material = $\dfrac{2}{3}\,\pi\,(R^3 - r^3)$.

Chapter 18. Trigonometry

1. Trigonometrical ratios :

   (i) $\sin \theta = \dfrac{\text{height}}{\text{hypotenuse}}$

   (ii) $\cos \theta = \dfrac{\text{base}}{\text{hypotenuse}}$

   (iii) $\tan \theta = \dfrac{\text{height}}{\text{base}}$

   (iv) $\cot \theta = \dfrac{\text{base}}{\text{height}}$

   (v) $\sec \theta = \dfrac{\text{hypotenuse}}{\text{base}}$

   (vi) $\csc \theta = \dfrac{\text{hypotenuse}}{\text{height}}$

2. Quotient relations :

   (i) $\tan \theta = \dfrac{\sin \theta}{\cos \theta}$

   (ii) $\cot \theta = \dfrac{\cos \theta}{\sin \theta}$

3. Square relations :

   (i) $\sin^2 \theta + \cos^2 \theta = 1$

   (ii) $1 + \tan^2 \theta = \sec^2 \theta$

   (iii) $1 + \cot^2 \theta = \csc^2 \theta$

4. Trigonometrical ratios of standard angles :

Angle → Ratio ↓	0°	30°	45°	60°	90°
$\sin \theta$	0	$\dfrac{1}{2}$	$\dfrac{1}{\sqrt{2}}$	$\dfrac{\sqrt{3}}{2}$	1
$\cos \theta$	1	$\dfrac{\sqrt{3}}{2}$	$\dfrac{1}{\sqrt{2}}$	$\dfrac{1}{2}$	0
$\tan \theta$	0	$\dfrac{1}{\sqrt{3}}$	1	$\sqrt{3}$	**not defined**

Chapter 19. Statistics

1. Mean :

   (i)   Mean (for ungrouped data) $= \dfrac{\Sigma x_i}{n}$, where

   $x_1, x_2, x_3, ..., x_n$ are the observations and n is the total number of observations.

   (ii) Mean (for grouped data) $= \dfrac{\Sigma f_i x_i}{\Sigma f_i}$, where

   $x_1, x_2, x_3, ..., x_n$ are different variates with frequencies $f_1, f_2, f_3, ..., f_n$ respectively.

   (iii) Mean for continuous distribution.

   Let there be n continuous classes and y_i be the class mark and f_i be the frequency of the ith class, then

   $$\text{Mean} = \dfrac{\Sigma f_i y_i}{\Sigma f_i} \quad \text{(Direct method)}$$

   Let A be the assumed mean, then

   $$\text{Mean} = A + \dfrac{\Sigma f_i d_i}{\Sigma f_i},$$

   where $d_i = y_i - A$ (Short cut method)

   If the classes are of equal size, say c, then

   $$\text{Mean} = A + c - 1 \text{ point } \dfrac{\Sigma f_i u_i}{\Sigma f_i},$$

   where $u_i = \dfrac{y_i - A}{c}$ (Step deviation method)

2. Median :

   Let n be the total number of observations, then Median

   $$= \begin{cases} \dfrac{n+1}{2} \text{th observation, if } n \text{ is odd} \\[2mm] \dfrac{\dfrac{n}{2} \text{th observation} + \left(\dfrac{n}{2}+1\right) \text{th observation}}{2} \\[2mm] \hfill \text{if } n \text{ is even.} \end{cases}$$

3. Quartiles :

   Lower quartile (Q_1)

   $$= \begin{cases} \dfrac{n+1}{4} \text{th observation, if } n \text{ is odd} \\[2mm] \dfrac{n}{4} \text{th observation, if } n \text{ is even} \end{cases}$$

   Upper quartile (Q_3)

   $$= \begin{cases} \dfrac{3(n+1)}{4} \text{th observation, if } n \text{ is odd} \\[2mm] \dfrac{3n}{4} \text{th observation, if } n \text{ is even} \end{cases}$$

   Interquartile range $= Q_3 - Q_1$ and

   semi-interquartile range $= \dfrac{Q_3 - Q_1}{2}$.

Chapter at a Glance

Chapter 20. Probability

1. If all the outcomes of an experiment are equally likely and E is an event, then probability of event E, written by P (E), is given by

$$P(E) = \frac{\text{number of outcomes favourable to } E}{\substack{\text{total number of possible outcomes} \\ \text{of the experiment}}}$$

2. $0 \leq P(E) \leq 1$

3. P (not E) = 1 – P (E)

4. P (E) = 1 – P (not E)

5. P (E) + P (not E) = 1

6. The sum of the probabilities of all the elementary events of an experiment = 1

7. The probability of a sure event = 1

8. The probability of an impossible event = 0.

□□

Formulae Based Questions | Set 2

Chapter 1. Goods and Services Tax (GST)

1. A wholesaler buys a TV from the manufacturer for ₹ 25,000. He marks the price of the TV 20% above his cost price and sells it to a retailer at a 10% discount on the marked price. If the rate of GST is 8%, Find the:

   (i) marked price.

   (ii) retailer's cost price inclusive of tax.

   (iii) GST paid by the wholesaler.

Sol. Given, wholesaler's C.P. of a T.V.

$$= ₹ 25,000$$

(i) Marked price of a T.V.

$$= ₹ 25,000 + 20\% \text{ of } ₹ 25,000$$

$$= ₹ 25,000 + ₹ 5,000$$

$$= ₹ 30,000. \quad \textbf{Ans.}$$

(ii) Discount = 10% of ₹ 30,000

$$= 30,000 \times \frac{10}{100} = ₹ 3,000$$

Discount price

$$= ₹ 30,000 - ₹ 3,000$$

$$= ₹ 27,000$$

Tax for the wholesaler

$$= 8\% \text{ of } 27,000$$

$$= ₹ 2160$$

Retailer's C.P. (inclusive of all taxes)

$$= ₹ 27,000 + ₹ 2160$$

$$= ₹ 29,160. \quad \textbf{Ans.}$$

(iii) Amount of GST to be paid by the wholesaler

$$= \text{Tax on the value added by the wholesaler}$$

$$= 8\% \text{ of } ₹ (27,000 - 25,000)$$

$$= \frac{8}{100} \times 2000$$

$$= ₹ 160. \quad \textbf{Ans.}$$

2. A shopkeeper bought a washing machine at a discount of 20% from a wholesaler, the printed price of the washing machine being ₹ 18,000. The shopkeeper sells it to a consumer at a discount of 10% on the printed price. If the rate of GST is 8%, find :

   (i) the GST paid by the shopkeeper.

   (ii) the total amount that the consumer pays for the washing machine.

Sol. Given,

$$\text{M.P.} = ₹ 18,000$$

$$\text{Discount} = 20\% \text{ for shop–owner.}$$

$$\text{Discount} = 10\% \text{ for consumer}$$

$$\text{GST} = 8\%$$

Discount for shop–owner

$$= 20\% \text{ of } 18,000$$

$$= \frac{20 \times 18000}{100}$$

$$= ₹ 3600$$

Cost for shop–owner

$$= ₹ 18000 - ₹ 3600$$

$$= ₹ 14400$$

Cost for consumer $= ₹ 18000 - 10\% \text{ of } ₹ 18000$

$$= ₹ 18000 - ₹ \frac{10 \times 18000}{100}$$

$$= ₹ 18000 - ₹ 1800$$

$$= ₹ 16,200$$

(i) ∴ GST paid by the shopkeeper

$$= \text{Tax on the value added by shopkeeper}$$

$$= 8\% \text{ of } (16,200 - 14,400)$$

$$= \frac{8}{100} \times 1800$$

$$= ₹ 144 \quad \textbf{Ans.}$$

(ii) Tax charged by the shopkeeper

$$= ₹ 16200 \times \frac{8}{100} = ₹ 1296$$

Amount paid by consumer

$$= ₹ (16200 + 1296)$$

$$= ₹ 17496. \quad \textbf{Ans.}$$

3. Mr. Bedi visits the market and buys the following articles :*

Medicines costing ₹ 950, GST @ 5%

A pair of shoes costing ₹ 3000, GST @ 18%

A laptop bag costing ₹ 1000 with a discount of 30%, GST @ 18%.

(i) Calculate the total amount of GST paid.

(ii) The total bill amount including GST paid by Mr. Bedi.

Sol. (i) Cost of medicines = ₹ 950

GST on medicines = 5% of 950

$= \dfrac{5}{100} \times 950$

$= ₹ 47.50$

Cost of a pair of shoes = ₹ 3000

GST on shoes = 18% of ₹ 3000

$= \dfrac{18}{100} \times 3000$

$= ₹ 540$

Cost of laptop bag = ₹ 1000

Discount on bag = 30% of 1000

$= \dfrac{30}{100} \times 1000$

$= ₹ 300$

∴ Cost of laptop bag after discount

$= ₹ (1000 - 300)$

$= ₹ 700$

GST on laptop bag = 18% of ₹ 700

$= \dfrac{18}{100} \times 700$

$= ₹ 126$

∴ Total GST on all items

$= ₹ (47.50 + 540 + 126)$

$= ₹ 713.50$ **Ans.**

(ii) Total bill including GST = cost of (medicines + shoes + laptop bag) + Total GST on all items.

$= ₹ (950 + 3000 + 700) + ₹ 713.50$

$= ₹ (4650 + 713.50)$

$= ₹ 5363.50$ **Ans.**

Chapter 2. Banking (Recurring Deposit Account)

1. Mr. Sonu has a recurring deposit account and deposits ₹ 750 per month for 2 years. If he gets ₹ 19125 at the time of maturity, find the rate of interest.*

Sol. Here, P = ₹ 750, n = 2 years = 24 months and M.V. = ₹ 19125

We know, $M.V. = P \times n + \dfrac{P \times n(n+1)}{2 \times 12} \times \dfrac{r}{100}$

$\Rightarrow 19125 = 750 \times 24$

$+ \dfrac{750 \times 24(24+1)}{2 \times 12} \times \dfrac{r}{100}$

$\Rightarrow 19125 = 18000 + 750 \times 25 \times \dfrac{r}{100}$

$\Rightarrow 19125 - 18000 = \dfrac{750 \times r}{4}$

$\Rightarrow 1125 = \dfrac{750 \times r}{4}$

$\Rightarrow r = \dfrac{1125 \times 4}{750} = 6$

Hence, the rate of interest is 6% p.a. **Ans.**

2. Naseem has a 5 years Recurring Deposit account in Punjab National Bank and deposit ₹ 240 per month. If she receives ₹ 17,694 at the time of maturity, find the rate of interest.

Sol. Here if r% be the rate of interest.

Maturity value

$= P \times n + P \times \dfrac{n(n+1)}{2 \times 12} \times \dfrac{r}{100}$

$= ₹(240 \times 12 \times 5)$

$+ ₹\left(240 \times \dfrac{60 \times 61}{2 \times 12} \times \dfrac{r}{100} \right)$

$17,694 = 14,400 + 366r$

$366r = 3,294$

$r = 9\%.$ **Ans.**

3. Zafarullah has a recurring deposit account in a bank for $3\dfrac{1}{2}$ years at 9.5% S.I. p.a. If he gets ₹ 78,638 at the time of maturity. Find the monthly instalment.

Sol. Let the monthly instalment be of ₹ x then,

Maturity value

$= ₹\left(x \times \dfrac{7}{2} \times 12 \right) + ₹\left(x \times \dfrac{42 \times 43}{2 \times 12} \times \dfrac{19}{200} \right)$

$\Rightarrow 78,638 = 42x + \dfrac{5,719x}{800}$

$\Rightarrow \dfrac{39,319}{800}x = 78,638$

$\Rightarrow x = 1600$

Hence, the monthly instalment is of ₹ 1600. **Ans.**

* Frequently asked previous years Board Exam Questions.

4. Priyanka has a recurring deposit account of ₹ 1000 per month at 10% per annum. If she gets ₹ 5550 as interest at the time of maturity, find the total time for which the account was held.*

Sol. Given, P = ₹ 1,000, r = 10%, I = ₹ 5,550, n = ?

$$\therefore \qquad I = P \times \frac{n(n+1)}{2 \times 12} \times \frac{r}{100}$$

$$\Rightarrow \qquad 5550 = 1000 \times \frac{n^2+n}{24} \times \frac{10}{100}$$

$$\Rightarrow \qquad 555 = \frac{5}{12}(n^2+n)$$

$$\Rightarrow \qquad 5n^2 + 5n = 6660$$

$$\Rightarrow \qquad 5(n^2+n) = 6660$$

$$\Rightarrow \qquad n^2 + n = 1332$$

$$\Rightarrow \qquad n^2 + n - 1332 = 0$$

$$\Rightarrow \qquad n^2 + 37n - 36n - 1332 = 0$$

$$\Rightarrow \qquad n(n+37) - 36(n+37) = 0$$

$$\Rightarrow \qquad (n+37)(n-36) = 0$$

$$\Rightarrow \qquad n + 37 = 0 \text{ or } n - 36 = 0$$

$$\Rightarrow \qquad n = -37 \text{ or } n = 36$$

$$\therefore \qquad n = 36$$

(∵ n cannot be negative)

Hence, total time for which amount was held is 36 months or 3 years. **Ans.**

5. Mohan saves ₹ 25 per month from his pocket allowance and puts this saving every month in a bank recurring deposit scheme for a period of 72 months at 5·25%. What amount does he get on maturity ?

Sol. Here, the monthly instalment is ₹ 25 per month

Maturity value = ₹ (25 × 72)

$$+ ₹\left(25 \times \frac{72 \times 73 \times 5·25}{2 \times 12 \times 100}\right)$$

= ₹ 1,800 + ₹ 287·4375

= ₹ 2,087·4   **Ans.**

6. Sonia had recurring deposit account in a bank and deposited ₹ 600 per month for $2\frac{1}{2}$ years. If the rate of interest was 10% p.a., find the maturity value of this account.*

Sol. Here, P = ₹ 600, n = $2\frac{1}{2}$ years = 30 months, r = 10%

$$\therefore \qquad \text{Interest, I} = P \times \frac{n(n+1)}{2 \times 12} \times \frac{r}{100}$$

$$= 600 \times \frac{30 \times 31}{2 \times 12} \times \frac{10}{100}$$

$$= ₹ 2325$$

$\therefore$ Maturity value,

M.V. = Pn + I

= 600 × 30 + 2325

= ₹ 20325.   **Ans.**

7. Kiran deposited ₹ 200 per month for 36 months in a bank's recurring deposit account. If the bank pays interest at the rate of 11% per annum, find the amount she gets on maturity.

Sol.

$$\text{Interest} = \frac{P \times n(n+1) \times R}{2,400}$$

$$= \frac{200 \times 36 \times 37 \times 11}{2,400}$$

$$= 3 \times 37 \times 11$$

$$= ₹ 1,221$$

Sum deposited = 36 × 200

= ₹ 7,200

Amount on maturity = ₹ 7,200 + ₹ 1,221

= ₹ 8,421.   **Ans.**

8. Katrina opened a recurring deposit account with a Nationalised Bank for a period of 2 years. If the bank pays interest at the rate of 6% per annum and the monthly installment is ₹ 1,000, find the:

(i) interest earned in 2 years.

(ii) matured value.

Sol. Since, money deposited = ₹ 1,000 per month *i.e.* P = ₹ 1,000

and number of months = 2 × 12 = 24 *i.e.*, n = 24 and r = 6%

(i) Interest earned in 2 years

$$= P \times \frac{n(n+1)}{2 \times 12} \times \frac{r}{100}$$

$$= 1000 \times \frac{24(24+1)}{2 \times 12} \times \frac{6}{100}$$

$$= ₹ 1,500.   \textbf{Ans.}$$

(ii) Matured value= Sum deposited + Interest

= ₹ (1,000 × 24) + ₹1,500

= ₹ 25,500.   **Ans.**

9. Mohan has a recurring deposit account in a bank for 2 years at 6% p.a. simple interest. If he gets ₹ 1200 as interest at the time of maturity, find :

(i) the monthly instalment

(ii) the amount of maturity.

Sol. (i) Since, number of months (n) = 24 and rate of interest (r) = 6%

---

* Frequently asked previous years Board Exam Questions.

$$I = P \times \frac{n(n+1)}{2 \times 12} \times \frac{r}{100}$$

$$1200 = P \times \frac{24(24+1)}{2 \times 12} \times \frac{6}{100}$$

$$P = \frac{1,200 \times 24 \times 100}{6 \times 24 \times 25}$$

$$= ₹\ 800$$

∴ Monthly instalment = ₹ 800 **Ans.**

(ii) Sum deposited = ₹ 800 × 24

$$= ₹\ 19200$$

Amount on maturity = ₹ 19,200 + ₹ 1,200

$$= ₹\ 20,400 \quad \textbf{Ans.}$$

10. Rekha opened a recurring deposit account for 20 months. The rate of interest is 9% per annum and Rekha receives ₹ 441 as interest at the time of maturity.

Find the amount Rekha deposited each month.*

Sol. Given, number of months (n) = 20

Rate of interest (r) = 9% p.a.

Interest received (I) = ₹ 441

Let the monthly deposit be ₹ P.

∴ $$I = P \times \frac{n(n+1)}{2 \times 12} \times \frac{r}{100}$$

⇒ $$441 = P \times \frac{20(20+1)}{2 \times 12} \times \frac{9}{100}$$

⇒ $$P = \frac{441 \times 2 \times 12 \times 100}{20 \times 21 \times 9}$$

$$= ₹\ 280$$

∴ The required monthly deposit is ₹ 280. **Ans.**

Chapter 3. Shares and Dividends

1. A man invests ₹ 22,500 in ₹ 50 shares available at 10% discount. If the dividend paid by the company is 12%, calculate :*

(i) The number of shares purchased

(ii) The annual dividend received

(iii) The rate of return he gets on his investment. Give your answer correct to the nearest whole number.

Sol. Given, investment = ₹ 22,500, N.V. = ₹ 50, discount = 10%

∴ $$\text{M.V.} = ₹\ \left(50 - \frac{10}{100} \times 50\right) = ₹\ 45$$

Rate of dividend = 12%

(i) Number of shares = $\dfrac{\text{Investment}}{\text{M.V.}}$

$$= \frac{22500}{45} = 500 \quad \textbf{Ans.}$$

(ii) Annual dividend = Dividend per share × No. of shares

$$= \frac{12}{100} \times 50 \times 500$$

$$= ₹\ 3000 \quad \textbf{Ans.}$$

(iii) Rate of return = $\dfrac{\text{Dividend}}{\text{Investment}} \times 100\%$

$$= \frac{3000}{22500} \times 100\%$$

$$= 13.3\% = 13\%$$

(correct to the nearest whole number)

Ans.

2. A man invested ₹ 45,000 in 15% ₹ 100 shares quoted at ₹ 125. When the market value of these share rose to ₹ 140. He sold same shares, just enough to raise ₹ 8,400 calculate.

(i) The number of shares he still holds.

(ii) The dividend due to him on these remaining shares.

Sol. Number of shares bought

$$= \frac{45,000}{125} = 360$$

Number of shares sold to raise ₹ 8,400.

$$= \frac{8,400}{140} = 60.$$

(i) Number of shares he still holds

$$= 360 - 60 = 300.$$

(ii) Dividend on these shares

$$= ₹\ (300 \times 15)$$

$$= ₹\ 4,500. \quad \textbf{Ans.}$$

3. A man invests ₹ 4500 in shares of a company which is paying 7.5% dividend. If ₹ 100 shares are available at a discount of 10%.*

Find :

(i) Number of shares he purchases.

(ii) His annual income.

Sol. Given, Investment = ₹ 4500

Rate of dividend = 7.5%

Nominal value = ₹ 100, Discount = 10%

---
* Frequently asked previous years Board Exam Questions.

$\therefore$ Market value $= ₹\left(100 - \dfrac{10}{100} \times 100\right) = ₹ 90$

(i) Number of shares purchased

$$= \dfrac{\text{Investment}}{\text{Market Value}}$$

$$= \dfrac{4500}{90} = ₹50 \qquad \textbf{Ans.}$$

(ii) Dividend per share $= \dfrac{7.5}{100} \times 100 = ₹ 7.50$

$\therefore$ Annual income $=$ Dividend per share

$$\times \text{ Number of shares}$$

$$= 7.50 \times 50$$

$$= ₹ 375 \qquad \textbf{Ans.}$$

4. Ashok invested ₹ 26,400 on 12%, ₹ 25 shares of a company. If he receives a dividend of ₹ 2,475, find the :

(i) Number of shares he bought

(ii) Market value of each share

Sol. (i) Given, nominal value of share

$$= ₹ 25$$

Rate of dividend $= 12\%$

Total dividend $= ₹ 2,475$

Dividend on each share

$$= \text{Rate of dividend} \times \text{N. V.}$$

$$= \dfrac{12}{100} \times 25 = ₹ 3$$

Number of shares $= \dfrac{\text{Total dividend}}{\text{Dividend on each share}}$

$$= \dfrac{2475}{3} = 825 \qquad \textbf{Ans.}$$

(ii) Market value of each share

$$= \dfrac{\text{Sum invested}}{\text{Number of shares}} = \dfrac{26,400}{825}$$

$$= ₹ 32. \qquad \textbf{Ans.}$$

5. Rohit invested ₹ 9,600 on ₹ 100 shares at ₹ 20 premium paying 8% dividend. Rohit sold the shares when the price rose to ₹ 160. He invested the proceeds (excluding dividend) in 10% ₹ 50 shares at ₹ 40. Find the :

(i) original number of shares.

(ii) sale proceeds.

(iii) new number of shares.

(iv) change in the two dividends.

Sol. Given,

Sum invested $= ₹ 9,600$

N.V. of each share $= ₹ 100$

M.V. of each share $= ₹ (100 + 20) = ₹ 120$

(i) No. of shares bought

$$= \dfrac{9600}{120} = 80 \qquad \textbf{Ans.}$$

(ii) Selling price of one share $= ₹ 160$

$\therefore$ Selling price of 80 shares

$$= ₹ 80 \times 160$$

$$= ₹ 12800$$

Hence, Rohit's sales produced

$$= ₹ 12800 \qquad \textbf{Ans.}$$

(iii) Market value of new share $= ₹ 40$

Investment $= ₹ 12800$

New no. of shares bought

$$= \dfrac{12800}{40} = 320 \qquad \textbf{Ans.}$$

(iv) Dividend from original shares $=$ Number of shares $\times$ rate of dividend$\times$ face value of one share

$$= ₹ 80 \times \dfrac{8}{100} \times 100$$

$$= ₹ 640$$

Annual dividend from new shares $=$ Number of shares $\times$ rate of dividend $\times$ face value of one share

$$= ₹ 320 \times \dfrac{10}{100} \times 50$$

$$= ₹ 1600$$

$\therefore$ Change in two dividend

$$= ₹ (1600 - 640)$$

$$= ₹ 960$$

Dividend increase $= ₹ 960 \qquad \textbf{Ans.}$

6. Sachin invests ₹ 8500 in 10%, ₹ 100 shares at ₹ 170. He sells the shares when the price of each share rises by ₹ 30. He invests the proceeds in 12% ₹ 100 shares at ₹ 125. Find :*

(i) the sale proceeds.

(ii) the number of ₹ 125 shares he buys.

(iii) the change in his annual income.

Sol. Given, Investment = ₹ 8500,

Rate of dividend = 10%

Nominal Value = ₹ 100,

Market Value = ₹ 170

∴ Number of shares = $\dfrac{\text{Investment}}{\text{Market Value}}$

$= \dfrac{8500}{170} = 50$

(i) Since the price of each share rises by ₹ 30,

Market Value of shares sold

= ₹ 170 + ₹ 30 = ₹ 200

∴ Sale proceeds = ₹ 200 × 50 = ₹ 10,000 **Ans.**

(ii) For new shares bought,

Investment = ₹ 10,000

Rate of dividend = 12%,

Nominal Value = ₹ 100,

and Market Value = ₹ 125.

∴ Number of shares bought

$= \dfrac{\text{Investment}}{\text{Market Value}}$

$= \dfrac{10,000}{125} = ₹ 80$ **Ans.**

(iii) Annual income from old shares

= Dividend per share × Number of shares

$= \dfrac{10}{100} × 100 × 50$

= ₹ 500

Annual income from new shares

$= \dfrac{12}{100} × 100 × 80$

= ₹ 960

∴ The change in his annual income

= ₹ 960 – ₹ 500

= ₹ 460 **Ans.**

7. Salman invests a sum of money in ₹ 50 shares, paying 15% dividend quoted at 20% premium. If his annual dividend is ₹ 600, calculate :

(i) the number of shares he bought.

(ii) his total investment.

(iii) the rate of return on his investment.

Sol. Face value = ₹ 50, Dividend % = 15%

Market value = 50 + 20% of 50

= 50 + 10

= ₹ 60

Annual dividend = ₹ 600

(i) As we know

Dividend % × (No. of shares × Face value)

= Dividend

$\dfrac{15}{100}$ × No. of shares × 50

= 600

No. of shares = $\dfrac{600 × 100}{15 × 50} = 80.$ **Ans.**

(ii) His total investment

= 80 × Market value

= 80 × 60 = ₹ 4800. **Ans.**

(iii) Rate of return on his investment

$= \left(\dfrac{\text{Total dividend}}{\text{Investment}} × 100\right)\%$

$= \left(\dfrac{600}{4800} × 100\right)\%$

$= \left(\dfrac{100}{8}\right)\% = 12.5\%.$ **Ans.**

8. (i) Which is better investment : 7% ₹ 100 shares at ₹ 120 or 8% ₹ 10 shares at ₹ 13·50.

(ii) Mamta invested ₹ 10,846 in buying the shares of a company at ₹ 17 each. If the face value of each share be ₹ 10 and company paid 15% dividend at the end of the year, find the dividend earned by her.

Sol. (i) Case I.

Income on ₹ 120 = 7% of ₹ 100

$= ₹ \dfrac{7 × 100}{100} = ₹ 7$

So, Income on ₹ 1 = ₹ $\dfrac{7}{120}$ = ₹ 0·058

Case II.

Income on ₹ 13·50 = 8% of ₹ 10

$= ₹ \dfrac{8 × 10}{100} = ₹ \dfrac{8}{10}$

So, Income on ₹ 1 = ₹ $\dfrac{\frac{8}{10}}{13·50}$

= ₹ 0·059

We find that investment in the second case is better than investment in the first case. **Ans.**

(ii) Market value of 1 share = ₹ 17

Total invested money = ₹ 10,846

Number of shares bought

$= \dfrac{10,846}{17} = 638$

Face value of 638 shares = 638 × ₹ 10

$$= ₹ 6,380$$

Dividend received by Mamta

$$= ₹ \left(6,380 \times \frac{15}{100}\right)$$

$$= ₹ 957. \qquad \textbf{Ans.}$$

9. A company with 500 shares of nominal value ₹ 120 declares an annual dividend of 15%. Calculate :*

(i) the total amount of dividend paid by the company.

(ii) annual income of Mr. Sharma who holds 80 shares of the company

If the return percent of Mr. Sharma from his shares is 10%, find the market value of each share.

Sol. (i) Total number of shares = 500

Nominal value of each share = ₹ 120

And, Dividend = 15%

Total value of shares = ₹ (500 × 120)

$$= ₹ 60,000$$

So, Total dividend = 15% of ₹ 60,000

$$= \frac{15}{100} \times 60,000$$

$$= ₹ 9,000 \qquad \textbf{Ans.}$$

(ii) Annual income of 80 shares

$$= 15\% \text{ of } (80 \times 120)$$

$$= \frac{15}{100} \times 9600$$

$$= ₹ 1,440 \qquad \textbf{Ans.}$$

Let the market value of each share be ₹ x.

So,   10% of 80x = 1440

$$\Rightarrow \qquad \frac{10}{100} \times 80x = 1440$$

$$\Rightarrow \qquad x = \frac{1440 \times 10}{80}$$

$$x = 180$$

So, the market value of each share is ₹ 180.

Ans.

10. Ajay owns 560 shares of a company. The face value of each share is ₹ 25. The company declares a dividend of 9%. Calculate :

(i) The dividend that Ajay will get.

(ii) The rate of interest on his investment, if Ajay had paid ₹ 30 for each share.

Sol. Number of shares = 560

N.V. of one share = ₹ 25

Rate of dividend = 9%

(i)   Dividend = Number of shares

$$\times \text{ N.V.} \times \text{Rate of divd.}$$

$$= 560 \times 25 \times \frac{9}{100}$$

$$= ₹ 1,260$$

(ii)   Investment = Number of shares × M.V.

$$= 560 \times 30$$

$$= ₹ 16,800$$

∴   Rate of interest on investment

$$= \frac{\text{Dividend}}{\text{Investment}} \times 100$$

$$= \frac{1,260}{16,800} \times 100$$

$$= 7 \cdot 5\%. \qquad \textbf{Ans.}$$

Chapter 6. Ratio and Proportion

1. If $(3a + 2b) : (5a + 3b) = 18 : 29$. Find $a : b$.

Sol. Here, $\dfrac{3a+2b}{5a+3b} = \dfrac{18}{29}$

$$\Rightarrow \qquad 29(3a + 2b) = 18(5a + 3b)$$

$$\Rightarrow \qquad 87a + 58b = 90a + 54b$$

$$\Rightarrow \qquad -90a + 87a = -58b + 54b$$

$$\Rightarrow \qquad -3a = -4b$$

$$\Rightarrow \qquad \frac{a}{b} = \frac{4}{3}$$

i.e., $a : b = 4 : 3$ **Ans.**

2. Given $= \dfrac{x^3 + 12x}{6x^2 + 8} = \dfrac{y^3 + 27y}{9y^2 + 27}$.

Using componendo and dividendo find $x : y$.

Sol. $\dfrac{x^3 + 12x}{6x^2 + 8} = \dfrac{y^3 + 27y}{9y^2 + 27}$

Applying componendo and dividendo, we get

$$\frac{x^3 + 12x + 6x^2 + 8}{x^3 + 12x - 6x^2 - 8} = \frac{y^3 + 27y + 9y^2 + 27}{y^3 + 27y - 9y^2 - 27}$$

* Frequently asked previous years Board Exam Questions.

$\Rightarrow \qquad \dfrac{(x+2)^3}{(x-2)^3} = \dfrac{(y+3)^3}{(y-3)^3}$

$\Rightarrow \qquad \dfrac{x+2}{x-2} = \dfrac{y+3}{y-3}$

Again using componendo and dividendo, we get

$$\dfrac{x+2+x-2}{x+2-x+2} = \dfrac{y+3+y-3}{y+3-y+3}$$

$\Rightarrow \qquad \dfrac{2x}{4} = \dfrac{2y}{6}$

$\Rightarrow \qquad \dfrac{x}{y} = \dfrac{2}{3}$

Hence, $\qquad x : y = 2 : 3.$ **Ans.**

3. If $\dfrac{x^2+y^2}{x^2-y^2} = \dfrac{17}{8}$, then find the value of :

(i) $x : y$.

(ii) $\dfrac{x^3+y^3}{x^3-y^3}$.

Sol. (i) $\qquad \dfrac{x^2+y^2}{x^2-y^2} = \dfrac{17}{8}$

Applying componendo and dividendo rule,

$$\dfrac{x^2+y^2+x^2-y^2}{x^2+y^2-x^2+y^2} = \dfrac{17+8}{17-8}$$

$\Rightarrow \qquad \dfrac{2x^2}{2y^2} = \dfrac{25}{9}$

$\Rightarrow \qquad \dfrac{x^2}{y^2} = \dfrac{25}{9}$

$\Rightarrow \qquad \dfrac{x}{y} = \dfrac{5}{3}$

$\Rightarrow \qquad x : y = 5 : 3.$ **Ans.**

(ii) $\dfrac{x}{y} = \dfrac{5}{3}$

Taking cube on both sides,

$$\dfrac{x^3}{y^3} = \dfrac{125}{27}$$

Applying componendo and dividendo rule,

$\Rightarrow \qquad \dfrac{x^3+y^3}{x^3-y^3} = \dfrac{125+27}{125-27}$

$\Rightarrow \qquad \dfrac{x^3+y^3}{x^3-y^3} = \dfrac{152}{98} = \dfrac{76}{49}$ **Ans.**

4. If $(x-9) : (3x+6)$ is the duplicate ratio of $4 : 9$, find the value of x.

Sol. As given $(x-9) : (3x+6)$ is duplicate ratio of $4 : 9$.

i.e., $\qquad \dfrac{x-9}{3x+6} = \left(\dfrac{4}{9}\right)^2$

$$\dfrac{x-9}{3x+6} = \dfrac{16}{81}$$

$\Rightarrow \qquad 81\,(x-9) = 16\,(3x+6)$

$\Rightarrow \qquad 81x - 729 = 48x + 96$

$\Rightarrow \qquad 81x - 48x = 96 + 729$

$\Rightarrow \qquad 33x = 825$

$\Rightarrow \qquad x = \dfrac{825}{33} = 25$

Thus, required value of x is 25. **Ans.**

5. Using the properties of proportion, solve for x, given $\dfrac{x^4+1}{2x^2} = \dfrac{17}{8}$.

Sol. Given, $\dfrac{x^4+1}{2x^2} = \dfrac{17}{8}$

Using Componendo and Dividendo,

$$\dfrac{x^4+1+2x^2}{x^4+1-2x^2} = \dfrac{17+8}{17-8}$$

$\Rightarrow \qquad \dfrac{(x^2+1)^2}{(x^2-1)^2} = \dfrac{25}{9}$

$\Rightarrow \qquad \dfrac{x^2+1}{x^2-1} = \dfrac{5}{3}$

{taking square root on both the sides}

Again applying Componendo and Dividendo,

$$\dfrac{x^2+1+x^2-1}{x^2+1-x^2+1} = \dfrac{5+3}{5-3}$$

$\Rightarrow \qquad \dfrac{2x^2}{2} = \dfrac{8}{2}$

$\Rightarrow \qquad x^2 = 4$

$\Rightarrow \qquad x = \pm 2$ **Ans.**

Chapter 9. Arithmetic Progression

1. Write down the first five terms of the A.P. with first term 8 and common difference 7.

Sol. Since arithmetic sequence is given by

$a, a + d, a + 2d, ...$, where a is the first term and d is the common difference

We have given that

$$a = 8, d = 7$$

Terms of A.P. are, 8, 15, 22, 29, 36, ... **Ans.**

2. Find the 17th term of the A.P. with first term 5 and common difference 2.

Sol. nth term of an A.P. is

$$a_n = a + (n - 1)\, d$$

∴ $$a_{17} = a + (17 - 1)\, d$$

$$= 5 + 16 \times 2 = 37. \quad \textbf{Ans.}$$

3. Find the 10th term and the general term for the sequence

$$9, 12, 15, 18, ...$$

Sol. We have first term

$$a = 9$$

and common difference

$$d = 12 - 9 = 3$$

$$a_{10} = a + 9d$$

$$= 9 + 9 \times 3$$

$$= 9 + 27 = 36$$

$$a_n = a + (n - 1)\, d$$

$$= 9 + (n - 1)\, 3$$

$$= 3n + 6. \quad \textbf{Ans.}$$

4. The third term of an A.P. is 16, and the 12th term is 79. Find the 41st term.

Sol. Let the first term be a and the common difference be d.

Since, $$a_3 = a + 2d = 16 \qquad ...(i)$$

and $$a_{12} = a + 11d = 79 \qquad ...(ii)$$

From equation (i) and (ii), we get

$$a = 2 \text{ and } d = 7$$

So, $$a_{41} = a + 40d$$

$$= 2 + 40 \times 7 = 282. \quad \textbf{Ans.}$$

5. Find the sum of the first 50 terms of the sequence.

$$1, 3, 5, 7, 9, ...$$

Sol. This is an A.P. with

$$a = 1, d = 2, n = 50$$

Using the formula,

$$S_n = \frac{n}{2} [2a + (n - 1)\, d]$$

$$S_{50} = \frac{50}{2} [2 \times 1 + (50 - 1) \times 2]$$

$$= 25 [2 + 49 \times 2]$$

$$= 25 [2 + 98] = 2500. \quad \textbf{Ans.}$$

6. Given the A.P. $40 + 37 + 34 + ...$, find S_{10}, a_n and expression for S_n.

Sol. Here $a = 40, d = -3$

Since $$S_n = \frac{n}{2} [2a + (n - 1)\, d]$$

So, $$S_{10} = 5 [80 + (- 27)]$$

$$= 265$$

Now, $$a_n = a + (n - 1)\, d$$

$$a_n = 40 + (n - 1)\, (- 3)$$

$$a_n = 40 - 3n + 3$$

$$a_n = 43 - 3n$$

also $$S_n = \frac{n}{2} [2 \times 40 + (n - 1)\, (- 3)]$$

$$= \frac{n}{2}\, (80 - 3n + 3)$$

$$= \frac{n}{2}\, (83 - 3n) \quad \textbf{Ans.}$$

7. Find the sum of all the integers from 100 to 200 inclusive.

Sol. The sequence 100, 101, ..., 200 is an A.P. with 101 terms, in which the first term, $a = 100$, and the last term, $l = 200$

So, $$S_{101} = \frac{n}{2}\, (a + l)$$

$$= \frac{101}{2} \times (100 + 200)$$

$$= 15150 \quad \textbf{Ans.}$$

8. Solve $1 + 6 + 11 + 16 + ... + x = 148$.

Sol. Since, the terms of the given series is an A.P. with $a = 1$ and the common difference $d = 5$.

Let there be n terms in this series.

Then,

$$1 + 6 + 11 + ... + x = 148$$

⇒ $$\frac{n}{2} [2a + (n - 1)\, d] = 148$$

$\Rightarrow \quad \dfrac{n}{2}[2 + (n-1)\,5] = 148$

$\Rightarrow \quad 5n^2 - 3n - 296 = 0$

$\Rightarrow \quad (n-8)(5n+37) = 0$

$\Rightarrow \qquad\qquad n = 8 \qquad (\because n \text{ is positive})$

Now, $\qquad\qquad x = n$th term

$\qquad\qquad\qquad = a + (n-1)\,d$

$\qquad\qquad\qquad = 1 + 7 \times 5 = 36$

$\Rightarrow \qquad\qquad x = 36.$ **Ans.**

Chapter 10. Geometric Progression

1. Write down the first five terms of the G.P. which has first term 1 and common ratio 1/2.

Sol. G.P. has the form, $a, ar, ar^2, \ldots\ldots$, where a is first term and r is the common ratio.

First five terms are a, ar, ar^2, ar^3, ar^4.

Here, $\qquad a = 1, r = 1/2$

So, $1, \dfrac{1}{2}, \dfrac{1}{4}, \dfrac{1}{8}, \dfrac{1}{16}, \ldots\ldots$ is the required G.P.

Ans.

2. Find a_n, a_6 and a_{15} for sequence $6, -18, 54, -162, \ldots\ldots$

Sol. The given sequence is a G.P. as

$$\dfrac{-18}{6} = \dfrac{54}{-18} = -3$$

where $a = 6$ and $r = -3$,

So, $\qquad a_n = ar^{n-1}$

$\qquad\qquad = 6 \times (-3)^{n-1}$

Therefore $\qquad a_6 = 6 \times (-3)^5 = -1458$

and $\qquad a_{15} = 6 \times (-3)^{14} = 6 \times 3^{14}$ **Ans.**

3. Find the 10th and 20th term of the G.P. with first term 3 and common ratio 2.

Sol. Here $a = 3, r = 2$, and $n = 10$ and 20.

Since nth term is given by $a_n = ar^{n-1}$

So, $\qquad a_{10} = 3\,(2)^9 = 1536$

and $\qquad a_{20} = 3\,(2)^{19} = 1572864.$ **Ans.**

4. Find the sum of six terms of G.P. $2, -6, +18 \ldots$

Sol. The series is a G.P. in which $a = 2, r = -3$.

So, $\qquad S_6 = \dfrac{a(1-r^6)}{1-r}$ as $(r < 1)$

$\qquad\qquad = \dfrac{2 \times \{1 - (-3)^6\}}{1+3}$

$\qquad\qquad S_6 = -364.$ **Ans.**

5. Find the sum of all the powers of 5 from 5^0 to 5^7.

Sol. The sum $5^0 + 5^1 + 5^2 + \ldots + 5^7$ is a G.P. with 8 terms, with $a = 1$ and $r = 5$,

So, $\qquad S_8 = \dfrac{a\,(r^8 - 1)}{r - 1}$ as $r > 1$

$\qquad\qquad = \dfrac{1 \cdot (5^8 - 1)}{5 - 1} = 97656.$ **Ans.**

6. Find the first term of the G.P. with second term 2 and the sum of infinite terms is 8.

Sol. Given, $ar = 2$ and $\dfrac{a}{1-r} = 8$

where a is the first term and r is the common ratio of the given G.P.

$$a = \dfrac{2}{r} \text{ and } a = 8 - 8r$$

$\Rightarrow \qquad \dfrac{2}{r} = 8 - 8r$

$\Rightarrow \qquad 2 = 8r - 8r^2$

$\Rightarrow \qquad 8r^2 - 8r + 2 = 0$

$\Rightarrow \qquad 4r^2 - 4r + 1 = 0$

$\Rightarrow \qquad (2r-1)^2 = 0$

$\Rightarrow \qquad (2r-1) = 0$

$\Rightarrow \qquad r = \dfrac{1}{2}$

Now, $ar = 2 \Rightarrow a = 4$

Hence, first term of the given G.P. is 4. **Ans.**

7. The 4th, 6th and the last term of a geometric progression are 10, 40 and 640 respectively. If the common ratio is positive, find the first term, common ratio and the number of terms of the series.*

Sol. Given : $\qquad a_4 = 10, a_6 = 40, a_n = 640$

$\therefore \qquad\qquad ar^3 = 10 \qquad\qquad \ldots\text{(i)}$

and $\qquad\qquad ar^5 = 40 \qquad\qquad \ldots\text{(ii)}$

On dividing (ii) by (i),

$$\dfrac{ar^5}{ar^3} = \dfrac{40}{10}$$

$\Rightarrow \qquad\qquad r^2 = 4$

$\Rightarrow \qquad\qquad r = 2 \qquad [\because r \text{ is positive}]$

Putting $r = 2$ in equation (i), we get

$$a \times 2^3 = 10$$

$\Rightarrow \qquad\qquad a = \dfrac{10}{8} = \dfrac{5}{4}$

---

* Frequently asked previous years Board Exam Questions.

Now, $\qquad a_n = 640$

$\Rightarrow \qquad ar^{n-1} = 640$

$\Rightarrow \qquad \dfrac{5}{4} \times (2)^{n-1} = 640$

$\Rightarrow \qquad 2^{n-1} = \dfrac{640 \times 4}{5} = 128 \times 4$

$\Rightarrow \qquad 2^{n-1} = 2^9$

$\therefore \qquad n - 1 = 9$

$\therefore \qquad n = 9 + 1 = 10$

Hence, $a = \dfrac{5}{4}$, $r = 2$ and $n = 10$ **Ans.**

8. The first and last term of a Geometrical Progression (G.P.) are 3 and 96 respectively. If the common ratio is 2, find :*

(i) 'n' the number of terms of the G.P.

(ii) Sum of the n terms.

Sol. Given, first term $(a) = 3$, Last term $(a_n) = 96$ and common ratio $(r) = 2$.

(i) $\because \qquad a_n = ar^{n-1}$

$\Rightarrow \qquad 96 = 3 \times 2^{n-1}$

$\Rightarrow \qquad \dfrac{96}{3} = 2^{n-1}$

$\Rightarrow \qquad 32 = 2^{n-1}$

$\Rightarrow \qquad 2^5 = 2^{n-1}$

$\Rightarrow \qquad n - 1 = 5 \Rightarrow n = 5 + 1 \Rightarrow n = 6.$ **Ans.**

(ii) Sum of n terms $(S_n) = \dfrac{a(r^n - 1)}{r - 1}$

$= \dfrac{3(2^6 - 1)}{2 - 1}$

$= 3 \times 63$

$= 189$ **Ans.**

9. Find the common ratio of an infinite G.P. whose each term is five times the sum of its succeeding terms.

Sol. Let a = first term of G.P.

and $\qquad r$ = common ratio

Given, $\qquad a = 5(ar + ar^2 + ar^3 + ...)$

$a = 5 \times \dfrac{ar}{1 - r}$

$5r = 1 - r$

$6r = 1$

$r = \dfrac{1}{6}.$ **Ans.**

10. Find geometric mean between :

(i) 3 and 27

(ii) 2 and 8

Sol. **(i)** Geometric mean between 3 and 27

$= \sqrt{3 \times 27} = 9$ **Ans.**

(ii) Geometric mean between 2 and 8

$= \sqrt{2 \times 8} = 4$ **Ans.**

Chapter 11. Co-ordinate Geometry

1. Find the co-ordinates of point P which divides the join of A $(6, -5)$ and B $(5, 3)$ in the ratio $2 : 5$.

Sol. Let the co-ordinates of P be (x, y)

$\therefore \qquad x = \dfrac{m_1 x_2 + m_2 x_1}{m_1 + m_2}$

A (6, –5)   P (x, y)   B (5, 3)

$= \dfrac{2 \times 5 + 5 \times 6}{2 + 5}$

$= \dfrac{10 + 30}{7}$

$= \dfrac{40}{7}$

$y = \dfrac{m_1 y_2 + m_2 y_1}{m_1 + m_2}$

$= \dfrac{2 \times 3 + 5 \times (-5)}{7}$

$= \dfrac{6 - 25}{7}$

$= -\dfrac{19}{7}$

Hence, the co-ordinates of P are $\left(\dfrac{40}{7}, \dfrac{-19}{7} \right)$.

Ans.

2. Find the ratio in which the point $(5, 4)$ divides the line joining points $(2, 1)$ and $(7, 6)$.

Sol. Let the required ratio be $m : n$

Let $\qquad (x_1, y_1) = (2, 1)$, $(x_2, y_2) = (7, 6)$,

$(x, y) = (5, 4)$

$x = \dfrac{m_1 x_2 + m_2 x_1}{m_1 + m_2}$

---

* **Frequently asked previous years Board Exam Questions.**

Formulae Based Questions

$$5 = \frac{m \times 7 + n \times 2}{m+n}$$

$\Rightarrow \quad 5m + 5n = 7m + 2n$

$\Rightarrow \quad 2m = 3n$

$\quad m : n = 3 : 2$ **Ans.**

3. In what ratio is the line joining P (5, 3) and Q (– 5, 3) divided by the *y*-axis ? Also find the coordinates of the point of intersection.*

Sol. Given points are $P(5, 3)$ and $Q(-5, 3)$

Let the coordinates of the point where this line meets *y*-axis be $A(0, y)$ and the ratio be $m : n$. Using section formula, we have

$$(x, y) = \left(\frac{m_1 x_2 + m_2 x_1}{m_1 + m_2}, \frac{m_1 y_2 + m_2 y_1}{m_1 + m_2}\right)$$

$\Rightarrow \quad 0 = \frac{-5m + 5n}{m+n}$

$\Rightarrow \quad 0 = -5m + 5n$

$\Rightarrow \quad 5m = 5n$

$\Rightarrow \quad m : n = 5 : 5 = 1 : 1$

Now, $\quad y = \frac{m \times 3 + 3 \times n}{m+n}$

$\quad = \frac{1 \times 3 + 1 \times 3}{1+1}$

$\quad = \frac{3+3}{2}$

$= \frac{6}{2} = 3$

Hence, the required ratio is 1 : 1 and the point of intersection is (0, 3). **Ans.**

4. The midpoint of the line segment joining $(2a, 4)$ and $(-2, 2b)$ is $(1, 2a + 1)$. Find the value of *a* and *b*.

Sol. Given, midpoint of line segment joining $(2a, 4)$ and $(-2, 2b)$ is $(1, 2a + 1)$

$$x = \frac{x_1 + x_2}{2} \qquad\qquad y = \frac{y_1 + y_2}{2}$$

$$1 = \frac{2a-2}{2} \qquad\qquad 2a+1 = \frac{4+2b}{2}$$

$$1 = a - 1 \qquad\qquad 2a+1 = 2+b$$

$\therefore \quad a = 2 \qquad\qquad \therefore \quad 5 - 2 = b$

$\qquad\qquad\qquad\qquad \therefore \quad b = 3$

Therefore, a = 2, b = 3. **Ans.**

5. Find the centroid of the triangle whose angular points are (3, – 6), (– 5, 2) and (10, – 2) respectively.

Sol. The co-ordinates of the centroid are

$$x = \frac{3-5+10}{3} = \frac{8}{3}$$

$$y = \frac{-6+2-2}{3} = \frac{-6}{3} = -2$$

∴ The centroid is (8/3, – 2). **Ans.**

Chapter 12. Reflection

1. Find the reflection of the point (7, – 4) in the point (3, – 1).

Sol. Let A' (x, y) be the reflection of the point (7, – 4) in the point (3, – 1) then, P is the midpoint of segment AA'.

By midpoint formula

$$3 = \frac{x+7}{2}$$

$6 = x + 7$

$x = -1$

$$-1 = \frac{-4+y}{2}$$

$-2 = -4 + y$

$y = 2$

Hence, the reflection of the point (7, – 4) in the point (3, – 1) is (– 1, 2). **Ans.**

Chapter 17. Mensuration

1. The circumference of the base of a cylindrical vessel is 132 cm and its height is 25 cm. Find the*

(i) radius of the cylinder

(ii) volume of cylinder.

$\left(use\ \pi = \dfrac{22}{7}\right)$

Sol. Given, circumference of base of cylinder = 132 cm, height of cylinder, h = 25 cm.

(i) Let r be the radius of cylinder

$$\therefore \qquad 2\pi r = 132$$

$$\Rightarrow \qquad 2 \times \frac{22}{7} \times r = 132$$

$$\Rightarrow \qquad r = \frac{132 \times 7}{2 \times 22} = 21 \text{ cm} \qquad \textbf{Ans.}$$

(ii) Volume of the cylinder

$$= \pi r^2 h$$
$$= \frac{22}{7} \times (21)^2 \times 25$$
$$= 34650 \text{ cm}^3. \qquad \textbf{Ans.}$$

2. The radius and height of a cylinder are in the ratio of 5 : 7 and its volume is 550 cm³. Find its radius. (Take $\pi = 22/7$)

Sol. Let the radius of the base and height of the cylinder be $5x$ cm and $7x$ cm respectively. Then,

Volume of the cylinder = 550 cm³

$$\Rightarrow \quad \frac{22}{7} \times (5x)^2 \times 7x = 550$$

$$\Rightarrow \quad \frac{22}{7} \times 25x^2 \times 7x = 550$$

$$\Rightarrow \qquad 22 \times 25x^3 = 550$$
$$\Rightarrow \qquad 550x^3 = 550$$
$$\Rightarrow \qquad x^3 = 1$$
$$\Rightarrow \qquad x = 1 \text{ cm}$$

Hence, radius of the cylinder

$$= 5x \text{ cm} = (5 \times 1) \text{ cm}$$
$$= 5 \text{ cm}. \qquad \textbf{Ans.}$$

3. The diameter of a garden roller is 1·4 m and it is 2 m long. How much area will it cover in 5 revolutions ? (Take $\pi = 22/7$)

Sol. Clearly,

Here, $\qquad r = \frac{1\cdot4}{2}$ m = 0·7 m and h = 2 m

$\therefore$ Curved surface area

$$= 2\pi r h = 2 \times \frac{22}{7} \times 0.7 \times 2 \text{ m}^2$$
$$= 8\cdot8 \text{ m}^2$$

Area covered = Curved surface area
$$\times \text{ No. of revolutions}$$

Hence, area covered
$$= 8\cdot8 \text{ m}^2 \times 5$$
$$= 44 \text{ m}^2. \qquad \textbf{Ans.}$$

4. Two cylinders have bases of same size. The diameter of each is 14 cm. One of the cylinders is 10 cm high and the other is 20 cm high. Find the ratio between their volumes.

Sol.

	Cylinder I	Cylinder II
Base diameter	14 cm	14 cm
Base radius	$r_1 = 7$ cm	$r_2 = 7$ cm
Height	$h_1 = 10$ cm	$h_2 = 20$ cm
Volume	$V_1 = \pi r_1^2 h_1$	$V_2 = \pi r_2^2 h_2$

$$V_1 : V_2 = \pi \times (7)^2 \times 10 \text{ cm}^3 : \pi \times (7)^2 \times 20 \text{ cm}^3$$

$$= 490\pi \text{ cm}^3 : 980\pi \text{ cm}^3$$

$$\therefore \qquad \frac{V_1}{V_2} = \frac{490\pi}{980\pi} = \frac{1}{2}$$

$$\Rightarrow \qquad V_1 : V_2 = 1 : 2. \qquad \textbf{Ans.}$$

5. A glass cylinder with diameter 20 cm has water to a height of 9 cm. A metal cube of 8 cm edge is immersed in it completely. Calculate the height by which water will rise in the cylinder. (Take $\pi = 3\cdot142$)

Sol. Suppose the water rises by h cm. Clearly water in the cylinder forms a cylinder of height h cm and radius 10 cm.

$\therefore$ Volume of the water displaced

$$= \text{Volume of the cube of edge 8 cm}$$
$$\Rightarrow \qquad \pi r^2 h = 8^3$$
$$\Rightarrow \quad 3\cdot142 \times 10^2 \times h = 8 \times 8 \times 8$$
$$\Rightarrow \qquad h = \frac{8 \times 8 \times 8}{3\cdot142 \times 10 \times 10} \text{ cm}$$
$$\Rightarrow \qquad h = 1\cdot6 \text{ cm}. \qquad \textbf{Ans.}$$

6. Water is being pumped out through a circular pipe whose external diameter is 7 cm. If the flow of water is 72 cm per second how many litres of water is being pumped out in one hour?

Sol. Volume of water that will be pumped out in 1 second

$$= \pi \left(\frac{7}{2}\right)^2 (72) \text{ cu. cm}$$

Volume of water that will be pumped out in one hour

$$= \pi \left(\frac{7}{2}\right)^2 (72)(3600) \text{ cu. cm}$$

$$= 99,79,200 \text{ cu. cm}$$

$$= 9979.2 \text{ litres.} \qquad \textbf{Ans.}$$

7. A well 28.8 m deep and of diameter 2 m is dug up. The soil dug out is spread all around the well to make a platform 1 m high considering the fact loose soil settled to a height in the ratio 6 : 5, find the width of the platform.

Sol. Volume of soil dug out

$$= \pi (1)^2 (28.8) \text{ cu. m.}$$

∴ Volume of soil that would be settled on the platform

$$= \frac{5 \times \pi \times 28.8}{6} \text{ cu. m.}$$

Let the width of the platform be r cm. Then,

$$\pi [(1 + r^2) - (1)^2 (1)] = \frac{5 \times \pi \times 28.8}{6}$$

$$\Rightarrow \quad (1 + r)^2 - 1 = \frac{5 \times 28.8}{6} = 24$$

$$\Rightarrow \quad (1 + r)^2 = 25$$

$$\Rightarrow \quad 1 + r = 5$$

$$\Rightarrow \quad r = 4 \text{ cm.} \qquad \textbf{Ans.}$$

8. The radius and height of cone are in the ratio 3 : 4. If its volume is 301.44 cu. cm. What is its radius ? What is its slant height ?(Take $\pi = 3.14$)

Sol. Let the radius of cone be $3x$ cm and the height $4x$ cm, then

$$\text{Volume of cone} = \frac{1}{3} \pi r^2 h$$

$$\Rightarrow \quad \frac{1}{3} \pi (3x)^2 (4x) = 301 \cdot 44$$

$$\Rightarrow \quad x^3 = 8 \Rightarrow x = 2$$

Thus, radius of cone is 6 cm and height 8 cm.

Now, slant height of cone

$$= \sqrt{(6)^2 + (8)^2}$$

$$= 10 \text{ cm.} \qquad \textbf{Ans.}$$

9. The diameter of two cones are equal. If their slant heights are in the ratio of 5 : 4. Find the ratio of their curved surface areas ?

Sol. Let their slant height be $5x$ and $4x$.

Given that diameter of two cones are equal

∴ $\qquad R_1 = R_2 = R$

$\qquad S_1 = \pi R l = \pi R (5x)$

$\qquad S_2 = \pi R l = \pi R (4x)$

∴ $\qquad \dfrac{S_1}{S_2} = \dfrac{\pi R (5x)}{\pi R (4x)} = \dfrac{5}{4}$

$\qquad S_1 : S_2 = 5 : 4 \qquad \textbf{Ans.}$

10. The ratio of the base area and curved surface of a conical tent is 40 : 41. If the height is 18 m, find the air capacity of tent in term of π.

Sol. Given, $\dfrac{\text{base area}}{\text{curved surface}} = \dfrac{40}{41}$

$$\Rightarrow \quad \frac{\pi r^2}{\pi r \sqrt{h^2 + r^2}} = \frac{40}{41}$$

$\left\{ \begin{array}{l} \text{where } h \text{ is the height and } r \text{ is} \\ \text{the radius of conical tent} \end{array} \right\}$

$$\Rightarrow \quad \frac{r}{\sqrt{18^2 + r^2}} = \frac{40}{41} \qquad (\because h = 18 \text{ m})$$

$$\Rightarrow \quad r = 80 \text{ m}$$

$$\text{Air capacity} = \frac{1}{3} \times \pi \times (80)^2 \times 18$$

$$= 38,400 \, \pi \text{ cu. m} \qquad \textbf{Ans.}$$

11. Find the volume and surface area of a sphere of diameter 21 cm.

Sol. Diameter of sphere = 21 cm

∴ Radius of sphere $= \dfrac{21}{2}$ cm

∴ Surface area of sphere $= 4 \pi r^2$

$$= 4 \times \frac{22}{7} \times \frac{21}{2} \times \frac{21}{2}$$

$$= 1386 \text{ cm}^2$$

$$\text{Volume of sphere} = \frac{4}{3} \pi r^3$$

$$= \frac{4}{3} \times \frac{22}{7} \times \frac{21}{2} \times \frac{21}{2} \times \frac{21}{2}$$

$$= 4851 \text{ cm}^3. \qquad \textbf{Ans.}$$

12. The volume of a sphere is $905\dfrac{1}{7}$ cm^3, find its diameter.

Sol. Volume of a sphere $= 905\dfrac{1}{7}$

$$\frac{4}{3} \pi r^3 = \frac{6336}{7}$$

$$\Rightarrow \quad r^3 = \frac{6336 \times 7 \times 3}{4 \times 22 \times 7}$$

$$\Rightarrow \quad r^3 = 216$$

$$\Rightarrow \quad r = \sqrt[3]{216}$$

$$\Rightarrow \quad r = 6 \text{ cm}$$

∴ Diameter of a sphere $= 2r = 2 \times 6 = 12$ cm.

$\textbf{Ans.}$

13. The surface area and volume of sphere are equal, find the radius of sphere.

Sol. Let the radius of sphere = r

$\because$ Volume of sphere = Surface area of sphere

$$\frac{4}{3}\pi r^3 = 4\pi r^2$$

$\Rightarrow$ $\qquad r^3 = 3r^2$

$\Rightarrow$ $\qquad r = 3$ cm

Hence, the radius of sphere = 3 cm. **Ans.**

14. There is a ratio of 1 : 4 between surface area of two spheres, find the ratio between their radius.

Sol. Let radius of spheres are r_1 and r_2.

So, surface area of spheres is $4\pi r_1^2$ and $4\pi r_2^2$

Ratio of surface area = $\dfrac{4\pi r_1^2}{4\pi r_1^2} = \dfrac{1}{4}$

$\therefore$ $\qquad \dfrac{r_1^2}{r_2^2} = \dfrac{1}{4}$

$\Rightarrow$ $\qquad \left(\dfrac{r_1}{r_2}\right)^2 = \dfrac{1}{4}$

$\Rightarrow$ $\qquad \dfrac{r_1}{r_2} = \sqrt{\dfrac{1}{4}}$

$\Rightarrow$ $\qquad \dfrac{r_1}{r_2} = \dfrac{1}{2}$

Hence, the ratio between their radius = 1 : 2.

Ans.

15. The radius of two spheres are in the ratio of 1 : 3. Find the ratio between their volume.

Sol. Let the radius of two sphere number is r_1 and r_2

$\because$ $\qquad \dfrac{r_1}{r_2} = \dfrac{1}{3}$

Volume of spheres,

$$V_1 = \frac{4}{3}\pi r_1^3$$

and $\qquad V_2 = \dfrac{4}{3}\pi r_2^3$

Now, $\qquad \dfrac{V_1}{V_2} = \dfrac{r_1^3}{r_2^3} = \left(\dfrac{r_1}{r_2}\right)^3$

$$= \left(\frac{1}{3}\right)^3 = \frac{1}{27}$$

$\therefore$ $\qquad V_1 : V_2 = 1 : 27$

Hence, the volume of two spheres are in the ratio of 1 : 27. **Ans.**

16. A sphere cut out from a side of 7 cm cube. Find the volume of this sphere ?

Sol. $\because$ Diameter of sphere equal to side of cube

$\therefore$ Radius of sphere = $\dfrac{7}{2}$ cm

Volume of sphere = $\dfrac{4}{3}\pi r^3$

$$= \frac{4}{3} \times \frac{22}{7} \times \frac{7}{2} \times \frac{7}{2} \times \frac{7}{2}$$

$$= \frac{539}{3}$$

$$= 179 \cdot 66 \text{ cm}^3. \qquad \textbf{Ans.}$$

17. A cone and a hemisphere have equal bases and equal volumes. Find the ratio of their heights.

Sol. Let, height of cone = h

and height of hemisphere = H

$\therefore$ Volume of cone = Volume of hemisphere

$$\frac{1}{3}\pi r^2 h = \frac{2}{3}\pi r^3$$

$\Rightarrow$ $\dfrac{1}{3}\pi r^2 h = \dfrac{2}{3}\pi r^3 H$ $\qquad (\because H = r)$

$\Rightarrow$ $\qquad \dfrac{h}{H} = \dfrac{2\pi r^2 \times 3}{3\pi r^2}$

$\Rightarrow$ $\qquad \dfrac{h}{H} = \dfrac{2}{1}$

$\Rightarrow$ $\qquad h : H = 2 : 1.$ **Ans.**

18. Marbles of diameter 1.4 cm dropped into a beaker containing some water are fully submerged. The diameter of beaker is 7 cm. Find how many marbles have been dropped in it if the water rises by 5.6 cm.

Sol. Volume of water that rises in putting marbles in the beaker.

$$= \pi \left(\frac{7}{2}\right)^2 \times (5.6) \text{ cu. cm}$$

Volume of one marble

$$= \frac{4}{3} \times (0.7)^3 \text{ cu. cm}$$

$\therefore$ Number of marbles

$$= \frac{\pi \left(\dfrac{7}{2}\right)^2 \times 5.6}{\dfrac{4}{3}\pi (0.7)^3} = 150 \quad \textbf{Ans.}$$

19. Find the weight of a lead pipe 35 cm long. The external diameter of the pipe is 2·4 cm and thickness of the pipe is 2 mm, given 1 cm^3 of lead weighs 10 gm.

Sol. External radius 'R' = 1·2 cm

Internal radius 'r' = 1·0 cm

[Since internal radius = external radius – thickness]

Height 'h' = 35 cm

$\therefore$ Volume of the pipe

$= \pi h [R^2 - r^2]$

$= \dfrac{22}{7} \times 35 \times [(1·2)^2 - (1·0)^2]$

$= 48·4$ cm^3

$\therefore$ Weight of lead pipe

$= 10 \times 48·4$

$= 484$ gm. **Ans.**

20. The total surface area of a hollow metal cylinder, open at both ends of external radius 8 cm and height 10 cm is 338 π cm^2. Taking r to be inner radius, write down an equation in r and use it to state the thickness of the metal in the cylinder.

Sol. Surface area of the hollow cylinder = 338π cm^2

$2\pi(8)10 + 2\pi(r)10 + 2[\pi(8)^2 - \pi(r)^2] = 338\pi$

$\Rightarrow \quad 160 + 20r + 2(64 - r^2) = 338$

$\Rightarrow \quad -2r^2 + 20r - 50 = 0$

$\Rightarrow \quad r^2 - 10r + 25 = 0$

$\Rightarrow \quad (r - 5)^2 = 0$

$\Rightarrow \quad r = 5$

$\therefore$ Thickness of the metal in the cylinder = 8 – r

$= 8 - 5 = 3$ cm. **Ans.**

21. A spherical cannon ball, 28 cm in diameter is melted and recast into a right circular conical mould, the base of which is 35 cm in diameter. Find the height of the cone, correct to one place of decimal.

Sol. Let h be the height of cone. Then

$$\dfrac{1}{3}\pi\left(\dfrac{35}{2}\right)^2 h = \dfrac{4}{3}\pi(14)^3$$

(Because the volume of conical mould is same as that of the spherical cannon ball.)

* Frequently asked previous years Board Exam Questions.

$\Rightarrow \qquad h = \dfrac{4 \times 14 \times 14 \times 14 \times 2 \times 2}{35 \times 35}$

$\Rightarrow \qquad h = \dfrac{896}{25} = 35.84$ cm. **Ans.**

22. A solid spherical ball of radius 6 cm is melted and recast into 64 identical spherical marbles. Find the radius of each marble.*

Sol. Let the radius of each spherical marble be r cm. Then, Volume of 64 spherical marbles

$= $ Volume of solid spherical ball

$\Rightarrow \quad 64 \times \dfrac{4}{3}\pi r^3 = \dfrac{4}{3} \times \pi \times 6^3$

$\Rightarrow \qquad r^3 = \dfrac{6 \times 6 \times 6}{64}$

$\Rightarrow \qquad r^3 = \left(\dfrac{6}{4}\right)^3$

or $\qquad r = \dfrac{6}{4} = 1.5$

Hence, the radius of each marble is 1.5 cm.

Ans.

23. A solid sphere of radius 15 cm is melted and recast into solid right circular cones of radius 2·5 cm and height 8 cm. Calculate the number of cones recast.

Sol. Number of cones

$= \dfrac{\text{Volume of solid sphere}}{\text{Volume of 1 cone}}$

$= \dfrac{\dfrac{4}{3}\pi(15)^3}{\dfrac{1}{3}\pi(2·5)^2 \times 8}$

$= \dfrac{4 \times 15 \times 15 \times 15}{2·5 \times 2·5 \times 8}$

$= 270$ **Ans.**

24. A hollow sphere of internal and external radii 6 cm and 8 cm respectively is melted and recast into small cones of base radius 2 cm and height 8 cm. Find the number of cones.

Sol. Volume of metal in hollow sphere

$= \dfrac{4}{3}\pi(8^3 - 6^3)$

$= \dfrac{1184}{3}\pi$ cm^3

Volume of metal in one cone

$$= \frac{1}{3} \pi r^2 h$$

$$= \frac{1}{3} \pi \times 2^2 \times 8$$

$$= \frac{32}{3} \pi \text{ cm}^3$$

Number of cones

$$= \frac{\text{Volume of metal in sphere}}{\text{Volume of metal in one cone}}$$

$$= \frac{\dfrac{1184}{3} \pi}{\dfrac{32}{3} \pi}$$

$$= \frac{1184}{32}$$

$$= 37 \qquad \textbf{Ans.}$$

25. How many spherical bullets can be made out of a solid cube of lead whose edge measures 44 cm, each bullet being 4 cm in diameter ?

Sol. Let the total number of bullets be x

Radius of a spherical bullet $= \dfrac{4}{2} = 2$ cm

Now, volume of a spherical bullet

$$= \frac{4}{3} \pi \times (2)^3 = \frac{4}{3} \times \frac{22}{7} \times 8$$

∴ Volume of x spherical bullets

$$= \frac{4}{3} \times \frac{22}{7} \ 8 \times x \text{ cm}^3$$

Volume of the solid cube $= (44)^3 \text{ cm}^3$

Clearly, volume of x spherical bullets

$$= \text{volume of cube}$$

$$\frac{4}{3} \times \frac{22}{7} \ 8 \times x = 44 \times 44 \times 44$$

$$x = \frac{44 \times 44 \times 44 \times 7 \times 3}{4 \times 22 \times 8}$$

$$x = 2541$$

Hence, total number of spherical bullets are 2541. **Ans.**

26. Two solid spheres of radii 2 cm and 4 cm are melted and recast into a cone of height 8 cm. Find the radius of the cone so formed.

Sol. Volume of solid sphere of radius 2 cm

$$= \frac{4}{3} \pi (2)^3 = \frac{32}{3} \pi \text{ cm}^3$$

Volume of solid sphere of radius 4 cm

$$= \frac{4}{3} \pi (4)^3$$

$$= \frac{256}{3} \text{ cm}^3$$

Total Volume $= \left(\dfrac{32}{3} \pi + \dfrac{256}{3} \pi \right) \text{cm}^3$

$$= 96 \pi \text{ cm}^3$$

Height of Cone = 8 cm

∴   Volume of Cone formed

$$= \frac{1}{3} \pi r^2 h$$

Volume of the two spheres = Volume of cone

$$\Rightarrow \qquad 96 \pi = \frac{1}{3} \pi r^2 \times 8$$

$$\Rightarrow \qquad r^2 = \frac{96 \times 3}{8}$$

$$\Rightarrow \qquad r = \sqrt{36}$$

$$\Rightarrow \qquad r = 6 \text{ cm}$$

Hence, the radius of the cone formed is 6 cm.
Ans.

27. A solid metallic sphere of radius 6 cm is melted and made into a solid cylinder of height 32 cm. Find the :

(i)   radius of the cylinder

(ii) curved surface area of the cylinder*

(*Take* $\pi = 3.1$)

Sol. Given, radius of sphere $(r_1) = 6$ cm

and height of cylinder $(h) = 32$ cm

∴   Volume of sphere $(V_1) = \dfrac{4}{3} \pi r_1^3$

$$= \frac{4}{3} \pi \times (6)^3 \text{ cm}^3$$

Let radius of cylinder be r_2.

∴   Volume of cylinder, $(V_2) = \pi r_2^2 h$

$$= \pi r_2^2 \times 32 \text{ cm}^3$$

∵ $\qquad\qquad V_1 = V_2$

$$\Rightarrow \qquad \frac{4}{3} \pi \times 6^3 = \pi r_2^2 \times 32$$

$$\Rightarrow \qquad r_2^2 = \frac{4 \times \pi \times 6^3}{3 \times \pi \times 32}$$

$$\Rightarrow \qquad r_2^2 = 9$$

$$\Rightarrow \qquad r_2 = 3$$

(i) Radius of the cylinder, $(r_2) = 3$ cm   **Ans.**

Formulae Based Questions

* Frequently asked previous years Board Exam Questions.

(ii) Curved surface area of the cylinder

$$= 2\pi r_2 h$$
$$= 2 \times 3.1 \times 3 \times 32$$
$$= 595.2 \text{ cm}^2 \qquad \textbf{Ans.}$$

28. A certain number of metallic cones, each of radius 2 cm and height 3 cm are melted and recast into a solid sphere of radius 6 cm. Find the number of cones.

Sol. Volume of metallic cone

$$= \frac{1}{3}\pi r^2 h$$
$$= \frac{1}{3}\pi \times (2)^2 \times 3$$
$$= 4\pi \text{ cm}^3$$

Volume of solid sphere

$$= \frac{4}{3}\pi r^3$$
$$= \frac{4}{3}\pi \times (6)^3$$
$$= 288\,\pi$$

∴ Number of cones

$$= \frac{\text{Volume of solid sphere}}{\text{Volume of metallic cone}}$$
$$= \frac{288\,\pi}{4\,\pi} = 72 \qquad \textbf{Ans.}$$

29. A hemispherical bowl of diameter 7·2 cm is filled completely with chocolate sauce. This sauce is poured into an inverted cone of radius 4·8 cm. Find the height of the cone.

Sol. Volume of hemispherical bowl

$$= \frac{2}{3}\pi r^3 = \frac{2}{3}\pi\,(3.6)^3$$

Volume of cone $= \dfrac{1}{3}\pi r^2 h$

$$= \frac{1}{3}\pi \times (4.8)^2 \times h$$

Volume of bowl = Volume of cone

$$\Rightarrow \quad \frac{2}{3}\pi \times (3.6)^3 = \frac{1}{3}\pi \times (4.8)^2 \times h$$

$$\Rightarrow \quad h = \frac{2 \times 3.6 \times 3.6 \times 3.6}{4.8 \times 4.8}$$

$$\Rightarrow \quad h = 4.05 \text{ cm} \qquad \textbf{Ans.}$$

30. A vessel is in the form of an inverted cone. Its height is 11 cm and the radius of its top which is open, is 2·5 cm. It is filled with water up to the rim. When lead shots, each of which is a sphere of radius 0·25 cm, are dropped into the vessel, $\dfrac{2}{5}$ th of the water flows out. Find the number of lead shots dropped into the vessel.

Sol. Volume of n lead shots

$$= \text{Volume of water displaced}$$

$$n \times \frac{4}{3}\pi r^3 = \frac{2}{5} \times \frac{1}{3}\pi R^2 H$$

$$\therefore \quad n = \frac{\dfrac{2}{5} \times \dfrac{1}{3}\pi R^2 H}{\dfrac{4}{3}\pi r^3}$$

$$= \frac{2R^2 H}{5 \times 4r^3}$$

$$= \frac{2 \times 2.5^2 \times 11}{5 \times 4 \times (0.25)^3}$$

$$= 440 \text{ shots} \qquad \textbf{Ans.}$$

31. A glass cylinder with diameter 20 cm has water to a height of 9 cm. A metal cube of 8 cm edge is immersed in it completely. Calculate the height by which the water will rise up in the cylinder. Answer correct to the nearest mm.

(Take $\pi = 3\cdot142$)

Sol. Let the height by which the water ups

$$= h \text{ cm}$$

Volume of the increase in water

$$= 3.142 \times 10 \times 10 \times h \text{ cm}^3$$

Volume of the cube $= 8 \times 8 \times 8 \text{ cm}^3$

Both the above volumes are equal

$$\therefore \quad 3.142 \times 10 \times 10 \times h = 8 \times 8 \times 8$$

$$h = \frac{8 \times 8 \times 8}{3.142 \times 10 \times 10}$$

$$= 1.6 \text{ cm}$$

$$h = 16 \text{ mm.} \qquad \textbf{Ans.}$$

32. A road roller is cylindrical in shape, its circular end has a diameter of 1·4 m and its width is 4 m. It is used to level a play ground measuring 70 m × 40 m. Find the minimum number of complete revolutions that the roller must take in order to cover the entire ground once.

Sol. Curved surface area of the road roller

$$= 2\pi rh$$

$$= 2 \times \frac{22}{7} \times 0.7 \times 4$$

$$= 17.6 \text{ m}^2$$

Area of the play ground $= 70 \times 40$

$$= 2800 \text{ m}^2$$

∴ Number of revolutions to cover the entire ground

$$= \frac{2800}{17.6} = 159\frac{1}{11}$$

∴ Number of complete revolutions = 160 **Ans.**

Chapter 19. Statistics

1. Find the mean of 4, 7, 12, 8, 11, 9, 13, 15, 2, 7.

Sol. Here, $n = 10$

and $\qquad \Sigma x = 4 + 7 + 12 + 8 + 11 + 9$
$$+ 13 + 15 + 2 + 7$$
$$= 88$$

∴ $\qquad$ Mean $\overline{X} = \dfrac{\Sigma x}{n}$

$$= \frac{88}{10} = 8.8. \qquad \textbf{Ans.}$$

2. Find the mean of first five natural numbers.

Sol. First five natural numbers are 1, 2, 3, 4 and 5

Hence,

Mean $\qquad \overline{X} = \dfrac{\Sigma x}{n}$

$$= \frac{1 + 2 + 3 + 4 + 5}{5} = \frac{15}{5}$$

∴ $\qquad \overline{X} = 3.$ $\qquad \textbf{Ans.}$

3. There are 45 students in a class, in which 15 are girls. The average weight of 15 girls is 45 kg and 30 boys is 52 kg. Find the mean weight in kg of the entire class.

Sol. Here, $n_1 = 15$, $n_2 = 30$, $\overline{X}_1 = 45$ kg and $\overline{X}_2 = 52$ kg.

∴ $\quad \overline{X} = \dfrac{n_1\overline{X}_1 + n_2\overline{X}_2}{n_1 + n_2} = \dfrac{15 \times 45 + 30 \times 52}{15 + 30}$

$$= \frac{2235}{45} \text{ kg}$$

$$= 49.67 \text{ kg.}$$

Hence, the mean weight of the entire class is 49.67 kg. $\qquad \textbf{Ans.}$

4. In X standard, there are three sections A, B and C with 25, 40 and 35 students, respectively. The average marks of section A is 70%, section B is 65% and of section C is 50%. Find the average marks of the entire X standard.

Sol. Here, $n_1 = 25$, $n_2 = 40$, $n_3 = 35$, $\overline{X}_1 = 70$, $\overline{X}_2 = 65$ and $\overline{X}_3 = 50$.

Let $\overline{X}$ denote the average marks of the entire X standard. Then,

$$\overline{X} = \frac{n_1\overline{X}_1 + n_2\overline{X}_2 + n_3\overline{X}_3}{n_1 + n_2 + n_3}$$

$$= \frac{25 \times 70 + 40 \times 65 + 35 \times 50}{25 + 40 + 35}$$

$$= \frac{1750 + 2600 + 1750}{100}$$

$$= \frac{6100}{100} = 61$$

Hence, the average marks of the entire X standard is 61%. $\qquad \textbf{Ans.}$

5. There are 50 students in a class in which 40 are boys and rest are girls. The average weight of the class is 44 kg and the average weight of the girls is 40 kg. Find the average weight of the boys.

Sol. We have

$$n = \text{No. of students in a class} = 50$$

$$n_1 = \text{No. of boys in a class} = 40$$

$$n_2 = \text{No. of girls in a class} = 10$$

$$\overline{X}_1 = \text{Average weight of boys} = ?$$

$$\overline{X}_2 = \text{Average weight of girls} = 40 \text{ kg.}$$

∴ $\qquad \overline{X} = \dfrac{n_1\overline{X}_1 + n_2\overline{X}_2}{n_1 + n_2}$

⇒ $\qquad 44 = \dfrac{40\overline{X}_1 + 10 \times 40}{40 + 10}$

⇒ $\quad 50 \times 44 = 40\overline{X}_1 + 400$

⇒ $\qquad 2200 = 40\overline{X}_1 + 400$

⇒ $\qquad 40\overline{X}_1 = 1800$

$\Rightarrow \qquad \overline{X}_1 = 45$

Hence, the average weight of boys is 45 kg.

Ans.

6. The average score of boys in an examination of a school is 71 and of girls is 73. The average score of school in that examination is 71·8. Find the ratio of the number of boys to the number of girls appeared in the examination.

Sol. Let $\overline{X}_1$ and $\overline{X}_2$ be the average scores of boys and girls respectively and $\overline{X}$ be the average of both boys and girls. Then

$$\overline{X}_1 = 71, \ \overline{X}_2 = 73, \ \overline{X} = 71\cdot8.$$

$\therefore \qquad \overline{X} = \dfrac{n_1 \overline{X}_1 + n_2 \overline{X}_2}{n_1 + n_2}$

$\Rightarrow \qquad 71\cdot8 = \dfrac{n_1 \times 71 + n_2 \times 73}{n_1 + n_2}$

$\Rightarrow \quad 71\cdot8 \, (n_1 + n_2) = 71 n_1 + 73 n_2$

$\Rightarrow \qquad 0\cdot8 n_1 = 1\cdot2 n_2$

$\Rightarrow \qquad 8 n_1 = 12 n_2$

$\Rightarrow \qquad \dfrac{n_1}{n_2} = \dfrac{12}{8} = \dfrac{3}{2}$

Hence, $\quad n_1 : n_2 = 3 : 2.$ **Ans.**

7. The mean of the following data is 16. Calculate the value of f.*

Marks	5	10	15	20	25
No. of Students	3	7	f	9	6

Sol.

Marks x_i	No. of students f_i	$f_i x_i$
5	3	15
10	7	70
15	f	$15f$
20	9	180
25	6	150
	$\sum f_i = 25 + f$	$\sum f_i x_i =$ $415 + 15f$

We know, $\quad \text{mean} = \dfrac{\sum f_i x_i}{\sum f_i}$

$\Rightarrow \qquad 16 = \dfrac{415 + 15f}{25 + f}$

$\Rightarrow \qquad 400 + 16f = 415 + 15f$

---
* Frequently asked previous years Board Exam Questions.

$\Rightarrow \qquad 16f - 15f = 415 - 400$

$\Rightarrow \qquad f = 15$ **Ans.**

8. From the following numbers find the median :

10, 75, 3, 81, 17, 27, 4, 48, 12, 47, 9, 15.

Sol. On arranging in ascending order

3, 4, 9, 10, 12, 15, 17, 27, 47, 48, 75, 81

Here, $\qquad n = 12$ which is even

Therefore,

$\text{Median} = \dfrac{\left(\dfrac{n}{2}\right)^{\text{th}} \text{term} + \left(\dfrac{n}{2}+1\right)^{\text{th}} \text{term}}{2}$

$= \dfrac{\left(\dfrac{12}{2}\right)^{\text{th}} \text{term} + \left(\dfrac{12}{2}+1\right)^{\text{th}} \text{term}}{2}$

$= \dfrac{6^{\text{th}} \text{term} + 7^{\text{th}} \text{term}}{2}$

$= \dfrac{15 + 17}{2} = \dfrac{32}{2} = 16$

Median = 16. **Ans.**

9. Find the median of the following values :

37, 31, 42, 43, 46, 25, 39, 45, 32.

Sol. Arranging the data in ascending order, we have

25, 31, 32, 37, 39, 42, 43, 45, 46

Here, the number of observations, n = 9(odd)

$\therefore \quad \text{Median} = \text{Value of} \left(\dfrac{9+1}{2}\right)^{\text{th}} \text{observation}$

$= \text{Value of } 5^{\text{th}} \text{ observation}$

$= 39.$ **Ans.**

10. The median of the following observation 11, 12, 14, 18, $(x + 4)$, 30, 32 35, 41 arranged in ascending order is 24. Find x.

Sol. The given observations are :

11, 12, 14, 18, $(x + 4)$, 30, 32, 35, 41

No. of terms are odd *i.e.*, 9

$\therefore \qquad \text{Median} = \left(\dfrac{n+1}{2}\right)^{\text{th}} \text{term}$

$= \left(\dfrac{9+1}{2}\right)^{\text{th}} \text{term}$

$= \text{5th term}$

∴   Median = $x + 4$

Given,   Median = 24

∴ $x + 4 = 24$

⇒ $x = 20$ **Ans.**

11. The median of the following observations arranged in ascending order is 24. Find x :

11, 12, 14, 18, $x + 2$, $x + 4$, 30, 32, 35, 41.

Sol. The given observations are :

11, 12, 14, 18, $x + 2$, $x + 4$, 30, 32, 35

$n = 10$ (even), Median = 24

∴ Median $= \dfrac{\left(\dfrac{n}{2}\right)^{th} term + \left(\dfrac{n}{2} + 1\right)^{th} term}{2}$

$= \dfrac{\left(\dfrac{10}{2}\right)^{th} term + \left(\dfrac{10}{2} + 1\right)^{th} term}{2}$

Median $= \dfrac{5^{th}\ term + 6^{th}\ term}{2}$

⇒ $24 = \dfrac{x + 2 + x + 4}{2}$

⇒ $2x + 6 = 24 \times 2$

⇒ $2x = 48 - 6$

⇒ $2x = 42$

⇒ $x = 21.$ **Ans.**

12. Find the mode from the following data :

110, 120, 130, 120, 110, 140, 130, 120, 140, 120.

Sol. Arranging the data in the form of a frequency table, we have :

Value	Tally bars	Frequency
110				2
120						4
130				2
140				2

Since, the value 120 occurs maximum number of times i.e., 4.

Hence, the modal value is 120.   **Ans.**

13. Find the mode for the following series :

2·5, 2·3, 2·2, 2·2, 2·4, 2·7, 2·7, 2·5, 2·3, 2·2, 2·6, 2·2.

Sol. Arranging the data in the form of a frequency table, we have :

Value	Tally bars	Frequency
2·2	||||	4
2·3	||	2
2·4			1
2·5	||	2
2·6			1
2·7	||	2

We see that the value 2·2 has the maximum frequency i.e., 4.

So, 2·2 is the mode for the given series.   **Ans.**

14. Find out the mode from the following data :

Wages (in ₹)	Number of persons
125	3
175	8
225	21
275	6
325	4
375	2

Sol. Clearly, the value 225 occurs maximum number of times. So, the modal wage is ₹ 225.   **Ans.**

15. Find the mean, median and mode of the following distribution :

8, 10, 7, 6, 10, 11, 6, 13, 10

Sol. Arranging the number of in ascending order 6, 6, 7, 8, 10, 10, 10, 11, 13

Mean $\overline{X} = \dfrac{\Sigma x}{n} = \dfrac{81}{9} = 9.$ **Ans.**

Median $= \left[\dfrac{n + 1}{2}\right]^{th}$ term

$= \left(\dfrac{9 + 1}{2}\right)^{th} = $ 5th term

∴   Median = 10   **Ans.**

As 10 is repeating 3 times which is highest frequency.

So, Mode is 10.   **Ans.**

Chapter 20. Probability

1. If the probability of winning a game is $\dfrac{5}{11}$, find the probability of losing the game.

Sol. Probability of winning the game,

$$P(E) = \dfrac{5}{11}$$

∴ Probability of losing the game

$$P(\bar{E}) = 1 - P(E)$$

$$= 1 - \frac{5}{11} = \frac{6}{11}$$ **Ans.**

2. If P (E) = 0·20, then what is the probability of 'not E' ?

Sol. $$P(E) = 0·20$$

$$P(\text{not } E) = 1 - P(E)$$

$$= 1 - 0·20$$

$$= 0·80$$ **Ans.**

3. Find the probability of an impossible event.

Sol. P (impossible event) = 0 **Ans.**

4. A die is thrown once. Find the probability of getting a prime number.

Sol. Total outcome = 6

Prime numbers = 2, 3, 5

∴ P (prime number) = $\frac{3}{6} = \frac{1}{2}$ **Ans.**

5. A die is thrown once. Find the probability of getting "at most 2."

Sol. Given,

Sample space S = {1, 2, 3, 4, 5, 6}

$$n(S) = 6$$

$$A = \{1, 2\}$$

$$n(A) = 2$$

∴ $$P(A) = \frac{n(A)}{n(S)} = \frac{2}{6} = \frac{1}{3}$$ **Ans.**

6. Two dice are thrown together. What is the probability of getting a doublet ?

Sol. Total number of possible outcomes = 36

E : doublets are (1, 1), (2, 2), (3, 3), (4, 4), (5, 5), (6, 6)

Outcomes favourable to E = 6

∴ P (a doublet)

$$= \frac{\text{Number of favourable outcomes}}{\text{Total number of outcomes}}$$

$$= \frac{6}{36} = \frac{1}{6}$$ **Ans.**

7. Two dice, one blue and one grey, are thrown at the same time. What is the probability that the sum of the two numbers appearing on the top of the dice is 8 ?

Sol. Total number of outcomes = 36

Favourable outcomes are

(2, 6), (3, 5), (4, 4), (5, 3), (6, 2) = 5

∴ Required probability = $\frac{5}{36}$ **Ans.**

8. Two different dice are tossed together. Find the probability that the product of the number on the top of the dice is 6.

Sol. Product of 6 are (1, 6), (2, 3), (6, 1), (3, 2)

No. of possible outcomes = 4

Total numbers of outcome = 6 × 6 = 36

P (Product of 6) $= \frac{4}{36} = \frac{1}{9}$ **Ans.**

9. Two coins are tossed together. Find the probability of getting both heads or both tails.

Sol. Possible cases are HH, HT, TH, TT

$$P(HH \text{ or } TT) = \frac{2}{4} = \frac{1}{2}$$ **Ans.**

10. Two unbaised coins are tossed simultaneously. Find the probability of getting :

(i) atleast one head,

(ii) atmost one head,

(iii) no head.

Sol. Sample space = {HH, HT, TH, TT}

(i) P(atleast one head) = $\frac{3}{4}$ **Ans.**

(ii) P(atmost one head) = $\frac{3}{4}$ **Ans.**

(iii) P(no head) = $\frac{1}{4}$ **Ans.**

11. Three coins are tossed simultaneously once. Find the probability of getting :

(i) atleast one tail

(ii) no tail

Sol. Sample space = {HHH, HTH, HHT, THH, TTH, THT, HTT, TTT}

(i) P (atleast one tail) = $\frac{7}{8}$ **Ans.**

(ii) P (number tail) = $\frac{1}{8}$ **Ans.**

12. A card is drawn at random from a well shuffled pack of 52 cards. Find the probability of getting neither a red card nor a queen.

Sol. Total number of cards = 52

Number of red cards = 26

Number of queens which are not red = 2

∴ Cards which are neither red nor queen

$$= 52 - [26 + 2] = 24$$

∴ Required probability

$$= \frac{24}{52} = \frac{6}{13}.$$ **Ans.**

13. One card is drawn from a well shuffled deck of 52 cards. Find the probability of getting :

(i) a non face card,

(ii) a black king.

Sol. We know that in a deck of cards total face cards

= 12

(i) P (non-face card) = $\frac{52-12}{52} = \frac{10}{13}$

(ii) P (black king) = $\frac{2}{52} = \frac{1}{26}$ **Ans.**

14. Five Cards, Ten, Jack, Queen, King and Ace of diamonds are well shuffled. One card is picked up from them.

(i) Find the probability that the drawn card is Queen.

(ii) If Queen is put aside, then find the probability that the second card drawn is an ace.

Sol. Total cards = 5

(i) P (Queen) = $\frac{1}{5}$ **Ans.**

(ii) Since, Queen was kept aside, 5 – 1 = 4

P (Ace) = $\frac{1}{4}$ **Ans.**

15. Out of 200 bulbs in a box, 12 bulbs are defective. One bulb is taken out at random from the box. What is the probability that the drawn bulb is not defective ?

Sol. Total number of bulbs

= 200

Total number of non defective bulbs

= 200 – 12 = 188

∴ Required probability

$$= \frac{188}{200}$$

$$= \frac{47}{50}$$ **Ans.**

16. A letter of English alphabet is chosen at random. Find the probability that the chosen letter is a consonant.

Sol. In the English language there are 26 alphabets in which consonants are 21.

The probability of chosen letter is a consonant = $\frac{21}{26}$

Ans.

17. A lot consists of 144 ball pens of which 20 are defective and others are good. Nuri will buy a pen if it is good, but will not buy if it is defective. The shopkeeper draws one pen at random and gives it to her. What is the probability that :

(i) She will buy it ?

(ii) She will not buy it ?

Sol. Total number of pens

= 144

Defective pens = 20

Good pens = 144 – 20 = 124

(i) Probability of purchasing pen

$$= \frac{124}{144} = \frac{31}{36}$$

(ii) Probability of not purchasing pen

$$= \frac{20}{144} = \frac{5}{36}$$ **Ans.**

18. A bag contains 5 red balls and some blue balls. If the probability of drawing a blue ball is double that of red ball, find number of blue balls in the bag.

Sol. Let the number of blue balls = x

Total number of balls = $x + 5$

Number of red balls = 5

$$\frac{x}{x+5} = 2\left(\frac{5}{x+5}\right)$$

$$x = 10$$ **Ans.**

19. A group consists of 12 persons, of which 3 are extremely patient, other 6 are extremely honest and rest are extremely kind. A person from the group is selected at random. Assuming that each person is equally likely to be selected, find the probability of selecting a person who is

(i) extremely patient

(ii) extremely kind or honest. Which of the almost values you prefer more ?

Formulae Based Questions

Sol. (i) P (extremely patient)

$$= \frac{3}{12} = \frac{1}{4} \quad \textbf{Ans.}$$

(ii) P (extremely kind or honest)

$$= \frac{6+3}{12} = \frac{9}{12} = \frac{3}{4}$$

Extremely Honest. **Ans.**

20. Cards marked with number 3, 4, 5, ..., 50 are placed in a box and mixed thoroughly. A card is drawn at random from the box. Find the probability that the selected card bears a perfect square number.

Sol. Possible favourable outcomes are 4, 9, 16, 25, 36, 49, i.e., 6.

$$\therefore \text{ P (perfect square number)} = \frac{6}{48} \text{ or } \frac{1}{8}. \quad \textbf{Ans.}$$

21. A bag contains cards numbered from 1 to 25. A card is drawn at random from the bag. Find the probability that number is divisible by both 2 and 3.

Sol. The numbers divisible by 2 and 3 both = 6, 12, 18, 24 = 4

$$\therefore \text{ P (number divisible by both 2 and 3)}$$
$$= \frac{4}{25} \quad \textbf{Ans.}$$

22. A number is selected at random from 1 to 30. Find the probability that it is a prime number.

Sol. Prime numbers are 2, 3, 5, 7, 11, 13, 17, 19, 23, 29 = 10

Number of possible outcomes = 30

$$\text{P (prime no.)} = \frac{10}{30} = \frac{1}{3} \quad \textbf{Ans.}$$

23. A box contains 90 discs, numbered from 1 to 90. If one disc is drawn at random from box, find the probability that it bears a prime number less than 23.

Sol. Number of possible outcomes = 90

Prime numbers less than 23

$$= 2, 3, 5, 7, 11, 13, 17, 19$$
$$= 8$$

P (prime number less than 23)

$$= \frac{8}{90} = \frac{4}{45} \quad \textbf{Ans.}$$

24. Each of the letters of the word 'AUTHORIZES' is written on identical circular discs and put in a bag. They are well shuffled. If a disc is drawn

at random from the bag, what is the probability that the letter is :*

(i) a vowel
(ii) one of the first 9 letters of the English alphabet which appears in the given word.
(iii) one of the last 9 letters of the English alphabet which appears in the given word ?

Sol. Letters are A, U, T, H, O, R, I, Z, E, S.

⇒ Total number of letters in the given word = 10.

(i) Here, vowels are A, U, O, I, E.

⇒ Number of vowels = 5

So, probability (a vowel) = $\frac{5}{10} = \frac{1}{2}$ **Ans.**

(ii) Letters in the given word which are in first 9 letters of english alphabets are A, I, E and H.

⇒ Number of such letters = 4

$$\therefore \text{ Probability} = \frac{4}{10} = \frac{2}{5} \quad \textbf{Ans.}$$

(iii) Letters in the given word which are in last 9 letters of english alphabets are U, T, R, Z and S.

⇒ Number of such letters = 5

$$\therefore \text{ Probability} = \frac{5}{10} = \frac{1}{2} \quad \textbf{Ans.}$$

25. There are 25 discs numbered 1 to 25. They are put in a closed box and shaken thoroughly. A disc is drawn at random from the box.*

Find the probability that the number on the disc is :

(i) an odd number
(ii) divisible by 2 and 3 both
(iii) a number less than 16.

Sol. Given, Total number of outcomes *i.e.*, $n(S) = 25$

(i) Let A be the event of getting an odd number.

$\therefore \quad A = \{1, 3, 5, 7, 9, 11, 13, 15, 17, 19, 21, 23, 25\}$

$\therefore \quad n(A) = 13$

$$\therefore \quad P(A) = \frac{n(A)}{n(S)} = \frac{13}{25} \quad \textbf{Ans.}$$

(ii) Let B be the event of getting a number divisible by 2 and 3 both.

$\therefore \quad\quad B = \{6, 12, 18, 24\}$

$\therefore \quad\quad n(B) = 4$

$$\therefore \quad\quad P(B) = \frac{n(B)}{n(S)} = \frac{4}{25} \quad \textbf{Ans.}$$

(iii) Let C be the event of getting a number less than 16.

$$\therefore \quad C = \{1, 2, 3, 4, 5, 6, 7, 8, 9, 10, 11, 12, 13, 14, 15\}$$

$$\therefore \quad n(C) = 15$$

$$\therefore \quad P(C) = \frac{n(C)}{n(S)} = \frac{15}{25} = \frac{3}{5} \quad \textbf{Ans.}$$

26. Cards bearing numbers 2, 4, 6, 8, 10, 12, 14, 16, 18 and 20 are kept in a bag. A card is drawn at random from the bag. Find the probability of getting a card which is:*

(i) a prime number.

(ii) a number divisible by 4.

(iii) a number that is a multiple of 6.

(iv) an odd number.

Sol. Here, Sample Space,

$$S = \{2, 4, 6, 8, 10, 12, 14, 16, 18, 20\}$$

$$\therefore \quad n(S) = 10$$

(i) Let A be the event of getting a prime number.

$$A = \{2\}$$

$$\therefore \quad n(A) = 1$$

$$\therefore \quad P(A) = \frac{n(A)}{n(S)} = \frac{1}{10} \quad \textbf{Ans.}$$

(ii) Let B be the event of getting a number divisible by 4.

$$\therefore \quad B = \{4, 8, 12, 16, 20\}$$

$$\therefore \quad n(B) = 5$$

$$\therefore \quad P(B) = \frac{n(B)}{n(S)} = \frac{5}{10} = \frac{1}{2} \quad \textbf{Ans.}$$

(iii) Let C be the event of getting a number which is multiple of 6.

$$\therefore \quad C = \{6, 12, 18\}$$

$$\therefore \quad n(C) = 3$$

$$\therefore \quad P(C) = \frac{n(C)}{n(S)} = \frac{3}{10} \quad \textbf{Ans.}$$

(iv) Let D be the event of getting an odd number.

$$\therefore \quad D = \{\ \}$$

$$\therefore \quad n(D) = 0$$

$$\therefore \quad P(D) = \frac{n(D)}{n(S)} = \frac{0}{10} = 0 \quad \textbf{Ans.}$$

27. Cards numbered 2 to 101 are placed in a box. A card is selected at random from the box, find the probability that the card selected :

(i) has a number which is a perfect square.

(ii) has an odd number which is not less than 70.

Sol. Total no. of cards = 100

(i) Perfect squares are 4, 9, 16, 25, 36, 49, 64, 81, 100.

$$P \text{ (Perfect square)} = \frac{9}{100} \quad \textbf{Ans.}$$

(ii) Let odd numbers not less than 70 = n

Since odd numbers are in A.P. : 71, 73, ..., 101 with $d = 2$

$$101 = 71 + (n - 1)(2)$$

$$\Rightarrow \quad n = 16$$

P (odd number not less than 70)

$$= \frac{16}{100} = \frac{4}{25} \quad \textbf{Ans.}$$

28. What is the probability that a non-leap year has 53 Mondays ?

Sol. There are 365 days in a non-leap year

$$\because \quad 365 \text{ days} = 52 \text{ weeks} + 1 \text{ day}$$

$$\therefore \quad \text{One day can be M, T, W, Th, F, S, S} = 7$$

$$\therefore \quad P \text{ (53 Mondays in non-leap year)}$$

$$= \frac{1}{7} \quad \textbf{Ans.}$$

29. What is the probability that there are 53 Wednesdays in a leap year ?

Sol. In a leap year number of days

$$= 366 \text{ days}$$

$$= 52 \text{ weeks} + 2 \text{ days}$$

$$\therefore \quad \text{Two days can be SM, MT, TW, WTh, ThF, FS, SS}$$

$$= 7$$

$$\therefore \quad \text{Out of these 7 calendars, two calendars will have 53 Wednesdays}$$

$$\therefore \quad P \text{ (53 Wednesdays in a leap year)} = \frac{2}{7} \quad \textbf{Ans.}$$

30. A game of chance consists of spinning an arrow which comes to rest pointing at one of the numbers 1, 2, 3, 4, 5, 6, 7, 8 and these are equally likely outcomes. Find the probability that the arrow will point at any factor of 8 ?

---

* Frequently asked previous years Board Exam Questions.

Sol. Total number of possible outcomes = 8

Favourable outcomes

$$= (1 \times 8), (2 \times 4), (8 \times 1), (4 \times 2)$$

$$= 4$$

∴ P (Factor of 8)

$$= \frac{\text{No. of favourable outcomes}}{\text{Total no. of possible outcomes}}$$

$$= \frac{4}{8} = \frac{1}{2}$$ **Ans.**

31. From the numbers 3, 5, 5, 7, 7, 7, 9, 9, 9, 9, one number is selected at random, what is the probability that the selected number is mean ?

Sol. Total outcome = 10

$$\text{Mean} = \frac{3+5+5+7+7+7+9+9+9+9}{10}$$

$$= \frac{70}{10} = 7$$

∴ $$P \text{ (Mean)} = \frac{3}{10}$$ **Ans.**

32. Cards numbered 1 to 30 are put in a bag. A card is drawn at random. Find the probability that the drawn cards is :

(i) prime number > 7.

(ii) not a perfect square

Sol. Number of possible outcomes = 30

(i) P (prime number > 7) = 11, 13, 17, 19, 23, 29

$$= 6$$

$$P(E_1) = \frac{6}{30} = \frac{1}{5}$$

(ii) No. of perfect squares = 5 (1, 4, 9, 16, 25)

P (not a perfect square)

$$= \frac{25}{30}$$ [∵ 30 − 5 = 25]

$$= \frac{5}{6}$$ **Ans.**

33. A bag contains cards numbered 1 to 49. Find the probability that the number on the drawn card is :

(i) an odd number

(ii) a multiple of 5

(iii) Even prime

Sol. Total cards = 49

(i) $$P \text{ (odd number)} = \frac{25}{49}$$ **Ans.**

(ii) $$P \text{ (multiple of 5)} = \frac{9}{49}$$ **Ans.**

(iii) $$P \text{ (even prime)} = \frac{1}{49}$$ **Ans.**

□□

Data Based Questions

1. Find the mean of the following distribution :

x	4	6	9	10	15
f	5	10	10	7	8

Sol. Calculation of Arithmetic Mean :

x_i	f_i	$f_i x_i$
4	5	20
6	10	60
9	10	90
10	7	70
15	8	120
	$\Sigma f_i = 40$	$\Sigma f_i x_i = 360$

$\therefore$ Mean = $\overline{X} = \dfrac{\Sigma f_i x_i}{\Sigma f_i} = \dfrac{360}{40} = 9$ **Ans.**

2. Find the mean of the following distribution :

x	10	30	50	70	89
f	7	8	10	15	10

Sol. Calculation of Mean :

x_i	f_i	$f_i x_i$
10	7	70
30	8	240
50	10	500
70	15	1050
89	10	890
	$\Sigma f_i = N = 50$	$\Sigma f_i x_i = 2750$

$\therefore$ Mean = $\dfrac{\Sigma f_i x_i}{N}$

$= \dfrac{2750}{50} = 55$ **Ans.**

3. The contents of 100 match box were checked to determine the number of match sticks they contained.

Number of match sticks	Number of boxes
35	6
36	10
37	18
38	25
39	21
40	12
41	8

(i) Calculate correct to one decimal place, the mean number of match sticks per box.

(ii) Determine how many matchsticks would have to be added to the total contents of the 100 boxes to bring the mean up exactly 39 match sticks.

Sol.

Number of match sticks (x_i)	Number of boxes (f_i)	$f_i x_i$
35	6	210
36	10	360
37	18	666
38	25	950
39	21	819
40	12	480
41	8	328
	$\Sigma f_i = 100$	$\Sigma f_i x_i = 3813$

(i) Mean = $\dfrac{\Sigma f_i x_i}{\Sigma f_i} = \dfrac{3813}{100}$

$= 38 \cdot 13 \approx 38 \cdot 1$ **Ans.**

(ii) Now, the number of extra sticks to be added.

$= 39 \times 100 - 38 \cdot 13 \times 100$

$= 3900 - 3813 = 87$ **Ans.**

4. The mean of the following distribution is 6. Find the value of P :

x	2	4	6	10	$P+5$
f	3	2	3	1	2

Sol. Calculation of Arithmetic Mean :

x_i	f_i	$f_i x_i$
2	3	6
4	2	8
6	3	18

10	1	10
$P+5$	2	$2P+10$
	$\Sigma f_i = 11$	$\Sigma f_i x_i = 2P+52$

30 – 40	10
40 – 50	5

We have,

$$\Sigma f_i = 11$$
$$\Sigma f_i x_i = 2P+52$$
$$\therefore \quad \text{Mean} = \frac{\Sigma f_i x_i}{\Sigma f_i}$$
$$6 = \frac{2P+52}{11}$$
$$\Rightarrow \quad 66 = 2P+52$$
$$\Rightarrow \quad 2P = 66-52$$
$$\Rightarrow \quad 2P = 14$$
$$\Rightarrow \quad P = 7. \qquad \textbf{Ans.}$$

5. If the mean of the following distribution is 24, find the value of 'a'.*

Marks	0–10	10–20	20–30	30–40	40–50
Number of students	7	a	8	10	5

Sol.

Marks	Mid values (x)	No. of students (f)	fx
0–10	5	7	35
10–20	15	a	$15a$
20–30	25	8	200
30–40	35	10	350
40–50	45	5	225
		$\Sigma f = 30+a$	$\Sigma fx = 15a+810$

$$\therefore \quad \text{Mean} = \frac{\Sigma fx}{\Sigma f}$$
$$\Rightarrow \quad 24 = \frac{15a+810}{a+30}$$
$$\Rightarrow \quad 24a+720 = 15a+810$$
$$\Rightarrow \quad 24a-15a = 810-720$$
$$\Rightarrow \quad 9a = 90$$
$$\Rightarrow \quad a = 10. \qquad \textbf{Ans.}$$

6. If the mean of the following distribution is 24, find the value of 'a'.

Marks	Number of students
0–10	7
10–20	a
20–30	8

Sol.

Marks	Mid values (x)	No. of students (f)	fx
0–10	5	7	35
10–20	15	a	$15a$
20–30	25	8	200
30–40	35	10	350
40–50	45	5	225
		$\Sigma f = 30+a$	$\Sigma fx = 15a+810$

$$\therefore \quad \text{Mean} = \frac{\Sigma fx}{\Sigma f}$$
$$\Rightarrow \quad 24 = \frac{15a+810}{a+30}$$
$$\Rightarrow \quad 24a+720 = 15a+810$$
$$\Rightarrow \quad 24a-15a = 810-720$$
$$\Rightarrow \quad 9a = 90$$
$$\Rightarrow \quad a = 10. \qquad \textbf{Ans.}$$

7. If the mean of the following distribution is 7·5, find the missing frequency 'f':

Variable	5	6	7	8	9	10	11	12
Frequency	20	17	f	10	8	6	7	6

Sol.

Variable	Frequency ($f_i x_i$)	fx
5	20	100
6	17	102
7	f	$7f$
8	10	80
9	8	72
10	6	60
11	7	77
12	6	72
	$\Sigma f_i = 74+f$	$563+7f$

$$\therefore \quad \text{Mean} = \frac{\Sigma f_i x_i}{\Sigma f_i}$$
$$\Rightarrow \quad 7{\cdot}5 = \frac{563+7f}{74+f}$$
$$\Rightarrow \quad 555+7{\cdot}5f = 563+7f$$
$$\Rightarrow \quad 0{\cdot}5f = 8$$
$$\Rightarrow \quad f = 16 \qquad \textbf{Ans.}$$

8. Marks obtained by 40 students in a short assesment is given below, where a and b are two missing data.

Marks	No. of Students
5	6
6	a
7	16
8	13
9	b

If the mean of the distribution is 7.2 find a & b.

Sol.

Marks (x)	No. of Students (f)	fx
5	6	30
6	a	6a
7	16	112
8	13	104
9	b	9b
Total	$\Sigma f = 35 + a + b$	$\Sigma fx = 246 + 6a + 9b$

Now, $\Sigma f = 40$

$35 + a + b = 40$

$a + b = 5$ …(i)

and $\overline{X} = \dfrac{\Sigma fx}{\Sigma f}$

$7 \cdot 2 = \dfrac{246 + 6a + 9b}{40}$

$\Rightarrow$ $6a + 9b + 246 = 288$

$\Rightarrow$ $6a + 9b = 42$

$\Rightarrow$ $2a + 3b = 14$ …(ii)

From (i) and (ii),

$a = 1, b = 4$ **Ans.**

9. The following table shows the weight of 12 students :

Weight in kg	67	70	72	73	75
Number of students	4	3	2	2	1

Find the mean weight.

Sol. Let the assumed mean be $A = 72$.

Weight in kgs. (x_i)	Number of students (f_i)	$d_i = x_i - A = x_i - 72$	$f_i d_i$
67	4	-5	-20
70	3	-2	-6
A = 72	2	0	0
73	2	1	2
75	1	3	3
	$N = \Sigma f_i = 12$		$\Sigma f_i d_i = -21$

We have, $N = 12, \Sigma f_i d_i = -21, A = 72$

$\therefore$ Mean $= A + \dfrac{1}{N}(\Sigma f_i d_i)$

$= 72 + \left(\dfrac{-21}{12}\right)$

$= 72 - \dfrac{7}{4} = \dfrac{288 - 7}{4} = \dfrac{281}{4} = 70 \cdot 25$ kgs

$\therefore$ Mean weight $= 70 \cdot 25$ kgs   **Ans.**

10. The data on the number of patients attending a hospital in a month are given below. Find the average (mean) number of patients attending the hospital in a month by using the shortcut method.*

Take the assumed mean as 45. Give your answer correct to 2 decimal places.

Number of patients	10-20	20-30	30-40	40-50	50-60	60-70
Number of Days	5	2	7	9	2	5

* **Frequently asked previous years Board Exam Questions.**

Data Based Questions

Sol. Given, assumed mean (A) = 45.

Number of patients	Mid-value (x_i)	$d_i = x_i - A$	Number of days (f_i)	$f_i d_i$
10 - 20	15	– 30	5	– 150
20 - 30	25	– 20	2	– 40
30 - 40	35	– 10	7	– 70
40 - 50	A = 45	0	9	0
50 - 60	55	10	2	20
60 - 70	65	20	5	100
			$\Sigma f_i = 30$	$\Sigma f_i d_i = -140$

$$\text{Mean} = A + \frac{\Sigma f_i d_i}{\Sigma f_i}$$

$$= 45 + \left(-\frac{140}{30}\right)$$

$$= 45 - 4.667$$

$$= 40.333$$

$$= 40.33$$

(Correct to 2 decimal places)

Ans.

11. Find the mean wage of a worker from the following data :

Wages (In ₹)	1400	1450	1500	1550	1600	1650	1700
Number of workers	15	20	18	27	15	3	2

Sol. Let the assumed mean be $A = 1550$. Thus

Wages (In ₹) x_i	Number of workers (f_i)	$d_i = x_i - 1550$	$f_i d_i$
1400	15	– 150	– 2250
1450	20	– 100	– 2000
1500	18	– 50	– 900
A = 1550	27	0	0
1600	15	50	750
1650	3	100	300
1700	2	150	300
	$\Sigma f_i = 100$		$\Sigma f_i d_i = -3800$

∴ Mean Wage $= A + \dfrac{\Sigma f_i d_i}{\Sigma f_i} = \left(1{,}550 - \dfrac{3{,}800}{100}\right)$

$$= 1{,}550 - 38$$

$$= ₹\, 1{,}512.$$

Ans.

12. Using the step deviation method find the arithmetic mean of the distribution :

Variate (x)	5	10	15	20	25	30	35	40	45	50
Frequency (f)	20	43	75	67	72	45	39	9	8	6

Sol. Let the assumed Mean be $A = 25$ and $h = 5$.

x_i	Frequencies f_i	Deviation $d_i = x_i - 25$	$u_i = \dfrac{x_i - 25}{5}$	$f_i u_i$
5	20	– 20	– 4	– 80
10	43	– 15	– 3	– 129
15	75	– 10	– 2	– 150
20	67	– 5	– 1	– 67
A = 25	72	0	0	0

30	45	5	1	45
35	39	10	2	78
40	9	15	3	27
45	8	20	4	32
50	6	25	5	30
	$N = \Sigma f_i = 384$			$\Sigma f_i u_i = -214$

We have, $N = 384$, $A = 25$, $h = 5$ and $\Sigma f_i u_i = -214$

$$\text{Mean } (\overline{X}) = A + h \left(\frac{1}{N} \Sigma f_i u_i \right) = 25 + 5 \times \left(\frac{-214}{384} \right)$$

$$= 25 - 2 \cdot 786$$

$$= 22 \cdot 214. \qquad \textbf{Ans.}$$

13. Find the mean of the following distribution :

Class interval	Frequency
0 – 10	10
10 – 20	6
20 – 30	8
30 – 40	12
40 – 50	5

Sol.

Class Interval	Frequency (f)	Mid value (x)	fx
0 – 10	10	5	50
10 – 20	6	15	90
20 – 30	8	25	200
30 – 40	12	35	420
40 – 50	5	45	225
	$\Sigma f = 41$		$\Sigma fx = 985$

$$\therefore \qquad \text{Mean} = \frac{\Sigma fx}{\Sigma f} = \frac{985}{11}$$

$$= 24 \cdot 02. \qquad \textbf{Ans.}$$

14. The following table gives the wages of worker in a factory :

Wages in ₹	45 – 50	50 – 55	55 – 60	60 – 65	65 – 70	70 – 75	75 – 80
No. of Worker's	5	8	30	25	14	12	6

Calculate the mean by the short cut method.

Sol.

Class Interval	Frequency f_i	Observation (mid value) x_i	$d_i = x_i - A$	$f_i d_i$
45 — 50	5	47·5	– 15	– 75
50 — 55	8	52·5	– 10	– 80
55 — 60	30	57·5	– 5	– 150
60 — 65	25	62·5 = A	0	0
65 — 70	14	67·5	5	70
70 — 75	12	72·5	10	120
75 — 80	6	77·5	15	90
	$\Sigma f_i = 100$			$\Sigma f_i d_i = -25$

$$\text{Mean } \overline{X} = A + \frac{\Sigma f_i d_i}{\Sigma f_i}$$

$$= 62 \cdot 5 + \left(\frac{-25}{100} \right) = 62 \cdot 25 \qquad \textbf{Ans.}$$

15. Find the mean of the following distribution by step deviation method :

Class interval	20−30	30−40	40−50	50−60	60−70	70−80
Frequency	10	6	8	12	5	9

Sol.

C.I.	f	(x) mid values	$u = \dfrac{x-A}{h}$	$f.u$
20−30	10	25	− 3	− 30
30−40	6	35	− 2	− 12
40−50	8	45	− 1	− 8
50−60	12	55 =A	0	0
60−70	5	65	1	5
70−80	9	75	2	18
	$\Sigma f = 50$			$\Sigma f\mu = -27$

Here, A = Assumed mean = 55

           $h = 10$

$\therefore$ Mean $(\overline{X})$ = $A + \dfrac{\Sigma fu}{\Sigma f} \times h$

               = $55 + \dfrac{(-27)}{50} \times 10$

               = $55 - 5{\cdot}4 = 49{\cdot}6$ **Ans.**

16. The weights of 50 apples were recorded as given below. Calculate the mean weight, to the nearest gram, by the Step Deviation Method.

Weights in grams	No. of apples
80−85	5
85−90	8
90−95	10
95−100	12
100−105	8
105−110	4
110−115	3

Sol.

Weight in gms.	No. of apples	x_i	$x_i - A$	$u_i = \dfrac{x_i - A}{5}$	$f_i u_i$
80−85	5	82·5	− 15	− 3	− 15
85−90	8	87·5	− 10	− 2	− 16
90−95	10	92·5	− 5	− 1	− 10
95−100	12	(97·5) = A	0	0	0
100−105	8	102·5	5	1	8
105−110	4	107·5	10	2	8
110−115	3	112·5	15	3	9
	$\Sigma f_i = 50$				$\Sigma f_i u_i = -16$

        $A = 97{\cdot}5, \Sigma f_i = 50, \Sigma f_i u_i = -16, h = 5.$

$\therefore$ Mean $(\overline{X})$ = $A + \dfrac{\Sigma f_i u_i}{\Sigma f_i} \times h$

$$= 97.5 + \left(\frac{-16}{50}\right) \times 5 = 95.9 \qquad \textbf{Ans.}$$

17. (i) Using step-deviation method, calculate the mean marks of the following distribution.

(ii) State the modal class.

Class interval	50–55	55–60	60–65	65–70	70–75	75–80	80–85	85–90
Frequency	5	20	10	10	9	6	12	8

Sol. (i)

C.I.	f	x	$u = \dfrac{x-A}{h}$	$f \cdot u$
50–55	5	52.5	– 3	– 15
55–60	20	57.5	– 2	– 40
60–65	10	62.5	– 1	– 10
65–70	10	67.5 = A	0	0
70–75	9	72.5	1	9
75–80	6	77.5	2	12
80–85	12	82.5	3	36
85–90	8	87.5	4	32
	$\Sigma f = 80$			$\Sigma f \cdot u = 24$

$$\therefore \quad \text{Mean } (\overline{X}) = A + \frac{\Sigma f \cdot u}{\Sigma f} \times h$$

$$= 67.5 + \frac{24}{80} \times 5 = 67.5 + 1.5 = 69 \qquad \textbf{Ans.}$$

(ii) Modal class = 55 – 60 **Ans.**

18. In a class of 40 students, marks obtained by the students in a class test (out of 10) are given below :

Marks	1	2	3	4	5	6	7	8	9	10
Number of Students	1	2	3	3	6	10	5	4	3	3

Calculate the following for the given distribution :

(i) Median

(ii) Mode*

Sol.

Marks	Number of Students	Cumulative Frequency
1	1	1
2	2	3
3	3	6
4	3	9
5	6	15
6	10	25
7	5	30
8	4	34
9	3	37
10	3	40
	$n = 40$	

Here, $n = 40$ (even)

(i) Median

$$= \dfrac{\dfrac{n}{2}^{\text{th}} \text{ observation} + \left(\dfrac{n}{2}+1\right)^{\text{th}} \text{ observation}}{2}$$

$$= \dfrac{20^{\text{th}} \text{ observation} + 21^{\text{st}} \text{ observation}}{2}$$

$$= \dfrac{6+6}{2} = 6 \qquad \textbf{Ans.}$$

(ii) $\because$ The highest frequency is 10.

$$\therefore \qquad \text{Mode} = 6 \qquad \textbf{Ans.}$$

19. Find the median of the following distribution :

x	3	5	10	12	8	15
f	2	4	6	10	8	7

Sol. Arranging the terms in ascending order and preparing the cumulative frequency table :

x	f	c.f.
3	2	2

Data Based Questions

---
* **Frequently asked previous years Board Exam Questions.**

5	4	6
8	8	14
10	6	20
12	10	30
15	7	37

Here, $n = 37$ which is odd.

So,   Median $= \left(\dfrac{n+1}{2}\right)^{th}$ term

$= \left(\dfrac{37+1}{2}\right)^{th}$ term

$= \left(\dfrac{38}{2}\right)^{th}$

$= 19^{th}$ term

Hence, Median is the value of the 19th term = 10.

Ans.

20. Obtain the median for the following frequency distribution :

x	1	2	3	4	5	6	7	8	9
f	8	10	11	16	20	25	15	9	6

Sol. Calculation of Median

x	f	c.f.
1	8	8
2	10	18
3	11	29
4	16	45
5	20	65
6	25	90
7	15	105
8	9	114
9	6	120
		$N = 120$

Here, $n = 120$, which is even

$\therefore$ Median

$= \dfrac{\dfrac{n}{2}\text{th observation} + \left(\dfrac{n}{2}+1\right)\text{th observation}}{2}$

$= \dfrac{60\text{th observation} + 61\text{th observation}}{2}$

$= \dfrac{5+5}{2}$

$\therefore$ Median = 5   **Ans.**

21. Find the mode and median of the following frequency distribution :

x	10	11	12	13	14	15
f	1	4	7	5	9	3

Sol.

x	f	c.f.
10	1	1
11	4	5
12	7	12
13	5	17
14	9	26
15	3	29

Since 14 has highest frequency

$\therefore$ Mode = 14   **Ans.**

Now, $n = 29$ (odd)

$\therefore$ Median $= \left(\dfrac{n+1}{2}\right)^{th}$ value

$= \left(\dfrac{29+1}{2}\right)^{th}$ value

$= 15^{th}$ value

$= 13$ **Ans.**

22. Calculate the mean of the distribution given below using the short cut method.

Marks	11–20	21–30	31–40	41–50	51–60	61–70	71–80
No. of students	2	6	10	12	9	7	4

Sol.

Class Interval (Inclusive form)	Class Interval (Exclusive form)	No. of Students (f_i)	x_i	$A_i = 45 \cdot 5$ $d_i = x - 45 \cdot 5$	$f_i d_i$
11—20	10·5 – 20·5	2	15·5	– 30	– 60
21—30	20·5 – 30·5	6	25·5	– 20	– 120
31—40	30·5 – 40·5	10	35·5	– 10	– 100
41—50	40·5 – 50·5	12	45·5	—	—
51—60	50·5 – 60·5	9	55·5	10	90

61—70	60·5 – 70·5	7	65·5	20	140
71—80	70·5 – 80·5	4	75·5	30	120
		$\Sigma f_i = 50$			$\Sigma f_i d_i = 70$

Assumed mean $(A_i) = 45\cdot5$

$$\Sigma f_i = 50, \Sigma f_i d_i = 70.$$

$$\text{Mean} = A_i + \frac{\Sigma f_i d_i}{\Sigma f_i} = 45\cdot5 + \frac{70}{50}$$

$$= 45\cdot5 + 1\cdot4 = 46\cdot9. \qquad \textbf{Ans.}$$

23. A study of the yield of 150 tomato plants, resulted in the record :

Tomatoes per Plant	1 – 5	6 – 10	11 – 15	16 – 20	21 – 25
Number of Plants	20	50	46	22	12

(i) Calculate the mean of the number of tomatoes per plant.

(ii) Name the modal class.

(iii) What is the frequency of the class preceding the modal class ?

Sol. (i)

Tomatoes per Plant	Mid-Point (x)	Number of Plants (f)	fx
1 – 5	3	20	60
6 – 10	8	50	400
11 – 15	13	46	598
16 – 20	18	22	396
21 – 25	23	12	276
Total		150	1730

$$\text{Mean} = \frac{\Sigma fx}{\Sigma f} = \frac{1730}{150} = \frac{173}{15} = 11\cdot53. \qquad \textbf{Ans.}$$

(ii) The modal class is 6 – 10. **Ans.**

(iii) The frequency of the class preceding the modal class is 20. **Ans.**

24. For the following frequency distribution find :

(i) Lower quartile   **(iii)** Inter quartile range

(ii) Upper quartile   **(iv)** Semi-inter quartile range.

x	1	2	3	4	5	6	7	8
f	3	5	9	15	20	16	10	2

Sol.

x	f	Cumulative Frequency
1	3	3
2	5	8
3	9	17
4	15	32
5	20	52
6	16	68
7	10	78
8	2	80
		$n = 20$

(i) Lower quartile (Q_1) = The value of $\left(\dfrac{n}{4}\right)^{th}$ observation

= The value of $\left(\dfrac{80}{4}\right)^{th}$ observation

= The value of 20th observation

$Q_1 = 4.$ **Ans.**

(ii) Upper quartile (Q_3) = The Value of $\left(\dfrac{3n}{4}\right)^{th}$ observation

= The value of $\left(\dfrac{3 \times 80}{4}\right)^{th}$ observation

$\therefore$ $Q_3 = 6.$ **Ans.**

(iii) Inter quartile range = $Q_3 - Q_1$

= $6 - 4 = 2.$ **Ans.**

(iv) Semi-quartile range = $\dfrac{Q_3 - Q_1}{2}$

= $\dfrac{2}{2} = 1.$ **Ans.**

❏❏

Chapter 4. Linear Inequations

1. For each inequality, determine which of the given numbers are in the solution set :

(i) $2x + 3 > 11; -3, 4, 5, 7$

(ii) $16 - 5x \leq -4; 4, -3, 10.$

Sol. (i) If $x = -3$

Then $2x + 3 = 2 \times (-3) + 3 = -3$

Since, $-3 > 11$ is false.

So, -3 is not in the solution of $2x + 3 > 11$

If, $x = 4$, then $2x + 3 = 2 \times 4 + 3 = 11$

Since $11 > 11$ is false.

So, 4 is not in the solution of $2x + 3 > 11$

If $x = 5$, then $2x + 3 = 2 \times 5 + 3 = 13$

Since, $13 > 11$ is true.

So, 5 is in the solution of $2x + 3 > 11$

Similarly, $x = 7$ is in the solution of $2x + 3 > 11$.

Ans.

(ii) If $x = 4$,

then $16 - 5x = 16 - 5 \times 4 = -4$

Since, $-4 \leq -4$ is true.

So, $x = 4$ is in the solution of $16 - 5x \leq -4$

If $x = -3$, then $16 - 5x = 16 - 5 \times (-3) = 31$

Since, $31 \leq -4$ is false.

So, $x = -3$ is not in the solution of $16 - 5x \leq -4$

If $x = 10$, then $16 - 5x = 16 - 5 \times 10 = -34$

Since, $-34 \leq -4$ is true.

So, $x = 10$ is in the solution of $16 - 5x \leq -4.$

Ans.

2. Graph the solution sets of the following inequalities :

(i) $2x - 4 > 3, x \in W$

(ii) $3x - 5 \leq -7, x \in I.$

Sol. (i) $2x - 4 > 3$

$2x > 3 + 4 \Rightarrow 2x > 7$

$$x > 7/2$$
$$\Rightarrow \quad x > 3 \cdot 5$$
$$x = \{4, 5, 6, \ldots\ldots\}$$

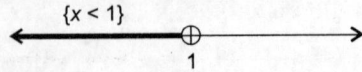

(ii) $3x - 5 \leq -7, x \in I$

$3x \leq 5 + (-7)$

$3x \leq -2$

$x \leq -2/3$

$x = \{\ldots\ldots, -3, -2, -1\}$

3. Solve the following inequalities and represent the solution on a number line where $(x \in R)$:

(i) $2x + 3 < 5$

(ii) $3x + 4 \leq x + 8$

(iii) $2x - 3 > 5x + 4$

(iv) $4 - 2x \geq 6 - 3x$

(v) $3(x - 2) > 1$

(vi) $\dfrac{2x + 5}{4} > \dfrac{4 - 3x}{6}$

(vii) $\dfrac{3x}{2} + \dfrac{1}{4} > \dfrac{5x}{8} - \dfrac{1}{2}.$

Sol. (i) We have, $2x + 3 < 5$

$$\Rightarrow \quad 2x < 5 - 3$$
$$\Rightarrow \quad 2x < 2$$
$$\Rightarrow \quad x < 1$$

The graph of the solution set $\{x : x < 1, x \in R\}$ is

$\{x < 1\}$

Ans.

(ii) We have, $3x + 4 \leq x + 8$

$$\Rightarrow \quad 3x - x \leq 8 - 4$$
$$\Rightarrow \quad 2x \leq 4$$
$$\Rightarrow \quad x \leq 2$$

The graph of the solution set $\{x : x \le 2, x \in R\}$ is

$x \le 2$

Ans.

(iii) We have the inequality

$2x - 3 > 5x + 4$

$\Rightarrow \quad -3 - 4 > 5x - 2x$

$\Rightarrow \quad -7 > 3x$ or $x < -7/3$

The graph of the solution set $\{x : x < -7/3, x \in R\}$ is

$x < -7/3$

$-7/3$

Ans.

(iv) We have the inequality

$4 - 2x \ge 6 - 3x$

$\Rightarrow \quad 3x - 2x \ge 6 - 4$

$\Rightarrow \quad x \ge 2$

The graph of the solution set $\{x : x \ge 2, x \in R\}$ is

$x \ge 2$

2

Ans.

(v) The given inequality is

$3(x - 2) > 1$

$\Rightarrow \quad 3x - 6 > 1$

$\Rightarrow \quad 3x > 7 \Rightarrow x > 7/3$

The graph of the solution set $\{x : x > 7/3, x \in R\}$ is

$x > 7/3$

$7/3$

Ans.

(vi) The given inequality is

$\dfrac{2x+5}{4} > \dfrac{4-3x}{6}$

$\Rightarrow \quad 6(2x + 5) > 4(4 - 3x)$

$\Rightarrow \quad 12x + 30 > 16 - 12x$

$\Rightarrow \quad 12x + 12x > 16 - 30$

$\Rightarrow \quad 24x > -14$

$\Rightarrow \quad x > \dfrac{-14}{24}$

$\Rightarrow \quad x > -7/12.$

The graph of solution set $\{x : x > -7/12, x \in R\}$ is

$x > -7/12$

$-7/12$

Ans.

(vii) The given inequality is

$\dfrac{3x}{2} + \dfrac{1}{4} > \dfrac{5x}{8} - \dfrac{1}{2}$

$\Rightarrow \quad \dfrac{3x}{2} - \dfrac{5x}{8} > -\dfrac{1}{2} - \dfrac{1}{4}$

$\Rightarrow \quad \dfrac{12x - 5x}{8} > \dfrac{-2 - 1}{4}$

$\Rightarrow \quad \dfrac{7x}{8} > \dfrac{-3}{4}$

$\Rightarrow \quad 4(7x) > (-3) \times 8$

$\Rightarrow \quad 28x > -24$

$\Rightarrow \quad x > \dfrac{-24}{28}$

$\Rightarrow \quad x > -6/7$

The graph of the solution set $\{x : x > -6/7, x \in R\}$ is

$x > -6/7$

$-6/7$

Ans.

4. Solve the following inequalities in the given universal set :

(i) $3x - 5 > x + 7; x \in N$

(ii) $4x + 2 \le 2x - 7; x \in I$

(iii) $5x - 3 < 6x - 2; x \in N$

(iv) $2x - 5 \le 5x + 4 < 11$, where $x \in I.$

Sol. (i) We have

$3x - 5 > x + 7, x \in N$

$\Rightarrow \quad 3x - x > 7 + 5$

$\Rightarrow \quad 2x > 12$

$\Rightarrow \quad x > 6$

As $x \in N$, x can take values 7, 8, 9, 10, ...

Solution set : $\{x : x > 6, x \in N\}$

This set is drawn on the number line as

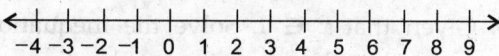

Ans.

(ii) We have

$4x + 2 \le 2x - 7; x \in I$

$\Rightarrow \quad 4x - 2x \le -7 - 2$

$\Rightarrow \quad 2x \le -9$

$\Rightarrow \quad x \le -9/2$

As $x \in I$, x can take values $-5, -6, -7, ...$,

So, Solution set $= \{x : x \le -9/2, x \in I\}$

This set can be drawn on number line as

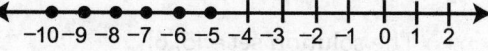

Ans.

(iii) We have

$$5x - 3 < 6x - 2; x \in N$$

$$\Rightarrow \quad 5x - 6x < -2 + 3$$

$$\Rightarrow \quad -x < 1$$

$$\Rightarrow \quad x > -1$$

As $x \in N$, so x can take value $\{1, 2, 3, 4, ...\}$

The solution set can be represented on number line as

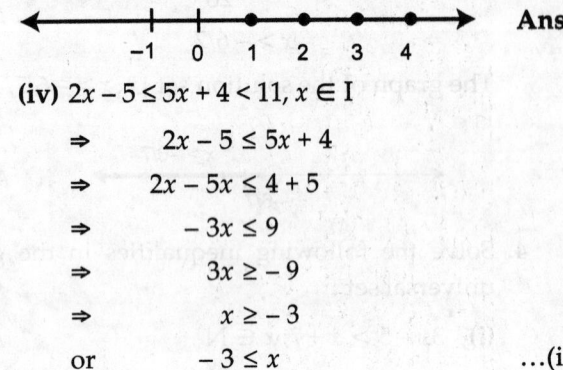

Ans.

(iv) $2x - 5 \le 5x + 4 < 11, x \in I$

$$\Rightarrow \quad 2x - 5 \le 5x + 4$$

$$\Rightarrow \quad 2x - 5x \le 4 + 5$$

$$\Rightarrow \quad -3x \le 9$$

$$\Rightarrow \quad 3x \ge -9$$

$$\Rightarrow \quad x \ge -3$$

or $\quad -3 \le x \qquad \qquad ...(i)$

$$\Rightarrow \quad 5x + 4 < 11$$

$$\Rightarrow \quad 5x < 11 - 4$$

$$\Rightarrow \quad 5x < 7$$

$$\Rightarrow \quad x < \frac{7}{5}$$

$$\Rightarrow \quad x < 1\frac{2}{5} \qquad \qquad ...(ii)$$

From (i) and (ii)

$$-3 \le x < 1\frac{2}{5}, x \in I$$

$\therefore$ Solution set = $\{-3, -2, -1, 0, 1\}$

Ans.

5. Given that $x \in I$. Solve the inequation and graph the solution on the number line :

$$3 \ge \frac{x-4}{2} + \frac{x}{3} \ge 2$$

Sol.

$$3 \ge \frac{x-4}{2} + \frac{x}{3} \ge 2$$

$$\Rightarrow \quad 3 \ge \frac{3(x-4) + 2x}{6} \ge 2$$

$$\Rightarrow \quad 18 \ge 5x - 12 \ge 12$$

$$\Rightarrow \quad 30 \ge 5x \ge 24$$

$$\Rightarrow \quad \frac{24}{5} \le x \le 6 \qquad \qquad (x \in I)$$

$\therefore$ The solution set = $\{5, 6\}$

Ans.

6. Given that $x \in R$, solve the following inequality and graph the solution on the number line :

$$-1 \le 3 + 4x < 23$$

Sol.

$$-1 \le 3 + 4x < 23$$

$$-1 - 3 \le 3 + 4x - 3 < 23 - 3$$

$$-4 \le 4x < 20$$

$$-\frac{4}{4} \le x < \frac{20}{4}$$

$$-1 \le x < 5.$$

Solution set = $\{x : -1 \le x < 5, x \in R\}$

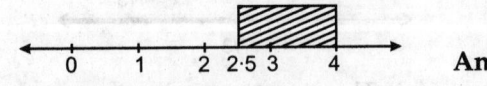

Ans.

7. Solve $2 \le 2x - 3 \le 5, x \in R$ and mark it on a number line.

Sol.

$$2 \le 2x - 3 \le 5, \qquad x \in R$$

$2 \le 2x - 3;$	$2x - 3 \le 5$
$2 + 3 \le 2x;$	$2x \le 5 + 3$
$5 \le 2x;$	$2x \le 8$
or $\quad 2x \ge 5;$	$x \le 4$
or $\quad x \ge \dfrac{5}{2}$	

$\therefore \qquad x \ge 2\frac{1}{2}$ and $x \le 4$

Solution set = $\{x : 2.5 \le x \le 4, x \in R\}$

Ans.

8. Solve the following inequation and write down the solution set :*

$$11x - 4 < 15x + 4 \le 13x + 14, x \in W$$

Represent the solution on a real number line.

Sol. Given, $11x - 4 < 15x + 4 \le 13x + 14, x \in W$.

$\therefore \quad 11x - 4 < 15x + 4$ and $15x + 4 \le 13x + 14$

$\Rightarrow \quad 11x - 15x < 4 + 4$ and $15x - 13x \le 14 - 4$

$\Rightarrow \quad -4x < 8$ and $2x \le 10$

$\Rightarrow \quad \dfrac{-4x}{-4} > \dfrac{8}{-4}$ and $\dfrac{2x}{2} \le \dfrac{10}{2}$

$\Rightarrow \quad x > -2$ and $x \le 5$

$\therefore \quad -2 < x \le 5$

$\therefore \quad$ Solution set = $\{0, 1, 2, 3, 4, 5\}$

9. Solve the following inequation, write down the solution set and represent it on the real number line :*

$$-2 + 10x \le 13x + 10 < 24 + 10x, x \in Z$$

Determine the Following

Sol. Given inequation is,

$$-2 + 10x \le 13x + 10 < 24 + 10x, x \in Z$$

$$\Rightarrow \quad -2 + 10x \le 13x + 10;$$

$$\Rightarrow \quad 10x - 13x \le 10 + 2;$$

$$\Rightarrow \quad -3x \le 12;$$

$$\Rightarrow \quad -x \le 4;$$

$$\Rightarrow \quad x \ge -4;$$

and $$13x + 10 < 24 + 10x$$

$$\Rightarrow \quad 13x - 10x < 24 - 10$$

$$\Rightarrow \quad 3x < 14$$

$$\Rightarrow \quad x < \frac{14}{3}$$

$$\therefore \quad -4 \le x < 4\frac{2}{3}$$

$\therefore$ Solution set = $\{-4, -3, -2, -1, 0, 1, 2, 3, 4\}$

number line from -5 to 6 with dots at $-4, -3, -2, -1, 0, 1, 2, 3, 4$

Ans.

10. Solve the following equation and represent the solution set on the number line.

$$-3 + x \le \frac{8x}{3} + 2 \le \frac{14}{3} + 2x, \text{ where } x \in I$$

Sol.

$$-3 + x \le \frac{8x}{3} + 2 \le \frac{14}{3} + 2x, \ x \in I,$$

$$-3 + x \le \frac{8x}{3} + 2, \qquad \frac{8x}{3} + 2 \le \frac{14}{3} + 2x$$

or $$\frac{8x}{3} - x \ge -3 - 2, \qquad \frac{8x}{3} - 2x \le \frac{14}{3} - 2$$

or $$\frac{5x}{3} \ge -5, \qquad \frac{2x}{3} \le \frac{8}{3}$$

$$5x \ge -15, \qquad 2x \le 8$$

$$x \ge -3, \qquad x \le 4$$

Solution set = $\{-3, -2, -1, 0, 1, 2, 3, 4\}$

Number line

number line from -4 to 5 with dots at $-3, -2, -1, 0, 1, 2, 3, 4$

Ans.

11. Solve the following inequation and represent the solution set on the number line.*

$$\frac{3x}{5} + 2 < x + 4 \le \frac{x}{2} + 5, x \in R$$

Sol. Given : $\frac{3x}{5} + 2 < x + 4 \le \frac{x}{2} + 5$

Now, $\frac{3x}{5} + 2 < x + 4$

* **Frequently asked previous years Board Exam Questions.**

$$\Rightarrow \quad \frac{3x}{5} - x < 4 - 2$$

$$\Rightarrow \quad \frac{3x - 5x}{5} < 2$$

$$\Rightarrow \quad -2x < 10$$

$$\Rightarrow \quad x > -\frac{10}{2}$$

$$\Rightarrow \quad x > -5$$

And, $$x + 4 \le \frac{x}{2} + 5$$

$$\Rightarrow \quad x - \frac{x}{2} \le 5 - 4$$

$$\Rightarrow \quad \frac{x}{2} \le 1$$

$$\Rightarrow \quad x \le 2$$

Hence, $$-5 < x \le 2$$

Solution set = $\{x : -5 < x \le 2, x \in R\}$

number line from -6 to 3 with open circle at -5 and filled dot at 2

12. Solve the following inequation and represent the solution set on the number line :

$$4x - 19 < \frac{3x}{5} - 2 \le \frac{-2}{5} + x, x \in R$$

Sol. $4x - 19 < \frac{3x}{5} - 2 \le \frac{-2}{5} + x , x \in R$

$$\therefore \quad 4x - 19 < \frac{3x}{5} - 2$$

$$4x - \frac{3x}{5} < -2 + 19$$

$$\frac{17x}{5} < 17$$

$$x < 5$$

and $$\frac{3x}{5} - 2 \le \frac{-2}{5} + x$$

$$\frac{3x}{5} - x \le \frac{-2}{5} + 2$$

$$-2x \le 8$$

$$x \ge -4$$

$$\Rightarrow \quad -4 \le x < 5$$

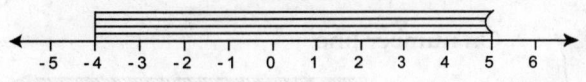

Ans.

13. Solve the following inequation and graph the solution set,

$$2x - 3 \le x + 2 \le 3x + 5; x \in R.$$

Sol. Here, $2x - 3 \le x + 2 \le 3x + 5$

$$\Rightarrow \quad 2x - 3 \le x + 2 \text{ and } x + 2 \le 3x + 5$$

$\Rightarrow \quad x \leq 5$ and $x \geq \dfrac{-3}{2}$

$\therefore \quad$ Solution set $= \left\{ x : \dfrac{-3}{2} \leq x \leq 5 \text{ and } x \in R \right\}$

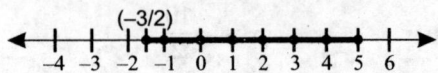

Ans.

14. Given :

$$P = \{x : 5 < 2x - 1 \leq 11, x \in R\}$$

$$Q = \{x : -1 \leq 3 + 4x < 23, x \in I\}$$

where R = (real numbers), I = (Integers). Represent P and Q on number lines. Write down the elements of P ∩ Q.

Sol. For P

$$5 < 2x - 1 \leq 11, x \in R$$

$\Rightarrow \quad 6 < 2x \leq 12, x \in R$

$\Rightarrow \quad 3 < x \leq 6, x \in R$

For Q $-1 \leq 3 + 4x < 23, x \in I$

$\Rightarrow \quad -4 \leq 4x < 20, x \in I$

$\Rightarrow \quad -1 \leq x < 5, x \in I$

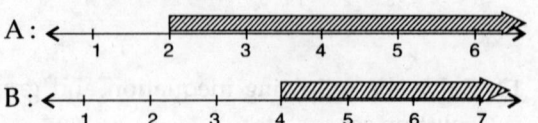

$$P \cap Q = \{4\}. \qquad \textbf{Ans.}$$

15. Solve the following inequalities and graph their solution set

$$A = \{x : 11x - 5 \geq 7x + 3, x \in R\}$$

and $\quad B = \{x : 18x - 9 \geq 15 + 12x, x \in R\}$

Sol. $\quad A = \{x : 11x - 5 \geq 7x + 3, x \in R\}$

$= \{x : 11x - 7x \geq 3 + 5, x \in R\}$

$= \{x : 4x \geq 8, x \in R\}$

$= \{x : x \geq 2, x \in R\} \qquad \dots(i)$

Also $\quad B = \{x : 18x - 9 \geq 15 + 12x, x \in R\}$

$= \{x : 18x - 12x \geq 15 + 9, x \in R\}$

$= \{x : 6x \geq 24, x \in R\}$

$= \{x : x \geq 4, x \in R\} \qquad \dots(ii)$

$\therefore$ On number line,

A :

B :

Ans.

16. Graph the solution set for each inequality :

  (i) $x \geq -3$ **(ii)** $x < 4$

  (iii) $-3 < x < 5$ **(v)** $-3 < x \leq 8$

  (iv) $5 \leq x < 10$ **(vi)** $-3 \leq x \leq 3$.

Sol. (i) We shade a number line to the right of -3. The darkened circle shows -3 is included.

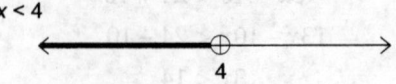

(ii) We shade a number line to the left of 4. The open circle shows that 4 is not included.

(iii) The graph of $-3 < x < 5$ is all the numbers between -3 and 5.

(iv) The graph of $5 \leq x < 10$ consists of all the numbers between 5 and 10 as well as 5.

(v) The graph of $-3 < x \leq 8$ consists of all the numbers between -3 and 8 as well as 8.

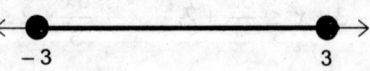

(vi) The graph of $-3 \leq x \leq 3$ consists of all the numbers between -3 and 3 as well as 3 and -3.

17. Solve the following inequalities and graph their solution set :

  (i) $\dfrac{2x - 5}{x + 2} < 2, x \in R$

  (ii) $\dfrac{x + 8}{x + 1} > 1, x \in R$

Sol. (i) Given $\dfrac{2x - 5}{x + 2} < 2$

$\Rightarrow \quad \dfrac{2x - 5}{x + 2} - 2 < 0$

$\Rightarrow \quad \dfrac{2x - 5 - 2x - 4}{x + 2} < 0$

$\Rightarrow \quad \dfrac{-9}{x + 2} < 0$

But $\quad \dfrac{a}{b} < 0, a < 0 \Rightarrow b > 0$

Thus, $\dfrac{-9}{x + 2} < 0, -9 < 0 \Rightarrow x + 2 > 0 \Rightarrow x > -2$

The graph of this solution set $\{x : x > -2, x \in R\}$ is

$$\xleftarrow{\qquad} \underset{-2}{\oplus} \xrightarrow{\quad x > -2 \quad}$$ **Ans.**

(ii) Given, $\dfrac{x+8}{x+1} > 1$

$\Rightarrow \qquad \dfrac{x+8}{x+1} - 1 > 0 \Leftrightarrow \dfrac{x+8-x-1}{x+1} > 0$

$\Rightarrow \qquad \dfrac{7}{x+1} > 0$

But $\qquad \dfrac{a}{b} > 0, a > 0 \Rightarrow b > 0$

Thus, $\dfrac{7}{x+1} > 0, 7 > 0 \Rightarrow x+1 > 0$ or $x > -1$

The graph of this solution set $\{x : > 1, x \in R\}$ is

$$\xleftarrow{\qquad} \underset{-1}{\bigcirc} \xrightarrow{\quad x > 1 \quad}$$

18. Find the solution set of the following inequalities and draw the graph of their solutions sets :

(i) $|x+5| < 8, x \in R$

(ii) $|x-1| > 3, x \in R$

(iii) $|3-2x| \geq 2, x \in R$

(iv) $\left|\dfrac{x-5}{3}\right| < 6, x \in R$

(v) $\dfrac{3}{|x-2|} > 5, x \in R.$

Sol. (i) We have

$$|x+5| < 8$$

Using property

$$|x| < a \Leftrightarrow -a < x < a$$

$\Rightarrow \qquad -8 < x+5 < 8$

$\Rightarrow \qquad -5-8 < x < 8-5$

$\Rightarrow \qquad -13 < x < 3$

The graph of this set is

$$\underset{-13}{\bigcirc} \xrightarrow{\hspace{3cm}} \underset{3}{\bigcirc}$$ **Ans.**

(ii) We have

$$|x-1| > 3$$

Using property,

$$|x| > a \Leftrightarrow x > a \text{ or } x < -a$$

Then, $|x-1| > 3 \Leftrightarrow x-1 > 3$

or $\qquad x-1 < (-3)$

$\Rightarrow \qquad x > 4 \text{ or } x < -2$

So, the solution set is $\{x : x < -2 \text{ or } x > 4, x \in R\}$

The graph of this set is

$$\xleftarrow{\quad x < -2 \quad} \underset{-2}{\bigcirc} \xrightarrow{\hspace{2cm}} \underset{4}{\bigcirc} \xrightarrow{\quad x > 4 \quad}$$ **Ans.**

(iii) We have

$$|3-2x| \geq 2$$

Using property

$$|x| \geq a \Leftrightarrow x \geq a \text{ or } x \leq -a$$

$$|3-2x| \geq 2$$

or $\quad 3-2x \leq -2 \text{ or } (3-2x) \geq 2$

$\Rightarrow \qquad -2x \leq -5 \text{ or } -2x \geq -1$

$\Rightarrow \qquad 2x \leq 1 \quad \text{or} \quad 2x \geq 5$

$\Rightarrow \qquad x \leq \dfrac{1}{2} \quad \text{or} \quad x \geq \dfrac{5}{2}$

The graph of this set is

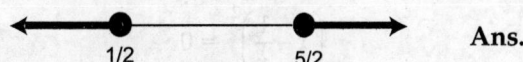
$$\xleftarrow{\hspace{1cm}} \underset{1/2}{\bullet} \xrightarrow{\hspace{2cm}} \underset{5/2}{\bullet} \xrightarrow{\hspace{1cm}}$$ **Ans.**

(iv) We have $\left|\dfrac{x-5}{3}\right| < 6$

Using property

$$|x| < a \Rightarrow -a < x < a$$

$$\left|\dfrac{x-5}{3}\right| < 6$$

$\Rightarrow \qquad -6 < \dfrac{x-5}{3} < 6$

$\Rightarrow \quad -18 < x-5 < 18$

$\Rightarrow 5-18 < x < 18+5$

$\Rightarrow \quad -13 < x < 23$

So the solution set is $\{x : -13 < x < 23, x \in R\}$

The graph of this set is

$$\underset{-13}{\bigcirc} \xrightarrow{\hspace{3cm}} \underset{23}{\bigcirc}$$ **Ans.**

(v) We have $\dfrac{3}{|x-2|} < 5$

$$\dfrac{1}{|x-2|} < \dfrac{5}{3}$$

$$|x-2| < \dfrac{3}{5}$$

Using property $|x| < a = -a < x < a$

$\therefore \qquad -\dfrac{3}{5} < x-2 < \dfrac{3}{5}$

$$\Rightarrow \quad -\frac{3}{5} + 2 < x < \frac{3}{5} + 2$$

$$\Rightarrow \quad \frac{7}{5} < x < \frac{13}{5}$$

So, the solution set is

$$\left\{ x : \frac{7}{5} < x < \frac{13}{5}, x \in R \right\}$$

The graph of this set is

7/5   13/5   **Ans.**

Chapter 5. Quadratic Equations

1. Which of the following are quadratic equations?

(i) $(2x - 3)(x + 5) = 2 - 3x$

(ii) $\left(x - \frac{1}{x} \right)^2 = 0.$

Sol. (i) Given equation is

$(2x - 3)(x + 5) = 2 - 3x$

$\Rightarrow \quad 2x^2 + 10x - 3x - 15 - 2 + 3x = 0$

$\Rightarrow \quad 2x^2 + 10x - 17 = 0$

∴   It is a quadratic equation.   **Ans.**

(ii) Given equation is

$$\left(x - \frac{1}{x} \right)^2 = 0$$

$\Rightarrow \quad x^2 + \frac{1}{x^2} - 2x \frac{1}{x} = 0$

$\Rightarrow \quad x^4 + 1 - 2x^2 = 0$

$\Rightarrow \quad x^4 - 2x^2 + 1 = 0$

∴   It is not a quadratic equation.   **Ans.**

2. Determine, if 3 is a root of the given equation $\sqrt{x^2 - 4x + 3} + \sqrt{x^2 - 9} = \sqrt{4x^2 - 14x + 16}$.

Sol. Substituting $x = 3$ in the given equation

$$\text{L.H.S.} = \sqrt{(3)^2 - 4 \times 3 + 3} + \sqrt{(3)^2 - 9}$$

$$= \sqrt{9 - 12 + 3} + \sqrt{9 - 9}$$

$$= 0 + 0 = 0$$

$$\text{R.H.S.} = \sqrt{4(3)^2 - 14 \times 3 + 16}$$

$$= \sqrt{36 - 42 + 16}$$

$$= \sqrt{52 - 42} = \sqrt{10}$$

Since,   L.H.S. ≠ R.H.S.

Therefore, $x = 3$ is not a root of the given equation.   **Ans.**

3. Examine whether the equation $5x^2 - 6x + 7 = 2x^2 - 4x + 5$ can be put in the form of a quadratic equation.

Sol. $5x^2 - 6x + 7 = 2x^2 - 4x + 5$

$\Rightarrow \quad 5x^2 - 6x + 7 - 2x^2 + 4x - 5 = 0$

$\Rightarrow \quad 3x^2 - 2x + 2 = 0$

∴   The given equation can be put in the form of a quadratic equation.   **Ans.**

4. Find if $x = -1$ is a root of the equation $2x^2 - 3x + 1 = 0$.

Sol. Given equation is $2x^2 - 3x + 1 = 0$.

Putting $x = -1$ in L.H.S. of equation

$$\text{L.H.S.} = 2(-1)^2 - 3 \times (-1) + 1$$

$$= 2 + 3 + 1 = 6 \neq 0 \neq \text{R.H.S.}$$

Hence, $x = -1$ is not a root of the equation.   **Ans.**

5. Determine the roots of the equation $(3x - 5)(2x + 7) = 0$

Sol. Given equation is

$(3x - 5)(2x + 7) = 0$

$\Rightarrow \quad 2x + 7 = 0$

$\Rightarrow \quad x = -\frac{7}{2}$

or $3x - 5 = 0$

or $x = \frac{5}{3}$

Hence, $x = \frac{5}{3}$ and $x = -\frac{7}{2}$ are two roots of the equation.   **Ans.**

6. Determine the roots of the equation

$$48x^2 - 13x - 1 = 0$$

Sol. Given equation is,

$$48x^2 - 13x - 1 = 0$$

$\Rightarrow \quad 48x^2 - 16x + 3x - 1 = 0$

$\Rightarrow \quad 16x(3x - 1) + 1(3x - 1) = 0$

$\Rightarrow \quad (3x - 1)(16x + 1) = 0$

$\Rightarrow \qquad 3x - 1 = 0$

or $\qquad 16x + 1 = 0$

$x = \dfrac{1}{3}$ or $x = \dfrac{-1}{16}$ are two roots of the equation.

Ans.

7. Determine the roots of the equation

$$10x - \dfrac{1}{x} = 3$$

Sol. Given equation is

$$10x - \dfrac{1}{x} = 3$$

$\Rightarrow \qquad \dfrac{10x^2 - 1}{x} = 3$

$\Rightarrow \qquad 10x^2 - 3x - 1 = 0$

$\Rightarrow \qquad 10x^2 - 5x + 2x - 1 = 0$

$\Rightarrow \qquad 5x(2x - 1) + 1(2x - 1) = 0$

$\Rightarrow \qquad (2x - 1)(5x + 1) = 0$

$\qquad 2x - 1 = 0$

or $\qquad 5x + 1 = 0$

$x = \dfrac{1}{2}$ or $x = -\dfrac{1}{5}$ are two roots of the equation.

Ans.

8. Determine the roots of the equation

$$\dfrac{2}{x^2} - \dfrac{5}{x} + 2 = 0$$

Sol. Given equation is

$$\dfrac{2}{x^2} - \dfrac{5}{x} + 2 = 0$$

$\Rightarrow \qquad \dfrac{2 - 5x + 2x^2}{x^2} = 0$

$\Rightarrow \qquad 2x^2 - 5x + 2 = 0$

$\Rightarrow \qquad 2x^2 - 4x - x + 2 = 0$

$\Rightarrow \qquad 2x(x - 2) - 1(x - 2) = 0$

$\Rightarrow \qquad (x - 2)(2x - 1) = 0$

$\Rightarrow \qquad x - 2 = 0$

or $\qquad 2x - 1 = 0$

$\Rightarrow x = 2$ or $x = \dfrac{1}{2}$ are two roots of the given equation. **Ans.**

9. Determine the roots of the equation

$$\sqrt{3}x^2 + 11x + 6\sqrt{3} = 0$$

Sol. Given equation is

$$\sqrt{3}x^2 + 11x + 6\sqrt{3} = 0$$

$\Rightarrow \quad \sqrt{3}x^2 + 9x + 2x + 6\sqrt{3} = 0$

$\Rightarrow \quad \sqrt{3}x(x + 3\sqrt{3}) + 2(x + 3\sqrt{3}) = 0$

$\Rightarrow \quad (x + 3\sqrt{3})(\sqrt{3}x + 2) = 0$

$\Rightarrow \qquad x + 3\sqrt{3} = 0$

or $\qquad \sqrt{3}x + 2 = 0$

$\Rightarrow \quad x = -3\sqrt{3}$ or $x = -\dfrac{2}{\sqrt{3}}$ are two roots of the given equation. **Ans.**

10. Determine the roots of the equation

$$ax^2 + (4a^2 - 3b)x - 12ab = 0$$

Sol. Given equation is,

$$ax^2 + (4a^2 - 3b)x - 12ab = 0$$

$\Rightarrow \qquad ax^2 + 4a^2x - 3bx - 12ab = 0$

$\Rightarrow \qquad ax(x + 4a) - 3b(x + 4a) = 0$

$\Rightarrow \qquad (ax - 3b)(x + 4a) = 0$

$\Rightarrow \qquad ax - 3b = 0$ or $x + 4a = 0$

$\Rightarrow x = \dfrac{3b}{a}$ or $-4a$ are two roots of the equation.

Ans.

11. Without solving the following quadratic equation, find the value of 'p' for which the given equation has real and equal roots :

$$x^2 + (p - 3)x + p = 0$$

Sol. Given equation is

$$x^2 + (p - 3)x + p = 0$$

Here, $a = 1$, $b = p - 3$ and $c = p$

For real and equal roots,

$\Rightarrow \qquad D = b^2 - 4ac = 0$

$\Rightarrow \qquad (p - 3)^2 - 4 \times 1 \times p = 0$

$\Rightarrow \qquad p^2 - 6p + 9 - 4p = 0$

$\Rightarrow \qquad p^2 - 10p + 9 = 0$

$\Rightarrow \qquad p^2 - p - 9p + 9 = 0$

$\Rightarrow \qquad p(p - 1) - 9(p - 1) = 0$

$\Rightarrow \qquad (p - 1)(p - 9) = 0$

$\Rightarrow \qquad p - 1 = 0$ or $p - 9 = 0$

$\Rightarrow \qquad p = 1$ or $p = +9$ **Ans.**

12. Find the value of k for which the following equation has equal roots :*

$$x^2 + 4kx + (k^2 - k + 2) = 0$$

Sol. Given equation is, $x^2 + 4k\ x + (k^2 - k + 2) = 0$

Comparing it with $ax^2 + bx + c = 0$, we have,

$\qquad a = 1, b = 4k, c = k^2 - k + 2.$

---

* Frequently asked previous years Board Exam Questions.

$\therefore$ $D = b^2 - 4ac = (4k)^2 - 4 \times 1$
$\times (k^2 - k + 2)$
$= 16k^2 - 4k^2 + 4k - 8$
$= 12k^2 + 4k - 8$

$\because$ The roots of given equation are equal, so

$$D = 0$$
$$\Rightarrow \quad 12k^2 + 4k - 8 = 0$$
$$\Rightarrow \quad 3k^2 + k - 2 = 0$$
$$\Rightarrow \quad 3k^2 + 3k - 2k - 2 = 0$$
$$\Rightarrow \quad 3k(k+1) - 2(k+1) = 0$$
$$\Rightarrow \quad (k+1)(3k-2) = 0$$
$$\Rightarrow \quad k + 1 = 0 \quad \text{or} \quad 3k - 2 = 0$$
$$\Rightarrow \quad k = -1 \text{ or} \quad k = \frac{2}{3}$$

$\therefore$ The value of k is -1 or $\frac{2}{3}$.   **Ans.**

13. Find the value of k for which the following equation has real and equal roots :
$$(k-12)x^2 + 2(k-12)x + 2 = 0.$$

Sol. The given equation is
$(k-12)x^2 + 2(k-12)x + 2 = 0$
Here, $a = k - 12$, $b = 2(k-12)$ and $c = 2$
For real and equal roots

$$b^2 - 4ac = 0$$
$$\Rightarrow \quad \{2(k-12)\}^2 - 4(k-12) \times 2 = 0$$
$$\Rightarrow \quad 4(k-12)^2 - 8(k-12) = 0$$
$$\Rightarrow \quad 4(k-12)\{k-12-2\} = 0$$
$$\Rightarrow \quad (k-12)(k-14) = 0$$
$$\Rightarrow \quad k - 12 = 0 \quad \text{or} \quad k - 14 = 0$$
$$\Rightarrow \quad k = 12 \quad \text{or} \quad k = 14.$$

Note : But at $k = 12$, terms of x^2 and x in the equation vanish hence only $k = 14$ is acceptable.
    Ans.

14. If one root of the equation $2x^2 - px + 4 = 0$ is 2, find the other root. Also find the value of p.

Sol. The given quadratic equation is
$$2x^2 - px + 4 = 0$$
one root = 2
Let the other root be α.
Then, sum of the roots
$$2 + \alpha = \frac{-(-p)}{2} = \frac{p}{2}$$
$$\Rightarrow \quad \alpha = \frac{p}{2} - 2 \qquad \text{...(i)}$$

The product of the roots
$$\alpha \times 2 = \frac{4}{2} = 2$$
$$\Rightarrow \quad \alpha = 1$$
Now, $2 + \alpha = \frac{p}{2}$
$$\Rightarrow \quad 2 + 1 = \frac{p}{2}$$
$$\Rightarrow \quad p = 6. \qquad \textbf{Ans.}$$

15. Solve the following quadratic equation :*
$$x^2 - 7x + 3 = 0$$
Give your answer correct to two decimal places.

Sol. Given : $x^2 - 7x + 3 = 0$
Here, $a = 1, b = -7$ and $c = 3$
$\therefore$
$$x = \frac{-b \pm \sqrt{b^2 - 4ac}}{2a}$$
$$= \frac{-(-7) \pm \sqrt{(-7)^2 - 4 \times 1 \times 3}}{2 \times 1}$$
$$= \frac{7 \pm \sqrt{49 - 12}}{2}$$
$$= \frac{7 \pm \sqrt{37}}{2} = \frac{7 \pm 6.08}{2}$$
Taking positive sign,
$$x = \frac{7 + 6.08}{2} = 6.541$$
Taking negative sign,
$$x = \frac{7 - 6.08}{2} = 0.458$$
Hence, $x = 6.54$ and 0.46 **Ans.**

16. Solve $x^{2/3} + x^{1/3} - 2 = 0$.

Sol. Given equation is $x^{2/3} + x^{1/3} - 2 = 0$
Putting $x^{1/3} = y$, the given equation becomes
$$y^2 + y - 2 = 0$$
$$\Rightarrow \quad y^2 + 2y - y - 2 = 0$$
$$\Rightarrow \quad y(y+2) - 1(y+2) = 0$$
$$\Rightarrow \quad (y+2)(y-1) = 0$$
$$\Rightarrow \quad y + 2 = 0 \text{ or } y - 1 = 0$$
$$\Rightarrow \quad y = -2 \text{ or } y = 1$$
But $x^{1/3} = y$
$\therefore$ $x^{1/3} = -2$ or $x^{1/3} = 1$
$$\Rightarrow \quad x = (-2)^3 \quad \text{or} \quad x = (1)^3$$
$$\Rightarrow \quad x = -8 \quad \text{or} \quad x = 1$$
Hence, roots are $-8, 1$.   **Ans.**

17. The sum of two numbers is 15. If the sum of their reciprocals is $\frac{3}{10}$, find the numbers.

Sol. Let the numbers be x and $15 - x$.

Then, according to problem

$$\frac{1}{x} + \frac{1}{15-x} = \frac{3}{10}$$

$$\Rightarrow \quad \frac{15-x+x}{x(15-x)} = \frac{3}{10}$$

$$\Rightarrow \quad 15 \times 10 = 3x(15-x)$$

$$\Rightarrow \quad 150 = 45x - 3x^2$$

$$\Rightarrow \quad 3x^2 - 45x + 150 = 0$$

$$\Rightarrow \quad x^2 - 15x + 50 = 0$$

$$\Rightarrow \quad x^2 - 10x - 5x + 50 = 0$$

$$\Rightarrow \quad x(x-10) - 5(x-10) = 0$$

$$\Rightarrow \quad x - 10 = 0 \text{ or } x - 5 = 0$$

$$\Rightarrow \quad x = 10 \text{ or } x = 5$$

Hence, the numbers are 10, 5.   **Ans.**

18. Find two consecutive natural numbers whose squares have the sum 221.

Sol. Let the number be $x, x + 1$

Then, $\quad x^2 + (x+1)^2 = 221$

$\Rightarrow \quad x^2 + x^2 + 1 + 2x - 221 = 0$

$\Rightarrow \quad 2x^2 + 2x - 220 = 0$

$\Rightarrow \quad x^2 + x - 110 = 0$

$\Rightarrow \quad x^2 + 11x - 10x - 110 = 0$

$\Rightarrow \quad x(x+11) - 10(x+11) = 0$

$\Rightarrow \quad (x+11)(x-10) = 0$

$\Rightarrow \quad x = -11 \text{ or } x = 10$

But $x = -11$ is rejected   [$\because$ It cannot be $-$ve as it is a natural number]

$\therefore \qquad\qquad x = 10$

Hence, required numbers are 10, 10 + 1.

i.e., 10 and 11.   **Ans.**

19. If an integer is added to its square the sum is 90. Find the integer with the help of a quadratic equation.

Sol. Let the required integer be x.

Then, according to the given condition

$\Rightarrow \qquad\qquad x + x^2 = 90$

$\Rightarrow \qquad\qquad x^2 + x - 90 = 0$

$\Rightarrow \qquad x^2 + 10x - 9x - 90 = 0$

$\Rightarrow \qquad x(x+10) - 9(x+10) = 0$

$\Rightarrow \qquad\qquad (x+10)(x-9) = 0$

$\Rightarrow \qquad x + 10 = 0 \text{ or } x - 9 = 0$

$\Rightarrow \qquad\qquad x = -10 \text{ or } x = 9$

Hence, the required integer is 9 or -10.   **Ans.**

20. The difference of two natural numbers is 7 and their product is 450. Find the numbers.*

Sol. Let the two natural numbers be x and y such that $x > y$.

Then, $\qquad\qquad x - y = 7$

$\Rightarrow \qquad\qquad x = 7 + y \qquad$ ...(i)

and $\qquad\qquad xy = 450$

$\Rightarrow \qquad\qquad (7+y)y = 450 \qquad$ [Using (i)]

$\Rightarrow \qquad\qquad y^2 + 7y - 450 = 0$

$\Rightarrow \quad y^2 + 25y - 18y - 450 = 0$ (on factorisation)

$\Rightarrow \quad y(y+25) - 18(y+25) = 0$

$\Rightarrow \qquad\qquad (y+25)(y-18) = 0$

$\Rightarrow \qquad\qquad\qquad y = -25 \qquad$ [Neglected]

or $\qquad\qquad\qquad\qquad y = 18$

$\therefore \qquad\qquad\qquad\qquad y = 18$

$\therefore \qquad\qquad\qquad x = 7 + 18 = 25$

Hence, the numbers are 25 and 18.   **Ans.**

21. Find two consecutive positive even integers whose squares have the sum 340.

Sol. Let two consecutive positive even integers be $2x, 2x + 2$

$\therefore \qquad (2x)^2 + (2x+2)^2 = 340$

$\Rightarrow \qquad 4x^2 + 4x^2 + 4 + 8x = 340$

$\Rightarrow \qquad\qquad 8x^2 + 8x - 336 = 0$

$\Rightarrow \qquad\qquad\qquad x^2 + x - 42 = 0$

$\Rightarrow \qquad\qquad x^2 + 7x - 6x - 42 = 0$

$\Rightarrow \qquad\qquad x(x+7) - 6(x+7) = 0$

$\Rightarrow \qquad\qquad\qquad (x+7)(x-6) = 0$

$\Rightarrow \qquad\qquad x + 7 = 0 \text{ or } x - 6 = 0$

$\Rightarrow \qquad\qquad\qquad x = -7 \text{ or } x = 6$

Negative integer is not required, therefore, $x = 6$.

Hence, integers are $6 \times 2, (6 \times 2) + 2$.

i.e., 12 and 14.   **Ans.**

22. Divide 29 into two parts so that the sum of the square of the parts is 425.

Sol. Let the parts be x and $29 - x$.

According to the problem

$$x^2 + (29 - x)^2 = 425$$

$$\Rightarrow \quad x^2 + 841 + x^2 - 58x - 425 = 0$$

$$\Rightarrow \quad 2x^2 - 58x + 416 = 0$$

$$\Rightarrow \quad x^2 - 29x + 208 = 0$$

$$\Rightarrow \quad x^2 - 16x - 13x + 208 = 0$$

$$\Rightarrow \quad x(x - 16) - 13(x - 16) = 0$$

$$\Rightarrow \quad (x - 16)(x - 13) = 0$$

$$\Rightarrow \quad x - 16 = 0 \text{ or } x - 13 = 0$$

$$\Rightarrow \quad x = 16 \text{ or } x = 13$$

When $x = 16$ and When $x = 13$

Then, $29 - x = 13$ Then, $29 - x = 16$

Hence, the parts are 16 and 13 or 13 and 16.

Ans.

23. In a two digit number, the unit's digit is twice the ten's digit. If 27 is added to the number, the digit interchange their places. Find the number.

Sol. Let ten's digit $= x$

Unit's digit $= 2x$

Required number $= 10x + 2x$

$$= 12x$$

On interchanging the digits

Number formed $= 10(2x) + x$

$$= 21x$$

According to the given condition

$$\Rightarrow \quad 12x + 27 = 21x$$

$$\Rightarrow \quad 27 = 21x - 12x$$

$$\Rightarrow \quad 27 = 9x$$

$$\Rightarrow \quad x = \frac{27}{9}$$

$$\therefore \quad x = 3$$

$$\therefore \quad \text{Required number} = 12 \times 3$$

$$= 36.$$ **Ans.**

24. A two digit positive number is such that the product of its digits is 6. If 9 is added to the number, the digits interchange their places. Find the number.

Sol. Let the unit's digit be x then, tens digit will be $\frac{6}{x}$, then two digit number is $\frac{60}{x} + x$.

From question,

$$\frac{60}{x} + x + 9 = 10x + \frac{6}{x}$$

$$\Rightarrow \quad 60 + x^2 + 9x = 10x^2 + 6$$

$$\Rightarrow \quad 9x^2 - 9x - 54 = 0$$

$$\Rightarrow \quad x^2 - x - 6 = 0$$

$$\Rightarrow \quad x^2 - 3x + 2x - 6 = 0$$

$$\Rightarrow \quad x(x - 3) + 2(x - 3) = 0$$

$$\Rightarrow \quad (x - 3)(x + 2) = 0$$

$$\Rightarrow \quad x = -2 \text{ or } 3$$

As x can't be $-$ve

So, required two digit number

$$= \frac{60}{3} + 3$$

$$= 23.$$ **Ans.**

25. Five years ago, a woman's age was the square of her son's age. Ten years later her age will be twice that of her son's age. Find :

(i) The age of the son five years ago.

(ii) The present age of the woman.

Sol. Let the age of son be x years five years ago.

$\therefore$ Mother's age will be x^2 years five years ago.

$\therefore$ Present age of son $= x + 5$

$\therefore$ Present age of mother $= x^2 + 5$

After ten years son's age be $(x + 15)$ years and woman's age be $(x^2 + 15)$

Given, $x^2 + 15 = 2(x + 15)$

$$\Rightarrow \quad x^2 + 15 = 2x + 30$$

$$\Rightarrow \quad x^2 - 2x - 15 = 0$$

$$\Rightarrow \quad (x - 5)(x + 3) = 0$$

$$\Rightarrow \quad x = 5$$

or $x = -3$ (not possible)

$\therefore$ **(i)** Son's age five years ago = 5 years. **Ans.**

(ii) Woman's present age = 25 + 5

$$= 30 \text{ years.}$$ **Ans.**

26. The length of verandah is 3 m more than its breadth. The numerical value of its area is equal to the numerical value of its perimeter.

(i) Taking x, breadth of the verandah write an equation in 'x' that represents the above statement.

(ii) Solve the equation obtained in above and hence find the dimension of verandah.

Sol. Let breadth = x m, length = $(x + 3)$ m.

Area = $x(x + 3)$ sq. m.

Perimeter = $2(x + x + 3) = (4x + 6)$ m.

(i) According to the question, $x(x + 3) = 4x + 6$

$\Rightarrow \qquad\qquad x^2 - x - 6 = 0$ **Ans.**

$\Rightarrow \qquad\qquad (x + 2)(x - 3) = 0$

(ii) $\qquad\qquad x^2 - x - 6 = 0$

$x^2 - 3x + 2x - 6 = 0$

$x(x - 3) + 2(x - 3) = 0$

(font ka dhyan rkhein)

$\therefore x = 3$ and $x = -2$ (inadmissible).

Hence, breadth = 3 m and length = 6 m. **Ans.**

27. In each of the following determine the value of k for which the given value is a solution of the equation :

(i) $kx^2 + 2x - 3 = 0; x = 2$

(ii) $3x^2 + 2kx - 3 = 0; x = -\dfrac{1}{2}$

(iii) $x^2 + 2ax - k = 0; x = -a.$

Sol. (i) Since, $x = 2$ is a root of the given equation, therefore, it satisfies the equation *i.e.,*

$k(2)^2 + 2 \times 2 - 3 = 0$

$\Rightarrow \qquad\qquad 4k + 1 = 0 \Rightarrow k = -\dfrac{1}{4}.$ **Ans.**

(ii) Since, $x = -\dfrac{1}{2}$ is a root of the given equation

$3x^2 + 2kx - 3 = 0$

Therefore, putting the value of x in equation

$3\left(-\dfrac{1}{2}\right)^2 + 2k\left(-\dfrac{1}{2}\right) - 3 = 0$

$\Rightarrow \qquad 3 \times \dfrac{1}{4} - k - 3 = 0$

$\Rightarrow \qquad k = \dfrac{3}{4} - 3 = -\dfrac{9}{4}$

$\Rightarrow \qquad k = -\dfrac{9}{4}.$ **Ans.**

(iii) Since, $x = -a$ is a root of the equation

Therefore, putting the value of x

$x^2 + 2ax - k = 0$

$\Rightarrow (-a)^2 + 2a \times (-a) - k = 0$

$\Rightarrow \qquad a^2 - 2a^2 - k = 0$

$\Rightarrow \qquad\qquad -k = a^2 \Rightarrow k = -a^2.$ **Ans.**

28. Solve for x the quadratic equation $x^2 - 4x - 8 = 0$. Give your answer correct to three significant figures. [2019]

Sol. Given quadratic equation is $x^2 - 4x - 8 = 0$.

Comparing it with $ax^2 + bx + c = 0$, we get

$a = 1, b = -4$ and $c = -8$

$\therefore \quad x = \dfrac{-b \pm \sqrt{b^2 - 4ac}}{2a}$

$= \dfrac{(-4) \pm \sqrt{(-4)^2 - 4 \times 1 \times (-8)}}{2 \times 1}$

$= \dfrac{4 \pm \sqrt{16 + 32}}{2} = \dfrac{4 \pm \sqrt{48}}{2} = \dfrac{4 \pm 6.928}{2}$

$= \dfrac{4 + 6.928}{2}$ or $\dfrac{4 - 6.928}{2}$

$= \dfrac{10.928}{2}$ or $\dfrac{-2.928}{2}$

$= 5.464$ or -1.464

$\therefore \quad x = 5.464$ or -1.464

(correct to 3 significant figures). **Ans.**

29. Solve $x^2 + 7x = 7$ and give your answer correct to two decimal places.*

Sol. We have, $\qquad x^2 + 7x = 7$

$\Rightarrow \qquad\qquad x^2 + 7x - 7 = 0$

Comparing it with $ax^2 + bx + c = 0$, we have

$a = 1, b = 7, c = -7$

$\therefore x = \dfrac{-b \pm \sqrt{b^2 - 4ac}}{2a}$

$= \dfrac{-7 \pm \sqrt{7^2 - 4 \times 1 \times (-7)}}{2 \times 1}$

$= \dfrac{-7 \pm \sqrt{49 + 28}}{2}$

$= \dfrac{-7 \pm \sqrt{77}}{2}$

$= \dfrac{-7 \pm 8.775}{2}$

$= \dfrac{-7 + 8.775}{2}$ or $\dfrac{-7 - 8.775}{2}$

$= \dfrac{1.775}{2}$ or $\dfrac{-15.775}{2}$

* **Frequently asked previous years Board Exam Questions.**

$= 0.8875$ or $- 7.8875$

$= 0.89$ or $- 7.89$

(correct to 2 decimal places) **Ans.**

30. Solve the following equation and give your answer up to two decimal places :

$$x^2 - 5x - 10 = 0$$

Sol. Given equation is

$$x^2 - 5x - 10 = 0$$

On comparing with

$$ax^2 + bx + c = 0$$

$$a = 1, b = -5, c = -10$$

$$\therefore \quad x = \frac{-b \pm \sqrt{b^2 - 4ac}}{2a}$$

$$\therefore \quad x = \frac{5 \pm \sqrt{25 + 40}}{2}$$

$$\Rightarrow \quad x = \frac{5 \pm \sqrt{65}}{2} = \frac{5 \pm 8.06}{2}$$

$$\Rightarrow \quad x = \frac{5 + 8.06}{2} = \frac{13.06}{2} = 6.53$$

and $$x = \frac{5 - 8.06}{2} = \frac{-3.06}{2} = -1.53$$

$$\Rightarrow \quad x = 6.53, x = -1.53 \qquad \textbf{Ans.}$$

31. Solve using the quadratic formula $x^2 - 4x + 1 = 0$.

Sol. We have, $x^2 - 4x + 1 = 0$

On comparing this equation with

$$ax^2 + bx + c = 0, \text{ we obtain}$$

$$a = 1, b = -4, c = 1$$

By using quadratic formula, we obtain

$$x = \frac{-b \pm \sqrt{b^2 - 4ac}}{2a}$$

$$= \frac{-(-4) \pm \sqrt{(-4)^2 - 4 \times 1 \times 1}}{2 \times 1}$$

$$= \frac{4 \pm \sqrt{16 - 4}}{2} = \frac{4 \pm \sqrt{12}}{2}$$

Taking (+) sign,

$$= \frac{4 + 2\sqrt{3}}{2} = 2 + \sqrt{3}$$

$$\therefore \quad x = 2 + 1.732 = 3.732$$

Taking (−) sign,

or $$x = \frac{4 - \sqrt{12}}{2} = \frac{4 - 2\sqrt{3}}{2} = 2 - \sqrt{3}$$

$$\therefore \quad x = 2 - 1.732 = 0.268$$

Hence, $x = 2 + \sqrt{3}$ and $2 - \sqrt{3}$

or 3.732 and 0.268 **Ans.**

32. Solve the quadratic equation

(i) $3a^2x^2 + 8abx + 4b^2 = 0$

(ii) $\left(x - \dfrac{a}{b}\right)^2 = \dfrac{a^2}{b^2}$

Sol. (i) We have

$$3a^2x^2 + 8abx + 4b^2 = 0$$

$$\Rightarrow \quad 3a^2x^2 + 6abx + 2abx + 4b^2 = 0$$

$$\Rightarrow \quad 3ax(ax + 2b) + 2b(ax + 2b) = 0$$

$$\Rightarrow \quad (3ax + 2b)(ax + 2b) = 0$$

$$\Rightarrow \quad x = -\frac{2b}{3a} \text{ or } -\frac{2b}{a}.$$

$$x = \left\{ -\frac{2b}{3a}, -\frac{2b}{a} \right\}$$

Ans.

(ii) We have

$$\left(x - \frac{a}{b}\right)^2 = \frac{a^2}{b^2}$$

$$\Rightarrow \quad x^2 + \frac{a^2}{b^2} - \frac{2ax}{b} = \frac{a^2}{b^2}$$

$$\Rightarrow \quad x^2 - \frac{2ax}{b} = 0$$

$$\Rightarrow \quad x\left(x - \frac{2a}{b}\right) = 0$$

$$\Rightarrow \quad x = 0 \text{ or } x - \frac{2a}{b} = 0$$

$$\Rightarrow \quad x = 0 \text{ or } x = \frac{2a}{b}.$$

$$\Rightarrow \quad x = \left\{ 0, \frac{2a}{b} \right\} \qquad \textbf{Ans.}$$

33. Solve the equation $2x - \dfrac{1}{x} = 7$. Write your answer correct upto two decimal places.

Sol. We have, $2x - \dfrac{1}{x} = 7$

$$\Rightarrow \quad 2x^2 - 1 = 7x$$

$$\Rightarrow \quad 2x^2 - 7x - 1 = 0$$

Determine the Following

By using formula,

$$x = \frac{-b \pm \sqrt{b^2 - 4ac}}{2a}$$

Here, $a = 2, b = -7, c = -1$

Therefore,

$$x = \frac{-(-7) \pm \sqrt{(-7)^2 - 4 \times 2 \times (-1)}}{2 \times 2}$$

$$x = \frac{7 \pm \sqrt{49 + 8}}{4} = \frac{7 \pm \sqrt{57}}{4}$$

$$x = \frac{7 + \sqrt{57}}{4}$$

or $\quad x = \frac{7 - \sqrt{57}}{4}$

$$x = \frac{7 + 7 \cdot 550}{4}$$

or $\quad x = \frac{7 - 7 \cdot 550}{4}$

$$x = 3 \cdot 64$$

or $\quad x = -\cdot 14$

$$x = \{3 \cdot 64, -0 \cdot 14\} \qquad \textbf{Ans.}$$

34. Form a quadratic equation whose roots are :

(i) $\sqrt{3}$ and $3\sqrt{3}$

(ii) $2 + \sqrt{5}$ and $2 - \sqrt{5}$

Sol. (i) Let α, β be the roots of the required quadratic equation :

Then, $\qquad \alpha = \sqrt{3}$ and $\beta = 3\sqrt{3}$

$\Rightarrow \qquad \alpha + \beta = \sqrt{3} + 3\sqrt{3}$

and $\qquad \alpha\beta = \sqrt{3} \times 3\sqrt{3}$

$\Rightarrow \qquad \alpha + \beta = 4\sqrt{3}$

and $\qquad \alpha\beta = 9$

Required quadratic equation is

$$x^2 - (\alpha + \beta)x + \alpha\beta = 0$$

$\Rightarrow \qquad x^2 - 4\sqrt{3}\,x + 9 = 0. \qquad \textbf{Ans.}$

(ii) Let α, β be the given roots of required quadratic equation.

Then, $\qquad \alpha = 2 + \sqrt{5}$

and $\qquad \beta = 2 - \sqrt{5}$

$$\alpha + \beta = 2 + \sqrt{5} + 2 - \sqrt{5} = 4$$

and $\qquad \alpha\beta = (2 + \sqrt{5})(2 - \sqrt{5})$

$\Rightarrow \qquad \alpha + \beta = 4$ and $\alpha\beta = (2)^2 - (\sqrt{5})^2$

$\Rightarrow \qquad \alpha + \beta = 4$ and $\alpha\beta = 4 - 5$

$\Rightarrow \qquad \alpha + \beta = 4$ and $\alpha\beta = -1$

Required quadratic equation is

$$x^2 - (\alpha + \beta)x + \alpha\beta = 0$$

$\Rightarrow \qquad x^2 - 4x - 1 = 0. \qquad \textbf{Ans.}$

35. Find the value of k for which the given quadratic equation has real roots :

(i) $kx^2 - 6x - 2 = 0$

(ii) $9x^2 + 3kx + 4 = 0.$

Sol. (i) We have,

$$kx^2 - 6x - 2 = 0$$

On comparing this equation with

$$ax^2 + bx + c = 0$$

We obtain, $a = k, b = -6$ and $c = -2$.

This equation has real roots if

$$b^2 - 4ac \geq 0$$

$\Rightarrow \quad (-6)^2 - 4 \times k \times (-2) \geq 0$

$\Rightarrow \qquad 36 + 8k \geq 0$

$\Rightarrow \qquad 8k \geq -36$

$\Rightarrow \qquad k \geq -\frac{36}{8} \Rightarrow k \geq -\frac{9}{2} .$

$$\textbf{Ans.}$$

(ii) We have,

$$9x^2 + 3kx + 4 = 0$$

On comparing this equation with $ax^2 + bx + c = 0$.

We have, $a = 9, b = 3k$ and $c = 4$.

This equation has real roots if

$$b^2 - 4ac \geq 0$$

$\Rightarrow \qquad (3k)^2 - 4 \times 9 \times 4 \geq 0$

$\Rightarrow \qquad 9k^2 - 144 \geq 0$

$\Rightarrow \qquad 9k^2 \geq 144$

$$\Rightarrow \qquad k^2 \geq \frac{144}{9} \Rightarrow k \geq \frac{12}{3}$$

$$\Rightarrow \qquad k \geq 4. \qquad \textbf{Ans.}$$

36. Without actually determining the roots comment upon the nature of the roots of each of the following equations :

(i) $3x^2 + 2x - 1 = 0$

(ii) $2\sqrt{3}x^2 - 2\sqrt{2}x - \sqrt{3} = 0$

(iii) $9a^2b^2x^2 - 48abcdx + 64c^2d^2 = 0, \ a \neq 0, \ b \neq 0$

(iv) $x^2 - 5x + 7 = 0$

(v) $x^2 - 4x + 1 = 0$

(vi) $x^2 + 5x + 15 = 0.$

Sol. (i) We have, $3x^2 + 2x - 1 = 0$.

Here, $a = 3$, $b = 2$ and $c = -1$

$$D = b^2 - 4ac = 4 - 4 \times 3 \times (-1)$$

$$\Rightarrow \qquad D = 4 + 12 = 16 > 0.$$

The given equation has real and distinct roots

Ans.

(ii) We have, $2\sqrt{3} x^2 - 2\sqrt{2} x - \sqrt{3} = 0$.

Here, $a = 2\sqrt{3}$, $b = -2\sqrt{2}$ and $c = -\sqrt{3}$

$$D = b^2 - 4ac$$

$$\Rightarrow \qquad D = 8 - 4 \times 2\sqrt{3} \times - \sqrt{3}$$

$$\Rightarrow \qquad D = 8 + 24 = 32 > 0$$

The given equation has real and distinct roots.

Ans.

(iii) We have, $9a^2b^2x^2 - 48abcdx + 64c^2d^2 = 0$.

Here, $\qquad D = b^2 - 4ac$

$$\Rightarrow \quad (-48abcd)^2 - 4 \times 9a^2b^2 \times 64c^2d^2$$

$$\Rightarrow \quad 2304 \, a^2b^2c^2d^2 - 2304 \, a^2b^2c^2d^2 = 0$$

$$\therefore \qquad D = 0$$

$\Rightarrow$ Roots are real and equal. **Ans.**

(iv) We have, $x^2 - 5x + 7 = 0$.

Here, $a = 1$, $b = -5$ and $c = 7$

$$D = b^2 - 4ac = 25 - 4 \times 1 \times 7.$$

$$\Rightarrow \qquad D = 25 - 28 = -3$$

Since, $D < 0$, roots are imaginary. **Ans.**

(v) We have, $x^2 - 4x + 1 = 0$.

Here, $a = 1$, $b = -4$ and $c = 1$

$$D = b^2 - 4ac = 16 - 4 \times 1 \times 1$$

$$\Rightarrow \qquad D = 16 - 4 = 12 > 0$$

The given equation has real and distinct roots.

Ans.

(vi) $x^2 + 5x + 15 = 0.$

Here, $a = 1$, $b = 5$ and $c = 15$

$$D = b^2 - 4ac = (5)^2 - 4 \times 1 \times 15$$

$$= 25 - 60 = -35$$

$$\Rightarrow \qquad D < 0$$

Roots are imaginary. **Ans.**

37. Solve for x using the quadratic formula. Write your answer correct upto two significant figures $(x - 1)^2 - 3x + 4 = 0.$

Sol. We have,

$$(x - 1)^2 - 3x + 4 = 0$$

$$\Rightarrow \qquad x^2 + 1 - 2x - 3x + 4 = 0$$

$$\Rightarrow \qquad x^2 - 5x + 5 = 0$$

Comparing it with

$$ax^2 + bx + c = 0$$

We get $\qquad a = 1, b = -5, c = 5$

By using the formula,

$$x = \frac{-b \pm \sqrt{b^2 - 4ac}}{2a}$$

$$= \frac{-(-5) \pm \sqrt{(-5)^2 - 4 \times 1 \times 5}}{1}$$

$$= \frac{5 + \sqrt{25 - 20}}{2}$$

$$= \frac{5 \pm \sqrt{5}}{2}$$

$$x = \frac{5 \pm 2 \cdot 24}{2}$$

Taking $+$ ve sign, $x = \frac{5 + 2 \cdot 24}{2}$

$$x = 3 \cdot 62$$

Taking $-$ ve sign, $x = \frac{5 - 2 \cdot 25}{2}$

$$= \frac{2 \cdot 75}{2} = 1 \cdot 38$$

Thus, required values are $3 \cdot 62$ and $1 \cdot 38$. **Ans.**

38. Without solving the following quadratic equation, find the value of 'm' for which the given equation has real and equal roots.

$$x^2 + 2(m - 1)x + (m + 5) = 0$$

Sol. We have,

$$x^2 + 2(m-1)x + (m+5) = 0$$

Comparing with

$$ax^2 + bx + c = 0$$

$$a = 1, b = 2(m-1), \ c = (m+5)$$

Since, equation has real and equal roots.

So, $D = 0$

$\Rightarrow$ $b^2 - 4ac = 0$

$\Rightarrow$ $[2(m-1)]^2 - 4 \times 1 \times (m+5) = 0$

$\Rightarrow$ $4(m-1)^2 - 4(m+5) = 0$

$\Rightarrow$ $4[(m-1)^2 - (m+5)] = 0$

$\Rightarrow$ $4[m^2 - 2m + 1 - m - 5] = 0$

$\Rightarrow$ $m^2 - 3m - 4 = 0$

$\Rightarrow$ $(m+1)(m-4) = 0$

Either $m + 1 = 0$

$\Rightarrow$ $m = -1$

or $m - 4 = 0$

$m = 4$

$m = \{-1, 4\}$ **Ans.**

39. Solve the following by reducing them into quadratic equations :

(i) $x^4 - 26x^2 + 25 = 0$

(ii) $z^4 - 10z^2 + 9 = 0$.

Sol. (i) Given equation is

$$x^4 - 26x^2 + 25 = 0$$

Putting, $x^2 = y$, the given equation reduces to the form $y^2 - 26y + 25 = 0$

$\Rightarrow$ $y^2 - 25y - y + 25 = 0$

$\Rightarrow$ $y(y-25) - 1(y-25) = 0$

$\Rightarrow$ $(y-25)(y-1) = 0$

$\Rightarrow$ $y - 25 = 0$ or $y - 1 = 0$

$\Rightarrow$ $y = 25$ or $y = 1$

$\therefore$ $x^2 = 25$

$\Rightarrow$ $x = \pm 5$

or $x^2 = 1$

$\Rightarrow$ $x = \pm 1$

Hence, the required roots are $\{\pm 5, \pm 1\}$.   **Ans.**

(ii) Given equation is

$$z^4 - 10z^2 + 9 = 0$$

Putting $z^2 = x$, then given equation reduces to the form $x^2 - 10x + 9 = 0$

$\Rightarrow$ $x^2 - 9x - x + 9 = 0$

$\Rightarrow$ $x(x-9) - 1(x-9) = 0$

$\Rightarrow$ $(x-9)(x-1) = 0$

$\Rightarrow$ $x - 9 = 0$ or $x - 1 = 1$

$\Rightarrow$ $x = 9$ or $x = 1$

But $z^2 = x$

$\therefore$ $z^2 = 9$

$\Rightarrow$ $z = \pm 3$

or $z^2 = 1$

$\Rightarrow$ $z = \pm 1$

Hence, the required roots are $\{\pm 3, \pm 1\}$.   **Ans.**

40. Solve for x : $9^{x+2} - 6.3^{x+1} + 1 = 0$.

Sol. Given equation is

$$9^{x+2} - 6.3^{x+1} + 1 = 0$$

$\Rightarrow$ $9^x.9^2 - 6.3^x.3^1 + 1 = 0$

$\Rightarrow$ $81.(3^2)^x - 18.3^x + 1 = 0$

$\Rightarrow$ $81.3^{2x} - 18.3^x + 1 = 0$

Putting $3^x = y$, then it becomes $81y^2 - 18y + 1 = 0$

$\Rightarrow$ $81y^2 - 9y - 9y + 1 = 0$

$\Rightarrow$ $9y(9y-1) - 1(9y-1) = 0$

$\Rightarrow$ $(9y-1)(9y-1) = 0$

$\Rightarrow$ $9y = 1 \Rightarrow y = \dfrac{1}{9}$

But $3^x = \dfrac{1}{9} = \dfrac{1}{3^2} = 3^{-2}$

$\therefore$ $x = -2$

Hence, the required root is -2.   **Ans.**

41. Solve for x :

$$(x^2 - 5x)^2 - 7(x^2 - 5x) + 6 = 0; \ x \in R.$$

Sol. Given equation is

$$(x^2 - 5x)^2 - 7(x^2 - 5x) + 6 = 0$$

Put $x^2 - 5x = y$

$\therefore$ The given equation becomes

$$y^2 - 7y + 6 = 0$$

$\Rightarrow$ $y^2 - 6y - y + 6 = 0$

$\Rightarrow$ $y(y-6) - 1(y-6) = 0$

$\Rightarrow$ $y = 1, 6$

But $x^2 - 5x = y$

$\therefore$ $x^2 - 5x = 1$

$x^2 - 5x = 6$

$\Rightarrow$ $x^2 - 5x - 1 = 0$

$\Rightarrow$ $x^2 - 5x - 6 = 0$

Here, $a = 1, b = -5, c = -1$

$\Rightarrow$ $x^2 - 6x + x - 6 = 0$

$\therefore$ $x = \dfrac{-b \pm \sqrt{b^2 - 4ac}}{2a}$

$\Rightarrow$ $x(x-6) + 1(x-6) = 0$

$\Rightarrow$ $x = \dfrac{-(-5) \pm \sqrt{25 + 4}}{2}$

$$\Rightarrow \qquad (x-6)(x+1) = 0$$

$$\Rightarrow \qquad x = \frac{5 \pm \sqrt{29}}{2}$$

$$\Rightarrow \qquad x = 6 \text{ or } x = -1$$

Hence, the roots are $\left\{-1, 6, \dfrac{5 \pm \sqrt{29}}{2}\right\}$ **Ans.**

42. Solve the following equation by reducing it to quadratic equation :

$$\sqrt{3x^2 - 2} + 1 = 2x.$$

Sol. Given equation is

$$\sqrt{3x^2 - 2} + 1 = 2x$$

$$\Rightarrow \qquad \sqrt{3x^2 - 2} = 2x - 1$$

On squaring both sides, we get

$$3x^2 - 2 = 4x^2 + 1 - 4x$$

$$\Rightarrow \qquad -x^2 + 4x - 3 = 0$$

$$\Rightarrow \qquad x^2 - 4x + 3 = 0$$

$$\Rightarrow \qquad x^2 - 3x - x + 3 = 0$$

$$\Rightarrow \qquad x(x-3) - 1(x-3) = 0$$

$$\Rightarrow \qquad (x-3)(x-1) = 0$$

$$\Rightarrow \qquad x = 3 \text{ or } x = 1$$

Hence, the roots are {3, 1}.   **Ans.**

43. Solve :

$$(x+2)(x-5)(x-6)(x+1) = 144.$$

Sol. Given equation is

$$(x+2)(x-5)(x-6)(x+1) = 144$$

$$\Rightarrow (x+2)(x-6)(x-5)(x+1) = 144$$

$$\Rightarrow (x^2 - 4x - 12)(x^2 - 4x - 5) = 144$$

Put $x^2 - 4x = y$

Then $\qquad (y-12)(y-5) = 144$

$$\Rightarrow \qquad y^2 - 17y + 60 - 144 = 0$$

$$\Rightarrow \qquad y^2 - 17y - 84 = 0$$

$$\Rightarrow \qquad y^2 - 21y + 4y - 84 = 0$$

$$\Rightarrow \qquad y(y-21) + 4(y-21) = 0$$

$$\Rightarrow \qquad (y-21)(y+4) = 0$$

$$\Rightarrow \qquad y - 21 = 0 \text{ or } y + 4 = 0$$

$$\Rightarrow \qquad y = 21 \text{ or } y = -4$$

But $x^2 - 4x = y$

$$\therefore \qquad x^2 - 4x = 21$$

or $\qquad x^2 - 4x = -4$

$$\Rightarrow \qquad x^2 - 4x - 21 = 0$$

or $\qquad x^2 - 4x + 4 = 0$

$$\Rightarrow \qquad x^2 - 7x + 3x - 21 = 0$$

or $\qquad (x-2)^2 = 0$

$$\Rightarrow \qquad x(x-7) + 3(x-7) = 0$$

or $\qquad x = 2, 2$

$$\Rightarrow \qquad (x-7)(x+3) = 0$$

$$\Rightarrow \qquad x = 7, -3$$

The roots are {7, −3, 2, 2}   **Ans.**

44. The side (in cm) of a triangle containing the right angle are $5x$ and $3x - 1$. If the area of the triangle is 60 cm². Find the sides of the triangle.

Sol. The area of right angle triangle ABC

$$= \frac{1}{2} \times \text{Base} \times \text{Height}$$

$$= \frac{5x(3x-1)}{2}$$

According to the question,

$$\therefore \qquad \frac{5x(3x-1)}{2} = 60$$

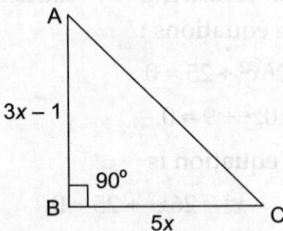

$$\Rightarrow \qquad 15x^2 - 5x = 120$$

$$\Rightarrow \qquad 3x^2 - x = 24$$

$$\Rightarrow \qquad 3x^2 - x - 24 = 0$$

$$\Rightarrow \qquad 3x^2 - 9x + 8x - 24 = 0$$

$$\Rightarrow \qquad 3x(x-3) + 8(x-3) = 0$$

$$\Rightarrow \qquad (x-3)(3x+8) = 0$$

$$\Rightarrow \qquad x - 3 = 0 \text{ or } 3x + 8 = 0$$

$$\Rightarrow \qquad x = 3 \quad \text{or} \quad x = \frac{-8}{3}$$

But $x = \dfrac{-8}{3}$ is not possible as side cannot be negative

Then $x = 3$.

Hence, sides are $AB = 3x - 1 = 8$ cm

$$BC = 5x = 15 \text{ cm}$$

In right angled Δ ABC, by Pythagoras theorem, we have

$$AC = \sqrt{(AB)^2 + (BC)^2}$$

$$= \sqrt{64 + 225}$$

$$= \sqrt{289} = 17 \text{ cm. } \textbf{Ans.}$$

45. ₹ 480 is divided equally among 'x' children. If the number of children were 20 more then each would have got ₹ 12 less. Find 'x'.

Sol. Share of each child = ₹ $\dfrac{480}{x}$

Now, Number of children = $x + 20$

∴ Share of each child = ₹ $\dfrac{480}{x + 20}$

Now, According to the question

$$\frac{480}{x} - \frac{480}{x + 20} = 12$$

$$\Rightarrow \frac{480x + 9,600 - 480x}{x(x + 20)} = 12$$

$$\Rightarrow 9,600 = 12x(x + 20)$$
$$\Rightarrow 800 = x^2 + 20x$$
$$\Rightarrow x^2 + 20x - 800 = 0$$
$$\Rightarrow x^2 + 40x - 20x - 800 = 0$$
$$\Rightarrow x(x + 40) - 20(x + 40) = 0$$
$$\Rightarrow (x - 20)(x + 40) = 0$$
$$\Rightarrow x - 20 = 0 \Rightarrow x = 20$$
or $x + 40 = 0 \Rightarrow x = -40$

(not possible)

∴ $x = 20$ **Ans.**

46. By increasing the speed of a car by 10 km/hr, the time of journey for a distance of 72 km. is reduced by 36 minutes. Find the original speed of the car.

Sol. Let original speed be x km/hr.

∴ Time = $\dfrac{72}{x}$ hr

and New speed = $(x + 10)$ km/hr

∴ New time = $\dfrac{72}{x + 10}$

Difference in time = 36 mins.

∴ $$\frac{72}{x} - \frac{72}{x + 10} = \frac{36}{60}$$

$$\Rightarrow \frac{72x + 720 - 72x}{x(x + 10)} = \frac{3}{5}$$

$$\Rightarrow 5 \times 720 = 3(x^2 + 10x)$$
$$\Rightarrow 1,200 = x^2 + 10x$$
$$\Rightarrow x^2 + 10x - 1,200 = 0$$

$$\Rightarrow x^2 + 40x - 30x - 1,200 = 0$$
$$\Rightarrow x(x + 40) - 30(x + 40) = 0$$
$$\Rightarrow (x - 30)(x + 40) = 0$$
$$\therefore x = 30$$

as $x = -40$ is not acceptable.

∴ Original speed = 30km/hr. **Ans.**

47. A car covers a distance of 400 km at a certain speed. Had the speed been 12 km/hr more, the time taken for the journey would have been 1 hour 40 minutes less. Find the original speed of the car.

Sol. Let the original speed of the car be x km/hr,

So, Time taken by car = $\dfrac{400}{x}$ hr

Again, Speed = $(x + 12)$ km/hr

Time taken by car = $\dfrac{400}{x + 12}$

So, $$\frac{400}{x} - \frac{400}{x + 12} = 1 \text{ hr} + \frac{40}{60}$$

$$\Rightarrow 400 \frac{(x + 12 - x)}{x(x + 12)} = \frac{5}{3}$$

$$\Rightarrow \frac{4800}{x^2 + 12x} = \frac{5}{3}$$

$$\Rightarrow 5(x^2 + 12x) = 14,400$$
$$\Rightarrow x^2 + 12x - 2,880 = 0$$
$$\Rightarrow x^2 + 60x - 48x - 2,880 = 0$$
$$\Rightarrow x(x + 60) - 48(x + 60) = 0$$
$$\Rightarrow (x + 60)(x - 48) = 0$$
Either, $x + 60 = 0$
$$\Rightarrow x = -60$$

(Neglect, as speed can't be negative)

or $x - 48 = 0$
$$\Rightarrow x = 48$$

⇒ Original speed of the car is 48 km/hr. **Ans.**

48. Some students planned a picnic. The budget for the food was ₹ 480. As eight of them failed to join the party, the cost of the food for each member increased by ₹ 10. Find how many students went for the picnic.

Sol. Let the total no. of students be x. Cost of food for each = ₹ $\dfrac{480}{x}$.

When 8 students failed to join, then cost of food for each = $\dfrac{480}{x - 8}$

According to question

$$\frac{480}{x-8} - \frac{480}{x} = 10$$

$$\Rightarrow \quad \frac{480x - 480(x-8)}{x(x-8)} = 10$$

$$\Rightarrow \quad \frac{480(x-x+8)}{x(x-8)} = 10$$

$$\Rightarrow \quad x^2 - 8x - 384 = 0$$

$$\Rightarrow \quad x^2 - 24x + 16x - 384 = 0$$

$$\Rightarrow \quad (x-24)(x+16) = 0$$

$\Rightarrow$ Since x can't be $-$ve, $x = 24$

The number of students went for picnic

$$= 24 - 8 = 16. \quad \textbf{Ans.}$$

49. Two pipes flowing together can fill a cistern in 6 minutes. If one pipe takes 5 minutes more than the other to fill the cistern, find the time in which each pipe would fill the cistern.

Sol. Let the time taken by the two pipes to fill the cistern be x and $x + 5$ min. respectively. In 1 min., the first pipe can fill $\frac{1}{x}$ of the cistern.

In 1 min., the second pipe can fill $\frac{1}{x+5}$ of the cistern.

Then

$$\frac{1}{x} + \frac{1}{x+5} = \frac{1}{6}$$

$$\Rightarrow \quad \frac{x+5+x}{x(x+5)} = \frac{1}{6}$$

$$\Rightarrow \quad \frac{2x+5}{x^2+5x} = \frac{1}{6}$$

$$\Rightarrow \quad x^2 + 5x = 12x + 30$$

$$\Rightarrow \quad x^2 - 7x - 30 = 0$$

$$\Rightarrow \quad x^2 - 10x + 3x - 30 = 0$$

$$\Rightarrow \quad x(x-10) + 3(x-10) = 0$$

$$\Rightarrow \quad (x-10)(x+3) = 0$$

$$\Rightarrow \quad x = 10 \text{ or } x = -3$$

Since, as time can not be negative.

So, $\qquad x = 10$ and $x + 5 = 10 + 5 = 15$.

Hence, the two pipes can fill the cistern in 10 min, and 15 min, respectively. **Ans.**

50. One-fourth of a herd of camels was seen in the forest. Twice the square root of the herd had gone to mountains and the remaining 15 camels were seen on the bank of a river. Find the total number of camels.

Sol. Let x be the total number of camels.

Number of camels seen in the forest $= \dfrac{x}{4}$

Number of camels gone to mountains $= 2\sqrt{x}$

Number of camels on the bank of river $= 15$

Total number of camels $= \dfrac{x}{4} + 2\sqrt{x} + 15 = x$

$$\Rightarrow \qquad x + 8\sqrt{x} + 60 = 4x$$

$$\Rightarrow \qquad 3x - 8\sqrt{x} - 60 = 0$$

Put $\sqrt{x} = y$

$$\Rightarrow \qquad 3y^2 - 8y - 60 = 0$$

$$\Rightarrow \quad 3y^2 - 18y + 10y - 60 = 0$$

$$\Rightarrow \quad 3y(y-6) + 10(y-6) = 0$$

$$\Rightarrow \qquad (y-6)(3y+10) = 0$$

$$\Rightarrow \quad y = 6 \quad \text{or} \quad y = -\frac{10}{3} \text{ (not possible)}$$

Now, $\qquad\qquad\qquad y = 6$

$$\Rightarrow \qquad\qquad \sqrt{x} = 6$$

On squaring both sides, we get

$$x = 36.$$

Hence, total number of camels $= 36$. **Ans.**

51. An aeroplane travelled a distance of 400 km at an average speed of x km/hr. On the return journey the speed was increased by 40 km/hr. Write down the expression for the time taken for

(i) The outward journey

(ii) The return journey.

If the return journey took 30 minutes less than the onward journey write down an equation in x and find its value.

Sol. (i) Time taken for the onward journey

$$= \frac{400}{x} \text{ hours.}$$

(ii) Time taken for the return journey

$$= \frac{400}{x+40} \text{ hours.}$$

According to the question,

$$\frac{400}{x+40} = \frac{400}{x} - \frac{1}{2}$$

$$\Rightarrow \qquad 800x = 800(x+40) - x(x+40)$$

$$\Rightarrow \quad x^2 + 40x - 32,000 = 0$$

$$\Rightarrow \quad (x+200)(x-160) = 0$$

$\Rightarrow$ $x = -200$ (inadmissible)
or 160

Hence, the required value of x is 160.   **Ans.**

52. Car A travels x km for every litre of petrol, while car B travels $(x + 5)$ km for every litre of petrol.

(i) Write down the number of litres of petrol used by car A and car B in covering a distance of 400 km.

(ii) If car A use 4 litre of petrol more than car B in covering the 400 km, write down the equation in x and solve it to determine the number of litre of petrol used by car B for the journey.

Sol. Given, Distance = 400 km.

Car A travels x km/litre.

Car B travels $(x + 5)$ km/litre.

(i) Number of litre used by car A = $\dfrac{\text{Distance}}{\text{Speed of car A}}$

$= \dfrac{400}{x}$ litre

Number of litre used by car B = $\dfrac{\text{Distance}}{\text{Speed of car B}}$

$= \dfrac{400}{x+5}$ litre.

(ii) Car A uses 4 litre more than car B

$\therefore$ $\dfrac{400}{x} - \dfrac{400}{x+5} = 4$

$\Rightarrow$ $400(x+5) - 400x = 4x(x+5)$

$\Rightarrow$ $400x + 2000 - 400x = 4x^2 + 20x$

$\Rightarrow$ $4x^2 + 20x - 2000 = 0$

$\Rightarrow$ $4(x^2 + 5x - 500) = 0$

$\Rightarrow$ $x^2 + 25x - 20x - 500 = 0$

$\Rightarrow$ $x(x+25) - 20(x+25) = 0$

$\Rightarrow$ $(x+25)(x-20) = 0$

$\therefore$ $x = -25$

(not acceptable)

or $x = 20$

Number of litre of petrol used by car B

$= \dfrac{400}{20+5} = \dfrac{400}{25} = 16$

Ans.

53. ₹ 7500 were divided equally among a certain number of children. Had there been 20 less

children, each would have received ₹ 100 more. Find the original number of children.*

Sol. Let the original number of children be x.

Total amount to be distributed = ₹ 7,500

$\therefore$ Each will receive = $\dfrac{7,500}{x}$

If the number of children are $(x - 20)$

Then,   Each will receive = $\dfrac{7,500}{x-20}$

According to question,

$\dfrac{7,500}{x-20} - \dfrac{7,500}{x} = 100$

$\Rightarrow$ $7,500\left(\dfrac{1}{x-20} - \dfrac{1}{x}\right) = 100$

$\Rightarrow$ $\dfrac{x-x+20}{x(x-20)} = \dfrac{100}{7,500}$

$\Rightarrow$ $\dfrac{20}{x^2-20x} = \dfrac{1}{75}$

$\Rightarrow$ $x^2 - 20x = 1,500$

$\Rightarrow$ $x^2 - 20x - 1,500 = 0$

$\Rightarrow$ $x^2 - (50-30)x - 1,500 = 0$

$\Rightarrow$ $x^2 - 50x + 30x - 1,500 = 0$

$\Rightarrow$ $x(x-50) + 30(x-50) = 0$

$\Rightarrow$ $(x-50)(x+30) = 0$

$\Rightarrow$ $x = 50$ or $x = -30$

$\therefore$ $x = 50$

($\because x$ cannot be negative)

$\therefore$ The original number of children = 50.   **Ans.**

54. A shopkeeper purchases a certain number of books for ₹ 960. If the cost per book was ₹ 8 less, the number of books that could be purchased for ₹ 960 would be 4 more. Write an equation, taking the original cost of each book to be ₹ x, and solve it to find the original cost of the books.

Sol. Original cost of each book = ₹ x

$\therefore$ Number of books for ₹ 960 = $\dfrac{960}{x}$

Now, If cost of each book = ₹ $(x-8)$

Number of books for ₹ 960 = $\dfrac{960}{x-8}$

According to the question

$\dfrac{960}{x} + 4 = \dfrac{960}{x-8}$

or $\dfrac{960}{(x-8)} - \dfrac{960}{x} = 4$

$$\Rightarrow \quad \frac{960x - 960x + 7{,}680}{x(x-8)} = 4$$

$$\Rightarrow \quad 7{,}680 = 4x^2 - 32x$$

$$\Rightarrow \quad x^2 - 8x - 1{,}920 = 0$$

$$\Rightarrow \quad x^2 + 40x - 48x - 1{,}920 = 0$$

$$\Rightarrow \quad x(x+40) - 48(x+40) = 0$$

$$(x+40)(x-48) = 0$$

$$\Rightarrow \quad x = -40, 48$$

$$\therefore \quad x = 48$$

(as cost can't be – ve) **Ans.**

55. Two pipes running together can fill a cistern in $11\dfrac{1}{9}$ minutes. If one pipe takes 5 minutes more than the other to fill the cistern find the time when each pipe would fill the cistern.

Sol. Let x minutes be time taken by the larger pipe to fill the cistern then the smaller pipe taken $(x + 5)$ minutes. These two pipes would fill $\dfrac{1}{x}$ and $\dfrac{1}{x+5}$ of the cistern in a minute, respectively.

$$\frac{1}{x} + \frac{1}{x+5} = \frac{9}{100}$$

$$\Rightarrow \quad 9x^2 - 155x - 500 = 0$$

$$\Rightarrow \quad 9x^2 + 25x - 180x - 500 = 0$$

$$\Rightarrow \quad x(9x+25) - 20(9x+25) = 0$$

$$\Rightarrow \quad (9x+25)(x-20) = 0$$

$$\Rightarrow \quad x = 20$$

and $\qquad x = -\dfrac{25}{9}$ (negligible)

Hence, the time taken by the pipes to fill the cistern in 20 minutes and 25 minutes. **Ans.**

56. Solve the following quadratic equation by factorisation method :

(i) $\dfrac{x}{x+1} + \dfrac{x+1}{x} = \dfrac{34}{15}$ $x \neq 0, x \neq -1$

(ii) $\dfrac{x+3}{x+1} - \dfrac{1-x}{x} = \dfrac{17}{4}$.

Sol. (i) We have

$$\frac{x}{x+1} + \frac{x+1}{x} = \frac{34}{15}$$

$$\Rightarrow \quad \frac{x^2 + (x+1)^2}{x(x+1)} = \frac{34}{15}$$

$$\Rightarrow \quad \frac{x^2 + x^2 + 1 + 2x}{x^2 + x} = \frac{34}{15}$$

$$\Rightarrow \quad \frac{2x^2 + 2x + 1}{x^2 + x} = \frac{34}{15}$$

$$\Rightarrow \quad 34x^2 + 34x = 30x^2 + 30x + 15$$

$$\Rightarrow \quad 4x^2 + 4x - 15 = 0$$

$$\Rightarrow \quad 4x^2 + 10x - 6x - 15 = 0$$

$$\Rightarrow \quad 2x(2x+5) - 3(2x+5) = 0$$

$$\Rightarrow \quad (2x+5)(2x-3) = 0$$

$$\Rightarrow \quad 2x = -5 \text{ and } 2x = 3$$

$$\Rightarrow \quad x = -\frac{5}{2} \text{ or } x = \frac{3}{2} .$$

$$\therefore \quad x = \left\{ -\frac{5}{2}, \frac{3}{2} \right\} \qquad \textbf{Ans.}$$

(ii) We have $\dfrac{x+3}{x-2} - \dfrac{1-x}{x} = \dfrac{17}{4}$

$$\Rightarrow \quad \frac{x^2 + 3x - (x-2)(1-x)}{x(x-2)} = \frac{17}{4}$$

$$\Rightarrow \quad \frac{x^2 + 3x - (x - x^2 - 2 + 2x)}{x^2 - 2x} = \frac{17}{4}$$

$$\Rightarrow \quad \frac{x^2 + 3x - (-x^2 + 3x - 2)}{x^2 - 2x} = \frac{17}{4}$$

$$\Rightarrow \quad \frac{x^2 + 3x + x^2 - 3x + 2)}{x^2 - 2x} = \frac{17}{4}$$

$$\Rightarrow \quad \frac{2x^2 + 2}{x^2 - 2x} = \frac{17}{4}$$

$$\Rightarrow \quad 17x^2 - 34x = 8x^2 + 8$$

$$\Rightarrow \quad 9x^2 - 34x - 8 = 0$$

$$\Rightarrow \quad 9x^2 - 36x + 2x - 8 = 0$$

$$\Rightarrow \quad 9x(x-4) + 2(x-4) = 0$$

$$\Rightarrow \quad (x-4)(9x+2) = 0$$

$$\Rightarrow \quad x = 4 \text{ or } x = -\frac{2}{9} .$$

$$\therefore \quad x = \left\{ 4, -\frac{2}{9} \right\} \qquad \textbf{Ans.}$$

57. Solve the following quadratic equation :

(i) $\dfrac{1}{a+b+x} = \dfrac{1}{a} + \dfrac{1}{b} + \dfrac{1}{x}$, $a + b \neq 0$

(ii) $4x^2 - 4ax + (a^2 - b^2) = 0$ where $a, b \in$ R.

Sol. (i) The given quadratic equation is

$$\frac{1}{a+b+x} = \frac{1}{a} + \frac{1}{b} + \frac{1}{x}$$

$$\Rightarrow \quad \frac{1}{a+b+x} - \frac{1}{x} = \frac{1}{a} + \frac{1}{b}$$

$$\Rightarrow \quad \frac{x-a-b-x}{x\,(a+b+x)} = \frac{1}{a} + \frac{1}{b}$$

$$\Rightarrow \quad \frac{-(a+b)}{x\,(a+b+x)} = \frac{(a+b)}{ab}$$

$$\Rightarrow \quad \frac{-1}{x\,(a+b+x)} = \frac{1}{ab}$$

$$\Rightarrow \quad -ab = ax + bx + x^2$$

$$\Rightarrow \quad x^2 + ax + bx + ab = 0$$

$$\Rightarrow \quad x\,(x+a) + b\,(x+a) = 0$$

$$\Rightarrow \quad (x+b)\,(x+a) = 0$$

$$\Rightarrow \quad x = -a \text{ or } x = -b$$

$$\therefore \quad x = \{-a, -b\} \qquad \textbf{Ans.}$$

(ii) The given quadratic equation is

$$4x^2 - 4ax + (a^2 - b^2) = 0$$

$$\text{where } a, b \in R$$

$$\Rightarrow \quad 4x^2 - \{2(a+b)x + 2(a-b)x\} + a^2 - b^2 = 0$$

$$\Rightarrow \quad \{4x^2 - 2(a+b)x\} - \{2(a-b)x - (a^2-b^2)\} = 0$$

$$\Rightarrow \quad 2x\{2x - (a+b)\} - (a-b)\{2x - (a+b)\} = 0$$

$$[\because (a^2 - b^2) = (a+b)\,(a-b)]$$

$$\Rightarrow \quad \{2x - (a+b)\}\{2x - (a-b)\} = 0$$

$$\Rightarrow \quad x = \frac{a+b}{2} \text{ or } x = \frac{a-b}{2}$$

$$\therefore \quad x = \left\{\left(\frac{a+b}{2}\right), \left(\frac{a-b}{2}\right)\right\} \qquad \textbf{Ans.}$$

58. Determine whether the given quadratic equations have equal roots and if so, find the roots :

(i) $x^2 + 5x + 5 = 0$

(ii) $x^2 + 2x + 4 = 0$

(iii) $\frac{4}{3}x^2 - 2x + \frac{3}{4} = 0$

(iv) $3x^2 - 6x + 5 = 0.$

Sol. (i) The given quadratic equation is

$$x^2 + 5x + 5 = 0$$

Here, $a = 1$, $b = 5$ and $c = 5$

$$\text{Discriminant} = b^2 - 4ac$$

$$= (5)^2 - 4 \times 1 \times 5$$

$$= 25 - 20 = 5 > 0$$

So, the given equation has two real and distinct roots **Ans.**

(ii) The given quadratic equation is

$$x^2 + 2x + 4 = 0$$

Here, $a = 1$, $b = 2$ and $c = 4$

$$\text{Descriminant} = b^2 - 4ac$$

$$= (2)^2 - 4 \times 1 \times 4$$

$$= 4 - 16 = -12 < 0$$

Hence, the given equation has no real roots.

Ans.

(iii) We have

$$\frac{4}{3}x^2 - 2x + \frac{3}{4} = 0$$

Here, $a = \frac{4}{3}$, $b = -2$ and $c = \frac{3}{4}$

$$\text{Discriminant} = b^2 - 4ac$$

$$= (-2)^2 - 4 \times \frac{4}{3} \times \frac{3}{4}$$

$$= 4 - 4 = 0$$

So, the given equation has two real and equal roots given by

$$\alpha, \beta = \frac{-b \pm \sqrt{b^2 - 4ac}}{2a} = \frac{+2 \pm 0}{2 \times \frac{4}{3}} = \frac{2}{2 \times 4/3}$$

$$= \frac{3}{4}$$

$$\alpha = \frac{3}{4}, \beta = \frac{3}{4}. \qquad \textbf{Ans.}$$

(iv) The given equation is

$$3x^2 - 6x + 5 = 0$$

Here, $a = 3$, $b = -6$ and $c = 5$

$$\text{Discriminant} = b^2 - 4ac$$

$$= (-6)^2 - 4 \times 3 \times 5$$

$$= 36 - 60 = -24 < 0$$

Imaginary roots or no real roots. **Ans.**

59. Find the value of k so that sum of the roots of the quadratic equation is equal to the product of the roots :

(i) $kx^2 + 6x - 3k = 0, k \neq 0$

(ii) $(k+1)x^2 + (2k+1)x - 9 = 0, k+1 \neq 0.$

Sol. (i) The given quadratic equation is

$$kx^2 + 6x - 3k = 0$$

Here, $a = k$, $b = 6$ and $c = -3k$

$$\text{Sum of the roots, } \alpha + \beta = \frac{-b}{a} = \frac{-6}{k}$$

$$\text{and product of the roots, } \alpha\beta = \frac{c}{a} = \frac{-3k}{k}$$

Since, Sum of the roots = Product of the roots

$$\Rightarrow \qquad \frac{-6}{k} = -3$$

$$\Rightarrow \qquad k = \frac{6}{3} \Rightarrow k = 2. \qquad \textbf{Ans.}$$

(ii) The given quadratic equation is

$$(k+1)x^2 + (2k+1)x - 9 = 0$$

Here, $a = k+1$, $b = (2k+1)$ and $c = -9$

Sum of the roots, $\alpha + \beta = \dfrac{-(2k+1)}{k+1}$

and $\qquad \alpha\beta = \dfrac{c}{a} = \dfrac{-9}{k+1}$

Since, Sum of the roots = Product of the roots

Then, $\qquad \left(\dfrac{-2k+1}{k+1}\right) = \dfrac{-9}{k+1}$

$$\Rightarrow \qquad 2k+1 = 9$$
$$\Rightarrow \qquad 2k = 9-1$$
$$\Rightarrow \qquad 2k = 8$$
$$\Rightarrow \qquad k = \frac{8}{2} = 4 \qquad \textbf{Ans.}$$

60. Solve the following by reducing them to quadratic equations :

(i) $\left(\dfrac{7y-1}{y}\right)^2 - 3\left(\dfrac{7y-1}{y}\right) - 18 = 0,\, y \neq 0$

(ii) $\sqrt{\dfrac{x}{1-x}} + \sqrt{\dfrac{1-x}{x}} = \dfrac{13}{6}$

Sol. (i) The given equation

$$\left(\dfrac{7y-1}{y}\right)^2 - 3\left(\dfrac{7y-1}{y}\right) - 18 = 0,\, y \neq 0$$

Putting $\dfrac{7y-1}{y} = z$, then the given equation becomes

$$z^2 - 3z - 18 = 0$$
$$\Rightarrow \qquad z^2 - 6z + 3z - 18 = 0$$
$$\Rightarrow \qquad z(z-6) + 3(z-6) = 0$$
$$\Rightarrow \qquad (z-6)(z+3) = 0$$
$$\Rightarrow \qquad z-6 = 0 \text{ or } z+3 = 0$$
$$\Rightarrow \qquad z = 6 \text{ or } z = -3$$

But $\dfrac{7y-1}{y} = z$

$$\therefore \qquad \dfrac{7y-1}{y} = 6 \Rightarrow 7y-1 = 6y$$

$$\Rightarrow \qquad 7y - 6y = 1$$

$$\Rightarrow \qquad y = 1$$

Also $\dfrac{7y-1}{y} = -3 \Rightarrow 7y - 1 = -3y$

$$\Rightarrow \qquad 7y + 3y - 1 = 0$$
$$\Rightarrow \qquad 10y = 1$$
$$\Rightarrow \qquad y = \frac{1}{10}$$

Hence, the required roots are $\left\{\dfrac{1}{10}, 1\right\}$. **Ans.**

(ii) Given equation is $\sqrt{\dfrac{x}{1-x}} + \sqrt{\dfrac{1-x}{x}} = \dfrac{13}{6}$

Putting $\sqrt{\dfrac{x}{1-x}} = y$, then given equation reducible to the form $y + \dfrac{1}{y} = \dfrac{13}{6}$

$$\Rightarrow \qquad \frac{y^2 + 1}{y} = \frac{13}{6}$$
$$\Rightarrow \qquad 6y^2 + 6 = 13y$$
$$\Rightarrow \qquad 6y^2 - 13y + 6 = 0$$
$$\Rightarrow \qquad 6y^2 - 9y - 4y + 6 = 0$$
$$\Rightarrow \qquad 3y(2y-3) - 2(2y-3) = 0$$
$$\Rightarrow \qquad (2y-3)(3y-2) = 0$$
$$\Rightarrow \qquad 2y-3 = 0 \text{ or } 3y-2 = 0$$
$$\Rightarrow \qquad y = 3/2 \text{ or } y = 2/3$$

But $\sqrt{\dfrac{x}{1-x}} = y$

$$\therefore \quad \sqrt{\dfrac{x}{1-x}} = \dfrac{3}{2} \qquad \text{or} \quad \sqrt{\dfrac{x}{1-x}} = \dfrac{2}{3}$$

Squaring both sides	Squaring both sides
$\dfrac{x}{1-x} = \dfrac{9}{4}$	$\dfrac{x}{1-x} = \dfrac{4}{9}$
$\Rightarrow \quad 4x = 9 - 9x$	$\Rightarrow \quad 9x = 4 - 4x$
$\Rightarrow \quad 13x = 9$	$\Rightarrow 9x + 4x = 4$
$\Rightarrow \quad x = \dfrac{9}{13}$	$\Rightarrow \quad 13x = 4$
	$\Rightarrow \quad x = \dfrac{4}{13}$

Hence, the required roots are $\left\{\dfrac{9}{13}, \dfrac{4}{13}\right\}$. **Ans.**

61. Solve the following by reducing them to quadratic form :

(i) $\sqrt{y+1} + \sqrt{2y-5} = 3, y \in R$

(ii) $\sqrt{x^2-16} - (x-4) = \sqrt{x^2-5x+4}$.

Sol. (i) Given equation is

$$\sqrt{y+1} + \sqrt{2y-5} = 3$$

$\Rightarrow$ $\qquad \sqrt{y+1} = 3 - \sqrt{2y-5}$

Squaring both sides, we get

$$y+1 = 9 + 2y - 5 - 6\sqrt{2y-5}$$

$\Rightarrow$ $\quad y - 2y + 1 - 4 = -6\sqrt{2y-5}$

$\Rightarrow$ $\qquad -y - 3 = -6\sqrt{2y-5}$

$\Rightarrow$ $\qquad y + 3 = 6\sqrt{2y-5}$

On squaring again, we get

$$y^2 + 9 + 6y = 36(2y-5)$$

$\Rightarrow$ $\quad y^2 + 9 + 6y = 72y - 180$

$\Rightarrow$ $\quad y^2 - 66y + 189 = 0$

$\therefore$ $\quad y^2 - 66y + 189 = 0$

Hence, $a = 1, b = -66, c = 189$

Then, $\qquad D = b^2 - 4ac$

$$= (66)^2 - 4(1)(189)$$

$$= 4356 - 756$$

$$= 3600 > 0$$

Roots are real.

$\therefore$ $\qquad y = \dfrac{-b \pm \sqrt{b^2-4ac}}{2a}$

$\Rightarrow$ $\qquad y = \dfrac{-(-66) \pm \sqrt{3600}}{2 \times 1}$

$\Rightarrow$ $\qquad y = \dfrac{66 \pm 60}{2}$

$\Rightarrow$ $\qquad y = \dfrac{66+60}{2} \text{ or } \dfrac{66-60}{2}$

$\Rightarrow$ $\qquad = \dfrac{126}{2} \text{ or } \dfrac{6}{2} = 63 \text{ or } 3$

$\Rightarrow$ $\qquad y = 3 \text{ or } 63$

But $x = 63$ does not satisfy the given equation.

Hence, the solution is 3. **Ans.**

(ii) Given equation is

$$\sqrt{x^2-16} - (x-4) = \sqrt{x^2-5x+4}$$

$\Rightarrow$ $\sqrt{(x+4)(x-4)} - (x-4) = \sqrt{(x-1)(x-4)}$

$\Rightarrow$ $\sqrt{x-4} \left[\sqrt{x+4} - \sqrt{x-4} - \sqrt{x-1} \right] = 0$

$\Rightarrow$ Either, $\sqrt{x-4} = 0$

(By squaring on both sides)

$\Rightarrow$ $\qquad\qquad x - 4 = 0$

$\Rightarrow$ $\qquad\qquad x = 4$

or $\sqrt{x+4} - \sqrt{x-4} - \sqrt{x-1} = 0$

$\Rightarrow$ $\qquad \sqrt{x+4} - \sqrt{x-4} = \sqrt{x-1}$

On squaring both sides, we get

$$x + 4 + x - 4 - 2\sqrt{(x+4)(x-4)} = x - 1$$

$\Rightarrow$ $\quad 2x - 2\sqrt{x^2-16} = x - 1$

$\Rightarrow$ $\; -2\sqrt{x^2-16} = x - 2x - 1 = -x-1$

$\Rightarrow$ $\qquad -2\sqrt{x^2-16} = -(x+1)$

$\Rightarrow$ $\qquad 2\sqrt{x^2-16} = x+1$

Squaring again, we get

$$4(x^2-16) = x^2 + 2x + 1$$

$\Rightarrow$ $4x^2 - 64 - x^2 - 2x - 1 = 0$

$\Rightarrow$ $\qquad 3x^2 - 2x - 65 = 0$

$\Rightarrow$ $\quad 3x^2 - 15x + 13x - 65 = 0$

$\Rightarrow$ $\quad 3x(x-5) + 13(x-5) = 0$

$\Rightarrow$ $\quad (x-5) + (3x+13) = 0$

$\Rightarrow$ $\qquad x = 5 \text{ or } x = \dfrac{-13}{3}$

But, $x = -13/3$ doesn't satisfy the given equation

Hence, the solutions are $\{4, 5\}$. **Ans.**

62. Solve the equation :

$$6\left(x^2 + \dfrac{1}{x^2}\right) - 25\left(x - \dfrac{1}{x}\right) + 12 = 0.$$

Sol. Given equation

$$6\left(x^2 + \dfrac{1}{x^2}\right) - 25\left(x - \dfrac{1}{x}\right) + 12 = 0$$

Put $x - \dfrac{1}{x} = y$, squaring both sides $\left(x - \dfrac{1}{x}\right)^2 = y^2$

$\Rightarrow$ $\qquad \dfrac{x^2+1}{x^2} - 2 = y^2$

$$\Rightarrow \qquad \frac{x^2+1}{x^2} = y^2 + 2$$

Now, given equation becomes

$$6(y^2+2) - 25y + 12 = 0$$

$$\Rightarrow \qquad 6y^2 + 12 - 25y + 12 = 0$$

$$\Rightarrow \qquad 6y^2 - 25y + 24 = 0$$

$$\Rightarrow \qquad 6y^2 - 16y - 9y + 24 = 0$$

$$\Rightarrow \quad 2y(3y-8) - 3(3y-8) = 0$$

$$\Rightarrow \qquad (3y-8)(2y-3) = 0$$

$$\Rightarrow \qquad 3y = 8 \text{ or } 2y = 3$$

$$\Rightarrow \qquad y = \frac{8}{3} \text{ or } y = \frac{3}{2}$$

But $x - \dfrac{1}{x} = y$

$$\therefore \qquad x - \frac{1}{x} = \frac{8}{3} \qquad\qquad \text{or } x - \frac{1}{x} = \frac{3}{2}$$

$$\Rightarrow \quad \frac{x^2-1}{x} = \frac{8}{3} \qquad \Rightarrow \frac{x^2-1}{x} = \frac{3}{2}$$

$$\Rightarrow \quad 3x^2 - 3 = 8x \quad \Rightarrow 2x^2 - 2 = 3x$$

$$\Rightarrow \quad 3x^2 - 8x - 3 = 0 \quad \Rightarrow 2x^2 - 3x - 2 = 0$$

$$\Rightarrow \quad 3x^2 - 9x + x - 3 = 0 \quad \Rightarrow 2x^2 - 4x + x - 2 = 0$$

$$\Rightarrow 3x(x-3) + 1(x-3) = 0 \quad \Rightarrow 2x(x-2) + 1(x-2) = 0$$

$$\Rightarrow \quad (x-3)(3x+1) = 0 \quad \Rightarrow (x-2)(2x+1) = 0$$

$$\Rightarrow \quad x = 3 \text{ or } x = \frac{-1}{3} \quad \Rightarrow x = 2 \text{ or } x = \frac{-1}{2}$$

Hence, $x = 3, \dfrac{-1}{3}, 2$ and $\dfrac{-1}{2}$.

Solutions are $\left\{3, \dfrac{-1}{3}, 2 \text{ and } \dfrac{-1}{2}\right\}$ **Ans.**

63. Solve for x :

$$\left(x+\frac{1}{x}\right)^2 - \frac{3}{2}\left(x-\frac{1}{x}\right) - 4 = 0.$$

Sol. Given equation is

$$\left(x+\frac{1}{x}\right)^2 - \frac{3}{2}\left(x-\frac{1}{x}\right) - 4 = 0$$

$$\Rightarrow \quad x^2 + \frac{1}{x^2} + 2 - \frac{3}{2}\left(x-\frac{1}{x}\right) - 4 = 0$$

Put $x - \dfrac{1}{x} = y$, squaring both sides $\dfrac{x^2+1}{x^2} - 2 = y^2$

$$\Rightarrow \qquad \frac{x^2+1}{x^2} = y^2 + 2$$

Then given equation becomes :

$$\Rightarrow \quad y^2 + 2 + 2 - \frac{3}{2}y - 4 = 0$$

$$\Rightarrow \qquad y^2 - \frac{3}{2}y = 0$$

$$\Rightarrow \qquad 2y^2 - 3y = 0$$

$$\Rightarrow \qquad y(2y-3) = 0$$

$$\Rightarrow \qquad y = 0 \text{ or } y = \frac{3}{2}$$

But $x - \dfrac{1}{x} = y$

Then, $x - \dfrac{1}{x} = 0$ or $\qquad\qquad x - \dfrac{1}{x} = \dfrac{3}{2}$

$$\Rightarrow x^2 - 1 = 0 \quad \Rightarrow \frac{x^2+1}{x^2} = \frac{3}{2}$$

$$\Rightarrow \qquad x^2 = 1 \quad \Rightarrow 2x^2 - 2 = 3x$$

$$\Rightarrow \qquad x = \pm 1 \quad \Rightarrow 2x^2 - 3x - 2 = 0$$

$$\Rightarrow \qquad 2x^2 - 4x + x - 2 = 0$$

$$\Rightarrow \quad 2x(x-2) + 1(x-2) = 0$$

$$\Rightarrow \qquad (x-2)(2x+1) = 0$$

$$\Rightarrow \qquad x = 2 \text{ or } x = -\frac{1}{2}$$

Hence, $x = \pm 1, 2, -\dfrac{1}{2}$.

Solution are $\left\{\pm 1, 2 - \dfrac{1}{2}\right\}$. **Ans.**

64. Solve the equation

$$x^4 + 2x^3 - 13x^2 + 2x + 1 = 0.$$

Sol. Given equation is

$$x^4 + 2x^3 - 13x^2 + 2x + 1 = 0$$

Dividing both sides by x^2, we get

$$x^2 + 2x - 13 + \frac{2}{x} + \frac{1}{x^2} = 0$$

$$\Rightarrow \quad \left(x^2 + \frac{1}{x^2}\right) + 2\left(x + \frac{1}{x}\right) - 13 = 0$$

Put $x + \dfrac{1}{x} = y$, squaring both sides

$$\frac{x^2+1}{x^2} + 2 = y^2$$

$\Rightarrow \qquad \dfrac{x^2+1}{x^2} = y^2-2$

Then, $\quad y^2-2+2y-13 = 0$

$\Rightarrow \qquad y^2+2y-15 = 0$

$\Rightarrow \qquad y^2+5y-3y-15 = 0$

$\Rightarrow \qquad y(y+5)-3(y+5) = 0$

$\Rightarrow \qquad (y+5)(y-3) = 0$

$\Rightarrow \qquad y = -5 \text{ or } y = 3$

But $\qquad x+\dfrac{1}{x} = y$

Then $\qquad x+\dfrac{1}{x} = -5$

$\Rightarrow \qquad x^2+1 = -5x$

$\Rightarrow \qquad x^2+5x+1 = 0$

We know that,

$$x = \dfrac{-b\pm\sqrt{b^2-4ac}}{2a}$$

Here, $\qquad a = 1, b = 5, c = 1$

$$x = \dfrac{-5\pm\sqrt{25-4\times1\times1}}{2\times1}$$

$\Rightarrow \qquad x = \dfrac{-5\pm\sqrt{25-4}}{2}$

$\Rightarrow \qquad x = \dfrac{-5\pm\sqrt{21}}{2}$

or $\qquad x+\dfrac{1}{x} = 3$

$\Rightarrow \qquad x^2+1 = 3x$

$\Rightarrow \qquad x^2-3x+1 = 0$

We know that,

$$x = \dfrac{-b\pm\sqrt{b^2-4ac}}{2a}$$

Here, $a = 1, b = -3, c = 1$

$\Rightarrow \qquad x = \dfrac{-(-3)\pm\sqrt{9-4\times1\times1}}{2}$

$\Rightarrow \qquad x = \dfrac{3\pm\sqrt{9-4}}{2}$

$\Rightarrow \qquad x = \dfrac{3\pm\sqrt{5}}{2}$

Hence, $\qquad x = \dfrac{-5\pm\sqrt{21}}{2} \text{ or } \dfrac{3\pm\sqrt{5}}{2}$

Solutions are $\left\{\dfrac{-5\pm\sqrt{21}}{2}, \dfrac{3\pm\sqrt{5}}{2}\right\}$ **Ans.**

65. The sum of the ages of Vivek and his younger brother Amit is 47 years. The product of their ages in year is 550. Find their ages.

Sol. Let Vivek 's age be x years.

∴ His brother's age $= (47-x) = 550$

According to question,

$\qquad x(47-x) = 550$

$\Rightarrow \qquad 47x-x^2 = 550$

$\Rightarrow \qquad x^2-47x+550 = 0$

$\Rightarrow \qquad x^2-25x-22x+550 = 0$

$\Rightarrow \qquad x(x-25)-22(x-25) = 0$

$\Rightarrow \qquad (x-25)(x-22) = 0$

$\Rightarrow \qquad x = 25 \text{ or } x = 22$

When $x = 25$, $47-x = 47-25 = 22$

When $x = 22$, $47-x = 47-22 = 25$ not possible since Amit is the younger brother

∴ Vivek's age $= x = 25$ years

Amit age $= 22$ years. **Ans.**

Chapter 6. Ratio and Proportion

1. Which is greater $4:5$ or $19:25$.

Sol. Let $a = 4, b = 5, c = 19$ and $d = 25$

then $\qquad ad = 4\times25 = 100$

and $\qquad bc = 5\times19 = 95$

Here, $\qquad 100 > 95 \Rightarrow ad > bc$

So, $\dfrac{a}{b} > \dfrac{c}{d}$

Hence, $\dfrac{4}{5}$ is greater. **Ans.**

2. Arrange $5:6, 8:9, 13:18$ and $7:12$ in ascending order of magnitude.

Sol. The given ratios are $5:6, 8:9, 13:18$ and $7:12$.

Now, L.C.M. of 6, 9, 18 and $12 = 36$

Now, $\qquad \dfrac{5}{6} = \dfrac{5\times6}{6\times6} = \dfrac{30}{36}$

$\dfrac{8}{9} = \dfrac{8\times4}{9\times4} = \dfrac{32}{36}$

$$\frac{13}{18} = \frac{13 \times 2}{18 \times 2} = \frac{26}{36}$$

and

$$\frac{7}{12} = \frac{7 \times 3}{12 \times 3} = \frac{21}{36}$$

Here,

$$\frac{21}{36} < \frac{26}{36} < \frac{30}{36} < \frac{32}{36}$$

Hence,

$$\frac{7}{12} < \frac{13}{18} < \frac{5}{6} < \frac{8}{9}$$

i.e., Ascending order

$$7 : 12 < 13 : 18 < 5 : 6 < 8 : 9. \textbf{ Ans.}$$

3. Determine

(i) The duplicate ratio of $7 : 9$

(ii) The triplicate ratio of $3 : 7$

(iii) The sub-duplicate ratio of $256 : 625$

(iv) The sub-triplicate ratio of $216 : 343$

(v) The reciprocal ratio of $8 : 15$.

Sol. (i) The duplicate ratio of $7 : 9$

$$= 7^2 : 9^2$$

$$= 49 : 81. \qquad \textbf{Ans.}$$

(ii) The triplicate ratio of $3 : 7 = 3^3 : 7^3$

$$= 27 : 343. \qquad \textbf{Ans.}$$

(iii) The sub-duplicate ratio of

$$256 : 625 = \sqrt{256} : \sqrt{625}$$

$$= 16 : 25. \qquad \textbf{Ans.}$$

(iv) The sub-triplicate ratio of

$$216 : 343 = \sqrt[3]{216} : \sqrt[3]{343}$$

$$= 6 : 7. \qquad \textbf{Ans.}$$

(v) The reciprocal ratio of

$$8 : 15 = 15 : 8. \qquad \textbf{Ans.}$$

4. Find :

(i) The sub-triplicate ratio of the sub-duplicate ratio of $729x^{18} : 64y^6$.

(ii) The sub-duplicate ratio of the sub-triplicate ratio of $4096x^6 : 729y^{12}$.

Sol. (i) The sub-duplicate ratio of $729x^{18} : 64y^6$

$$= \sqrt{729x^{18}} : \sqrt{64y^6} = 27x^9 : 8y^3$$

∴ The sub-triplicate ratio of $27x^9 : 8y^3$

$$= \sqrt[3]{27x^9} : \sqrt[3]{8y^3}$$

$$= 3x^3 : 2y. \qquad \textbf{Ans.}$$

(ii) The sub-triplicate ratio of $4096x^6 : 729y^{12}$

$$= \sqrt[3]{4096x^6} : \sqrt[3]{729y^{12}}$$

$$= 16x^2 : 9y^4$$

∴ The sub-duplicate ratio of $16x^2 : 9y^4$

$$= \sqrt{16x^2} : \sqrt{9y^4}$$

$$= 4x : 3y^2. \qquad \textbf{Ans.}$$

5. The following numbers, $K + 3, K + 2, 3K - 7$ and $2K - 3$ are in proportion. Find K.*

Sol. Given, $K + 3, K + 2, 3K - 7$ and $2K - 3$ are in proportion.

∴

$$\frac{K + 3}{K + 2} = \frac{3K - 7}{2K - 3}$$

$$\Rightarrow \quad (K + 2)(3K - 7) = (K + 3)(2K - 3)$$

$$\Rightarrow \quad 3K^2 - 7K + 6K - 14 = 2K^2 - 3K + 6K - 9$$

$$\Rightarrow \quad K^2 - 4K - 5 = 0$$

$$\Rightarrow \quad K^2 - 5K + K - 5 = 0$$

$$\Rightarrow \quad K(K - 5) + 1(K - 5) = 0$$

$$\Rightarrow \quad (K - 5)(K + 1) = 0$$

$$\Rightarrow \quad K - 5 = 0 \text{ or } K + 1 = 0$$

∴

$$K = 5 \text{ or } -1. \quad \textbf{Ans.}$$

6. Two numbers are in the ratio of $3 : 5$. If 8 is added to each number, the ratio becomes $2 : 3$. Find the numbers.

Sol. Let the numbers be $3x$ and $5x$

$$3x + 8 : 5x + 8 = 2 : 3$$

$$\Rightarrow \quad \frac{3x + 8}{5x + 8} = \frac{2}{3}$$

$$\Rightarrow \quad 2(5x + 8) = 3(3x + 8)$$

$$\Rightarrow \quad 10x + 16 = 9x + 24$$

$$\Rightarrow \quad x = 8$$

∴ The numbers are 24 and 40. **Ans.**

7. Divide ₹ 720 between Sunil, Sohil and Akhil. So that Sunil gets $\frac{4}{5}$ of Sohil's and Akhil's share together and Sohil gets $\frac{2}{3}$ of Akhil's share.

Sol. Let Akhil's share be ₹ x then

Sohil's share = ₹ $\frac{2}{3} x$

and Sunil's share = ₹ $\frac{4}{5}\left(\frac{2}{3}x + x\right)$

$$= ₹ \frac{4}{5}\left(\frac{2x + 3x}{3}\right)$$

$$= ₹ \frac{4}{5}\left(\frac{5x}{3}\right)$$

Determine the Following

$$= ₹ \frac{4}{3}x.$$

According to the question

$$\frac{4}{3}x + \frac{2}{3}x + x = 720$$

$$\Rightarrow \quad \frac{4x + 2x + 3x}{3} = 720$$

$$\Rightarrow \quad 9x = 720 \times 3$$

$$\Rightarrow \quad x = \frac{720 \times 3}{9} = 240$$

Hence, putting the value of x in Sunil, Sohil and Akhil's share.

∴ Their respective shares are ₹ 320, ₹ 160 and ₹ 240. **Ans.**

8. (i) What number must be added to each of the numbers 6, 15, 20 and 43 to make them proportional ?

(ii) What least number must be added to each of the numbers 5, 11, 19 and 37, so that they are in proportion ?

Sol. (i) Let the number be 'x'

$$\therefore \quad \frac{6+x}{15+x} = \frac{20+x}{43+x}$$

$$\Rightarrow \quad (6+x)(43+x) = (20+x)(15+x)$$

$$\Rightarrow \quad 258 + 43x + 6x + x^2 = 300 + 15x + 20x + x^2$$

$$\Rightarrow \quad 258 + 49x + x^2 = 300 + 35x + x^2$$

$$\Rightarrow \quad 14x = 42$$

$$\Rightarrow \quad x = 3$$

∴ The required no. is 3. **Ans.**

(ii) Let x be the number added to 5, 11, 19, 37.

$$\therefore \quad \frac{5+x}{11+x} = \frac{19+x}{37+x}$$

Applying componendo and dividendo rule

$$\frac{5+x+11+x}{5+x-11-x} = \frac{19+x+37+x}{19+x-37-x}$$

$$\Rightarrow \quad \frac{16+2x}{-6} = \frac{56+2x}{-18}$$

$$\Rightarrow \quad 4x = 8$$

$$\Rightarrow \quad x = 2. \quad \textbf{Ans.}$$

9. What quantity must be added to each term of the ratio $a + b : a - b$ to make it equal to $(a + b)^2 : (a - b)^2$?

Sol. Let the quantity to be added be x. Then

$$\frac{(a+b)+x}{(a-b)+x} = \frac{(a+b)^2}{(a-b)^2}$$

$$\Rightarrow \quad (a+b)(a-b)^2 + (a-b)^2.x$$
$$= (a+b)^2(a-b) + (a+b)^2.x$$

$$\Rightarrow \quad [(a+b)^2 - (a-b)^2]x$$
$$= (a^2-b^2)(a-b) - (a^2-b^2)(a+b)$$

$$\Rightarrow \quad (4abx) = (a^2-b^2)[(a-b)-(a+b)]$$

$$\Rightarrow \quad x = \frac{-2b(a^2-b^2)}{4ab} = \frac{b^2-a^2}{2a}$$

Ans.

10. Determine the fourth proportional to :

(i) $2xy, x^2, y^2$

(ii) $x^3 - y^3, x^4 + x^2y^2 + y^4, x - y.$

Sol. (i) Let A be the fourth proportional then

$$2xy : x^2 = y^2 : A$$

$$\Rightarrow \quad \frac{2xy}{x^2} = \frac{y^2}{A}$$

$$\Rightarrow \quad A = \frac{xy}{2}. \quad \textbf{Ans.}$$

(ii) Let A be the fourth proportional then

$$x^3 - y^3 : x^4 + x^2y^2 + y^4 = x - y : A$$

$$\Rightarrow \quad \frac{x^3 - y^3}{x^4 + x^2y^2 + y^4} = \frac{x-y}{A}$$

$$\Rightarrow \quad A(x^3 - y^3) = (x-y)(x^4 + x^2y^2 + y^4)$$

$$\Rightarrow \quad A = \frac{(x-y)(x^4 + x^2y^2 + y^4)}{x^3 - y^3}$$

$$\Rightarrow \quad A = \frac{(x-y)(x^2 + y^2 + xy)(x^2 + y^2 - xy)}{(x-y)(x^2 + xy + y^2)}$$

$$\Rightarrow \quad A = x^2 + y^2 - xy. \quad \textbf{Ans.}$$

11. Determine the third proportional to :

(i) $x - y, x^2 - y^2$

(ii) $\frac{a}{b} + \frac{b}{c}, \sqrt{a^2 + b^2}$

Sol. (i) Let A be the third proportional then

$$(x-y) : (x^2-y^2) = (x^2-y^2) : A$$

$$\Rightarrow \quad \frac{x-y}{x^2-y^2} = \frac{x^2-y^2}{A}$$

$$\Rightarrow \quad \frac{(x-y)}{x^2-y^2} = \frac{(x+y)(x-y)}{A}$$

$$\Rightarrow \quad A = (x+y)(x^2-y^2). \quad \textbf{Ans.}$$

(ii) Let x be the third proportional then

$$\frac{a}{b} + \frac{b}{a} : \sqrt{a^2 + b^2} = \sqrt{a^2 + b^2} : x$$

$$\Rightarrow \quad \frac{a^2 + b^2}{ab} : \sqrt{a^2 + b^2} = \sqrt{a^2 + b^2} : x$$

$$\Rightarrow \quad \frac{a^2 + b^2}{ab\sqrt{a^2 + b^2}} = \frac{\sqrt{a^2 + b^2}}{x}$$

$$\Rightarrow \quad x = \frac{ab(a^2 + b^2)}{(a^2 + b^2)}$$

$$\Rightarrow \quad x = ab. \qquad \textbf{Ans.}$$

12. Determine the two numbers such that their mean proportional is 24 and the third proportional is 1,536.

Sol. Let x and y be two numbers

Mean proportional = 24

$$\Rightarrow \qquad \sqrt{xy} = 24$$

$$\Rightarrow \qquad xy = 24 \times 24 = 576$$

$$\Rightarrow \qquad x = \frac{576}{y} \qquad \text{...(i)}$$

Also, 1,536 is the third proportional then

$$x : y = y : 1{,}536$$

$$\Rightarrow \qquad \frac{x}{y} = \frac{y}{1{,}536}$$

From (i), $\qquad y^2 = 1{,}536 \times \dfrac{576}{y}$

$$\Rightarrow \qquad y^3 = 1{,}536 \times 576$$

$$\Rightarrow \qquad y^3 = 24 \times 24 \times 24 \times 64$$

$$\Rightarrow \qquad y = 24 \times 4$$

$$\Rightarrow \qquad y = 96$$

Again, from (i), we get

$$x = \frac{576}{96} = 6.$$

Hence, the required numbers are 6 and 96. **Ans.**

13. Determine the compound ratio of the following :

(i) If $A : B = 4 : 5$, $B : C = 6 : 7$ and $C : D = 14 : 15$. Find $A : D$.

(ii) If $P : Q = 6 : 7$, $Q : R = 8 : 9$ find $P : Q : R$.

(iii) $(a + b) : (a - b)$, $a^2 + b^2 : (a + b)^2$ and

$$(a^2 - b^2)^2 : (a^4 - b^4).$$

Sol. (i) Given $A : B = 4 : 5$, $B : C = 6 : 7$

and $C : D = 14 : 15$

or $\qquad \dfrac{A}{B} = \dfrac{4}{5}, \dfrac{B}{C} = \dfrac{6}{7}, \dfrac{C}{D} = \dfrac{14}{15}$

Multiply all $\dfrac{A}{B} \times \dfrac{B}{C} \times \dfrac{C}{D} = \dfrac{4}{5} \times \dfrac{6}{7} \times \dfrac{14}{15}$

$$\therefore \qquad \frac{A}{D} = \frac{16}{25}$$

$$\Rightarrow \qquad A : D = 16 : 25 \qquad \textbf{Ans.}$$

(ii) Given $P : Q = 6 : 7$ and $Q : R = 8 : 9$

$$\frac{P}{Q} = \frac{6}{7} \times \frac{8}{8}, \frac{Q}{R} = \frac{8}{9} \times \frac{7}{7}$$

$$\frac{P}{Q} = \frac{48}{56}, \frac{Q}{R} = \frac{56}{63}$$

$$\therefore \qquad P : Q : R = 48 : 56 : 63 \qquad \textbf{Ans.}$$

(iii) The compound ratio is

$$= \frac{(a+b)}{(a-b)} \times \frac{(a^2+b^2)}{(a+b)^2} \times \frac{(a^2-b^2)^2}{(a^4-b^4)}$$

$$= \frac{(a+b)(a^2+b^2)(a^2-b^2)(a^2-b^2)}{(a-b)(a+b)(a+b)(a^2-b^2)(a^2+b^2)}$$

$$= \frac{(a-b)(a+b)}{(a-b)(a+b)} = \frac{1}{1} = 1 : 1. \qquad \textbf{Ans.}$$

14. The ratio between two numbers is $3 : 4$. If their L.C.M. is 180. Determine the numbers.

Sol. Let the required numbers be $3x$ and $4x$.

The L.C.M. of $3x$ and $4x = 12x$

then $\qquad 12x = 180 \Rightarrow x = 15$

Hence, the required numbers are

$$3x = 3 \times 15 = 45$$

and $\qquad 4x = 4 \times 15 = 60.$

Hence, the numbers are (45, 60). **Ans.**

15. If $(3a + 2b) : (5a + 3b) = 18 : 29$. Find $a : b$.

Sol. Here,

$$\Rightarrow \qquad \frac{3a + 2b}{5a + 3b} = \frac{18}{29}$$

$$\Rightarrow \qquad 87a + 58b = 90a + 54b$$

$$\Rightarrow \qquad -3a = -4b$$

$$\Rightarrow \qquad \frac{a}{b} = \frac{4}{3}$$

i.e., $\qquad a : b = 4 : 3 \qquad \textbf{Ans.}$

16. If $x : y = 2 : 3$, find the value of

$(3x + 2y) : (2x + 5y)$.

Sol. We have

$$\frac{x}{y} = \frac{2}{3}$$

Now, $\dfrac{3x+2y}{2x+5y} = \dfrac{y\left(\dfrac{3x}{y}+2\right)}{y\left(\dfrac{2x}{y}+5\right)}$

(Both numerator and denominator are divided by y)

Now, putting the value $\dfrac{x}{y} = \dfrac{2}{3}$

$= \dfrac{3\times\dfrac{2}{3}+2}{2\times\dfrac{2}{3}+5} = \dfrac{4}{\dfrac{19}{3}}$

$= \dfrac{4\times 3}{19} = 12 : 19.$ **Ans.**

17. The work done by $(x-3)$ men in $(2x+1)$ days and the work done by $(2x+1)$ men in $(x+4)$ days are in the ratio of $3 : 10$. Determine the value of x.

Sol. $(x-3)$ men do a work in $(2x+1)$ day

∴ 1 man does it in $(2x+1)(x-3)$ days

$(2x+1)$ men do other work in $(x+4)$ days

∴ 1 man does it in $(x+4)(2x+1)$ days

$\dfrac{(2x+1)(x-3)}{(x+4)(2x+1)} = \dfrac{3}{10}$

$\Rightarrow \quad \dfrac{x-3}{x+4} = \dfrac{3}{10}$

$\Rightarrow \quad 10x - 30 = 3x + 12$

$\Rightarrow \quad 10x - 3x = 12 + 30$

$\Rightarrow \quad 7x = 42$

$\Rightarrow \quad x = \dfrac{42}{7}$

$\Rightarrow \quad x = 6.$ **Ans.**

18. Using properties of proportion, solve for x. Given that x is positive :*

$$\dfrac{2x+\sqrt{4x^2-1}}{2x-\sqrt{4x^2-1}} = 4$$

Sol. Given, $\dfrac{2x+\sqrt{4x^2-1}}{2x-\sqrt{4x^2-1}} = \dfrac{4}{1}$

$\Rightarrow \dfrac{2x+\sqrt{4x^2-1}+2x-\sqrt{4x^2-1}}{2x+\sqrt{4x^2-1}-2x+\sqrt{4x^2-1}} = \dfrac{4+1}{4-1}$

(using componendo and dividendo)

$\Rightarrow \quad \dfrac{4x}{2\sqrt{4x^2-1}} = \dfrac{5}{3}$

$\Rightarrow \quad 10\sqrt{4x^2-1} = 12x$

$\Rightarrow \quad 100(4x^2-1) = 144x^2$

(On squaring both sides)

$\Rightarrow \quad 400x^2 - 100 = 144x^2$

$\Rightarrow \quad 400x^2 - 144x^2 = 100$

$\Rightarrow \quad 256x^2 = 100$

$\Rightarrow \quad x^2 = \dfrac{100}{256}$

$\Rightarrow \quad x^2 = \left(\dfrac{10}{16}\right)^2$

$\Rightarrow \quad x = \pm\dfrac{10}{16} = \pm\dfrac{5}{8}$

$\therefore \quad x = \dfrac{5}{8}$ ($\because x$ is positive)

Ans.

19. Using properties of proportion solve for x, given

$$\dfrac{\sqrt{5x}+\sqrt{2x-6}}{\sqrt{5x}-\sqrt{2x-6}} = 4\,*$$

Sol. Given, $\dfrac{\sqrt{5x}+\sqrt{2x-6}}{\sqrt{5x}-\sqrt{2x-6}} = \dfrac{4}{1}$

Applying componendo and dividendo,

$\dfrac{(\sqrt{5x}+\sqrt{2x-6})+(\sqrt{5x}-\sqrt{2x-6})}{(\sqrt{5x}+\sqrt{2x-6})-(\sqrt{5x}-\sqrt{2x-6})} = \dfrac{4+1}{4-1}$

$\Rightarrow \dfrac{\sqrt{5x}+\sqrt{2x-6}+\sqrt{5x}-\sqrt{2x-6}}{\sqrt{5x}+\sqrt{2x-6}-\sqrt{5x}+\sqrt{2x-6}} = \dfrac{5}{3}$

$\Rightarrow \quad \dfrac{2\sqrt{5x}}{2\sqrt{2x-6}} = \dfrac{5}{3}$

$\Rightarrow \quad \dfrac{\sqrt{5x}}{\sqrt{2x-6}} = \dfrac{5}{3}$

Squaring both sides, we get

$$\dfrac{5x}{2x-6} = \dfrac{25}{9}$$

$\Rightarrow \quad 25(2x-6) = 9\times 5x$

$\Rightarrow \quad 50x - 150 = 45x$

$\Rightarrow \quad 50x - 45x = 150$

$\Rightarrow \quad 5x = 150$

$\Rightarrow \quad x = 3$ **Ans.**

20. Using componendo and dividendo, find the value of x

$$\dfrac{\sqrt{3x+4}+\sqrt{3x-5}}{\sqrt{3x+4}-\sqrt{3x-5}} = 9$$

* Frequently asked previous years Board Exam Questions.

Sol. $\dfrac{\sqrt{3x+4}+\sqrt{3x-5}}{\sqrt{3x+4}-\sqrt{3x-5}}=\dfrac{9}{1}$

Using componendo and dividendo

$\dfrac{\sqrt{3x+4}+\sqrt{3x-5}+\sqrt{3x+4}-\sqrt{3x-5}}{\sqrt{3x+4}+\sqrt{3x-5}-\sqrt{3x+4}+\sqrt{3x-5}}$

$=\dfrac{9+1}{9-1}=\dfrac{10}{8}=\dfrac{5}{4}$

$\Rightarrow \quad \dfrac{2\sqrt{3x+4}}{2\sqrt{3x-5}}=\dfrac{5}{4}$

$\Rightarrow \quad \dfrac{3x+4}{3x-5}=\dfrac{25}{16}$ (Squaring both sides)

$\Rightarrow \quad 48x+64=75x-125$

$\Rightarrow \quad 27x=189 \Rightarrow x=\dfrac{189}{27}=7$ **Ans.**

21. Using properties of proportion find $x:y$, given :

$$\dfrac{x^2+2x}{2x+4}=\dfrac{y^2+3y}{3y+9} *$$

Sol. Given : $\dfrac{x^2+2x}{2x+4}=\dfrac{y^2+3y}{3y+9}$

Using componendo and dividendo,

$\dfrac{x^2+2x+2x+4}{x^2+2x-2x-4}=\dfrac{y^2+3y+3y+9}{y^2+3y-3y-9}$

$\Rightarrow \quad \dfrac{x^2+4x+4}{x^2-4}=\dfrac{y^2+6y+9}{y^2-9}$

$\Rightarrow \quad \dfrac{(x+2)^2}{(x-2)(x+2)}=\dfrac{(y+3)^2}{(y-3)(y+3)}$

$\Rightarrow \quad \dfrac{x+2}{x-2}=\dfrac{y+3}{y-3}$

Again, using componendo and dividendo

$\dfrac{x+2+x-2}{x+2-x+2}=\dfrac{y+3+y-3}{y+3-y+3}$

$\Rightarrow \quad \dfrac{2x}{4}=\dfrac{2y}{6}$

$\Rightarrow \quad \dfrac{x}{y}=\dfrac{4}{6}=\dfrac{2}{3}$

Hence, $x:y=2:3$ **Ans.**

22. If $\dfrac{7m+2n}{7m-2n}=\dfrac{5}{3}$, use properties of proportion to find :

(i) $m:n$

(ii) $\dfrac{m^2+n^2}{m^2-n^2}$

Sol. (i) Given, $\dfrac{7m+2n}{7m-2n}=\dfrac{5}{3}$

Using componendo and dividendo,

$\dfrac{(7m+2n)+(7m-2n)}{(7m+2n)-(7m-2n)}=\dfrac{5+3}{5-3}$

$\Rightarrow \quad \dfrac{7m+7m}{2n+2n}=\dfrac{8}{2}$

$\Rightarrow \quad \dfrac{14m}{4n}=\dfrac{4}{1}$

$\Rightarrow \quad \dfrac{7m}{2n}=\dfrac{4}{1}$

$\Rightarrow \quad \dfrac{m}{n}=\dfrac{4}{1}\times\dfrac{2}{7}$

$\Rightarrow \quad m:n=8:7$ **Ans.**

(ii) $\dfrac{m}{n}=\dfrac{8}{7} \Rightarrow \dfrac{m^2}{n^2}=\dfrac{64}{49}$

Using componendo and dividendo,

$\dfrac{m^2+n^2}{m^2-n^2}=\dfrac{64+49}{64-49}=\dfrac{113}{15}$ **Ans.**

23. Given that $\dfrac{a^3+3ab^2}{b^3+3a^2b}=\dfrac{63}{62}$.

Using componendo and dividendo find $a:b$.

Sol. We have

$$\dfrac{a^3+3ab^2}{b^3+3a^2b}=\dfrac{63}{62}.$$

Applying componendo and dividendo rule,

$\dfrac{a^3+3ab^2+b^3+3a^2b}{a^3+3ab^2-b^3-3a^2b}=\dfrac{63+62}{63-62}$

$\Rightarrow \quad \dfrac{a^3+b^3+3ab^2+3a^2b}{a^3-b^3+3ab^2-3a^2b}=\dfrac{125}{1}$

$\Rightarrow \quad \dfrac{(a+b)^3}{(a-b)^3}=\dfrac{125}{1}$

$\Rightarrow \quad \dfrac{a+b}{a-b}=\dfrac{5}{1}$

Again, applying componendo and dividendo rule

$\dfrac{a+b+a-b}{a+b-a+b}=\dfrac{5+1}{5-1}$

$\Rightarrow \quad \dfrac{2a}{2b}=\dfrac{6}{4}$

$\Rightarrow \quad a:b=3:2$ **Ans.**

Determine the Following

---

* Frequently asked previous years Board Exam Questions.

24. If $\dfrac{3x+5y}{3x-5y} = \dfrac{7}{3}$, determine $x:y$.

Sol. Given, $\dfrac{3x+5y}{3x-5y} = \dfrac{7}{3}$

Applying componendo and dividendo rule

$\dfrac{3x+5y+3x-5y}{3x+5y-3x+5y} = \dfrac{7+3}{7-3}$

$\Rightarrow \qquad \dfrac{6x}{10y} = \dfrac{10}{4}$

$\Rightarrow \qquad \dfrac{x}{y} = \dfrac{10 \times 10}{4 \times 6}$

$\Rightarrow \qquad \dfrac{x}{y} = \dfrac{25}{6}$

$\therefore \qquad\qquad x:y = 25:6$ **Ans.**

25. Using properties of proportion, solve for x. Given that x is positive :

$$\dfrac{2x+\sqrt{4x^2-1}}{2x-\sqrt{4x^2-1}} = 4$$

Sol. Given,

$$\dfrac{2x+\sqrt{4x^2-1}}{2x-\sqrt{4x^2-1}} = \dfrac{4}{1}$$

$\Rightarrow \dfrac{2x+\sqrt{4x^2-1}+2x-\sqrt{4x^2-1}}{2x+\sqrt{4x^2-1}-2x-\sqrt{4x^2-1}} = \dfrac{4+1}{4-1}$

[Using componendo and dividendo]

$\Rightarrow \qquad \dfrac{4x}{2\sqrt{4x^2-1}} = \dfrac{5}{3}$

$\Rightarrow \qquad 10\sqrt{4x^2-1} = 12x$

$\Rightarrow \qquad 100(4x^2-1) = 144x^2$ (squaring both sides)

$\Rightarrow \qquad 400x^2 - 100 = 144x^2$

$\Rightarrow \qquad 400x^2 - 144x^2 = 100$

$\Rightarrow \qquad 256x^2 = 100$

$\Rightarrow \qquad x^2 = \dfrac{100}{256}$

$\Rightarrow \qquad x^2 = \left(\dfrac{10}{16}\right)^2$

$\Rightarrow \qquad x = \pm\dfrac{10}{16} = \pm\dfrac{5}{8}$

$\therefore \qquad x = \dfrac{5}{8}$ $(\because x$ is positive) **Ans.**

26. Solve for x :

$$\dfrac{3x^2+5x+18}{5x^2+6x+12} = \dfrac{3x+5}{5x+6}.$$

Sol. Given,

$$\dfrac{3x^2+5x+18}{5x^2+6x+12} = \dfrac{3x+5}{5x+6}$$

Multiplying the numerator and denominator of R.H.S. by $-x$

$$\dfrac{3x^2+5x+18}{5x^2+6x+12} = \dfrac{-3x^2-5x}{-5x^2-6x}$$

Since, Each ratio $= \dfrac{\text{Sum of antecedents}}{\text{Sum of consequents}}$

So, $\dfrac{3x^2+5x+18-3x^2-5x}{5x^2+6x+12-5x^2-6x} = \dfrac{-3x^2-5x}{-5x^2-6x}$

$\Rightarrow \qquad \dfrac{18}{12} = \dfrac{-3x^2-5x}{-5x^2-6x}$

$\Rightarrow \qquad \dfrac{3}{2} = \dfrac{-3x^2-5x}{-5x^2-6x}$

$\Rightarrow \qquad \dfrac{3}{2} = \dfrac{3x+5}{5x+6}$

$\Rightarrow \qquad 15x + 18 = 6x + 10$

$\Rightarrow \qquad 9x = -8$

$\Rightarrow \qquad x = \dfrac{-8}{9}$ **Ans.**

27. Solve for x : $\dfrac{1-px}{1+px} = \sqrt{\dfrac{1-qx}{1+qx}}$

Sol. Given $\dfrac{1-px}{1+px} = \sqrt{\dfrac{1-qx}{1+qx}}$

Squaring both sides

$$\left(\dfrac{1-px}{1+px}\right)^2 = \dfrac{1-qx}{1+qx}$$

$\Rightarrow \qquad \dfrac{1+p^2x^2-2px}{1+p^2x^2+2px} = \dfrac{1-qx}{1+qx}$

Applying componendo and dividendo rule

$\dfrac{1+p^2x^2-2px+1+p^2x^2+2px}{1+p^2x^2-2px-1-p^2x^2-2px}$

$\qquad = \dfrac{1-qx+1+qx}{1-qx-1-qx}$

$\Rightarrow \qquad \dfrac{2(1+p^2x^2)}{2(-2px)} = \dfrac{2}{-2qx}$

$$\Rightarrow \qquad \frac{1+p^2x^2}{2px} = \frac{1}{qx}$$

$$\Rightarrow \qquad qx\,(1+p^2x^2) = 2px$$

$$\Rightarrow x\,(p^2qx^2 - 2p + q) = 0$$

Either $\qquad x = 0$

or $\qquad p^2qx^2 = 2p - q$

$$\Rightarrow \qquad x^2 = \frac{2p-q}{p^2q}$$

$$\Rightarrow \qquad x = 0 \text{ or } x = \pm\frac{1}{p}\sqrt{\frac{2p-q}{q}} \qquad \textbf{Ans.}$$

28. Find the value of

$$\frac{x+\sqrt{3}}{x-\sqrt{3}} + \frac{x+\sqrt{2}}{x-\sqrt{2}}, \text{ if } x = \frac{2\sqrt{6}}{\sqrt{3}+\sqrt{2}}$$

Sol. We have

$$x = \frac{2\sqrt{6}}{\sqrt{3}+\sqrt{2}}$$

or $\qquad x = \dfrac{2\times\sqrt{3}\times\sqrt{2}}{\sqrt{3}+\sqrt{2}}$

$$\Rightarrow \qquad \frac{x}{\sqrt{3}} = \frac{2\sqrt{2}}{\sqrt{3}+\sqrt{2}}$$

Applying componendo and dividendo rule

$$\frac{x+\sqrt{3}}{x-\sqrt{3}} = \frac{2\sqrt{2}+\sqrt{3}+\sqrt{2}}{2\sqrt{2}-\sqrt{3}-\sqrt{2}}$$

$$= \frac{3\sqrt{2}+\sqrt{3}}{\sqrt{2}-\sqrt{3}}$$

$$\Rightarrow \qquad \frac{x+\sqrt{3}}{x-\sqrt{3}} = \frac{3\sqrt{2}+\sqrt{3}}{-(\sqrt{3}-\sqrt{2})} \qquad \text{...(i)}$$

Also $\qquad \dfrac{x}{\sqrt{2}} = \dfrac{2\sqrt{3}}{\sqrt{3}+\sqrt{2}}$

Applying componendo and dividendo rule

$$\frac{x+\sqrt{2}}{x-\sqrt{2}} = \frac{2\sqrt{3}+\sqrt{3}+\sqrt{2}}{2\sqrt{3}-\sqrt{3}-\sqrt{2}}$$

$$\Rightarrow \qquad \frac{x+\sqrt{2}}{x-\sqrt{2}} = \frac{3\sqrt{3}+\sqrt{2}}{\sqrt{3}-\sqrt{2}} \qquad \text{...(ii)}$$

Adding (i) and (ii)

$$\frac{x+\sqrt{3}}{x-\sqrt{3}} + \frac{x+\sqrt{2}}{x-\sqrt{2}} = \frac{-3\sqrt{2}-\sqrt{3}+3\sqrt{3}+\sqrt{2}}{\sqrt{3}-\sqrt{2}}$$

$$= \frac{-2\sqrt{2}+2\sqrt{3}}{\sqrt{3}-\sqrt{2}}$$

$$= \frac{2(\sqrt{3}-\sqrt{2})}{(\sqrt{3}-\sqrt{2})}$$

$$= 2. \qquad \textbf{Ans.}$$

Chapter 7. Factorization

1. Use remainder theorem to factorize the following polynomial :*

$$2x^3 + 3x^2 - 9x - 10.$$

Sol. Let $\qquad f(x) = 2x^3 + 3x^2 - 9x - 10$

For $x = 2$,

$$f(2) = 2\times 2^3 + 3\times 2^2 - 9\times 2 - 10$$

$$= 16 + 12 - 18 - 10$$

$$= 28 - 28 = 0.$$

$\therefore$ $(x - 2)$ is a factor of $f(x)$

$$x-2\overline{)\;2x^3 + 3x^2 - 9x - 10\;}\,(2x^2 + 7x + 5$$

$$\underline{2x^3 - 4x^2}$$

$$\quad - \quad +$$

$$7x^2 - 9x$$

$$7x^2 - 14x$$

$$\underline{\quad - \quad + \quad}$$

$$5x - 10$$

$$5x - 10$$

$$\underline{\;-\quad +\;}$$

$$\times$$

Now, $2x^2 + 7x + 5 = 2x^2 + 5x + 2x + 5$

$$= x\,(2x + 5) + 1\,(2x + 5)$$

$$= (2x + 5)\,(x + 1)$$

$\therefore \qquad f(x) = (x + 1)\,(x - 2)\,(2x + 5)$ **Ans.**

2. Use remainder theorem and find the remainder when the polynomial $g(x) = x^3 + x^2 - 2x + 1$ is divided by $x - 3$.

Sol. If $\qquad x - 3 = 0$

$$\Rightarrow \qquad x = 3$$

By the remainder theorem, required remainder is

$$g(3) = (3)^3 + (3)^2 - 2\times 3 + 1$$

$$= 27 + 9 - 6 + 1 = 31. \qquad \textbf{Ans.}$$

---

* **Frequently asked previous years Board Exam Questions.**

Determine the Following

3. Find the remainder when the polynomial $f(x) = 2x^4 - 6x^3 + 2x^2 - x + 2$ is divided by $x + 2$.

Sol. If $\quad x + 2 = 0$

$$x = -2$$

By the remainder theorem, required remainder is

$$f(-2) = 2(-2)^4 - 6(-2)^3 + 2(-2)^2 - (-2) + 2$$

$$= 2(16) - 6(-8) + 2(4) + 2 + 2$$

$$= 32 + 48 + 8 + 2 + 2 = 92$$

Hence, required remainder = 92.   **Ans.**

4. Using the Remainder Theorem find the remainders obtained when $x^3 + (kx + 8)x + k$ is divided by $x + 1$ and $x - 2$.

Hence find k if the sum of the two remainders is 1.*

Sol. Let $\quad\quad f(x) = x^3 + (kx + 8)x + k$

when $f(x)$ is divided by $(x + 1)$ then by remainder theorem, $x + 1 = 0 \Rightarrow x = -1$

Remainder, $f(-1) = (-1)^3 + \{k(-1) + 8\}(-1) + k$

$$= -1 + (-k + 8)(-1) + k$$

$$= -1 + k - 8 + k$$

$$= 2k - 9$$

Similarly when $f(x)$ is divided by $(x - 2)$,

Remainder, $\quad f(2) = (2)^3 + (k.2 + 8)2 + k$

$$= 8 + 4k + 16 + k$$

$$= 5k + 24$$

Also, sum of remainders = 1

$$f(-1) + f(2) = 1$$

$$\Rightarrow 2k - 9 + 5k + 24 = 1$$

$$\Rightarrow \quad\quad 7k + 15 = 1$$

$$\Rightarrow \quad\quad 7k = 1 - 15$$

$$\Rightarrow \quad\quad k = \frac{-14}{7} = -2 \quad\quad\textbf{Ans.}$$

5. In the following problems use the factor 'theorem' to find if $g(x)$ is a factor of $p(x)$:

(i) $p(x) = x^3 - 3x^2 + 4x - 4$ and $g(x) = x - 2$

(ii) $p(x) = 2x^3 + 4x + 6$ and $g(x) = x + 1$

(iii) $p(x) = x^3 + x^2 + 3x + 175$ and $g(x) = x + 5$.

Sol. (i)

$$p(x) = x^3 - 3x^2 + 4x - 4$$

and $\quad\quad g(x) = x - 2$

To check whether $x - 2$ is a factor of $p(x)$ now put $x = 2$ in equation (i), we get

$$p(2) = (2)^3 - 3(2)^2 + 4(2) - 4$$

$$= 8 - 3 \times 4 + 8 - 4$$

$$= 8 - 12 + 8 - 4$$

$$= 16 - 16 = 0$$

Since, $p(2) = 0$, so by factor theorem $(x - 2)$ is a factor of $p(x)$.   **Ans.**

(ii) $\quad\quad p(x) = 2x^3 + 4x + 6$

and $\quad\quad g(x) = x + 1$

Now, put $x = -1$ in equation (i), we get

$$p(-1) = 2(-1)^3 + 4(-1) + 6$$

$$= 2 \times -1 - 4 + 6$$

$$= -2 - 4 + 6$$

$$= -6 + 6 = 0$$

Since, $p(-1) = 0$, so by factor theorem $(x + 1)$ is a factor of $p(x)$.   **Ans.**

(iii) $\quad\quad p(x) = x^3 + x^2 + 3x + 175 \quad\quad...(i)$

and $\quad\quad g(x) = x + 5$

To check whether $(x + 5)$ is a factor of $p(x)$, put $x = -5$ in equation (i), we get

$$p(-5) = (-5)^3 + (-5)^2 + 3(-5) + 175$$

$$= -125 + 25 - 15 + 175$$

$$= -140 + 200 = 60$$

Since, $p(-5) \neq 0$, so by factor theorem $(x + 5)$ is not a factor of $p(x)$.   **Ans.**

6. Use the factor theorem to determine that $x - 1$ is a factor of $x^6 - x^5 + x^4 - x^3 + x^2 - x + 1$.

Sol. Let $f(x) = x^6 - x^5 + x^4 - x^3 + x^2 - x + 1$, to check whether $x - 1$ is a factor of $x^6 - x^5 + x^4 - x^3 + x^2 - x + 1$, we find $f(1)$.

Put $x = 1$ in equation (i) we get

$$f(1) = (1)^6 - (1)^5 + (1)^4 - (1)^3 + (1)^2 - (1) + 1$$

$$= 1 - 1 + 1 - 1 + 1 - 1 + 1$$

$$= 4 - 3 = 1.$$

Since, $f(1) \neq 0$. So by factor theorem $(x - 1)$ is not a factor of $f(x)$.   **Ans.**

Determine the Following

7. (i) When $x^3 + 3x^2 - kx + 4$ is divided by $(x - 2)$, the remainder is k. Find the value of k.

(ii) Find the value of p if the division of $px^3 + 9x^2 + 4x - 10$ by $(x + 3)$ leaves the remainder 5.

Sol. (i) Here, $P(2) = k$

$\Rightarrow$ $2^3 + 3(2)^2 - k(2) + 4 = k$

$\Rightarrow$ $8 + 12 - 2k + 4 = k$

$\Rightarrow$ $3k = 24$

$\Rightarrow$ $k = 8$ **Ans.**

(ii) Here, $P(-3) = 5$

$\Rightarrow$ $p(-3)^3 + 9(-3)^2 + 4(-3) - 10 = 5$

$\Rightarrow$ $-27p + 81 - 12 - 10 = 5$

$\Rightarrow$ $-27p = -54$

$\Rightarrow$ $p = 2$ **Ans.**

8. Find the value of a, if $(x - a)$ is a factor of $x^3 - a^2x + x + 2$.

Sol. Let $f(x) = x^3 - a^2x + x + 2$

Put $x - a = 0$

$\therefore$ $x = a$

$f(a) = a^3 - a^2 \cdot a + a + 2$

$\Rightarrow$ $0 = a^3 - a^3 + a + 2$

$\Rightarrow$ $a + 2 = 0$

$\therefore$ $a = -2$ **Ans.**

9. If $x - 2$ is a factor of each of the following three polynomials. Find the value of 'a' in each case :

(i) $x^2 - 3x + 5a$

(ii) $x^3 + 2ax^2 + ax - 1$

(iii) $x^5 - 3x^4 - ax^3 + 3ax^2 + 2ax + 4$.

Sol. (i) Let

$p(x) = x^2 - 3x + 5a$ ...(i)

Since, $(x - 2)$ is a factor of $p(x)$, so $p(2) = 0$

(by factor theorem)

Put $x = 2$ in equation (i), we get

$p(2) = (2)^2 - 3 \times 2 + 5a$

$= 4 - 6 + 5a$

$= 5a - 2$

But $p(2) = 0$

$\Rightarrow$ $5a - 2 = 0$

$\Rightarrow$ $5a = 2$

$\Rightarrow$ $a = \dfrac{2}{5}$.

Ans.

(ii) Let $p(x) = x^3 + 2ax^2 + ax - 1$ ...(i)

Since, $(x - 2)$ is a factor of $p(x)$, so $p(2) = 0$

Put $x = 2$ in equation (i), we get

$p(2) = (2)^3 - 2a(2)^2 + a(2) - 1$

$= 8 - 2a \times 4 + 2a - 1$

$= 8 - 8a + 2a - 1$

$= 7 - 6a$

But $p(2) = 0$

$7 - 6a = 0$

$\Rightarrow$ $-6a = -7$

$\Rightarrow$ $a = \dfrac{7}{6}$.   **Ans.**

(iii)   Let $p(x) = x^5 - 3x^4 - ax^3 + 3ax^2 + 2ax + 4$ ...(i)

Since, $(x - 2)$ is factor of $p(x)$, so $p(2) = 0$

Put $x = 2$ in equation (i) we get

$p(2) = (2)^5 - 3(2)^4 - a(2)^3 + 3a(2)^2 + 2a(2) + 4$

$= 32 - 3 \times 16 - a \times 8 + 3a \times 4 + 4a + 4$

$= 32 - 48 - 8a + 12a + 4a + 4$

$= 8a - 12$

But $p(2) = 0$

$\Rightarrow$ $8a - 12 = 0$

$\Rightarrow$ $8a = 12$

$\Rightarrow$ $a = \dfrac{12}{8}$

$\Rightarrow$ $a = \dfrac{3}{2}$.   **Ans.**

10. Find the value of the constant a and b, if $(x - 2)$ and $(x + 3)$ are both factors of expression $x^3 + ax^2 + bx - 12$.

Sol. Expression $x^3 + ax^2 + bx - 12$

$(x - 2)$ is a factor *i.e.*, at $x = 2$

the remainder will be zero

$\Rightarrow$ $(2)^3 + a(2)^2 + b(2) - 12 = 0$

$\Rightarrow$ $8 + 4a + 2b - 12 = 0$

$\Rightarrow$ $4a + 2b = 4$

$\Rightarrow$ $2a + b = 2$ ...(i)

when $x + 3$ is a factor *i.e.*, at $x = -3$, the remainder will be zero.

$\Rightarrow$ $(-3)^3 + a(-3)^2 + b(-3) - 12 = 0$

$\Rightarrow$ $-27 + 9a - 3b - 12 = 0$

$$\Rightarrow \quad 9a - 3b = 39$$

$$\Rightarrow \quad 3a - b = 13 \qquad ...(ii)$$

Adding (i) and (ii),

$$5a = 15$$

$$\Rightarrow \quad a = 3$$

Substituting the value of a in the equation (i)

$$\Rightarrow \quad 2 \times 3 + b = 2$$

$$\Rightarrow \quad 6 + b = 2$$

$$\Rightarrow \quad b = 2 - 6 = -4$$

$$\Rightarrow \quad a = 3, b = -4 \text{ Ans.}$$

11. If $(x - 2)$ is a factor of the expression $2x^3 + ax^2 + bx - 14$ and when the expression is divided by $(x - 3)$, it leaves a remainder 52, find the values of a and b.

Sol. Let $\qquad f(x) = 2x^3 + ax^2 + bx - 14 \qquad ...(i)$

as $(x - 2)$ is factor of (i)

Put $\qquad x - 2 = 0$

$$\Rightarrow \quad x = 2 \text{ in (i)}$$

$$f(2) = 2\,(2)^3 + a\,(2)^2 + b\,(2) - 14$$

$$0 = 16 + 4a + 2b - 14$$

$$\Rightarrow \quad 4a + 2b = -2$$

$$\Rightarrow \quad 2a + b = -1 \qquad ...(ii)$$

Again when $f(x)$ is divided by $(x - 3)$, it leaves remainder 52.

Put $\qquad x - 3 = 0$

$$\Rightarrow \quad x = 3$$

$$f(3) = 2\,(3)^3 + a\,(3)^2 + b\,(3) - 14$$

$$52 = 54 + 9a + 3b - 14$$

$$52 = 9a + 3b + 40$$

$$52 - 40 = 9a + 3b$$

$$12 = 9a + 3b$$

or $\qquad 4 = 3a + b \qquad ...(iii)$

Solving (ii) and (iii)

$$3a + b = 4$$

$$2a + b = -1$$

By subtracting $\quad \underline{- \quad - \quad +}$

$$a = 5$$

Substitute $a = 5$ in $3a + b = 4$

$$\Rightarrow \quad 3 \times 5 + b = 4$$

$$15 + b = 4$$

$$\Rightarrow \quad b = 4 - 15$$

$$b = -11$$

$$\Rightarrow \quad a = 5, b = -11 \qquad \textbf{Ans.}$$

12. Find the value of a and b so that the polynomial $x^3 - ax^2 - 13x + b$ has $(x - 1)\,(x + 3)$ as factor.

Sol. Let $p(x) = x^3 - ax^2 - 13x + b$ be the given polynomial.

If $(x - 1)$ and $(x + 3)$ are the factors of $p(x)$ then

$$p(1) = 0$$

and $\qquad p(-3) = 0$

$$p(1) = (1)^3 - a(1)^2 - 13(1) + b = 0$$

$$= 1 - a - 13 + b = 0$$

$$a - b = -12 \qquad ...(i)$$

$$p(-3) = (-3)^3 - a(-3)^2 - 13(-3) + b = 0$$

$$= -27 - 9a + 39 + b = 0$$

$$9a - b = 12 \qquad ...(ii)$$

Solving (i) and (ii), we get

$$a = 3$$

and $\qquad b = 15$. $\qquad\qquad$ **Ans.**

13. If the polynomials $ax^3 + 4x^2 + 3x - 4$ and $x^3 - 4x + a$ leave the same remainder when divided by $(x - 3)$, find the value of a.

Sol. Let $p(x) = ax^3 + 4x^2 + 3x - 4$ and $q(x) = x^3 - 4x + a$ be the given polynomials.

When $p(x)$ and $q(x)$ are divided by $(x - 3)$, the remainder are $p(3)$ and $q(3)$ respectively.

$$p(3) = q(3) \qquad \text{(given)}$$

$$a(3)^3 + 4(3)^2 + 3 \times 3 - 4 = 3^3 - 4 \times 3 + a$$

$$\Rightarrow \quad 27a + 36 + 9 - 4 = 27 - 12 + a$$

$$\Rightarrow \quad 26a = 15 - 41$$

$$\Rightarrow \quad 26a = -26$$

$$\therefore \qquad a = -\frac{26}{26} = -1. \quad \textbf{Ans.}$$

14. Use factor theorem to factorize $6x^3 + 17x^2 + 4x - 12$ completely.*

Sol. Let $p(x) = 6x^3 + 17x^2 + 4x - 12$

$$\because p(-2) = 6 \times (-2)^3 + 17 \times (-2)^2 + 4(-2) - 12$$

$$= 6 \times (-8) + 17 \times 4 - 8 - 12$$

$$= -48 + 68 - 20$$

$$= -68 + 68 = 0$$

$$\therefore (x + 2) \text{ is a factor of } p(x)$$

---

* **Frequently asked previous years Board Exam Questions.**

Determine the Following

Dividing $p(x)$ by $(x + 2)$, see get

$$x + 2 \overline{)6x^3 + 17x^2 + 4x - 12} \, (6x^2 + 5x - 6$$
$$\underline{6x^3 + 12x^2}$$
$$\,\, -\quad\,\, -$$
$$5x^2 + 4x$$
$$5x^2 + 10x$$
$$\,\, -\quad\,\, -$$
$$-6x - 12$$
$$-6x - 12$$
$$\,\, +\quad\,\, +$$
$$0$$

Now for the quotients

$\because 6x^2 + 5x - 6 = 6x^2 + 9x - 4x - 6$

$\qquad = 3x(2x + 3) - 2(2x + 3)$

$\qquad = (3x - 2)(2x + 3)$

Therefore,

$6x^3 + 17x^2 + 4x - 12 = (x + 2)(6x^2 + 5x - 6)$

$\qquad\qquad = (x + 2)(2x + 3)(3x - 2)$ **Ans.**

15. Use the factor theorem to factorize completely $x^3 + x^2 - 4x - 4$.

Sol. $x^3 + x^2 - 4x - 4$

Let $\qquad x + 1 = 0$

$\therefore \qquad\qquad x = -1$

On substituting value of x in the expression

$\because \qquad f(-1) = (-1)^3 + (-1)^2 - 4(-1) - 4 = 0$

Clearly $x + 1$ is a factor of

$\qquad f(x) = x^3 + x^2 - 4x - 4$

$\therefore \qquad f(x) = (x + 1)(x^2 - 4)$

(By actual division)

$\qquad = (x + 1)(x - 2)(x + 2)$ **Ans.**

16. Show that $(x - 1)$ is a factor of $x^3 - 7x^2 + 14x - 8$. Hence, completely factorise the above expression.

Sol. If $(x - 1)$ is a factor of $x^3 - 7x^2 + 14x - 8$ then on putting $x - 1 = 0$.

$\qquad\qquad x = 1$

$\qquad\qquad f(1) = 0$

$\qquad\qquad = 1^3 - 7(1)^2 + 14(1) - 8$

$\qquad\qquad = 1 - 7 + 14 - 8 = 0$

Hence, $x - 1$ is one factor.

To find other factors

$\qquad\qquad = x^3 - 7x^2 + 14x - 8$

$\qquad\qquad = x^2(x - 1) - 6x(x - 1) + 8(x - 1)$

$\qquad = (x - 1)(x^2 - 6x + 8)$

$\qquad = (x - 1)(x^2 - 4x - 2x + 8)$

$\qquad = (x - 1)\{x(x - 4) - 2(x - 4)\}$

$\qquad = (x - 1)(x - 2)(x - 4)$.   **Ans.**

17. What must be added to the polynomial $2x^3 - 3x^2 - 8x$, so that it leaves a remainder 10 when divided by $2x + 1$?*

Sol. Let k be the required term to be added.

So, $\qquad\qquad p(x) = 2x^3 - 3x^2 - 8x + k$

$\because$ $p(x)$ leaves remainder 10 when divided by $2x + 1$,

$\therefore \qquad\qquad p\left(-\dfrac{1}{2}\right) = 10$

$\Rightarrow\ 2 \times \left(-\dfrac{1}{2}\right)^3 - 3 \times \left(-\dfrac{1}{2}\right)^2 - 8 \times \left(-\dfrac{1}{2}\right) + k = 10$

$\Rightarrow\ 2 \times \left(-\dfrac{1}{8}\right) - 3 \times \dfrac{1}{4} + 4 + k = 10$

$\Rightarrow\qquad\qquad -\dfrac{1}{4} - \dfrac{3}{4} + 4 + k = 10$

$\Rightarrow\qquad\qquad k = 10 - 4 + \dfrac{1 + 3}{4}$

$\Rightarrow\qquad\qquad k = 6 + 1 = 7$

$\therefore\qquad\qquad k = 7$ **Ans.**

18. The expression $2x^3 + ax^2 + bx - 2$ leaves the remainder 7 and 0 when divided by $(2x - 3)$ and $(x + 2)$ respectively calculate the value of a and b. With these value of a and b factorise the expression completely.

Sol. Let $P(x) = 2x^3 + ax^2 + bx - 2$

when $P(x)$ is divided by $2x - 3$

$$P\left(\dfrac{3}{2}\right) = 2\left(\dfrac{3}{2}\right)^3 + a\left(\dfrac{3}{2}\right)^2 + b\left(\dfrac{3}{2}\right) - 2 = 7$$

$$= \dfrac{27}{4} + \dfrac{9}{4}a + \dfrac{3}{2}b - 2 = 7$$

$$= \dfrac{27 + 9a + 6b - 8}{4}$$

$$= 9a + 6b = 28 + 8 - 27$$

$$= 9a + 6b = 9$$

$$= 3a + 2b = 3 \qquad\qquad …(i)$$

Similarly when $P(x)$ is divided by $x + 2$

$\Rightarrow\qquad\qquad x = -2$

$\therefore\qquad 2(-2)^3 + a(-2)^2 + b(-2) - 2 = 0$

$\Rightarrow\qquad\qquad -16 + 4a - 2b - 2 = 0$

$\Rightarrow\qquad\qquad 4a - 2b = 18 \qquad …(ii)$

---

* **Frequently asked previous years Board Exam Questions.**

On solving equations (i) and (ii)

$$3a + 2b = 3$$
$$\underline{4a - 2b = 18} \quad \text{(On adding (ii)}$$
$$7a = 21$$
$$a = 3$$

On substituting value of a in equation (i)

$$3 \times 3 + 2b = 3$$
$$2b = 3 - 9$$
$$b = \frac{-6}{2} = -3$$
$$b = -3$$
$$a = 3, b = -3 \quad \textbf{Ans.}$$

On substituting value of a and b

$$2x^3 + 3x^2 - 3x - 2$$

When $x + 2$ is a factor

$$
\begin{array}{r}
2x^2 - x - 1 \\
x + 2)\overline{2x^3 + 3x^2 - 3x - 2}(\\
2x^3 + 4x^2 \\
\underline{- \quad -} \\
-x^2 - 3x \\
-x^2 - 2x \\
\underline{+ \quad +} \\
-x - 2 \\
-x + 2 \\
\underline{+ \quad +} \\
\times
\end{array}
$$

$$2x^2 - x - 1 = 2x^2 - 2x + x - 1$$
$$= 2x(x - 1) + 1\,(x - 1)$$
$$= (x - 1)\,(2x + 1)$$

Hence, required factors are

$$(x - 1)\,(x + 2)\,(2x + 1) \quad \textbf{Ans.}$$

19. If $x - 2$ is a factor of

$$2x^3 - x^2 - px - 2.$$

(i) find the value of p

(ii) with the value of p, factorize the above expression completely.

Sol. Given expression is $2x^3 - x^2 - px - 2$ and $x - 2$ is the factor.

(i) $x - 2 = 0$, $x = 2$ in expression

$$2\,(2)^3 - (2)^2 - p\,(2) - 2 = 0$$
$$\Rightarrow \qquad 16 - 4 - 2p - 2 = 0$$
$$\Rightarrow \qquad 10 - 2p = 0$$
$$\Rightarrow \qquad p = 5$$

(ii) Putting the value of p

$$
\begin{array}{r}
2x^2 + 3x + 1 \\
x - 2)\overline{2x^3 - x^2 - 5x - 2}(\\
2x^3 - 4x^2 \\
\underline{- \quad +} \\
3x^2 - 5x \\
3x^2 - 6x \\
\underline{- \quad +} \\
x - 2 \\
x - 2 \\
\underline{- \quad +} \\
\times
\end{array}
$$

$$\therefore \ 2x^3 - x^2 - 5x - 2 = (x - 2)\,(2x^2 + 3x + 1)$$

The expression can be the written as

$$(2x^2 + 3x + 1)\,(x - 2) \text{ or } (2x + 1)\,(x + 1)\,(x - 2).$$

$$\textbf{Ans.}$$

Chapter 8. Matrices

---

1. Simplify :*

$$\sin A \begin{bmatrix} \sin A & -\cos A \\ \cos A & \sin A \end{bmatrix} + \cos A \begin{bmatrix} \cos A & \sin A \\ -\sin A & \cos A \end{bmatrix}$$

Sol. $\sin A \begin{bmatrix} \sin A & -\cos A \\ \cos A & \sin A \end{bmatrix} + \cos A \begin{bmatrix} \cos A & \sin A \\ -\sin A & \cos A \end{bmatrix}$

$$= \begin{bmatrix} \sin^2 A & -\sin A \cos A \\ \sin A \cos A & \sin^2 A \end{bmatrix}$$

$$+ \begin{bmatrix} \cos^2 A & \sin A \cos A \\ -\sin A \cos A & \cos^2 A \end{bmatrix}$$

$$= \begin{bmatrix} \sin^2 A + \cos^2 A & \\ \sin A \cos A - \sin A \cos A & \end{bmatrix}$$

$$\begin{bmatrix} & -\sin A \cos A + \sin A \cos A \\ & \sin^2 A + \cos^2 A \end{bmatrix}$$

$$= \begin{bmatrix} 1 & 0 \\ 0 & 1 \end{bmatrix} \qquad [\because \sin^2 A + \cos^2 A = 1]$$

$$\textbf{Ans.}$$

2. Construct a 2×2 matrix whose elements a_{ij} are given by

(i) $a_{ij} = 2i - j$

(ii) $\dfrac{(i + 2j)^2}{2}$.

* Frequently asked previous years Board Exam Questions.

Sol. (i) We have

$$a_{ij} = 2i - j$$

Now

$$a_{11} = 2 \times 1 - 1 = 1$$
$$a_{12} = 2 \times 1 - 2 = 0$$
$$a_{21} = 2 \times 2 - 1 = 3$$
$$a_{22} = 2 \times 2 - 2 = 2$$

So, the required matrix

$$A = \begin{bmatrix} a_{11} & a_{12} \\ a_{21} & a_{22} \end{bmatrix}$$

$$A = \begin{bmatrix} 1 & 0 \\ 3 & 2 \end{bmatrix}.$$ **Ans.**

(ii) We have

$$a_{ij} = \frac{(i+2j)^2}{2}$$

$$a_{11} = \frac{(1+2\times1)^2}{2} = \frac{9}{2}$$

$$a_{12} = \frac{(1+2\times2)^2}{2} = \frac{25}{2}$$

$$a_{21} = \frac{(2+2\times1)^2}{2} = \frac{16}{2} = 8$$

$$a_{22} = \frac{(2+2\times2)^2}{2} = \frac{36}{2} = 18.$$

The required matrix

$$A = \begin{bmatrix} a_{11} & a_{12} \\ a_{21} & a_{22} \end{bmatrix}$$

$$A = \begin{bmatrix} 9/2 & 25/2 \\ 8 & 18 \end{bmatrix}$$ **Ans.**

3. Find the value of 'x' and 'y' if :

$$2\begin{bmatrix} x & 7 \\ 9 & y-5 \end{bmatrix} + \begin{bmatrix} 6 & -7 \\ 4 & 5 \end{bmatrix} = \begin{bmatrix} 10 & 7 \\ 22 & 15 \end{bmatrix}$$

Sol. We have,

$$2\begin{bmatrix} x & 7 \\ 9 & y-5 \end{bmatrix} + \begin{bmatrix} 6 & -7 \\ 4 & 5 \end{bmatrix} = \begin{bmatrix} 10 & 7 \\ 22 & 15 \end{bmatrix}$$

$$\Rightarrow \begin{bmatrix} 2x & 14 \\ 18 & 2y-10 \end{bmatrix} + \begin{bmatrix} 6 & -7 \\ 4 & 5 \end{bmatrix} = \begin{bmatrix} 10 & 7 \\ 22 & 15 \end{bmatrix}$$

$$\Rightarrow \begin{bmatrix} 2x+6 & 7 \\ 22 & 2y-5 \end{bmatrix} = \begin{bmatrix} 10 & 7 \\ 22 & 15 \end{bmatrix}$$

On comparing both sides, we get

$$\Rightarrow \quad 2x + 6 = 10, \qquad 2y - 5 = 15$$
$$\Rightarrow \quad 2x = 10 - 6, \qquad 2y = 15 + 5$$
$$\Rightarrow \quad 2x = 4, \qquad 2y = 20$$

$$\Rightarrow \quad x = \frac{4}{2}, \qquad y = \frac{20}{2}$$

$$\therefore x = 2 \text{ and } y = 10.$$ **Ans.**

4. Determine the value of p and q if :

$$\begin{bmatrix} 2p+1 & q^2-2 \\ 6 & 0 \end{bmatrix} = \begin{bmatrix} p+3 & 3q-4 \\ 5q-q^2 & 0 \end{bmatrix}$$

Sol. On comparing both sides

$$2p + 1 = p + 3$$
$$\Rightarrow \quad 2p - p = 3 - 1$$
$$\Rightarrow \quad p = 2 \qquad \dots(i)$$

and

$$q^2 - 2 = 3q - 4$$
$$\Rightarrow \quad q^2 - 3q + 2 = 0$$
$$\Rightarrow \quad q^2 - 2q - q + 2 = 0$$
$$\Rightarrow \quad q(q-2) - (q-2) = 0$$
$$\Rightarrow \quad (q-2)(q-1) = 0 \qquad \dots \text{(ii)}$$
$$\Rightarrow \quad 5q - q^2 = 6$$
$$\Rightarrow \quad q^2 - 5q + 6 = 0$$
$$\Rightarrow \quad q^2 - 3q - 2q + 6 = 0$$
$$\Rightarrow \quad (q-3)(q-2) = 0 \qquad \dots \text{(iii)}$$

By equation (ii) and (iii)

$$q = 2$$
$$\Rightarrow \quad p = 2, q = 2$$ **Ans.**

5. Given

$$A = \begin{bmatrix} 2 & -6 \\ 2 & 0 \end{bmatrix}, B = \begin{bmatrix} -3 & 2 \\ 4 & 0 \end{bmatrix}, C = \begin{bmatrix} 4 & 0 \\ 0 & 2 \end{bmatrix}$$

Determine the matrix X such that

$$A + 2X = 2B + C.$$

Sol. Given,

$$A = \begin{bmatrix} 2 & -6 \\ 2 & 0 \end{bmatrix}, B = \begin{bmatrix} -3 & 2 \\ 4 & 0 \end{bmatrix}$$

and

$$C = \begin{bmatrix} 4 & 0 \\ 0 & 2 \end{bmatrix}$$

Given, $A + 2X = 2B + C$

$$\begin{bmatrix} 2 & -6 \\ 2 & 0 \end{bmatrix} + 2X = 2\begin{bmatrix} -3 & 2 \\ 4 & 0 \end{bmatrix} + \begin{bmatrix} 4 & 0 \\ 0 & 2 \end{bmatrix}$$

$$2X = \begin{bmatrix} -6 & 4 \\ 8 & 0 \end{bmatrix} + \begin{bmatrix} 4 & 0 \\ 0 & 2 \end{bmatrix} - \begin{bmatrix} 2 & -6 \\ 2 & 0 \end{bmatrix}$$

$$2X = \begin{bmatrix} -6+4-2 & 4+0+6 \\ 8+0-2 & 0+2-0 \end{bmatrix} = \begin{bmatrix} -4 & 10 \\ 6 & 2 \end{bmatrix}$$

$$2X = 2\begin{bmatrix} -2 & 5 \\ 3 & 1 \end{bmatrix}$$

Determine the Following

$$X = \begin{bmatrix} -2 & 5 \\ 3 & 1 \end{bmatrix}$$ **Ans.**

6. If $A = \begin{bmatrix} 9 & 1 \\ 7 & 8 \end{bmatrix}$, $B = \begin{bmatrix} 1 & 5 \\ 7 & 12 \end{bmatrix}$ find matrix C such that $5A + 5B + 2C$ is a null matrix.

Sol. Let $C = \begin{bmatrix} a & b \\ c & d \end{bmatrix}$

We have $A = \begin{bmatrix} 9 & 1 \\ 7 & 8 \end{bmatrix}$ and $B \begin{bmatrix} 1 & 5 \\ 7 & 12 \end{bmatrix}$

Now, $5A + 3B + 2C = 0$

$\Rightarrow 5\begin{bmatrix} 9 & 1 \\ 7 & 8 \end{bmatrix} + 3\begin{bmatrix} 1 & 5 \\ 7 & 12 \end{bmatrix} + 2\begin{bmatrix} a & b \\ c & d \end{bmatrix} = \begin{bmatrix} 0 & 0 \\ 0 & 0 \end{bmatrix}$

$\Rightarrow \begin{bmatrix} 45 & 5 \\ 35 & 40 \end{bmatrix} + \begin{bmatrix} 3 & 15 \\ 21 & 36 \end{bmatrix} + \begin{bmatrix} 2a & 2b \\ 2c & 2d \end{bmatrix} = \begin{bmatrix} 0 & 0 \\ 0 & 0 \end{bmatrix}$

$\Rightarrow \begin{bmatrix} 45+3+2a & 5+15+2b \\ 35+21+2c & 40+36+2d \end{bmatrix} = \begin{bmatrix} 0 & 0 \\ 0 & 0 \end{bmatrix}$

$\Rightarrow \begin{bmatrix} 48+2a & 20+2b \\ 56+2c & 76+2d \end{bmatrix} = \begin{bmatrix} 0 & 0 \\ 0 & 0 \end{bmatrix}$

$48 + 2a = 0 \Rightarrow 2a = -48 \Rightarrow a = -24$

$20 + 2b = 0 \Rightarrow 2b = -20 \Rightarrow b = -10$

$56 + 2c = 0 \Rightarrow 2c = -56 \Rightarrow c = -28$

$76 + 2d = 0 \Rightarrow 2d = -76 \Rightarrow d = -38$

Thus, $C = \begin{bmatrix} -24 & -10 \\ -28 & -38 \end{bmatrix}$. **Ans.**

7. If $A = \begin{bmatrix} 9 & 1 \\ 5 & 3 \end{bmatrix}$ and $B = \begin{bmatrix} 1 & 5 \\ 7 & -11 \end{bmatrix}$, find matrix X such that $3A + 5B - 2X = 0$.

Sol. Let $X = \begin{bmatrix} x & y \\ z & u \end{bmatrix}$

We have $A = \begin{bmatrix} 9 & 1 \\ 5 & 3 \end{bmatrix}$ and $B = \begin{bmatrix} 1 & 5 \\ 7 & -11 \end{bmatrix}$

$3A = 3\begin{bmatrix} 9 & 1 \\ 5 & 3 \end{bmatrix} = \begin{bmatrix} 27 & 3 \\ 15 & 9 \end{bmatrix}$

$5B = 5\begin{bmatrix} 1 & 5 \\ 7 & -11 \end{bmatrix} = \begin{bmatrix} 5 & 25 \\ 35 & -55 \end{bmatrix}$

Now, $3A + 5B - 2X = 0$

$\Rightarrow \begin{bmatrix} 27 & 3 \\ 15 & 9 \end{bmatrix} + \begin{bmatrix} 5 & 25 \\ 35 & -55 \end{bmatrix} + \begin{bmatrix} -2x & -2y \\ -2z & -2u \end{bmatrix} = \begin{bmatrix} 0 & 0 \\ 0 & 0 \end{bmatrix}$

$\Rightarrow \begin{bmatrix} 27+5-2x & 3+25-2y \\ 15+35-2z & 9-55-2u \end{bmatrix} = \begin{bmatrix} 0 & 0 \\ 0 & 0 \end{bmatrix}$

$\Rightarrow \begin{bmatrix} 32-2x & 28-2y \\ 50-2z & -46-2u \end{bmatrix} = \begin{bmatrix} 0 & 0 \\ 0 & 0 \end{bmatrix}$

Comparing both sides,

$32 - 2x = 0 \Rightarrow 2x = 32 \Rightarrow x = 16$

$28 - 2y = 0 \Rightarrow 2y = 28 \Rightarrow y = 14$

$50 - 2z = 0 \Rightarrow 2z = 50 \Rightarrow z = 25$

$-46 - 2u = 0 \Rightarrow 2u = -46 \Rightarrow u = -23$

Hence, $X = \begin{bmatrix} 16 & 14 \\ 25 & -23 \end{bmatrix}$ **Ans.**

8. If $A = \begin{bmatrix} 3 & 5 \\ 4 & -2 \end{bmatrix}$ and $B = \begin{bmatrix} 2 \\ 4 \end{bmatrix}$, is the product AB possible ? Give a reason. If yes, find AB.

Sol. $A = \begin{bmatrix} 3 & 5 \\ 4 & -2 \end{bmatrix}_{2\times2}$ and $B = \begin{bmatrix} 2 \\ 4 \end{bmatrix}_{2\times1}$

The product AB is possible as the number of columns in A are equal to the number of rows in B.

Now $AB = \begin{bmatrix} 3 & 5 \\ 4 & -2 \end{bmatrix}\begin{bmatrix} 2 \\ 4 \end{bmatrix}$

$= \begin{bmatrix} 3\times2 + 5\times4 \\ 4\times2 + (-2)\times4 \end{bmatrix}$

$= \begin{bmatrix} 26 \\ 0 \end{bmatrix}$ **Ans.**

9. Determine the multiplication of the given 'matrices' : $\begin{bmatrix} 2\sin30° & -2\cos60° \\ -\cot45° & \sin90° \end{bmatrix}$ $\begin{bmatrix} \tan45° & \sec60° \\ \operatorname{cosec}30° & \cos0° \end{bmatrix}$

Sol. $\begin{bmatrix} 2\sin30° & -2\cos60° \\ -\cot45° & \sin90° \end{bmatrix}\begin{bmatrix} \tan45° & \sec60° \\ \operatorname{cosec}30° & \cos0° \end{bmatrix}$

$= \begin{bmatrix} 2\times\dfrac{1}{2} & -2\times\dfrac{1}{2} \\ -1 & 1 \end{bmatrix}\begin{bmatrix} 1 & 2 \\ 2 & 1 \end{bmatrix}$

$= \begin{bmatrix} 1 & -1 \\ -1 & 1 \end{bmatrix}\begin{bmatrix} 1 & 2 \\ 2 & 1 \end{bmatrix} = \begin{bmatrix} -1 & 1 \\ 1 & -1 \end{bmatrix}$ **Ans.**

10. Given $A = \begin{bmatrix} p & 0 \\ 0 & 2 \end{bmatrix}$, $B = \begin{bmatrix} 0 & -q \\ 1 & 0 \end{bmatrix}$

$C = \begin{bmatrix} 2 & -2 \\ 2 & 2 \end{bmatrix}$ and $BA = C^2$. Find the values of p and q.

Sol. $A = \begin{bmatrix} p & 0 \\ 0 & 2 \end{bmatrix}$, $B = \begin{bmatrix} 0 & -q \\ 1 & 0 \end{bmatrix}$

$$C = \begin{bmatrix} 2 & -2 \\ 2 & 2 \end{bmatrix}$$

$$BA = \begin{bmatrix} 0 & -q \\ 1 & 0 \end{bmatrix}\begin{bmatrix} p & 0 \\ 0 & 2 \end{bmatrix} = \begin{bmatrix} 0 & -2q \\ p & 0 \end{bmatrix}$$

$$C^2 = \begin{bmatrix} 2 & -2 \\ 2 & 2 \end{bmatrix}\begin{bmatrix} 2 & -2 \\ 2 & 2 \end{bmatrix} = \begin{bmatrix} 0 & -8 \\ 8 & 0 \end{bmatrix}$$

Since, $BA = C^2$

$\Rightarrow \qquad -2q = -8$

$\Rightarrow \qquad q = 4,$

$\qquad\qquad p = 8$ **Ans.**

11. Find x, y if

$$\begin{bmatrix} -2 & 0 \\ 3 & 1 \end{bmatrix}\begin{bmatrix} -1 \\ 2x \end{bmatrix} + 3\begin{bmatrix} -2 \\ 1 \end{bmatrix} = 2\begin{bmatrix} y \\ 3 \end{bmatrix}.$$

Sol. $\begin{bmatrix} -2 & 0 \\ 3 & 1 \end{bmatrix}\begin{bmatrix} -1 \\ 2x \end{bmatrix} + 3\begin{bmatrix} -2 \\ 1 \end{bmatrix} = 2\begin{bmatrix} y \\ 3 \end{bmatrix}$

$$\Rightarrow \qquad \begin{bmatrix} 2+0 \\ -3+2x \end{bmatrix} + \begin{bmatrix} -6 \\ 3 \end{bmatrix} = \begin{bmatrix} 2y \\ 6 \end{bmatrix}$$

$$\Rightarrow \qquad \begin{bmatrix} -4 \\ 2x \end{bmatrix} = \begin{bmatrix} 2y \\ 6 \end{bmatrix}$$

$\Rightarrow \qquad 2y = -4, \ 2x = 6$

$\Rightarrow \qquad y = -2, x = 3$

Thus, required values are $x = 3$ and $y = -2$. **Ans.**

12. Given that $A = \begin{bmatrix} 3 & 0 \\ 0 & 4 \end{bmatrix}$ and $B \begin{bmatrix} a & b \\ 0 & c \end{bmatrix}$ and that

$AB = A + B$, find the values of a, b and c.

Sol. $\qquad AB = A + B$

$$\begin{bmatrix} 3 & 0 \\ 0 & 4 \end{bmatrix}\begin{bmatrix} a & b \\ 0 & c \end{bmatrix} = \begin{bmatrix} 3 & 0 \\ 0 & 4 \end{bmatrix} + \begin{bmatrix} a & b \\ 0 & c \end{bmatrix}$$

$$\begin{bmatrix} 3a & 3b \\ 0 & 4c \end{bmatrix} = \begin{bmatrix} 3+a & b \\ 0 & 4+c \end{bmatrix}$$

$3a = 3 + a \qquad 3b = b$

$2a = 3 \qquad\qquad 2b = 0$

$a = \dfrac{3}{2} \qquad\qquad b = 0$

$4c = 4 + c$

$3c = 4$

$c = \dfrac{4}{3}$.

$\Rightarrow \qquad a = \dfrac{3}{2}, b = 0$ and $c = \dfrac{4}{3}$. **Ans.**

13. Determine the value of x given that $A^2 = B$, where

$$A = \begin{bmatrix} 2 & 12 \\ 0 & 1 \end{bmatrix}, B = \begin{bmatrix} 4 & x \\ 0 & 1 \end{bmatrix}$$

Sol. $\qquad A = \begin{bmatrix} 2 & 12 \\ 0 & 1 \end{bmatrix}$

$\therefore \qquad A^2 = \begin{bmatrix} 2 & 12 \\ 0 & 1 \end{bmatrix}\begin{bmatrix} 2 & 12 \\ 0 & 1 \end{bmatrix}$

$$= \begin{bmatrix} 4 & 36 \\ 0 & 1 \end{bmatrix}$$

$\therefore \qquad A^2 = B$ (given)

$\therefore \qquad \begin{bmatrix} 4 & 36 \\ 0 & 1 \end{bmatrix} = \begin{bmatrix} 4 & x \\ 0 & 1 \end{bmatrix}$

$\therefore \qquad x = 36$ **Ans.**

14. Given $\qquad A = \begin{bmatrix} x & 3 \\ y & 3 \end{bmatrix}$

If $A^2 = 3I$, where I is the identity matrix of order 2, find x and y.*

Sol. Given : $\qquad A = \begin{bmatrix} x & 3 \\ y & 3 \end{bmatrix}$

Also, $\qquad A^2 = 3I$

$\Rightarrow \quad \begin{bmatrix} x & 3 \\ y & 3 \end{bmatrix}\begin{bmatrix} x & 3 \\ y & 3 \end{bmatrix} = 3\begin{bmatrix} 1 & 0 \\ 0 & 1 \end{bmatrix}$

$\Rightarrow \quad \begin{bmatrix} x^2 + 3y & 3x + 9 \\ xy + 3y & 3y + 9 \end{bmatrix} = \begin{bmatrix} 3 & 0 \\ 0 & 3 \end{bmatrix}$

Comparing both sides, we get

$\qquad\qquad 3x + 9 = 0$

$\Rightarrow \qquad x = -\dfrac{9}{3} = -3$

and $\qquad 3y + 9 = 3$

$\Rightarrow \qquad 3y = 3 - 9 = -6$

$\Rightarrow \qquad y = -\dfrac{6}{3} = -2$

$\therefore \qquad x = -3$ and $y = -2$ **Ans.**

15. Determine x and y, if :

$$\begin{bmatrix} 3 & -2 \\ -1 & 4 \end{bmatrix}\begin{bmatrix} 2x \\ 1 \end{bmatrix} + 2\begin{bmatrix} -4 \\ 5 \end{bmatrix} = 4\begin{bmatrix} 2 \\ y \end{bmatrix}$$

*** Frequently asked previous years Board Exam Questions.**

Determine the Following

Sol. $\begin{bmatrix} 3 & -2 \\ -1 & 4 \end{bmatrix}\begin{bmatrix} 2x \\ 1 \end{bmatrix} + 2\begin{bmatrix} -4 \\ 5 \end{bmatrix} = 4\begin{bmatrix} 2 \\ y \end{bmatrix}$

$$\begin{bmatrix} 6x-2 \\ -2x+4 \end{bmatrix} + \begin{bmatrix} -8 \\ 10 \end{bmatrix} = \begin{bmatrix} 8 \\ 4y \end{bmatrix}$$

$$\begin{bmatrix} 6x-2-8 \\ -2x+4+10 \end{bmatrix} = \begin{bmatrix} 8 \\ 4y \end{bmatrix}$$

Now, $\qquad 6x - 10 = 8$

$\Rightarrow \qquad\qquad 6x = 18$

$\Rightarrow \qquad\qquad x = \dfrac{18}{6} = 3$

and $\qquad -2x + 14 = 4y$

$\Rightarrow \qquad -2 \times 3 + 14 = 4y$

$\Rightarrow \qquad\qquad 4y = 14 - 6 = 8$

$\Rightarrow \qquad\qquad y = \dfrac{8}{4} = 2$

$\therefore$ $x = 3$ and $y = 2$. **Ans.**

16. If $A = \begin{bmatrix} 3 & 1 \\ -1 & 2 \end{bmatrix}$ and $B = \begin{bmatrix} 7 \\ 0 \end{bmatrix}$, find matrix C if

AC = B.

Sol. Let $\qquad C = \begin{bmatrix} a \\ b \end{bmatrix}$ then

$$AC = B$$

$\Rightarrow \begin{bmatrix} 3 & 1 \\ -1 & 2 \end{bmatrix}\begin{bmatrix} a \\ b \end{bmatrix} = \begin{bmatrix} 7 \\ 0 \end{bmatrix}$

$\Rightarrow \qquad \begin{bmatrix} 3a+b \\ -a+2b \end{bmatrix} = \begin{bmatrix} 7 \\ 0 \end{bmatrix}$

$\Rightarrow \qquad\qquad 3a + b = 7 \qquad\qquad …(i)$

$\qquad\qquad -a + 2b = 0 \qquad\qquad …(ii)$

From equation (i),

$\qquad\qquad 6a + 2b = 14 \qquad\qquad …(iii)$

Subtracting (ii) from (iii)

$\qquad\qquad 7a = 14$

$\Rightarrow \qquad\qquad a = 2$

Put $a = 2$ in equation (i), we get

$\qquad\qquad 6 + b = 7$

$\Rightarrow \qquad\qquad b = 7 - 6 = 1$

$\therefore \qquad\qquad C = \begin{bmatrix} 2 \\ 1 \end{bmatrix}$. **Ans.**

17. Determine : x and y, if

$$\begin{bmatrix} 2x & x \\ y & 3y \end{bmatrix}\begin{bmatrix} 3 \\ 2 \end{bmatrix} = \begin{bmatrix} 16 \\ 9 \end{bmatrix}$$

Sol. $\begin{bmatrix} 2x & x \\ y & 3y \end{bmatrix}\begin{bmatrix} 3 \\ 2 \end{bmatrix} = \begin{bmatrix} 16 \\ 9 \end{bmatrix}$

$\Rightarrow \qquad \begin{bmatrix} 6x+2x \\ 3y+6y \end{bmatrix} = \begin{bmatrix} 16 \\ 9 \end{bmatrix}$

$\Rightarrow \qquad \begin{bmatrix} 8x \\ 9y \end{bmatrix} = \begin{bmatrix} 16 \\ 9 \end{bmatrix}$

$\therefore \qquad\qquad 8x = 16 \Rightarrow x = 2$

and $\qquad\qquad 9y = 9 \Rightarrow y = 1$ **Ans.**

18. Determine x and y if

$$\begin{bmatrix} x & 3x \\ y & 4y \end{bmatrix}\begin{bmatrix} 2 \\ 1 \end{bmatrix} = \begin{bmatrix} 5 \\ 12 \end{bmatrix}.$$

Sol. $\begin{bmatrix} x & 3x \\ y & 4y \end{bmatrix}\begin{bmatrix} 2 \\ 1 \end{bmatrix} = \begin{bmatrix} 5 \\ 12 \end{bmatrix}$

$\Rightarrow \qquad \begin{bmatrix} 2x+3x \\ 2y+4y \end{bmatrix} = \begin{bmatrix} 5 \\ 12 \end{bmatrix}$

$\Rightarrow \qquad \begin{bmatrix} 5x \\ 6y \end{bmatrix} = \begin{bmatrix} 5 \\ 12 \end{bmatrix}$

$\Rightarrow \qquad\qquad 5x = 5$

$\Rightarrow \qquad\qquad x = 1$

and $\qquad\qquad 6y = 12$

$\Rightarrow \qquad\qquad y = 2.$

Hence, $x = 1$ and $y = 2$. **Ans.**

19. Determine x and y if :

$$\begin{bmatrix} -3 & 2 \\ 0 & -5 \end{bmatrix}\begin{bmatrix} x \\ 2 \end{bmatrix} = \begin{bmatrix} -5 \\ y \end{bmatrix}$$

Sol. $\begin{bmatrix} -3 & 2 \\ 0 & -5 \end{bmatrix}\begin{bmatrix} x \\ 2 \end{bmatrix} = \begin{bmatrix} -5 \\ y \end{bmatrix}$

$\Rightarrow \qquad \begin{bmatrix} -3x+4 \\ 0-10 \end{bmatrix} = \begin{bmatrix} -5 \\ y \end{bmatrix}$

$\Rightarrow \qquad\qquad -3x + 4 = -5$

$\Rightarrow \qquad\qquad -3x = -5 - 4$

$\Rightarrow \qquad\qquad -3x = -9$

$\Rightarrow \qquad\qquad x = 3$

and $\qquad\qquad y = -10$

Hence, $x = 3$ and $y = 10$. **Ans.**

20. Given $\begin{bmatrix} 2 & 1 \\ -3 & 4 \end{bmatrix} X = \begin{bmatrix} 7 \\ 6 \end{bmatrix}$.

Determine :

(i) the order of the matrix X.

(ii) the matrix X.

Sol. (i) Given, $\begin{bmatrix} 2 & 1 \\ -3 & 4 \end{bmatrix} X = \begin{bmatrix} 7 \\ 6 \end{bmatrix}$

The order of matrix $X = 2 \times 1$

(ii) Let $X = \begin{bmatrix} a \\ b \end{bmatrix}$

So $\begin{bmatrix} 2 & 1 \\ -3 & 4 \end{bmatrix}\begin{bmatrix} a \\ b \end{bmatrix} = \begin{bmatrix} 7 \\ 6 \end{bmatrix}$

$\Rightarrow \begin{bmatrix} 2a+b \\ -3a+4b \end{bmatrix} = \begin{bmatrix} 7 \\ 6 \end{bmatrix}$

$\Rightarrow \qquad 2a + b = 7 \qquad \qquad ...(i)$

$\qquad \qquad -3a + 4b = 6 \qquad \qquad ...(ii)$

From (i) and (ii)

$a = 2, b = 3$

$\Rightarrow \qquad X = \begin{bmatrix} 2 \\ 3 \end{bmatrix}$ **Ans.**

21. Find the 2×2 matrix X which satisfies the equation.

$\begin{bmatrix} 3 & 7 \\ 2 & 4 \end{bmatrix}\begin{bmatrix} 0 & 2 \\ 5 & 3 \end{bmatrix} + 2X = \begin{bmatrix} 1 & -5 \\ -4 & 6 \end{bmatrix}$

Sol. $\begin{bmatrix} 3 & 7 \\ 2 & 4 \end{bmatrix}\begin{bmatrix} 0 & 2 \\ 5 & 3 \end{bmatrix} + 2X = \begin{bmatrix} 1 & -5 \\ -4 & 6 \end{bmatrix}$

$\Rightarrow \begin{bmatrix} 0+35 & 6+21 \\ 0+20 & 4+12 \end{bmatrix} + 2X = \begin{bmatrix} 1 & -5 \\ -4 & 6 \end{bmatrix}$

$\Rightarrow \begin{bmatrix} 35 & 27 \\ 20 & 16 \end{bmatrix} + 2X = \begin{bmatrix} 1 & -5 \\ -4 & 6 \end{bmatrix}$

$\Rightarrow \qquad 2X = \begin{bmatrix} 1 & -5 \\ -4 & 6 \end{bmatrix} - \begin{bmatrix} 35 & 27 \\ 20 & 16 \end{bmatrix}$

$\Rightarrow \qquad 2X = \begin{bmatrix} -34 & -32 \\ -24 & -10 \end{bmatrix}$

$\Rightarrow \qquad X = \begin{bmatrix} \dfrac{-34}{2} & \dfrac{-32}{2} \\ \dfrac{-24}{2} & \dfrac{-10}{2} \end{bmatrix}$

$\Rightarrow \qquad X = \begin{bmatrix} -17 & -16 \\ -12 & -5 \end{bmatrix}$ **Ans.**

22. Determine matrices X and Y, if

$X + Y = \begin{bmatrix} 5 & 2 \\ 0 & 9 \end{bmatrix}$ and $X - Y = \begin{bmatrix} 3 & 6 \\ 0 & -1 \end{bmatrix}$.

Sol. We have

$X + Y = \begin{bmatrix} 5 & 2 \\ 0 & 9 \end{bmatrix}$

and $\qquad X - Y = \begin{bmatrix} 3 & 6 \\ 0 & -1 \end{bmatrix}$

Now $(X + Y) + (X - Y) = \begin{bmatrix} 5 & 2 \\ 0 & 9 \end{bmatrix} + \begin{bmatrix} 3 & 6 \\ 0 & -1 \end{bmatrix}$

$2X = \begin{bmatrix} 8 & 8 \\ 0 & 8 \end{bmatrix}$

$X = \dfrac{1}{2}\begin{bmatrix} 8 & 8 \\ 0 & 8 \end{bmatrix} = \begin{bmatrix} 4 & 4 \\ 0 & 4 \end{bmatrix}$

Also, $(X + Y) - (X - Y) = \begin{bmatrix} 5 & 2 \\ 0 & 9 \end{bmatrix} + \begin{bmatrix} -3 & -6 \\ 0 & 1 \end{bmatrix}$

$\Rightarrow \qquad 2Y = \begin{bmatrix} 2 & -4 \\ 0 & 10 \end{bmatrix}$

$\Rightarrow \qquad Y = \dfrac{1}{2}\begin{bmatrix} 2 & -4 \\ 0 & 10 \end{bmatrix} = \begin{bmatrix} 1 & -2 \\ 0 & 5 \end{bmatrix}$

Thus, $X = \begin{bmatrix} 4 & 4 \\ 0 & 4 \end{bmatrix}$ and $Y = \begin{bmatrix} 1 & -2 \\ 0 & 5 \end{bmatrix}$

Ans.

23. If $A = \begin{bmatrix} 3 & 1 \\ -1 & 2 \end{bmatrix}$ and $I = \begin{bmatrix} 1 & 0 \\ 0 & 1 \end{bmatrix}$,

Determine $A^2 - 5A + 7I$.

Sol. $\qquad A^2 = A \cdot A$

$= \begin{bmatrix} 3 & 1 \\ -1 & 2 \end{bmatrix}\begin{bmatrix} 3 & 1 \\ -1 & 2 \end{bmatrix}$

$= \begin{bmatrix} 9-1 & 3+2 \\ -3-2 & -1+4 \end{bmatrix}$

$= \begin{bmatrix} 8 & 5 \\ -5 & 3 \end{bmatrix}$

$\therefore \quad A^2 - 5A + 7I$

$= \begin{bmatrix} 8 & 5 \\ -5 & 3 \end{bmatrix} - 5\begin{bmatrix} 3 & 1 \\ -1 & 2 \end{bmatrix} + 7\begin{bmatrix} 1 & 0 \\ 0 & 1 \end{bmatrix}$

$= \begin{bmatrix} 8 & 5 \\ -5 & 3 \end{bmatrix} - \begin{bmatrix} 15 & 5 \\ -5 & 10 \end{bmatrix} + \begin{bmatrix} 7 & 0 \\ 0 & 7 \end{bmatrix}$

$= \begin{bmatrix} 8-15 & 5-5 \\ -5+5 & 3-10 \end{bmatrix} + \begin{bmatrix} 7 & 0 \\ 0 & 7 \end{bmatrix}$

$= \begin{bmatrix} -7 & 0 \\ 0 & -7 \end{bmatrix} + \begin{bmatrix} 7 & 0 \\ 0 & 7 \end{bmatrix}$

$= \begin{bmatrix} -7+7 & 0+0 \\ 0+0 & -7+7 \end{bmatrix}$

$= \begin{bmatrix} 0 & 0 \\ 0 & 0 \end{bmatrix}$

$= 0$ **Ans.**

Determine the Following

24. Given,

$$A = \begin{bmatrix} 1 & 1 \\ 8 & 3 \end{bmatrix} \text{ Determine } A^2 - 4A.$$

Sol.

$$A = \begin{bmatrix} 1 & 1 \\ 8 & 3 \end{bmatrix}$$

$$A^2 = A \times A = \begin{bmatrix} 1 & 1 \\ 8 & 3 \end{bmatrix}\begin{bmatrix} 1 & 1 \\ 8 & 3 \end{bmatrix}$$

$$= \begin{bmatrix} 1+8 & 1+3 \\ 8+24 & 8+9 \end{bmatrix} - \begin{bmatrix} 9 & 4 \\ 32 & 17 \end{bmatrix}$$

$$4A = 4\begin{bmatrix} 1 & 1 \\ 8 & 3 \end{bmatrix} = \begin{bmatrix} 4 & 4 \\ 32 & 12 \end{bmatrix}$$

$$A^2 - 4A = \begin{bmatrix} 9 & 4 \\ 32 & 17 \end{bmatrix} - \begin{bmatrix} 4 & 4 \\ 32 & 12 \end{bmatrix}$$

$$= \begin{bmatrix} 9-4 & 4-4 \\ 32-32 & 17-12 \end{bmatrix}$$

$$A^2 - 4A = \begin{bmatrix} 5 & 0 \\ 0 & 5 \end{bmatrix}. \qquad \textbf{Ans.}$$

25. If $A = \begin{bmatrix} 2 & 3 \\ 5 & 7 \end{bmatrix}$, $B = \begin{bmatrix} 0 & 4 \\ -1 & 7 \end{bmatrix}$ and $C = \begin{bmatrix} 1 & 0 \\ -1 & 4 \end{bmatrix}$, find $AC + B^2 - 10C$.*

Sol. Given, $A = \begin{bmatrix} 2 & 3 \\ 5 & 7 \end{bmatrix}$, $B = \begin{bmatrix} 0 & 4 \\ -1 & 7 \end{bmatrix}$, $C = \begin{bmatrix} 1 & 0 \\ -1 & 4 \end{bmatrix}$

$$\therefore \quad AC + B^2 - 10C = \begin{bmatrix} 2 & 3 \\ 5 & 7 \end{bmatrix}\begin{bmatrix} 1 & 0 \\ -1 & 4 \end{bmatrix}$$

$$+ \begin{bmatrix} 0 & 4 \\ -1 & 7 \end{bmatrix}\begin{bmatrix} 0 & 4 \\ -1 & 7 \end{bmatrix} - 10\begin{bmatrix} 1 & 0 \\ -1 & 4 \end{bmatrix}$$

$$= \begin{bmatrix} 2-3 & 0+12 \\ 5-7 & 0+28 \end{bmatrix} + \begin{bmatrix} 0-4 & 0+28 \\ 0-7 & -4+49 \end{bmatrix}$$

$$- \begin{bmatrix} 10 & 0 \\ -10 & 40 \end{bmatrix}$$

$$= \begin{bmatrix} -1 & 12 \\ -2 & 28 \end{bmatrix} + \begin{bmatrix} -4 & 28 \\ -7 & 45 \end{bmatrix} - \begin{bmatrix} 10 & 0 \\ -10 & 40 \end{bmatrix}$$

$$= \begin{bmatrix} -5 & 40 \\ -9 & 73 \end{bmatrix} - \begin{bmatrix} 10 & 0 \\ -10 & 40 \end{bmatrix}$$

$$= \begin{bmatrix} -15 & 40 \\ 1 & 33 \end{bmatrix} \qquad \textbf{Ans.}$$

26. Let $A = \begin{bmatrix} 2 & 1 \\ 0 & -2 \end{bmatrix}$, $B = \begin{bmatrix} 4 & 1 \\ -3 & -2 \end{bmatrix}$

and $C = \begin{bmatrix} -3 & 2 \\ -1 & 4 \end{bmatrix}$

Determine $A^2 + AC - 5B$.

Sol.

$$A = \begin{bmatrix} 2 & 1 \\ 0 & -2 \end{bmatrix}, B = \begin{bmatrix} 4 & 1 \\ -3 & -2 \end{bmatrix} \text{ and } C = \begin{bmatrix} -3 & 2 \\ -1 & 4 \end{bmatrix}$$

$$A^2 = \begin{bmatrix} 2 & 1 \\ 0 & -2 \end{bmatrix}\begin{bmatrix} 2 & 1 \\ 0 & -2 \end{bmatrix}$$

$$= \begin{bmatrix} 4+0 & 2-2 \\ 0 & 0+4 \end{bmatrix} = \begin{bmatrix} 4 & 0 \\ 0 & 4 \end{bmatrix}$$

$$5B = \begin{bmatrix} 20 & 5 \\ -15 & -10 \end{bmatrix}$$

$$AC = \begin{bmatrix} 2 & 1 \\ 0 & -2 \end{bmatrix}\begin{bmatrix} -3 & 2 \\ -1 & 4 \end{bmatrix}$$

$$= \begin{bmatrix} -6-1 & 4+4 \\ 0+2 & 0-8 \end{bmatrix} = \begin{bmatrix} -7 & 8 \\ 2 & -8 \end{bmatrix}$$

$$\therefore \quad A^2 + AC - 5B$$

$$= \begin{bmatrix} 4 & 0 \\ 0 & 4 \end{bmatrix} + \begin{bmatrix} -7 & 8 \\ 2 & -8 \end{bmatrix} - \begin{bmatrix} 20 & 5 \\ -15 & -10 \end{bmatrix}$$

$$= \begin{bmatrix} 4-7-20 & 0+8-5 \\ 0+2+15 & 4-8+10 \end{bmatrix}$$

$$= \begin{bmatrix} -23 & 3 \\ 17 & 6 \end{bmatrix} \qquad \textbf{Ans.}$$

27. If $A = \begin{bmatrix} 4 & -2 \\ 6 & -3 \end{bmatrix}$, $B = \begin{bmatrix} 0 & 2 \\ 1 & -1 \end{bmatrix}$

and $C = \begin{bmatrix} -2 & 3 \\ 1 & -1 \end{bmatrix}$. Find $A^2 - A + BC$

Sol. $A = \begin{bmatrix} 4 & -2 \\ 6 & -3 \end{bmatrix}$, $B = \begin{bmatrix} 0 & 2 \\ 1 & -1 \end{bmatrix}$

and $\qquad C = \begin{bmatrix} -2 & 3 \\ 1 & -1 \end{bmatrix}$.

$$\therefore \quad A^2 = \begin{bmatrix} 4 & -2 \\ 6 & -3 \end{bmatrix}\begin{bmatrix} 4 & -2 \\ 6 & -3 \end{bmatrix}$$

$$= \begin{bmatrix} 16-12 & -8+6 \\ 24-18 & -12+9 \end{bmatrix}$$

$$\therefore \quad A^2 = \begin{bmatrix} 4 & -2 \\ 6 & -3 \end{bmatrix}$$

$$BC = \begin{bmatrix} 0 & 2 \\ 1 & -1 \end{bmatrix}\begin{bmatrix} -2 & 3 \\ 1 & -1 \end{bmatrix}$$

$$= \begin{bmatrix} 0+2 & 0-2 \\ -2-1 & 3+1 \end{bmatrix}$$

* Frequently asked previous years Board Exam Questions.

$$= \begin{bmatrix} 2 & -2 \\ -3 & 4 \end{bmatrix}$$

Now, $A^2 - A + BC$

$$= \begin{bmatrix} 4 & -2 \\ 6 & -3 \end{bmatrix} - \begin{bmatrix} 4 & -2 \\ 6 & -3 \end{bmatrix} + \begin{bmatrix} 2 & -2 \\ -3 & 4 \end{bmatrix}$$

$$= \begin{bmatrix} 0 & 0 \\ 0 & 0 \end{bmatrix} + \begin{bmatrix} 2 & -2 \\ -3 & 4 \end{bmatrix} = \begin{bmatrix} 2 & -2 \\ -3 & 4 \end{bmatrix} \qquad \textbf{Ans.}$$

28. Let $A = \begin{bmatrix} 1 & 0 \\ 2 & 1 \end{bmatrix}$, $B = \begin{bmatrix} 2 & 3 \\ -1 & 0 \end{bmatrix}$.

Find $A^2 + AB + B^2$.

Sol. $A = \begin{bmatrix} 1 & 0 \\ 2 & 1 \end{bmatrix}$, $B = \begin{bmatrix} 2 & 3 \\ -1 & 0 \end{bmatrix}$

$$A^2 = A \times A = \begin{bmatrix} 1 & 0 \\ 2 & 1 \end{bmatrix} \times \begin{bmatrix} 1 & 0 \\ 2 & 1 \end{bmatrix}$$

$$= \begin{bmatrix} 1 \times 1 + 0 \times 2 & 1 \times 0 + 0 \times 1 \\ 2 \times 1 + 1 \times 2 & 2 \times 0 + 1 \times 1 \end{bmatrix}$$

$$= \begin{bmatrix} 1 & 0 \\ 4 & 1 \end{bmatrix}$$

$$AB = A \times B = \begin{bmatrix} 1 & 0 \\ 2 & 1 \end{bmatrix} \times \begin{bmatrix} 2 & 3 \\ -1 & 0 \end{bmatrix}$$

$$= \begin{bmatrix} 1 \times 2 + 0 \times -1 & 1 \times 3 + 0 \times 0 \\ 2 \times 2 + 1 \times -1 & 2 \times 3 + 1 \times 0 \end{bmatrix}$$

$$= \begin{bmatrix} 2 & 3 \\ 3 & 6 \end{bmatrix}$$

$$B^2 = B \times B = \begin{bmatrix} 2 & 3 \\ -1 & 0 \end{bmatrix} \times \begin{bmatrix} 2 & 3 \\ -1 & 0 \end{bmatrix}$$

$$= \begin{bmatrix} 2 \times 2 + 3 \times -1 & 2 \times 3 + 3 \times 0 \\ -1 \times 2 + 0 \times -1 & -1 \times 3 + 0 \times 0 \end{bmatrix}$$

$$= \begin{bmatrix} 1 & 6 \\ -2 & -3 \end{bmatrix}$$

$$\therefore A^2 + AB + B^2 = \begin{bmatrix} 1 & 0 \\ 4 & 1 \end{bmatrix} + \begin{bmatrix} 2 & 3 \\ 3 & 6 \end{bmatrix} + \begin{bmatrix} 1 & 6 \\ -2 & -3 \end{bmatrix}$$

$$= \begin{bmatrix} 4 & 9 \\ 5 & 4 \end{bmatrix} \qquad \textbf{Ans.}$$

29. If $A = \begin{bmatrix} 1 & 0 \\ -1 & 7 \end{bmatrix}$ and $I = \begin{bmatrix} 1 & 0 \\ 0 & 1 \end{bmatrix}$

then determine k so that $A^2 = 8A + kI$.

Sol. We have

$$A = \begin{bmatrix} 1 & 0 \\ -1 & 7 \end{bmatrix}$$

$$A^2 = AA = \begin{bmatrix} 1 & 0 \\ -1 & 7 \end{bmatrix} \begin{bmatrix} 1 & 0 \\ -1 & 7 \end{bmatrix}$$

$$= \begin{bmatrix} 1 & 0 \\ -8 & 49 \end{bmatrix}$$

and $\qquad 8A + kI = 8 \begin{bmatrix} 1 & 0 \\ -1 & 7 \end{bmatrix} + k \begin{bmatrix} 1 & 0 \\ 0 & 1 \end{bmatrix}$

$$= \begin{bmatrix} 8 & 0 \\ -8 & 56 \end{bmatrix} + \begin{bmatrix} k & 0 \\ 0 & k \end{bmatrix}$$

$$= \begin{bmatrix} 8+k & 0 \\ -8 & 56+k \end{bmatrix}$$

Thus, $\qquad A^2 = 8A + kI$

$\Rightarrow \qquad \begin{bmatrix} 1 & 0 \\ -8 & 49 \end{bmatrix} = \begin{bmatrix} 8+k & 0 \\ -8 & 56+k \end{bmatrix}$

$\Rightarrow \qquad 1 = 8+k$

$\Rightarrow \qquad k = -7$

Also, $\qquad 56 + k = 49$

$\Rightarrow \qquad k = -7 \qquad \textbf{Ans.}$

30. If $A = \begin{bmatrix} 3 & 0 \\ 5 & 1 \end{bmatrix}$ and $B = \begin{bmatrix} -4 & 2 \\ 1 & 0 \end{bmatrix}$.

Find $A^2 - 2AB + B^2$

Sol. Given : $A = \begin{bmatrix} 3 & 0 \\ 5 & 1 \end{bmatrix}$ and $B = \begin{bmatrix} -4 & 2 \\ 1 & 0 \end{bmatrix}$

Now, $A^2 - 2AB + B^2 = \begin{bmatrix} 3 & 0 \\ 5 & 1 \end{bmatrix} \begin{bmatrix} 3 & 0 \\ 5 & 1 \end{bmatrix}$

$$-2 \begin{bmatrix} 3 & 0 \\ 5 & 1 \end{bmatrix} \begin{bmatrix} -4 & 2 \\ 1 & 0 \end{bmatrix} + \begin{bmatrix} -4 & 2 \\ 1 & 0 \end{bmatrix} \begin{bmatrix} -4 & 2 \\ 1 & 0 \end{bmatrix}$$

$$= \begin{bmatrix} 9+0 & 0+0 \\ 15+5 & 0+1 \end{bmatrix} - 2 \begin{bmatrix} -12+0 & 6+0 \\ -20+1 & 10+0 \end{bmatrix}$$

$$+ \begin{bmatrix} 16+2 & -8+0 \\ -4+0 & 2+0 \end{bmatrix}$$

$$= \begin{bmatrix} 9 & 0 \\ 20 & 1 \end{bmatrix} - 2 \begin{bmatrix} -12 & 6 \\ -19 & 10 \end{bmatrix} + \begin{bmatrix} 18 & -8 \\ -4 & 2 \end{bmatrix}$$

$$= \begin{bmatrix} 9 & 0 \\ 20 & 1 \end{bmatrix} + \begin{bmatrix} 24 & -12 \\ 38 & -20 \end{bmatrix} + \begin{bmatrix} 18 & -8 \\ -4 & 2 \end{bmatrix}$$

$$= \begin{bmatrix} 9+24+18 & 0-12-8 \\ 20+38-4 & 1-20+2 \end{bmatrix}$$

$$= \begin{bmatrix} 51 & -20 \\ 54 & -17 \end{bmatrix} \qquad \textbf{Ans.}$$

Determine the Following

Chapter 9. Arithmetic Progression

1. Show that the sequence $\log a$, $\log (ab)$, $\log (ab^2)$, $\log (ab^3)$, ... is an A.P., also determine its nth term.

Sol. We have,

$$\log (ab) - \log a = \log \left(\frac{ab}{a} \right) = \log b$$

$$\log (ab^2) - \log (ab) = \log \left(\frac{ab^2}{ab} \right) = \log b$$

$$\log (ab^3) - \log (ab^2) = \log \left(\frac{ab^3}{ab^2} \right) = \log b$$

Therefore, we can conclude from the above, that the difference of a term and the preceeding is always same. So, the given sequence is an A.P.

Now, nth term $= a_n = a + (n-1) d$

$$\Rightarrow \qquad a_n = \log a + (n-1) \log b$$

$$= \log a + \log b^{n-1}$$

$$a_n = \log (ab^{n-1}) \qquad \textbf{Ans.}$$

2. Determine the A.P. whose 2nd term is 5 and the 5th term is 9.

Sol. We know that

$$a_n = a + (n-1) d$$

where a is first term, a_n is nth term and d is the common difference of the given A.P.

$$a_2 = a + (2-1)d$$

$$= a + d = 5 \qquad \text{...(i)}$$

and $\qquad a_5 = a + (5-1) d$

$$= a + 4d = 9 \qquad \text{...(ii)}$$

Subtracting (i) from (ii)

$$3d = 4$$

$$\Rightarrow \qquad d = \frac{4}{3}$$

Putting $d = \frac{4}{3}$ in (i), we get

$$a + \frac{4}{3} = 5$$

$$\Rightarrow \qquad a = \frac{11}{3}$$

$$\therefore \qquad a = \frac{11}{3}, d = \frac{4}{3}$$

Hence, the required A.P. is $\frac{11}{3}, 5, \frac{19}{3}, \frac{23}{3}$. **Ans.**

3. Determine the 10th term from the last term (towards the first term) of the A.P. 10, 7, 4, ..., -62.

Sol. Here $a = 10$, $d = 7 - 10 = -3$

and last term $l = -62$

10th term from the last term

$$i.e., \qquad n = 10$$

Required term $= l - (n-1) d$

$$= -62 - (10 - 1) (-3)$$

$$= -62 + 27$$

$$= -35$$

Therefore, the 10th term from the last term is -35. **Ans.**

4. Determine which term of the sequence 4, 9, 14, 19, ... is 129 ?

Sol. The given sequence is an A.P. with first term $a = 4$ and the common difference $d = 9 - 4 = 5$.

Let 129 be the nth term of the sequence.

Then $\qquad a_n = 129 = a + (n-1) d$

$$\Rightarrow \qquad 129 = 4 + (n-1) 5$$

$$= 4 + 5n - 5$$

$$\Rightarrow \qquad 129 = 5n - 1$$

$$\Rightarrow \qquad 5n = 130$$

$$\Rightarrow \qquad n = 26$$

Hence, 26th term of the sequence is 129. **Ans.**

5. Determine which term of the A.P. 121, 117, 113, ... is its first negative term ?

Sol. To find the first negative term, we find the together as 'number' of terms till we get zero, the next term will be its first negative term.

So, here $a = 121$, $d = 117 - 121 = (-4)$

Let $\qquad a_n = 0$

$$\because \qquad a_n = a + (n-1) d$$

$$\Rightarrow \qquad 0 = 121 + (n-1) (-4)$$

$$\Rightarrow \qquad 0 = 121 - 4n + 4$$

$$\Rightarrow \qquad 4n = 125$$

$$\Rightarrow \qquad n = 31 \cdot 25$$

So, 32th term will be first negative term of the given A.P. **Ans.**

6. Determine the sum of 15 terms of the A.P. 1, 4, 7, 10, ...

Sol. $a = $ first term $= 1$

and $\qquad d = $ common difference

$$= 4 - 1 = 7 - 4 = 3$$

Sum of n terms of an A.P. is given by

---

* **Frequently asked previous years Board Exam Questions.**

$$S_n = \frac{n}{2} [2a + (n-1)d]$$

∴ Sum of 15 terms is

$$S_{15} = \frac{15}{2} [2 \times 1 + (15-1) 3]$$

$$= \frac{15}{2} [2 + 42]$$

$$= \frac{15 \times 44}{2} = 15 \times 22$$

$$= 330$$

∴ Sum of 15 terms is 330. **Ans.**

7. Determine the sum of all natural numbers 'between' 2 and 100 which are exactly divisible by 3.

Sol. The numbers between 2 and 100 which are together as 'exactly' divisible by 3 are 3, 6, 9, 12, …… 99.

This sequence is an A.P. with first term $a = 3$ and common difference $d = 3$.

Let there are n terms in this A.P. then,

$$a + (n-1) d = 99$$
$$\Rightarrow \quad 3 + (n-1) 3 = 99$$
$$\Rightarrow \quad 3n = 99$$
$$\Rightarrow \quad n = 33$$

$$\therefore \quad S_n = \frac{n}{2} (a + l)$$

$$= \frac{33}{2} (3 + 99)$$

$$= \frac{33 \times 102}{2}$$

$$= 1683. \quad \textbf{Ans.}$$

8. Determine how many two digit numbers are divisible by 5 ?

Sol. The list of 2-digit numbers divisible by 5 is 10, 15, 20, ……, 95.

Since this is an A.P.,

Here $a = 10$, $d = 5$ and $a_n = 95$

as $\quad a_n = a + (n-1) d$
$$\Rightarrow \quad 95 = 10 + (n-1) 5$$
$$\Rightarrow \quad 85 = (n-1) 5$$
$$\Rightarrow \quad 17 = n-1$$
$$\Rightarrow \quad n = 18$$

Hence, there are 18 two digit numbers divisible by 5. **Ans.**

9. The income of a person is ₹ 3,00,000, in the first year and he receives an increase of ₹ 10,000 to his income per year for the next 9

years. Determine the total amount, he received in 10 years.

Sol. Here $a = 3,00,000$ and $d = 10,000$ and $n = 10$.

Since, the sum of n terms

$$S_n = \frac{n}{2} [2a + (n-1) d]$$

$$\therefore \quad S_{10} = \frac{10}{2} [6,00,000 + (10-1) \times 10,000]$$

$$= 5 \times 6,90,000$$

$$= 34,50,000$$

Hence, the person received ₹ 34,50,000 as the total amount at the end of 10 years. **Ans.**

10. In a shop, there are 22 rose plants in the first row, 20 in the second row, 18 in the third row and so on. There are 6 rose plants in the last row. Find the number of rows in the shop ?

Sol. The number of rose plants in the 1st, 2nd, 3rd, … n^{th}, rows are :

$$22, 20, 18, ……… 6.$$

Since it forms an A.P. (Because the difference between two terms is same).

Let the number of rows in the shop be n.

Here, $a = 22$, $d = -2$ and $a_n = 6$.

As, $\quad a_n = a + (n-1) d$

we have, $\quad 6 = 22 + (n-1) (-2)$
$$\Rightarrow \quad 6 = 24 - 2n$$
$$\Rightarrow \quad 2n = 18$$
$$\Rightarrow \quad n = 9$$

So, there are 9 rows in the shop. **Ans.**

11. If the sum of the first 10 terms of an A.P. is 1050 and its first term is 5, determine the 20th term.

Sol. Given, $S_{10} = 1050$, $a = 5$ and $n = 10$

As $\quad S_n = \frac{n}{2} [2a + (n-1) d]$

So, $\quad 1050 = \frac{10}{2} [2 \times 5 + (10-1)d]$

$$\Rightarrow \quad \frac{1050}{5} = [10 + 9d]$$

$$\Rightarrow \quad 210 = 10 + 9d$$

$$\Rightarrow \quad 200 = 9d$$

$$\Rightarrow \quad d = \frac{200}{9}$$

As, nth term is

$$a_n = a + (n-1) d$$

$$\Rightarrow \quad a_{20} = 5 + (19) \times \frac{200}{9}$$

Determine the Following

$$\Rightarrow \qquad a_{20} = \frac{3845}{9}$$

i.e., 20th term is $\dfrac{3845}{9}$. **Ans.**

12. Find the sum of first 20 terms of an A.P. in which $d = 5$ and 20th term is 149.

Sol. Here,

$$a_{20} = 149 = a + (20 - 1)\,5$$

$$\Rightarrow \qquad 149 = a + 95$$

$$\Rightarrow \qquad a = 54$$

Now, $\qquad S_n = \dfrac{n}{2}\,[2a + (n - 1)\,d]$

$$= \frac{20}{2}\,[2 \times 54 + (20 - 1) \times 5]$$

$$= 10\,[108 + 95]$$

$$= 2030$$

Hence, the sum is 2030. **Ans.**

13. If the 6th term of an A.P. is equal to four times its first term and the sum of first six terms is 75, find the first term and the common difference.*

Sol. Let the first term of an A.P. be a and the common difference be d.

$$\because \qquad a_6 = 4a \qquad \text{[Given]}$$

$$\Rightarrow \qquad a + 5d = 4a$$

$$\Rightarrow \qquad 5d = 3a$$

$$\therefore \qquad a = \frac{5d}{3} \qquad \text{...(i)}$$

Also, $\qquad S_6 = 75 \qquad$ [Given]

$$\Rightarrow \qquad \frac{6}{2}[2a + (6 - 1)d] = 75$$

$$\Rightarrow \qquad 3\left[2 \times \frac{5d}{3} + 5d\right] = 75 \qquad \text{[Using (i)]}$$

$$\Rightarrow \qquad 3\left[\frac{10d + 15d}{3}\right] = 75$$

$$\Rightarrow \qquad 25d = 75$$

$$\therefore \qquad d = \frac{75}{25} = 3$$

$$\therefore \qquad a = \frac{5d}{3} = \frac{5 \times 3}{3} = 5$$

Hence, $\qquad a = 5$ and $d = 3$ **Ans.**

14. The first term of an A.P. is 5, the last term is 45 and the sum of its terms is 400. Determine the number of terms and the common difference.

Sol. Given, $a = 5$, last term $= l = 45$

$$S_n = 400$$

$$\because \qquad S_n = \frac{n}{2}\,[a + l]$$

$$\Rightarrow \qquad 400 = \frac{n}{2}\,[5 + 45]$$

$$\Rightarrow \qquad 800 = n\,(50)$$

$$\Rightarrow \qquad n = 16.$$

$\because$ last term $l = a_n = a_{16} = 45$

$$\therefore \qquad 45 = a + (16 - 1)\,d$$

$$\Rightarrow \qquad 45 = 5 + (16 - 1)\,d$$

$$\Rightarrow \qquad 40 = 15d$$

$$\Rightarrow \qquad d = \frac{40}{15} = \frac{8}{3}$$

Hence, $n = 15$ and $d = \dfrac{8}{3}$. **Ans.**

15. In an Arithmetic Progression (A.P.) the fourth and sixth terms are 8 and 14 respectively. Find the :*

(i) first term

(ii) common difference

(iii) sum of the first 20 terms

Sol. Let a and d be the first term and common difference of the given A.P. respectively

Then, $\qquad a_4 = 8$ and $a_6 = 14$

$$\Rightarrow \qquad a + 3d = 8 \qquad \text{...(i)}$$

and $\qquad a + 5d = 14 \qquad \text{...(ii)}$

Subtracting equation (i) from (ii), we get

$$2d = 6$$

$$\Rightarrow \qquad d = 3$$

Putting $d = 3$ in equation (i), we get

$$a + 3 \times 3 = 8$$

$$\Rightarrow \qquad a = 8 - 9 = -1$$

(i) First term $(a) = -1$. **Ans.**

(ii) Common difference $(d) = 3$. **Ans.**

(iii) Sum of first 20 terms (S_{20})

$$\because \qquad S_n = \frac{n}{2}[2a + (n - 1)d]$$

$$\therefore \qquad S_{20} = \frac{20}{2}[2 \times (-1) + (20 - 1) \times 3]$$

$$= 10\,(-2 + 57)$$

$$= 550 \qquad \textbf{Ans.}$$

16. Determine the sum of first 15 terms of the list of numbers whose nth term is given by

$$a_n = 2 + 3n$$

Sol. Given, $\qquad a_n = 2 + 3n$

So, $\qquad a_1 = 2 + 3 \times 1 = 5$

$$a_2 = 2 + 3 \times 2 = 8$$

$$a_3 = 2 + 3 \times 3 = 11$$

So, list of numbers becomes 5, 8, 11, ...

---
* Frequently asked previous years Board Exam Questions.

Here, $a = 5$ and $d = 8 - 5 = 11 - 8 = 3$.

we know

$$S_n = \frac{n}{2}[2a + (n-1)d]$$

$$S_{15} = \frac{15}{2}[2 \times 5 + (15-1)3]$$

$$= \frac{15}{2}[10 + 42]$$

$$= \frac{15}{2} \times 52 = 15 \times 26$$

$$S_{15} = 390.$$

So, sum of first 15 terms of the list of numbers is 390. **Ans.**

17. Determine the number of terms of the A.P. : 5, 7, 9, ... so that their sum is 672 ?

Sol. Here, $a = 5$, $d = 7 - 5 = 9 - 7 = 2$,

$$S_n = 672$$

We know that, $S_n = \frac{n}{2}[2a + (n-1)d]$

So, $\quad 672 = \frac{n}{2}[2 \times 5 + (n-1)2]$

$\Rightarrow \quad 1344 = n[10 + 2n - 2]$

$\Rightarrow \quad 1344 = n[2n + 8]$

$\Rightarrow \quad 2n^2 + 8n - 1344 = 0$

$\Rightarrow \quad n^2 + 4n - 672 = 0$

$\Rightarrow \quad n^2 - 24n + 28n - 672 = 0$

$\Rightarrow \quad (n-24)(n+28) = 0$

So, $\quad n = 24$ or -28

Since, number of terms cannot be negative therefore, n cannot be -28.

Hence, $n = 24$. **Ans.**

18. The sum of n terms of two A.P.'s are in the ratio $(3n + 8) : (7n + 15)$. Determine the ratio of their 10th terms.

Sol. Let a_1, a_2 and d_1, d_2 be the first term and common difference of the first and second A.P., respectively. According to the given condition, we have

$$\frac{\text{Sum of } n \text{ terms of first A.P.}}{\text{Sum of } n \text{ terms of second A.P.}} = \frac{3n+8}{7n+15}$$

$$\Rightarrow \quad \frac{\frac{n}{2}[2a_1 + (n-1)d_1]}{\frac{n}{2}[2a_2 + (n-1)d_2]} = \frac{3n+8}{7n+15}$$

$$\Rightarrow \quad \frac{2a_1 + (n-1)d_1}{2a_2 + (n-1)d_2} = \frac{3n+8}{7n+15}$$

Now, $\dfrac{10^{\text{th}} \text{ term of first A.P.}}{10^{\text{th}} \text{ term of second A.P.}}$

$$= \frac{a_1 + (10-1)d_1}{a_2 + (10-1)d_2}$$

$$= \frac{a_1 + 9d_1}{a_2 + 9d_2}$$

$$= \frac{2a_1 + 18d_1}{2a_2 + 18d_2}$$

$$= \frac{2a_1 + (19-1)d_1}{2a_2 + (19-1)d_2}$$

Now, $\dfrac{2a_1 + (19-1)d_1}{2a_2 + (19-1)d_2} = \dfrac{3 \times 19 + 8}{7 \times 19 + 15}$

$$\therefore \quad \frac{2a_1 + 18d_1}{2a_2 + 18d_2} = \frac{57 + 8}{133 + 15}$$

$$= \frac{65}{148}$$

Therefore, the required ratio is 65 : 148. **Ans.**

Chapter 10. Geometric Progression

1. If third term of a G.P. is 4. Determine the product of its first five terms.

Sol. Let a be first term and r be the common ratio.

Then, the third term

$$a_3 = ar^2 = 4 \quad [\text{From } a^n = ar^{n-1}]$$

$\therefore$ Product of five terms

$$= a_1 a_2 a_3 a_4 a_5$$

$$= a(ar)(ar^2)(ar^3)(ar^4)$$

$$= a^5 r^{10}$$

$$= (ar^2)^5 = (4)^5$$

$$= 1024. \quad \textbf{Ans.}$$

2. Determine the G.P. whose 3rd term is 8 and 7th term is $\dfrac{128}{625}$.

Sol. Given : $a_3 = 8$ and $a_7 = \dfrac{128}{625}$.

Let a, ar, ar^2, ... be the G.P.

Then, $\qquad a_3 = ar^2$ and $a_7 = ar^6$

Now, $\qquad \dfrac{a_7}{a_3} = \dfrac{ar^6}{ar^2} = r^4$

and $\dfrac{a_7}{a_3} = \dfrac{128}{625 \times 8} = \dfrac{16}{625}$

$\therefore \qquad r^4 = \dfrac{16}{625} = \left(\dfrac{2}{5}\right)^4$

$\Rightarrow \qquad r = \pm\dfrac{2}{5}.$

As $\qquad ar^2 = 8$

$\Rightarrow \qquad a = 8 \times \left(\dfrac{5}{2}\right)^2$

$\qquad\qquad = \dfrac{8 \times 25}{4} = 50$

$\therefore$ G.P. is 50, 20, 8, ... (when $r = 2/5$).
or 50, – 20, 8, ... (when $r = -2/5$). **Ans.**

3. Determine which term of the G.P. 2, 1, $\dfrac{1}{2}, \dfrac{1}{4}$,

...... is $\dfrac{1}{128}$?

Sol. Here, first term $a = 2$ and common ratio

$r = \dfrac{1}{2}$

Let n^{th} term be $\dfrac{1}{128}$

Then, $\qquad a_n = ar^{n-1}$

$\Rightarrow \qquad \dfrac{1}{128} = 2 \cdot \left(\dfrac{1}{2}\right)^{n-1}$

$\Rightarrow \qquad \left(\dfrac{1}{2}\right)^7 = \left(\dfrac{1}{2}\right)^{n-2}$

$\Rightarrow \qquad 7 = n - 2$

$\Rightarrow \qquad n = 9$

Thus, 9th term of the given G.P. is $\dfrac{1}{128}$. **Ans.**

4. Determine the sum of the series

$x(x+y) + x^2(x^2+y^2) + x^3(x^3+y^3) + ... +$ to n terms.

Sol. Let S_n denote the sum of n terms of the given series. Then

$S_n = x(x+y) + x^2(x^2+y^2) + x^3(x^3+y^3)$
$\qquad\qquad + ... + x^n(x^n+y^n)$

$S_n = (x^2 + x^4 + x^6 + ... + x^{2n})$
$\qquad\qquad + (xy + x^2y^2 + x^3y^3 + ... + x^ny^n)$

$\Rightarrow S_n = x^2(1 + x^2 + x^4 + ... + x^n)$
$\qquad\qquad + xy[1 + xy + (xy)^2 + ... + (xy)^{n-1}]$

$\because$ Sum of G.P. series

$\qquad = \dfrac{a(1-r^n)}{1-r}$

$\therefore S_n = x^2 \cdot \left(\dfrac{(x^2)^n - 1}{x^2 - 1}\right) + xy\left(\dfrac{(xy)^n - 1}{xy - 1}\right)$

$\Rightarrow S_n = x^2\left(\dfrac{x^{2n} - 1}{x^2 - 1}\right) + xy\left(\dfrac{(xy)^n - 1}{xy - 1}\right)$ **Ans.**

5. Find the sum of n terms of the series :
11 + 105 + 1007 + ...

Sol. Let

$S = 11 + 105 + 1007 + ...$ to n terms
$S = (10 + 1) + (10^2 + 5) + (10^3 + 7)$
$\qquad\qquad + ...$ to n terms

$\Rightarrow S = \underbrace{(10 + 10^2 + 10^3 + ... + 10^n)}_{\text{G.P.}}$
$\qquad\qquad \underbrace{+ (1 + 5 + 7 + ...\text{ to } n \text{ terms})}_{\text{A.P.}}$

$\Rightarrow S = \dfrac{10 \cdot (10^n - 1)}{10 - 1} + \dfrac{n}{2}[2 \cdot 1 + (n-1)4]$

$\qquad = \dfrac{10}{9}(10^n - 1) + \dfrac{n}{2}[2 + 4n - 4]$

$\therefore S = \dfrac{10}{9}(10n - 1) + n(2n - 1).$ **Ans.**

6. Determine the sum of the series
5 + 55 + 555 + ... + to n terms

Sol. $S_n = 5 + 55 + 555 + ... +$ to n terms

$\qquad = 5(1 + 11 + 111 + ... +$ to n terms$)$

$\qquad = \dfrac{5}{9}(9 + 99 + 999 + ... +$ to n terms$)$

$\qquad = \dfrac{5}{9}[(10 - 1) + (100 - 1) + (1000 - 1)$
$\qquad\qquad\qquad + ... +$ to n terms$]$

$\qquad = \dfrac{5}{9}[\underbrace{(10 + 10^2 + 10^3 + ... + 10^n)}_{\text{G.P.}}$
$\qquad\qquad\qquad \underbrace{- (1 + 1 + 1 + ... + 1)}_{n\text{ terms}}]$

$\qquad = \dfrac{5}{9}\left[\dfrac{10 \cdot (10^n - 1)}{10 - 1} - n\right]$

$\qquad = \dfrac{5}{9}\left[\dfrac{10^{n+1} - 10}{9} - n\right]$

$\Rightarrow S_n = \dfrac{5}{81}[10^{n+1} - 10 - 9n].$ **Ans.**

7. Determine $\sum_{k=11}^{11} (5 + 3^k)$

Sol. $\sum_{k=11}^{11} (5 + 3^k) = (5 + 3^1) + (5 + 3^2)$

$$+ (5 + 3^3) + \dots + (5 + 3^{11})$$

$\Rightarrow \sum_{k=11}^{11} (5 + 3^k) = \underbrace{(5 + 5 + 5 + \dots + 5)}_{11 \text{ times}}$

$$\underbrace{+ (3 + 3^2 + 3^3 + \dots + 3^{11})}_{\text{G.P.}}$$

Since $S_n = \dfrac{a(r^n - 1)}{r - 1}$; $|r| > 1$

$\Rightarrow \sum_{k=11}^{11} (5 + 3^k) = 5 \times 11 + \dfrac{3 \cdot (3^{11} - 1)}{3 - 1}$

$\Rightarrow \sum_{k=11}^{11} (5 + 3^k) = 55 + \dfrac{3}{2}(3^{11} - 1)$ **Ans.**

8. The sum of first three terms of a G.P. is 16 and the sum of next three terms is 128. Determine the sum of n terms of the G.P.

Sol. Let a be the first term and r be the common ratio of the G.P. Then, according to given condition,

$$a + ar + ar^2 = 16 \qquad \dots(i)$$
$$\text{and} \quad ar^3 + ar^4 + ar^5 = 128 \qquad \dots(ii)$$
$$\Rightarrow \quad a(1 + r + r^2) = 16$$
$$\text{and} \quad ar^3(1 + r + r^2) = 128$$
$$\Rightarrow \quad \dfrac{ar^3(1 + r + r^2)}{a(1 + r + r^2)} = \dfrac{128}{16}$$
$$\Rightarrow \quad r^3 = \dfrac{128}{16}$$
$$\Rightarrow \quad r^3 = 8$$
$$\Rightarrow \quad r = 2$$

Putting $r = 2$ in equation (i), we get

$$a + 2a + 4a = 16$$
$$\Rightarrow \quad 7a = 16$$
$$\Rightarrow \quad a = \dfrac{16}{7}$$

$\therefore$ Sum of n terms, $S_n = \dfrac{a(r^n - 1)}{r - 1}$

$\Rightarrow \quad S_n = \dfrac{16}{7}\left(\dfrac{2^n - 1}{2 - 1}\right)$

$$= \dfrac{16}{7}(2^n - 1) \qquad \textbf{Ans.}$$

9. Determine how many terms of the Geometric series $1 + 4 + 16 + 64 + \dots$ will make the sum 5461 ?

Sol. Let the sum of n terms of the given series is 5461.

Here, $a = 1$, $r = 4$ and $S_n = 5461$.

Since, $S_n = 5461 = \dfrac{a(r^n - 1)}{r - 1}$

$\Rightarrow \quad 5461 = \dfrac{1 \cdot (4^n - 1)}{3}$

$\Rightarrow \quad 4^n - 1 = 16383$

$\Rightarrow \quad 4^n = 16384 = 4^7$

$\Rightarrow \quad n = 7$

Hence, sum of 7 terms is equal to 5461.   **Ans.**

10. Determine the least value of n for which the sum $1 + 5 + 5^2 + \dots\dots$ to n terms is greater than 7000.

Sol. Since,

$$S_n = 1 + 5 + 5^2 + \dots + 5^{n-1}$$

$$= \dfrac{1(5^n - 1)}{5 - 1}$$

$$= \dfrac{5^n - 1}{4}$$

$\Rightarrow \qquad \dfrac{5^n - 1}{4} > 7000$

$\Rightarrow \qquad 5^n > 28001$

Since, $5^6 = 15625$

and $5^7 = 78,125$

$\therefore$ n lies between 6 and 7.

Therefore least value of n is 7.   **Ans.**

Chapter 11. Co-ordinate Geometry

1. The line segment joining A (2, 3) and B (6, – 5) is intersected by the X-axis at the point K. Write the ordinate of the point K. Hence, find the ratio in which K divides AB.

Sol. A (2, 3) and B (6, – 5)

AB is intersected by X-axis at K.

$\therefore$ Ordinate of K = 0

Let required ratio be $a : 1$

$$\Rightarrow \quad 0 = \frac{a \times (-5) + 1 \times 3}{a + 1}$$

$$\Rightarrow \quad 0 = -5a + 3$$

$$\Rightarrow \quad 5a = 3$$

$$\Rightarrow \quad a = \frac{3}{5}$$

∴ K divides AB in ratio of 3 : 5.   **Ans.**

2. Find the value of x so that the line passing through $(3, 4)$ and $(x, 5)$ makes an angle $135°$ with positive direction of X-axis.

Sol. Slope of the line which makes an angle $135°$ with X-axis,

$$m = \tan 135°$$
$$= -1.$$

Also,   slope $m = \dfrac{5 - 4}{x - 3} = \dfrac{1}{x - 3}$

Then, $\dfrac{1}{x - 3} = -1$

$$\Rightarrow \quad x - 3 = -1$$

$$\therefore \quad x = 2.$$ **Ans.**

3. If the straight lines $3x - 5y = 7$ and $4x + ay + 9 = 0$ are perpendicular to one another, find the value of a.*

Sol. Given equation of lines are $3x - 5y = 7$ and $4x + ay + 9 = 0$

$$\Rightarrow \quad -5y = -3x + 7$$

and $ay = -4x - 9$

$$\Rightarrow \quad y = \frac{3}{5}x - \frac{7}{5}$$

and $y = -\dfrac{4}{a}x - \dfrac{9}{a}$

Comparing both equations with $y = mx + c$, we get

$$m_1 = \frac{3}{5}$$

$$m_2 = -\frac{4}{a}$$

The lines are perpendicular to each other,

$$\therefore \quad m_1 \times m_2 = -1$$

$$\Rightarrow \quad \frac{3}{5} \times \left(-\frac{4}{a}\right) = -1$$

$$\Rightarrow \quad -\frac{12}{5} = -a$$

$$\Rightarrow \quad a = \frac{12}{5}$$

$$\Rightarrow \quad a = 2\frac{2}{5}.$$ **Ans.**

4. Find the value of k, if the line represented by $kx - 5y + 4 = 0$ and $4x - 2y + 5 = 0$ are perpendicular to each other.

Sol. Here, $kx - 5y + 4 = 0$

$$\Rightarrow \quad y = \frac{kx}{5} + \frac{4}{5}$$

∴ The slope of the line is $\dfrac{k}{5}$.

Also $4x - 2y + 5 = 0$

$$\Rightarrow \quad y = 2x + \frac{5}{2}$$

∴ The slope of line is 2.

Since, the given lines are perpendicular to each other, we have

$$\left(\frac{k}{2}\right)(2) = -1 \Rightarrow k = \frac{-5}{2}.$$ **Ans.**

5. Find the value of 'p' if the lines, $5x - 3y + 2 = 0$ and $6x - py + 7 = 0$ are perpendicular to each other. Hence, find the equation of a line passing through $(-2, -1)$ and parallel to $6x - py + 7 = 0$.*

Sol. Given lines are,

$$5x - 3y + 2 = 0$$

and $6x - py + 7 = 0$

Now, $5x - 3y + 2 = 0$

$$\Rightarrow \quad 3y = 5x + 2$$

$$\Rightarrow \quad y = \frac{5}{3}x + \frac{2}{3}$$

$$\therefore \quad \text{Slope } (m_1) = \frac{5}{3}$$

and $6x - py + 7 = 0$

$$\Rightarrow \quad py = 6x + 7$$

$$\Rightarrow \quad y = \frac{6}{p}x + \frac{7}{p}$$

$$\therefore \quad \text{Slope } (m_2) = \frac{6}{p}$$

Since, given lines are perpendicular to each other,

So, $m_1 \times m_2 = -1$

$$\frac{5}{3} \times \frac{6}{p} = -1$$

$$\Rightarrow \quad p = -10$$

Now, slope $(m_2) = \dfrac{6}{p} = \dfrac{6}{-10} = -\dfrac{3}{5}$

∵ Slopes of parallel lines are equal.

So, slope of required line is $\left(-\dfrac{3}{5}\right)$.

Now, equation of required line is

$$\frac{y - y_1}{x - x_1} = m$$

$$\Rightarrow \qquad \frac{y + 1}{x + 2} = -\frac{3}{5}$$

$$\Rightarrow \qquad 5y + 5 = -3x - 6$$

$$\Rightarrow \quad 3x + 5y + 5 + 6 = 0$$

$$\Rightarrow \quad 3x + 5y + 11 = 0 \qquad \textbf{Ans.}$$

6. Find the equation of a line which is inclined to X-axis at an angle of 60° and its y-intercept is 2.

Sol. Hence, $\qquad m = \tan 60° = \sqrt{3}$

and $\qquad c = 2$

The equation of line is given by

$$y = mx + c$$

$$\Rightarrow \qquad y = \sqrt{3} \cdot x + 2$$

$$\Rightarrow \qquad y = \sqrt{3}\, x + 2$$

$$\Rightarrow \qquad \sqrt{3}\, x - y + 2 = 0. \qquad \textbf{Ans.}$$

7. Find the equation of a line with slope 1 and cutting off an intercept of 5 units on Y-axis.

Sol. We have

Slope of the line, $m = 1$

and Y-intercept, $c = 5$ units

The equation of line is given by

$$y = mx + c$$

i.e., $\qquad y = 1.x + 5$

$$\Rightarrow \qquad y = x + 5$$

or $\qquad x - y + 5 = 0. \qquad \textbf{Ans.}$

8. Find the equations of a line passing through the point (2, 3) and having the x-intercept of 4 units.

Sol. Since x-intercept is 4 units coordinates of point are (4, 0). Equation of a line passing through (2, 3) and (4, 0) is

$$y - y_1 = \frac{y_2 - y_1}{x_2 - x_1}\,(x - x_1)$$

$$\Rightarrow \qquad y - 3 = \frac{0 - 3}{4 - 2}\,(x - 2)$$

$$\Rightarrow \qquad y - 3 = \frac{-3}{2}\,(x - 2)$$

$$\Rightarrow \qquad 2y - 6 = -3x + 6$$

$$\Rightarrow \qquad 3x + 2y = 12. \qquad \textbf{Ans.}$$

9. The vertices of a $\triangle ABC$ are A (3, 8), B (– 1, 2) and C(6, – 6). Find :*

(i) Slope of *BC*.

(ii) Equation of a line perpendicular to *BC* and passing through *A*.

Sol. Given, *A* (3, 8), *B* (– 1, 2) and *C*(6, – 6)

(i) Slope of *BC* $(m_1) = \dfrac{y_2 - y_1}{x_2 - x_1} = \dfrac{-6 - 2}{6 - (-1)}$

$$= \frac{-8}{7} \qquad \textbf{Ans.}$$

(ii) Slope of a line perpendicular to *BC* (m)

$$= -\frac{1}{m_1}$$

$$= -\frac{1}{-8/7} = \frac{7}{8}$$

Let the equation of the line perpendicular to *BC* and through *A* be

$$y - y_1 = m\,(x - x_1)$$

$$\Rightarrow \qquad y - 8 = \frac{7}{8}\,(x - 3)$$

$$\Rightarrow \qquad 8\,(y - 8) = 7\,(x - 3)$$

$$\Rightarrow \qquad 8y - 64 = 7x - 21$$

$$\Rightarrow \quad 7x - 8y - 21 + 64 = 0$$

$$\Rightarrow \qquad 7x - 8y + 43 = 0$$

which is the required equation. $\qquad \textbf{Ans.}$

10. The line through A (– 2, 3) and B (4, b) is perpendicular to the line 2x – 4y = 5. Find the value of b.

Sol. Slope of $\qquad AB = \dfrac{b - 3}{4 + 2}$

$$\Rightarrow \qquad m_1 = \frac{b - 3}{6}$$

$$\Rightarrow \qquad 2x - 4y = 5$$

$$\Rightarrow \qquad 4y = 2x - 5$$

$$\Rightarrow \qquad y = \frac{1}{2}x - \frac{5}{4}$$

$$\therefore \qquad \text{Slope } (m_2) = \frac{1}{2}$$

Since, both lines are perpendicular to each other

So, $\qquad m_1 \cdot m_2 = -1$

$$\Rightarrow \qquad \frac{b - 3}{6} \cdot \frac{1}{2} = -1$$

$$\Rightarrow \qquad b - 3 = -12$$

$$\Rightarrow \qquad b = -9. \qquad \textbf{Ans.}$$

11. Given that $(a, 2a)$ lies on line $\dfrac{y}{2} = 3x - 6$. Find the value of a.

Sol. Point $(a, 2a)$ lies on the line

$$\frac{y}{2} = 3x - 6$$

$\therefore \qquad \frac{2a}{2} = 3a - 6$

$\Rightarrow \qquad a = 3a - 6$

$\Rightarrow \qquad 2a = 6$

$\Rightarrow \qquad a = 3.$ **Ans.**

12. Find the equation of a straight line which cuts an intercept of 5 units on Y-axis and is parallel to the line joining the points $(3, -2)$ and $(1, 4)$.

Sol. Let m be the slope of the required line and since the required line is parallel to the line joining the points $(3, -2)$ and $(1, 4)$.

Hence, slope of the line

$$m = \frac{4+2}{1-3}$$

$$= \frac{6}{-2}$$

$$= -3.$$

Also, Y-intercept, $c = 5$ units.

So, equation of the required line be

$$y = mx + c$$

$\Rightarrow \qquad y = -3x + 5$

$\Rightarrow \qquad 3x + y - 5 = 0.$ **Ans.**

13. Find the equation of a line that has Y-intercept 3 units and is perpendicular to the line joining $(2, -3)$ and $(4, 2)$.

Sol. Let m be the slope of required line

Slope of the given line $= \frac{2+3}{4-2} = \frac{5}{2}$.

But the required line is perpendicular to the given line.

Hence,

$m \times$ Slope of the given line $= -1$

$\Rightarrow \qquad m \times \frac{5}{2} = -1$

$\Rightarrow \qquad m = \frac{-2}{5}$

$\therefore$ Y-intercept, $c = 3$

Hence, equation of the required line is given by

$$y = mx + c$$

i.e., $\qquad y = \frac{-2}{5}x + 3$

$\Rightarrow \qquad 5y = -2x + 15$

$\Rightarrow \qquad 2x + 5y - 15 = 0.$ **Ans.**

14. Find a general equation of a line which passes through :

(i) $(0, -5)$ and $(3, 0)$

(ii) $(2, 3)$ and $(-1, 2)$.

Sol. We have the equation of a line which passes through (x_1, y_1) and (x_2, y_2) is

$$y - y_1 = \frac{y_2 - y_1}{x_2 - x_1}(x - x_1)$$

(i) Putting $x_1 = 0$, $y_1 = -5$ and $x_2 = 3$, $y_2 = 0$

$$y - (-5) = \frac{0-(-5)}{3-0}(x-0)$$

$\Rightarrow \qquad y + 5 = \frac{5}{3}(x - 0)$

$\Rightarrow \qquad 3y + 15 = 5x$

$\Rightarrow \qquad 5x - 3y - 15 = 0$

which is the required equation. **Ans.**

(ii) Putting $x_1 = 2$, $y_1 = 3$ and $x_2 = -1$, $y_2 = 2$

$$y - 3 = \frac{2-3}{-1-2}(x-2)$$

$\Rightarrow \qquad y - 3 = \frac{-1}{-3}(x - 2)$

$\Rightarrow \qquad 3y - 9 = (x - 2)$

$\Rightarrow \qquad x - 2 - 3y + 9 = 0$

$\Rightarrow \qquad x - 3y + 7 = 0$

which is the equation of the required line. **Ans.**

15. Find the equation of the line passing through $(0, 4)$ and parallel to the line $3x + 5y + 15 = 0$.

Sol. Since line is parallel to

$$3x + 5y + 15 = 0$$

$\Rightarrow \qquad 5y = -3x - 15$

$\Rightarrow \qquad y = \frac{-3}{5}x - 3$

$\therefore \qquad m_1 = \frac{-3}{5}$

We have $\qquad m_1 = m_2 \quad (\because$ lines are parallel$)$

$\therefore \qquad m_2 = \frac{-3}{5}$

and passing through the point $(0, 4)$.

Equation of line

$$y - y_1 = m(x - x_1)$$

$$\Rightarrow \qquad y - 4 = \frac{-3}{5}(x - 0)$$

$$\Rightarrow \qquad 5y - 20 = -3x$$

$$\Rightarrow \qquad 3x + 5y = 20. \qquad \textbf{Ans.}$$

16. Find the equation of a line passing through $(3, -2)$ and perpendicular to the line $x - 3y + 5 = 0$.

Sol. $\qquad x - 3y + 5 = 0$

$$\Rightarrow \qquad 3y = x + 5$$

$$\Rightarrow \qquad y = \frac{x}{3} + \frac{5}{3}$$

$$\Rightarrow \qquad m_1 = \frac{1}{3}$$

Since, lines are perpendicular to each other

$$\Rightarrow \qquad m_1 \times m_2 = -1$$

$$\Rightarrow \qquad \frac{1}{3} \times m_2 = -1$$

$$\Rightarrow \qquad m_2 = -1 \times 3$$

$$\Rightarrow \qquad m_2 = -3$$

Passing through the point is $(3, -2)$

∴ Equation of line

$$y - y_1 = m(x - x_1)$$

$$\Rightarrow \qquad y + 2 = -3(x - 3)$$

$$\Rightarrow \qquad y + 2 = -3x + 9$$

$$\Rightarrow \qquad 3x + y + 2 - 9 = 0$$

$$\Rightarrow \qquad 3x + y = 7. \qquad \textbf{Ans.}$$

17. Find the equation of the straight line which has Y-intercept equal to $\frac{4}{3}$ and is perpendicular to $3x - 4y + 11 = 0$.

Sol. Equation of the given line is

$$3x - 4y + 11 = 0$$

Slope form of the line is $y = mx + c$

$$\Rightarrow \qquad 4y = 3x + 11$$

$$\Rightarrow \qquad y = \frac{3}{4}x + \frac{11}{4}$$

$$\Rightarrow \qquad m_1 = \frac{4}{3}$$

Let m_2 be the slope of the line which is perpendicular to the given line then

$$m_1 m_2 = -1$$

$$\frac{3}{4}\, m_2 = -1$$

$$\Rightarrow \qquad m_2 = -\frac{4}{3}$$

Also Y-intercept, $c = \frac{4}{3}$.

Equation of the required line

$$y = m_2 x + c$$

$$\Rightarrow \qquad y = \frac{-4}{3}x + \frac{4}{3}$$

$$\Rightarrow \qquad 3y = -4x + 4$$

$$\Rightarrow \qquad 4x + 3y - 4 = 0. \qquad \textbf{Ans.}$$

18. Find the equation of the straight line perpendicular to $5x - 2y = 8$ and which passes through the midpoint of the line segment joining $(2, 3)$ and $(4, 5)$.

Sol. $\qquad 5x - 2y = 8$

$$\Rightarrow \qquad 2y = 5x - 8$$

$$\Rightarrow \qquad y = \frac{5}{2}x - 4$$

$$\Rightarrow \qquad y = mx + c$$

$$\therefore \qquad m_1 = \frac{5}{2}$$

Since, lines are perpendicular to each other

$$\therefore \qquad m_1 \times m_2 = -1$$

$$\Rightarrow \qquad \frac{5}{2} \times m_2 = -1$$

$$\Rightarrow \qquad m_2 = -1 \div \frac{2}{5}$$

$$\Rightarrow \qquad m_2 = -\frac{2}{5}$$

Coordinates of midpoints

$$= \frac{2+4}{2}, \frac{3+5}{2}$$

Passing point $= (3, 4)$

∴ Equation of line,

$$y - y_1 = m(x - x_1)$$

$$\Rightarrow \qquad y - 4 = \frac{-2}{5}(x - 3)$$

$$\Rightarrow \qquad 5y - 20 = -2x + 6$$

$$\Rightarrow \qquad 2x + 5y = 26. \qquad \textbf{Ans.}$$

19. A line passing through the points $(a, 2a)$ and $(-2, 3)$ is perpendicular to the line $4x + 3y + 5 = 0$. Find the value of a.

Sol. Let m_1 be the slope of the line joining at the points $(a, 2a)$ and $(-2, 3)$, then

$$m_1 = \frac{2a - 3}{a + 2}$$

Also, slope of the line $4x + 3y + 5 = 0$

$$m_2 = -\frac{4}{3}$$

Since, both the lines are perpendicular.

So, $\qquad m_1 m_2 = -1$

$\Rightarrow \qquad \dfrac{2a-3}{a+2} \times \dfrac{(-4)}{3} = -1$

$\Rightarrow \qquad 8a - 12 = 3a + 6$

$\Rightarrow \qquad 8a - 3a = 18$

$\Rightarrow \qquad 5a = 18$

$\Rightarrow \qquad a = \dfrac{18}{5}$

$\Rightarrow \qquad a = 3\dfrac{3}{5}.$ **Ans.**

20. $A(2, 5)$, $B(-1, 2)$ and $C(5, 8)$ are the vertices of a tirangle ABC, 'M' is a point on AB such that $AM : MB = 1 : 2$. Find the coordinates of 'M'. Hence find the equation of the line passing through the points C and M.*

Sol. Given vertices of triangle are, $A(2, 5)$, $B(-1, 2)$, $C(5, 8)$, $AM : MB = 1 : 2$.

$\because$ M is a point on AB.

$\therefore$ Coordinates of $M = \left(\dfrac{m_1 x_2 + m_2 x_1}{m_1 + m_2} + \dfrac{m_1 y_2 + m_2 y_1}{m_1 + m_2} \right)$

Here, $m_1 : m_2 = 1 : 2$, $x_1 = 2$, $y_1 = 5$, $x_2 = -1$, $y_2 = 2$

$\therefore$ Coordinates of $M = \left(\dfrac{1 \times (-1) + 2 \times 2}{1+2}, \dfrac{1 \times 2 + 2 \times 5}{1+2} \right)$

$= \left(\dfrac{-1+4}{3}, \dfrac{14}{3} \right) = (1, 4)$ **Ans.**

The equation of line passing through $C(5, 8)$ and $M(1, 4)$ is

$$y - y_1 = \dfrac{y_2 - y_1}{x_2 - x_1}(x - x_1)$$

Here, $\qquad x_1 = 5$, $y_1 = 8$, $x_2 = 1$, $y_2 = 4$

$\therefore \qquad y - 8 = \dfrac{4-8}{1-5}(x-5)$

$\Rightarrow \qquad y - 8 = \dfrac{-4}{4}(x-5)$

$\Rightarrow \qquad y - 8 = x - 5$

$\Rightarrow \qquad x - y + 3 = 0.$ **Ans.**

Chapter 12. Reflection

1. The triangle $A(1, 2)$, $B(4, 4)$ and $C(3, 7)$ is first reflected in the line $y = 0$ onto triangle $A'B'C'$ and then triangle $A'B'C'$ is reflected in the origin onto triangle $A''B''C''$. Write down the coordinates of :

(i) A', B', C',

(ii) A'', B'', C''.

Sol. (i) $\qquad\qquad A' \rightarrow (1, -2)$,

$\qquad\qquad\qquad B' \rightarrow (4, -4)$,

$\qquad\qquad\qquad C' \rightarrow (3, -7).$ **Ans.**

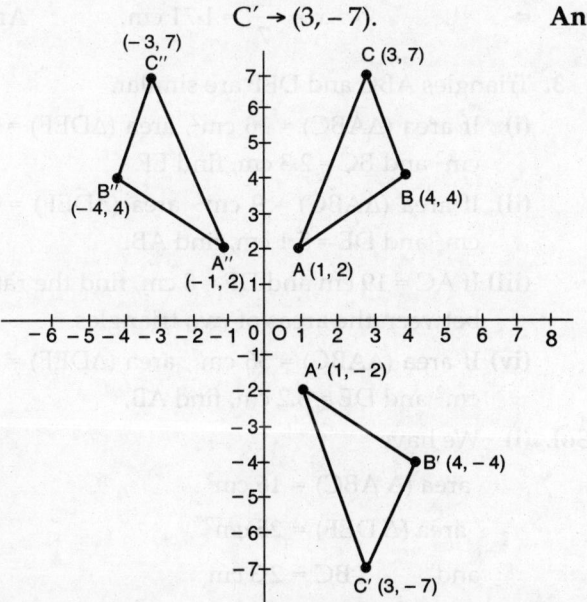

(ii) $\qquad\qquad A'' \rightarrow (-1, 2)$,

$\qquad\qquad\qquad B'' \rightarrow (-4, 4)$,

$\qquad\qquad\qquad C'' \rightarrow (-3, 7).$ **Ans.**

2. The point $P(a, b)$ is first reflected in the origin and then reflected on the Y-axis to p'. If P' has coordinates $(3, -4)$, evaluate a, b.

Sol. $P(a, b)$ after reflection at the origin $= (-a, -b)$,

$(-a, -b)$ after reflection on the Y-axis $= p'(a, -b)$

According to question,

$\Rightarrow \qquad (a, -b) = (3, -4)$

$\Rightarrow \qquad a = 3, -b = -4$

$\Rightarrow \qquad a = 3, b = 4.$ **Ans.**

---

* Frequently asked previous years Board Exam Questions.

Chapter 13. Similarity

1. In the figure, FG = EG, BE = 30, CF = 40, AE = 18 and DF = 24. Determine which triangle in the figure are similar.

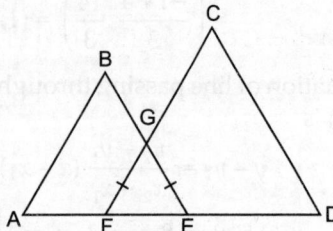

Sol. Since Δ FGE is an isosceles triangle

$$(\because FG = EG)$$

So, $\angle GFE = \angle GEF$.

Now, $\dfrac{AE}{DF} = \dfrac{18}{24} = \dfrac{3}{4}$

and $\dfrac{BE}{CF} = \dfrac{30}{40} = \dfrac{3}{4}$

∴ By substitution,

$$\dfrac{AE}{DF} = \dfrac{BE}{CF}$$

If the measures of the corresponding sides that includes the angles are proportional, then the triangles are similar.

∴ By SAS similarity, Δ ABE ~ Δ DCF.   **Ans.**

2. Determine the values of x and y of Δ ABC ~ Δ PQR in the following figure

(a)

(b)

(c)

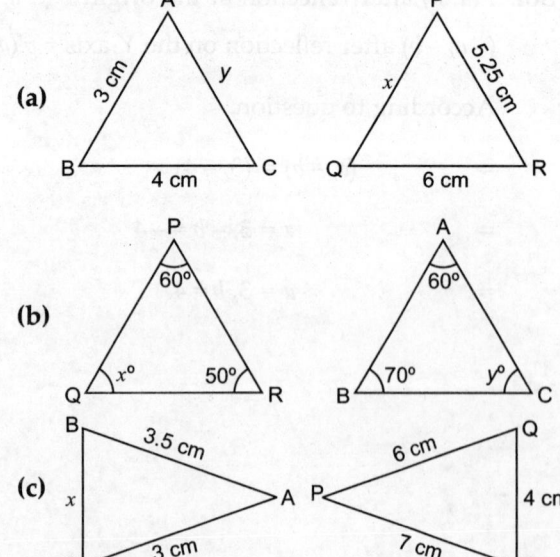

Sol. (a) Since, Δ ABC ~ Δ PQR

Therefore, corresponding sides are proportional

∴ $\dfrac{AB}{PQ} = \dfrac{AC}{PR} = \dfrac{BC}{QR}$

Now,

$$\dfrac{AB}{PQ} = \dfrac{BC}{QR}$$

⇒ $\dfrac{3}{x} = \dfrac{4}{6}$

⇒ $x = \dfrac{18}{4} = \dfrac{9}{2} = 4\cdot5$

$$\dfrac{AC}{PQ} = \dfrac{BC}{QR}$$

⇒ $\dfrac{y}{5\cdot25} = \dfrac{4}{6}$

⇒ $y = \dfrac{5\cdot25 \times 4}{6} = 3\cdot5$

Hence, $x = 4\cdot5$ and $y = 3\cdot5$ **Ans.**

(b) Since triangles ABC and PQR are similar therefore corresponding angles are equal.

∴ $x = 70°$ and $y = 50°$.   **Ans.**

(c) Since triangles are similar,

∴ corresponding sides are proportional

$$\dfrac{BC}{QR} = \dfrac{AC}{PR}$$

⇒ $\dfrac{x}{4} = \dfrac{3}{7}$

⇒ $x = \dfrac{12}{7} = 1\cdot71$ cm.   **Ans.**

3. Triangles ABC and DEF are similar.

(i) If area (ΔABC) = 16 cm², area (ΔDEF) = 25 cm² and BC = 2.3 cm, find EF.

(ii) If area (ΔABC) = 9 cm², area (ΔDEF) = 64 cm² and DE = 5.1 cm, find AB.

(iii) If AC = 19 cm and DF = 8 cm, find the ratio between the areas of two triangles.

(iv) If area (ΔABC) = 36 cm², area (ΔDEF) = 64 cm² and DE = 6.2 cm, find AB.

Sol. (i)   We have

area (Δ ABC) = 16 cm²

area (Δ DEF) = 25 cm²

and   BC = 2·3 cm

Since, $\dfrac{\text{area (ΔABC)}}{\text{area (ΔDEF)}} = \dfrac{BC^2}{EF^2}$

$$\Rightarrow \quad \frac{16}{25} = \frac{(2.3)^2}{EF^2}$$

$$\Rightarrow \quad \frac{2.3}{EF} = \frac{4}{5}$$

$$\Rightarrow \quad 4\,EF = 5 \times 2.3$$

$$\Rightarrow \quad EF = \frac{11.5}{4}$$

$$\Rightarrow \quad EF = 2.875 \text{ cm.} \qquad \textbf{Ans.}$$

(ii) We have

$$\text{area } (\Delta \, ABC) = 9 \text{ cm}^2$$

$$\text{area } (\Delta \, DEF) = 64 \text{ cm}^2$$

$$\text{and} \qquad DE = 5.1 \text{ cm}$$

Since, $\dfrac{\text{area } (\Delta ABC)}{\text{area } (\Delta DEF)} = \dfrac{AB^2}{DE^2}$

$$\Rightarrow \quad \frac{9}{64} = \frac{AB^2}{DE^2}$$

$$\Rightarrow \quad \frac{AB}{DE} = \frac{3}{8}$$

$$\Rightarrow \quad \frac{AB}{5.1} = \frac{3}{8}$$

$$\Rightarrow \quad AB = \frac{3}{8} \times 5.1 = \frac{15.3}{8}$$

$$\Rightarrow \quad AB = 1.9125 \text{ cm.} \qquad \textbf{Ans.}$$

(iii) In Δ ABC and Δ DEF, AC = 19 cm, DF = 8 cm.

Since, $\dfrac{\text{area } (\Delta ABC)}{\text{area } (\Delta DEF)} = \dfrac{AC^2}{DF^2} = \dfrac{(19)^2}{(8)^2} = \dfrac{361}{64}$

Hence, the required ratio is 361 : 64. **Ans.**

(iv) Area (Δ ABC) = 36 cm^2

Area (Δ DEF) = 64 cm^2.

$$DE = 6.2 \text{ cm}$$

$$AB = ?$$

We have

$$\frac{\text{area } (\Delta ABC)}{\text{area } (\Delta DEF)} = \frac{AB^2}{DE^2}$$

$$\Rightarrow \quad \frac{36}{64} = \frac{AB^2}{(6.2)^2}$$

$$\Rightarrow \quad \frac{AB}{6.2} = \frac{6}{8}$$

$$\Rightarrow \quad AB = \frac{6 \times 6.2}{8}$$

$$\Rightarrow \quad AB = 4.65 \text{ cm.} \qquad \textbf{Ans.}$$

4. Determine the ratio of the area of two similar triangles if one pair of their corresponding sides are 3 cm and 5 cm.

Sol. Let the two triangles be ABC and DEF

Let BC = 3 cm and EF = 5 cm.

Then $\dfrac{\text{Area } (\Delta \, ABC)}{\text{Area } (\Delta \, DEF)} = \dfrac{(BC)^2}{(EF)^2}$

$$= \frac{3^2}{5^2} = 9 : 25. \qquad \textbf{Ans.}$$

5. In a Δ ABC, PQ ∥ BC and intersects AB and AC at P and Q respectively. If $= \dfrac{AP}{BP} = \dfrac{3}{5}$. Find the ratio of areas Δ APQ and Δ ABC.

Sol. Since $\qquad$ PQ ∥ BC

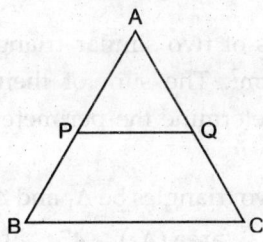

$$\therefore \quad \frac{AP}{BP} = \frac{AQ}{CQ} = \frac{3}{5}$$

$$\therefore \quad \frac{BP}{AP} = \frac{QC}{AQ} = \frac{5}{3}$$

$$\therefore \quad 1 + \frac{BP}{AP} = 1 + \frac{QC}{AQ}$$

$$= 1 + \frac{5}{3} = \frac{8}{3}$$

$$\Rightarrow \quad \frac{AB}{AP} = \frac{AC}{AQ}$$

$$= \frac{8}{3}$$

$$\Rightarrow \quad \frac{AP}{AB} = \frac{AQ}{AC} = \frac{3}{8}$$

$$\Rightarrow \quad \Delta \, ABC \sim \Delta \, APQ$$

$$\Rightarrow \quad \frac{\text{area } \Delta ABC}{\text{area } \Delta APQ} = \frac{AB^2}{AP^2}$$

$$= \left(\frac{8}{3}\right)^2 = \frac{64}{9}$$

$$\text{or} \quad \frac{\text{area } \Delta APQ}{\text{area } \Delta ABC} = 9 : 64. \qquad \textbf{Ans.}$$

6. If the ratio of the areas of two similar triangles is 16 : 25, determine the ratio of their corresponding sides.

Sol. Let Δ ABC and Δ PQR are similar and given $\dfrac{\text{area }\Delta ABC}{\text{area }\Delta PQR} = \dfrac{16}{25}$.

Since, $\dfrac{\text{area }\Delta ABC}{\text{area }\Delta PQR} = \left(\dfrac{AB}{PQ}\right)^2 = \left(\dfrac{BC}{QR}\right)^2 = \left(\dfrac{AC}{PR}\right)^2$

$\Rightarrow \quad \left(\dfrac{AB}{PQ}\right)^2 = \left(\dfrac{BC}{QR}\right)^2 = \left(\dfrac{AC}{PR}\right)^2$

$= \dfrac{16}{25} = \left(\dfrac{4}{5}\right)^2$

$\Rightarrow \quad \dfrac{AB}{PQ} = \dfrac{BC}{QR} = \dfrac{AC}{PR} = 4:5.$ **Ans.**

7. The areas of two similar triangles are 45 cm² and 80 cm². The sum of their perimeters is 35 cm. Determine the perimeter of each triangle.

Sol. Let the two triangles be Δ_1 and Δ_2.

Since, $\dfrac{\text{area }(\Delta_1)}{\text{area }(\Delta_2)} = \dfrac{45}{80} = \dfrac{9}{16}$

Since, $\dfrac{\text{area }\Delta_1}{\text{area }\Delta_2} = \dfrac{9}{16} = \left(\dfrac{a}{b}\right)^2$

where a and b are corresponding sides of triangle.

$\Rightarrow \quad \dfrac{a}{b} = \dfrac{3}{4}.$

Since, $\dfrac{\text{Perimeter }\Delta_1}{\text{Perimeter }\Delta_2} = \dfrac{a}{b}$

Let $\quad 3x = \text{Perimeter of }\Delta_1$

and $\quad 4x = \text{Perimeter of }\Delta_2$

Then, $\quad 3x + 4x = 35$

($\because$ sum of perimeters is 35)

$\Rightarrow \quad x = 5$

So, Perimeter of $\Delta_1 = 3 \times 5 = 15$ cm

and Perimeter of $\Delta_2 = 4 \times 5 = 20$ cm. **Ans.**

8. On a map drawn to a scale of 1 : 50,000, a rectangular plot of land *ABCD* has the following dimensions. $AB = 6$ cm; $BC = 8$ cm and all angles are right angles. Find:*

(i) the actual length of the diagonal distance AC of the plot in km.

* Frequently asked previous years Board Exam Questions.

(ii) the actual area of the plot in sq. km.

Sol. Here, $\quad 1 : k = 1 : 50,000$

and $\quad AB = 6$ cm, $BC = 8$ cm

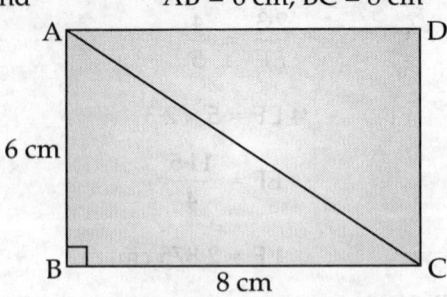

$\therefore \quad AC = \sqrt{AB^2 + BC^2}$

$= \sqrt{6^2 + 8^2}$

$= \sqrt{36 + 64}$

$= \sqrt{100} = 10$ cm

(i) Actual length of $AC = k \times AC$

$= 50,000 \times 10$ cm

$= 5,00,000$ cm

$= \dfrac{500000}{100000}$ km $= 5$ km. **Ans.**

(ii) Area of rectangle ABCD

$= 6 \times 8 = 48$ cm²

$\therefore \quad$ Actual area $= k^2 \times$ Area of ABCD

$= (50,000)^2 \times 48$ cm²

$= \dfrac{50,000 \times 50,000 \times 48}{1,00,000 \times 1,00,000}$ km²

$= 12$ km². **Ans.**

9. The model of a building is constructed with scale factor 1 : 30.

(i) If the height of the model is 80 cm, find the actual height of the building in metres.

(ii) If the actual volume of a tank at the top of the building is 27 m³, find the volume of the tank on the top of the model.

Sol. (i) $\dfrac{\text{Height of model}}{\text{Height of actual building}} = \dfrac{1}{30}$

$\Rightarrow \quad \dfrac{80}{H} = \dfrac{1}{30}$

$\Rightarrow \quad H = 2,400$ cm $= 24$ m. **Ans.**

(ii) $\dfrac{\text{Volume of model}}{\text{Volume of tank}} = \left(\dfrac{1}{30}\right)^3$

$\Rightarrow \quad \dfrac{V}{27} = \dfrac{1}{27,000}$

$\Rightarrow \quad V = \dfrac{1}{1,000}$ m³ $= 1,000$ cm³. **Ans.**

Chapter 17. Mensuration

1. Inner and outer radii of a pipe are 2 cm and 3 cm respectively. If the length of the pipe is 45 cm, find its total surface area.   [Use $\pi = 3.14$]

Sol. Inner curved surface area of the pipe

$$= 2\pi rh$$
$$= 2\pi \times 2 \times 45 \text{ cm}^2$$
$$= 180\,\pi \text{ cm}^2 \qquad \dots (i)$$

Outer curved surface area of the pipe

$$= 2\pi \times 3 \times 45 \text{ cm}^2$$
$$= 270\,\pi \text{ cm}^2 \qquad \dots (ii)$$

Area of two ends $= 2\pi\,[(3)^2 - 2^2]$ cm^2

$$= 2\pi\,(5) \text{ cm}^2$$
$$= 10\,\pi \text{ cm}^2 \qquad \dots (iii)$$

∴ Total surface area = sum of (i), (ii), and (iii)

$$= (180\,\pi + 270\,\pi + 10\,\pi) \text{ cm}^2$$
$$= 460\,\pi \text{ cm}^2$$
$$= 460 \times 3.14 \text{ cm}^2$$
$$= 1444.4 \text{ cm}^2. \qquad \textbf{Ans.}$$

2. The curved surface area of a right circular cylinder of length 15 cm is 90 cm^2. Determine the diameter of the base of the cylinder.

Sol. Since, curved surface area of right circular cylinder $= 2\pi rh = 90$ cm^2

$$\Rightarrow \qquad 90 \text{ cm}^2 = 2\pi r\,(15) \text{ cm}^2$$
$$\Rightarrow \qquad r = \frac{90}{30\pi} = \frac{3}{\pi} = \frac{3 \times 7}{22} = \frac{21}{22}$$

∴   Diameter $= 2r = 2\left(\dfrac{21}{22}\right)$

$$= \frac{21}{11} = 1.90 \text{ cm} \qquad \textbf{Ans.}$$

3. A medicine capsule is in the shape of a cylinder with two hemisphere stuck to each of its ends. The length of the entire capsule is 14 mm and the diameter of the capsule is 4 mm. Find its surface area.

Sol. We know that, the curved surface area of cylinder is $2\pi rh$ and the hemisphere is $2\pi r^2$.

Since,   diameter $= 2r = 4$ mm

$$\Rightarrow \qquad r = 2 \text{ mm}$$

Since, entire length is 14 mm

∴ Length of cylinder

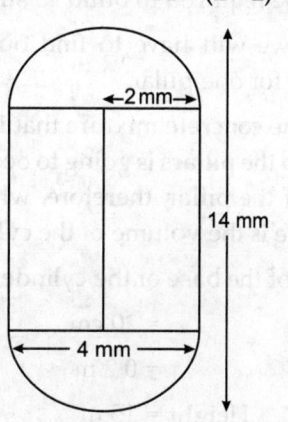

$$= 14 - (2 + 2) = 10 \text{ mm}$$

∴ Total surface area

$$= \text{(Curved surface area of cylinder)}$$
$$+ \text{(Surface area of 2 hemispheres)}$$
$$= 2\pi\,(2)\,(10) \text{ mm}^2 + 2 \times [2\pi\,(2)^2] \text{ mm}^2$$
$$= 40\,\pi \text{ mm}^2 + 16\,\pi \text{ mm}^2$$
$$= 56\,\pi \text{ mm}^2$$
$$= 56 \times 3.14 \text{ mm}^2$$
$$= 175.84 \text{ mm}^2 \qquad \textbf{Ans.}$$

4. Rakesh made a bird-bath for his garden in the shape of a cylinder with a hemispherical depression at one end. The height of the cylinder is 1.50 m and its radius is 50 cm. Find the total surface area of the birth-bath.

$$\left(\text{Take } \pi = \frac{22}{7} \right)$$

Sol. Let h be the height of the cylinder and r be the common radius of cylinder and hemisphere. We know that

Curved surface area of cylinder $= 2\pi rh$

and curved surface area of hemisphere $= 2\pi r^2$

Therefore, the total surface area

$$= \text{C.S.A. of cylinder} + \text{C.S.A. of hemisphere}$$
$$= 2\pi rh + 2\pi r^2$$
$$= 2\pi\,(50)\,150 \text{ cm}^2 + 2\pi\,(50)^2 \text{ cm}^2$$
$$= 2\pi \times 50\,(150 + 50) \text{ cm}^2$$
$$= 100\,\pi\,(200) \text{ cm}^2$$
$$= 20000\,\pi \text{ cm}^2 = 20000 \times \frac{22}{7} \text{ cm}^2$$
$$= 62857.14 \text{ cm}^2 \qquad \textbf{Ans.}$$

5. The pillars of a temple are cylindrically shaped. If each pillar has a circular base of radius 20 cm and height 15 cm, how much concrete mixture would be required to build 15 such pillars.

Sol. Firstly, we will have to find out the concrete mixture for one pillar.

Since, the concrete mixture that is to be used to build up the pillars is going to occupy the entire space of the pillar, therefore, what we need to find here is the volume of the cylinders.

Radius of the base of the cylinder

$$= 20 \text{ cm}$$
$$= 0.2 \text{ m}$$

and   Height = 15 m

So, volume of each cylinder

$$= \pi r^2 h$$
$$= \frac{22}{7} (0.2)^2 = 15 \text{ m}^3$$
$$= 1.88 \text{ m}^3 = \frac{13.2}{7} \text{ m}^3$$

Therefore, Volume of 15 pillars

$$= 15 \times \text{Volume of each pillar}$$
$$= 15 \times \frac{13.2}{7} \text{ m}^3 = 28.28 \text{ m}^3$$

So, 15 pillars would be needed 28.28 m³ for concrete mixture. **Ans.**

6. If the internal radius of the pipe is 2 cm, the external radius is 2.5 cm and the length of the pipe is 10 cm. Find the volume of the metal used.

Sol. Since, the volume of the right circular hollow cylinder $= \pi (R^2 - r^2) h$.

Here, R = outer radius = 2.5 cm and r = inner radius = 2 cm

and   Height, h = 10 cm

$\therefore$ Volume $= \pi (R^2 - r^2)h$
$$= \pi [(2.5)^2 - (2)^2] \ 10 \text{ cm}^3$$
$$= \pi (22.5) \text{ cm}^3$$
$$= 70.7 \text{ cm}^3 \ \left(\text{Using } \pi = \frac{22}{7} \right)$$

Ans.

7. A rectangular piece of paper of width 20 cm and length 45 cm is rolled along its width to form a cylinder. Determine the curved surface area of the cylinder so formed ?

Sol. The length of the rectangle becomes the circumference of the base of the cylinder.

$\therefore$ $2\pi r = 45,$

where r = Radius of cylinder

$\Rightarrow$ $r = \dfrac{45}{2\pi}$

The width of the rectangle becomes the height of the cylinder, *i.e.*, $h = 20$ cm.

$\therefore$ Curved surface area of the cylinder

$$= 2\pi rh$$
$$= 2\pi \left(\frac{45}{2\pi} \right) 20 \text{ cm}^2$$
$$= 900 \text{ cm}^2. \qquad \textbf{Ans.}$$

8. A circus tent consists of cylindrical base surmounted by a conical roof. The radius of the cylinder is 10 m. The height of the tent is 60 m and that of the cone is 20 m. Find the volume of the tent and the area of the canvas used for making it.

Sol. Height of the tent

$$= \text{Height of cone} + \text{Height of the cylinder}$$

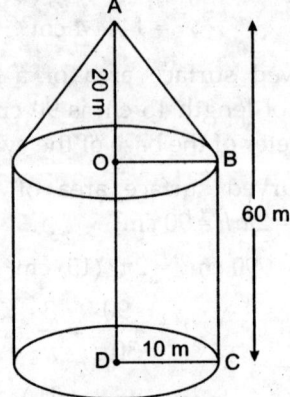

Given, height of tent = 60 m

$$H = \text{height of cone} \ = 20 \text{ m}$$

$\therefore$ Height of cylinder

$$= h = 60 - 20 = 40 \text{ m}$$

and Radius of cone = Radius of cylinder

$$r = 10 \text{ m}$$

$\therefore$ Volume of the tent = Volume of cylinder

$$+ \text{Volume of the cone}$$
$$= \pi r^2 h + \frac{1}{3} \pi r^2 H$$
$$= \pi r^2 \left(h + \frac{H}{3} \right)$$
$$= \pi (10)^2 \left(40 + \frac{20}{3} \right)$$

$$= 100 \times \frac{22}{7}\left(\frac{140}{3}\right)$$

$$= 14666 \cdot 6 \text{ m}^3$$

Slant height of the cone is

$$l = \sqrt{H^2 + r^2}$$

$$= \sqrt{400 + 100}$$

$$= \sqrt{500} = 10\sqrt{5} \text{ m}$$

Since, curved surface area of cone

$$= \pi r l$$

$$= \frac{22}{7} \times 10 \times 10\sqrt{5} \text{ m}^2$$

and curved surface area of cylinder

$$= 2\pi r h$$

$$= 2 \times \frac{22}{7} \times 10 \times 40$$

∴ Total surface area of the canvas in making the tent

$$= \text{C.S.A. of cylinder} + \text{C.S.A. of cone}$$

$$= 2\pi r h + \pi r l$$

$$= \pi r (2h + l)$$

$$= \frac{22}{7} \times 10 (2 \times 40 + 10\sqrt{5}) \text{ m}^2$$

$$= \frac{220}{7}(80 + 10\sqrt{5}) \text{ m}^2$$

Total Surface Area = 3217·04 m² **Ans.**

9. The surface area of a sphere and the curved surface area of cylinder are in the ratio 2 : 1. Find the ratio of their volumes, if their radii are equal.

Sol. Given

$$\frac{\text{Surface area of sphere}}{\text{Curved surface area of cylinder}} = \frac{2}{1}$$

$$\Rightarrow \frac{4\pi r^2}{2\pi r h} = \frac{2}{1} \Rightarrow r = h$$

Also, we have given radii of both are equal.

The ratio of their volumes

$$= \frac{\text{Volume of sphere}}{\text{Volume of cylinder}}$$

$$= \frac{\frac{4}{3}\pi r^3}{\pi r^2 h}$$

$$= \frac{4\pi r^3}{\pi r^3} \qquad (\because h = r)$$

$$= \frac{4}{3}$$

∴ Ratio of their volumes 4 : 3. **Ans.**

10. A right circular cylinder just encloses a sphere of radius *r*. Determine :

(i) surface area of the sphere.

(ii) curved surface area of the cylinder.

(iii) ratio of the areas obtained in (i) and (ii).

Sol. (i) Surface area of the sphere

$$= 4\pi r^2 \qquad \textbf{Ans.}$$

(ii) For cylinder,

Radius = *r* and Height = 2*r*

∴ C.S.A. of cylinder

$$= 2\pi r h$$

$$= 2\pi r (2r)$$

$$= 4\pi r^2 \qquad \textbf{Ans.}$$

(iii) Ratio of the areas obtained in (i) and (ii).

$$= \frac{\text{Surface area of sphere}}{\text{Curved surface area of cylinder}}$$

$$= \frac{4\pi r^2}{4\pi r^2} = 1 : 1 \qquad \textbf{Ans.}$$

11. The inner diameter of a cylindrical wooden pipe is 22 cm and its outer diameter is 24 cm. The length of the pipe is 30 cm. Find the mass of the pipe, if 1 cm³ of wood has a mass of 0·6g.

Sol. Inner radius

$$r = \frac{\text{Inner diameter}}{2}$$

$$\Rightarrow r = \frac{22}{2} = 11 \text{ cm}$$

and Outer radius

$$R = \frac{\text{Outer diameter}}{2}$$

$$\Rightarrow R = \frac{24}{2} = 12 \text{ cm}$$

and length of the pipe

$$= h = 30 \text{ cm}$$

∴ Outer volume

$$\pi R^2 h = \frac{22}{7} \times 12 \times 12 \times 30$$

$$= 95040/7 \text{ cm}^3$$

and inner volume

$= \pi r^2 h$

$= \dfrac{22}{7} \times 11 \times 11 \times 30$

$= \dfrac{79860}{7}$ cm^3

∴ Volume of wood used

= Outer volume – Inner volume

= 15180/7 cm^3

∴ Mass of the pipe

= (15180/7) × 0·6

= 1301·1 g = 1·30 kg. **Ans.**

12. A patient in a hospital is given soup daily in a cylindrical bowl of diameter 6 cm. If the bowl is filled with soup to a height of 4 cm, how much soup the hospital has to prepare daily to serve 250 patients ?

Sol. Dimension of cylindrical bowl

Diameter = 6 cm, Height = 4 cm

∴ $r = \dfrac{6}{2} = 3$ cm

∴ Volume of the soup in the cylindrical bowl

$= \pi r^2 h = \pi (3)^2 \, 4 = 36\pi$ cm^3

∴ Volume of soup to be prepared daily to serve 250 patients

= 250 × 36 π cm^3

= 9000 π cm^2

= 9π litre

= 28·26 litre (or 28260 cm^3)

Therefore, the hospital has to prepare 28,260 cm^3 (or 28·26 *l*) of soup daily to serve 250 patients. **Ans.**

13. A juice seller was serving his customers using glasses as shown in figure. The inner diameter of the cylindrical glass was 5 cm, but the bottom of the glass has a hemispherical raised portion which reduced the capacity of the glass. If the height of a glass was 15 cm, find the apparent capacity of the glass and its actual capacity (use π = 3·14).

Sol. Since, the inner diameter of the glass

= 5 cm and height = 15 cm

∴ The apparent capacity of the glass

= Volume of cylinder

$= \pi r^2 h$

$= \pi (2\cdot5)^2 \, 15$ cm^3

= 294·37 cm^3

But the actual capacity of the glass is less by the volume of the hemisphere at the base of the glass.

i.e., it is less by $\dfrac{2}{3} \times \pi r^3$

$= \dfrac{2}{3} \times 3\cdot14 \times (2\cdot5)^3$ cm^3

= 32·71 cm^3

So, the actual capacity of the glass

= Apparent capacity of the glass

– Volume of the hemisphere

= (294·37 – 32·71) cm^3

= 261·66 cm^3. **Ans.**

14. Determine :

(i) The curved or lateral surface area of a cylindrical petrol storage tank that is 4·0 m in diameter and 4·4 m high.

(ii) How much steel was actually used, if $\dfrac{1}{2}$ of the steel actually used was wasted in making the closed tank.

Sol. (i) Here,

$r = \dfrac{4\cdot0}{2} = 2$ m and $h = 4\cdot4$ m

Curved surface area $= 2\pi r h$ m^2

$= 2 \times \dfrac{22}{7} \times 2 \times 4\cdot4$ cm^2

= 55·31 m^2 **Ans.**

(ii) Since $\dfrac{1}{12}$ of the actual steel used was wasted, the area of the steel which has gone into the tank $= \left(1 - \dfrac{1}{12}\right) = \dfrac{11}{12}$ of *x*, where

x = total area of steel used.

Steel used $= (2\pi r h + 2\pi r^2)$ m^2

$= \left(55\cdot31 + 2 \times \dfrac{22}{7} \times 4\right)$ m^2

= (55·31 + 25·14) m^2

= 80·45 m^2

∴ $\dfrac{11}{12} x = 80\cdot45$

⇒ $x = 87\cdot76$ m^2

Hence, the actual area of the steel used = 87·76 m^2.

Ans.

Chapter 18. Trigonometry

1. If $5 \tan \theta = 4$, find the value of

$$\frac{5 \sin \theta + 3 \cos \theta}{5 \sin \theta + 2 \cos \theta}.$$

Sol. $\qquad 5 \tan \theta = 4$

$\Rightarrow \qquad \tan \theta = \dfrac{4}{5}$

$\Rightarrow \qquad \dfrac{\sin \theta}{\cos \theta} = \dfrac{4}{5}$

$$\frac{5 \sin \theta + 3 \cos \theta}{5 \sin \theta + 2 \cos \theta} = \frac{5 \dfrac{\sin \theta}{\cos \theta} + 3 \dfrac{\cos \theta}{\cos \theta}}{5 \dfrac{\sin \theta}{\cos \theta} + 2 \dfrac{\cos \theta}{\cos \theta}}$$

[Dividing Numerator and Denominator by $\cos \theta$]

$$= \frac{5 \times \dfrac{4}{5} + 3}{5 \times \dfrac{4}{5} + 2} = \frac{4 + 3}{4 + 2} = \frac{7}{6}. \textbf{ Ans.}$$

2. Given that

$$\tan (\theta_1 + \theta_2) = \frac{\tan \theta_1 + \tan \theta_2}{1 - \tan \theta_1 \tan \theta_2}.$$

Determine $(\theta_1 + \theta_2)$, when $\tan \theta_1 = \dfrac{1}{2}$, $\tan \theta_2 = \dfrac{1}{3}$.

Sol. We have,

$$\tan \theta_1 = \frac{1}{2}$$

and $\qquad \tan \theta_2 = \dfrac{1}{3}$

$\therefore \qquad \tan (\theta_1 + \theta_2) = \dfrac{\tan \theta_1 + \tan \theta_2}{1 - \tan \theta_1 \tan \theta_2}$

$$= \frac{\dfrac{1}{2} + \dfrac{1}{3}}{1 - \dfrac{1}{2} \times \dfrac{1}{3}} = \frac{\dfrac{5}{6}}{1 - \dfrac{1}{6}}$$

$\Rightarrow \qquad \tan (\theta_1 + \theta_2) = \dfrac{\dfrac{5}{6}}{\dfrac{5}{6}}$

$\Rightarrow \qquad \tan (\theta_1 + \theta_2) = 1 = \tan 45°$

$\Rightarrow \qquad \theta_1 + \theta_2 = 45°. \qquad$ **Ans.**

3. (i) $\dfrac{\sin 40° + \cos 50°}{\tan 38° \, 20'}$

(ii) $\dfrac{\sin 20° \, 50' + \tan 67° \, 40'}{\cos 32° \, 20' - \sin 15° \, 10'}$.

Sol. (i) $\dfrac{\sin 40° + \cos 50°}{\tan 38°20'}$

$$= \frac{0 \cdot 6428 + 0 \cdot 6428}{0 \cdot 7907}$$

$$= \frac{1 \cdot 2856}{0 \cdot 7907}$$

$$= 1 \cdot 6259. \qquad \textbf{Ans.}$$

(ii) $\dfrac{\sin 20° \, 50' + \tan 67° \, 40'}{\cos 32° \, 20' - \sin 15° \, 10'}$

$$= \frac{0 \cdot 3557 + 2 \cdot 4340}{0 \cdot 8450 - 0 \cdot 2616}$$

$$= \frac{2 \cdot 7897}{0 \cdot 5834}$$

$$= \frac{27897}{5834}$$

$$= 4 \cdot 7818. \qquad \textbf{Ans.}$$

4. The string of a kite is 150 m long and it makes an angle of 60° with the horizontal. Determine the height of the kite from the ground.

Sol. Let h be the height of the kite. PB be the length of string such that PB = 150 m

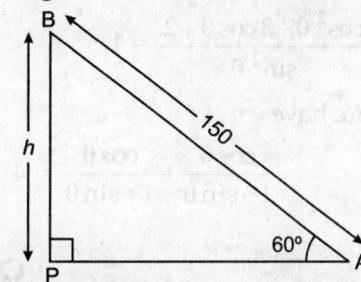

In right angled $\triangle$BPA,

$$\sin 60° = \frac{h}{150}$$

$\Rightarrow \qquad \dfrac{\sqrt{3}}{2} = \dfrac{h}{150}$

$\Rightarrow \qquad h = \dfrac{150\sqrt{3}}{2}$

$\qquad\qquad = 75\sqrt{3}$

$\Rightarrow \qquad h = 1 \cdot 732 \times 75$

$\qquad\qquad = 129 \cdot 9$ m

Hence, the height of kite above the ground

$$= 129 \cdot 9 \text{ m.} \qquad \textbf{Ans.}$$

5. Solve : $2 \cos^2 \theta + \sin \theta - 2 = 0$.

Sol.
$$2 \cos^2 \theta + \sin \theta - 2 = 0$$
$$\Rightarrow \quad 2(1 - \sin^2 \theta) + \sin \theta - 2 = 0$$
$$\Rightarrow \quad 2 - 2 \sin^2 \theta + \sin \theta - 2 = 0$$
$$\Rightarrow \quad -\sin \theta (2 \sin \theta - 1) = 0$$
$$\Rightarrow \quad \sin \theta (2 \sin \theta - 1) = 0$$
$$\Rightarrow \quad \sin \theta = 0 \text{ or } 2 \sin \theta - 1 = 0$$
$$\Rightarrow \quad \sin \theta = 0 \text{ or } \sin \theta = \frac{1}{2}$$
$$\Rightarrow \quad \theta = 0° \text{ or } \theta = 30° \qquad \textbf{Ans.}$$

6. Solve : $\sin^2 \theta - 3 \sin \theta + 2 = 0$.

Sol.
$$\sin^2 \theta - 3 \sin \theta + 2 = 0$$
$$\Rightarrow \quad \sin^2 \theta - 2 \sin \theta - \sin \theta + 2 = 0$$
$$\Rightarrow \sin \theta (\sin \theta - 2) - 1(\sin \theta - 2) = 0$$
$$\Rightarrow \quad (\sin \theta - 2)(\sin \theta - 1) = 0$$
$$\Rightarrow \quad \sin \theta - 2 = 0$$
$$\Rightarrow \quad \sin \theta = 2$$
Not possible since $-1 \le \sin \theta \le 1$
or $\quad \sin \theta - 1 = 0$
$$\Rightarrow \quad \sin \theta = 1$$
$$\Rightarrow \quad \theta = 90°. \qquad \textbf{Ans.}$$

7. Solve the following equations :

(i) $\dfrac{\cos \theta}{1 - \sin \theta} + \dfrac{\cos \theta}{1 + \sin \theta} = 4$

(ii) $\dfrac{\cos^2 \theta - 3 \cos \theta + 2}{\sin^2 \theta} = 1$.

Sol. (i) We have
$$\frac{\cos \theta}{1 - \sin \theta} + \frac{\cos \theta}{1 + \sin \theta} = 4$$

$$\Rightarrow \quad \cos \theta \left\{ \frac{1}{1 - \sin \theta} + \frac{1}{1 + \sin \theta} \right\} = 4$$
$$\Rightarrow \quad \cos \theta \left\{ \frac{1 + \sin \theta + 1 - \sin \theta}{(1 - \sin \theta)(1 + \sin \theta)} \right\} = 4$$
$$\Rightarrow \quad 2 \cos \theta = 4(1 - \sin \theta)(1 + \sin \theta)$$
$$\Rightarrow \quad 2 \cos \theta = 4(1 - \sin^2 \theta)$$
$$\Rightarrow \quad 2 \cos \theta = 4 \cos^2 \theta$$
$$\Rightarrow \quad 4 \cos^2 \theta - 2 \cos \theta = 0$$
$$\Rightarrow \quad 2 \cos \theta (2 \cos \theta - 1) = 0$$
$$\Rightarrow 2 \cos \theta = 0 \text{ or } 2 \cos \theta - 1 = 0$$
$$\Rightarrow \quad \cos \theta = 0 \text{ or } \cos \theta = \frac{1}{2}$$
$$\Rightarrow \quad \theta = 90° \text{ or } 60° \qquad \textbf{Ans.}$$

(ii) We have, $\dfrac{\cos^2 \theta - 3 \cos \theta + 2}{\sin^2 \theta} = 1$

$$\Rightarrow \quad \cos^2 \theta - 3 \cos \theta + 2 = \sin^2 \theta$$
$$\Rightarrow \quad \cos^2 \theta - 3 \cos \theta + 2 - \sin^2 \theta = 0$$
$$\Rightarrow \quad \cos^2 \theta - 3 \cos \theta + 1 + \cos^2 \theta = 0$$
$$\Rightarrow \quad 2 \cos^2 \theta - 3 \cos \theta + 1 = 0$$
$$\Rightarrow \quad 2 \cos^2 \theta - 2 \cos \theta - \cos \theta + 1 = 0$$
$$\Rightarrow \quad 2 \cos \theta (\cos \theta - 1) - 1(\cos \theta - 1) = 0$$
$$\Rightarrow \quad (\cos \theta - 1)(2 \cos \theta - 1) = 0$$
$$\Rightarrow \quad \cos \theta - 1 = 0 \text{ or } 2 \cos \theta - 1 = 0$$
$$\Rightarrow \quad \cos \theta = 1 \text{ or } \cos \theta = \frac{1}{2}$$
$$\Rightarrow \quad \theta = 0° \text{ or } \theta = 60° \textbf{ Ans.}$$

Chapter 20. Probability

Determine the Following

1. Three different coins are tossed together. Determine the probability of getting :

(i) exactly two heads.

(ii) atleast two heads.

(iii) atleast two tails.

Sol. Sample space for three coins tossed is

{HHH, HHT, HTH, THH, HTT, THT, TTH, TTT}

$$\Rightarrow \quad n(S) = 8$$

(i) Exactly two heads = {HHT, HTH, THH}

$$\Rightarrow \quad n(P_1) = 3$$

$$\therefore \quad P_1 = \frac{n(P_1)}{n(S)} = \frac{3}{8} \qquad \textbf{Ans.}$$

(ii) Atleast two heads {HHT, HTH, THH, HHH}

$$\Rightarrow \quad n(P_2) = 4$$

$$\therefore \quad P_2 = \frac{n(P_1)}{n(S)} = \frac{4}{8} = \frac{1}{2} \qquad \textbf{Ans.}$$

(iii) Atleast two tails {TTH, THT, HTT, TTT}

$$n(P_3) = 4$$

$$P_3 = \frac{n(P_3)}{n(S)} = \frac{4}{8} = \frac{1}{2} \qquad \textbf{Ans.}$$

2. Three unbiased coins are tossed together. Determine the probability of getting :

(i) atleast two heads,

(ii) atmost two heads.

Sol. Sample space

$$S = \{(H, H, H), (H, H, T), (H, T, H),$$
$$(T, H, H), (T, H, T), (T, T, H),$$
$$(T, T, T), (H, T, H)\}$$

The total number of possible outcomes = 8

(i) E_1 = atleast 2 heads

$$= \{(H, H, H), (H, H, T), (H, T, H)$$
$$(T, H, H)\}$$

$$P(E_1) = \frac{4}{8} = \frac{1}{2} \qquad \textbf{Ans.}$$

(ii) E_2 : atmost 2 heads

$$= \{(H, H, T), (H, T, H), (T, T, T)$$
$$(T, H, H), (T, H, T), (T, T, H),$$
$$(H, T, T)\}$$

$$P(E_2) = \frac{7}{8} \qquad \textbf{Ans.}$$

3. From a pack of 52 playing cards, Jacks, Queens and Kings of red colour are removed. From the remaining, a card is drawn at random. Determine the probability that drawn card is :

(i) a black king.

(ii) a card of red colour.

(iii) a card of black colour.

Sol. Total cards in pack = 52

Jacks, Queens and Kings of red colour = 6

∴ Card remaining in pack = 52 – 6 = 46

(i) Number of black kings = 2

∴ Probability of black king = $\frac{2}{46} = \frac{1}{23}$ **Ans.**

(ii) Number of red cards = 20

∴ Probability of red card = $\frac{20}{46} = \frac{10}{23}$ **Ans.**

(iii) Number of black cards = 26

∴ Probability of black card = $\frac{26}{46} = \frac{13}{23}$ **Ans.**

4. One card is drawn from a well shuffled deck of 52 cards. Determine the probability of getting

(a) Non face card,

(b) Black king or a Red queen,

(c) Spade card.

Sol. Total number of cards = 52

(a) Number of non-face cards = 52 – 12 = 40

$$P \text{ (non-face cards)} = \frac{40}{52} = \frac{10}{13} \qquad \textbf{Ans.}$$

(b) Number of black kings = 2

Number of red queens = 2

$$P \text{ (a black king or a red queen)} = \frac{4}{52} \qquad \textbf{Ans.}$$

(c) Number of spade cards = 13

$$P \text{ (Spade cards)} = \frac{13}{52} \qquad \textbf{Ans.}$$

5. All the red face cards are removed from a pack of 52 playing cards. A card is drawn at random, determine the probability that a drawn card is :

(i) red colour   **(ii)** a queen

(iii) an ace   **(iv)** a face card

Sol. Since, the red face cards are removed, number of cards = 46.

∴ **(i)** P (of red colour)

$$= \frac{20}{46} = \frac{10}{23} \qquad \textbf{Ans.}$$

(ii) $P \text{ (a queen)} = \frac{2}{46} = \frac{1}{23}$ **Ans.**

(iii) $P \text{ (an ace)} = \frac{4}{46} = \frac{2}{23}$ **Ans.**

(iv) $P \text{ (a face card)} = \frac{6}{46} = \frac{3}{23}$ **Ans.**

6. A bag contains 15 balls of which x are blue and the remaining are red. If the number of red balls increased by 5, the probability of drawing the red balls doubles. Determine :

(i) P (red ball)   **(ii)** P (blue ball)

(iii) P (blue ball is of 5 extra red balls are actually added)

Sol. According to the question,

$$\frac{20-x}{20} = 2\left(\frac{15-x}{15}\right)$$

$$\Rightarrow \qquad 1 - \frac{x}{20} = 2 - \frac{2x}{15}$$

$$\Rightarrow \qquad \frac{2x}{15} - \frac{x}{20} = 2 - 1$$

$$\Rightarrow \qquad \frac{8x - 3x}{60} = 1$$

$$\Rightarrow \qquad 5x = 60$$

$$\therefore \qquad x = 12$$

$$\therefore \qquad \text{Blue ball = 12 and red ball = 3}$$

(i) $P \text{ (red ball)} = \frac{3}{15} = \frac{1}{5}$ **Ans.**

(ii) $P \text{ (blue ball)} = \frac{12}{15} = \frac{4}{5}$ **Ans.**

(iii) P (blue ball if 5 red balls are added)

$$= \frac{12}{20} = \frac{3}{5} \qquad \textbf{Ans.}$$

7. A bag contains 20 balls out of which x balls are red :

(i) If one ball is drawn at random from the bag, find the probability that it is not red.

(ii) If 4 more red balls are out into the bag, the probability of drawing a red ball will be $\frac{5}{4}$ times the probability of drawing a red ball in the first case. Determine the value of x.

Sol. (i) P (ball not red)

$$= 1 - \frac{x}{20} \text{ or } \frac{20-x}{20} \qquad \textbf{Ans.}$$

(ii) Total number of balls = 24

red balls = $x + 4$

$$P \text{ (red ball)} = \frac{x+4}{24}$$

According to the question,

$$= \frac{x+4}{24} = \frac{5}{4} \times \frac{x}{20}$$

$$x = 8 \qquad \textbf{Ans.}$$

8. A bag contains 18 balls out of which x balls are red :

(i) If one ball is drawn at random from the bag, what is the probability that it is not red ?

(ii) If 2 more red balls are put in the bag, the probability of drawing a red ball will be $\frac{9}{8}$ times the probability of drwing a red ball in the first case. Determine the value of x.

Sol. $P \text{ (red ball)} = \frac{x}{18}$

(i) P (no red ball) $= 1 - \frac{x}{18} = \frac{18-x}{18}$ **Ans.**

(ii) Total number of balls = 18 + 2 = 20

red balls are = $x + 2$

$$P \text{ (red balls)} = \frac{x+2}{20}$$

Now, According to the question,

$$\frac{x+2}{20} = \frac{9}{8} \times \frac{x}{18}$$

$$\Rightarrow \qquad 180x = 144x + 288$$

$$\Rightarrow \qquad 36x = 288$$

$$\Rightarrow \qquad x = \frac{288}{36} = 8. \qquad \textbf{Ans.}$$

9. The probability of selecting a red ball at random from a jar that contains only red, blue and orange balls is $\frac{1}{4}$. The probability of selecting a blue ball at random from the same jar is $\frac{1}{3}$. If the jar contains 10 orange balls, determine the total number of ball in the jar.

Sol. $$P \text{ (red ball)} = \frac{1}{4}$$

$$P \text{ (blue ball)} = \frac{1}{3}$$

$$\Rightarrow \quad P \text{ (orange ball)} = 1 - \left(\frac{1}{4} + \frac{1}{3}\right) = \frac{5}{12}$$

$$\Rightarrow \quad \frac{5}{12} \times \text{(Total no. of balls)} = 10$$

$$\Rightarrow \quad \text{Total numbers of balls} = \frac{10 \times 12}{5} = 24.$$

$$\textbf{Ans.}$$

10. Cards marked with numbers 3, 4, 5..., 50 are placed in a bag and mixed thoroughly. One card is drawn at random from the bag. Determine the probability that number on the card drawn is :

(a) Divisible by 7.

(b) A perfect square.

(c) A multiple of 6.

Sol. Total number of cards = 48

Probability of an event

$$= \frac{\text{Total number of favourable outcomes}}{\text{Total number of outcomes}}$$

(a) Number of cards divisible by 7 = 7

P (cards divisible by 7)

$$= \frac{7}{48} \qquad \textbf{Ans.}$$

(b) Number of cards having a perfect square

$$= 6$$

P (cards having a perfect square)

$$= \frac{6}{48} = \frac{1}{8} \qquad \textbf{Ans.}$$

(c) Number of multiples of 6 from 3 to 50

$$= 8$$

P (multiple of 6 from 3 to 50)

$$= \frac{8}{48} = \frac{1}{6} \qquad \textbf{Ans.}$$

11. A game of chance consists of spinning an arrow on a circular board, divided into 8 equal parts, which comes to rest pointing at one of the numbers 1, 2, 3,... 8, which are equally likely outcomes. What is the probability that the arrow will piont at

(i) an odd number

(ii) a number greater than 3

(iii) a number less than 9.

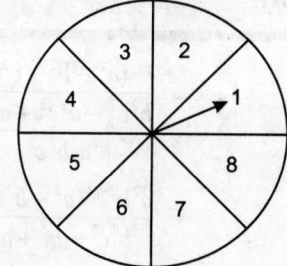

Sol. (i) Favourable outcomes are 1, 3, 5, 7, *i.e.*, 4 outcomes.

∴　P (an odd number)

$$= \frac{4}{8} \text{ or } \frac{1}{2} \qquad \textbf{Ans.}$$

(ii) Favourable outcomes are 4, 5, 6, 7, 8 *i.e.*, 5 outcomes

P (a number greater than 3)

$$= \frac{5}{8} \qquad \textbf{Ans.}$$

(iii) Favourable outcomes are 1, 2, 3, ... 8

P (a number less than 9)

$$= \frac{8}{8} = 1. \qquad \textbf{Ans.}$$

12. A box consists of 100 shirts of which 88 are good, 8 have minor defects and 4 have major defects. Ramesh, a shopkeeper will buy only those shirts which are good but 'Kewal' another shopkeeper will not buy shirts with major defects. A shirt is taken out of the box at random. Determine the probability that :

(i) Ramesh will buy the selected shirt ?

(ii) 'Kewal' will buy the selected shirt ?

Sol. (i) Number of good shirts = 88

$$P \text{ (Ramesh buys the shirt)} = \frac{88}{100} \text{ or } \frac{22}{25} \textbf{ Ans.}$$

(ii) Number of shirts without Major defect = 96

$$P \text{ (Kewal buys a shirt)} = \frac{96}{100} \text{ or } \frac{24}{25} \qquad \textbf{Ans.}$$

13. A number x is chosen from 25, 24, 23, − 2, − 1, 0, 1, 2, 3. Determine the probability that $|x| < 3$.

Sol. Favourable outcome = 5

$$[|-2|, |-1|, |0|, |1|, |2|] < 3$$

Total outcomes = 9

$$P (|x| < 3) = \frac{5}{9} \qquad \textbf{Ans.}$$

□□

Prove the Following

Chapter 6. Ratio and Proportion

1. Let $(a-x):(b-x)$ be the duplicate ratio of $a:b$ show that :

$$\frac{1}{x}=\frac{1}{a}+\frac{1}{b}.$$

Sol. Here, $(a-x):(b-x)$ is duplicate ratio of $a:b$

$$\therefore \quad \frac{a^2}{b^2}=\frac{a-x}{b-x}$$

$$\Rightarrow \quad a^2b-a^2x=b^2a-b^2x$$

$$\Rightarrow \quad a^2b-b^2a=a^2x-b^2x$$

$$\Rightarrow \quad ab(a-b)=x(a-b)(a+b)$$

$$\Rightarrow \quad ab=x(a+b)$$

$$\Rightarrow \quad \frac{1}{x}=\frac{a+b}{ab}$$

$$\Rightarrow \quad \frac{1}{x}=\frac{1}{a}+\frac{1}{b} \quad \textbf{Hence Proved.}$$

2. If $a:b$ with $a\neq b$ is the duplicate ratio of $a+c:b+c$, show that $c^2=ab$.

Sol. The duplicate ratio of

$$\frac{a}{b}=\frac{(a+c)^2}{(b+c)^2}$$

$$\Rightarrow \quad \frac{a}{b}=\frac{a^2+c^2+2ac}{b^2+c^2+2bc}$$

$$\Rightarrow \quad ab^2+ac^2+2abc=a^2b+bc^2+2abc$$

$$\Rightarrow \quad ac^2-bc^2=a^2b-ab^2$$

$$\Rightarrow \quad c^2(a-b)=ab(a-b)$$

Hence, $\quad c^2=ab.$ **Hence Proved.**

3. If b is the mean proportional between a and c, prove that $\dfrac{a^2-b^2+c^2}{a^{-2}-b^{-2}+c^{-2}}=b^4.$

Sol. Since, b is the mean proportion between a and c. So, $b^2=ac$.

$$\text{L.H.S.}=\frac{a^2-b^2+c^2}{a^{-2}-b^{-2}+c^{-2}}$$

$$=\frac{a^2-b^2+c^2}{\dfrac{1}{a^2}-\dfrac{1}{b^2}+\dfrac{1}{c^2}}$$

$$=\frac{(a^2-b^2+c^2)}{\dfrac{b^2c^2-a^2c^2+a^2b^2}{a^2b^2c^2}}$$

$$=\frac{a^2b^2c^2(a^2-b^2+c^2)}{b^2c^2-b^4+a^2b^2}$$

$$=\frac{b^4\times b^2(a^2-b^2+c^2)}{b^2(c^2-b^2+a^2)}$$

$$=b^4$$

$$=\text{R.H.S.} \quad \textbf{Hence Proved.}$$

4. Let x and y be unequal and $x:y$ be the duplicate ratio of $(x+z)$ and $(y+z)$ prove that z is mean proportional between x and y.

Sol. Since, $x:y$ is duplicate ratio of $(x+z)$ and $(y+z)$

$$\therefore \quad x:y=(x+z)^2:(y+z)^2$$

$$x(y+z)^2=y(x+z)^2$$

On simplifying, we get

$$xy^2+xz^2+2xyz=yx^2+yz^2+2xyz$$

$$\Rightarrow \quad x^2y-xy^2=xz^2-yz^2$$

$$\Rightarrow \quad xy(x-y)=z^2(x-y)$$

$$\Rightarrow \quad xy=z^2 \qquad (x\neq y)$$

$$\Rightarrow \quad x:z::z:y. \quad \textbf{Hence Proved.}$$

5. If a,b,c are in continued proportion, prove that $a:c=(a^2+b^2):(b^2+c^2)$.

Sol. a,b and c are the continued proportion

$$a:b=b:c$$

$$\Rightarrow \quad \frac{a}{b}=\frac{b}{c}$$

$$\Rightarrow \quad b^2=ac$$

Now let,

$$\Rightarrow \quad a(b^2+c^2)=c(a^2+b^2)$$

$$\therefore \quad \text{L.H.S.}=a(b^2+c^2)=a(ac+c^2)=ac(a+c)$$

$$\text{R.H.S.}=c(a^2+b^2)=c(a^2+ac)=ac(a+c)$$

$$\text{L.H.S.}=\text{R.H.S.}$$

$$\Rightarrow \quad a(b_2+c_2)=c(a_2+b_2)$$

$$\Rightarrow \quad a:c=(a_2+b_2):(b_2+c_2)$$

Hence Proved.

6. If a, b, c, d are in continued proportion, prove that

$$(b-c)^2 + (c-a)^2 + (d-b)^2 = (d-a)^2.$$

Sol. Since, a, b, c, d are in continued proportion, we have

$$\frac{a}{b} = \frac{b}{c} = \frac{c}{d} = K \text{ (say)}$$

∴ $c = dK$, $b = cK = dK^2$ and $a = bK = dK^3$.

L.H.S.

$= (b-c)^2 + (c-a)^2 + (d-b)^2$

$= (dK^2 - dK)^2 + (dK - dK^3)^2 + (d - dK^2)^2$

$= d^2K^2(K-1)^2 + d^2K^2(1-K^2)^2 + d^2(1-K^2)^2$

$= d^2[K^2(K-1)^2 + K^2(K^2-1)^2 + d^2(K^2-1)^2]$

$= d^2[K^2(K-1)^2 + K^2(K-1)^2(K+1)^2 + (K-1)^2(K+1)^2]$

$= d^2(K-1)^2[K^2 + K^2(K+1)^2 + (K+1)^2]$

$= d^2(K-1)^2[K^2 + K^2(K^2+2K+1) + K^2+2K+1]$

$= d^2(K-1)^2[K^4 + 2K^3 + 3K^2 + 2K + 1]$

$= d^2(K-1)^2(K^2+K+1)^2$

$= d^2[(K-1)(K^2+K+1)]^2$

$= d^2(K^3-1)^2 = (dK^3-d)^2 = (a-d)^2 = (d-a)^2$

$=$ R.H.S.

Hence, $(b-c)^2 + (c-a)^2 + (d-b)^2 = (d-a)^2.$

Hence Proved.

7. If q is the mean proportional between p and r, prove that

$$p^2 - q^2 + r^2 = q^4\left[\frac{1}{p^2} - \frac{1}{q^2} + \frac{1}{r^2}\right].$$

Sol. Since, q is the mean proportional of p and r.

Hence, $q^2 = pr.$

$$\text{R.H.S.} = q^4\left[\frac{1}{p^2} - \frac{1}{q^2} + \frac{1}{r^2}\right]$$

$$= q^4\left[\frac{1}{p^2} - \frac{1}{pr} + \frac{1}{r^2}\right]$$

$$= q^4\left[\frac{r^2 - pr + p^2}{p^2r^2}\right]$$

$$= q^4\left[\frac{p^2 - pr + r^2}{(pr)^2}\right]$$

$$= q^4\left[\frac{p^2 - pr + r^2}{q^4}\right]$$

$$= p^2 - pr + r^2$$

$$= p^2 - q^2 + r^2 = \text{L.H.S.}$$

Hence Proved.

8. If a, b, c, d are in continued proportion, prove that

(i) $\sqrt{ab} - \sqrt{bc} + \sqrt{cd} = \sqrt{(a-b+c)(b-c+d)}$

(ii) $(a^2 + b^2 + c^2)(b^2 + c^2 + d^2) = (ab + bc + cd)^2.$

Sol. (i) Since a, b, c, d are in continued proportion then

$$\frac{a}{b} = \frac{b}{c} = \frac{c}{d} = k$$

⇒ $a = bk$, $b = ck$, $c = dk$

⇒ $a = ck^2$

⇒ $a = dk^3$, $b = dk^2$ and $c = dk$

L.H.S. $= \sqrt{ab} - \sqrt{bc} + \sqrt{cd}$

$= \sqrt{dk^3 \cdot dk^2} - \sqrt{dk^2 \cdot dk} + \sqrt{dk \cdot d}$

$= dk^2\sqrt{k} - dk\sqrt{k} + d\sqrt{k}$

$= (k^2 - k + 1)d\sqrt{k}$

R.H.S. $= \sqrt{(a-b+c)(b-c+d)}$

$= \sqrt{(dk^3 - dk^2 + dk)(dk^2 - dk + d)}$

$= \sqrt{d \times d \times k(k^2 - k + 1)(k^2 - k + 1)}$

$= (k^2 - k + 1)d\sqrt{k}$

∴ L.H.S. = R.H.S. **Hence Proved.**

(ii) L.H.S. $= (d^2k^6 + d^2k^4 + d^2k^2)(d^2k^4 + d^2k^2 + d^2)$

$= d^2k^2(k^4 + k^2 + 1)\cdot d^2(k^4 + k^2 + 1)$

$= d^4k^2(k^4 + k^2 + 1)^2$

R.H.S. $= (ab + bc + cd)^2$

$= (dk^3 \cdot dk^2 + dk^2 \cdot dk + dk \cdot d)^2$

$= d^4k^2(k^4 + k^2 + 1)^2$

L.H.S. = R.H.S. **Hence Proved.**

9. If $\dfrac{8a-5b}{8c-5d} = \dfrac{8a+5b}{8c+5d}$, prove that

$$\frac{a}{b} = \frac{c}{d}.$$

Sol. Given, $\dfrac{8a-5b}{8c-5d} = \dfrac{8a+5b}{8c+5d}$

Applying alternendo, we get

$$\frac{8a-5b}{8a+5b} = \frac{8c-5d}{8c+5d}$$

Applying componendo and dividendo, we get

$$\frac{8a-5b+8a+5b}{8a-5b-8a-5b} = \frac{8c-5d+8c+5d}{8c-5d-8c-5d}$$

$$\Rightarrow \quad \frac{16a}{-10b} = \frac{16c}{-10d}$$

$$\therefore \quad \frac{a}{b} = \frac{c}{d} \qquad \textbf{Hence Proved.}$$

10. If $a : b = 5 : 3$, show that

$$(5a + 8b) : (6a - 7b) = 49 : 9.$$

Sol. Given $a : b = 5 : 3$

$$\Rightarrow \quad \frac{a}{b} = \frac{5}{3}$$

$$\therefore \quad \frac{5a + 8b}{6a - 7b} = \frac{5\left(\dfrac{a}{b}\right) + 8}{6\left(\dfrac{a}{b}\right) - 7}$$

[Numerator and denominator are divided by 'b']

$$= \frac{5 \times \dfrac{5}{3} + 8}{6 \times \dfrac{5}{3} - 7} = \frac{49}{9} = 49 : 9. \qquad \textbf{Hence Proved.}$$

11. If $\dfrac{a}{b} = \dfrac{c}{d}$, show that

$$(9a + 13b)(9c - 13d) = (9c + 13b)(9a - 13d).$$

Sol. We have $\dfrac{a}{b} = \dfrac{c}{d}$

$$\frac{9a}{13b} = \frac{9c}{13d}$$

$$\left[\text{Multiplying both sides by } \frac{9}{13}\right]$$

By componendo and dividendo, we get

$$\frac{9a + 13b}{9a - 13b} = \frac{9c + 13d}{9c - 13d}$$

$$\Rightarrow (9a + 13b)(9c - 13d) = (9a - 13b)(9c + 13d).$$

(By cross multiplication)

Hence Proved.

12. If $\dfrac{p}{q} = \dfrac{r}{s}$, prove that

$$\frac{2p + 3q}{2p - 3q} = \frac{2r + 3s}{2r - 3s}.$$

Sol. We have

$$\frac{p}{q} = \frac{r}{s}$$

$$\frac{2p}{3q} = \frac{2r}{3s}$$

[Multiplying both sides by 2/3]

By componendo and dividendo, we get

$$\therefore \quad \frac{2p + 3q}{2p - 3q} = \frac{2r + 3s}{2r - 3s}. \qquad \textbf{Hence Proved.}$$

13. Show that a, b, c, d are in proportion if :

(i) $(6a + 7b) : (6c + 7d) :: (6a - 7b) : (6c - 7d)$

(ii) $(a + b + c + d)(a - b - c + d)$
$$= (a + b - c - d)(a - b + c - d).$$

Sol. (i) $\quad \dfrac{a}{b} = \dfrac{c}{d}$

$$\Rightarrow \quad \frac{6a}{7b} = \frac{6c}{7d}$$

$$\left(\text{Both sides are multiplied by } \frac{6}{7}\right)$$

Applying componendo and dividendo, we get

$$\frac{6a + 7b}{6a - 7b} = \frac{6c + 7d}{6c - 7d}$$

Applying alternendo, we get

$$\frac{6a + 7b}{6c + 7b} = \frac{6a - 7b}{6c - 7d}$$

$(6a + 7b) : (6c + 7d) :: (6a - 7b) : (6c - 7d).$

Hence, a, b, c, d are in proportion if

$(6a + 7b) : (6c + 7d) :: (6a - 7b) : (6c - 7d)$

Hence Proved.

(ii) We have

$$\frac{a}{b} = \frac{c}{d}$$

Applying componendo and dividendo, we get

$$\frac{a + b}{a - b} = \frac{c + d}{c - d}$$

Applying alternendo, we get

$$\frac{a + b}{c + d} = \frac{a - b}{c - d}$$

Again, applying componendo and dividendo, we get

$$\frac{a + b + c + d}{a + b - c - d} = \frac{a - b + c - d}{a - b - c + d}$$

$$\Rightarrow \quad (a + b + c + d)(a - b - c + d)$$
$$= (a + b - c - d)(a - b + c - d).$$

Hence, a, b, c, d are in proportion if

$(a + b + c + d)(a - b - c + d)$
$$= (a + b - c - d)(a - b + c - d).$$

Hence Proved.

14. If $y = \dfrac{\sqrt{a + 3b} + \sqrt{a - 3b}}{\sqrt{a + 3b} - \sqrt{a - 3b}}$, show that

$$3by^2 - 2ay + 3b = 0.$$

Sol. We have

$$\frac{y}{1} = \frac{\sqrt{a+3b} + \sqrt{a-3b}}{\sqrt{a+3b} - \sqrt{a-3b}}$$

Applying componendo and dividendo, we get

$$\frac{y+1}{y-1} = \frac{\sqrt{a+3b} + \sqrt{a-3b} + \sqrt{a+3b} - \sqrt{a-3b}}{\sqrt{a+3b} + \sqrt{a-3b} - \sqrt{a+3b} + \sqrt{a-3b}}$$

$$\Rightarrow \quad \frac{y+1}{y-1} = \frac{2\sqrt{a+3b}}{2\sqrt{a-3b}}$$

Squaring both sides,

$$\frac{(y+1)^2}{(y-1)^2} = \frac{a+3b}{a-3b}$$

$$\Rightarrow \quad \frac{y^2 + 1 + 2y}{y^2 + 1 - 2y} = \frac{a+3b}{a-3b}$$

Again, applying componendo and dividendo, we get

$$\frac{y^2 + 1 + 2y + y^2 + 1 - 2y}{y^2 + 1 + 2y - y^2 - 1 + 2y} = \frac{a + 3b + a - 3b}{a + 3b - a + 3b}$$

$$\Rightarrow \quad \frac{2(y^2 + 1)}{4y} = \frac{2a}{6b}$$

$$\Rightarrow \quad 3by^2 + 3b = 2ay$$

$$\Rightarrow \quad 3by^2 - 2ay + 3b = 0. \qquad \textbf{Hence Proved.}$$

15. If $y = \dfrac{(p+1)^{1/3} + (p-1)^{1/3}}{(p+1)^{1/3} - (p-1)^{1/3}}$, show that

$$y^3 - 3py^2 + 3y - p = 0.$$

Sol. We have

$$\frac{y}{1} = \frac{(p+1)^{1/3} + (p-1)^{1/3}}{(p+1)^{1/3} - (p-1)^{1/3}}$$

Applying componendo and dividendo, we get

$$\frac{y+1}{y-1} = \frac{(p+1)^{1/3} + (p-1)^{1/3} + (p+1)^{1/3} - (p-1)^{1/3}}{(p+1)^{1/3} + (p-1)^{1/3} - (p+1)^{1/3} + (p-1)^{1/3}}$$

$$\Rightarrow \quad \frac{y+1}{y-1} = \frac{2(p+1)^{1/3}}{2(p-1)^{1/3}}$$

Cubing both sides,

$$\frac{(y+1)^3}{(y-1)^3} = \frac{p+1}{p-1}$$

$$\Rightarrow \quad \frac{y^3 + 1 + 3y^2 + 3y}{y^3 - 1 - 3y^2 + 3y} = \frac{p+1}{p-1}$$

Again, applying componendo and dividendo, we get

$$\frac{y^3 + 1 + 3y^2 + 3y + y^3 - 1 - 3y^2 + 3y}{y^3 + 1 + 3y^2 + 3y - y^3 + 1 + 3y^2 - 3y} = \frac{p+1+p-1}{p+1-p+1}$$

$$\Rightarrow \quad \frac{2y^3 + 6y}{6y^2 + 2} = \frac{2p}{2}$$

$$\Rightarrow \quad \frac{2(y^3 + 3y)}{2(3y^2 + 1)} = p$$

$$\Rightarrow \quad y^3 + 3y = 3py^2 + p$$

$$\Rightarrow \quad y^3 - 3py^2 + 3y - p = 0. \qquad \textbf{Hence Proved.}$$

16. If $x = \dfrac{\sqrt{2a+1} + \sqrt{2a-1}}{\sqrt{2a+1} - \sqrt{2a-1}}$, prove that $x^2 - 4ax + 1 = 0$*

Sol. Given : $\qquad x = \dfrac{\sqrt{2a+1} + \sqrt{2a-1}}{\sqrt{2a+1} - \sqrt{2a-1}}$

Using componendo and dividendo,

$$\frac{x+1}{x-1} = \frac{\sqrt{2a+1} + \sqrt{2a-1} + \sqrt{2a+1} - \sqrt{2a-1}}{\sqrt{2a+1} + \sqrt{2a-1} - \sqrt{2a+1} + \sqrt{2a-1}}$$

$$\Rightarrow \quad \frac{x+1}{x-1} = \frac{2\sqrt{2a+1}}{2\sqrt{2a-1}}$$

$$\Rightarrow \quad \left(\frac{x+1}{x-1}\right)^2 = \left(\frac{\sqrt{2a+1}}{\sqrt{2a-1}}\right)^2$$

[Squaring on both sides]

$$\Rightarrow \quad \frac{x^2 + 1 + 2x}{x^2 + 1 - 2x} = \frac{2a+1}{2a-1}$$

Again, using componendo and dividendo,

$$\frac{x^2 + 1 + 2x + x^2 + 1 - 2x}{x^2 + 1 + 2x - x^2 - 1 + 2x} = \frac{2a + 1 + 2a - 1}{2a + 1 - 2a + 1}$$

$$\Rightarrow \quad \frac{2(x^2 + 1)}{4x} = \frac{4a}{2}$$

$$\Rightarrow \quad \frac{x^2 + 1}{2x} = 2a$$

$$\Rightarrow \quad x^2 + 1 = 4ax$$

$$\Rightarrow \quad x^2 - 4ax + 1 = 0 \qquad \textbf{Hence Proved.}$$

17. Given : $x = \dfrac{\sqrt{a^2 + b^2} + \sqrt{a^2 - b^2}}{\sqrt{a^2 + b^2} - \sqrt{a^2 - b^2}}$

Use componendo and dividendo to prove that

$$b^2 = \frac{2a^2 x}{x^2 + 1}.$$

Sol. Given, $\qquad x = \dfrac{\sqrt{a^2 + b^2} + \sqrt{a^2 - b^2}}{\sqrt{a^2 + b^2} - \sqrt{a^2 - b^2}}$

By componendo and dividendo, we get

$$\frac{x+1}{x-1} = \frac{2\sqrt{a^2+b^2}}{2\sqrt{a^2-b^2}}$$

Squaring both sides,

$$\frac{x^2+2x+1}{x^2-2x+1} = \frac{a^2+b^2}{a^2-b^2}$$

By componendo and dividendo, we get

$$\frac{2(x^2+1)}{4x} = \frac{2a^2}{2b^2}$$

$$\Rightarrow \quad \frac{x^2+1}{2x} = \frac{a^2}{b^2}$$

$$\Rightarrow \quad b^2 = \frac{2a^2 x}{x^2+1}. \quad \textbf{Hence Proved.}$$

18. If $\dfrac{by+cz}{b^2+c^2} = \dfrac{cz+ax}{c^2+a^2} = \dfrac{ax+by}{a^2+b^2}$ then show that

each ratio is equal to $\dfrac{x}{a} = \dfrac{y}{b} = \dfrac{z}{c}$.

Sol. Each of the given ratio

$$= \frac{(by+cz)+(cz+ax)+(ax+by)}{(b^2+c^2)+(c^2+a^2)+(a^2+b^2)}$$

$$= \frac{ax+by+cz}{a^2+b^2+c^2}$$

Now, $\dfrac{by+cz}{b^2+c^2} = \dfrac{ax+by+cz}{a^2+b^2+c^2}$

$$\Rightarrow \quad \frac{a^2+b^2+c^2}{b^2+c^2} = \frac{ax+by+cz}{by+cz}$$

$$\Rightarrow \quad \frac{a^2}{b^2+c^2} + \frac{b^2+c^2}{b^2+c^2} = \frac{ax}{by+cz} + \frac{by+cz}{by+cz}$$

$$\Rightarrow \quad \frac{a^2}{b^2+c^2} = \frac{ax}{by+cz} \quad \text{(App. dividendo)}$$

$$\Rightarrow \quad \frac{b^2+c^2}{a^2} = \frac{by+cz}{ax} \quad \text{(App. invertendo)}$$

$$\Rightarrow \quad \frac{a^2+b^2+c^2}{a^2} = \frac{ax+by+cz}{ax}$$

$$\text{(by componendo)}$$

$$\Rightarrow \quad \frac{x}{a} = \frac{ax+by+cz}{a^2+b^2+c^2}$$

$$\therefore \quad \frac{x}{a} = \frac{y}{b} = \frac{z}{c} = \frac{ax+by+cz}{a^2+b^2+c^2}$$

$$\textbf{Hence Proved.}$$

19. If $\dfrac{a}{b} = \dfrac{c}{d} = \dfrac{e}{f}$, prove that each of these ratios is

equal to $\dfrac{a+c+e}{b+d+f}$.

Sol. Let $\dfrac{a}{b} = \dfrac{c}{d} = \dfrac{e}{f} = k$, then

$$a = bk, \ c = dk \text{ and } e = fk.$$

Now, $\dfrac{a+c+e}{b+d+f} = \dfrac{bk+dk+fk}{b+d+f}$

$$= \frac{k(b+d+f)}{(b+d+f)} = k$$

Hence, $\dfrac{a}{b} = \dfrac{c}{d} = \dfrac{e}{f} = \dfrac{a+c+e}{b+d+f}$.

$$\textbf{Hence Proved.}$$

20. If $ax = by = cz$, prove that

$$\frac{x^2}{yz} + \frac{y^2}{zx} + \frac{z^2}{xy} = \frac{bc}{a^2} + \frac{ca}{b^2} + \frac{ab}{c^2}.$$

Sol. Let $ax = by = cz = k$, then

$$x = \frac{k}{a}, \ y = \frac{k}{b} \text{ and } z = \frac{k}{c}$$

$$\text{L.H.S.} = \frac{x^2}{yz} + \frac{y^2}{zx} + \frac{z^2}{xy}$$

$$= \frac{k^2}{a^2 \times \dfrac{k}{b} \times \dfrac{k}{c}} + \frac{k^2}{b^2 \times \dfrac{k}{c} \times \dfrac{k}{a}} + \frac{k^2}{c^2 \times \dfrac{k}{a} \times \dfrac{k}{b}}$$

$$= \frac{bc}{a^2} + \frac{ca}{b^2} + \frac{ab}{c^2}$$

$$= \text{R.H.S.} \quad \textbf{Hence Proved.}$$

21. If $\dfrac{x}{b+c-a} = \dfrac{y}{c+a-b} = \dfrac{z}{a+b-c}$, then show that

$(b-c)x + (c-a)y + (a-b)z = 0$.

Sol. Let

$$\frac{x}{b+c-a} = \frac{y}{c+a-b} = \frac{z}{a+b-c} = k$$

$$x = (b+c-a)\,k,$$
$$y = (c+a-b)\,k,$$
$$z = (a+b-c)\,k$$

$(b-c)x + (c-a)y + (a-b)z = (b-c)(b+c-a)\,k$

$$+ (c-a)(c+a-b)\,k + (a-b)(a+b-c)\,k$$

$\Rightarrow k\,(b^2 + bc - ab - bc - c^2 + ca + c^2 + ca - bc - ac -$
$$a^2 + ab + a^2 + ab - ac - ab - b^2 + bc) = 0.$$

$$\textbf{Hence Proved.}$$

22. If $p + r = 2q$ and $\dfrac{1}{q} + \dfrac{1}{s} = \dfrac{2}{r}$, then prove that $p : q$

$= r : s$.

Sol. Given $\dfrac{1}{q} + \dfrac{1}{s} = \dfrac{2}{r}$

$\Rightarrow \qquad \dfrac{s+q}{qs} = \dfrac{2}{r}$

$\Rightarrow \qquad 2qs = r(s+q)$

$\Rightarrow \qquad (p+r)s = r(s+q)$

$\Rightarrow \qquad ps + rs = rs + rq$

$\Rightarrow \qquad ps = rq$

$\Rightarrow \qquad \dfrac{p}{q} = \dfrac{r}{s}.$ **Hence Proved.**

23. If $\dfrac{a}{b} = \dfrac{c}{d}$, show that

$a + b : c + d = \sqrt{a^2 + b^2} : \sqrt{c^2 + d^2}$.

Sol. Let $\dfrac{a}{b} = \dfrac{c}{d} = k$

$\Rightarrow \qquad a = bk$ and $c = dk$

L.H.S. $= \dfrac{a+b}{c+d} = \dfrac{bk+b}{dk+d}$

$= \dfrac{b(k+1)}{d(k+1)} = \dfrac{b}{d}$

R.H.S. $= \dfrac{\sqrt{a^2+b^2}}{\sqrt{c^2+d^2}} = \dfrac{\sqrt{b^2k^2+b^2}}{\sqrt{d^2k^2+d^2}}$

$= \dfrac{b(\sqrt{k^2+1})}{d(\sqrt{k^2+1})} = \dfrac{b}{d}$

L.H.S. = R.H.S. **Hence Proved.**

24. If $a : b = c : d$, show that

$(a-c)b^2 : (b-d)cd = (a^2 - b^2 - ab) : (c^2 - d^2 - cd)$.

Sol. Let $\dfrac{a}{b} = \dfrac{c}{d} = k$

$\Rightarrow \qquad a = bk$ and $c = dk$

L.H.S. $= \dfrac{(a-c)b^2}{(b-d)cd} = \dfrac{(bk-dk)b^2}{(b-d)dk.d}$

$= \dfrac{b^2.k(b-d)}{d^2k(b-d)} = \dfrac{b^2}{d^2}.$

R.H.S. $= \dfrac{a^2 - b^2 - ab}{c^2 - d^2 - cd}$

$= \dfrac{b^2k^2 - b^2 - bk.b}{d^2k^2 - d^2 - dk.d}$

$= \dfrac{b^2(k^2-k-1)}{d^2(k^2-k-1)}$

$= \dfrac{b^2}{d^2}$

L.H.S. = R.H.S. **Hence Proved.**

25. If $\dfrac{a}{b} = \dfrac{c}{d} = \dfrac{e}{f}$, prove that

$(ab + cd + ef)^2 = (a^2 + c^2 + e^2)(b^2 + d^2 + f^2)$.

Sol. Let $\dfrac{a}{b} = \dfrac{c}{d} = \dfrac{e}{f} = k$, then

$a = bk, c = dk$ and $e = fk$

L.H.S. $= (ab + cd + ef)^2$

$= (bk.b + dk.d + fk.f)^2$

$= k^2(b^2 + d^2 + f^2)^2$

R.H.S. $= (a^2 + c^2 + e^2)(b^2 + d^2 + f^2)$

$= (b^2k^2 + d^2k^2 + f^2k^2)(b^2 + d^2 + f^2)$

$= k^2(b^2 + d^2 + f^2)(b^2 + d^2 + f^2)$

$= k^2(b^2 + d^2 + f^2)^2$

L.H.S. = R.H.S. **Hence Proved.**

26. If $\dfrac{a}{b} = \dfrac{c}{d} = \dfrac{e}{f}$, prove that

$\left(\dfrac{a^2b^2 + c^2d^2 + e^2f^2}{ab^3 + cd^3 + ef^3}\right)^{3/2} = \sqrt{\dfrac{ace}{bdf}}$

Sol. Let $\dfrac{a}{b} = \dfrac{c}{d} = \dfrac{e}{f} = k$

$\therefore \qquad a = bk, c = dk, e = fk$

L.H.S. $= \left(\dfrac{a^2b^2 + c^2d^2 + e^2f^2}{ab^3 + cd^3 + ef^3}\right)^{3/2}$

$= \left(\dfrac{b^2k^2.b^2 + d^2k^2.d^2 + f^2k^2.f^2}{bk.b^3 + dk.d^3 + fk.f^3}\right)^{3/2}$

$= \left[\dfrac{k^2(b^4 + d^4 + f^4)}{k(b^4 + d^4 + f^4)}\right]^{3/2}$

$= k^{3/2}$

R.H.S. $= \sqrt{\dfrac{ace}{bdf}} = \sqrt{\dfrac{bk.dk.fk}{bdf}} = k^{3/2}$

$\therefore \qquad$ L.H.S. = R.H.S. **Hence Proved.**

27. If $\dfrac{x}{a} = \dfrac{y}{b} = \dfrac{z}{c}$, show that

$\dfrac{x^3}{a^3} = \dfrac{y^3}{b^3} + \dfrac{z^3}{c^3} = \dfrac{xyz}{abc}.$

Sol Let $\dfrac{x}{a} = \dfrac{y}{b} = \dfrac{z}{c} = k$

$$x = ak, \; y = bk, \; z = ck$$

L.H.S. $= \dfrac{x^3}{a^3} - \dfrac{y^3}{b^3} + \dfrac{z^3}{c^3} = \dfrac{a^3 k^3}{a^3} - \dfrac{b^3 k^3}{b^3} + \dfrac{c^3 k^3}{c^3}$

$$= k^3 - k^3 + k^3 = k^3$$

R.H.S. $= \dfrac{xyz}{abc} = \dfrac{ak \cdot bk \cdot ck}{abc} = \dfrac{k^3 abc}{abc} = k^3$

$\therefore$ L.H.S. = R.H.S. **Hence Proved.**

28. If $\dfrac{x}{a} = \dfrac{y}{b} = \dfrac{z}{c}$, prove that

$$\dfrac{x^3}{a^2} + \dfrac{y^3}{b^2} + \dfrac{z^3}{c^2} = \dfrac{(x+y+z)^3}{(a+b+c)^2}.$$

Sol. Let $\dfrac{x}{a} = \dfrac{y}{b} = \dfrac{z}{c} = k$,   [By k method]

$$x = ak, \; y = bk \text{ and } z = ck.$$

L.H.S. $= \dfrac{a^3 k^3}{a^2} + \dfrac{b^3 k^3}{b^2} + \dfrac{c^3 k^3}{c^2} = k^3 [a+b+c]$

R.H.S. $= \dfrac{\big[ak + bk + ck\big]^3}{[a+b+c]^2} = \dfrac{k^3 \big[a+b+c\big]^3}{[a+b+c]^2}$

$= k^3 (a+b+c)$

$\therefore$ L.H.S. = R.H.S.

Hence Proved.

29. If $a = \dfrac{b+c}{2}, c = \dfrac{a+b}{2}$ and b is mean proportional between a and c, prove that

$$\dfrac{1}{a} + \dfrac{1}{c} = \dfrac{2}{b}.$$

Sol. b is the mean proportional of a and c,

$\therefore$ $b^2 = ac$

$\Rightarrow$ $b^2 = \left(\dfrac{b+c}{2}\right) \cdot \left(\dfrac{a+b}{2}\right)$

$\Rightarrow$ $4b^2 = ab + ac + b^2 + bc$

$\Rightarrow$ $4b^2 = ab + 2b^2 + bc$ $[\because b^2 = ac]$

$\Rightarrow$ $2b^2 = ab + bc$

$\Rightarrow$ $\dfrac{2b^2}{abc} = \dfrac{ab}{abc} + \dfrac{bc}{abc}$

[Dividing both sides by abc]

$\Rightarrow$ $\dfrac{2}{b} = \dfrac{1}{c} + \dfrac{1}{a}$ $[\because b^2 = ac]$

Hence Proved.

Chapter 7. Factorization

1. Show that $x^2 - 9$ is a factor of

$$x^3 + 5x^2 - 9x - 45.$$

Sol. We know that

$$x^2 - 9 = (x+3)(x-3)$$

$x^2 - 9$ will be a factor of

$$f(x) = x^3 + 5x^2 - 9x - 45$$

Only when both $(x+3)$ and $(x-3)$ are factors of this polynomial.

Now, $f(-3) = (-3)^3 + 5(-3)^2 - 9(-3) - 45$

$$= -27 + 45 + 27 - 45 = 0$$

and $f(3) = (3)^3 + 5(3)^2 - 9(3) - 45$

$$= 27 + 45 - 27 - 45 = 0$$

So, both $x + 3$ and $x - 3$ are factors of

$$x^3 + 5x^2 - 9x - 45.$$

Hence, $x^2 - 9$ is a factor of the given polynomial.   **Hence Proved.**

2. Using the factor theorem, show that $(x - 2)$ is a factor of $x^3 + x^2 - 4x - 4$. Hence factorise the polynomial completely.*

Sol. Let $f(x) = x^3 + x^2 - 4x - 4$

If $(x - 2)$ is a factor of $f(x)$, then

$$f(2) = 0$$

Now, $f(2) = 2^3 + 2^2 - 4 \times 2 - 4$

$$= 8 + 4 - 8 - 4$$

$$= 0$$

$\therefore (x - 2)$ is a factor of $f(x)$.

$$\begin{array}{r} x^2 + 3x + 2 \\ x-2\overline{)x^3 + x^2 - 4x - 4(} \\ x^3 - 2x^2 \\ \underline{- +} \\ 3x^2 - 4x \\ 3x^2 + 6x \\ \underline{- +} \\ 2x - 4 \\ 2x - 4 \\ \underline{- +} \\ \times \end{array}$$

Now, $x^2 + 3x + 2 = x^2 + 2x + x + 2$

$$= x(x+2) + 1(x+2)$$

$$= (x+2)(x+1)$$

$\therefore$ $f(x) = (x+1)(x+2)(x-2)$ **Ans.**

3. Show that $2x + 7$ is a factor of $2x^3 + 5x^2 - 11x - 14$. Hence, factorize the given expression completely, using the factor theorem.

* Frequently asked previous years Board Exam Questions.

Prove the Following

Sol. If $2x + 7$ is a factor of $2x^3 + 5x^2 - 11x - 14$

then on putting $2x + 7 = 0$

$$x = -7/2$$

$$f(-7/2)$$

$$= 2\left(-\frac{7}{2}\right)^3 + 5\left(-\frac{7}{2}\right)^2 - 11\left(-\frac{7}{2}\right) - 14$$

$$= \frac{-343}{4} + \frac{245}{4} + \frac{77}{2} - 14$$

$$= \frac{-399}{4} + \frac{245 + 154}{4}$$

$$= \frac{-399 + 399}{4} = 0$$

Hence, $2x + 7$ is one factor.

Now, $2x^3 + 5x^2 - 11x - 14$

$$= x^2(2x + 7) - x(2x + 7) - 2(2x + 7)$$

$$= (2x + 7)(x^2 - x - 2)$$

$$= (2x + 7)(x^2 + x - 2x - 2)$$

$$= (2x + 7)[x(x + 1) - 2(x + 1)]$$

$$= (2x + 7)(x - 2)(x + 1) \textbf{ Hence Proved.}$$

4. Using factor theorem, show that $(x - 3)$ is a factor of $x^3 - 7x^2 + 15x - 9$. Hence, factorise the given expression completely.

Sol. Let $p(x) = x^3 - 7x^2 + 15x - 9$

For checking that $(x - 3)$ is a factor of $p(x)$, we find $p(3)$.

$$p(3) = (3)^3 - 7(3)^2 + 15(3) - 9$$

$$= 27 - 63 + 45 - 9$$

$$= 72 - 72$$

$$= 0.$$

Hence, $(x - 3)$ is a factor of $p(x)$.

By division of $p(x)$ by $x - 3$, we get the quotient

$$= x^2 - 4x + 3.$$

$$\therefore \quad x^3 - 7x^2 + 15x - 9 = (x - 3)(x^2 - 4x + 3)$$

$$= (x - 3)(x - 3)(x - 1)$$

$$= (x - 3)^2(x - 1). \textbf{Hence Proved.}$$

Chapter 8. Matrices

1. If $A = \begin{bmatrix} a & b \\ c & d \end{bmatrix}$ and $I = \begin{bmatrix} 1 & 0 \\ 0 & 1 \end{bmatrix}$, show that

$A_2 - (a + d)A = (bc - ad)I$.

Sol. Here, $A^2 - (a + d)A$

$$= \begin{bmatrix} a & b \\ c & d \end{bmatrix}\begin{bmatrix} a & b \\ c & d \end{bmatrix} - (a + d)\begin{bmatrix} a & b \\ c & d \end{bmatrix}$$

$$= \begin{bmatrix} a^2 + bc & ab + bd \\ ac + dc & cb + d^2 \end{bmatrix} - \begin{bmatrix} a^2 + ad & ab + bd \\ ac + dc & ad + d^2 \end{bmatrix}$$

$$= \begin{bmatrix} bc - ad & 0 \\ 0 & bc - ad \end{bmatrix} = (bc - ad)\begin{bmatrix} 1 & 0 \\ 0 & 1 \end{bmatrix}$$

$$= (bc - ad)I. \qquad \textbf{Hence Proved.}$$

2. If $A = \begin{bmatrix} 1 & 2 \\ -2 & 3 \end{bmatrix}$, $B = \begin{bmatrix} 2 & 1 \\ 2 & 3 \end{bmatrix}$ and $C = \begin{bmatrix} -3 & 1 \\ 2 & 0 \end{bmatrix}$

verify that

(i) $(AB)C = A(BC)$

(ii) $A(B + C) = AB + AC$.

Sol. (i)

$$AB = \begin{bmatrix} 1 & 2 \\ -2 & 3 \end{bmatrix}\begin{bmatrix} 2 & 1 \\ 2 & 3 \end{bmatrix}$$

$$= \begin{bmatrix} 2 + 4 & 1 + 6 \\ -4 + 6 & -2 + 9 \end{bmatrix} = \begin{bmatrix} 6 & 7 \\ 2 & 7 \end{bmatrix}$$

$$(AB)C = \begin{bmatrix} 6 & 7 \\ 2 & 7 \end{bmatrix}\begin{bmatrix} -3 & 1 \\ 2 & 0 \end{bmatrix}$$

$$= \begin{bmatrix} -18 + 14 & 6 + 0 \\ -6 + 14 & 2 + 0 \end{bmatrix} = \begin{bmatrix} -4 & 6 \\ 8 & 2 \end{bmatrix}$$

Now, $\quad BC = \begin{bmatrix} 2 & 1 \\ 2 & 3 \end{bmatrix}\begin{bmatrix} -3 & 1 \\ 2 & 0 \end{bmatrix}$

$$= \begin{bmatrix} -6 + 2 & 2 + 0 \\ -6 + 6 & 2 + 0 \end{bmatrix} = \begin{bmatrix} -4 & 2 \\ 0 & 2 \end{bmatrix}$$

$$A(BC) = \begin{bmatrix} 1 & 2 \\ -2 & 3 \end{bmatrix}\begin{bmatrix} -4 & 2 \\ 0 & 2 \end{bmatrix}$$

$$= \begin{bmatrix} -4 + 0 & 2 + 4 \\ 8 + 0 & -4 + 6 \end{bmatrix} = \begin{bmatrix} -4 & 6 \\ 8 & 2 \end{bmatrix}$$

Hence, $(AB)C = A(BC)$. **Hence Proved.**

(ii) $\quad B + C = \begin{bmatrix} 2 & 1 \\ 2 & 3 \end{bmatrix} + \begin{bmatrix} -3 & 1 \\ 2 & 0 \end{bmatrix}$

$$= \begin{bmatrix} 2 - 3 & 1 + 1 \\ 2 + 2 & 3 + 0 \end{bmatrix} = \begin{bmatrix} -1 & 2 \\ 4 & 3 \end{bmatrix}$$

$$A(B + C) = \begin{bmatrix} 1 & 2 \\ -2 & 3 \end{bmatrix}\begin{bmatrix} -1 & 2 \\ 4 & 3 \end{bmatrix}$$

$$= \begin{bmatrix} -1+8 & 2+6 \\ 2+12 & -4+9 \end{bmatrix} = \begin{bmatrix} 7 & 8 \\ 14 & 5 \end{bmatrix}$$

Now, $AB = \begin{bmatrix} 6 & 7 \\ 2 & 7 \end{bmatrix}$

$$AC = \begin{bmatrix} 1 & 2 \\ -2 & 3 \end{bmatrix}\begin{bmatrix} -3 & 1 \\ 2 & 0 \end{bmatrix}$$

$$= \begin{bmatrix} -3+4 & 1+0 \\ 6+6 & -2+0 \end{bmatrix} = \begin{bmatrix} 1 & 1 \\ 12 & -2 \end{bmatrix}$$

$$AB + AC = \begin{bmatrix} 6 & 7 \\ 2 & 7 \end{bmatrix} + \begin{bmatrix} 1 & 1 \\ 12 & -2 \end{bmatrix}$$

$$= \begin{bmatrix} 6+1 & 7+1 \\ 2+12 & 7-2 \end{bmatrix}$$

$$\therefore \quad AB + AC = \begin{bmatrix} 7 & 8 \\ 14 & 5 \end{bmatrix}$$

Hence, $A(B + C) = AB + AC$. **Hence Proved.**

3. If $A = \begin{bmatrix} 3 & 1 \\ 2 & 1 \end{bmatrix}$ and $B = \begin{bmatrix} 1 & -2 \\ 5 & 3 \end{bmatrix}$, then show that

$(A - B)^2 \neq A^2 - 2AB + B^2$.

Sol. $A - B = \begin{bmatrix} 3 & 1 \\ 2 & 1 \end{bmatrix} - \begin{bmatrix} 1 & -2 \\ 5 & 3 \end{bmatrix}$

$$= \begin{bmatrix} 3-1 & 1+2 \\ 2-5 & 1-3 \end{bmatrix} = \begin{bmatrix} 2 & 3 \\ -3 & -2 \end{bmatrix}$$

$$(A - B)^2 = (A - B)(A - B)$$

$$\Rightarrow \quad (A - B)^2 = \begin{bmatrix} 2 & 3 \\ -3 & -2 \end{bmatrix}\begin{bmatrix} 2 & 3 \\ -3 & -2 \end{bmatrix}$$

$$= \begin{bmatrix} 4-9 & 6-6 \\ -6+6 & -9+4 \end{bmatrix}$$

$$= \begin{bmatrix} -5 & 0 \\ 0 & -5 \end{bmatrix}$$

and $A^2 = \begin{bmatrix} 3 & 1 \\ 2 & 1 \end{bmatrix}\begin{bmatrix} 3 & 1 \\ 2 & 1 \end{bmatrix}$

$$= \begin{bmatrix} 9+2 & 3+1 \\ 6+2 & 2+1 \end{bmatrix} = \begin{bmatrix} 11 & 4 \\ 8 & 3 \end{bmatrix}$$

and $B^2 = \begin{bmatrix} 1 & -2 \\ 5 & 3 \end{bmatrix}\begin{bmatrix} 1 & -2 \\ 5 & 3 \end{bmatrix}$

$$= \begin{bmatrix} 1-10 & -2-6 \\ 5+15 & -10+9 \end{bmatrix}$$

$$= \begin{bmatrix} -9 & -8 \\ 20 & -1 \end{bmatrix}$$

and $AB = \begin{bmatrix} 3 & 1 \\ 2 & 1 \end{bmatrix}\begin{bmatrix} 1 & -2 \\ 5 & 3 \end{bmatrix}$

$$= \begin{bmatrix} 3+5 & -6+3 \\ 2+5 & -4+3 \end{bmatrix} = \begin{bmatrix} 8 & -3 \\ 7 & -1 \end{bmatrix}$$

Now, $A^2 - 2AB + B^2$

$$= \begin{bmatrix} 11 & 4 \\ 8 & 3 \end{bmatrix} - 2\begin{bmatrix} 8 & -3 \\ 7 & -1 \end{bmatrix} + \begin{bmatrix} -9 & -8 \\ 20 & -1 \end{bmatrix}$$

$$= \begin{bmatrix} 11 & 4 \\ 8 & 3 \end{bmatrix} - \begin{bmatrix} 16 & -6 \\ 14 & -2 \end{bmatrix} + \begin{bmatrix} -9 & -8 \\ 20 & -1 \end{bmatrix}$$

$$= \begin{bmatrix} 11-16-9 & 4+6-8 \\ 8-14+20 & 3+2-1 \end{bmatrix}$$

$$= \begin{bmatrix} -14 & 2 \\ 14 & 4 \end{bmatrix}$$

Hence, from above calculations, we get

$(A - B)^2 \neq A^2 - 2AB + B^2$. **Hence Proved.**

4. $A = \begin{bmatrix} 3 & 1 \\ -1 & 2 \end{bmatrix}$, show that

$$A^2 - 5A + 7I_2 = 0.$$

Sol. We have

$$A = \begin{bmatrix} 3 & 1 \\ -1 & 2 \end{bmatrix}$$

$$A^2 = \begin{bmatrix} 3 & 1 \\ -1 & 2 \end{bmatrix}\begin{bmatrix} 3 & 1 \\ -1 & 2 \end{bmatrix}$$

$$= \begin{bmatrix} 9-1 & 3+2 \\ -3-2 & -1+4 \end{bmatrix}$$

$$= \begin{bmatrix} 8 & 5 \\ -5 & 3 \end{bmatrix}$$

$$-5A = \begin{bmatrix} (-5)\cdot 3 & (-5)\cdot 1 \\ (-5)\cdot(-1) & (-5)\cdot 2 \end{bmatrix}$$

$$= \begin{bmatrix} -15 & -5 \\ 5 & -10 \end{bmatrix}$$

$$7I_2 = 7\begin{bmatrix} 1 & 0 \\ 0 & 1 \end{bmatrix} = \begin{bmatrix} 7 & 0 \\ 0 & 7 \end{bmatrix}$$

So, $A^2 - 5A + 7I_2$

$$= \begin{bmatrix} 8 & 5 \\ -5 & 3 \end{bmatrix} + \begin{bmatrix} -15 & -5 \\ 5 & -10 \end{bmatrix} + \begin{bmatrix} 7 & 0 \\ 0 & 7 \end{bmatrix}$$

$$= \begin{bmatrix} 8-15+7 & 5-5+0 \\ -5+5+0 & 3-10+7 \end{bmatrix} = \begin{bmatrix} 0 & 0 \\ 0 & 0 \end{bmatrix}$$

So, $A^2 - 5A + 7I_2 = 0$.   **Hence Proved.**

5. If $X = \begin{bmatrix} 4 & 1 \\ -1 & 2 \end{bmatrix}$, show that $6X - X^2 = 9I$, where I is unit matrix.

Sol. Here

$$X^2 = X \cdot X$$

$$= \begin{bmatrix} 4 & 1 \\ -1 & 2 \end{bmatrix} \begin{bmatrix} 4 & 1 \\ -1 & 2 \end{bmatrix}$$

$$= \begin{bmatrix} 16-1 & 4+2 \\ -4-2 & -1+4 \end{bmatrix} = \begin{bmatrix} 15 & 6 \\ -6 & 3 \end{bmatrix}$$

L.H.S. $= 6X - X^2$

$$= 6 \begin{bmatrix} 4 & 1 \\ -1 & 2 \end{bmatrix} - \begin{bmatrix} 15 & 6 \\ -6 & 3 \end{bmatrix}$$

$$= \begin{bmatrix} 24 & 6 \\ -6 & 12 \end{bmatrix} - \begin{bmatrix} 15 & 6 \\ -6 & 3 \end{bmatrix}$$

$$= \begin{bmatrix} 24-15 & 6-6 \\ -6+6 & 12-3 \end{bmatrix}$$

$$= \begin{bmatrix} 9 & 0 \\ 0 & 9 \end{bmatrix}$$

$$= 9 \begin{bmatrix} 1 & 0 \\ 0 & 1 \end{bmatrix}$$

$$= 9I = \text{R.H.S.}   \textbf{Hence Proved.}$$

Chapter 9. Arithmetic Progression

1. Show that $a_1, a_2, \ldots, a_n, \ldots$ form an A.P. where a_n is defined as below :

(i) $a_n = 3 + 4n$

(ii) $a_n = 9 - 5n$

Also, find S_{15} for both A.P.

Sol. (i) Given,

$$a_n = 3 + 4n$$

when $n = 1$

$$a_1 = 3 + 4 (1)$$

$$= 3 + 4 = 7$$

when $n = 2$,

$$a_2 = 3 + 4 (2)$$

$$= 3 + 8 = 11$$

when $n = 3$,

$$a_3 = 3 + 4 (3)$$

$$= 3 + 12 = 15$$

Since, $a_2 - a_1 = 11 - 7$

$$= 4$$

and $a_3 - a_2 = 15 - 11 = 4$

i.e., $a_{k+1} - a_k$ is same every time, the given list forms an A.P. with the common difference $(d) = 4$.

Also $S_n = \dfrac{n}{2} [2a + (n-1) d]$

$$S_{15} = \dfrac{15}{2} [2 (7) + (15 - 1) 4]$$

$$= \dfrac{15}{2} [14 + (14) 4]$$

$$= \dfrac{15}{2} [14 + 56]$$

$$= \dfrac{15}{2} [70] = 525$$

Thus, this is in an A.P. with $a = 7$, $d = 4$, $S_{15} = 525$.

Hence Proved.

(ii) Given, $a_n = 9 - 5n$

when $n = 1$,

$$a_1 = 4$$

when $n = 2$,

$$a_2 = 9 - 10 = -1$$

when $n = 3$,

$$a_3 = 9 - 15$$

$$= -6$$

Since, $a_2 - a_1 = -1 - 4 = -5$

and $a_3 - a_2 = -6 + 1 = -5$.

i.e., $a_{k+1} - a_k$ is same every time, the given list forms an A.P. with the common difference $(d) = -5$.

Prove the Following

Also $\qquad S_n = \dfrac{n}{2}[2a + (n-1)d]$

$$S_{15} = \dfrac{15}{2}[2(4) + (15-1)(-5)]$$

$$= \dfrac{15}{2}[8 + (14)(-5)]$$

$$= \dfrac{15}{2}[8 + (-70)]$$

$$= \dfrac{15}{2}[-62]$$

$$= -465.$$

This is an A.P. with $a = 4$, $d = -5$, $S_{15} = -465$.

Hence Proved.

2. Let the mth term of an A.P. be $\dfrac{1}{n}$ and the nth term be $\dfrac{1}{m}$, then show that its (mn)th term is 1.

Sol. Let a and d be the first term and common difference, respectively of the given A.P., then

$$\dfrac{1}{n} = m\text{th term} = a + (m-1)d \qquad ...(i)$$

$$\dfrac{1}{m} = n\text{th term} = a + (n-1)d. \qquad ...(ii)$$

On subtracting (ii) from (i), we get

$$\dfrac{1}{n} - \dfrac{1}{m} = (m-n)d$$

$$\Rightarrow \qquad d = \dfrac{1}{mn}$$

Putting $\qquad d = \dfrac{1}{mn}$ in (i), we get

$$\dfrac{1}{n} = a + \dfrac{(m-1)}{mn}$$

$$\Rightarrow \qquad a = \dfrac{1}{mn}$$

So, (mn)th term $= a + (mn-1)d$

$$= \dfrac{1}{mn} + (mn-1) \cdot \dfrac{1}{mn}$$

$$= 1$$

Hence, (mn)th term is 1. **Hence Proved.**

3. If m times the mth term of an A.P. is equal to n times its nth term, show that the $(m+n)$th term of the A.P. is zero.

Sol. Let a be the first term and d be the common difference of the given A.P.

Then, m times mth term $= n$ times nth term

$$\Rightarrow \qquad ma_m = na_n$$

$$\Rightarrow \quad m[a + (m-1)d] = n[a + (n-1)d]$$

$$\Rightarrow \quad m[a + (m-1)d] - n[a + (n-1)d] = 0$$

$$\Rightarrow \quad a(m-n) + [m(m-1) - n(n-1)]d = 0$$

$$\Rightarrow \quad a(m-n) + [(m^2 - n^2) - (m-n)]d = 0$$

$$\Rightarrow \quad a(m-n) + (m-n)(m+n-1)d = 0$$

$$\Rightarrow \quad (m-n)[a + (m+n-1)d] = 0$$

$$\Rightarrow \qquad a + (m+n-1)d = 0$$

$$\Rightarrow \qquad a_{m+n} = 0$$

Hence, the $(m+n)$th term of the given A.P. is zero. **Hence Proved.**

4. If the mth term of an A.P. is $\dfrac{1}{n}$ and the nth term of an A.P. is $\dfrac{1}{m}$, show that the sum of mn terms is $\dfrac{1}{2}(mn+1)$.

Sol. Let a be the first term and d be the common difference of the given A.P., then

$$a_m = \dfrac{1}{n}$$

$$\Rightarrow \qquad a + (m-1)d = \dfrac{1}{n} \qquad ...(i)$$

and $\qquad a_n = \dfrac{1}{m}$

$$\Rightarrow \qquad a + (n-1)d = \dfrac{1}{m} \qquad ...(ii)$$

Subtracting (ii) from (i), we get

$$\dfrac{1}{n} - \dfrac{1}{m} = (m-n)d$$

$$\Rightarrow \qquad d = \dfrac{1}{mn}.$$

Putting $d = \dfrac{1}{mn}$ in (i), we get

$$a + (m-1)\dfrac{1}{mn} = \dfrac{1}{n}$$

$$\Rightarrow \qquad a = \dfrac{1}{mn}$$

Now, $\qquad S_{mn} = \dfrac{mn}{2} + \left[\dfrac{2}{mn} + (mn-1)\dfrac{1}{mn}\right]$

$$S_{mn} = \dfrac{1}{2}(mn+1)$$

Hence Proved.

5. Prove that a sequence is an A.P. if the sum of its n terms is of the form $An^2 + Bn$, where A, B are constants.

Sol. Let S_n be the sum of n terms of an A.P. with first term a and common difference d. Then,

$$S_n = \frac{n}{2}[2a + (n-1)d]$$

$$\Rightarrow \quad S_n = a \cdot n + \frac{n^2}{2}d - \frac{n}{2}d$$

$$= \left(\frac{d}{2}\right)n^2 + \left(a - \frac{d}{2}\right)n$$

$$\Rightarrow \quad S_n = An^2 + Bn,$$

where $A = \dfrac{d}{2}$ and $B = a - \dfrac{d}{2}$ constants.

Thus, the sum of n terms of an A.P. is of the form $An^2 + Bn$. **Hence Proved.**

Conversely, Let S_n the sum of n terms of a sequence $a_1, a_2, \ldots a_n, \ldots$ be of the form $An^2 + Bn$. Then, we have to show that the sequence is an A.P.

We have $S_n = An^2 + Bn$.

$\Rightarrow \quad S_{n-1} = A(n-1)^2 + B(n-1)$.

Now, $a_n = S_n - S_{n-1}$

$\qquad = An^2 + Bn - A(n-1)^2 - B(n-1)$

$a_n = 2An + (B - A)$

$\Rightarrow \quad a_{n+1} = 2A(n+1) + (B - A)$

$\therefore \quad a_{n+1} - a_n = 2A(n+1) - 2An = 2A$

Since, $a_{n+1} - a_n = 2A \ \forall \ n \in N$.

So, the sequence is an A.P. with common difference $2A$. **Hence Proved.**

6. The pth term of an A.P. is a and qth term is b. Prove that the sum of its $(p+q)$th term is :

$$\frac{p+q}{2}\left[a + b + \frac{a-b}{p-q}\right].$$

Sol. Let the first term $= A$, common difference $= D$

Then, $\quad S_{p+q} = \dfrac{p+q}{2}[2A + (p+q-1)D]$ ...(i)

It is given that $t_p = a$ and $t_q = b$

$\therefore \quad t_p = A + (p-1)D = a$ ...(ii)

$\qquad t_q = A + (q-1)D = b$ ...(iii)

Subtracting (iii) from (ii), we have

$(p - q)D = a - b$

$\therefore \quad D = \dfrac{a-b}{p-q}$ ...(iv)

Adding (ii) and (iii), we have

$2A + (p+q-2)D = a + b$

or $\quad 2A + (p+q-1)D = a + b + D$

$$= a + b + \frac{a-b}{p-q} \qquad \text{...(v)}$$

$$\left[\because D = \frac{a-b}{p-q}\right]$$

Putting (v) in (i), we get

$$S_{p+q} = \frac{p+q}{2}\left[a + b + \frac{a-b}{p-q}\right]$$

Hence Proved.

7. If the sum of p, q, r terms of an A.P. be a, b, c respectively, then prove that

$$\frac{a}{p}(q-r) + \frac{b}{q}(r-p) + \frac{c}{r}(p-q) = 0.$$

Sol. Let first term $= A$ and common difference $= D$

Then, $\quad S_p = \dfrac{p}{2}[2A + (p-1)D] = a$

$\therefore \quad \dfrac{2a}{p} = 2A + (p-1)D$ ...(i)

Similarly,

$\dfrac{2b}{q} = 2A + (q-1)D$ ...(ii)

and $\quad \dfrac{2c}{r} = 2A + (r-1)D$ ...(iii)

Multiplying (i), (ii) and (iii) by $(q-r)$, $(r-p)$ and $(p-q)$ respectively and adding, we have

$$\frac{2a}{p}(q-r) + \frac{2b}{q}(r-p) + \frac{2c}{r}(p-q)$$

$$= 2A[q - r + r - p + p - q]$$
$$+ D[(p-1)(q-r) + (q-1)(r-p)$$
$$+ (r-1)(p-q)]$$
$$= 2A \times 0 + D[pq - pr - q + r + qr$$
$$- pq - r + p + pr - qr - p + q]$$
$$= 0 + D \times 0$$
$$= 0. \qquad \textbf{Hence Proved.}$$

8. If there are $(2n+1)$ terms in an A.P., then prove that the ratio of the sum of odd terms and the sum of even terms is $(n+1):n$.

Sol. Let a be the first term and d be the common difference of the given A.P. Let a_p denote the pth term of the given A.P.

Then $\quad a_p = a + (p-1)d$.

Now, $\quad S_1 = $ sum of odd terms

$$S_1 = a_1 + a_3 + a_5 + \ldots + a_{2n+1}$$

$$\Rightarrow \quad S_1 = \frac{n+1}{2}[a_1 + a_{2n+1}]$$

$$= \frac{n+1}{2}[a + a(2n+1-1)d]$$

$$= (n+1)(a+nd).$$

and

$$S_2 = \text{Sum of even terms}$$

$$= a_2 + a_4 + a_6 + \ldots + a_{2n}$$

$$\Rightarrow \quad S_2 = \frac{n}{2}[a_2 + a_{2n}]$$

$$= \frac{n}{2}[(a+d) + a + (2n-1)d]$$

$$\Rightarrow \quad S_2 = n(a+nd)$$

$$\therefore \quad S_1 : S_2 = \frac{(n+1)(a+nd)}{n(a+nd)}$$

$$= (n+1) : n. \quad \textbf{Hence Proved.}$$

9. If the ratio of the sum of m terms and n terms of an A.P. be $m^2 : n^2$, prove that the ratio of its mth and nth terms will be $2m-1 : 2n-1$.

Sol. Given,

$$\frac{S_m}{S_n} = \frac{m^2}{n^2}$$

$$\therefore \quad \frac{S_m}{m^2} = \frac{S_n}{n^2} = k \text{ (say)} \quad \ldots\text{(i)}$$

or

$$S_m = km^2, \ S_n = kn^2$$

Now,

$$\frac{t_m}{t_n} = \frac{S_m - S_{m-1}}{S_n - S_{n-1}}$$

$$= \frac{k[m^2 - (m-1)^2]}{k[n^2 - (n-1)^2]}$$

$$= \frac{m^2 - m^2 + 2m - 1}{n^2 - n^2 + 2n - 1}$$

$$= \frac{2m-1}{2n-1} \quad [\because t_m = S_m - S_{m-1}]$$

$$\therefore \quad t_m : t_n = 2m - 1 : 2n - 1$$

Hence Proved.

10. If a, b, c are in A.P., prove that the following are also in A.P. :

(a) $b + c, c + a, a + b$.

(b) $\dfrac{1}{bc}, \dfrac{1}{ca}, \dfrac{1}{ab}$

(c) $\dfrac{1}{\sqrt{b}+\sqrt{c}}, \dfrac{1}{\sqrt{c}+\sqrt{a}}, \dfrac{1}{\sqrt{a}+\sqrt{b}}$

Sol. (a) $b + c, c + a, a + b$ will be in A.P.

$$\text{if}\,(c+a) - (b+c) = (a+b) - (c+a)$$

i.e., if $\qquad a - b = b - c$

i.e., if $\qquad 2b = a + c$

i.e., if a, b, c are in A.P.

Thus, if a, b, c are in A.P.

$\Rightarrow$ $b + c, c + a, a + b$ are in A.P. **Hence Proved.**

(b) Given, a, b, c are in A.P.

$$\Rightarrow \quad \frac{a}{abc}, \frac{b}{abc}, \frac{c}{abc} \text{ are in A.P.}$$

[on dividing each term by abc]

$$\Rightarrow \quad \frac{1}{bc}, \frac{1}{ca}, \frac{1}{ab} \text{ are in A.P.} \quad \textbf{Hence Proved.}$$

(c) $\dfrac{1}{\sqrt{b}+\sqrt{c}}, \dfrac{1}{\sqrt{c}+\sqrt{a}}, \dfrac{1}{\sqrt{a}+\sqrt{b}}$ will be in A.P.

if

$$\frac{1}{\sqrt{c}+\sqrt{a}} - \frac{1}{\sqrt{b}+\sqrt{c}} = \frac{1}{\sqrt{a}+\sqrt{b}} - \frac{1}{\sqrt{c}+\sqrt{a}}$$

i.e., if

$$\frac{\sqrt{b}-\sqrt{a}}{(\sqrt{c}+\sqrt{a})(\sqrt{b}+\sqrt{c})} = \frac{\sqrt{c}-\sqrt{b}}{(\sqrt{a}+\sqrt{b})(\sqrt{c}+\sqrt{a})}$$

i.e., if

$$\frac{\sqrt{b}-\sqrt{a}}{\sqrt{b}+\sqrt{c}} = \frac{\sqrt{c}-\sqrt{b}}{\sqrt{b}+\sqrt{a}}$$

i.e., if $\qquad b - a = c - b$

i.e., if $\qquad 2b = a + c$

i.e., if a, b, c are in A.P. **Hence Proved.**

11. If a^2, b^2, c^2 are in A.P. then prove that the following are also in A.P. :

(a) $\dfrac{a}{b+c}, \dfrac{b}{c+a}, \dfrac{c}{a+b}$

(b) $\dfrac{a}{b+c}, \dfrac{b}{c+a}, \dfrac{c}{a+b}$

Sol. (a) $\dfrac{a}{b+c}, \dfrac{b}{c+a}, \dfrac{c}{a+b}$ will be in A.P.

if

$$\frac{1}{c+a} - \frac{1}{b+c} = \frac{1}{a+b} - \frac{1}{c+a}$$

i.e., if

$$\frac{b-a}{(c+a)(b+c)} = \frac{c-b}{(a+b)(c+a)}$$

i.e., if

$$\frac{b-a}{b+c} = \frac{c-b}{a+b}$$

i.e., if $\qquad b^2 - a^2 = c^2 - b^2$

i.e., if $\qquad 2b^2 = a^2 + c^2$

i.e., if a^2, b^2, c^2 are in A.P.

Thus, a^2, b^2, c^2 are in A.P.

$$\Rightarrow \quad \frac{a}{b+c}, \frac{b}{c+a}, \frac{c}{a+b} \text{ are in A.P.} \quad \textbf{Hence Proved.}$$

Prove the Following

(b) $\dfrac{a}{b+c}, \dfrac{b}{c+a}, \dfrac{c}{a+b}$ will be in A.P.

if $\dfrac{a}{b+c}+1, \dfrac{b}{c+a}+1, \dfrac{c}{a+b}+1$ are in A.P.

[On adding 1 to each term]

i.e., if $\dfrac{a+b+c}{b+c}, \dfrac{a+b+c}{c+a}, \dfrac{a+b+c}{a+b}$ are in A.P.

i.e., if $\dfrac{a}{b+c}, \dfrac{b}{c+a}, \dfrac{c}{a+b}$ are in A.P.

[On dividing each term of $a + b + c$]

i.e., if $\dfrac{1}{c+a} - \dfrac{1}{b+c} = \dfrac{1}{a+b} - \dfrac{1}{c+a}$

i.e., if $\dfrac{b-a}{b+c} = \dfrac{c-b}{a+b}$

i.e., if $b^2 - a^2 = c^2 - b^2$

i.e, if $2b^2 = a^2 + c^2$

i.e., if a^2, b^2, c^2 are in A.P.

Thus, if a^2, b^2, c^2 are in A.P.

$\Rightarrow \dfrac{a}{b+c}, \dfrac{b}{c+a}, \dfrac{c}{a+b}$ are in A.P. **Hence Proved.**

12. If $\dfrac{b+c-a}{a}, \dfrac{c+a-b}{b}, \dfrac{a+b-c}{c}$ are in A.P., prove

that $\dfrac{1}{a}, \dfrac{1}{b}, \dfrac{1}{c}$ are also in A.P.

Sol. Given, $\dfrac{b+c-a}{a}, \dfrac{c+a-b}{b}, \dfrac{a+b-c}{c}$ are in A.P.

$\Rightarrow \dfrac{b+c-a}{a}+2, \dfrac{c+a-b}{b}+2, \dfrac{a+b-c}{c}+2$ are in A.P.

[Adding 2 to each term]

$\Rightarrow \dfrac{b+c-a}{a}, \dfrac{c+a-b}{b}, \dfrac{a+b-c}{c}$ are in A.P.

$\Rightarrow \dfrac{1}{a}, \dfrac{1}{b}, \dfrac{1}{c}$ are in A.P.

$\left(\text{Dividing each term by } \dfrac{1}{a+b+c}\right)$

Hence Proved.

13. If $a^2(b+c), b^2(c+a), c^2(a+b)$ are in A.P., show that either a, b, c are in A.P. or $ab + bc + ca = 0$.

Sol. Given $a^2(b+c), b^2(c+a), c^2(a+b)$ are in A.P.

$\Rightarrow \quad b^2(c+a) - a^2(b+c) = c^2(a+b) - b^2(c+a)$

$\Rightarrow \quad (b^2a - a^2b) + (b^2c - a^2c) = (c^2b - b^2c) + (c^2a - b^2a)$

$\Rightarrow \quad (b-a)(ab+bc+c) = (c-b)(ab+bc+ca)$

$\Rightarrow \quad (ab+bc+ca)(2b-a-c) = 0$

$\Rightarrow \quad\quad\quad\quad\quad ab+bc+ca = 0$

or $\quad\quad\quad\quad\quad 2b-a-c = 0$

$\Rightarrow \quad\quad\quad\quad\quad ab+bc+ca = 0$

or a, b, c are in A.P. **Hence Proved.**

14. If x, y, z are in A.P., show that

$(x+2y-z)(2y+z-x)(z+x-y) = 4xyz$.

Sol. Given x, y, z are in A.P.

$\therefore \quad\quad\quad y = \dfrac{x+z}{2}$ ...(i)

$\therefore (x+2y-z)(2y+z-x)(z+x-y)$

$= (x+x+z-z)(x+z+z-x)(2y-y)$

[From (i)]

$= (2x)(2z)(y)$

$= 4xyz$

$= \text{R.H.S.}$ **Hence Proved.**

Chapter 10. Geometric Progression

1. The $(m+n)$th and $(m-n)$th terms of a G.P. are p and q respectively. Show that the mth and nth terms are $\sqrt{pq}$ and $p\left(\dfrac{q}{p}\right)^{m/2n}$ respectively.

Sol. Let a be the first term and r be the common ratio. Then

$a_{m+n} = p$ and $a_{m-n} = q$

$\Rightarrow \quad ar^{m+n-1} = p$ and $ar^{m-n-1} = q$

$\Rightarrow \quad \dfrac{ar^{m+n-1}}{ar^{m-n-1}} = \dfrac{p}{q}$

$\Rightarrow \quad\quad r^{2n} = \dfrac{p}{q}$

$\Rightarrow \quad\quad r = \left(\dfrac{p}{q}\right)^{1/2n}$

$\Rightarrow \quad\quad \dfrac{1}{r} = \left(\dfrac{q}{p}\right)^{1/2n}$

Now, $\quad a_m = ar^{m-1}$

$= ar^{m+n-1} \cdot \left(\dfrac{1}{r}\right)^n$

$\Rightarrow \qquad a_m = a_{m+n} \left(\dfrac{1}{r}\right)^n \quad [\because a_{m+n} = ar^{m+n-1}]$

$\Rightarrow \qquad a_m = p \cdot \left(\dfrac{q}{p}\right)^{1/2n}$

$\qquad = p \left(\dfrac{q}{p}\right)^{1/2}$

$\Rightarrow \qquad a_m = \sqrt{pq}$ \hfill **Hence Proved.**

and $\qquad a_n = ar^{n-1}$

$\Rightarrow \qquad a_n = ar^{m+n-1} \left(\dfrac{1}{r}\right)^m$

$\qquad = a_{m+n} \left(\dfrac{1}{r}\right)^m$

$\Rightarrow \qquad a_n = p \cdot \left(\dfrac{q}{p}\right)^{m/2n}$ \hfill **Hence Proved.**

2. If the first and the nth terms of a G.P. are a and b respectively and if P is the product of the first n terms, prove that $P^2 = (ab)^n$.

Sol. Let r be the common ratio of the given G.P. then,

$\qquad b = n\text{th term} = ar^{n-1}$

$\Rightarrow \qquad r^{n-1} = \dfrac{b}{a}$

$\Rightarrow \qquad r = \left(\dfrac{b}{a}\right)^{\frac{1}{n-1}}$

Now,

$\Rightarrow \qquad$ P = Product of the first n terms

$\qquad$ P = $a.\,ar.\,ar^2.\,\dots\,ar^{n-1}$

$\qquad = a^n.r^{1+2+3+\dots+(n-1)}$

$\qquad = a^n. \, r^{\frac{n(n-1)}{2}}$

$\qquad = a^n \left[\left(\dfrac{b}{a}\right)^{\frac{1}{n-1}}\right]^{\frac{n(n-1)}{2}}$

$\qquad = a^n \cdot \left(\dfrac{b}{a}\right)^{\frac{n}{2}}$

$\qquad = a^n \cdot \dfrac{b^{n/2}}{a^{n/2}}$

$\qquad = a^{n/2} b^{n/2}$

$\qquad = (ab)^{n/2}$

$\Rightarrow \qquad P^2 = (ab)^n.$ \hfill **Hence Proved.**

3. Prove that the sum of n terms of the series $11 + 103 + 1005 + \dots$ is $\dfrac{10}{9}(10^n - 1) + n^2$.

Sol. Let S_n denote the sum to n terms of the given series. Then,

$\qquad S_n = 11 + 103 + 1005 + \dots \text{ to } n \text{ terms}$

$\Rightarrow \qquad S_n = (10 + 10^2 + 10^3 + \dots + 10^n)$

$\qquad \qquad + [1 + 3 + 5 + \dots + (2n - 1)]$

$\Rightarrow \qquad S_n = \dfrac{10(10^n - 1)}{10 - 1} + \dfrac{n}{2}[1 + (2n - 1)]$

$\Rightarrow \qquad S_n = \dfrac{10}{9}(10^n - 1) + n^2.$

\hfill **Hence Proved.**

4. If S be the sum, P be the product and R be the sum of the reciprocals of n terms of a G.P., prove that

$$\left(\dfrac{S}{R}\right)^n = P^2.$$

Sol. Let a be the first term and r be the common ratio of the G.P.

Then, $\qquad S = a + ar + ar^2 + \dots + ar^{n-1}$

$\qquad = \dfrac{a(r^n - 1)}{r - 1}$

$\qquad$ P = $a.\,ar.\,ar^2\dots\dots ar^{n-1}$

$\qquad = a^n.\,r^{1+2+3+\dots+(n-1)}$

$\Rightarrow \qquad$ P = $a^n \, r^{\frac{n(n-1)}{3}}$

and $\qquad R = \dfrac{1}{a} + \dfrac{1}{ar} + \dfrac{1}{ar^2} + \dots + \dfrac{1}{ar^{n-1}}$

$\Rightarrow \qquad R = \dfrac{1}{a}\left\{\dfrac{(1/r)^n - 1}{1/r - 1}\right\}$

$\qquad = \dfrac{1}{a}\left(\dfrac{1 - r^n}{1 - r}\right)\dfrac{1}{r^{n-1}}$

$\Rightarrow \qquad R = \dfrac{1}{a}\left(\dfrac{r^n - 1}{r - 1}\right)\dfrac{1}{r^{n-1}}$

$\therefore \qquad \dfrac{S}{R} = a\left(\dfrac{r^n - 1}{r - 1}\right)\bigg/\dfrac{1}{a}\left(\dfrac{r^n - 1}{r - 1}\right).\dfrac{1}{r^{n-1}}$

$\qquad = a^2 . \, r^{n-1}$

$\Rightarrow \qquad \left(\dfrac{S}{R}\right)^n = a^{2n} \, r^{n(n-1)}$

$\qquad = \left[a^n . r^{\frac{n(n-1)}{2}}\right]^2$

$\qquad = P^2.$ \hfill **Hence Proved.**

5. Prove the following :

If the pth, qth and rth terms of G.P. are a, b, c respectively, prove that

$$a^{q-r} \cdot b^{r-p} \cdot c^{p-q} = 1.$$

Sol. Let A be the first term and R be the common ratio of the given G.P.

Then $\qquad a = p$th term

$\Rightarrow \qquad a = AR^{p-1}$

$\qquad b = q$th term

$\Rightarrow \qquad b = AR^{q-1}$

$\qquad c = r$th term

$\Rightarrow \qquad c = AR^{r-1}$

Now, $a^{q-r} \cdot b^{r-p} \cdot c^{p-q}$

$= (AR^{p-1})^{q-r} \cdot (AR^{q-1})^{r-p} \cdot (AR^{r-1})^{p-q}$

$= A^{(q-r)} R^{(p-1)(q-r)} \cdot A^{(r-p)} \cdot R^{(q-1)(r-p)} \cdot A^{(p-q)} R^{(r-1)(p-q)}$

$= A^{(q-r+r-p+p-q)} \cdot R^{(p-1)(q-r)+(q-1)(r-p)+(r-1)(p-q)}$

$= A^0 \cdot R^0 = 1.$ $\qquad$ **Hence Proved.**

6. If a, b, c are in G.P., then prove that $\log a^n$, $\log b^n$, $\log c^n$ are in A.P.

Sol. As a, b, c are in G.P.

$\Rightarrow \qquad b^2 = ac$

$\Rightarrow \qquad (b^2)^n = (ac)^n = a^n c^n$

$\Rightarrow \qquad \log b^{2n} = \log (a^n c^n)$

$\qquad \qquad = \log a^n + \log c^n$

$\Rightarrow \qquad 2 \log b^n = \log a^n + \log c^n$

$\Rightarrow \qquad \log a^n, \log b^n, \log c^n$ are in A.P.

$\qquad \qquad$ **Hence Proved.**

7. If pth, qth, rth and sth terms of a G.P. are in G.P., prove that :

$(p-q)$, $(q-r)$ and $(r-s)$ are also in G.P.

Sol. Let for the given G.P., first term = A and common ratio = R

$\therefore \qquad t_p = AR^{p-1}, t_q = AR^{q-1},$

$\qquad \qquad t_r = AR^{n-1}$

and $\qquad t_s = AR^{s-1}$ are in G.P.

$\Rightarrow \qquad \dfrac{AR^{q-1}}{AR^{p-1}} = \dfrac{AR^{r-1}}{AR^{q-1}} = \dfrac{AR^{s-1}}{AR^{r-1}}$

$\Rightarrow \qquad R^{q-p} = R^{r-q} = R^{s-r}$

$\Rightarrow \qquad q-p = r-q = s-r$

$\Rightarrow \qquad q-p = r-q$ and $r-q = s-r$

$\Rightarrow \qquad \dfrac{q-p}{r-q} = 1$ and $\dfrac{r-q}{s-r} = 1$

$\Rightarrow \qquad \dfrac{q-p}{r-q} = \dfrac{r-q}{s-r}$

$\Rightarrow \qquad (r-q)^2 = (q-p)(s-r)$

$\Rightarrow \qquad (q-r)^2 = (p-q)(r-s)$

$\Rightarrow (p-q), (q-r), (r-s)$ is also in G.P.

$\qquad \qquad$ **Hence Proved.**

8. Prove the following :

If a, b, c, d are in G.P., show that :

(a) $(b-c)^2 + (c-a)^2 + (d-b)^2 = (a-d)^2$

(b) $a+b, b+c, c+d$ are also in G.P.

Sol. Let r be the common ratio of the G.P. a, b, c, d.

Then $\qquad b = ar$, $c = ar^2$ and $d = ar^3$.

(a) $\therefore$ L.H.S. $= (b-c)^2 + (c-a)^2 + (d-b)^2$

$= (ar - ar^2)^2 + (ar^2 - a)^2 + (ar^3 - ar)^2$

$= a^2r^2(1-r)^2 + a^2(r^2-1)^2 + a^2r^2(r^2-1)^2$

$= a^2(r^6 - 2r^3 + 1)$

$= a^2(1-r^3)^2$

$= (a - ar^3)^2$

$= (a-d)^2 =$ R.H.S. $\quad$ **Hence Proved.**

(b) $\qquad a + b = a + ar = a(1+r),$

$\qquad \qquad b + c = ar + ar^2 = ar(1+r),$

and $\qquad c + d = ar^2 + ar^3 = ar^2(1+r),$

Now, $(b+c)^2 = a^2r^2(1+r)^2$

$\qquad \qquad = a(1+r) \cdot ar^2(1+r)$

$\qquad \qquad = (a+b)(c+d)$

Hence, $a+b, b+c, c+d$ are in G.P. **Hence Proved.**

9. If $a^2 + b^2$, $ab + bc$ and $b^2 + c^2$ are in G.P., prove that a, b, c are also in G.P.

Sol. $a^2 + b^2$, $ab + bc$, $b^2 + c^2$ are in G.P.

$\Rightarrow \qquad (ab+bc)^2 = (a^2+b^2)(b^2+c^2)$

$\Rightarrow \quad a^2b^2 + b^2c^2 + 2ab^2c = a^2b^2 + a^2c^2 + b^2c^2 + b^4$

$\Rightarrow \qquad b^4 + a^2c^2 - 2ab^2c = 0$

$\Rightarrow \qquad (b^2 - ac)^2 = 0$

$\Rightarrow \qquad b^2 = ac$

$\Rightarrow \qquad a, b, c$ are in G.P. $\qquad$ **Hence Proved.**

Chapter 11. Co-ordinate Geometry

1. Show that the points A(–2, 5), B(2, –3) and C(0, 1) are collinear.

Sol. m_1 = Slope of AB

$$= \frac{-3-5}{2-(-2)} = -\frac{8}{4} = -2$$

m_2 = Slope of BC

$$= \frac{1-(-3)}{0-2} = \frac{4}{-2} = -2.$$

Hence, $m_1 = m_2 = -2$

So, AB is parallel to BC.

But B is common to AB and BC.

Hence, A, B and C must lies on the same line.

∴ A, B and C are collinear. **Hence Proved.**

2. Show that the line joining (2, –3) and (–5, 1) is :

(i) Parallel to line joining (7, –1) and (0, 3).

(ii) Perpendicular to the line joining (4, 5) and (0, –2).

Sol. Let m_1 be the slope of the line joining (2, –3) and (–5, 1), then

$$m_1 = \frac{y_2 - y_1}{x_2 - x_1}$$

$$= \frac{1-(-3)}{-5-2} = -\frac{4}{7}$$

(i) Let m_2 be the slope of the line joining (7, –1) and (0, 3), then

$$m_2 = \frac{3-(-1)}{0-7} = -\frac{4}{7}$$

Since, $m_1 = m_2$, the two lines are parallel.

Hence Proved.

(ii) Let m_3 be the slope of the line joining (4, 5) and (0, –2), then

$$m_3 = \frac{-2-5}{0-4} = \frac{7}{4}$$

Now, $m_1 m_3 = -\frac{4}{7} \times \frac{7}{4} = -1$

Hence, the two lines are perpendicular.

Hence Proved.

3. Without using Pythagoras theorem, show that A(4, 4), B(3, 5) and C(– 1, – 1) are the vertices of a right angled triangle.

Sol. Slope of BC = $m_1 = \frac{-1-5}{-1-3} = \frac{3}{2}$

Slope of CA = $m_2 = \frac{4-(-1)}{4-(-1)} = 1$

Also, Slope of AB = $m_3 = \frac{5-4}{3-4} = -1$

Since, $m_2 m_3 = 1 \times (-1) = -1$. So, AB and CA are perpendicular to each other.

Thus, ΔABC is a right angled triangle at A.

Hence Proved.

Chapter 13. Similarity

1. In figure ABC and DBC are two triangles on the same base BC. Prove that

$$\frac{\text{Area } (\Delta \text{ ABC})}{\text{Area } (\Delta \text{ DBC})} = \frac{\text{AO}}{\text{DO}}.$$

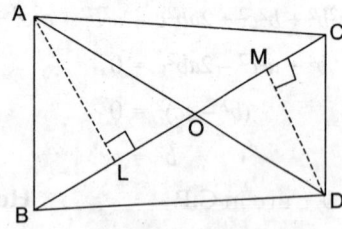

Sol. In Δ AOL and Δ DOM,

∠ ALO = ∠ DMO   (90° each)

∠ AOL = ∠ DOM

(Vertically opposite angles)

∴   Δ AOL ~ Δ DOM

∴ $\frac{\text{AL}}{\text{DM}} = \frac{\text{AO}}{\text{DO}}$ ...(i)

If two Δ's are similar then ratio between their corresponding sides is the same.

Now, $\dfrac{\text{area } (\Delta \text{ ABC})}{\text{area } (\Delta \text{ DBC})} = \dfrac{\frac{1}{2} \times \text{BC} \times \text{AL}}{\frac{1}{2} \times \text{BC} \times \text{DM}} = \dfrac{\text{AL}}{\text{DM}}$

From (i), we get

$\dfrac{\text{area } (\Delta \text{ ABC})}{\text{area } (\Delta \text{ DBC})} = \dfrac{\text{AO}}{\text{DO}}.$ **Hence Proved.**

2. In the following figure, the medians BD and CE of a Δ ABC meet at G. Prove that

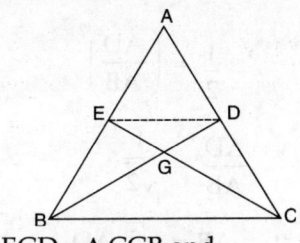

(i) △ EGD ~ △ CGB and

(ii) BG = 2GD for (i) above.

Sol. Since D and E are midpoint of AC and AB respectively in △ ABC, ED is parallel to BC.

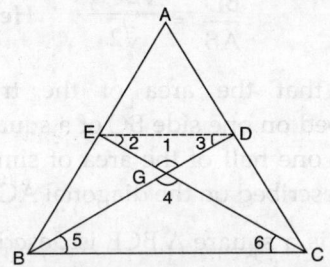

(i) In △'s EGD and CGB,

$$\angle EGD = \angle CGB$$

(Vertically opp. angles)

$$\angle EDG = \angle CBG \quad \text{(Alternate angles)}$$

So, △EGD ~ △CGB. **Hence Proved.**

(ii) ∴

$$\frac{BG}{GD} = \frac{BC}{DE}$$

But

$$\frac{BC}{DE} = 2$$

So,

$$\frac{BG}{GD} = 2$$

⇒ BG = 2GD. **Hence Proved.**

3. In the given figure, $\angle PQR = \angle PST = 90°$, $PQ = 5$ cm and $PS = 2$ cm.*

(i) Prove that $\triangle PQR \sim \triangle PST$.

(ii) Find-Area of $\triangle PQR$: Area of quadrilateral *SRQT*.

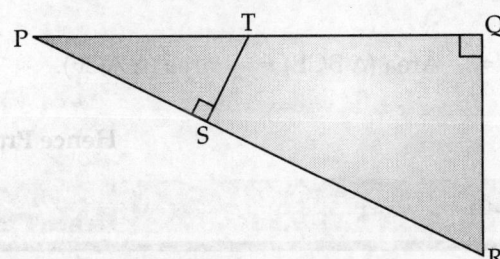

Sol. Given, $\angle PQR = \angle PST = 90°,$

$PQ = 5$ cm and $PS = 2$ cm

* Frequently asked previous years Board Exam Questions.
* Frequently asked previous years Board Exam Questions.

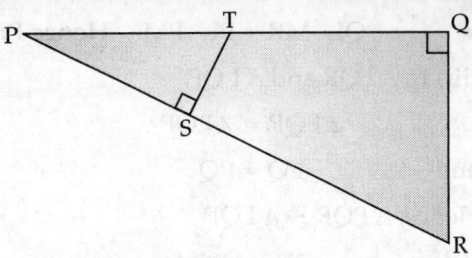

(i) In $\triangle PQR$ and $\triangle PST$,

$$\angle PQR = \angle PST = 90° \quad \text{(Given)}$$
$$\angle QPR = \angle SPT \quad \text{(Common)}$$
∴ $$\triangle PQR \sim \triangle PST \quad \text{(By AA axiom)}$$

Hence Proved.

(ii) $\dfrac{\text{Area of } \triangle PQR}{\text{Area of } \triangle PST} = \dfrac{PQ^2}{PS^2}$ ($\because \triangle PQR \sim \triangle PST$)

$$= \frac{5^2}{2^2} = \frac{25}{4}$$

Now,

$$\frac{\text{Area of } \triangle PQR}{\text{Area of quadrilateral } SRQT}$$

$$= \frac{\text{Area of } \triangle PQR}{\text{Area of } \triangle PQR - \text{Area of } \triangle PST}$$

$$= \frac{25\,K}{25K - 4K} = \frac{25}{21} \quad \textbf{Ans.}$$

4. In $\triangle PQR$, L and M are two points on the base QR, such that $\angle LPQ = \angle QRP$ and $\angle RPM = \angle RQP$.

Prove that : **(i)** $\triangle PQL \sim \triangle RPM$

(ii) QL. RM = PL. PM

(iii) $PQ^2 = QR.\ QL$.

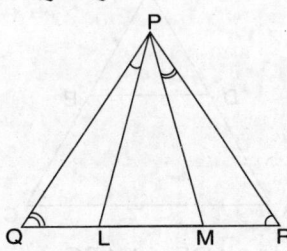

Sol. (i) Consider

△ PQL and △ RPM

Since $\angle PQL = \angle RPM$

and $\angle QPL = \angle PRM$ (By A. A. criterion)

∴ △PQL ~ △ RPM. **Hence Proved.**

(ii) In △ PQL ~ △ RPM,

$$\frac{PQ}{RP} = \frac{QL}{PM} = \frac{PL}{MR}$$

then $$\frac{QL}{PM} = \frac{PL}{MR}$$

$\Rightarrow \qquad \text{QL} \cdot \text{MR} = \text{PL} \cdot \text{PM}.$ **Hence Proved.**

(iii) In Δ PQR and Δ LQP,

$$\angle \text{PQR} = \angle \text{LQP}$$

and $\qquad \text{PQ} = \text{PQ}$

Hence, Δ PQR $\sim$ Δ LQP

$$\frac{\text{QR}}{\text{PQ}} = \frac{\text{PQ}}{\text{LQ}}$$

$\Rightarrow \qquad \text{PQ}^2 = \text{QR} \cdot \text{QL}.$ **Hence Proved.**

5. D and E are points on the sides AB and AC respectively of a Δ ABC such that DE $\parallel$ BC and divides Δ ABC into two parts, equal in area. Prove that

$$\frac{\text{BD}}{\text{AB}} = \frac{\sqrt{2}-1}{\sqrt{2}}.$$

Sol. We have

area (Δ ADE) = area (trapezium BCED)

$\Rightarrow$ area (Δ ADE) + area (Δ ADE)

$\qquad$ = area (trapezium BCED)

$\qquad\qquad$ + area (Δ ADE)

$\Rightarrow$ 2 area (Δ ADE) = area (Δ ABC) ...(i)

In Δ ADE and Δ ABC, we have

$$\angle \text{ADE} = \angle \text{B} \qquad [\because \text{DE} \parallel \text{BC}]$$
$$\therefore \qquad \angle \text{AED} = \angle \text{C}$$

$\qquad\qquad$ (Corresponding angles)

and $\qquad \angle \text{A} = \angle \text{A} \qquad$ [Common]

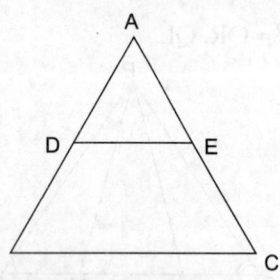

$\therefore \qquad \Delta$ ADE $\sim$ Δ ABC

$$\Rightarrow \frac{\text{area } (\Delta \text{ADE})}{\text{area } (\Delta \text{ABC})} = \frac{\text{AD}^2}{\text{AB}^2}$$

$$\Rightarrow \frac{\text{area } (\Delta \text{ADE})}{2 \text{ area } (\Delta \text{ADE})} = \frac{\text{AD}^2}{\text{AB}^2}$$

$$\Rightarrow \qquad \frac{1}{2} = \left(\frac{\text{AD}}{\text{AB}}\right)^2$$

$$\Rightarrow \qquad \frac{\text{AD}}{\text{AB}} = \frac{1}{\sqrt{2}}$$

$$\Rightarrow \qquad \text{AB} = \sqrt{2} \text{ AD}$$

$$\Rightarrow \qquad \text{AB} = \sqrt{2} \text{ (AB} - \text{BD)}$$

$$\Rightarrow \quad (\sqrt{2} - 1) \text{ AB} = \sqrt{2} \text{ BD}$$

$$\Rightarrow \qquad \frac{\text{BD}}{\text{AB}} = \frac{\sqrt{2}-1}{\sqrt{2}}.$$ **Hence Proved.**

6. Prove that the area of the triangle BCE described on one side BC of a square ABCD as base is one half of the area of similar triangle ACF described on the diagonal AC as base.

Sol. ABCD is a square Δ BCE is described on side BC is similar to Δ ACF described on diagonal AC.

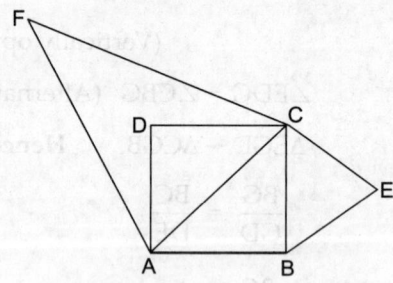

Since, ABCD is a square. Therefore

$$\text{AB} = \text{BC} = \text{CD} = \text{DA}$$

and $\qquad \text{AC} = \sqrt{2} \text{ BC}$

$\qquad\qquad$ [$\because$ Diagonal $= \sqrt{2}$ (side)]

Now, $\qquad \Delta$ BCE $\sim$ Δ ACF

$$\Rightarrow \frac{\text{Area } (\Delta \text{ BCE})}{\text{Area } (\Delta \text{ ACF})} = \frac{\text{BC}^2}{\text{AC}^2}$$

$$\Rightarrow \frac{\text{Area } (\Delta \text{ BCE})}{\text{Area } (\Delta \text{ ACF})} = \frac{\text{BC}^2}{(\sqrt{2}\text{BC})^2} = \frac{1}{2}$$

$$\Rightarrow \quad \text{Area } (\Delta \text{ BCE}) = \frac{1}{2} \text{ area } (\Delta \text{ ACF}).$$

$\qquad\qquad\qquad\qquad\qquad$ **Hence Proved.**

Chapter 14. Loci

1. The bisector of $\angle$ B and $\angle$ C of a quadrilateral ABCD intersect in P, show that P is equidistant from the opposite sides AB and CD.

Sol. Given, in quadrilateral ABCD, bisectors of $\angle$ B and $\angle$ C meet in P. PM $\perp$ AB and PN $\perp$ CD.

To prove that :

PM = PN ...(i)

Construction : Draw PL ⊥ BC

Proof : P lies on bisector or of ∠ B

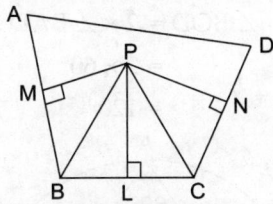

∴ PM = PL

P lies on bisector of ∠ C

PL = PN ...(ii)

From (i) and (ii), we have

PM = PN. **Hence Proved.**

2. Prove that the common chord of two intersecting circles is bisected at right angles by the line of centres.

Sol. Given, two intersecting circles with centres C and D.

AB is their common chord.

To prove : AB bisected by CD at right angles.

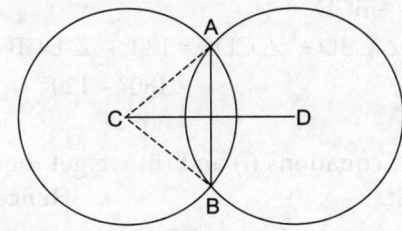

Proof : CA = CB (radii)

∴ C lies on the right bisector of AB.

Similarly, D lies on the right bisector of AB.

Therefore, CD is the right bisector of AB.

Hence Proved.

3. In ∆ABC, the bisector AX of ∠A intersects BC at X. XL ⊥ AB and XM ⊥ AC are drawn (Fig.) is XL = XM ? Why or why not ?

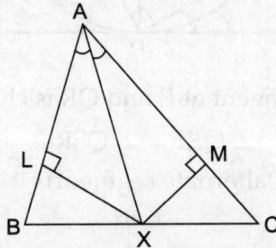

Sol. Since, every point on the bisectors of the angles between two intersecting lines is equidistant from the lines. Here, X lies on the bisector of

∠ BAC. Therefore, X is equidistant from AB and AC. It is given that XL ⊥ AB and XM ⊥ AC. Therefore, distance of X from AB and AC are XL and XM respectively.

Hence, XL = XM. **Ans.**

4. In Fig. ABCD is a quadrilateral in which AB = BC. E is the point of intersection of the right bisectors of AD and CD. Prove that BE bisects ∠ ABC.

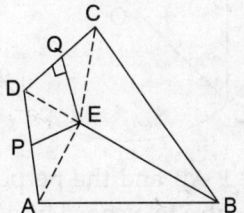

Sol. Given, a quadrilateral ABCD in which AB = BC. PE and QE are right bisectors of AD and CD respectively such that they meet at E.

To prove : BE bisects ∠ ABC.

Construction : Join AE, DE and CE.

Proof : Since, PE is the right bisector of AD and E lies on it.

∴ AE = ED ...(i)

[∵ Points on the right bisector of a line segment are equidistant from the ends of the segment]

Also, QE is the right bisector of CD and E lies on it.

∴ ED = EC ...(ii)

From equations (i) and (ii), we get

AE = EC ...(iii)

Now, in triangles ABE and CBE, we have

AB = BC [Given]

BE = BE [Common]

and AE = EC [From (iii)]

So, by SSS criterion of congruence

∆ ABE = ∆ ACE

⇒ ∠ ABE = ∠ CBE

⇒ BE bisects ∠ ABC.

Hence, BE is the bisector of ∠ ABC.

Hence Proved.

Chapter 15. Circles

1. In the given figure, OD is perpendicular to the chord AB of a circle whose centre is O. If BC is a diameter, show that CA = 2.OD.

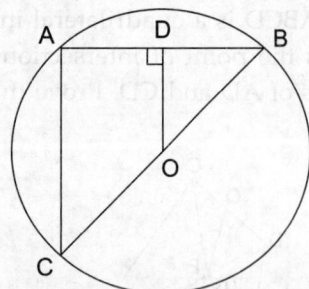

Sol. Since, OD ⊥ AB and the perpendicular drawn from the centre to a chord bisects the chord.

∴ D is the midpoint of AB.

Also, O being the centre, is the midpoint of BC.

Thus, in ΔABC, D and O are midpoints of AB and BC respectively. Therefore, OD ∥ AC

and   OD = $\frac{1}{2}$ CA

[∵ Segment joining the midpoints of two sides of a triangle is half of the third side]

⇒   CA = 2OD.   **Hence Proved.**

2. In the given below figure, O is the centre of the circle and ∠AOC = 160°. Prove that 3∠y − 2∠x = 140°.

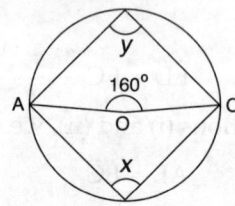

Sol. We know that angle by same arc at circle *i.e.,* on circumference is half of the angle by same arc at centre.

∴   ∠x = $\frac{1}{2}$ × 160° = 80°

(Opposite angles of a cyclic quadrilateral are supplementary)

∴   ∠x + ∠y = 180°

∴   ∠y = 100°

∴   3∠y − 2∠x = 3 × 100° − 2 × 80°

                    = 300° − 160°

                    = 140°   **Hence Proved.**

3. ABCD is quadrilateral inscribed in circle, having ∠A = 60°, O is the centre of the circle, show that

∠OBD + ∠ODB = ∠CBD + ∠CDB

Sol. Here,   ∠BOD = 2 × ∠BAD

                    = 2 × 60°

                    = 120°

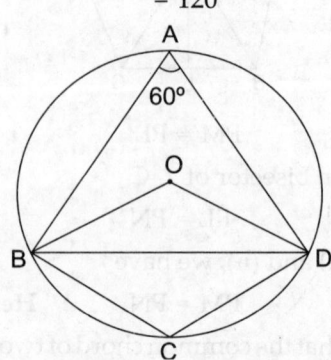

Now in Δ BOD,

∠OBD + ∠ODB = 180° − 120°

                    = 60°   ...(i)

Also ∠DAB + ∠DCB = 180°

                    (ABCD is a cyclic quadrilateral)

⇒   ∠DCB = 180° − 60° = 120°

∴ In Δ BCD,

∠CBD + ∠CDB = 180° − ∠DCB

                    = 180° − 120°

                    = 60°   ... (ii)

From equations (i) and (ii) we get the required result.   **Hence Proved.**

4. In the given figure, PT touches a circle with centre O at R. Diameter SQ when produced meets PT at P. If ∠ SPR = x° and ∠ QRP = y°, show that x° + 2y° = 90°.

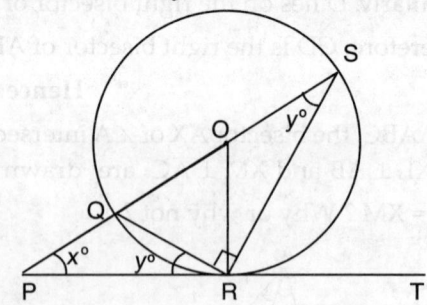

Sol PRT is tangent at R and QR is chord.

∴   ∠ QRP = ∠ QSR

(Angle in alternate segment)

                    = y°

and   ∠ QRS = 90°

(∵ QS is diameter and angle in semicircle is right angle)

Now, in ΔPRS,

$$\angle \text{SPR} + \angle \text{PRS} + \angle \text{RSP} = 180°$$
$$\Rightarrow \qquad x° + y° + 90 + y° = 180°$$
$$\Rightarrow \qquad x° + 2y° = 180° - 90°$$
$$\Rightarrow \qquad x° + 2y° = 90° \qquad \textbf{Hence Proved.}$$

5. In Fig. ABC is a triangle in which $\angle \text{BAC} = 30°$. Show that BC is the radius of the circumcircle of $\triangle$ ABC, whose centre is O.

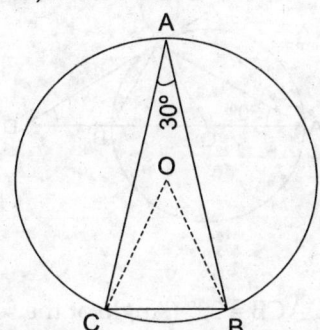

Sol. Join OB and OC. Since, the angle subtended by an arc of a circle at its centre is twice the angle subtended by the same arc at a point on the circumference.

$$\therefore \qquad \angle \text{BOC} = 2 \angle \text{BAC}$$
$$\Rightarrow \qquad \angle \text{BOC} = 2 \times 30° = 60°$$

Now, in $\triangle \text{BOC}$, we have

$$\text{OB} = \text{OC}$$

[Each equal to radius of the circle]

$$\Rightarrow \qquad \angle \text{OBC} = \angle \text{OCB}$$

[$\because$ Angles opposite to equal sides of a triangle are equal]

But $\quad \angle \text{OBC} + \angle \text{OCB} + \angle \text{BOC} = 180°$

$$\therefore \qquad 2 \angle \text{OBC} + 60° = 180°$$
$$\Rightarrow \qquad 2 \angle \text{OBC} = 120°$$
$$\Rightarrow \qquad \angle \text{OBC} = 60°$$

Thus, $\qquad \angle \text{OBC} = \angle \text{OCB}$
$$= \angle \text{BOC} = 60°$$

$\Rightarrow \triangle$ OBC is an equilateral triangle

$$\Rightarrow \qquad \text{OB} = \text{BC}$$

$\Rightarrow$ BC is the radius of the circumcircle of $\triangle$ ABC.

Hence Proved.

6. If O is the circumcentre of a $\triangle$ ABC and OD $\perp$ BC, prove that $\angle$ BOD = $\angle$A.

Sol. Join OB and OC.

In $\triangle$ OBD and $\triangle$ OCD, we have

$$\text{OB} = \text{OC}$$

[Each equal to the radius of circumcircle]

$$\angle \text{ODB} = \angle \text{ODC}$$

[Each equal to 90°]

and $\qquad \text{OD} = \text{OD} \qquad$ [Common]

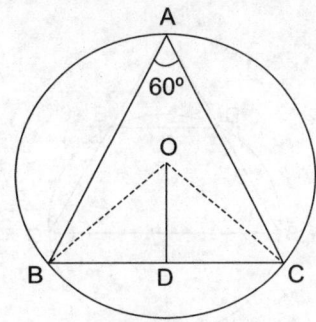

$$\therefore \qquad \triangle \text{OBD} \cong \triangle \text{OCD}$$
$$\Rightarrow \qquad \angle \text{BOD} = \angle \text{COD}$$
$$\Rightarrow \qquad \angle \text{BOC} = 2 \angle \text{BOD} = 2 \angle \text{COD}$$

Now, arc BC subtends $\angle \text{BOC}$ at the centre and $\angle \text{BAC} = \angle \text{A}$ at a point in the remaining part of the circle.

$$\therefore \qquad \angle \text{BOC} = 2\angle \text{A}$$
$$\Rightarrow \qquad 2 \angle \text{BOD} = 2\angle \text{A}$$

$$[\because \angle \text{BOC} = 2 \angle \text{BOD}]$$

$$\Rightarrow \qquad \angle \text{BOD} = \angle \text{A}. \qquad \textbf{Hence Proved.}$$

7. ABCD is a cyclic quadrilateral AB and DC are produced to meet in E. Prove that

$$\triangle \text{EBC} \sim \triangle \text{EDA}.$$

Sol. In triangles EBC and EDA, we have

$$\angle \text{EBC} = \angle \text{EDA}$$

[$\because$ Exterior angle in a cyclic quadrilateral is equal to opposite interior angle]

$$\angle \text{ECB} = \angle \text{EAD}$$

[$\because$ Exterior angle in a cyclic quadrilateral is equal to opposite interior angle]

and $\qquad \angle \text{E} = \angle \text{E}$

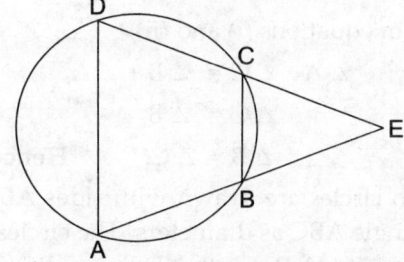

So, by AAA enterior of similarly, we get

$$\triangle \text{EBC} \sim \triangle \text{EDA}. \qquad \textbf{Hence Proved.}$$

8. In an isosceles triangle ABC with AB = AC, a circle passing through B and C intersects the sides AB and AC at D and E respectively. Prove that DE $\parallel$ BC.

Sol. In order to prove that DE $\parallel$ BC, it is sufficient to show that $\angle$ B = $\angle$ ADE.

In $\triangle$ ABC, we have

$$\text{AB} = \text{AC} \Rightarrow \angle \text{B} = \angle \text{C} \qquad ...(i)$$

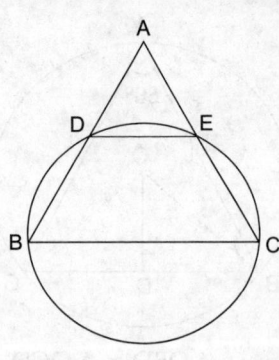

In the cyclic quadrilateral CBDE, side BD is produced to A.

∴   ∠ ADE = ∠ C   ...(ii)

[∵ Exterior angle = Opposite interior angle]

From (i) and (ii), we get

∠ B = ∠ ADE.

Hence,   DE ‖ BC.   **Hence Proved.**

9. If ABCD is a cyclic quadrilateral in which AD ‖ BC, prove that ∠ B = ∠ C.

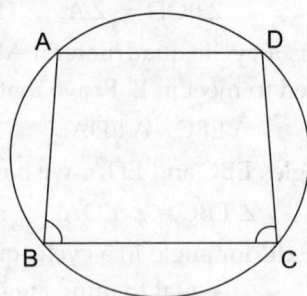

Sol. ABCD is a cyclic quadrilateral.

So,   ∠ A + ∠ C = 180°   ...(i)

Since   AD ‖ BC

So,   ∠ B + ∠ A = 180°   ...(ii)

From equations (i) and (ii),

∠ A + ∠ C = ∠ B + ∠ A

⇒   ∠ C = ∠ B

or   ∠ B = ∠ C.   **Hence Proved.**

10. Two circles are drawn with sides AB, AC of a triangle ABC as diameters. The circles intersect at a point D. Prove that D lies on BC.

Sol. Join AD.

Since, angle in a semicircle is a right angle.

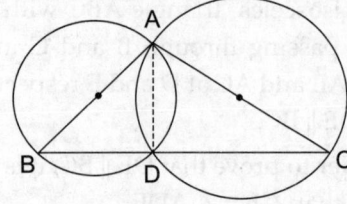

∴   ∠ ADB = 90° and ∠ ADC = 90°

⇒   ∠ADB + ∠ADC = 90° + 90°

⇒   ∠ADB + ∠ADC = 180°

BDC is a straight line

⇒ D lies on BC.   **Hence Proved.**

11. In the figure AB is a diameter and AC is a chord of a circle such that ∠ BAC = 30°. The tangent at C intersect AB produced at D. Prove that BC = BD.

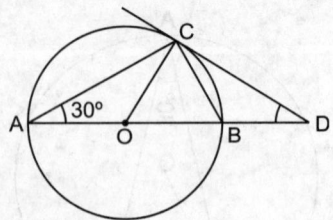

Sol. Join OC.

∠ ACB = 90° (Angle of the semicircle)

∠ ABC = 60°   (Angle sum property)

∠ CBD = 120° (∠ CBD = 180° − ∠ CBA)

∠ OCD = 90°

∠ COB = 60°

(Angle at the centre is equal to twice the that of circumference)

∠ OCB = 60°   (Angle sum property)

∠ BCD = ∠ OCD − ∠ OCB = 30°

∴   ∠ BDC = ∠ BDC = 30°

BD = BC   **Hence Proved.**

12. In an equilateral triangle, prove that the centroid and centre of the circumcircle (circumcentre) coincide.

Sol. Given, an equilateral triangle ABC in which D, E and F are the midpoints of sides BC, CA and AB respectively.

To prove : The centroid and circumcentre are coincident.

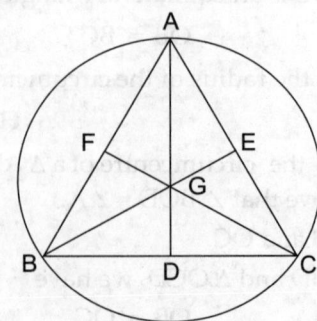

Construction : Draw medians AD, BE and CF.

Proof : Let G be the centroid of ΔABC i.e., the point of intersection of AD, BE and CF. In triangles BEC and BFC, we have

$$\angle B = \angle C = 60°$$
$$BC = BC$$
and $$BF = CE$$

$$\left[\because AB = AC \Rightarrow \frac{1}{2}AB = \frac{1}{2}AC \Rightarrow BF = CE\right]$$

$$\therefore \qquad \Delta BEC \cong \Delta BFC$$
$$\Rightarrow \qquad BE = CF \qquad\qquad ...(i)$$
Similarly, $\quad \Delta CAF \cong \Delta CAD$
$$CF = AD \qquad\qquad ...(ii)$$
From equations (i) and (ii),
$$AD = BE = CF$$
$$\Rightarrow \qquad \frac{2}{3}AD = \frac{2}{3}BE = \frac{2}{3}CF$$
$$CG = \frac{2}{3}CF$$
$$GA = \frac{2}{3}AD,$$
$$GB = \frac{2}{3}BE$$
$$\Rightarrow \qquad GA = GB = GC$$

⇒ G is equidistant from the vertices.

⇒ G is the circumcentre of ΔABC.

Hence, the centroid and circumcentre are coincident. **Hence Proved.**

13 Prove that the angle bisectors of the angles formed by producing opposite sides of a cyclic quadrilateral (provided they are not parallel) intersect at right angle.

Sol. Here, ABCD is a cyclic quadrilateral. PM is bisector of ∠ APB and QM is bisector of ∠AQD.

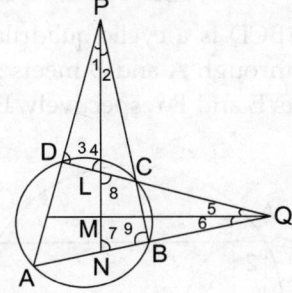

In Δ PDL and Δ PBN,
$$\angle 1 = \angle 2$$

(PM is the bisector of ∠ P)
$$\angle 3 = \angle 9$$

(Exterior angle of a cyclic quadrilateral is equal to the interior opposite angle)
$$\therefore \qquad \angle 4 = \angle 7$$

But $$\angle 4 = \angle 8$$

(Vertically opposite angles)
$$\therefore \qquad \angle 7 = \angle 8$$
Now, in Δ QMN and Δ QML,
$$\angle 7 = \angle 8 \qquad \text{(Proved above)}$$
$$\angle 5 = \angle 6 \quad \text{(QM is bisector of Q)}$$
$$\Delta QMN \sim \Delta QML$$
$$\therefore \qquad \angle QMN = \angle QML$$
But ∠ QMN + ∠ QML = 180°
$$\therefore \qquad \angle QMN = \angle QML = 90°$$
Hence, $\quad \angle PMQ = 90°$ (∵ ∠ PMQ = ∠ QML)

Hence Proved.

14. In figure given below, P is any point on the chord BC of a circle such that AB = AP. Prove that CP = CQ.

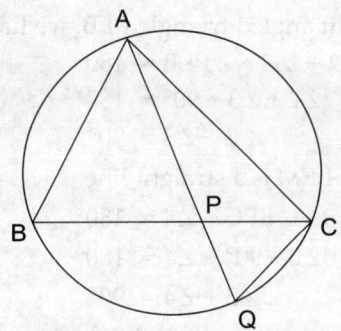

Sol. We have to prove that CP = CQ *i.e.,* ΔCPQ is an isosceles triangle. For this it is sufficient to prove that ∠CPQ = ∠CQP.

In ΔABP, we have
$$AB = AP$$
$$\Rightarrow \qquad \angle APB = \angle ABP$$
$$\Rightarrow \qquad \angle CPQ = \angle APB \qquad\qquad ...(i)$$
[∵ ∠APB and ∠CPQ are vertically opposite angles]

Now, consider arc AC, clearly, it subtends ∠ABC and ∠AQC at points B and Q.
$$\therefore \qquad \angle ABC = \angle AQC$$
[∵ Angles in the same segment]
$$\Rightarrow \qquad \angle ABP = \angle PQC$$
[∵ ∠ABC = ∠ABP and ∠AQC = ∠PQC]
$$\Rightarrow \qquad \angle ABP = \angle CQP \qquad\qquad ...(ii)$$
[∵ ∠PQC = ∠CQP]
From equations (i) and (ii), we get
$$\angle CPQ = \angle CQP$$
$$\Rightarrow \qquad CQ = CP. \qquad \textbf{Hence Proved.}$$

15. The diagonals of a cyclic quadrilateral are at right angles. Prove that the perpendicular from the point of their intersection on any side when produced backward bisects the opposite side.

Sol. Let ABCD be a cyclic quadrilateral such that its diagonals AC and BD intersect in P at right angles. Let PL ⊥ AB such that LP produced to meet CD in M. We have to prove that M bisects CD *i.e.*,

$$CM = MD.$$

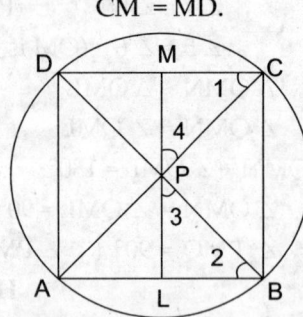

Consider arc AD. Clearly, it makes angles ∠1 and ∠2 in the same segment.

$$∠1 = ∠2 \qquad ...(i)$$

In right angled triangle PLB, we have

$$∠2 + ∠3 + ∠PLB = 180°$$
$$⇒ \qquad ∠2 + ∠3 + 90° = 180°$$
$$⇒ \qquad ∠2 + ∠3 = 90° \qquad ...(ii)$$

Since, LPM is a straight line.

$$∴ \quad ∠3 + ∠BPC + ∠4 = 180°$$
$$⇒ \qquad ∠3 + 90° + ∠4 = 180°$$
$$⇒ \qquad ∠3 + ∠4 = 90° \qquad ...(iii)$$

From equations (ii) and (iii), we get

$$∠2 + ∠3 = ∠3 + ∠4$$
$$⇒ \qquad ∠2 = ∠4 \qquad ...(iv)$$

From equations (i) and (iv), we get

$$∠1 = ∠4 \qquad ...(v)$$
$$⇒ \qquad PM = CM$$

Similarly, $\qquad$ PM = DM.

Hence, $\qquad$ CM = MD. $\quad$ **Hence Proved.**

16. In a circle with centre O, chords AB and CD intersect inside the circumference at E. Prove that ∠AOC + ∠BOD = 2∠AEC.

Sol. Consider arc AC of the circle with centre at O. Clearly, arc AC subtends ∠AOC at the centre and ∠ABC at the remaining part of the circle.

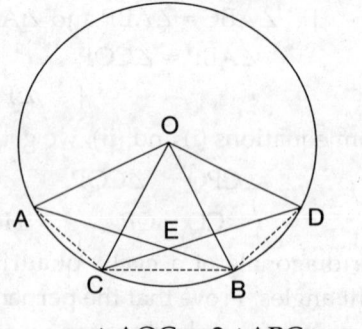

$$∴ \qquad ∠AOC = 2∠ABC \qquad ...(i)$$

Similarly, arc BD subtends ∠BOD at the centre

and ∠BCD at the remaining part of the circle.

$$∴ \qquad ∠BOD = 2∠BCD \qquad ...(ii)$$

Adding equations (i) and (ii), we get

$$∠AOC + ∠BOD = 2(∠ABC + ∠BCD)$$
$$⇒ \quad ∠AOC + ∠BOD = 2∠AEC$$

[∵ ∠AEC is the exterior angle and ∠ABC and ∠BCD are other interior angles of Δ BEC

∴ ∠ABC + ∠BCD = ∠AEC]

Hence Proved.

17. Prove that the circle drawn on any one of the equal sides of an isosceles triangles as diameter bisects the base.

Sol. Given, in isosceles Δ ABC. A circle is drawn taken AB as diameter which intersect BC at D.

To prove : BD = DC.

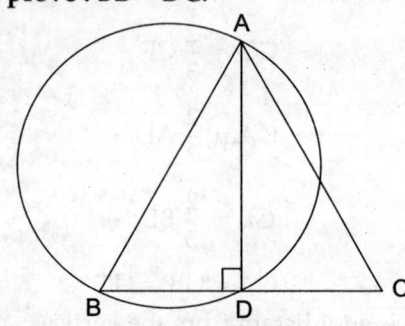

Construction : Join AD.

Proof : $\qquad$ ∠ADB = 90°

(Angle of semi-circle)

In Δ ABD and Δ ACD,

$$AB = AC \qquad \text{(Given)}$$
$$∠ADB = ∠ADC \qquad (90°)$$
$$AD = AD \qquad \text{(Common)}$$
$$∴ \qquad Δ ABD ≅ Δ ADC$$

Hence, $\qquad$ BD = DC. $\quad$ **Hence Proved.**

18. In Fig. ABCD is a cyclic quadrilateral. A circle passing through A and B meets AD and BC in the points E and F respectively. Prove that EF ∥ DC.

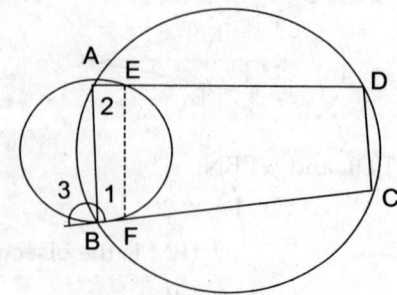

Sol. In order to prove that EF ∥ DC. It is sufficient to show that ∠2 = ∠3.

Since, ABCD is a cyclic quadrilateral.

$$∴ \qquad ∠1 + ∠3 = 180° \qquad ...(i)$$

Similarly, in the cyclic quadrilateral ABFE, we have

$$\angle 1 + \angle 2 = 180° \qquad \text{...(ii)}$$

From equations (i) and (ii), we get

$$\angle 1 + \angle 3 = \angle 1 + \angle 2$$
$$\Rightarrow \qquad \angle 2 = \angle 3.$$

Hence, $\qquad$ EF $\parallel$ DC. **Hence Proved.**

19. If $A = \begin{bmatrix} 3 & 0 \\ 5 & 1 \end{bmatrix}$ and $B = \begin{bmatrix} -4 & 2 \\ 1 & 0 \end{bmatrix}$*

Find $A^2 - 2AB + B^2$

Sol. Given : $\qquad A = \begin{bmatrix} 3 & 0 \\ 5 & 1 \end{bmatrix}$ and $B = \begin{bmatrix} -4 & 2 \\ 1 & 0 \end{bmatrix}$

Now, $A^2 - 2AB + B^2 = \begin{bmatrix} 3 & 0 \\ 5 & 1 \end{bmatrix}\begin{bmatrix} 3 & 0 \\ 5 & 1 \end{bmatrix}$

$$-2\begin{bmatrix} 3 & 0 \\ 5 & 1 \end{bmatrix}\begin{bmatrix} -4 & 2 \\ 1 & 0 \end{bmatrix} + \begin{bmatrix} -4 & 2 \\ 1 & 0 \end{bmatrix}\begin{bmatrix} -4 & 2 \\ 1 & 0 \end{bmatrix}$$

$$= \begin{bmatrix} 9+0 & 0+0 \\ 15+5 & 0+1 \end{bmatrix} - 2\begin{bmatrix} -12+0 & 6+0 \\ -20+1 & 10+0 \end{bmatrix}$$

$$+ \begin{bmatrix} 16+2 & -8+0 \\ -4+0 & 2+0 \end{bmatrix}$$

$$= \begin{bmatrix} 9 & 0 \\ 20 & 1 \end{bmatrix} - 2\begin{bmatrix} -12 & 6 \\ -19 & 10 \end{bmatrix} + \begin{bmatrix} 18 & -8 \\ -4 & 2 \end{bmatrix}$$

$$= \begin{bmatrix} 9 & 0 \\ 20 & 1 \end{bmatrix} + \begin{bmatrix} 24 & -12 \\ 38 & -20 \end{bmatrix} + \begin{bmatrix} 18 & -8 \\ -4 & 2 \end{bmatrix}$$

$$= \begin{bmatrix} 9+24+18 & 0-12-8 \\ 20+38-4 & 1-20+2 \end{bmatrix}$$

$$= \begin{bmatrix} 51 & -20 \\ 54 & -17 \end{bmatrix} \qquad \textbf{Ans.}$$

20. In Fig. AB and CD are two chords of a circle intersecting each other at P such that AP = CP. Show that AB = CD.

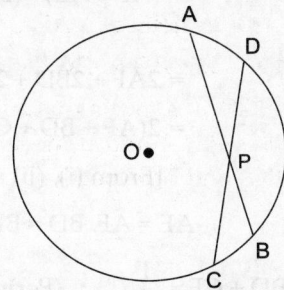

Sol. In order to prove the desired result, we shall first prove that Δ PAD $\sim \Delta$ PCB.

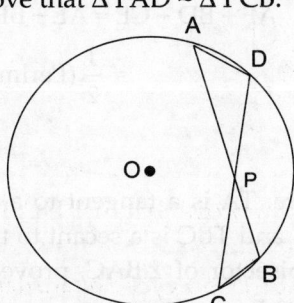

In triangles PAD and PCB, we have

$$\angle PAD = \angle PCB$$

[Angles in the same segment of arc BD]

$$\angle APD = \angle CPB$$

[Vertically opposite angles]

So, by AA criterion of similarity, we have

$$\Delta PAD \sim \Delta PCB$$

$$\Rightarrow \qquad \frac{PA}{PC} = \frac{PD}{PB}$$

[∵ Corresponding sides of similar triangles are in the same ratio]

$$\Rightarrow \qquad \frac{AP}{CP} = \frac{PD}{PB}$$

$$\Rightarrow \qquad 1 = \frac{PD}{PB} \qquad \left[\because AP = CP, \therefore \frac{AP}{CP} = 1\right]$$

$$\Rightarrow \qquad PB = PD$$

$$\Rightarrow \qquad AP + PB = AP + PD$$

[Adding AP on both sides]

$$\Rightarrow \qquad AP + PB = CP + PD \qquad [\because AP = CP]$$

$$\Rightarrow \qquad AB = CD. \qquad \textbf{Hence Proved.}$$

21. If PA and PB are two tangent drawn from a point P to a circle with centre C touching it A and B, prove that CP is the perpendicular bisector of AB.

Sol. We shall prove that

$$\angle ACP = \angle BCP = 90°$$

and $\qquad\qquad$ AC = BC

Now, $\qquad\qquad \angle APC = \angle BPC$

Since O lies on the bisector of $\angle APB$.

Triangles ACP and BCP are congruent traingles by SAS congruence criterion.

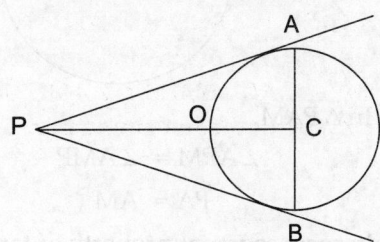

$\therefore \qquad\qquad$ AC = BC

and $\qquad\qquad \angle ACP = \angle BCP$

Since $\angle ACP + \angle BCP = 180°$

$$\Rightarrow \qquad\qquad 2 \angle ACP = 180°$$

$$\Rightarrow \qquad\qquad \angle ACP = 90°$$

$$\therefore \qquad\qquad \angle ACP = \angle BCP = 90°$$

Hence Proved.

22. If AB and CD are two chords which when produced meet at P and if AP = CP, show that AB = CD.

Sol. Here, chords AB and CD of the circle intersect at P.

$$\therefore \qquad PA \times PB = PC \times PD$$

$$\Rightarrow \qquad PB = \frac{PC \times PD}{PA}$$

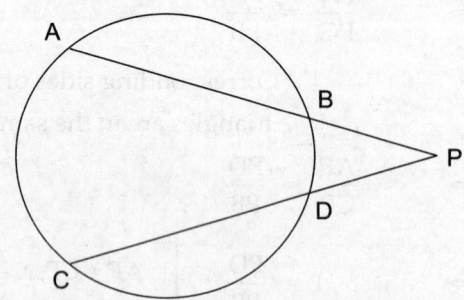

$$\Rightarrow \qquad PB = \frac{AP \times PD}{AP}$$

$$\{\because PC = AP \text{ (given)}\}$$

$$\Rightarrow \qquad PB = PD \qquad \ldots(i)$$

Now, $\qquad AB = AP - BP$

$$\Rightarrow \qquad AB = CP - PD$$

$$[\because AP = CP \text{ (given)}, BP = PD \text{ {From (i)}}]$$

But $\qquad CD = PC - CP$

Hence, $\qquad AB = CD.$ **Hence Proved.**

23. In the figure, PM is a tangent to the circle and PA = AM. Prove that :

(i) ΔPMB is isosceles.

(ii) PA × PB = MB².

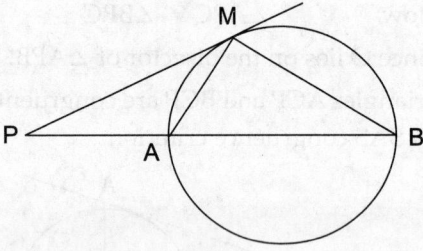

Sol. (i) In Δ PAM,

$$\angle APM = \angle AMP \qquad \ldots (i)$$

$$PA = AM \qquad \text{(Given)}$$

by alternate segment property of tangent

$$\angle ABM = \angle AMP$$

$$\therefore \qquad \angle APM = \angle ABM$$

$$[\text{from (i) and (ii)}]$$

$$\therefore \qquad PM = MB$$

i.e. Δ PMB is an isosceles. **Hence Proved.**

(ii) By rectangle property of tangent and chord

$$PM^2 = PA \times PB$$

$$\therefore \qquad MB^2 = PA \times PB \quad [\because PM = MB]$$

Hence Proved.

24. In figure the incircle of ΔABC, touches the sides BC, CA and AB at D, E respectively. Show that :

$$AF + BD + CE = AE + BF + CD$$

$$= \frac{1}{2} \text{ (Perimeter of ΔABC).}$$

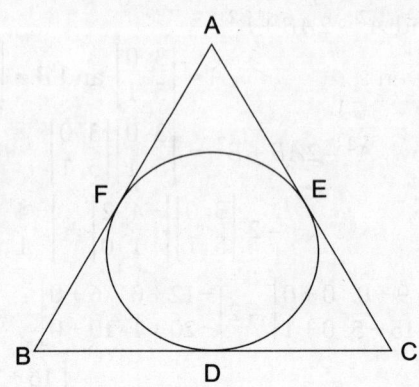

Sol. Since, lengths of the tangents drawn from an exterior point to a circle are equal.

$$\therefore \qquad AF = AE \qquad \ldots(i)$$

$$BD = BF \qquad \ldots(ii)$$

and $\qquad CE = CD \qquad \ldots(iii)$

Adding equations (i), (ii) and (iii), we get

$$AF + BD + CE = AE + BF + CD$$

Now, perimeter of Δ ABC

$$= AB + BC + AC$$

$$= (AF + FB) + (BD + CD)$$

$$+ (AE + EC)$$

$$= (AF + AE) + (BF + BD)$$

$$+ (CD + CE)$$

$$= 2AF + 2BD + 2CE$$

$$= 2(AF + BD + CE)$$

$$[\text{From (i), (ii) and (iii), we get}$$

$$AE = AF, BD = BF \text{ and } CD = CE]$$

$$\therefore AF + BD + CE = \frac{1}{2} \qquad \text{(Perimeter of ΔABC)}$$

Hence, $AF + BD + CE = AE + BF + CD$

$$= \frac{1}{2} \text{ (Perimeter of Δ ABC).}$$

Hence Proved.

25. In figure, TA is a tangent to a circle from the point T and TBC is a secant to the circle. If AD is the bisector of ∠BAC, prove that Δ ADT is isosceles.

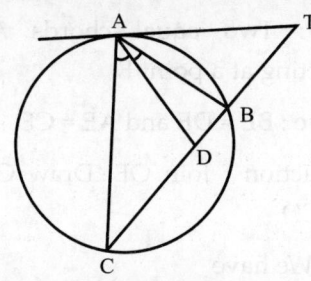

Sol. In order to prove that Δ ADT is isosceles *i.e.*, TA = TD, it is sufficient to show that

$$\angle TAD = \angle TDA.$$

Since ∠TAB and ∠BCA are angles in the alternate segments of chord AB.

∴   ∠TAB = ∠BCA   …(i)

It is given that AD is the bisector of ∠BAC.

∴   ∠BAD = ∠CAD   …(ii)

Now,   ∠TAD = ∠TAB + ∠BAD

⇒   ∠TAD = ∠BCA + ∠CAD

[Using (i) and (ii)]

⇒   ∠TAD = ∠DCA + ∠CAD

[∵ ∠BCA = ∠DCA]

⇒   ∠TAD = 180° − ∠CDA

[In ΔCAD, ∠CAD + ∠DCA + ∠CDA = 180°

∴ ∠CAD + ∠BCA = 180° − ∠CDA]

⇒   ∠TAD = ∠TDA

[∵ ∠CDA + ∠TDA = 180°]

⇒   TD = TA

Hence, ΔADT is isosceles.   **Hence Proved.**

26. In figure AP is a tangent to the circle at P, ABC is a secant and PD is the bisector of ∠BPC.

Prove that $\angle BPD = \dfrac{1}{2} (\angle ABP - \angle APB)$.

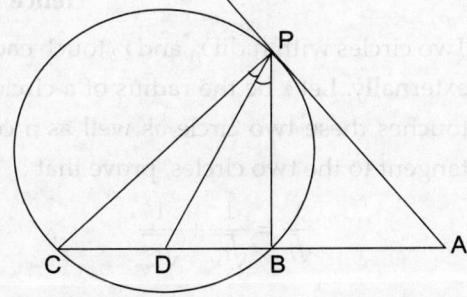

Sol. Since, ∠APB and ∠BCP are angles in alternate segments of chord PB.

∴   ∠APB = ∠BCP   …(i)

Since, PD is bisector of ∠BPC

∴   ∠CPB = 2 ∠BPD   …(ii)

In ΔPCB, side CB has been produced to A, forming exterior angle ∠ABP.

∴   ∠ABP = ∠BCP + ∠CPB

⇒   ∠ABP = ∠APB + 2 ∠BPD

[Using (i) and (ii)]

⇒   2∠BPD = ∠ABP − ∠APB

⇒ $\angle BPD = \dfrac{1}{2} (\angle ABP - \angle APB)$.

Hence Proved.

27. In figure, *n* and *m* are two parallel tangents at A and B. The tangent at C makes an intercept DE between *n* and *m*. Prove that ∠DFE = 90°.

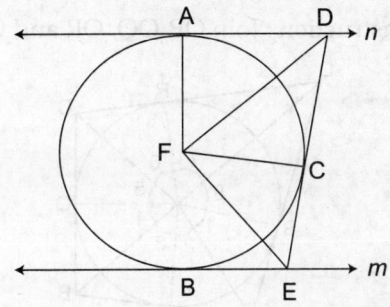

Sol. In triangles ADF and DFC, we have

DA = DC

[Tangents drawn from an external point are equal in length]

DF = DF   [Common]

AF = CF

[Radii of the same circle]

So, by SSS criterion of congruence, we get

Δ ADF ≅ Δ DFC

⇒   ∠ ADF = ∠CDF

⇒   ∠ADC = 2 ∠CDF   …(i)

Similarly, we can prove that

∠BEF = ∠CEF

⇒   ∠CEB = 2 ∠CEF   …(ii)

Now, ∠ADC + ∠CEB = 180°

[Sum of the interior angles on the same side of transversal is 180°]

⇒ 2 (∠CDF + ∠CEF) = 180°

⇒ $\angle CDF + \angle CEF = \dfrac{180°}{2}$

⇒   ∠CDF + ∠CEF = 90°

Now, in Δ DEF,

∠DFE + ∠CDF + ∠CEF = 180°

$\Rightarrow \quad \angle DFE + 90° = 180°$

$\Rightarrow \quad \angle DFE = 180° - 90°$

$\Rightarrow \quad \angle DFE = 90°.$ **Hence Proved.**

28. A circle touches the sides of a quadrilateral ABCD at P, Q, R, S respectively. Show that the angles subtended at the centre by a pair of opposite sides are supplementary.

Sol. Given, a circle with centre O touches the sides AB, BC, CD and DA of a quadrilateral ABCD at the points P, Q, R and S respectively.

To prove :

$\angle AOB + \angle COD = 180°$

and $\angle AOD + \angle BOC = 180°$

Construction : Join OP, OQ, OR and OS.

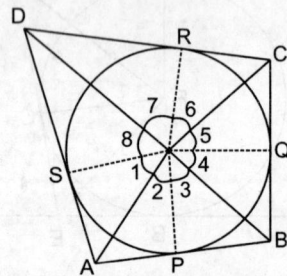

Proof : Since, the two tangents drawn from an external point to a circle subtend equal angles at the centre.

$\therefore \angle 1 = \angle 2, \angle 3 = \angle 4, \angle 5 = \angle 6$ and $\angle 7 = \angle 8$ ...(i)

Now,

$\angle 1 + \angle 2 + \angle 3 + \angle 4 + \angle 5 + \angle 6 + \angle 7 + \angle 8 = 360°$

[Sum of all the angles subtended at a point is 360°]

$\Rightarrow \quad 2(\angle 2 + \angle 3 + \angle 6 + \angle 7) = 360°$

and $2(\angle 1 + \angle 8 + \angle 4 + \angle 5) = 360°$

$\Rightarrow \quad (\angle 2 + \angle 3) + (\angle 6 + \angle 7) = 180°$

and $(\angle 1 + \angle 8) + (\angle 4 + \angle 5) = 180°$

$\Rightarrow \quad \angle AOB + \angle COD = 180°$

[$\because \angle 2 + \angle 3 = \angle AOB, \angle 6 + \angle 7 = \angle COD, \angle 1 + \angle 8 = \angle AOD$ and $\angle 4 + \angle 5 = \angle BOC$]

and $\angle AOD + \angle BOC = 180°$.

Hence Proved.

29. Two equal chords AB and CD of a circle with centre O, when produced meet at a point E, as shown in fig. Prove that BE = DE and AE = CE.

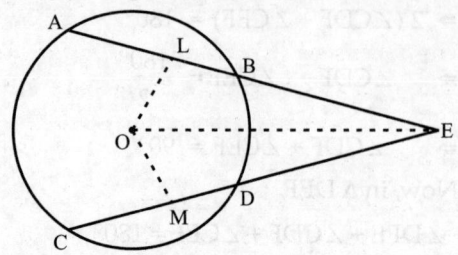

Sol. Given : Two equal chords AB and CD intersecting at a point E.

To prove : BE = DE and AE = CE

Construction : Join OE. Draw OL ⊥ AB and OM ⊥ CD.

Proof : We have

$AB = CD$

$\Rightarrow \quad OL = OM$

[∵ Equal chords are equidistant from the centre]

In triangles OLE and OME, we have

$OL = OM$

$\angle OLE = \angle OM$

[Each equal to 90°]

and $OE = OE$ [Common]

So, by SAS criterion of congruence, we get

$\Delta OLE \cong \Delta OME$

$\Rightarrow \quad LE = ME$ ...(i)

Now, $AB = CD$

$\Rightarrow \quad \frac{1}{2} AB = \frac{1}{2} CD \Rightarrow BL = DM$ ...(ii)

Subtracting (ii) from (i), we get

$LE - BL = ME - DM$

$\Rightarrow \quad BE = DE$

Again, $AB = CD$ and $BE = DE$

$\Rightarrow \quad AB + BE = CD + DE$

$\Rightarrow \quad AE = CE$

Hence, $BE = DE$ and $AE = CE$.

Hence Proved.

30. Two circles with radii r_1 and r_2 touch each other externally. Let r be the radius of a circle which touches these two circle as well as a common tangent to the two circles, prove that :

$$\frac{1}{\sqrt{r}} = \frac{1}{\sqrt{r_1}} + \frac{1}{\sqrt{r_2}}$$

Sol. From the following figure,

$$PQ = SY = \sqrt{XY^2 - XS^2}$$

$$= \sqrt{(r_1 + r_2)^2 - (r_1 - r_2)^2}$$

$$= \sqrt{4r_1 r_2} = 2\sqrt{r_1 r_2}$$

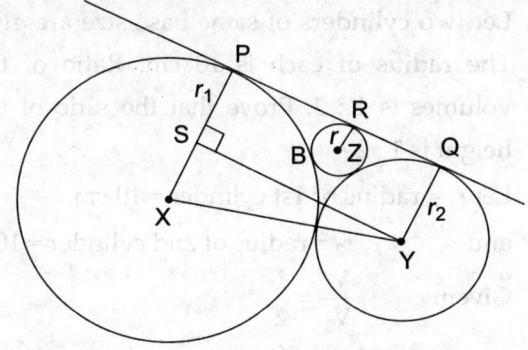

Similarly, $\quad PR = 2\sqrt{r_1 r}$ and $RQ = 2\sqrt{r r_2}$

Now, $\quad\quad\quad\quad PQ = PR + RQ$

$$\therefore \quad\quad 2\sqrt{r_1 r_2} = 2\sqrt{r r_1} + 2\sqrt{r r_2}$$

$$\Rightarrow \quad\quad \sqrt{r_1 r_2} = \sqrt{r r_1} + \sqrt{r r_2}$$

Dividing by $\sqrt{r r_1 r_2}$ on both sides,

$$\Rightarrow \quad\quad \frac{1}{\sqrt{r}} = \frac{1}{\sqrt{r_1}} + \frac{1}{\sqrt{r_2}} \text{ Hence Proved.}$$

31. Prove that the quadrilateral formed by angle bisectors of a cyclic quadrilateral ABCD is also cyclic.

Sol. Given, in cyclic quadrilateral ABCD, the angle bisectors formed a quadrilateral ABCD.

To prove : PQRS is a cyclic quadrilateral.

Proof : In cyclic quadrilateral ABCD, AR and BS

be the bisectors of $\angle A$ and $\angle B$.

So, $\quad\quad \angle 1 = \angle A/2$ and $\angle 2 = \angle B/2$

In Δ ASB, $\angle RSP$ is the exterior angle,

So, $\quad\quad\quad\quad \angle RSP = \angle 1 + \angle 2$

$$\angle RSP = \frac{\angle A}{2} + \frac{\angle B}{2} \quad\quad \text{...(i)}$$

Similarly, $\quad \angle PQR = \frac{\angle C}{2} + \frac{\angle D}{2} \quad \text{...(ii)}$

Adding equations (i) and (ii),

$$\angle PQR + \angle RSP = \frac{1}{2}(\angle A + \angle B + \angle C + \angle D)$$

$$= \frac{1}{2} \times 360° = 180°$$

$$\Rightarrow \quad \angle PQR + \angle RSP = 180°$$

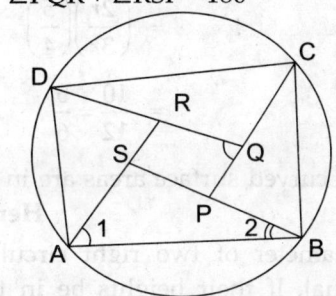

But these are the opposite angles of quadrilateral PQRS.

Hence, PQRS is a cyclic quadrilateral.

Hence Proved.

Chapter 17. Mensuration

1. The circumference of the base of a 10 m high conical tent is 44 metre. Prove that the length of canvas used in making the tent is approximately 134 metres if width of canvas is 2 m. (Take π = 22/7)

Sol. Let r m be the radius of the base, h m be the height and l m be the slant height of the cone. Then,

$$\text{Circumference} = 44 \text{ metres}$$

$$\Rightarrow \quad\quad\quad 2\pi r = 44$$

$$\Rightarrow \quad\quad 2 \times \frac{22}{7} \times r = 44$$

$$\Rightarrow \quad\quad\quad\quad r = 7 \text{ metres}$$

It is given that $h = 10$ metres

$$\therefore \quad\quad\quad\quad l^2 = r^2 + h^2$$

$$\Rightarrow \quad\quad\quad l = \sqrt{r^2 + h^2}$$

$$l = \sqrt{49 + 100} = \sqrt{149}$$

$$= 12 \cdot 2 \text{ m}$$

Now, surface area of the tent

$$= \pi r l \text{ m}^2$$

$$= \frac{22}{7} \times 7 \times 12 \cdot 2 \text{ m}^2$$

$$= 268 \cdot 4 \text{ m}^2$$

$\therefore$ Area of the canvas used $= 268 \cdot 4$ m²

It is given that the width of the canvas is 2 m.

$\therefore$ Length of the canvas used

$$= \frac{\text{Area}}{\text{Width}}$$

$$= \frac{268 \cdot 4}{2}$$

$$= 134 \cdot 2 \text{ metres} \approx 134 \text{ metres}$$

Hence Proved.

2. The radius of two circular cylinder are in the ratio of 2 : 3 and their volumes are in the ratio of 5 : 9. Prove that the curved surface areas are in the ratio 5 : 6.

Sol. Let $2r$ and $3r$ be the radius of two cylinders, respectively. Let $5V_1$ and $9V_2$ be the volumes of two cylinders respectively.

$$\frac{V_1}{V_2} = \frac{5}{9} = \frac{\pi r_1^2 h_1}{\pi r_2^2 h_2}$$

$$\Rightarrow \qquad \frac{4r^2 h_1}{9r^2 h_2} = \frac{5}{9}$$

$$\Rightarrow \qquad \frac{h_1}{h_2} = \frac{9 \times 5}{4 \times 9} = \frac{5}{4}.$$

Then, let S_1 and S_2 be curved surface areas of both cylinders, respectively.

Then, $$\frac{S_1}{S_2} = \frac{2\pi r_1 h_1}{2\pi r_2 h_2}$$

$$= \left(\frac{2r}{3r}\right)\left(\frac{5}{4}\right)$$

$$= \frac{10}{12} = \frac{5}{6}$$

Hence, curved surface areas are in the ratio of 5 : 6. **Hence Proved.**

3. The diameter of two right circular cylinder are equal. If their heights be in the ratio of 2 : 5. Prove that the ratio of curved surface area is 2 : 5.

Sol. Let $d_1 = d_2 = d$,

$$\therefore \qquad r_1 = r_2 = r$$

and height be $2x$ and $5x$ respectively.

Then, $$\frac{S_1}{S_2} = \frac{2\pi r_1 h_1}{2\pi r_2 h_2}$$

$$= \frac{2\pi r \cdot 2x}{2\pi r \cdot 5x} = \frac{2}{5}$$

Hence, required ratio is 2 : 5. **Hence Proved.**

4. The radius of two cylinders are in the ratio of 1 : 4. Heights of both are equal. Prove that the ratio between their volume is 1 : 16.

Sol. Let r_1 and r_2 be the radius of two cylinders.

$$\therefore \qquad \frac{r_1}{r_2} = \frac{1}{4}$$

and $$h_1 = h_2 = h.$$

$$\frac{\text{Vol. of cylinder 1st}}{\text{Vol. of cylinder 22nd}} = \frac{\pi r_1^2 h_1}{\pi r_2^2 h_2}$$

$$= \left(\frac{r_1}{r_2}\right)^2 = \left(\frac{1}{4}\right)^2 = \frac{1}{16}$$

Hence, ratio of their volume is 1 : 16.
Hence Proved.

5. Let two cylinders of same base size are given. The radius of each is 10 cm. Ratio of their volumes is 1 : 2. Prove that the ratio of their height is 1 : 2.

Sol. Let r_1 = radius of 1st cylinder = 10 cm

and r_2 = radius of 2nd cylinder = 10 cm

Given, $$\frac{V_1}{V_2} = \frac{1}{2}$$

Now, $$\frac{V_1}{V_2} = \frac{\text{Vol. of lst cylinder}}{\text{Vol. of 2nd cylinder}} = \frac{1}{2}$$

$$\Rightarrow \qquad \frac{\pi r_1^2 h_1}{\pi r_2^2 h_2} = \frac{1}{2}$$

$$\Rightarrow \qquad \frac{(10)^2 h_1}{(10)^2 h_2} = \frac{1}{2}$$

$$\Rightarrow \qquad \frac{h_1}{h_2} = \frac{1}{2}.$$

Hence, ratio of height is 1 : 2. **Hence Proved.**

6. Two cylinders have bases of same size. The diameter of each is 15 cm one of the cylinder is 12 cm high and the other is 24 cm high. Prove that the ratio of their volumes is 1 : 2.

Sol. Let r_1 = radius of 1st cylinder

$$= \frac{15}{2} \text{ cm}$$

r_2 = Radius of 2nd cylinder

$$= \frac{15}{2} \text{ cm}$$

Height h_1 = Height of 1st cylinder

$$= 12 \text{ cm}$$

h_2 = Height of 2nd cylinder

$$= 24 \text{ cm}.$$

Now $$\frac{\text{Vol. of 1st cylinder}}{\text{Vol. of 2nd cylinder}} = \frac{\pi r_1^2 h_1}{\pi r_2^2 h_2}$$

$$= \frac{\pi \times (15/2)^2 \times 12}{\pi \times (15/2)^2 \times 24}$$

$$= \frac{12}{24}$$

$$= 1 : 2$$

$\therefore$ Ratio of volumes is 1 : 2. **Hence Proved.**

Chapter 18. Trigonometry

1. Prove that :*

$$\frac{\sin A}{1 + \cot A} - \frac{\cos A}{1 + \tan A} = \sin A - \cos A$$

Sol. To prove :

$$\frac{\sin A}{1 + \cot A} - \frac{\cos A}{1 + \tan A} = \sin A - \cos A$$

Taking, L.H.S.$= \dfrac{\sin A}{1 + \cot A} - \dfrac{\cos A}{1 + \tan A}$

$$= \frac{\sin A \times \sin A}{\sin A + \cos A} - \frac{\cos A \times \cos A}{\cos A + \sin A}$$

$$= \frac{\sin^2 A - \cos^2 A}{\sin A + \cos A}$$

$$= \frac{(\sin A - \cos A)(\sin A + \cos A)}{(\sin A + \cos A)}$$

$$[\because a^2 - b^2 = (a - b)(a + b)]$$

$$= \sin A - \cos A = \text{R.H.S.}$$

Hence Proved.

2. Prove that :*

$(\operatorname{cosec} \theta - \sin \theta)(\sec \theta - \cos \theta)(\tan \theta + \cot \theta) = 1$

Sol. To prove :

$(\operatorname{cosec} \theta - \sin \theta)(\sec \theta - \cos \theta)(\tan \theta + \cot \theta) = 1$

L.H.S.$= (\operatorname{cosec} \theta - \sin \theta)(\sec \theta - \cos \theta)$

$$(\tan \theta + \cot \theta)$$

$$= \left(\frac{1}{\sin \theta} - \sin \theta\right)\left(\frac{1}{\cos \theta} - \cos \theta\right)\left(\frac{\sin \theta}{\cos \theta} + \frac{\cos \theta}{\sin \theta}\right)$$

$$= \left(\frac{1 - \sin^2\theta}{\sin \theta}\right)\left(\frac{1 - \cos^2\theta}{\cos \theta}\right)\left(\frac{\sin^2 \theta + \cos^2 \theta}{\sin \theta \cos \theta}\right)$$

$$= \frac{\cos^2 \theta}{\sin \theta} \times \frac{\sin^2 \theta}{\cos \theta} \times \frac{1}{\sin \theta \cos \theta}$$

$$= \frac{\cos^2 \theta}{\cos^2 \theta} \times \frac{\sin^2 \theta}{\sin^2 \theta}$$

$$= 1 = \text{R.H.S.}$$

Hence Proved.

3. Prove that $\dfrac{\cos \theta}{1 - \sin \theta} = \dfrac{1 + \sin \theta}{\cos \theta}.$

Sol. L.H.S. $= \dfrac{\cos \theta}{1 - \sin \theta}$

$$= \frac{\cos \theta\,(1 + \sin \theta)}{(1 - \sin \theta)(1 + \sin \theta)}$$

$$= \frac{\cos \theta\,(1 + \sin \theta)}{1 - \sin^2 \theta}$$

$$= \frac{\cos \theta\,(1 + \sin \theta)}{\cos^2 \theta}$$

$$= \frac{1 + \sin \theta}{\cos \theta}. \quad \textbf{Hence Proved.}$$

4. Prove that

$$\sin^2 \theta + \cos^4 \theta = \cos^2 \theta + \sin^4 \theta.$$

Sol. L.H.S. $= \sin^2 \theta + \cos^4 \theta$

$$= 1 - \cos^2 \theta + \cos^4 \theta$$

$$= 1 - \cos^2 \theta\,(1 - \cos^2 \theta)$$

$$= 1 - (1 - \sin^2 \theta)\sin^2 \theta$$

$$= 1 - \sin^2 \theta + \sin^4 \theta$$

$$= \cos^2 \theta + \sin^4 \theta = \text{R.H.S.}$$

Hence Proved.

5. Prove that

$$\sin^4 \theta - \cos^4 \theta = \sin^2 \theta - \cos^2 \theta$$

$$= 2 \sin^2 \theta - 1$$

$$= 1 - 2 \cos^2 \theta.$$

Sol. Consider, $\sin^4 \theta - \cos^4 \theta$

$$= (\sin^2 \theta)^2 - (\cos^2 \theta)^2$$

$$= (\sin^2 \theta - \cos^2 \theta)(\sin^2 \theta + \cos^2 \theta)$$

$$= (\sin^2 \theta - \cos^2 \theta) \times 1$$

$$= \sin^2 \theta - \cos^2 \theta$$

$$= \sin^2 \theta - (1 - \sin^2 \theta)$$

$$= \sin^2 \theta - 1 + \sin^2 \theta$$

$$= 2 \sin^2 \theta - 1$$

$$= 2(1 - \cos^2 \theta) - 1$$

$$= 2 - 2 \cos^2 \theta - 1$$

$$= 1 - 2 \cos^2 \theta \quad \textbf{Hence Proved.}$$

6. Prove that

$$\tan^2 \phi + \cot^2 \phi + 2 = \sec^2 \phi \cdot \operatorname{cosec}^2 \phi.$$

Sol. L.H.S. $= \tan^2 \phi + \cot^2 \phi + 2$

$$= \tan^2 \phi + 1 + \cot^2 \phi + 1$$

$$= \sec^2 \phi + \operatorname{cosec}^2 \phi$$

$$= \frac{1}{\cos^2 \phi} + \frac{1}{\sin^2 \phi}$$

---

* **Frequently asked previous years Board Exam Questions.**

$$= \frac{\sin^2 \phi + \cos^2 \phi}{\sin^2 \phi . \cos^2 \phi}$$

$$= \frac{1}{\sin^2 \phi . \cos^2 \phi}$$

$$= \cosec^2 \phi . \sec^2 \phi = \text{R.H.S.}$$

Hence Proved.

7. Prove that

$$\sqrt{2 + \tan^2 \theta + \cot^2 \theta} = \tan \theta + \cot \theta.$$

Sol. L.H.S. $= \sqrt{2 + \tan^2 \theta + \cot^2 \theta}$

$$= \sqrt{\tan^2 \theta + \cot^2 \theta + 2\tan\theta.\cot\theta}$$

$$= \sqrt{(\tan \theta + \cot \theta)^2}$$

$$[\because \tan \theta \cot \theta = 1]$$

$$= \tan \theta + \cot \theta = \text{R.H.S.}$$

Hence Proved.

8. Prove that $\dfrac{\sec\theta - 1}{\sec\theta + 1} = \left(\dfrac{\sin\theta}{1 + \cos\theta}\right)^2$.

Sol. L.H.S. $= \dfrac{\sec\theta - 1}{\sec\theta + 1}$

$$= \frac{\dfrac{1}{\cos\theta} - 1}{\dfrac{1}{\cos\theta} + 1}$$

$$= \frac{1 - \cos\theta}{1 + \cos\theta}$$

$$= \frac{(1 - \cos\theta) \times (1 + \cos\theta)}{(1 + \cos\theta) \times (1 + \cos\theta)}$$

$$= \frac{1 - \cos^2 \theta}{(1 + \cos\theta)^2}$$

$$= \frac{\sin^2 \theta}{(1 + \cos\theta)^2}$$

$$= \left(\frac{\sin\theta}{1 + \cos\theta}\right)^2 = \text{R.H.S.}$$

Hence Proved.

9. Prove that

$$\frac{\sin\theta \tan\theta}{1 - \cos\theta} = 1 + \sec\theta.$$

Sol. L.H.S. $= \dfrac{\sin\theta \tan\theta}{1 - \cos\theta} = \dfrac{\sin\theta . \dfrac{\sin\theta}{\cos\theta}}{1 - \cos\theta}$

$$= \frac{\sin^2 \theta}{\cos\theta (1 - \cos\theta)}$$

$$= \frac{1 - \cos^2 \theta}{\cos\theta (1 - \cos\theta)}$$

$$= \frac{(1 - \cos\theta)(1 + \cos\theta)}{\cos\theta (1 - \cos\theta)}$$

$$= \frac{1 + \cos\theta}{\cos\theta} = \frac{1}{\cos\theta} + \frac{\cos\theta}{\cos\theta}$$

$$= \sec\theta + 1$$

$$= \text{R.H.S.} \qquad \textbf{Hence Proved.}$$

10. Prove that $(1 + \cot\theta - \cosec\theta)(1 + \tan\theta + \sec\theta) = 2$*

Sol. To prove, $(1 + \cot\theta - \cosec\theta)(1 + \tan\theta + \sec\theta) = 2$

$\therefore$ L.H.S.$= (1 + \cot\theta - \cosec\theta)$

$$(1 + \tan\theta + \sec\theta)$$

$$= \left(1 + \frac{\cos\theta}{\sin\theta} - \frac{1}{\sin\theta}\right)$$

$$\left(1 + \frac{\sin\theta}{\cos\theta} + \frac{1}{\cos\theta}\right)$$

$$= \left(\frac{\sin\theta + \cos\theta - 1}{\sin\theta}\right)$$

$$\left(\frac{\cos\theta + \sin\theta + 1}{\cos\theta}\right)$$

$$= \frac{(\sin\theta + \cos\theta)^2 - (1)^2}{\sin\theta\cos\theta}$$

$$[\because (a + b)(a - b) = a^2 - b^2]$$

$$= \frac{\sin^2\theta + \cos^2\theta + 2\sin\theta\cos\theta - 1}{\sin\theta\cos\theta}$$

$$= \frac{1 + 2\sin\theta\cos\theta - 1}{\sin\theta\cos\theta} \quad [\because \sin^2\theta + \cos^2\theta = 1]$$

$$= \frac{2\sin\theta\cos\theta}{\sin\theta\cos\theta}$$

$$= 2 = \text{R.H.S.} \qquad \textbf{Hence Proved.}$$

11. Prove that

$$\frac{\sec\theta - \tan\theta}{\sec\theta + \tan\theta} = 1 - 2\sec\theta.\tan\theta + 2\tan^2\theta.$$

Sol. L.H.S. $= \dfrac{\sec\theta - \tan\theta}{\sec\theta + \tan\theta}$

$$= \frac{\sec\theta - \tan\theta}{\sec\theta + \tan\theta} \times \frac{\sec\theta - \tan\theta}{\sec\theta - \tan\theta}$$

Prove the Following

---

* **Frequently asked previous years Board Exam Questions.**

$$= \frac{(\sec\theta - \tan\theta)^2}{\sec^2\theta + \tan^2\theta}$$

$$= \frac{\sec^2\theta + \tan^2\theta - 2\sec\theta.\tan\theta}{1}$$

$$= 1 + 2\tan^2\theta - 2\sec\theta.\tan\theta$$

$$= \text{R.H.S.} \qquad \textbf{Hence Proved.}$$

12. Prove that :

$$(1+\tan A)^2 + (1-\tan A)^2 = 2\sec^2 A.$$

Sol. $\quad$ L.H.S. $= (1+\tan A)^2 + (1-\tan A)^2$

$$= 1 + 2\tan A + \tan^2 A$$

$$+ 1 - 2\tan A + \tan^2 A$$

$$= 2(1 + \tan^2 A)$$

$$= 2\sec^2 A = \text{R.H.S.}$$

$$\textbf{Hence Proved.}$$

13. Prove that

$$\frac{1}{\sec A - 1} + \frac{1}{\sec A + 1} = 2\,\text{cosec}\,A.\cot A.$$

Sol. $\quad$ L.H.S. $= \dfrac{1}{\sec A - 1} + \dfrac{1}{\sec A + 1}$

$$= \frac{\sec A + 1 + \sec A - 1}{\sec^2 A - 1} = \frac{2\sec A}{\tan^2 A}$$

$$= 2\frac{1}{\cos A} \times \frac{1}{\dfrac{\sin^2 A}{\cos^2 A}} = 2\frac{1}{\cos A} \times \frac{\cos^2 A}{\sin^2 A}$$

$$= 2\,\text{cosec}\,A.\cot A$$

$$= \text{R.H.S.} \qquad \textbf{Hence Proved.}$$

14. Prove that

$$\frac{1 + \sin\theta}{1 - \sin\theta} = 1 + 2\frac{\tan\theta}{\cos\theta} + 2\tan^2\theta.$$

Sol. $\quad$ R.H.S. $= 1 + 2\dfrac{\tan\theta}{\cos\theta} + 2\tan^2\theta$

$$= 1 + 2\frac{\sin\theta}{\cos^2\theta} + 2\frac{\sin^2\theta}{\cos^2\theta}$$

$$= \frac{\cos^2\theta + 2\sin\theta + 2\sin^2\theta}{\cos^2\theta}$$

$$= \frac{1 - \sin^2\theta + 2\sin\theta + 2\sin^2\theta}{1 - \sin^2\theta}$$

$$= \frac{1 - \sin^2\theta + 2\sin\theta}{1 - \sin^2\theta}$$

$$= \frac{(1 + \sin\theta)^2}{(1 + \sin\theta)(1 - \sin\theta)}$$

$$= \frac{1 + \sin\theta}{1 - \sin\theta}$$

$$= \text{L.H.S.} \qquad \textbf{Hence Proved.}$$

15. Prove that

$$1 - \frac{\cos^2\theta}{1 + \sin\theta} = \sin\theta$$

Sol. $\quad$ L.H.S. $= 1 - \dfrac{\cos^2\theta}{1 + \sin\theta} = 1 - \dfrac{(1 - \sin^2\theta)}{1 + \sin\theta}$

$$= 1 - \frac{(1 - \sin\theta)(1 + \sin\theta)}{1 + \sin\theta}$$

$$= 1 - (1 - \sin\theta) = 1 - 1 + \sin\theta$$

$$= \sin\theta = \text{R.H.S.} \qquad \textbf{Hence Proved.}$$

16. Prove that :

(i) $\quad \sqrt{\dfrac{1 - \cos\theta}{1 + \cos\theta}} = \text{cosec}\,\theta - \cot\theta$

(ii) $\quad \sqrt{\dfrac{1 + \sin\theta}{1 - \sin\theta}} = \sec\theta + \tan\theta$

Sol. (i) $\quad$ L.H.S. $= \sqrt{\dfrac{1 - \cos\theta}{1 + \cos\theta} \times \dfrac{1 - \cos\theta}{1 - \cos\theta}}$

$$= \sqrt{\frac{(1 - \cos\theta)^2}{1 - \cos^2\theta}}$$

$$= \frac{1 - \cos\theta}{\sqrt{1 - \cos^2\theta}}$$

$$= \frac{1 - \cos\theta}{\sqrt{\sin^2\theta}}$$

$$= \frac{1 - \cos\theta}{\sin\theta}$$

$$= \frac{1}{\sin\theta} - \frac{\cos\theta}{\sin\theta}$$

$$= \text{cosec}\,\theta - \cot\theta$$

$$= \text{R.H.S.} \qquad \textbf{Hence Proved.}$$

(ii) $\quad$ L.H.S. $= \sqrt{\dfrac{1 + \sin\theta}{1 - \sin\theta} \times \dfrac{1 + \sin\theta}{1 + \sin\theta}}$

$$= \sqrt{\frac{(1 + \sin\theta)^2}{1 - \sin^2\theta}}$$

$$= \sqrt{\frac{(1 + \sin\theta)^2}{\cos^2\theta}}$$

$$= \frac{1+\sin\theta}{\cos\theta} = \frac{1}{\cos\theta} + \frac{\sin\theta}{\cos\theta}$$

$$= \sec\theta + \tan\theta = \text{R.H.S.}$$

Hence Proved.

17. Prove that

$(\csc A - \sin A)(\sec A - \cos A)\sec^2 A = \tan A.$

Sol. L.H.S. $= (\csc A - \sin A)(\sec A - \cos A) \cdot \sec^2 A$

$$= \left(\frac{1}{\sin A} - \sin A\right) \cdot \left(\frac{1}{\cos A} - \cos A\right) \cdot \frac{1}{\cos^2 A}$$

$$= \left(\frac{1-\sin^2 A}{\sin A}\right) \times \left(\frac{1-\cos^2 A}{\cos A}\right) \times \frac{1}{\cos^2 A}$$

$$= \frac{\cos^2 A}{\sin A} \times \frac{\sin^2 A}{\cos A} \times \frac{1}{\cos^2 A}$$

$$\left[\begin{array}{l} \because \ (1-\sin^2 A) = \cos^2 A \\ \text{and } 1-\cos^2 A = \sin^2 A \end{array}\right]$$

$$= \frac{\sin A}{\cos A} = \tan A$$

$$= \text{R.H.S.}$$ 　　**Hence Proved.**

18. Prove that

$$\frac{\sin\theta \tan\theta}{1-\cos\theta} = 1 + \sec\theta.$$

Sol. 　　L.H.S. $= \dfrac{\sin\theta \cdot \tan\theta}{1-\cos\theta}$

$$= \frac{\sin\theta \cdot \dfrac{\sin\theta}{\cos\theta}}{1-\cos\theta}$$

$$= \frac{\sin^2\theta}{\cos\theta\,(1-\cos\theta)}$$

$$= \frac{1-\cos^2\theta}{\cos\theta\,(1-\cos\theta)}$$

$$= \frac{(1+\cos\theta)\,(1-\cos\theta)}{\cos\theta\,(1-\cos\theta)}$$

$$= \frac{1+\cos\theta}{\cos\theta}$$

$$= \frac{1}{\cos\theta} + \frac{\cos\theta}{\cos\theta}$$

$$= \sec\theta + 1 = \text{R.H.S.}$$

Hence Proved.

19. Prove that

$$\frac{\tan^2\theta}{(\sec\theta-1)^2} = \frac{1+\cos\theta}{1-\cos\theta}.$$

Sol. 　　L.H.S. $= \dfrac{\tan^2\theta}{(\sec\theta-1)^2}$

$$= \frac{\dfrac{\sin^2\theta}{\cos^2\theta}}{\left(\dfrac{1}{\cos\theta}-1\right)^2}$$

$$\left(\begin{array}{l} \because \tan\theta = \dfrac{\sin\theta}{\cos\theta} \\ \text{and } \sec\theta = \dfrac{1}{\cos\theta} \end{array}\right)$$

$$= \frac{\dfrac{\sin^2\theta}{\cos^2\theta}}{\dfrac{(1-\cos\theta)^2}{\cos^2\theta}}$$

$$= \frac{\sin^2\theta}{(1-\cos\theta)^2}$$

$$= \frac{1-\cos^2\theta}{(1-\cos\theta)^2}$$

$$[\because \ \sin^2\theta = 1 - \cos^2\theta]$$

$$= \frac{(1-\cos\theta)\,(1+\cos\theta)}{(1-\cos\theta)}$$

$$\left[\because a^2 - b^2 = (a+b)\,(a-b)\right]$$

$$= \frac{1+\cos\theta}{1-\cos\theta} = \text{R.H.S.}$$

Hence Proved.

20. Prove that

$$\left(\frac{1-\cos^2\theta}{\cos\theta}\right)\left(\frac{1-\sin^2\theta}{\sin\theta}\right) = \frac{1}{\tan\theta + \cot\theta}.$$

Sol. 　　L.H.S. $= \left(\dfrac{1-\cos^2\theta}{\cos\theta}\right)\left(\dfrac{1-\sin^2\theta}{\sin\theta}\right)$

$$= \frac{\sin^2\theta}{\cos\theta} \cdot \frac{\cos^2\theta}{\sin\theta}$$

$$= \sin\theta \cdot \cos\theta$$

R.H.S. $= \dfrac{1}{\tan\theta + \cot\theta}$

$$= \frac{1}{\dfrac{\sin\theta}{\cos\theta} + \dfrac{\cos\theta}{\sin\theta}}$$

Prove the Following

$$= \frac{1}{\dfrac{\sin^2\theta + \cos^2\theta}{\sin\theta\cos\theta}}$$

$$= \frac{\sin\theta\cos\theta}{\sin^2\theta + \cos^2\theta}$$

$$= \sin\theta\cos\theta \quad \textbf{Hence Proved.}$$

21. Prove the following identities :

(i) $\dfrac{\cos\theta}{1+\sin\theta} = \dfrac{1-\sin\theta}{\cos\theta}$

(ii) $\sec^2\theta + \text{cosec}^2\theta = \sec^2\theta\,\text{cosec}^2\theta$

(iii) $\dfrac{1+\sin\theta}{\cos\theta} + \dfrac{\cos\theta}{1+\sin\theta} = 2\sec\theta$

(iv) $\cot\theta - \tan\theta = \dfrac{2\cos^2\theta - 1}{\sin\theta\cos\theta}$

(v) $\dfrac{1}{\sin\theta + \cos\theta} + \dfrac{1}{\sin\theta - \cos\theta} = \dfrac{2\sin\theta}{1 - 2\sin^2\theta}$

Sol. (i) L.H.S. $= \dfrac{\cos\theta}{1+\sin\theta}$

Multiplying numerator and denominator by $1-\sin\theta$,

$$= \frac{\cos\theta\,(1-\sin\theta)}{(1+\sin\theta)\,(1-\sin\theta)}$$

$$= \frac{\cos\theta\,(1-\sin\theta)}{1-\sin^2\theta}$$

$$= \frac{\cos\theta\,(1-\sin\theta)}{\cos^2\theta}$$

$$= \frac{1-\sin\theta}{\cos\theta}$$

$$= \text{R.H.S.} \quad \textbf{Hence Proved.}$$

(ii) L.H.S. $= \sec^2\theta + \text{cosec}^2\theta$

$$= \frac{1}{\cos^2\theta} + \frac{1}{\sin^2\theta}$$

$$= \frac{\sin^2\theta + \cos^2\theta}{\sin^2\theta\cos^2\theta}$$

$$= \frac{1}{\sin^2\theta\cos^2\theta}$$

$$= \frac{1}{\sin^2\theta} \times \frac{1}{\cos^2\theta}$$

$$= \text{cosec}^2\theta \cdot \sec^2\theta = \text{R.H.S.}$$

$$\textbf{Hence Proved.}$$

(iii) L.H.S. $= \dfrac{1+\sin\theta}{\cos\theta} + \dfrac{\cos\theta}{1+\sin\theta}$

$$= \frac{(1+\sin\theta)^2 + \cos^2\theta}{\cos\theta\,(1+\sin\theta)}$$

$$= \frac{1 + \sin^2\theta + 2\sin\theta + \cos^2\theta}{\cos\theta\,(1+\sin\theta)}$$

$$= \frac{1 + (\sin^2\theta + \cos^2\theta) + 2\sin\theta}{\cos\theta\,(1+\sin\theta)}$$

$$= \frac{1 + 1 + 2\sin\theta}{\cos\theta\,(1+\sin\theta)}$$

$$= \frac{2\,(1+\sin\theta)}{\cos\theta\,(1+\sin\theta)}$$

$$= 2\sec\theta = \text{R.H.S.}$$

$$\textbf{Hence Proved.}$$

(iv) L.H.S. $= \cot\theta - \tan\theta$

$$= \frac{\cos\theta}{\sin\theta} - \frac{\sin\theta}{\cos\theta}$$

$$= \frac{\cos^2\theta - \sin^2\theta}{\sin\theta\cos\theta}$$

$$= \frac{\cos^2\theta - (1-\cos^2\theta)}{\sin\theta\cos\theta}$$

$$= \frac{2\cos^2\theta - 1}{\sin\theta\cos\theta} = \text{R.H.S.}$$

$$\textbf{Hence Proved.}$$

(v) L.H.S. $= \dfrac{1}{\sin\theta + \cos\theta} + \dfrac{1}{\sin\theta - \cos\theta}$

$$= \frac{(\sin\theta - \cos\theta) + (\sin\theta + \cos\theta)}{\sin^2\theta - \cos^2\theta}$$

$$= \frac{2\sin\theta}{(1-\cos^2\theta) - \cos^2\theta}$$

$$= \frac{2\sin\theta}{1 - 2\cos^2\theta} = \text{R.H.S.}$$

$$\textbf{Hence Proved.}$$

22. Prove the following identities :

(i) $\dfrac{1-\cos\theta}{1+\cos\theta} = (\cot\theta - \text{cosec}\,\theta)^2$

(ii) $\dfrac{1-\tan^2\theta}{\cot^2\theta - 1} = \tan^2\theta$

(iii) $\sec A\,(1+\sin A)\,(\sec A - \tan A) = 1$

(iv) $\dfrac{1+\cos\theta}{1-\cos\theta} = \dfrac{\tan^2\theta}{(\sec\theta - 1)^2}.$

Prove the Following

Sol. (i)   L.H.S. $= \dfrac{1-\cos\theta}{1+\cos\theta}$

$= \dfrac{1-\cos\theta}{1+\cos\theta} \times \dfrac{(1-\cos\theta)}{(1-\cos\theta)}$

$= \dfrac{(1-\cos\theta)^2}{1-\cos^2\theta}$

$= \dfrac{(1-\cos\theta)^2}{\sin^2\theta}$

$= \left[\dfrac{1-\cos\theta}{\sin\theta}\right]^2$

$= \left[\dfrac{1}{\sin\theta} - \dfrac{\cos\theta}{\sin\theta}\right]^2$

$= [\operatorname{cosec}\theta - \cot\theta]^2$

$= [-(\cot\theta - \operatorname{cosec}\theta)]^2$

$= (\cot\theta - \operatorname{cosec}\theta)^2$

$= $ R.H.S.　　**Hence Proved.**

(ii)　L.H.S. $= \dfrac{1-\tan^2\theta}{\cot^2\theta-1} = \dfrac{1-\tan^2\theta}{\dfrac{1}{\tan^2\theta}-1}$

$= \dfrac{1-\tan^2\theta}{\dfrac{1-\tan^2\theta}{\tan^2\theta}}$

$= \tan^2\theta = $ R.H.S.

　　　　　　　Hence Proved.

(iii) L.H.S. $= \sec A\,(1+\sin A)\,(\sec A - \tan A)$

$= \dfrac{1}{\cos A}(1+\sin A)\left(\dfrac{1}{\cos A} - \dfrac{\sin A}{\cos A}\right)$

$= \dfrac{1}{\cos A}(1+\sin A)\left(\dfrac{1-\sin A}{\cos A}\right)$

$= \dfrac{1-\sin^2 A}{\cos^2 A} = \dfrac{\cos^2 A}{\cos^2 A}$

$= 1 = $ R.H.S.　　**Hence Proved.**

(iv) R.H.S. $= \dfrac{\tan^2\theta}{(\sec\theta-1)^2} = \dfrac{\dfrac{\sin^2\theta}{\cos^2\theta}}{\left(\dfrac{1}{\cos\theta}-1\right)^2}$

$= \dfrac{\dfrac{\sin^2\theta}{\cos^2\theta}}{\dfrac{(1-\cos\theta)^2}{\cos^2\theta}} = \dfrac{1-\cos^2\theta}{(1-\cos\theta)^2}$

$= \dfrac{(1+\cos\theta)(1-\cos\theta)}{(1-\cos\theta)^2}$

$= \dfrac{1+\cos\theta}{1-\cos\theta} = $ L.H.S.　　**Hence Proved.**

23. Prove that :

(i)　$(\sec\theta - \tan\theta)^2 = \dfrac{1-\sin\theta}{1+\sin\theta}$

(ii)　$\sin^4\theta + \cos^4\theta = 1 - 2\sin^2\theta\cos^2\theta$

(iii) $(1-\sin^2 A)\sec^2 A = 1$

(iv)　$\cos^2 A + \dfrac{1}{1+\cot^2 A} = 1$

(v)　$\dfrac{\sec A-1}{\sec A+1} = \dfrac{1-\cos A}{1+\cos A}$.

Sol. (i)　　L.H.S. $= (\sec\theta - \tan\theta)^2$

$= \left(\dfrac{1}{\cos\theta} - \dfrac{\sin\theta}{\cos\theta}\right)^2$

$= \left(\dfrac{1-\sin\theta}{\cos\theta}\right)^2$

$= \dfrac{(1-\sin\theta)^2}{\cos^2\theta}$

$= \dfrac{(1-\sin\theta)^2}{1-\sin^2\theta}$

$= \dfrac{(1-\sin\theta)^2}{(1+\sin\theta)(1-\sin\theta)}$

$= \dfrac{1-\sin\theta}{1+\sin\theta} = $ R.H.S.

　　　　　　　Hence Proved.

(ii)　L.H.S. $= (\sin^2\theta)^2 + (\cos^2\theta)^2$

$\qquad + 2\sin^2\theta\cos^2\theta - 2\sin^2\theta\cos^2\theta$

$= (\sin^2\theta + \cos^2\theta)^2 - 2\sin^2\theta\cos^2\theta$

$= 1 - 2\sin^2\theta\cos^2\theta = $ R.H.S. **Hence Proved.**

(iii)　　L.H.S. $= (1-\sin^2 A)\sec^2 A$

$= \cos^2 A \times \dfrac{1}{\cos^2 A}$

$= 1 = $ R.H.S.　**Hence Proved.**

(iv)　　L.H.S. $= \cos^2 A + \dfrac{1}{\operatorname{cosec}^2 A}$

$= \cos^2 A + \sin^2 A$

$= 1 = $ R.H.S.　**Hence Proved.**

(v)　　L.H.S. $= \dfrac{\sec A-1}{\sec A+1}$

$= \dfrac{\dfrac{1}{\cos A}-1}{\dfrac{1}{\cos A}+1}$

$$= \frac{\dfrac{1-\cos A}{\cos A}}{\dfrac{1+\cos A}{\cos A}}$$

$$= \frac{1-\cos A}{1+\cos A}$$

$$= \text{R.H.S.} \qquad \textbf{Hence Proved.}$$

24. Prove that :

(i) $\dfrac{1}{\sec\theta - \tan\theta} = \sec\theta + \tan\theta$

(ii) $\dfrac{\sin\theta - 2\sin^3\theta}{2\cos^3\theta - \cos\theta} = \tan\theta$

(iii) $\dfrac{\tan\theta + \sin\theta}{\tan\theta - \sin\theta} = \dfrac{\sec\theta + 1}{\sec\theta - 1}$

Sol. (i) $\text{L.H.S.} = \dfrac{1}{\sec\theta - \tan\theta}$

$$= \frac{1}{\dfrac{1}{\cos\theta} - \dfrac{\sin\theta}{\cos\theta}}$$

$$= \frac{\cos\theta \times (1+\sin\theta)}{(1-\sin\theta) \times (1+\sin\theta)}$$

$$= \frac{\cos\theta\,(1+\sin\theta)}{1-\sin^2\theta}$$

$$= \frac{\cos\theta\,(1+\sin\theta)}{\cos^2\theta}$$

$$= \frac{1}{\cos\theta} + \frac{\sin\theta}{\cos\theta}$$

$$= \sec\theta + \tan\theta = \text{R.H.S.}$$

$$\textbf{Hence Proved.}$$

(ii) $\text{L.H.S.} = \dfrac{\sin\theta - 2\sin^3\theta}{2\cos^3\theta - \cos\theta}$

$$= \frac{\sin\theta\,(1-2\sin^2\theta)}{\cos\theta\,(2\cos^2\theta - 1)}$$

$$= \frac{\tan\theta\,[1-2\,(1-\cos^2\theta)]}{2\cos^2\theta - 1}$$

$$= \frac{\tan\theta\,(1-2+2\cos^2\theta)}{2\cos^2\theta - 1}$$

$$= \frac{\tan\theta\,(2\cos^2\theta - 1)}{(2\cos^2\theta - 1)}$$

$$= \tan\theta = \text{R.H.S.}$$

$$\textbf{Hence Proved.}$$

(iii) $\text{L.H.S.} = \dfrac{\dfrac{\sin\theta}{\cos\theta} + \sin\theta}{\dfrac{\sin\theta}{\cos\theta} - \sin\theta} = \dfrac{\sin\theta\left(\dfrac{1}{\cos\theta} + 1\right)}{\sin\theta\left(\dfrac{1}{\cos\theta} - 1\right)}$

$$= \frac{\sec\theta + 1}{\sec\theta - 1} = \text{R.H.S.} \quad \textbf{Hence Proved.}$$

25. Prove that :

(i) $1 + \dfrac{\cot^2\theta}{1+\operatorname{cosec}\theta} = \operatorname{cosec}\theta$

(ii) $\dfrac{\sin A + \cos A}{\sin A - \cos A} + \dfrac{\sin A - \cos A}{\sin A + \cos A}$

$$= \frac{2}{\sin^2 A - \cos^2 A}$$

(iii) $\dfrac{(1+\tan^2 A)\cot A}{\operatorname{cosec}^2 A} = \tan A$

(iv) $(\sin\theta + \operatorname{cosec}\theta)^2 + (\cos\theta + \sec\theta)^2$

$$= 7 + \tan^2\theta + \cot^2\theta.$$

Sol. (i) $\text{L.H.S.} = 1 + \dfrac{\cot^2\theta}{1+\operatorname{cosec}\theta}$

$$= \frac{1+\operatorname{cosec}\theta + \operatorname{cosec}^2\theta - 1}{1+\operatorname{cosec}\theta}$$

$$= \frac{\operatorname{cosec}\theta\,(1+\operatorname{cosec}\theta)}{(1+\operatorname{cosec}\theta)}$$

$$= \operatorname{cosec}\theta = \text{R.H.S.}$$

$$\textbf{Hence Proved.}$$

(ii) $\text{L.H.S.} = \dfrac{\sin A + \cos A}{\sin A - \cos A} + \dfrac{\sin A - \cos A}{\sin A + \cos A}$

$$= \frac{(\sin A + \cos A)^2}{(\sin A - \cos A)} + \frac{(\sin A - \cos A)^2}{(\sin A + \cos A)}$$

$$= \frac{\sin^2 A + \cos^2 A + 2\sin A\cos A + \sin^2 A + \cos^2 A - 2\sin A\cos A}{\sin^2 A - \cos^2 A}$$

$$= \frac{2\,(\sin^2 A + \cos^2 A)}{\sin^2 A - \cos^2 A} = \frac{2}{\sin^2 A - \cos^2 A}$$

$$= \text{R.H.S.} \qquad \textbf{Hence Proved.}$$

(iii) $\text{L.H.S.} = \dfrac{(1+\tan^2 A)\cot A}{\operatorname{cosec}^2 A}$

$$= \frac{\sec^2 A \cot A}{\operatorname{cosec}^2 A} = \frac{\dfrac{1}{\cos^2 A} \cdot \cot A}{\dfrac{1}{\sin^2 A}}$$

$$= \frac{\sin^2 A}{\cos^2 A} \cdot \frac{\cos A}{\sin A}$$

$$= \frac{\sin A}{\cos A} = \tan A = \text{R.H.S.} \qquad \textbf{Hence Proved.}$$

(iv) L.H.S.

$$= (\sin\theta + \text{cosec}\,\theta)^2 + (\cos\theta + \sec\theta)^2$$

$$= \sin^2\theta + \text{cosec}^2\theta + 2\sin\theta\,\text{cosec}\,\theta + \cos^2\theta$$
$$+ \sec^2\theta + 2\cos\theta.\sec\theta$$

$$= (\sin^2\theta + \cos^2\theta) + 1 + \cot^2\theta + 2\sin\theta \times \frac{1}{\sin\theta}$$

$$+ 1 + \tan^2\theta + 2\cos\theta \times \frac{1}{\cos\theta}$$

$$= 1 + 1 + 1 + 2 + 2 + \tan^2\theta + \cot^2\theta$$

$$= 7 + \tan^2\theta + \cot^2\theta = \text{R.H.S. } \textbf{Hence Proved.}$$

26. Prove that :

(i) $\dfrac{1}{\text{cosec}\,A - \cot A} - \dfrac{1}{\sin A}$

$$= \frac{1}{\sin A} - \frac{1}{\text{cosec}\,A + \cot A}$$

(ii) $\sin^6\theta + \cos^6\theta = 1 - 3\sin^2\theta\cos^2\theta$

(iii) $\dfrac{\cos^3\theta + \sin^3\theta}{\cos\theta + \sin\theta} + \dfrac{\cos^3\theta - \sin^3\theta}{\cos\theta - \sin\theta} = 2.$

Sol. (i) $\dfrac{1}{\text{cosec}\,A - \cot A} - \dfrac{1}{\sin A}$

$$= \frac{1}{\sin A} - \frac{1}{\text{cosec}\,A + \cot A}$$

or $\dfrac{1}{\text{cosec}\,A - \cot A} + \dfrac{1}{\text{cosec}\,A + \cot A}$

$$= \frac{1}{\sin A} + \frac{1}{\sin A} = \frac{2}{\sin A}$$

$$\text{L.H.S.} = \frac{(\text{cosec}\,A + \cot A) + (\text{cosec}\,A - \cot A)}{(\text{cosec}\,A - \cot A)(\text{cosec}\,A + \cot A)}$$

$$= \frac{2\,\text{cosec}\,A}{\text{cosec}^2 A - \cot^2 A} = \frac{2\,\text{cosec}\,A}{1}$$

$$= \frac{2}{\sin A} = \text{R.H.S.} \qquad \textbf{Hence Proved.}$$

(ii) $\qquad$ L.H.S. $= \sin^6\theta + \cos^6\theta$

$$= (\sin^2\theta)^3 + (\cos^2\theta)^3$$

$$= (\sin^2\theta + \cos^2\theta)(\sin^4\theta + \cos^4\theta$$
$$- \sin^2\theta\cos^2\theta)$$

$$= 1.\{(\sin^2\theta)^2 + (\cos^2\theta)^2$$
$$+ 2\sin^2\theta\cos^2\theta - 3\sin^2\theta\cos^2\theta\}$$

$$= (\sin^2\theta + \cos^2\theta)^2 - 3\sin^2\theta\cos^2\theta$$

$$= 1 - 3\sin^2\theta\cos^2\theta = \text{R.H.S. } \textbf{Hence Proved.}$$

(iii) L.H.S. $= \dfrac{\cos^3\theta + \sin^3\theta}{\cos\theta + \sin\theta} + \dfrac{\cos^3\theta - \sin^3\theta}{\cos\theta - \sin\theta}$

$$= \frac{(\cos\theta + \sin\theta)(\cos^2\theta + \sin^2\theta - \cos\theta\sin\theta)}{(\cos\theta + \sin\theta)}$$

$$+ \frac{(\cos\theta - \sin\theta)(\cos^2\theta + \sin^2\theta + \sin\theta\cos\theta)}{(\cos\theta - \sin\theta)}$$

$$= 1 - \sin\theta\cos\theta + 1 + \sin\theta\cos\theta$$

$$= 2 = \text{R.H.S.} \qquad \textbf{Hence Proved.}$$

27. Prove that

(i) $\dfrac{\cot A + \text{cosec}\,A - 1}{\cot A - \text{cosec}\,A + 1} = \dfrac{1 + \cos A}{\sin A}$

(ii) $\dfrac{\tan A + \sec A - 1}{\tan A - \sec A + 1} = \dfrac{1 + \sin A}{\cos A}.$

Sol. (i) L. H. S. $= \dfrac{\cot A + \text{cosec}\,A - 1}{\cot A - \text{cosec}\,A + 1}$

$$= \frac{(\cot A + \text{cosec}\,A) - (\text{cosec}^2 A - \cot^2 A)}{\cot A - \text{cosec}\,A + 1}$$

$$= \frac{(\cot A + \text{cosec}\,A)[\{1 - (\text{cosec}\,A - \cot A)\}]}{\cot A - \text{cosec}\,A + 1}$$

$$= \cot A + \text{cosec}\,A = \frac{\cos A}{\sin A} + \frac{1}{\sin A}$$

$$= \frac{\cos A + 1}{\sin A} = \text{R.H.S.} \qquad \textbf{Hence Proved.}$$

(ii) L. H. S. $= \dfrac{\tan A + \sec A - 1}{\tan A - \sec A + 1}$

$$= \frac{(\tan A + \sec A) - (\sec^2 A - \tan^2 A)}{(\tan A - \sec A) + 1}$$

$$= \frac{(\tan A + \sec A)(1 - \sec A + \tan A)}{\tan A - \sec A + 1}$$

$$= \tan A + \sec A$$

$$= \frac{\sin A}{\cos A} + \frac{1}{\cos A} = \frac{1 + \sin A}{\cos A} = \text{R. H. S.}$$

$$\textbf{Hence Proved.}$$

28. Prove that

$$\sqrt{\frac{1 + \cos A}{1 - \cos A}} = \frac{\tan A + \sin A}{\tan A \sin A}.$$

Sol. L.H.S. $= \sqrt{\dfrac{(1+\cos A)(1+\cos A)}{(1-\cos A)(1+\cos A)}}$

$= \sqrt{\dfrac{(1+\cos A)^2}{1-\cos^2 A}}$

$= \sqrt{\dfrac{1+\cos^2 A+2\cos A}{\sin^2 A}}$

$= \dfrac{1+\cos A}{\sin A}$

R.H.S. $= \dfrac{\tan A+\sin A}{\tan A \sin A}$

$= \dfrac{\sin A\left(\dfrac{1}{\cos A}+1\right)}{\dfrac{\sin A}{\cos A}\times \sin A}$

$= \dfrac{\dfrac{\sin A(1+\cos A)}{\cos A}\times \dfrac{\cos A}{\sin A \sin A}}$

$= \dfrac{1+\cos A}{\sin A}$ **Hence Proved.**

29. Prove that

$\dfrac{\sin A+\cos A}{\sin A-\cos A}+\dfrac{\sin A-\cos A}{\sin A+\cos A}=\dfrac{2}{2\sin^2 A-1}.$

Sol. L.H.S.

$= \dfrac{\sin A+\cos A}{\sin A-\cos A}+\dfrac{\sin A-\cos A}{\sin A+\cos A}$

$= \dfrac{(\sin A+\cos A)^2+(\sin A-\cos A)^2}{(\sin A-\cos A)(\sin A+\cos A)}$

$= \dfrac{\begin{matrix}\sin^2 A+\cos^2 A+2\sin A\cos A\\+\sin^2 A+\cos^2 A-2\sin A\cos A\end{matrix}}{\sin^2 A-\cos^2 A}$

$= \dfrac{2(\sin^2 A+\cos^2 A)}{\sin^2 A-\cos^2 A}=\dfrac{2\times 1}{\sin^2 A-(1-\sin^2 A)}$

$= \dfrac{2}{\sin^2 A-1+\sin^2 A}=\dfrac{2}{2\sin^2 A-1}=$ R.H.S.

Hence Proved.

30. Prove that

$\dfrac{\sin^2 \theta}{\cos^2 \theta}+\dfrac{\cos^2 \theta}{\sin^2 \theta}=\dfrac{1}{\sin^2 \theta.\cos^2 \theta}-2.$

Sol. L.H.S. $= \dfrac{\sin^2 \theta}{\cos^2 \theta}+\dfrac{\cos^2 \theta}{\sin^2 \theta}=\dfrac{\sin^4 \theta+\cos^4 \theta}{\sin^2 \theta.\cos^2 \theta}$

$= \dfrac{(\sin^2 \theta+\cos^2 \theta)^2-2\sin^2 \theta.\cos^2 \theta}{\sin^2 \theta.\cos^2 \theta}$

$= \dfrac{(1)^2-2\sin^2 \theta.\cos^2 \theta}{\sin^2 \theta \cos^2 \theta}$

$= \dfrac{1}{\sin^2 \theta.\cos^2 \theta}-\dfrac{2\sin^2 \theta.\cos^2 \theta}{\sin^2 \theta.\cos^2 \theta}$

$= \dfrac{1}{\sin^2 \theta \cos^2 \theta}-2=$ R.H.S.

Hence Proved.

31. Prove that

$\dfrac{\tan A}{(1+\tan^2 A)^2}+\dfrac{\cot A}{(1+\cot^2 A)^2}=\sin A.\cos A$

Sol. L.H.S. $= \dfrac{\tan A}{(1+\tan^2 A)^2}+\dfrac{\cot A}{(1+\cot^2 A)^2}$

$= \dfrac{\tan A}{(\sec^2 A)^2}+\dfrac{\cot A}{(\text{cosec}^2 A)^2}$

$= \dfrac{\sin A}{\cos A}\times \cos^2 A\times \cos^2 A$

$\quad +\dfrac{\cos A}{\sin A}\times \sin^2 A\times \sin^2 A$

$= \sin A.\cos^3 A+\sin^3 A.\cos A$

$= \sin A\cos A(\cos^2 A+\sin^2 A)$

$= \sin A.\cos A\times 1=\sin A.\cos A$

$= $ R.H.S. **Hence Proved.**

32. Prove that

$\dfrac{\sin A}{(\sec A+\tan A-1)}+\dfrac{\cos A}{(\text{cosec }A+\cot A-1)}=1.$

Sol. L.H.S.

$= \dfrac{\sin A}{(\sec A+\tan A-1)}+\dfrac{\cos A}{(\text{cosec }A+\cot A-1)}$

$= \dfrac{\sin A}{\dfrac{1}{\cos A}+\dfrac{\sin A}{\cos A}-1}+\dfrac{\cos A}{\dfrac{1}{\sin A}+\dfrac{\cos A}{\sin A}-1}$

$= \dfrac{\sin A}{\dfrac{1+\sin A-\cos A}{\cos A}}+\dfrac{\cos A}{\dfrac{1+\cos A-\sin A}{\sin A}}$

$= \dfrac{\sin A.\cos A}{1+\sin A-\cos A}+\dfrac{\sin A.\cos A}{1+\cos A-\sin A}$

$= \dfrac{\sin A.\cos A(1+\cos A-\sin A+1+\sin A-\cos A)}{[1+(\sin A-\cos A)][1-(\sin A-\cos A)]}$

$= \dfrac{2\sin A.\cos A}{(1)^2-(\sin A-\cos A)^2}$

$$= \frac{2\sin A.\cos A}{1-(\sin^2 A + \cos^2 A - 2\sin A\cos A)}$$

$$= \frac{2\sin A.\cos A}{1-1+2\sin A.\cos A}$$

$$= \frac{2}{2} = 1 = \text{R.H.S.} \qquad \textbf{Hence Proved.}$$

33. Prove that

$$\frac{\tan^3 \theta}{1+\tan^2 \theta} + \frac{\cot^3 \theta}{1+\cot^2 \theta} = \sec \theta.\operatorname{cosec}\theta - 2\sin\theta\cos\theta.$$

Sol. L.H.S. $= \dfrac{\tan^3 \theta}{1+\tan^2 \theta} + \dfrac{\cot^3 \theta}{1+\cot^2 \theta}$

$$= \frac{\tan^3 \theta}{\sec^2 \theta} + \frac{\cot^3 \theta}{\operatorname{cosec}^2 \theta}$$

$$= \frac{\sin^3 \theta}{\cos^3 \theta} \times \cos^2 \theta + \frac{\cos^3 \theta}{\sin^3 \theta} \times \sin^2 \theta$$

$$= \frac{\sin^3 \theta}{\cos^3 \theta} + \frac{\cos^3 \theta}{\sin \theta} = \frac{\sin^4 \theta + \cos^4 \theta}{\sin\theta.\cos\theta}$$

$$= \frac{[\sin^2 \theta + \cos^2 \theta]^2 - 2\sin^2 \theta.\cos^2 \theta}{\sin\theta.\cos\theta}$$

$$= \frac{(1)^2 - 2\sin^2 \theta.\cos^2 \theta}{\sin\theta.\cos\theta}$$

$$= \frac{1 - 2\sin^2 \theta.\cos^2 \theta}{\sin\theta.\cos\theta}$$

$$= \frac{1}{\sin\theta.\cos\theta} - \frac{2\sin^2 \theta.\cos^2 \theta}{\sin\theta.\cos\theta}$$

$$= \sec\theta.\operatorname{cosec}\theta - 2\sin\theta\cos\theta$$

$$= \text{R.H.S.} \qquad \textbf{Hence Proved.}$$

34. Prove that

$$\left(\frac{1+\sin\theta-\cos\theta}{1+\sin\theta+\cos\theta}\right)^2 = \frac{1-\cos\theta}{1+\cos\theta}.$$

Sol. L.H.S. $= \left(\dfrac{1+\sin\theta-\cos\theta}{1+\sin\theta+\cos\theta}\right)^2$

$$= \frac{1+\sin^2 \theta+\cos^2 \theta+2(\sin\theta-\cos\theta-\sin\theta.\cos\theta)}{1+\sin^2 \theta+\cos^2 \theta+2(\sin\theta+\cos\theta+\sin\theta.\cos\theta)}$$

$$= \frac{1+1+2(\sin\theta-\cos\theta-\sin\theta\cos\theta)}{1+1+2(\sin\theta+\cos\theta+\sin\theta\cos\theta)}$$

$$= \frac{2(1+\sin\theta-\cos\theta-\sin\theta\cos\theta)}{2(1+\sin\theta+\cos\theta+\sin\theta\cos\theta)}$$

$$= \frac{1+\sin\theta-\cos\theta(1+\sin\theta)}{1+\sin\theta+\cos\theta(1+\sin\theta)}$$

$$= \frac{(1+\sin\theta)(1-\cos\theta)}{(1+\sin\theta)(1+\cos\theta)} = \frac{1-\cos\theta}{1+\cos\theta}$$

$$= \text{R.H.S.} \qquad \textbf{Hence Proved.}$$

35. Prove that

$$\frac{\cos A}{1-\tan A} + \frac{\sin A}{1-\cot A} = \cos A + \sin A.$$

Sol. L. H. S. $= \dfrac{\cos A}{1-\tan A} + \dfrac{\sin A}{1-\cot A}$

$$= \frac{\cos A}{1-\dfrac{\sin A}{\cos A}} + \frac{\sin A}{1-\dfrac{\cos A}{\sin A}}$$

$$= \frac{\cos A}{\dfrac{\cos A - \sin A}{\cos A}} + \frac{\sin A}{\dfrac{\sin A - \cos A}{\sin A}}$$

$$= \frac{\cos^2 A}{\cos A - \sin A} + \frac{\sin^2 A}{\sin A - \cos A}$$

$$= \frac{\cos^2 A - \sin^2 A}{(\cos A - \sin A)}$$

$$= \frac{(\cos A + \sin A)(\cos A - \sin A)}{(\cos A - \sin A)}$$

$$= \cos A + \sin A$$

$$= \text{R.H.S.} \qquad \textbf{Hence Proved.}$$

36. Prove that

$$\left[\frac{1}{\sec^2 \theta - \cos^2 \theta} + \frac{1}{\operatorname{cosec}^2 \theta - \sin^2 \theta}\right] \sin^2 \theta.\cos^2 \theta$$

$$= \frac{1-\sin^2 \theta.\cos^2 \theta}{2+\sin^2 \theta.\cos^2 \theta}$$

Sol. L.H.S.

$$= \left[\frac{1}{\sec^2 \theta - \cos^2 \theta} + \frac{1}{\operatorname{cosec}^2\theta - \sin^2 \theta}\right] \sin^2 \theta.\cos^2 \theta$$

$$= \left[\frac{1}{\dfrac{1}{\cos^2 \theta} - \cos^2 \theta} + \frac{1}{\dfrac{1}{\sin^2 \theta} - \sin^2 \theta}\right] \sin^2 \theta \cos^2 \theta$$

$$= \left[\frac{1}{\dfrac{1-\cos^4 \theta}{\cos^2 \theta}} + \frac{1}{\dfrac{1-\sin^4 \theta}{\sin^2 \theta}}\right] \sin^2 \theta.\cos^2 \theta$$

$$= \left[\frac{\cos^2 \theta}{1-\cos^4 \theta} + \frac{\sin^2 \theta}{1-\sin^4 \theta}\right] \sin^2 \theta \cos^2 \theta$$

$$= \left[\frac{\cos^2 \theta(1-\sin^4 \theta) + \sin^2 \theta(1-\cos^4 \theta)}{(1-\cos^4 \theta)(1-\sin^4 \theta)}\right] \sin^2 \theta.\cos^2 \theta$$

$$= \left[\frac{\cos^4 \theta(1+\sin^4 \theta) + \sin^4 \theta(1+\cos^2 \theta)}{\sin^2 \theta\cos^2 \theta(1+\cos^2 \theta)(1+\sin^2 \theta)}\right] \sin^2 \theta\cos^2 \theta$$

Prove the Following

$= \dfrac{\cos^4\theta + \cos^4\theta.\sin^2\theta + \sin^4\theta + \sin^4\theta.\cos^2\theta}{1 + \sin^2\theta + \cos^2\theta + \sin^2\theta.\cos^2\theta}$

$= \dfrac{(\cos^4\theta + \sin^4\theta) + \sin^2\theta.\cos^2\theta\,(\sin^2\theta + \cos^2\theta)}{1 + 1 + \sin^2\theta.\cos^2\theta}$

$= \dfrac{(\cos^2\theta + \sin^2\theta)^2 - 2\sin^2\theta.\cos^2\theta + \sin^2\theta.\cos^2\theta \times 1}{2 + \sin^2\theta.\cos^2\theta}$

$= \dfrac{(1)^2 - 2\sin^2\theta.\cos^2\theta + \sin^2\theta.\cos^2\theta}{2 + \sin^2\theta.\cos^2\theta}$

$= \dfrac{1 - \sin^2\theta.\cos^2\theta}{2 + \sin^2\theta.\cos^2\theta} = $ R.H.S. **Hence Proved.**

37. Prove that

$\dfrac{\tan A}{1 - \cot A} + \dfrac{\cot A}{1 - \tan A} = \sec A.\operatorname{cosec} A + 1.$

Sol. L.H.S.

$= \dfrac{\dfrac{\sin A}{\cos A}}{1 - \dfrac{\cos A}{\sin A}} + \dfrac{\dfrac{\cos A}{\sin A}}{1 - \dfrac{\sin A}{\cos A}}$

$= \dfrac{\sin A}{\cos A} \times \dfrac{\sin A}{\sin A - \cos A} + \dfrac{\cos A}{\sin A} \times \dfrac{\cos A}{\cos A - \sin A}$

$= \dfrac{\sin^2 A}{\cos A\,(\sin A - \cos A)} + \dfrac{\cos^2 A}{\sin A\,(\cos A - \sin A)}$

$= \dfrac{\sin^2 A}{\cos A\,(\sin A - \cos A)} - \dfrac{\cos^2 A}{\sin A\,(\sin A - \cos A)}$

$= \dfrac{\sin^3 A - \cos^3 A}{\sin A.\cos A.(\sin A - \cos A)}$

$= \dfrac{(\sin A - \cos A)\,(\sin^2 A + \cos^2 A + \sin A.\cos A)}{\sin A.\cos A.(\sin A - \cos A)}$

$= \dfrac{1 + \sin A.\cos A}{\sin A.\cos A} = \dfrac{1}{\sin A.\cos A} + \dfrac{\sin A.\cos A}{\sin A.\cos A}$

$= \operatorname{cosec} A.\sec A + 1 = $ R.H.S. **Hence Proved.**

38. Prove that :

$\dfrac{\sin A}{1 + \cos A} + \dfrac{1 + \cos A}{\sin A} = 2\operatorname{cosec} A$

Sol. L. H. S. $= \dfrac{\sin^2 A + (1 + \cos A)^2}{(1 + \cos A)\sin A}$

$= \dfrac{\sin^2 A + 1 + \cos^2 A + 2\cos A}{(1 + \cos A)\sin A}$

$= \dfrac{1 + 1 + 2\cos A}{(1 + \cos A)\sin A}$

$= \dfrac{2\,(1 + \cos A)}{(1 + \cos A)\sin A}$

$= 2\operatorname{cosec} A = $ R. H. S. **Hence Proved.**

39. Prove that
$2(\sin^6\theta + \cos^6\theta) - 3\,(\sin^4\theta + \cos^4\theta) + 1 = 0.$

Sol. L.H.S. $= 2(\sin^6\theta + \cos^6\theta) - 3\,(\sin^4\theta + \cos^4\theta) + 1$

$= 2\,(\sin^2\theta + \cos^2\theta)\,[\sin^4\theta + \cos^4\theta - \sin^2\theta.\cos^2\theta]$
$\quad - 3[(\sin^2\theta + \cos^2\theta)^2 - 2\sin^2\theta.\cos^2\theta] + 1$

$= 2 \times 1\,[(\sin^2\theta + \cos^2\theta)^2 - 2\sin^2\theta.\cos^2\theta$
$\quad - \sin^2\theta.\cos^2\theta] - 3[(1)^2 - 2\sin^2\theta\cos^2\theta] + 1$

$= 2\,[(1)^2 - 3\sin^2\theta\cos^2\theta] - 3$
$\quad [1 - 2\sin^2\theta.\cos^2\theta] + 1$

$= 2 - 6\sin^2\theta.\cos^2\theta - 3 + 6\sin^2\theta.\cos^2\theta + 1$

$= -1 + 1 = 0 = $ R.H.S. **Hence Proved.**

40. If $\cos\theta + \sin\theta = \sqrt{2}\,\cos\theta$, show that

$\cos\theta - \sin\theta = \sqrt{2}\,\sin\theta.$

Sol. We have

$\cos\theta + \sin\theta = \sqrt{2}\,\cos\theta$

Squaring both sides, we get

$(\cos\theta + \sin\theta)^2 = 2\cos^2\theta$

$\Rightarrow \cos^2\theta + \sin^2\theta + 2\sin\theta\cos\theta = 2\cos^2\theta$

$\Rightarrow 2\sin\theta\cos\theta = 2\cos^2\theta - \cos^2\theta - \sin^2\theta$

$\Rightarrow 2\sin\theta\cos\theta = \cos^2\theta - \sin^2\theta$

$\Rightarrow 2\sin\theta\cos\theta = (\cos\theta + \sin\theta)(\cos\theta - \sin\theta)$

$\Rightarrow 2\sin\theta\cos\theta = (\cos\theta - \sin\theta) \times \sqrt{2}\,\cos\theta$

(Given)

$\Rightarrow \cos\theta - \sin\theta = \sqrt{2}\,\sin\theta.$ **Hence Proved.**

41. If $x = r\sin\theta\cos\phi$, $y = r\sin\theta\sin\phi$ and $z = r\cos\theta$, prove that $x^2 + y^2 + z^2 = r^2$.

Sol. We have

$x = r\sin\theta\cos\phi$
$y = r\sin\theta\sin\phi$
$z = r\cos\theta$

Squaring and adding,
$x^2 + y^2 + z^2$
$= r^2\sin^2\theta\cos^2\phi + r^2\sin^2\theta\sin^2\phi + r^2\cos^2\theta$
$= r^2\sin^2\theta\,(\cos^2\phi + \sin^2\phi) + r^2\cos^2\theta$
$= r^2\sin^2\theta \times 1 + r^2\cos^2\theta$
$= r^2\,(\sin^2\theta + \cos^2\theta)$
$= r^2 \times 1 = r^2.$

Hence, $x^2 + y^2 + z^2 = r^2.$ **Hence Proved.**

42. If $x = a \sec \theta + b \tan \theta$ and $y = a \tan \theta + b \sec \theta$ prove that

$$x^2 - y^2 = a^2 - b^2.$$

Sol. Here, $x^2 = a^2 \sec^2 \theta + 2ab \sec \theta \tan \theta + b^2 \tan^2 \theta$

$$y^2 = a^2 \tan^2 \theta + 2ab \sec \theta \tan \theta + b^2 \sec^2 \theta$$

$$\Rightarrow \quad x^2 - y^2 = a^2 (\sec^2 \theta - \tan^2 \theta) - b^2 (\sec^2 \theta - \tan^2 \theta)$$

$$= a^2 - b^2 \qquad (\because \sec^2 \theta - \tan^2 \theta = 1)$$

Hence Proved.

43. If $\tan A + \sin A = m$ and $\tan A - \sin A = n$, then show that

$$m^2 - n^2 = 4\sqrt{mn}$$

Sol. Here,

$$m^2 - n^2 = (\tan A + \sin A)^2 - (\tan A - \sin A)^2$$

$$= (\tan A + \sin A + \tan A - \sin A)$$

$$(\tan A + \sin A - \tan A + \sin A)$$

$$= (2 \tan A)(2 \sin A)$$

$$= 4 \tan A \sin A \qquad \dots \text{(i)}$$

Also,

$$4\sqrt{mn} = 4\sqrt{(\tan A + \sin A)(\tan A - \sin A)}$$

$$= 4\sqrt{\tan^2 A - \sin^2 A}$$

$$= 4\sqrt{\frac{\sin^2 A}{\cos^2 - A} - \sin^2 A}$$

$$= 4 \sin A \sqrt{\frac{1 - \cos^2 A}{\cos^2 A}}$$

$$= 4 \sin A \sqrt{\frac{\sin^2 A}{\cos^2 A}}$$

$$= 4 \sin A \cdot \frac{\sin A}{\cos A}$$

$$= 4 \sin A \cdot \tan A \qquad \dots \text{(ii)}$$

Using equations (i) and (ii), we get the required conditions. **Hence Proved.**

44. If $\tan \alpha = n \tan \beta$, $\sin \alpha = m \sin \beta$, prove that $\cos^2 \alpha = \dfrac{m^2 - 1}{n^2 - 1}$.

Sol. We have,

$$\tan \alpha = n \tan \beta$$

$$\Rightarrow \quad \tan \beta = \frac{\tan \alpha}{n}$$

$$\Rightarrow \quad \cot \beta = \frac{n}{\tan \alpha}$$

$$\Rightarrow \quad \sin \alpha = m \sin \beta$$

$$\Rightarrow \quad \sin \beta = \frac{\sin \alpha}{m}$$

$$\Rightarrow \quad \csc \beta = \frac{m}{\sin \alpha}$$

Since, $\csc^2 \beta - \cot^2 \beta = 1$

$$\Rightarrow \quad \frac{m^2}{\sin^2 \alpha} - \frac{n^2}{\tan^2 \alpha} = 1$$

$$\Rightarrow \quad \frac{m^2}{\sin^2 \alpha} - \frac{n^2 \cos^2 \alpha}{\sin^2 \alpha} = 1$$

$$\Rightarrow \quad m^2 - n^2 \cos^2 \alpha = \sin^2 \alpha$$

$$\Rightarrow \quad m^2 - n^2 \cos^2 \alpha = 1 - \cos^2 \alpha$$

$$\Rightarrow \quad m^2 - 1 = (n^2 - 1) \cos^2 \alpha$$

$$\Rightarrow \quad \cos^2 \alpha = \frac{m^2 - 1}{n^2 - 1}.$$

Hence Proved.

45. If $\sec \theta + \tan \theta = p$, then prove that

$$\sin \theta = \frac{p^2 - 1}{p^2 + 1}.$$

Sol. Given, $\sec \theta + \tan \theta = p$

$$\Rightarrow \quad \frac{1}{\cos \theta} + \frac{\sin \theta}{\cos \theta} = p$$

$$\Rightarrow \quad \frac{1 + \sin \theta}{\cos \theta} = p$$

$$\Rightarrow \quad \frac{(1 + \sin \theta)^2}{\cos^2 \theta} = p^2, \quad \text{[Squaring both sides]}$$

$$\Rightarrow \quad \frac{1 + \sin^2 \theta + 2 \sin \theta}{\cos^2 \theta} = p^2$$

$$\Rightarrow \quad \frac{1 + \sin^2 \theta + 2 \sin \theta + \cos^2 \theta}{1 + \sin^2 \theta + 2 \sin \theta - \cos^2 \theta} = \frac{p^2 + 1}{p^2 - 1}$$

[Applying componendo and dividendo]

$$\Rightarrow \quad \frac{1 + 1 + 2 \sin \theta}{\sin^2 \theta + \sin^2 \theta + 2 \sin \theta} = \frac{p^2 + 1}{p^2 - 1}$$

$$\Rightarrow \quad \frac{2(1 + \sin \theta)}{2 \sin \theta (1 + \sin \theta)} = \frac{p^2 + 1}{p^2 - 1}$$

$\Rightarrow \qquad \dfrac{1}{\sin\theta} = \dfrac{p^2+1}{p^2-1}$

Taking reciprocals, we get

$\Rightarrow \qquad \sin\theta = \dfrac{p^2-1}{p^2+1}$.

Hence Proved.

46. If $x\sin^3\theta + y\cos^3\theta = \sin\theta\cos\theta$ and $x\sin\theta = y\cos\theta$, then show that $x^2 + y^2 = 1$.

Sol. Given, $x\sin^3\theta + y\cos^3\theta = \sin\theta\cos\theta$

$\Rightarrow (x\sin\theta)\sin^2\theta + (y\cos\theta)\cos^2\theta = \sin\theta\cos\theta$

$\Rightarrow (x\sin\theta)\sin^2\theta + (x\sin\theta)\cos^2\theta = \sin\theta\cos\theta$

$(\because\ y\cos\theta = x\sin\theta)$

$\Rightarrow x\sin\theta\,(\sin^2\theta + \cos^2\theta) = \sin\theta\cos\theta$

$\Rightarrow \qquad\qquad x\sin\theta = \sin\theta\cos\theta$

$\Rightarrow \qquad\qquad x = \cos\theta \qquad\qquad \dots\text{(i)}$

Again $\quad x\sin\theta = y\cos\theta$

$\Rightarrow \qquad \cos\theta\sin\theta = y\cos\theta$

$\Rightarrow \qquad\qquad y = \sin\theta \qquad\qquad \dots\text{(ii)}$

Squaring and adding (i) and (ii), we get

$\qquad x^2 + y^2 = \cos^2\theta + \sin^2\theta$

$\Rightarrow \qquad x^2 + y^2 = 1.$ **Hence Proved.**

47. If $x = h + a\cos\theta$, $y = k + b\sin\theta$, prove that

$\left(\dfrac{x-h}{a}\right)^2 + \left(\dfrac{y-k}{b}\right)^2 = 1.$

Sol. It is given that

$\qquad\qquad x = h + a\cos\theta$

and $\qquad\quad y = k + b\sin\theta$

$\qquad\qquad x - h = a\cos\theta \qquad\qquad \dots\text{(i)}$

$\qquad\qquad y - k = b\sin\theta \qquad\qquad \dots\text{(ii)}$

The given equation is

$\left(\dfrac{x-h}{a}\right)^2 + \left(\dfrac{y-k}{b}\right)^2 = 1$

L.H.S. $= \left(\dfrac{a\cos\theta}{a}\right)^2 + \left(\dfrac{b\sin\theta}{b}\right)^2$

[Putting the values of (i) and (ii)]

$= \cos^2\theta + \sin^2\theta = 1 = \text{R.H.S.}$

Hence Proved.

48. If $\dfrac{x}{a}\cos\theta + \dfrac{y}{b}\sin\theta = 1$ and $\dfrac{x}{a}\sin\theta$

$-\dfrac{y}{b}\cos\theta = 1$, prove that $\dfrac{x^2}{a^2} + \dfrac{y^2}{b^2} = 2$.

Sol. It is given that :

$\dfrac{x}{a}\cos\theta + \dfrac{y}{b}\sin\theta = 1 \qquad\qquad \dots\text{(i)}$

and $\dfrac{x}{a}\sin\theta - \dfrac{y}{b}\cos\theta = 1 \qquad\qquad \dots\text{(ii)}$

On squaring equation (i), we get

$\left(\dfrac{x}{a}\cos\theta + \dfrac{y}{b}\sin\theta\right)^2 = (1)^2$

$\Rightarrow \quad \dfrac{x^2}{a^2}\cos^2\theta + \dfrac{y^2}{b^2}\sin^2\theta$

$+ 2\,\dfrac{x}{a}\cdot\dfrac{y}{b}\sin\theta.\cos\theta = 1 \qquad \dots\text{(iii)}$

On squaring equation (ii), we get

$\left(\dfrac{x}{a}\sin\theta - \dfrac{y}{b}\cos\theta\right)^2 = (1)^2$

$\Rightarrow \quad \dfrac{x^2}{a^2}\sin^2\theta + \dfrac{y^2}{b^2}\cos^2\theta$

$- 2\,\dfrac{x}{a}\cdot\dfrac{y}{b}\sin\theta.\cos\theta = 1 \qquad \dots\text{(iv)}$

Adding equations (iii) and (iv), we get

$\Rightarrow \quad \dfrac{x^2}{a^2}\cos^2\theta + \dfrac{y^2}{b^2}\sin^2\theta + 2\,\dfrac{x}{a}\cdot\dfrac{y}{b}\cdot\sin\theta.\cos\theta$

$+ \dfrac{x^2}{a^2}\sin^2\theta + \dfrac{y^2}{b^2}\cos^2\theta - 2\,\dfrac{x}{a}\cdot\dfrac{y}{b}\cdot\sin\theta.\cos\theta$

$= 1 + 1$

$\Rightarrow \quad \dfrac{x^2}{a^2}(\sin^2\theta + \cos^2\theta)$

$+ \dfrac{y^2}{b^2}(\sin^2\theta + \cos^2\theta) = 2$

$\Rightarrow \qquad \dfrac{x^2}{a^2}\times 1 + \dfrac{y^2}{b^2}\times 1 = 2$

$\Rightarrow \qquad \dfrac{x^2}{a^2} + \dfrac{y^2}{b^2} = 2.$

Hence Proved.

49. The length of a shadow of a tower standing on level plane is found to be $2y$ metres longer when the sun's altitude is $30°$ than when it was 45° prove that the height of the tower is y $(\sqrt{3}+1)$ metre.

Sol. In right angled $\triangle$ BCD.

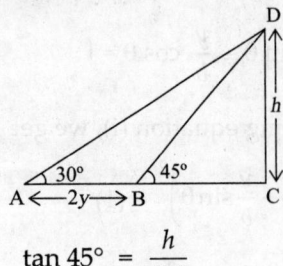

$$\tan 45° = \frac{h}{BC} \qquad (\tan 45° = 1)$$

$$h = BC \qquad \dots \text{(i)}$$

In right angled $\triangle$ ACD,

$$\tan 30° = \frac{h}{2y + BC}$$

$$\Rightarrow \qquad \frac{1}{\sqrt{3}} = \frac{h}{2y + h}$$

$$\Rightarrow \qquad h(\sqrt{3}-1) = 2y$$

$$\Rightarrow \qquad h = y\,(\sqrt{3}+1) \text{ m.}$$

Hence Proved.

Chapter 19. Statistics

1. If the mean of n observations $ax_1, ax_2, ax_3,\dots, ax_n$ is $a\overline{X}$, show that

$$(ax_1 - a\overline{X}) + (ax_2 - a\overline{X}) + \dots + (ax_n - a\overline{X}) = 0.$$

Sol. We have

$$a\overline{X} = \frac{ax_1 + ax_2 + \dots + ax_n}{n}$$

$$\Rightarrow \qquad ax_1 + ax_2 + \dots + ax_n = n(a\overline{X}) \qquad \dots \text{(i)}$$

Now, $(ax_1 - a\overline{X}) + (ax_2 - a\overline{X}) + \dots + (ax_n - a\overline{X})$

$$= (ax_1 + ax_2 + \dots + ax_n) - (a\overline{X} + a\overline{X} + \dots$$

$$+ a\overline{X} \; n\text{-times})$$

$$= n(a\overline{X}) - n(a\overline{X}) = 0. \qquad \text{[Using (i)]}$$

Hence Proved.

2. The mean of n observations $x_1, x_2,\dots, x_n$ is $\overline{X}$. If $(a-b)$ is added to each of the observation, show

that the mean of the new set of observations is $\overline{X} + (a-b)$.

Sol. We have

$$\overline{X} = \frac{x_1 + x_2 + \dots + x_n}{n} \qquad \dots \text{(i)}$$

Let $\overline{X}$ be the mean of $x_1 + (a-b), x_2 + (a-b),\dots,$ $x_n + (a-b)$. Then

$$\overline{X} = \frac{[x_1 + (a-b)] + [x_2 + (a-b)] + \dots + [x_n + (a-b)]}{n}$$

$$= \frac{x_1 + x_2 + \dots + x_n + n(a-b)}{n}$$

$$= \frac{x_1 + x_2 + \dots + x_n}{n} + \frac{n(a-b)}{n}$$

$$= \overline{X} + (a-b). \quad \text{[Using (i)]} \qquad \textbf{Hence Proved.}$$

❑❑

Prove the Following

Chapter 11. Coordinate Geometry

1. If the line joining the points A(4, – 5) and B(4, 5) is divided by the point P such that $\dfrac{AP}{AB} = \dfrac{2}{5}$, find the coordinates of P.

Sol. Given, A(4, – 5), B(4, 5) and

$$\frac{AP}{AB} = \frac{2}{5}$$

$$\therefore \qquad \frac{AP}{PB} = \frac{2}{3}$$

```
       2   P   3
  A |———————————| B
 (4,–5)        (4, 5)
```

Let coordinates of P be (x, y).

So, $\qquad x = \dfrac{mx_2 + nx_1}{m+n}, \; y = \dfrac{my_2 + ny_1}{m+n}$

Here, $\qquad m = 2, n = 3$

$$x_1 = 4, x_2 = 4$$

$$y_1 = -5, y_2 = 5$$

$$\therefore \qquad x = \frac{2 \times 4 + 3 \times 4}{2+3}$$

$$= \frac{8+12}{5} = \frac{20}{5} = 4$$

$$y = \frac{2 \times 5 + 3\,(-5)}{2+3}$$

$$= \frac{10-15}{5} = \frac{-5}{5} = -1$$

∴ Coordinates of P are (4, – 1).　　**Ans.**

2. Determine the ratio in which the line $3x + y - 9 = 0$ divides the line joining (1, 3) and (2, 7).

Sol. Suppose the line $3x + y - 9 = 0$ divides the line joining A(1, 3) and B(2, 7) in the ratio of $\lambda : 1$ at point C.

Coordinates of C $= \left(\dfrac{2\lambda+1}{\lambda+1}, \dfrac{7\lambda+3}{\lambda+1} \right)$

But point C lies on the line $3x + y - 9 = 0$.

$$\therefore \quad 3\left(\frac{2\lambda+1}{\lambda+1} \right) + \left(\frac{7\lambda+3}{\lambda+1} \right) - 9 = 0$$

$$\Rightarrow \quad 6\lambda + 3 + 7\lambda + 3 - 9\lambda - 9 = 0$$

$$\Rightarrow \quad 4\lambda - 3 = 0$$

$$\Rightarrow \quad \lambda = \frac{3}{4}$$

The required ratio $= \lambda : 1$

$$= 3 : 4. \qquad \textbf{Ans.}$$

3. The midpoint of the line segment AB shown in the diagram is (4, – 3). Write down the coordinates of A and B.

Sol. Let the coordinates of A and B are $(x, 0)$ and $(0, y)$.

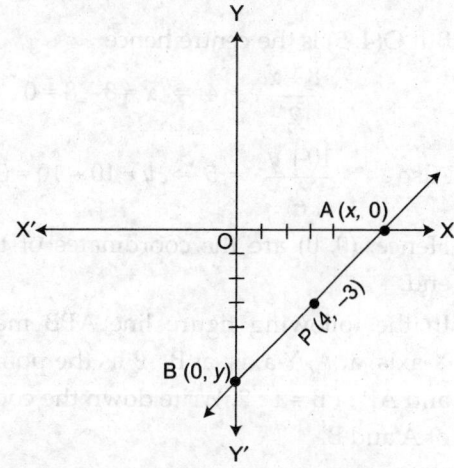

Thus, the coordinates of midpoint of

$$AB = \left(\frac{x+0}{2}, \frac{y+0}{2} \right)$$

$$= \left(\frac{x}{2}, \frac{y}{2}\right)$$

According to question, the coordinates of mid-point of AB are (4, – 3)

∴ $\frac{x}{2} = 4 \Rightarrow x = 8$

and $\frac{y}{2} = -3 \Rightarrow y = -6$

∴ The required points are (8, 0) and (0, – 6).

Ans.

4. The centre 'O' of a circle has the coordinates (4, 5) and one point on the circumference is (8, 10). Find the coordinates of the other end of the diameter of the circle through this point.

Sol. Let (x, y) be the coordinates of the other end of the diameter of the circle.

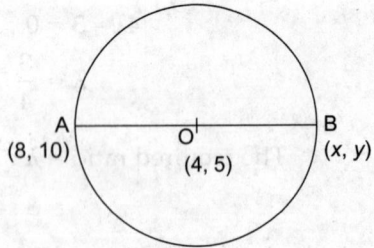

Since, centre is the midpoint of the diameter of the circle.

So, coordinates of midpoint of diameter

$$AB = \left(\frac{8+x}{2}, \frac{10+y}{2}\right)$$

But O(4, 5) is the centre hence

$$\frac{8+x}{2} = 4 \Rightarrow x = 8 - 8 = 0$$

Also $\frac{10+y}{2} = 5 \Rightarrow y = 10 - 10 = 0$

Hence, (0, 0) are the coordinates of the other end. **Ans.**

5. In the following figure line APB meets the X-axis at A, Y-axis at B. P is the point (4, – 2) and AP : PB = 1 : 2. Write down the coordinates of A and B.

Sol. Let $(x, 0)$ and $(0, y)$ be the coordinates of A and B respectively.

Point P divides AB in the ratio of 1 : 2.

So, coordinates of P

$$4 = \frac{1 \times 0 + 2 \times x}{1 + 2}$$

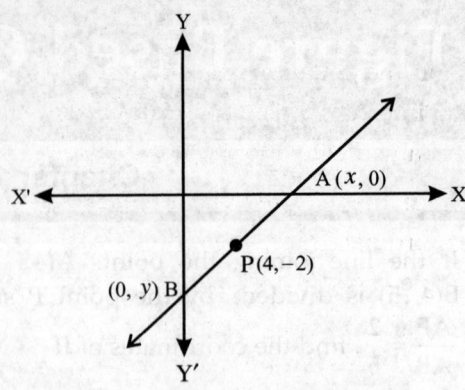

⇒ $2x = 4 \times 3$

⇒ $x = 6$

Also $-2 = \frac{2 \times 0 + 1 \times y}{1 + 2}$

⇒ $-6 = y$

⇒ $y = -6$

Hence, the coordinates of A and B are (6, 0) and (0, – 6) respectively. **Ans.**

6. The three vertices of a parallelogram taken in order are (– 1, 0), (3, 1) and (2, 2) respectively. Find the coordinates of the fourth vertex.

Sol. Let A (– 1, 0), B (3, 1), C (2, 2) and D (x, y) be the vertices of a parallelogram ABCD taken in order.

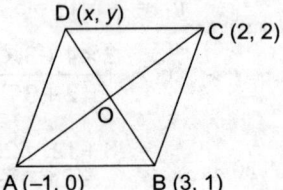

Since, the diagonals of a parallelogram bisect each other.

So, coordinates of the midpoint of AC

= coordinates of midpoint of BD

⇒ $\left(\frac{-1+2}{2}, \frac{0+2}{2}\right) = \left(\frac{3+x}{2}, \frac{y+1}{2}\right)$

⇒ $\left(\frac{1}{2}, 1\right) = \left(\frac{3+x}{2}, \frac{y+1}{2}\right)$

⇒ $\frac{3+x}{2} = \frac{1}{2} \Rightarrow x = -2$

and $\frac{y+1}{2} = 1 \Rightarrow y + 1 = 2$

$\Rightarrow \qquad y = 1$

The fourth vertex of parallelogram = $(-2, 1)$.

Ans.

7. Find the equation of a straight line which cuts an intercept -2 units from Y-axis and being equally inclined to the axis.

Sol. Since, the required line is equally inclined with co-ordinate axis, therefore, it makes either an angle of $45°$ or $135°$ with the X-axis.

So, its slope is $m = \tan 45° \Rightarrow m = 1$

or $\qquad m = \tan 135° \Rightarrow m = -1$

Y-intercept, $c = -2$

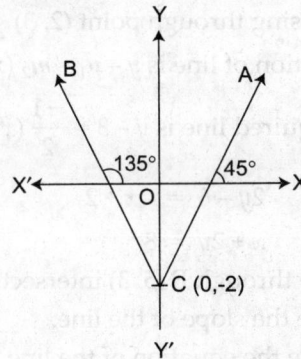

Hence, the equation of required lines are

$$y = mx + c$$

i.e., $\qquad y = 1 \cdot x - 2$ or $y = -1 \cdot x - 2$

$\Rightarrow \qquad y = x - 2$ or $y = -x - 2$

$\Rightarrow \qquad x - y - 2 = 0$ or $x + y + 2 = 0$. **Ans.**

8. $A(2, 5)$, $B(-1, 2)$ and $C(5, 8)$ are the vertices of a triangle ABC, 'M' is a point on AB such that $AM : MB = 1 : 2$. Find the coordinates of 'M'. Hence, find the equation of the line passing through the points C and M.*

Sol. Given, vertices of triangle are, A $(2, 5)$, B $(-1, 2)$, C $(5, 8)$, AM : MB = 1 : 2.

$\because$ M is a point on AB.

$$\underset{\substack{A \\ (2,5)}}{\rule{0pt}{0pt}} \overset{\substack{1:2 \\ \rule{3cm}{0.4pt}}}{\underset{\substack{M\,(a,\,b)}}{\rule{0pt}{0pt}}} \underset{\substack{B \\ (-1,\,2)}}{\rule{0pt}{0pt}}$$

$\therefore$ Coordinates of

$$M = \left(\frac{m_1 x_2 + m_2 x_1}{m_1 + m_2}, \frac{m_1 y_2 + m_2 y_1}{m_1 + m_2} \right)$$

Here, $m_1 : m_2 = 1 : 2$, $x_1 = 2$, $y_1 = 5$, $x_2 = -1$, $y_2 = 2$

$\therefore$ Coordinates of M

$$= \left(\frac{1 \times (-1) + 2 \times 2}{1 + 2}, \frac{1 \times 2 + 2 \times 5}{1 + 2} \right)$$

$$= \left(\frac{-1 + 4}{3}, \frac{12}{3} \right) = (1, 4) \qquad \textbf{Ans.}$$

The equation of line passing through C $(5, 8)$ and M $(1, 4)$ is

$$y - y_1 = \frac{y_2 - y_1}{x_2 - x_1} (x - x_1)$$

Here, $x_1 = 5$, $y_1 = 8$, $x_2 = 1$, $y_2 = 4$

$\therefore \qquad y - 8 = \dfrac{4 - 8}{1 - 5}(x - 5)$

$\Rightarrow \qquad y - 8 = \dfrac{-4}{-4}(x - 5)$

$\Rightarrow \qquad y - 8 = x - 5$

$\Rightarrow \qquad x - y + 3 = 0.$ **Ans.**

9. In $\triangle ABC$, A $(3, 5)$, B $(7, 8)$ and C $(1, -10)$. Find the equation of the median through A.

Sol. Coordinates of

$$D\left(\frac{7 + 1}{2}, \frac{8 - 10}{2} \right) = (4, -1)$$

(Midpoint formula)

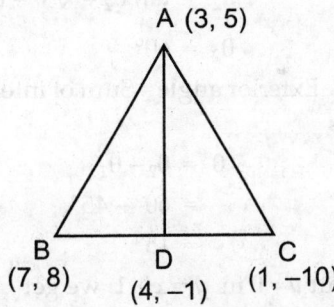

Now, equation of AD (Median through A)

$$y - 5 = \frac{-1 - 5}{4 - 3}(x - 3)$$

(Two point form)

$\Rightarrow \qquad y - 5 = -6(x - 3)$

$\Rightarrow \qquad y - 5 = -6x + 18$

or $\qquad 6x + y - 23 = 0.$ **Ans.**

10. The figure alongside (not drawn to scale) represents the lines $y = x + 1$ and $y = \sqrt{3}x - 1$.

(i) Find the angle which the line $y = x + 1$ makes with X-axis.

---

* Frequently asked previous years Board Exam Questions.

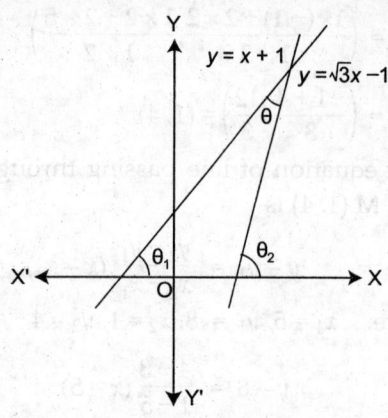

(ii) Find the angle which the line $y = \sqrt{3}x - 1$ makes with X-axis.

(iii) Determine angle θ.

(iv) Find the point where the line $y = x + 1$ meets X-axis.

(v) Find the point where the line $y = \sqrt{3}x - 1$ meets Y-axis.

Sol. (i)
$$y = x + 1$$
$$\Rightarrow \quad m_1 = \tan \theta_1 = 1 = \tan 45°$$
$$\Rightarrow \quad \theta_1 = 45°. \qquad \textbf{Ans.}$$

(ii)
$$y = \sqrt{3}x - 1$$
$$\Rightarrow \quad m_2 = \tan \theta_2 = \sqrt{3} = \tan 60°$$
$$\Rightarrow \quad \theta_2 = 60°. \qquad \textbf{Ans.}$$

(iii) ∵ Exterior angle = Sum of interior opposite angles

∴
$$\theta = \theta_2 - \theta_1$$
$$= 60° - 45°$$
$$= 15°. \qquad \textbf{Ans.}$$

(iv) Put $y = 0$ in $y = x + 1$, we get
$$0 = x + 1$$
$$\Rightarrow \quad x = -1$$

∴ The required point is $(-1, 0)$. **Ans.**

(v) Put $x = 0$ in $y = \sqrt{3}x - 1$, we get $y = -1$

∴ The required point is $(0, -1)$. **Ans.**

11. In the adjoining figure, write

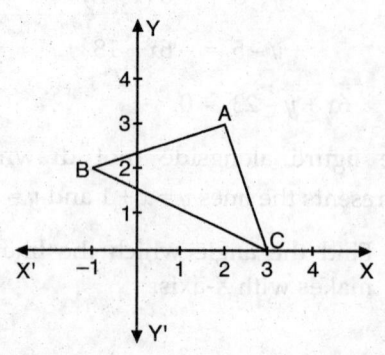

(i) The co-ordinates of A, B and C.

(ii) The equation of the line through A and ∥ to BC.

Sol. (i) A = (2, 3), B = (-1, 2), C = (3, 0). **Ans.**

(ii) Slope of BC $= \dfrac{y_2 - y_1}{x_2 - x_1} = \dfrac{2 - 0}{-1 - 3} = \dfrac{2}{-4}$

$$m_1 = \frac{-1}{2}$$

Since lines are parallel

∴
$$m_1 = m_2$$

Hence,
$$m_2 = -\frac{1}{2}$$

and passing through point (2, 3)

∵ Equation of line is $y - y_1 = m_2(x - x_1)$

∴ Required line is $y - 3 = \dfrac{-1}{2}(x - 2)$

$$\Rightarrow \qquad 2y - 6 = -x + 2$$
$$\Rightarrow \qquad x + 2y = 8. \qquad \textbf{Ans.}$$

12. The line through P (5, 3) intersects Y- axis at Q.
(i) Write the slope of the line.
(ii) Write the equation of the line.
(iii) Find the coordinates of Q.

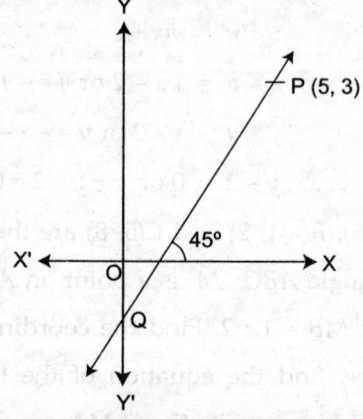

Sol. (i)
$$m = \tan \theta = \tan 45°$$
$$m = 1$$

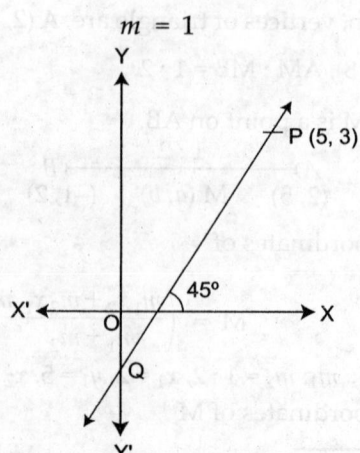

(ii) Equation of line PQ

$$y - y_1 = m(x - x_1)$$
$$\Rightarrow \qquad y - 3 = 1(x - 5)$$
$$\Rightarrow \qquad y - 3 = x - 5$$
$$\Rightarrow \qquad x - y - 2 = 0$$

(iii) Equation of PQ is

$$x - y - 2 = 0$$

Put $x = 0$ (coordinates of Q)

$$-y - 2 = 0$$
$$\Rightarrow \qquad y = -2$$

So, co-ordinates of Q $(0, -2)$.   **Ans.**

13. Find the value of 'a' for which the following points A $(a, 3)$, B $(2, 1)$ and C $(5, a)$ are collinear. Hence find the equation of the line.

Sol. Equation of line passing through AC is

$$(y - 3) = \left(\frac{a-3}{5-a}\right)(x - a)$$

As if A, B and C are collinear then B will satisfy it, *i.e.*,

A $(a, 3)$ B $(2, 1)$ C $(5, a)$

$$(1 - 3) = \left(\frac{a-3}{5-a}\right)(2 - a)$$

$$\Rightarrow \qquad -2(5 - a) = (a - 3)(2 - a)$$
$$\Rightarrow \qquad -10 + 2a = 2a - 6 - a^2 + 3a$$
$$\Rightarrow \qquad a^2 - 3a - 4 = 0$$
$$\Rightarrow \qquad a^2 - 4a + a - 4 = 0$$
$$\Rightarrow \qquad a(a - 4) + 1(a - 4) = 0$$
$$\Rightarrow \qquad (a - 4)(a + 1) = 0$$
$$\Rightarrow \qquad a = 4 \text{ or } -1.$$ **Ans.**

Thus, required equation of straight line is

$$(y - 3) = \left(\frac{4-3}{5-4}\right)(x - 4)$$

$$\Rightarrow \qquad y - 3 = \left(\frac{1}{1}\right)(x - 4)$$

$$\Rightarrow \qquad x - y - 1 = 0$$

or $\qquad (y - 3) = \left(\frac{-1-3}{5+1}\right)(x + 1)$

$$\Rightarrow \qquad (y - 3) = \left(\frac{-4}{6}\right)(x + 1)$$

$$\Rightarrow \qquad y - 3 = \frac{-2}{3}(x + 1)$$

$$\Rightarrow \qquad 3y - 9 = -2x - 2$$

$$\Rightarrow \qquad 2x + 3y - 7 = 0$$ **Ans.**

14. The vertices of a triangle are A$(10, 4)$, B$(-4, 9)$ and C$(-2, -1)$. Find the equation of its altitudes.

Sol. Let AD, BE and CF be the three altitudes of $\triangle$ABC, then

$$AD \perp BC$$
$$BE \perp CA$$
and $$CF \perp AB.$$

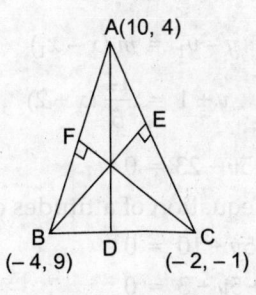

$$\text{Slope of BC} = \frac{-1-9}{-2+4} = -5$$

Since $AD \perp BC$

Slope of BC × Slope of AD $= -1$

$$\text{Slope of AD} = \frac{-1}{-5} = \frac{1}{5}$$

$$\therefore \qquad AD \perp BC$$

Since, AD passes through A$(10, 4)$.

So, equation of AD is

$$y - y_1 = m(x - x_1)$$

$$\Rightarrow \qquad y - 4 = \frac{1}{5}(x - 10)$$

$$\Rightarrow \qquad 5y - 20 = x - 10$$

$$\Rightarrow \qquad x - 5y + 10 = 0 \qquad \ldots(i)$$

Now, Slope of AC $= \frac{4+1}{10+2} = \frac{5}{12}$

Since $BE \perp AC$

Slope of BE × Slope of AC $= -1$

So, Slope of BE $= \frac{-1 \times 12}{5} = -\frac{12}{5}$.

Equation of BE which passes through B$(-4, 9)$ is

$$y - y_1 = m(x - x_1)$$

$$y - 9 = -\frac{12}{5}(x + 4)$$

or $\quad 12x + 5y + 3 = 0 \qquad \ldots(ii)$

Now, Slope of $AB = \frac{4-9}{10+4} = \frac{-5}{14}$

Since $CF \perp AB$.

So,

Slope of AB × Slope of CF = – 1

$\Rightarrow \quad -\dfrac{5}{14} \times$ Slope of CF = – 1

$\Rightarrow \quad$ Slope of CF $= \dfrac{14}{5}$

Equation of CF which passes through C(–2, –1) is

$$y - y_1 = m(x - x_1)$$

$\Rightarrow \qquad y + 1 = \dfrac{14}{5}(x + 2)$

$\Rightarrow \quad 14x - 5y + 23 = 0 \qquad \qquad …(iii)$

Thus, the equation of altitudes of ΔABC are

$$x - 5y + 10 = 0$$
$$12x + 5y + 3 = 0$$

and $14x - 5y + 23 = 0$. **Ans.**

15. Given equation of line L_1 is $y = 4$.

(i) Write the slope of line L_2, if L_2 is the bisector of angle O.

(ii) Write the co-ordinates of point P.

(iii) Find the equation of L_2.

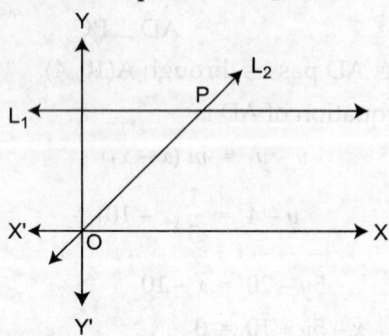

Sol. Equation of L_1 is $y = 4$ (given)

(i) As L_2 is bisector of O

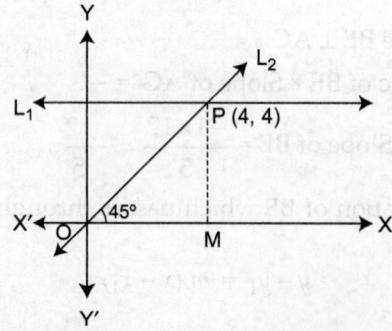

$\Rightarrow \quad L_2$ is inclined at an angle of 45° with XX′

∴ Slope of $L_2 = m = \tan 45° = 1$ **Ans.**

(ii) Slope of $L_2 = \dfrac{4-0}{x-0} \Rightarrow 1 = \dfrac{4}{x} \Rightarrow x = 4$

So, co-ordinates of P are (4, 4).

(Since the slope of L_2 is 1, $L_2 \Rightarrow$ PM = OM) **Ans.**

(iii) L_2 passes through O (0, 0), P (4, 4) and has slope $m = 1$

∴ Equation of L_2 is

$$y - y_1 = m(x - x_1)$$
$$y - 0 = 1(x - 0)$$

or $\qquad \qquad y = x$

or $\qquad \qquad x - y = 0.$ **Ans.**

16. From the adjacent figure :

(i) Write the coordinates of the points A, B and C

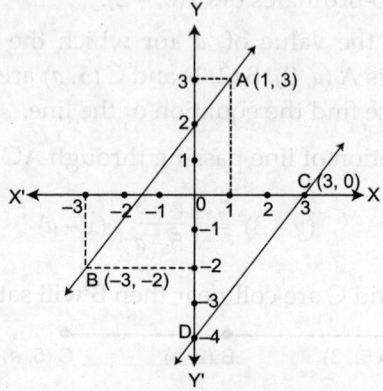

(ii) Write the slope of the line AB.

(iii) Line through C, drawn parallel to AB, intersects Y-axis at D. Calculate the coordintes of D.

Sol. (i) Co-ordinates of the points A, B and C are (1, 3), (– 3, – 2) and (3, 0) respectively.

(ii) Slope of AB $= \dfrac{-2-3}{-3-1} = \dfrac{5}{4}$.

(iii) Line through C (3, 0) and parallel to AB

∴ $\qquad \qquad$ Slope $= \dfrac{5}{4}$.

∴ Equation to the line is

$$y - y_1 = m(x - x_1)$$

$\Rightarrow \qquad y - 0 = \dfrac{5}{4}(x - 3)$

$\Rightarrow \qquad 4y = 5x - 15$

This line intersects Y-axis at D.

∴ On solving

$$4y = 5x - 15$$

and $\qquad \qquad x = 0 \qquad$ (Equation to Y-axis)

we get, $\qquad 4y = -15$

$\Rightarrow \qquad \qquad y = -\dfrac{15}{4}$

∴ Co-ordinates of point D are $\left(0, \dfrac{-15}{4}\right)$. **Ans.**

17. A line AB meets X-axis at A and Y-axis at B. P (4, –1) divides AB in the ratio 1 : 2.

   (i) Find the co-ordinates of A and B.

   (ii) Find the equation of the line through P and perpendicular to AB.

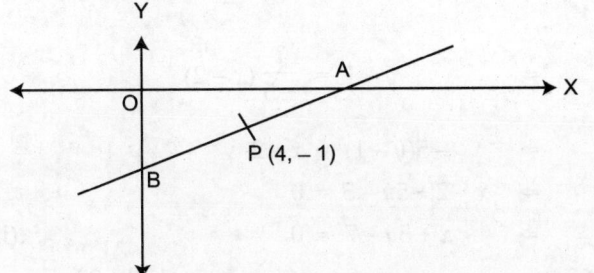

Sol. (i) Let the co-ordinates of A be $(x, 0)$ and B be $(0, y)$.

Given, P = (4, – 1) divides AB in the ratio 1 : 2.

Now, $\qquad x = \dfrac{m_1 x_2 + m_2 x_1}{m_1 + m_2}$

$\Rightarrow \qquad 4 = \dfrac{1 \times 0 + 2 \times x}{1 + 2}$

$\Rightarrow \qquad 4 = \dfrac{2x}{3}$

$\therefore \qquad x = 6$

and $\qquad y = \dfrac{m_1 y_2 + m_2 y_1}{m_1 + m_2}$

$\Rightarrow \qquad -1 = \dfrac{1 \times y + 2 \times 0}{1 + 2}$

$\Rightarrow \qquad -1 = \dfrac{y}{3}$

$\therefore \qquad y = -3$

$\therefore$ Coordinates of A = (6, 0) and coordinates of B = (0, – 3).

(ii) Slope of AB = $\dfrac{y_2 - y_1}{x_2 - x_1} = \dfrac{-3 - 0}{0 - 6} = \dfrac{-3}{-6} = \dfrac{1}{2}$

Now, slope of the line perpendicular to AB

$= -\dfrac{1}{\text{slope of AB}}$

$= -\dfrac{1}{1/2} = -2$

which passes through P (4, – 1).

Equation of line is,

$\qquad y - y_1 = m (x - x_1)$

$\Rightarrow \qquad y - (-1) = -2 (x - 4)$

Hence, $\qquad y = -2x + 7$ **Ans.**

18. Three vertices of a parallelogram ABCD taken in order are A (3, 6), B (5, 10) and C (3, 2) find :

   (i) the coordinates of the fourth vertex D.

   (ii) length of diagonal BD.

   (iii) equation of side AB of the parallelogram ABCD.

Sol. (i) Let the coordinates of the fourth vertex of a parallelogram be D (x, y).

Since, diagonals of a parallelogram bisects each other

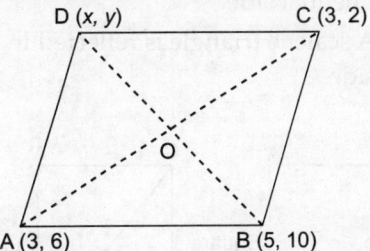

$\therefore$ Midpoint of AC = Midpoint of BD

$\Rightarrow \left(\dfrac{3+3}{2}, \dfrac{6+2}{2} \right) = \left(\dfrac{5+x}{2}, \dfrac{10+y}{2} \right)$

$\Rightarrow \qquad (3, 4) = \left(\dfrac{5+x}{2}, \dfrac{10+y}{2} \right)$

$\Rightarrow \qquad \dfrac{5+x}{2} = 3$ and $\dfrac{10+y}{2} = 4$

$\Rightarrow \qquad 5 + x = 6$ and $10 + y = 8$

$\Rightarrow \qquad x = 1$ and $y = -2$

$\therefore$ The coordinates of the fourth vertex

$\qquad\qquad D = (1, -2)$ **Ans.**

(ii) Length of BD $= \sqrt{(10+2)^2 + (5-1)^2}$

$\qquad\qquad = \sqrt{12^2 + 4^2}$

$\qquad\qquad = \sqrt{160}$

$\qquad\qquad = 4\sqrt{10}$ units   **Ans.**

(iii) Here, A = (3, 6) and B (5, 10)

$\therefore \qquad m = \dfrac{y_2 - y_1}{x_2 - x_1}$

$\qquad\qquad = \dfrac{10 - 6}{5 - 3} = 2$

$\therefore$ Equation of side AB of the parallelogram ABCD is

$\qquad\qquad y - y_1 = m (x - x_1)$

$\Rightarrow \qquad y - 6 = 2 (x - 3)$

$\Rightarrow \qquad y - 6 = 2x - 6$

$\Rightarrow \qquad y = 2x.$ **Ans.**

Chapter 12. Reflection

1. Name the figure formed by a triangle and its reflection, when :

   (i) An isosceles right-angled triangle is reflected in its hypotenuse.

   (ii) A right-angled triangle is reflected in its hypotenuse.

   (iii) An isosceles triangle is reflected in its unequal side.

   (iv) A scalene triangle is reflected in its greatest side.

Sol.

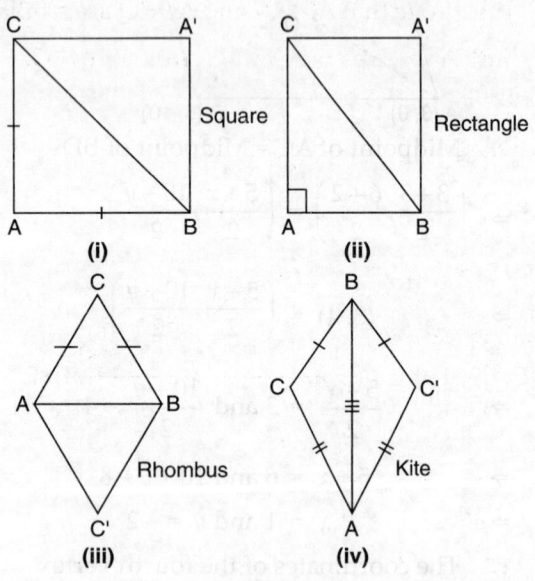

2. Find the image of a point $(-1, 2)$ in the line joining $(2, 1)$ and $(-3, 2)$.

Sol. Let $D(\alpha, \beta)$ be the image of point $C(-1, 2)$ in the line joining the points $A(2, 1)$ and $B(-3, 2)$.

Since, AB is the perpendicular bisector of CD.

So, Slope of AB × Slope of CD = -1

$$\Rightarrow \quad \frac{2-1}{-3-2} \times \frac{\beta-2}{\alpha+1} = -1$$

$$\Rightarrow \quad \frac{1}{-5} \times \frac{\beta-2}{\alpha+1} = -1$$

$$\Rightarrow \quad \beta - 2 = 5\alpha + 5$$

$$\Rightarrow \quad 5\alpha - \beta + 7 = 0 \qquad \ldots(i)$$

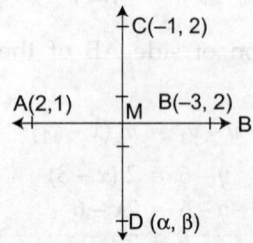

Equation of line AB,

$$y - 1 = \frac{2-1}{-3-2}(x-2)$$

$$\Rightarrow \quad y - 1 = \frac{1}{-5}(x-2)$$

$$\Rightarrow \quad -5(y-1) = x - 2$$

$$\Rightarrow \quad x - 2 + 5y - 5 = 0$$

$$\Rightarrow \quad x + 5y - 7 = 0 \qquad \ldots(ii)$$

Since, midpoint M of CD $\left(\dfrac{\alpha-1}{2}, \dfrac{\beta+2}{2}\right)$ lies on AB.

$$\frac{\alpha-1}{2} + 5\left(\frac{\beta+2}{2}\right) - 7 = 0$$

$$\Rightarrow \quad \alpha - 1 + 5\beta + 10 - 14 = 0$$

$$\Rightarrow \quad \alpha + 5\beta - 5 = 0 \qquad \ldots(iii)$$

Solving (i) and (iii), we get

$$\alpha = \frac{-15}{13} \text{ and } \beta = \frac{16}{13}$$

Hence, coordinates of D are $\left(-\dfrac{15}{13}, \dfrac{16}{13}\right)$. **Ans.**

3. If the image of the point $(2, 1)$ with respect to the line mirror be $(5, 2)$. Find the equation of the mirror.

Sol. Let CD be the line mirror with slope m_1.

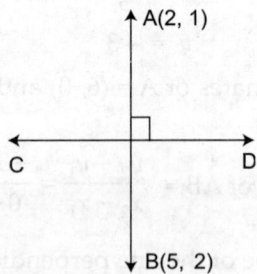

Now, the slope of the line joining $A(2, 1)$ and $B(5, 2)$.

$$m_2 = \frac{2-1}{5-2} = \frac{1}{3}$$

Since   CD ⊥ AB

So, $m_1 m_2 = -1$

$$\Rightarrow \quad m_1 \times \frac{1}{3} = -1$$

$$\Rightarrow \quad m_1 = -3.$$

Now, midpoint of $AB = \left(\dfrac{2+5}{2}, \dfrac{1+2}{2}\right) = \left(\dfrac{7}{2}, \dfrac{3}{2}\right)$

$\Rightarrow \qquad y - \dfrac{3}{2} = -3x + \dfrac{21}{2}$

Equation of the mirror CD,

$$y - y_1 = m(x - x_1)$$

$\Rightarrow \qquad 2y - 3 = -6x + 21$

$\Rightarrow \qquad y - \dfrac{3}{2} = -3\left(x - \dfrac{7}{2}\right)$

$\Rightarrow \quad 6x + 2y - 3 - 21 = 0$

$\Rightarrow \qquad 6x + 2y - 24 = 0$

or $\qquad 3x + y - 12 = 0.$ **Ans.**

Chapter 13. Similarity

1. In the given figure, AB and DE are perpendicular to BC.

(i) Prove that $\triangle ABC \sim \triangle DEC$

(ii) If AB = 6 cm, DE = 4 cm and AC = 15 cm. Calculate CD.

(iii) Find the ratio of the area of $\triangle ABC$: area of $\triangle DEC$.

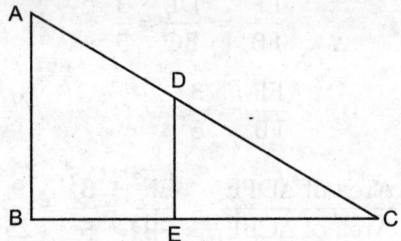

Sol. (i) Given, $AB \perp BC$

$DE \perp BC$

To prove : $\triangle ABC \sim \triangle DEC$

Proof : In $\triangle ABC$ and $\triangle DEC$,

$\angle ABC = \angle DEC = 90°$ (given)

$\angle C = \angle C$ {common}

$\therefore \qquad \triangle ABC \sim \triangle DEC$ {A.A criteria}

Hence Proved.

(ii) Given, $AB = 6$ cm, $DE = 4$ cm

$AC = 15$ cm, $CD = ?$

Since $\triangle ABC \sim \triangle DEC$

$\Rightarrow \qquad \dfrac{AB}{DE} = \dfrac{AC}{CD}$

{Corresponding sides of similar $\triangle$'s are proportional}

$\therefore \qquad \dfrac{6}{4} = \dfrac{15}{CD}$

$\Rightarrow \qquad CD = \dfrac{15 \times 4}{6} = 10.$ **Ans.**

(iii) $\dfrac{\text{area } \triangle ABC}{\text{area } \triangle DEC} = \dfrac{AB^2}{DE^2}$ {Area theorem}

$= \dfrac{36}{16} = \dfrac{9}{4}$ or $9 : 4.$ **Ans.**

---

2. In $\triangle PQR$, MN is parallel to QR and $\dfrac{PM}{MQ} = \dfrac{2}{3}$ *

(i) Find $\dfrac{MN}{QR}$

(ii) Prove that $\triangle OMN$ and $\triangle ORQ$ are similar.

(iii) Find, Area of $\triangle OMN$: Area of $\triangle ORQ$.

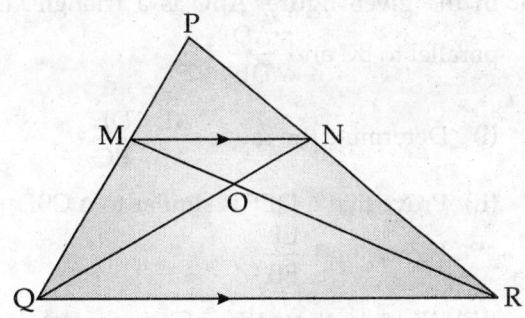

Sol. Given, MN ∥ QR, and $\dfrac{PM}{MQ} = \dfrac{2}{3}$.

Now, $\dfrac{PM}{MQ} = \dfrac{2}{3}$

$\Rightarrow \qquad \dfrac{PM}{PM + MQ} = \dfrac{2}{2+3}$

$\Rightarrow \qquad \dfrac{PM}{PQ} = \dfrac{2}{5}$

(i) In $\triangle PMN$ and $\triangle PQR$,

$\angle P = \angle P$ (common angle)

$\angle PMN = \angle PQR$

(corresponding angles, MN ∥ QR)

$\therefore \qquad \triangle PMN \sim \triangle PQR$ (AA axiom)

$\therefore \qquad \dfrac{MN}{QR} = \dfrac{PM}{PQ}$ (corresponding sides of similar $\triangle$s)

$\dfrac{MN}{QR} = \dfrac{2}{5}.$ **Ans.**

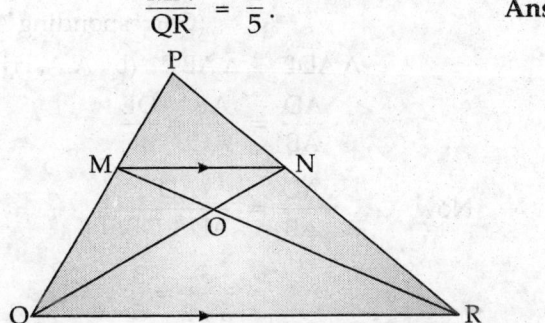

(ii) In $\triangle OMN$ and $\triangle ORQ$,

$$\angle MON = \angle QOR$$

(vertically opposite angles)

$$\angle OMN = \angle ORQ$$

(Alternate angles, MN ‖ QR)

$\therefore \quad \triangle OMN \sim \triangle ORQ \quad$ (By AA axiom)

Ans.

(iii) $\dfrac{\text{Area of } (\triangle OMN)}{\text{Area of } (\triangle ORQ)} = \dfrac{MN^2}{QR^2}$

(Area of similar triangles are proportional to the square of their corresponding sides)

$$= \dfrac{2^2}{5^2} = \dfrac{4}{25}$$

$\Rightarrow$ Area of $\triangle OMN$: Area of $\triangle ORQ = 4 : 25$.

Ans.

3. In the given figure, ABC is a triangle. DE is parallel to BC and $\dfrac{AD}{DB} = \dfrac{3}{2}$.

(i) Determine the ratios $\dfrac{AD}{AB}, \dfrac{DE}{BC}$.

(ii) Prove that $\triangle DEF$ is similar to $\triangle CBF$.

Hence, find $\dfrac{EF}{FB}$.

(iii) What is the ratio of the areas of $\triangle DEF$ and $\triangle BFC$?

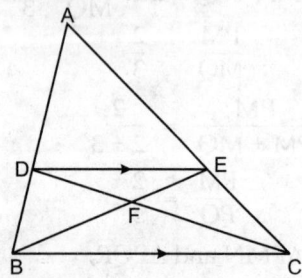

Sol. (i) Given

$$DE \parallel BC$$

and $\quad \dfrac{AD}{DB} = \dfrac{3}{2}$

In $\triangle ADE$ and $\triangle ABC$,

$$\angle A = \angle A \quad \text{(Common Angles)}$$

$$\angle D = \angle B$$

(Corresponding Angles)

$\therefore \quad \triangle ADE \sim \triangle ABC \quad$ (by A.A. criterion)

$\therefore \quad \dfrac{AD}{AB} = \dfrac{AE}{AC} = \dfrac{DE}{BC}$

Now, $\quad \dfrac{AD}{AB} = \dfrac{AD}{AD+DB}$

$$= \dfrac{3}{3+2} = \dfrac{3}{5}$$

$\therefore \quad \dfrac{AD}{AB} = \dfrac{3}{5} = \dfrac{DE}{BC}.$ **Ans.**

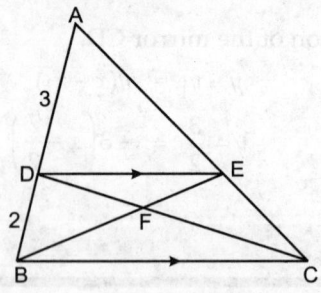

(ii) In $\triangle DEF$ and $\triangle CBF$,

$$\angle FDE = \angle FCB \quad \text{(Alternate Angles)}$$

$$\angle DFE = \angle BFC$$

(Vertically Opposite Angles)

$\therefore \quad \triangle DEF \sim \triangle CBF \quad$ (by A.A. criterion)

Hence Proved.

$$\dfrac{EF}{FB} = \dfrac{DE}{BC} = \dfrac{3}{5}$$

$\therefore \quad \dfrac{EF}{FB} = \dfrac{3}{5}.$ **Ans.**

(iii) $\dfrac{\text{Area of } \triangle DFE}{\text{Area of } \triangle CBF} = \dfrac{EF^2}{FB^2} = \dfrac{3^2}{5^2} = \dfrac{9}{25}.$ **Ans.**

4. In the given figure $\triangle ABC$ and $\triangle AMP$ are right angled at B and M respectively.

Given AC = 10 cm, AP = 15 cm and PM = 12 cm.

(i) Prove $\triangle ABC \sim \triangle AMP$.

(ii) Find AB and BC.

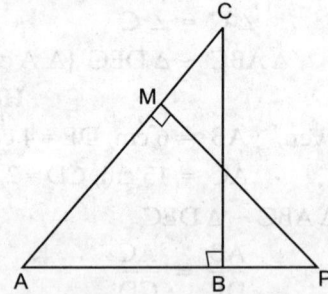

Sol. (i) In $\triangle ABC$ and $\triangle AMP$,

$$\angle ABC = \angle AMP \quad \text{(90° each)}$$

$$\angle A = \angle A \quad \text{(common)}$$

$\Rightarrow \quad \triangle ABC \sim \triangle AMP \quad$ (by AA similarity)

Hence proved.

(ii) Since, $\triangle ABC \sim \triangle AMP$

$\Rightarrow \quad \dfrac{AB}{AM} = \dfrac{BC}{PM} = \dfrac{AC}{AP}$

$\Rightarrow \quad \dfrac{BC}{PM} = \dfrac{AC}{AP}$

$\Rightarrow \qquad \dfrac{BC}{12} = \dfrac{10}{15}$

$\Rightarrow \qquad BC = \dfrac{10}{15} \times 12$

$\Rightarrow \qquad BC = 8$

Now, $\qquad AB^2 = AC^2 - BC^2$

$\qquad\qquad\quad = 10^2 - 8^2$

$\qquad\qquad\quad = 100 - 64 = 36$

$\therefore \qquad\qquad AB = 6 \text{ cm}.$ **Ans.**

5. In the adjoining figure, Δ ACB ~ Δ APQ. If BC = 10 cm, PQ = 5 cm, BA = 6·5 cm and AP = 2·8 cm. Find the area (Δ ACB) : area (Δ APQ).

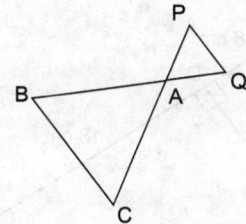

Sol. Given $\quad \Delta$ ACB ~ Δ APQ.

Then, $\quad \dfrac{\text{area }(\Delta ACB)}{\text{area }(\Delta APQ)} = \dfrac{BC^2}{PQ^2}$

$\qquad\qquad = \dfrac{(10)^2}{(5)^2}$

$\qquad\qquad = \dfrac{100}{25}$

$\qquad\qquad = \dfrac{4}{1}$

Hence, Required ratio is 4 : 1. **Ans.**

6. Triangles ABC and DEF are similar.

(i) If area (ΔABC) = 16 cm², area (ΔDEF) = 25 cm² and BC = 2.3 cm, find EF.

(ii) If area (ΔABC) = 9 cm², area (ΔDEF) = 64 cm² and DE = 5.1 cm, find AB.

(iii) If AC = 19 cm and DF = 8 cm, find the ratio between the areas of two triangles.

(iv) If area (ΔABC) = 36 cm², area (ΔDEF) = 64 cm² and DE = 6.2 cm, find AB.

Sol. **(i)** We have

$\qquad$ area (ΔABC) = 16 cm²

$\qquad$ area (ΔDEF) = 25 cm²

and $\qquad\qquad BC = 2\cdot3$ cm

Since, $\dfrac{\text{area }(\Delta ABC)}{\text{area }(\Delta DEF)} = \dfrac{BC^2}{EF^2}$

$\Rightarrow \qquad \dfrac{16}{25} = \dfrac{(2\cdot3)^2}{EF^2}$

$\Rightarrow \qquad \dfrac{2\cdot3}{EF} = \dfrac{4}{5}$

$\Rightarrow \qquad 4\,EF = 5 \times 2\cdot3$

$\Rightarrow \qquad EF = \dfrac{11\cdot5}{4}$

$\Rightarrow \qquad EF = 2\cdot875$ cm. **Ans.**

(ii) We have

$\qquad$ area (ΔABC) = 9 cm²

$\qquad$ area (ΔDEF) = 64 cm²

and $\qquad\qquad DE = 5\cdot1$ cm

Since, $\dfrac{\text{area }(\Delta ABC)}{\text{area }(\Delta DEF)} = \dfrac{AB^2}{DE^2}$

$\Rightarrow \qquad \dfrac{9}{64} = \dfrac{AB^2}{DE^2}$

$\Rightarrow \qquad \dfrac{AB}{DE} = \dfrac{3}{8}$

$\Rightarrow \qquad \dfrac{AB}{5\cdot1} = \dfrac{3}{8}$

$\Rightarrow \qquad AB = \dfrac{3}{8} \times 5\cdot1 = \dfrac{15\cdot3}{8}$

$\Rightarrow \qquad AB = 1\cdot9125$ cm. **Ans.**

(iii) In ΔABC and ΔDEF, AC = 19 cm, DF = 8 cm.

Since, $\dfrac{\text{area }(\Delta ABC)}{\text{area }(\Delta DEF)} = \dfrac{AC^2}{DF^2} = \dfrac{(19)^2}{(8)^2} = \dfrac{361}{64}$

Hence, the required ratio is 361 : 64. **Ans.**

(iv) area (ΔABC) = 36 cm²

$\qquad$ area (ΔDEF) = 64 cm².

$\qquad\qquad DE = 6\cdot2$ cm

$\qquad\qquad AB = ?$

We have

$\dfrac{\text{area }(\Delta ABC)}{\text{area }(\Delta DEF)} = \dfrac{AB^2}{DE^2}$

$\Rightarrow \qquad \dfrac{36}{64} = \dfrac{AB^2}{(6\cdot2)^2}$

$\Rightarrow \qquad \dfrac{AB}{6.2} = \dfrac{6}{8}$

$\Rightarrow \qquad AB = \dfrac{6 \times 6 \cdot 2}{8}$

$\Rightarrow \qquad AB = 4 \cdot 65$ cm. **Ans.**

7. Two isosceles triangles have equal vertical angles and their areas are in the ratio of 36 : 25. Find the ratio between their corresponding heights.

Sol. $\triangle ABC$ and $\triangle PQR$ be the two isosceles triangles such that

$$\angle A = \angle P.$$

Then $\quad \triangle ABC \sim \triangle PQR.$

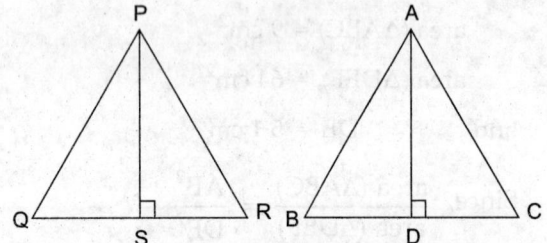

Let AD and PS be their heights then

$$\dfrac{\text{area } (\triangle ABC)}{\text{area } (\triangle PQR)} = \dfrac{AD^2}{PS^2}$$

$\Rightarrow \qquad \dfrac{36}{25} = \dfrac{AD^2}{PS^2}$

$\Rightarrow \qquad \dfrac{AD}{PS} = \dfrac{6}{5}$

$\Rightarrow \qquad AD : PS = 6 : 5.$ **Ans.**

8. In $\triangle ABC$, D and E are the midpoints of AB and AC respectively. Find the ratio of the areas of $\triangle$ ADE and $\triangle$ ABC.

Sol. Since, D and E are the midpoints of AB and AC respectively.

Therefore, $\quad DE \parallel BC.$

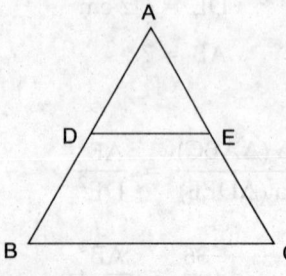

Consequently,

$$\triangle ADE \sim \triangle ABC$$

$\Rightarrow \qquad \dfrac{\text{area } (\triangle ADE)}{\text{area } (\triangle ABC)} = \dfrac{AD^2}{AB^2}$

$$= \dfrac{AD^2}{(2AD^2)}$$

$$= \dfrac{1}{4} \qquad (\because AB = 2AD) \text{ **Ans.**}$$

9. In the adjoining figure ABC is a right angled triangle with $\angle$ BAC = 90°, and AD $\perp$ BC.

(i) Prove $\triangle$ ADB $\sim$ $\triangle$ CDA.

(ii) If BD = 18 cm, CD = 8 cm find AD.

(iii) Find the ratio of the area of $\triangle$ ADB is to area of $\triangle$ CDA.

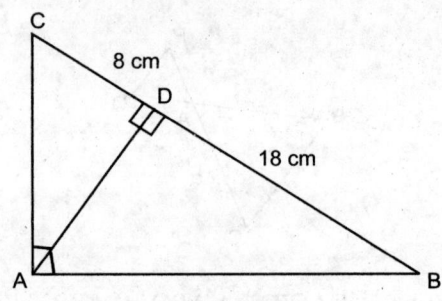

Sol. **(i)** In $\triangle$ ADB and $\triangle$ ADC,

Let $\qquad \angle CAD = x$

$\Rightarrow \qquad \angle DAB = 90° - x$

$\Rightarrow \qquad \angle DBA = 180° - 90° - 90° + x$

$\Rightarrow \qquad \angle DBA = x$

$\therefore \qquad \angle DBA = \angle CAD$

$\angle ADC = 90° \qquad (AD \perp BC)$

$\angle ADB = 90° \qquad (AD \perp BC)$

$\therefore \qquad \angle ADC = \angle ADB$

So, $\qquad \triangle ADB \sim \triangle ADC$

(By AAA similarity)

or $\qquad \triangle ADB \sim \triangle CDA$ **Hence Proved.**

(ii) $\because \qquad \triangle ADB \sim \triangle CDA$

$\therefore \qquad \dfrac{AD}{BD} = \dfrac{CD}{AD}$

$\begin{bmatrix} \text{corresponding parts of similar} \\ \triangle\text{'s are proportional} \end{bmatrix}$

or $\qquad AD^2 = BD \times CD$

$\Rightarrow \qquad AD^2 = 18 \times 8 \qquad \begin{bmatrix} BD = 18 \\ CD = 8 \end{bmatrix}$ (given)

$\Rightarrow \qquad AD^2 = 144$

$\qquad\qquad AD = 12$ cm **Ans.**

(iii) $\dfrac{\text{Area of } \triangle ADB}{\text{Area of } \triangle CDA} = \dfrac{BD^2}{AD^2}$

$\left[\begin{array}{c}\text{Area theorem of}\\\text{similar triangles}\end{array}\right]$

$\qquad = \dfrac{18^2}{12^2} = \dfrac{18 \times 18}{12 \times 12}$

$\qquad = \dfrac{3 \times 3}{2 \times 2} = \dfrac{9}{4}$

$\Rightarrow$ area ($\triangle$ ADB) : area ($\triangle$ CDA) = 9 : 4.   **Ans.**

10. Equilateral triangles are drawn on the sides of a right angled triangle. Show that the area of the triangle on the hypotenuse is equal to the sum of the areas of triangles on the other two sides.

Sol. Given, a right angled triangle ABC with right angle at B. Equilateral triangles PAB, QBC and RAC are described on sides AB, BC and CA respectively.

To Prove :

Area ($\triangle$PAB) + Area ($\triangle$QBC) = Area ($\triangle$RAC).

Proof : Since, triangles PAB, QBC and RAC are equilateral. Therefore, they are equiangular and hence similar.

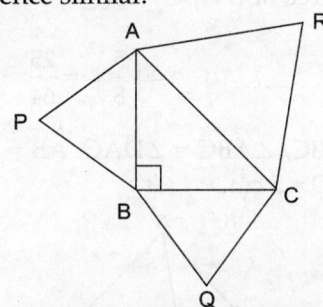

$\therefore \quad \dfrac{\text{area } (\triangle PAB)}{\text{area } (\triangle RAC)} + \dfrac{\text{area } (\triangle QBC)}{\text{area } (\triangle RAC)}$

$\qquad = \dfrac{AB^2}{AC^2} + \dfrac{BC^2}{AC^2}$

$\qquad = \dfrac{AB^2 + BC^2}{AC^2}$

$\qquad = \dfrac{AC^2}{AC^2} = 1,$

$\left[\begin{array}{l}\because \triangle \text{ ABC is a right angled with } \angle B = 90°\\ \therefore AC^2 = AB^2 + BC^2\end{array}\right]$

$\Rightarrow \dfrac{\text{area } (\triangle PAB) + \text{area } (\triangle QBC)}{\text{area } (\triangle RAC)} = 1$

$\Rightarrow$ area ($\triangle$PAB) + area ($\triangle$QBC)

$\qquad\qquad = $ area ($\triangle$RAC) **Hence Proved.**

11. In the adjoining figure, BC is parallel to DE, area of $\triangle$ABC = 25 sq. cm, area of trapezium BCED = 24 sq. cm, DE = 14 cm. Calculate the length of BC.

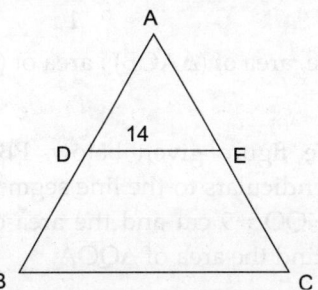

Sol. Given, area of $\triangle$ ABC = 25 cm^2,

area of trapezium BCED = 24 cm^2

and $\qquad\qquad$ DE = 14 cm

$\therefore \quad$ Area of $\triangle$ ADE = area of $\triangle$ ABC

$\qquad\qquad\qquad$ – area of trap. BCED

$\qquad\qquad = 25 - 24$

$\qquad\qquad = 1 \text{ cm}^2$

$\because \qquad \triangle$ ABC ~ $\triangle$ ADE

$\therefore \quad \dfrac{\text{Area of } (\triangle ABC)}{\text{Area of } (\triangle ADE)} = \dfrac{BC^2}{DE^2}$

$\Rightarrow \qquad\qquad \dfrac{25}{1} = \dfrac{BC^2}{14^2}$

$\Rightarrow \qquad\qquad \dfrac{BC}{14} = \dfrac{5}{1}$

$\Rightarrow \qquad\qquad BC = 5 \times 14 = 70 \text{ cm}$ **Ans.**

12. In figure ABCD is a trapezium in which AB || DC and AB = 2DC. Determine the ratio between the areas of $\triangle$AOB and $\triangle$COD.

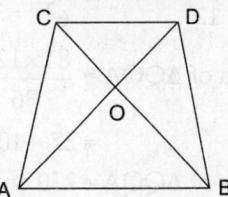

Sol. In triangles AOB and COD, we have

$\qquad\qquad \angle AOB = \angle COD,$

$\qquad\qquad$ [Vertically opposite angles]

and $\qquad \angle OAB = \angle OCD,$

$\qquad\qquad$ [Corresponding angles]

So, by AA-criterion of similarity, we have

$\qquad\qquad \triangle AOB \sim \triangle COD$

$\Rightarrow \dfrac{\text{Area of } (\triangle AOB)}{\text{Area of } (\triangle COD)} = \dfrac{AB^2}{DC^2}$

$$\Rightarrow \quad \frac{\text{Area of } (\Delta \text{ AOB})}{\text{Area of } (\Delta \text{ COD})} = \frac{(2\text{DC})^2}{(\text{DC})^2}$$

$$= \frac{4}{1}$$

Hence, area of (ΔAOB) : area of (ΔCOD) = 4 : 1.

Ans.

13. In the figure given below, PB and QA are perpendiculars to the line segment AB. If PO = 6 cm, QO = 9 cm and the area of ΔPOB = 120 cm², find the area of ΔQOA.

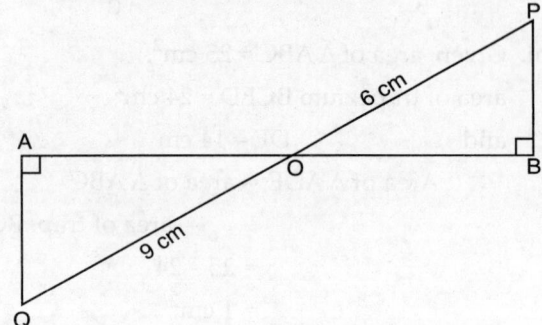

Sol. PO = 6 cm, QO = 9 cm.

Area of ΔPOB = 120 cm²

In ΔPOB and ΔQOB,

$$\angle B = \angle A \qquad \text{(each 90°)}$$

$$\angle POB = \angle QOA$$

(Opposite vertical angles)

$$\Rightarrow \qquad \angle POB \sim \angle QOA$$

In similar Δ's

$$\frac{\text{Area of } \Delta \text{ QOA}}{\text{Area of } \Delta \text{ POB}} = \frac{OQ^2}{OP^2}$$

$$\Rightarrow \quad \frac{\text{Area of } \Delta \text{ QOA}}{12} = \frac{9^2}{6^2}$$

$$\Rightarrow \quad \text{Area of } \Delta \text{QOA} = \frac{81 \times 120}{36}$$

$$= 27 \times 10$$

$$\therefore \quad \text{Area of } \Delta \text{QOA} = 270 \text{ cm}^2. \qquad \textbf{Ans.}$$

14. In the given figure, ABC and CEF are two triangles where BA is parallel to CE and AF : AC = 5 : 8.

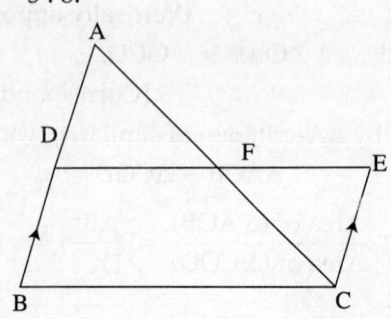

(i) Prove that Δ ADF ~ ΔCEF.

(ii) Find AD if CE = 6 cm.

(iii) If DF is parallel to BC, find area of ΔADF : area of ΔABC.

Sol. (i) In Δ ADF and Δ CFE,

$$\angle DAF = \angle FCE \quad \text{(Alternate angles)}$$

$$\angle AFD = \angle CFE$$

(Vertically opp. angles)

$$\angle ADF = \angle CEF$$

$$\Rightarrow \qquad \Delta \text{ADF} \sim \Delta \text{CEF} \quad \text{(by A.A. criterion)}$$

Hence Proved

(ii) $$\Delta \text{ADF} \sim \Delta \text{CEF}$$

$$\Rightarrow \qquad \frac{AD}{CE} = \frac{AF}{FC}$$

$$\Rightarrow \qquad FC = AC - AF$$

$$= 8 - 5 = 3$$

$$\Rightarrow \qquad \frac{AD}{6} = \frac{5}{3}$$

$$\Rightarrow \qquad AD = 10 \text{ cm.} \qquad \textbf{Ans.}$$

(iii) DF || BC

$$\therefore \quad \Delta \text{ ADF} \sim \Delta \text{ ABC}$$

$$\because \quad \angle D = \angle B \text{ and } \angle F = \angle C.$$

$$\Rightarrow \quad \frac{\text{Area of } \Delta \text{ ADF}}{\text{Area of } \Delta \text{ ABC}} = \frac{AF^2}{AC^2}$$

$$= \left(\frac{5}{8}\right)^2 = \frac{25}{64} \qquad \textbf{Ans.}$$

15. In ΔABC, ∠ABC = ∠DAC, AB = 8 cm, AC = 4 cm, AD = 5 cm.

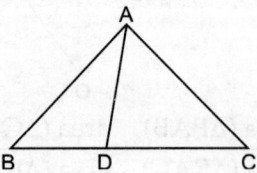

(i) Prove that ΔACD is similar to Δ BCA.

(ii) Find BC and CD.

(iii) Find area of ΔACD : area of ΔABC.

Sol. $$\angle ABC = \angle DAC = x \text{ (say)}$$

$$AB = 8 \text{ cm, } AC = 4 \text{ cm,}$$

$$AD = 5 \text{ cm.}$$

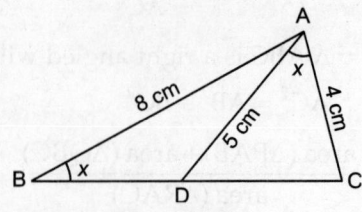

(i) In Δ ACD and Δ BCA,

$$\angle ABC = \angle DAC \qquad \text{(Given)}$$

$\angle ACD = \angle BCA$ (Common)

$\therefore$ $\triangle ACD \sim \triangle BCA$ (By AA axiom)

Hence, $\triangle ACD$ is similar to $\triangle BCA$.

                    Hence Proved.

(ii) As we have,

$$\frac{AC}{BC} = \frac{CD}{CA} = \frac{AD}{BA}$$

$\Rightarrow$ $\frac{4}{BC} = \frac{CD}{4} = \frac{5}{8}$

$\Rightarrow$ $\frac{4}{BC} = \frac{5}{8}$

$\Rightarrow$ $BC = \frac{8 \times 4}{5} = \frac{32}{5}$

             $= 6.4$ cm.

and $\frac{CD}{4} = \frac{5}{8}$

$\Rightarrow$ $CD = \frac{5 \times 4}{8}$

$\Rightarrow$ $CD = 2.5$ cm.   **Ans.**

(iii) $\frac{\text{area of } \triangle ACD}{\text{area of } \triangle ABC} = \left(\frac{AC}{AB}\right)^2$

               $= \left(\frac{4}{8}\right)^2 = \frac{1}{4}$

Thus, area of $\triangle ACD$: area of $\triangle ABC = 1 : 4$.

                    Ans.

16. If the areas of two similar triangles are equal, then the two triangles are congruent.

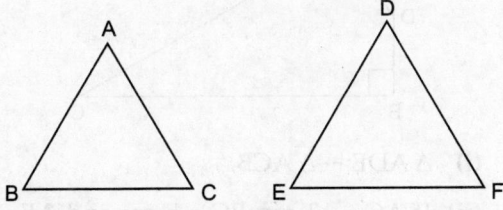

Sol. Given, $\triangle ABC \sim \triangle DEF$

and area $(\triangle ABC)$ = area $(\triangle DEF)$

To Prove : $\triangle ABC \cong \triangle DEF$

$$\frac{\text{area } (\triangle ABC)}{\text{area } (\triangle DEF)} = \frac{AB^2}{DE^2} = \frac{BC^2}{EF^2} = \frac{AC^2}{DF^2}$$

             $= 1$ ($\because$ both area are equal)

$\Rightarrow$ $AB = DE$, $BC = EF$ and $AC = DF$

$\therefore$ $\triangle ABC \cong \triangle DEF$ (By SSS congruence)

                  Hence Proved.

17. If $\triangle ABC \sim \triangle DEF$ such that BC = 3 cm and EF = 4 cm and the area of $\triangle ABC = 54$ cm². Find the area of $\triangle DEF$.

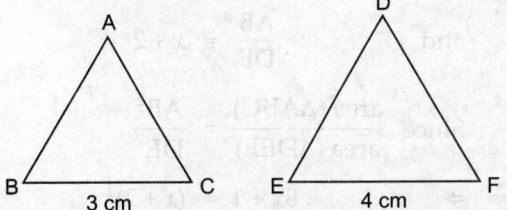

Sol. Since the ratio of the areas of two similar triangles are equal to the ratio of the squares of any two corresponding sides.

$\therefore$ $\frac{\text{Area } (\triangle ABC)}{\text{Area } (\triangle DEF)} = \frac{BC^2}{EF^2}$

$\Rightarrow$ $\frac{54}{\text{Area } (\triangle DEF)} = \frac{3^2}{4^2}$

$\Rightarrow$ Area $(\triangle DEF) = \frac{54 \times 16}{9}$

$\Rightarrow$ Area $(\triangle DEF) = 96$ cm².   **Ans.**

18. If $\triangle XYZ$ is similar to $\triangle JKL$, and the area of $\triangle XYZ$ is 9 times the area of $\triangle JKL$, then how many times the length of JK is XY ?

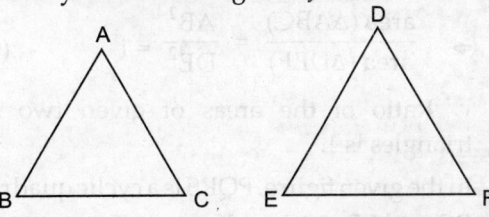

Sol. Given,

     area (DXYZ) = 9 area (JKL)

$\Rightarrow$ $\frac{\text{area } (\triangle XYZ)}{\text{area } (\triangle JKL)} = \frac{9}{1}$

Since, $\frac{\text{area } (\triangle XYZ)}{\text{area } (\triangle JKL)} = \frac{XY^2}{JK^2}$

$\Rightarrow$ $\frac{9}{1} = \frac{(XY)^2}{(JK)^2}$

$\therefore$ $XY = 3 JK$

$\therefore$ Length of XY is 3 times of the length of JK.

                    Ans.

19. The ratio of the areas of two similar triangles is $8x + 1$ and the ratio of their corresponding sides is $x + 2$. What is the value of x ?

Sol. Let $\triangle ABC$ and $\triangle DEF$ are similar.

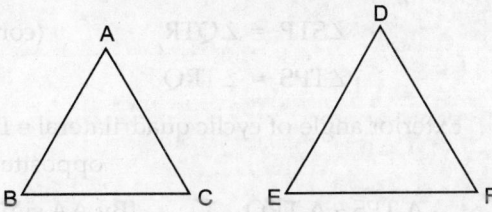

Since, we have given that

$$\frac{\text{area } (\Delta ABC)}{\text{area } (\Delta DEF)} = 8x + 1$$

and

$$\frac{AB}{DE} = x + 2$$

Since

$$\frac{\text{area } (\Delta ABC)}{\text{area } (\Delta DEF)} = \frac{AB^2}{DE^2}$$

$\Rightarrow \qquad 8x + 1 = (x + 2)^2$

$\Rightarrow \qquad 8x + 1 = x^2 + 4 + 4x$

$\Rightarrow \qquad x^2 - 4x + 3 = 0$

$\Rightarrow \qquad (x - 3)(x - 1) = 0$

$\Rightarrow \qquad x = 3 \text{ or } x = 1.$ **Ans.**

20. If the ratio of the corresponding sides of two similar triangles is 1, what is the ratio of the areas of triangles ?

Sol. Let ΔABC and ΔDEF be the similar triangles.

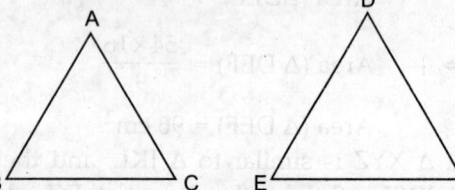

Given, ratio of corresponding sides is 1.

$$\Rightarrow \quad \frac{\text{area } (\Delta ABC)}{\text{area } (\Delta DEF)} = \frac{AB^2}{DE^2} = 1 \qquad \text{(Given)}$$

∴ Ratio of the areas of given two similar triangles is 1. **Ans.**

21. In the given figure, PQRS is a cyclic quadrilateral PQ and SR produced meet at T.

(i) Prove $\Delta TPS \sim \Delta TRQ$.

(ii) Find SP if TP = 18 cm, RQ = 4 cm and TR = 6 cm.

(iii) Find area of quadrilateral PQRS if area of Δ PTS = 27 cm^2.

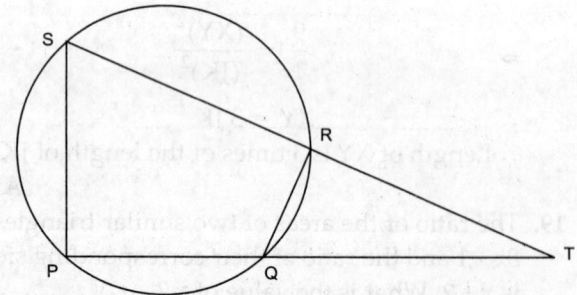

Sol. (i) In Δ TPS and Δ TRQ,

$\angle STP = \angle QTR$ \qquad (common)

$\angle TPS = \angle TRQ$

(∵ Exterior angle of cyclic quadrilateral = Interior

opposite angle)

∴ Δ TPS ~ Δ TRQ \qquad [By AA similarity]

(ii) Since Δ TPS ~ Δ TRQ

$$\therefore \qquad \frac{TR}{TP} = \frac{RQ}{SP}$$

$$\Rightarrow \qquad \frac{6}{18} = \frac{4}{SP}$$

$$\therefore \qquad SP = \frac{4 \times 18}{6} = 12 \qquad \textbf{Ans.}$$

(iii) We know that, the ratio between the areas of two similar triangles = ratio between the squares of its corresponding sides.

$$\frac{\text{Ar } (\Delta PTS)}{\text{Ar } (\Delta RTQ)} = \frac{(SP)^2}{(QR)^2}$$

$$= \frac{(12)^2}{(4)^2} = \frac{9}{1}$$

$$\frac{\text{Ar } (\Delta PTS)}{\text{Ar } (\Delta PTS) - \text{Ar } (\Delta RTQ)} = \frac{9}{9 - 1}$$

$$\frac{\text{Ar } (\Delta PTS)}{\text{Ar (quadrilateral PQRS)}} = \frac{9}{8}$$

$$\therefore \text{Ar (quadrilateral PQRS)} = \frac{8 \times 27}{9} = 24 \text{ cm}^2$$

Ans.

22. ABC is a right angled triangle with $\angle ABC = 90°$. D is any point on AB and DE is perpendicular to AC. Prove that :

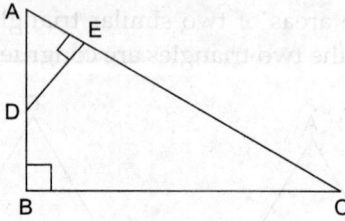

(i) $\Delta ADE \sim \Delta ACB$.

(ii) If AC = 13 cm, BC = 5 cm and AE = 4 cm, find DE and AD.

(iii) Find area of Δ ADE : area of quadrilateral BCED.

Sol. (i) In Δ ADE and Δ ACB,

$\angle ABC = \angle AED = 90°$

$\angle A = \angle A$ \qquad (Common)

∴ By AA axiom, Δ ADE ~ Δ ACB.

Hence Proved

(ii) Given , AC = 13 cm, BC = 5 cm and AE = 4 cm

In right angled triangle ABC,

$$AB^2 + BC^2 = AC^2$$
$$\Rightarrow \quad AB^2 + (5)^2 = (13)^2$$
$$\Rightarrow \quad AB = \sqrt{169 - 25}$$
$$= 12 \text{ cm}$$

Since, they are similar triangles, the sides are proportional.

Now, $\dfrac{AC}{AD} = \dfrac{AB}{AE} \Rightarrow \dfrac{13}{AD} = \dfrac{12}{4}$

$$\Rightarrow \quad AD = \dfrac{13 \times 4}{12} = 4.33 \text{ cm}$$

and $\dfrac{BC}{DE} = \dfrac{AB}{BE} \Rightarrow \dfrac{5}{DE} = \dfrac{12}{4}$

$$\Rightarrow \quad DE = \dfrac{5 \times 4}{12} = 1.67 \text{ cm.} \qquad \textbf{Ans.}$$

(iii) $\dfrac{\text{Ar of } (\triangle ABC)}{\text{Ar of } (\triangle ADE)} = \dfrac{AB^2}{AE^2}$

$$= \dfrac{144}{16} = \dfrac{9}{1}$$

$$\Rightarrow \dfrac{\text{Ar of } (\triangle ADE) + \text{Ar of (quadrilateral BCED)}}{\text{Ar of } (\triangle ADE)} = 9$$

$$\Rightarrow \quad 1 + \dfrac{\text{Ar of (quadrilateral BCED)}}{\text{Ar of } (\triangle ADE)} = 9$$

$$\Rightarrow \quad \dfrac{\text{Ar of (quadrilateral BCED)}}{\text{Ar of } (\triangle ADE)} = 8$$

$$\Rightarrow \quad \dfrac{\text{Ar of } (\triangle ADE)}{\text{Ar of (quadrilateral BCED)}} = \dfrac{1}{8} \textbf{ Ans.}$$

23. In $\triangle ABC$, $\angle ABC = \angle DAC$, $AB = 8$ cm, $AC = 4$ cm, $AD = 5$ cm.

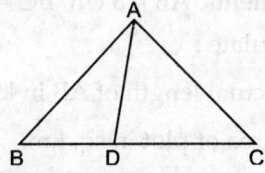

(i) Prove that $\triangle ACD$ is similar to $\triangle BCA$.

(ii) Find BC and CD.

(iii) Find area of $\triangle ACD$: area of $\triangle ABC$.

Sol. $\qquad \angle ABC = \angle DAC = x$ (say)

Given, $AB = 8$ cm, $AC = 4$ cm and $AD = 5$ cm.

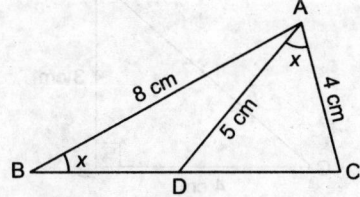

(i) In $\triangle ACD$ and $\triangle BCA$,

$$\angle ABC = \angle DAC \qquad \text{(Given)}$$
$$\angle ACD = \angle BCA \qquad \text{(Common)}$$
$$\Rightarrow \quad \triangle ACD \sim \triangle BCA \qquad \text{(By AA axiom)}$$

Hence, $\triangle ACD$ is similar to $\triangle BCA$.

Hence Proved.

(ii) As we have,

$$\dfrac{AC}{BC} = \dfrac{CD}{CA} = \dfrac{AD}{BA}$$

$$\Rightarrow \quad \dfrac{4}{BC} = \dfrac{CD}{4} = \dfrac{5}{8}$$

$$\Rightarrow \quad \dfrac{4}{BC} = \dfrac{5}{8}$$

$$\Rightarrow \quad BC = \dfrac{8 \times 4}{5} = \dfrac{32}{5} = 6.4 \text{ cm.}$$

and $\qquad \dfrac{CD}{4} = \dfrac{5}{8}$

$$\Rightarrow \quad CD = \dfrac{5 \times 4}{8} = 2.5 \text{ cm.} \qquad \textbf{Ans.}$$

(iii) $\dfrac{\text{Area of } \triangle ACD}{\text{Area of } \triangle ABC} = \left(\dfrac{AC}{AB}\right)^2$

$$= \left(\dfrac{4}{8}\right)^2 = \dfrac{1}{4}$$

Thus, area of $\triangle ACD$: area of $\triangle ABC = 1 : 4$.

Ans.

24. In $\angle PQR$, MN is parallel to QR and $\dfrac{PM}{MQ} = \dfrac{2}{3}$

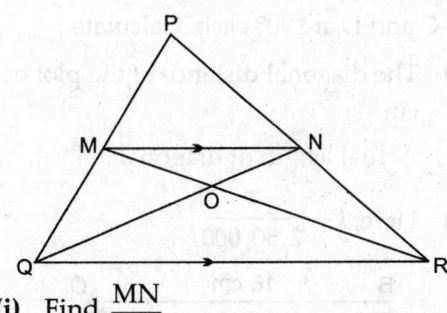

(i) Find $\dfrac{MN}{QR}$.

(ii) Prove that $\triangle OMN$ and $\triangle ORQ$ are similar.

(iii) Find, Area of $\triangle OMN$: Area of $\triangle ORQ$.

Sol. Given, MN || QR, and $\dfrac{PM}{MQ} = \dfrac{2}{3}$

Now, $\qquad \dfrac{PM}{MQ} = \dfrac{2}{3}$

$$\Rightarrow \quad \dfrac{PM}{PM + MQ} = \dfrac{2}{2 + 3}$$

$$\Rightarrow \quad \frac{PM}{PQ} = \frac{2}{5}$$

(i) In $\triangle PMN$ and $\triangle PQR$,

$$\angle P = \angle P \quad \text{(common)}$$
$$\angle PMN = \angle PQR$$
(correspondinig angles, $MN \parallel QR$)

$\therefore \quad \triangle PMN \sim \triangle PQR$ (AA axiom)

$\therefore$
$$\frac{MN}{QR} = \frac{PM}{PQ}$$

$$\frac{MN}{QR} = \frac{2}{5} \qquad \textbf{Ans.}$$

(ii) In $\triangle OMN$ and $\triangle ORQ$,
$$\angle MON = \angle QOR$$
(vertically opposite angles)
$$\angle OMN = \angle ORQ$$
(Alternate angles, $MN \parallel QR$)

$\therefore \quad \triangle OMN \sim \triangle ORQ \qquad$ (AA axiom)

Hence Proved.

(iii) $\dfrac{\text{Area of } \triangle OMN}{\text{Area of } \triangle ORQ} = \dfrac{MN^2}{QR^2}$

(Area of similar triangles are proportional to the square of their corresponding sides)

$$= \frac{2^2}{5^2} = \frac{4}{25}$$

$\Rightarrow$ Area of $\triangle OMN$: Area of $\triangle ORQ = 4 : 25$.

Ans.

25. On a map drawn to scale of 1 : 2,50,000 a rectangular plot of land ABCD has the following measurement AB = 12 cm, BC = 16 cm, angles A, B, C and D are 90° each. Calculate :

(i) The diagonal distance of the plot of land in cm.

(ii) Actual length of diagonal .

Sol. (i) Here, $k = \dfrac{1}{2,50,000}$

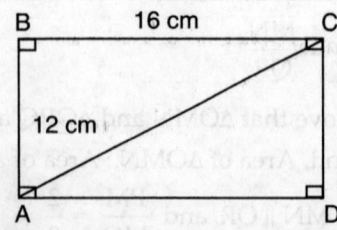

Length of diagonal (on map)

$$= \sqrt{AB^2 + BC^2}$$
$$= \sqrt{12^2 + 16^2}$$

$$= \sqrt{400} = 20 \text{ cm} \qquad \textbf{Ans.}$$

(ii) Length of diagonal on map
$$= k \times \text{Actual length of the diagonal}$$
$$\Rightarrow 20 = \frac{1}{2,50,000} \times \text{Actual length of the diagonal}$$

$\Rightarrow$ Actual length of diagonal
$$= 20 (2,50,000) \text{ cm}$$
$$= 50,00,000 \text{ cm}$$
$$= 50 \text{ km} \qquad \textbf{Ans.}$$

26. A model of a high rise building is made to a scale of 1 : 50.*

(i) If the height of the model is 0.8 m, find the height of the actual building.

(ii) If the floor area of a flat in the building is 20 m² , find the floor area of that in the model.

Sol. Given : Scale = 1 : 50

(i) Let the actual height of the building be h m.

$\therefore \quad \dfrac{0.8}{h} = \dfrac{1}{50}$

$\Rightarrow \quad h = 50 \times 0.8 = 40 \text{ m} \qquad \textbf{Ans.}$

(ii) Let the floor area of the model be x m² .

$\therefore \qquad \dfrac{x}{20} = \left(\dfrac{1}{50}\right)^2$

$\Rightarrow \qquad \dfrac{x}{20} = \dfrac{1}{2500}$

$\Rightarrow \qquad x = \dfrac{20}{2500} \text{ m}^2$

$$= 0.008 \text{ m}^2 \text{ or } 80 \text{ cm}^2 \qquad \textbf{Ans.}$$

27. On a map drawn to a scale of 1 : 2,50,000, a triangular plot of land has the following measurements, AB = 3 cm, BC = 4 cm, $\angle ABC = 90°$. Calculate :

(i) The actual length of AB in km.

(ii) The area of plot in sq. km.

Sol. The scale of a map = 1 : 2,50,000 that is

$$1 \text{ cm} = \frac{2,50,000}{1,000 \times 1000}$$
$$= 2\cdot 5 \text{ km}$$

(i) Actual length of AB

$$= 3 \text{ cm} = 3 \times 2 \cdot 5 \text{ km}$$
$$= 7 \cdot 5 \text{ km} \qquad \textbf{Ans.}$$

(ii) Area of triangular plot

$$= \frac{1}{2} \times AB \times BC$$
$$= \frac{1}{2} \times 3 \times 4$$
$$= 6 \text{ cm}^2$$
$$= 6 \times 2 \cdot 5 \times 2 \cdot 5 \text{ km}^2$$
$$= 37 \cdot 5 \text{ km}^2. \qquad \textbf{Ans.}$$

Chapter 14. Loci

1. Without using set squares and the protractor construct the quadrilateral ABCD in which ∠ BAD = 45°, AD = AB = 6 cm, BC = 3·6 cm, CD = 5 cm.

   (i) Measure ∠ BCD.

   (ii) Locate point P on BD which is equidistant from BC and CD.

   Sol. (i) ∠ BCD = 62°. **Ans.**

   (ii) Draw angle bisector of ∠BCD. Join BD. The point of intersection of the bisector and BD is P. P is equidistant from BC and CD.

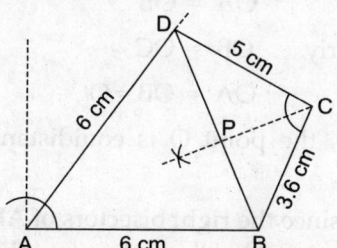

2. Without using set squares or protractor, construct a triangle ABC in which AB = 4 cm, BC = 5 cm and ∠ ABC = 120°.

   (i) Locate the point P such that ΔBAP = 90° and BP = CP.

   (ii) Measure the length of BP.

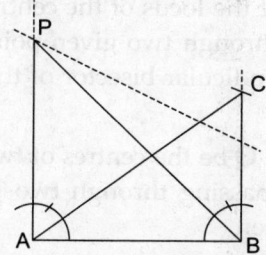

   Sol. (i) Draw ⊥ bisector of BC. Draw AP at A such that ∠ PAB = 90°. The point of intersection P of bisector and AP is the required point. **Ans.**

   (ii) BP = 6·5 cm. **Ans.**

3. State and draw the locus of a swimmer maintaining the same distance from a light house.

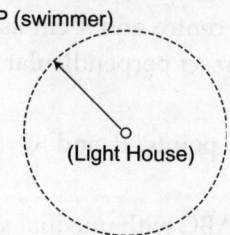

(Light House)

Proof : The locus of the swimmer will be a circle with light house as the centre and the same distane between the light house and the swimmer as radius. **Ans.**

4. State and draw the locus of a point equidistant from two given parallel lines.

   Sol.

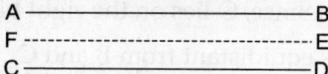

   The locus of a point equidistant from two given parallel lines AB and CD is the line EF parallel to AB or CD exactly mid-way between AB and CD.

   Ans.

5. *l* is the perpendicular bisector of line segment PQ and R is a point on the same side of *l* as P. The segment QR intersects *l* at X. Prove that PX + XR = QR.

   Sol. Since, line *l* is the perpendicular bisector of PQ and X lies on *l*. Therefore, X is equidistant from P and Q.

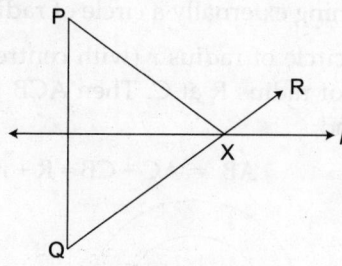

   i.e., $\qquad PX = QX$

   ⇒ $\qquad PX + XR = QX + XR$

   ⇒ $\qquad PX + XR = QR.$ **Hence Proved.**

6. Construct a ΔABC, with AB = 6 cm, AC = BC = 9 cm; find a point 4 cm from A and equidistant from B and C.

Sol. Construct the △ABC with given measurements. Draw perpendicular bisector of BC.

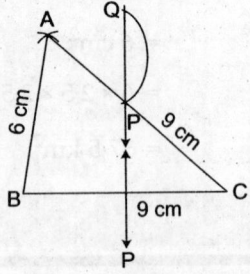

With A as centre and 4 cm as radius, draw an arc to intersect perpendicular bisector at P and Q.

Then, the points P and Q are the requisite points. **Ans.**

7. Given a △ABC with unequal sides. Find a point which is equidistant from B and C as well as from AB and AC.

Sol. Draw the angular bisector of ∠A and perpendicular bisector of side BC of △ ABC. Let these two bisectors meet at point O. Hence 'O' is our required point.

Proof : Since, O lies on the right bisector of BC.

∴ O is equidistant from B and C.

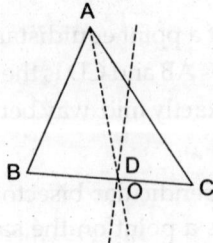

Again, since O lies on the bisector of ∆ A, formed by AB and AC.

So, O is equidistant from AB and AC. **Ans.**

8. Find the locus of the centre of a circle of radius r touching externally a circle of radius R.

Sol. Let a circle of radius r (with centre B) touch a circle of radius R at C. Then ACB is a straight line and

$$AB = AC + CB = R + r$$

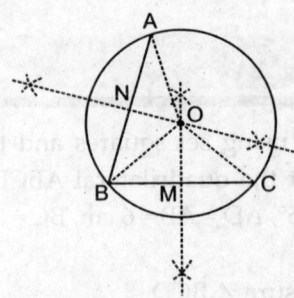

Thus, B moves such that its distance from fixed point A remains constant and is equal to R + r.

Hence, the locus of B is a circle whose centre is A and radius equal to R + r. **Ans.**

9. What is the locus of points which are equidistant from the given non-collinear point A, B and C ? Justify your answer.

Sol. Let A, B, C be three non-collinear points.

Join AB and BC.

Draw the perpendicular bisectors of AB and BC.

Let they meet each other at O.

∵ O lies on the right bisector of AB.

∴   OA = OB

Similarly,   OB = OC

∴   OA = OB = OC

Hence, the point O is equidistant from A, B and C.

Now, since the right bisectors of AB and BC are two non-parallel lines, therefore they have only one point in common and the point is O.

∴ O is the only point equidistant from A, B and C.

Hence, the required locus is the centre of the circle through three given non-collinear points. **Ans.**

10. Show that the locus of the centres of all circles passing through two given points A and B, is the perpendicular bisector of the line segment AB.

Sol. Let P and Q be the centres of two circles S and S', each passing through two given points A and B. Then,

       PA = PB   [Radii of the same circle]

⇒ P lies on the perpendicular bisector of AB

                               ...(i)

Again, QA = QB   [Radii of the same circle]

⇒ Q lies on the perpendicular bisector of AB

                                 ...(ii)

Figure Based Questions

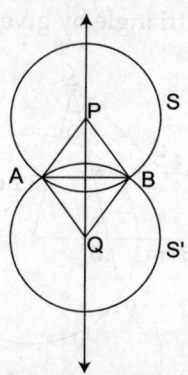

From (i) and (ii), it follows that P and Q both lies on the perpendicular bisector of AB.

Hence, the locus of the centres of all the circles passing through A and B is the perpendicular bisector of AB. **Hence Proved.**

11. Use ruler and compass for this question. Construct a circle of radius 4.5 cm. Draw a chord AB = 6 cm.*

   (i) Find the locus of points equidistant from A and B. Mark the point where it meets the circle as D.

   (ii) Join AD and find the locus of points which are equidistant from AD and AB. Mark the point where it meets the circle as C.

   (iii) Join BC and CD. Measure and write down the length of side CD of the quadrilateral ABCD.

Sol. Steps of construction :

   1. Draw a circle of radius 4.5 cm.

   2. Take a point *A* on the circle. Taking *A* as centre, draw an arc of radius 6 cm, which cuts circle at *B*.

   3. Join *AB*.

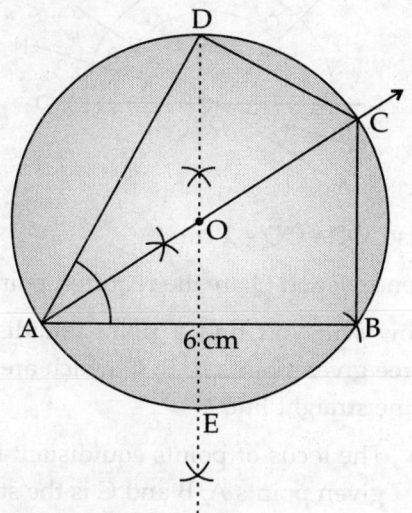

   (i) Draw perpendicular bisector of *AB* which

---

meets the circle at *D* and *E*.

Thus, *DE* is the required locus.

   (ii) Join *AD* and draw angle bisector of ∠*DAB* which meets the circle at *C*.

   Thus, *AC* is the required locus.

   (iii) Length of side *CD* = 5 cm.

12. Using ruler and compass construct :

   (i) a triangle ABC in which AB = 5·5 cm, BC = 3·4 cm and CA = 4·9 cm.

   (ii) the locus of point equidistant from A and C.

   (iii) a circle touching AB at A and passing through C.

Sol. Steps of construction :

   (i) Draw AC = 4·9 cm, AB = 5·5 cm and AC = 4·9 cm.

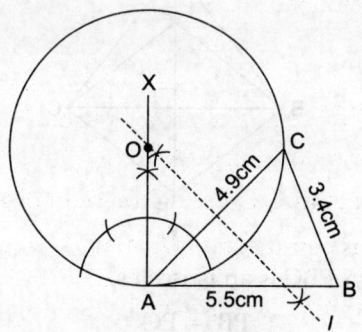

   (ii) Draw bisector *l* ⊥ AC.

   (iii) Draw AX ⊥ AB.

   (iv) Intersection of AX and *l* i.e., O is centre of circle. **Ans.**

13. Using only a ruler and compass construct ∠ABC = 120°, where AB = BC = 5 cm.

   (i) Mark two points D and E which satisfy the condition that they are equidistant from both BA and BC.

   (ii) In the above figure, join AD, DC, AE and EC. Describe the figures :

   (a) AECB, **(b)** ABD, **(c)** ABE.

Sol. (i) and (ii)

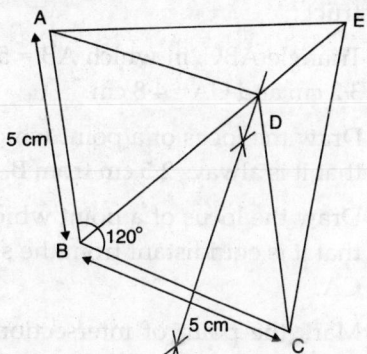

(a) A quadrilateral

(b) A triangle

(c) A triangle. **Ans.**

14. $\triangle PBC$, $\triangle QBC$ and $\triangle RBC$ are three isosceles triangles on the same base BC. Show that P, Q and R are collinear.

Sol. Given, three isosceles triangles PBC, QBC and RBC on the same base BC such that PB = PC, QB = QC and RB = RC.

To prove : P, Q, R are collinear.

Proof : Let l be the perpendicular bisector of BC. Since, the locus of points equidistant from B and C is the perpendicular of the segment joining them. Therefore,

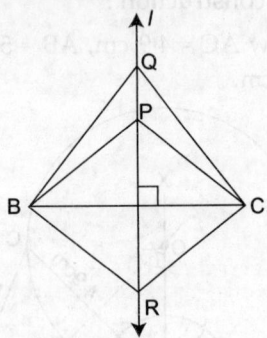

$\triangle$ PBC is an isosceles.

$\Rightarrow$ PB = PC

$\Rightarrow$ P lies on l …(i)

$\triangle$ QBC is isosceles.

$\Rightarrow$ QB = QC

$\Rightarrow$ Q lies on l …(ii)

$\triangle$ RBC is an isoscles.

$\Rightarrow$ RB = RC

$\Rightarrow$ R lies on l …(iii)

From (i), (ii) and (iii), it follows that P, Q and R lie on L.

Hence, P, Q and R are collinear. **Hence Proved.**

15. Without using set squares or protractor construct :

(i) Triangle ABC, in which AB = 5·5 cm, BC = 3·2 cm and CA = 4·8 cm.

(ii) Draw the locus of a point which moves so that it is always 2·5 cm from B.

(iii) Draw the locus of a point which moves so that it is equidistant from the sides BC and CA.

(iv) Mark the point of intersection of the loci with the letter P and measure PC.

Sol. (i) Draw a triangle by given measurements.

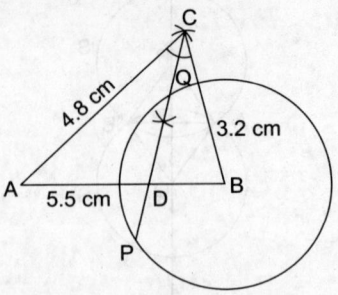

(ii) The locus of a point which moves so that it is always 2·5 cm from B is a circle as shown in the figure. **Ans.**

(iii) The locus of a point is bisector of $\triangle ACB$. **Ans.**

(iv) The circle and bisector intersect in two points PD = 0·9 cm and PC = 3·4 cm. **Ans.**

16. Draw two intersecting lines to include an angle of 30°. Use ruler and compass to locate points, which are equidistant from these lines and also 2 cm away from these points of intersection. How many such points exist ?

Sol. AB and CD are two intersecting lines at an angle of 30°. Their point of intersection is O.

Draw MON and ROS, the bisector of angles between AB and CD. On ON, locate a point P such that OP = 2 cm.

On OR locate a point Q such that OQ = 2 cm.

Since, P and Q are on the angle bisectors of angles between AB and CD, hence each of P and Q is equidistant from AB and CD.

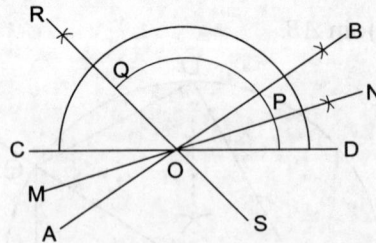

Also, OP = OQ = 2 cm

Hence, P and Q are the required points. **Ans.**

17. How will you find a point equidistant from three given points A, B, C which are not in the same straight line ?

Sol. (i) The locus of points equidistant from three given points A, B and C is the straight line PQ, which bisects AB at right angles.

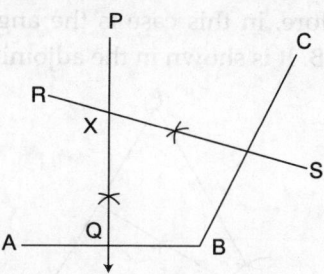

(ii) Similarly, the locus of points equidistant from B and C is the straight line RS which bisects BC at right angles.

Hence, the point common to PQ and RS must satisfy both conditions; that is to say, X, the point of intersection of PQ and RS will be equidistant from A, B and C. **Ans.**

18. Without using set squares or protactor :

   (i) Construct a △ ABC, given BC = 4 cm, ∠B = 75° and CA = 6 cm.

   (ii) Find the point P such that PB = PC and P is equidistant from the side BC and BA. Measure AP.

Sol. (i) Draw BC = 4 cm. Draw BA at B such that △ABC = 75°. Cut CA = 6 cm. Then △ ABC is the required triangle.

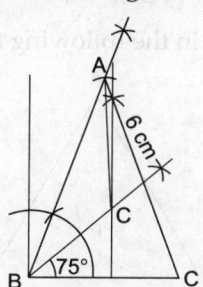

   (ii) Draw single bisector of ∠B. Draw ⊥ bisector of BC. Their point of intersection (P) is the requisite point.

$$AP = 3·9 \text{ cm.} \quad \textbf{Ans.}$$

19. Given, ∠ BAC, a line intersects the arms of ∠ BAC at P and Q. How will you locate a point on line segment PQ, which is equidistant from AB and AC ? Does such a point always exist ?

Sol. Since, locus of points equidistant from AB and AC is the bisector of ∠ BAC. Draw the bisector of ∠BAC intersecting PQ at R.

Since, R is on the bisector, so it is equidistant from AB and AC.

Yes, such a point always exists as there will be definitely a point where angular bisector and line will intersect.

Hence, R is the required point. **Ans.**

20. The bisectors of ∠ B and ∠ C of a quadrilateral ABCD intersect at P. Show that P is equidistant from the opposite sides AB and CD.

Sol. Given, a quadrilateral ABCD in which bisectors of ∠B and ∠C meet at P. PM ⊥ AB and PN ⊥ CD.

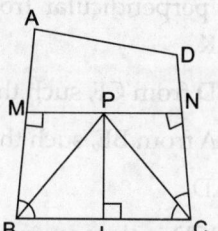

To prove :   PM = PN

Construction : Draw PL ⊥ BC.

Proof : Since, P lies on the bisector of ∠B.

∴ P is equidistant from BC and BA

⇒   PL = PM   ...(i)

Also, P lies on the bisector of ∠C   [Given]

∴ P is equidistant from CB and CD

⇒   PL = PN   ...(ii)

From (i) and (ii), we have

           PL = PM

and   PL = PN

⇒   PM = PN.   **Hence Proved.**

21. Use ruler and compasses only for the following questions :

Construct triangle BCP, when CB = 5 cm, BP = 4 cm, ∠ PBC = 45°.

Complete the rectangle ABCD such that :

   (i) P is equidistant from AB and BC and

   (ii) P is equidistant from C and D. Measure and write down the length of AB.

Sol. Given, BC = 5 cm, BP = 4 cm and ∠ PBC = 45°.

Steps of construction :

   (i) Construct △ BCP with BC = 5 cm, BP = 4 cm and ∠ PBC = 45°.

   (ii) Draw perpendiculars BE and CF and B and C respectively.

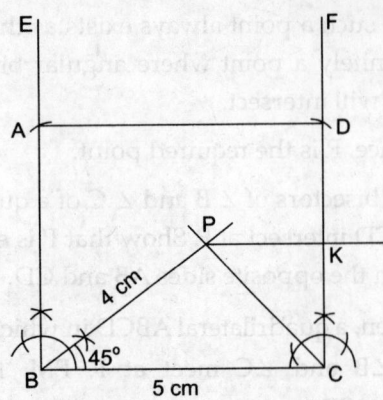

(iii) Draw perpendicular from on CF meeting CF at K.

(iv) Cut CD from CF, such that CK = KD.

(v) Cut BA from BE, such that BA = CD.

(vi) Join AD.

Hence, ABCD is the required rectangle and AB = 5·7 cm.   **Ans.**

22. Ruler and compass only be used in this question. All construction lines and arcs must be clearly shown, and be of sufficient length and clarity to permit assessment.

    (i)   Construct △ ABC, in which BC = 8 cm, AB = 5 cm, ∠ ABC = 60°.

    (ii) Construct the locus of points inside the triangle which are equidistant from BA and BC.

    (iii) Construct the locus of points inside the triangle which are equidistant from B and C.

    (iv) Mark as P, the point which is equidistant from AB, BC and also equidistant from B and C.

    (v)   Measure and record the length of PB.

Sol. (i) Steps of Construction :

1. Draw a line segment BC = 8 cm.
2. Make ∠ CBX = 60°.
3. Set off BA = 5 cm, along BX.
4. Join CA.

Then, △ ABC is the required triangle.

(ii) We know that the locus of point equidistant from two intersecting straight lines consist of a pair of straight lines that bisect the angles between the given straight lines.

Therefore, in this case is the angle bisector of angle B. It is shown in the adjoining figure.

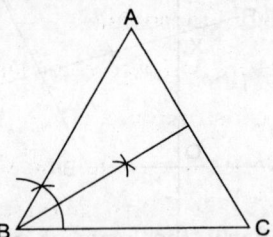

(iii) We know that the locus of a point equidistant from two fixed points is the right bisector of the straight line joining the two fixed points.

Therefore, in this case the right bisector of side BC of △ ABC. It is shown in the given figure.

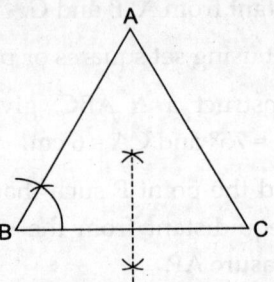

(iv) The point P, is the point in intersecting of angle bisector of ∠ ABC and the right bisector of BC.

It is shown in the following figure :

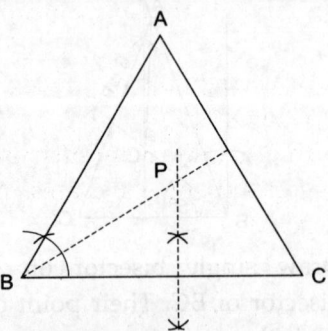

(v) On measuring, we find the length of PB = 3 cm.   **Ans.**

23. Ruler and compasses only be used in this question. All construction lines and arcs must be clearly shown, and be of sufficient length and clarity to permit assessment.

    (i) Construct a △ ABC, in which BC = 6 cm, AB = 9 cm and ∠ ABC = 60°.

    (ii) Construct the locus of the vertices of the triangles with BC as base, which are equal in area to △ ABC.

(iii) Mark the point Q, in your construction, which would make △ QBC equal in area to △ABC, and isosceles.

(iv) Measure and record the length of CQ.

Sol. Steps of construction :

(i) 1. Mark a horizontal line XY on your paper and take BC = 6 cm on it.

2. Construct ∠ ABC = 60° with arm AB = 9 cm.

3. Join A and C to get the required △ ABC.

(ii) 1. Draw AD ⊥ BC.

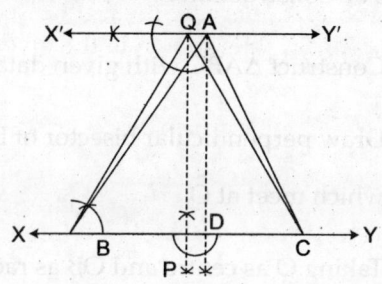

2. Construct a line X′Y′, perpendicular to AD, parallel to XY and passing through A.

3. X′Y′ is the required locus of the vertices of triangles with base BC and area to △ ABC.

[∵ triangles having same base and height are equal in area]

(iii) 1. Draw right bisector PQ of BC, meeeting X′Y′ in Q.

2. Then Q is the point such that △ QBC is an isosceles triangle and area (△ QBC) = area (△ ABC).

(iv) On measuring, we find CQ = 8·4 cm. **Ans.**

24. Use ruler and compasses only for the following question. All construction lines and arcs must be clearly shown.

(i) Construct a △ ABC in which BC = 6·5 cm, ∠ ABC = 60°, AB = 5 cm.

(ii) Construct the locus of points at a distance of 3·5 cm from A.

(iii) Construct the locus of points equidistant from AC and BC.

(iv) Mark 2 points X and Y which are at a distance of 3·5 cm from A and also equidistant from AC and BC. Measure XY.

Sol. Steps of construction :

(i) 1. Draw a line BC = 6·5 cm.

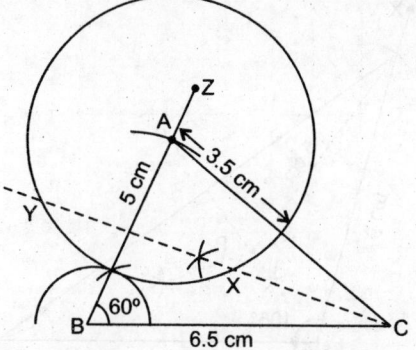

2. At B, draw BZ making an angle of 60° with BC.

3. With B as centre, draw an arc of 5 cm. It cuts BZ at point A.

4. Join AC.

(ii) Taking A as centre and 3·5 cm as radius, draw a circle which is the required locus of points.

(iii) Draw the bisector of angle of vertex ACB, which is the required locus of points equidistant from AC and BC.

(iv) Length of XY = 5 cm.

25. Construct a triangle ABC with AB = 5·5 cm, AC = 6 cm and ∠ BAC = 105°. Hence

(i) Construct the locus of points equidistant from BA and BC.

(ii) Construct the locus of points equidistant from B and C.

(iii) Mark the point which satisfies the above two loci as P. Measure and write the length of PC.

Sol. (i) Draw a line AB = 5·5 cm.

(ii) Now, from point A draw ∠ XAB = 105°.

(iii) Taking A as centre and 6 cm as radius draw arc on AX mark this point as C.

(iv) Join BC.

(v) Draw bisector of ∠ ABC and perpendicular bisector of BC, both intersecting at P. P is the required point.

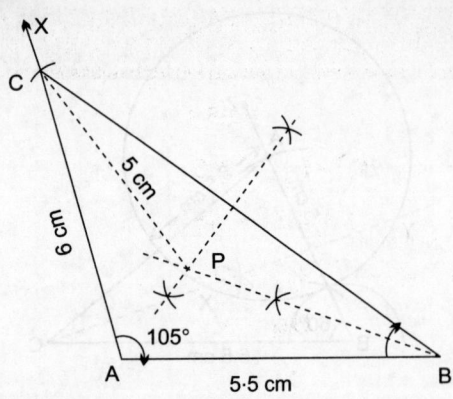

Reason :

Since, **(i)** P is on bisector of angle ABC, P is equidistant from BA and BC. **Ans.**

(ii) P is on perpendicular bisector of BC, P is equidistant from B and C. **Ans.**

(iii) Length of PC is 5 cm. **Ans.**

26. Determine the locus of the centre of a circle. Determine the locus of the centre of a circular disk.

(i) moving so that it touches each of two parallel lines.

(ii) moving tangentially to two concentric circles.

(iii) moving so that its rim passes through a fixed point.

(iv) rolling along a large fixed circular hoop.

Sol. (i)

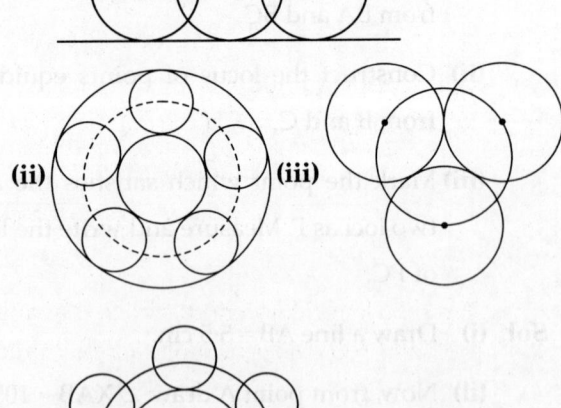

(ii) **(iii)**

(iv)

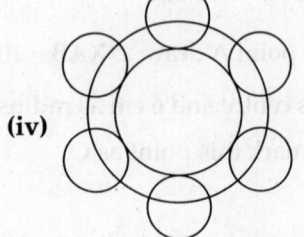

27. Using ruler and compass only, construct a △ABC such that BC = 5 cm and AB = 6·5 cm and ∠ABC = 120°.

(i) Construct a circumcircle of △ABC.

(ii) Construct a cyclic quadrilateral ABCD, such that D is equidistant from AB and BC.

Sol. Given, BC = 5 cm, AB = 6·5 cm, ABC = 120°.

Steps of Construction :

(i) Construct △ABC with given data.

(ii) Draw perpendicular bisector of BC and AB which meet at O.

(iii) Taking O as centre and OB as radius, draw circumcircle of ∠ABC passing through A, B and C.

(iv) Draw angle bisector of ABC as BD which meets circle at D.

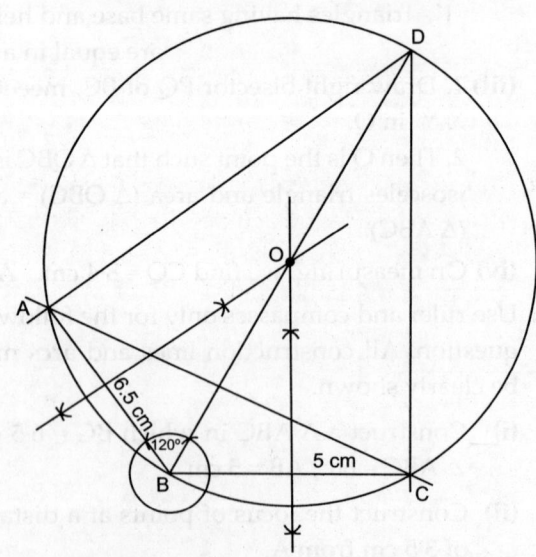

(v) Join AD and CD.

ABCD is the required cyclic quadrilateral.

Ans.

Chapter 15. Circles

1. Two concentric circles with centre O have A, B, C, D as the points of intersection with the lines L shown in figure. If AD = 12 cm and BC = 8 cm, find the lengths of AB, CD, AC and BD.

Sol. Since, OM ⊥ BC

$$BM = CM = \frac{1}{2} BC = 4 \text{ cm}$$

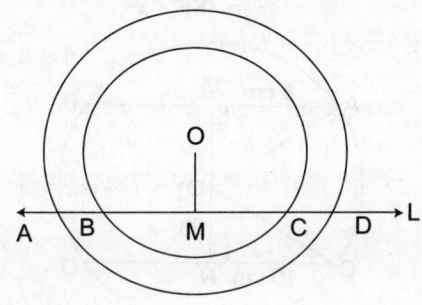

Also   OM ⊥ AD

So, $AM = DM = \frac{1}{2} AD = 6$ cm

Now,   AB = AM − BM = (6 − 4) cm = 2 cm

CD = DM − CM = (6 − 4) cm = 2 cm

∴   AC = AB + BC = (2 + 8) cm = 10 cm

and   BD = BC + CD = (8 + 2) cm = 10 cm.

Ans.

2. In the given figure, the area enclosed between the two concentric circles is 770 cm². If the radius of outer circle is 21 cm, calculate the radius of the inner circle.

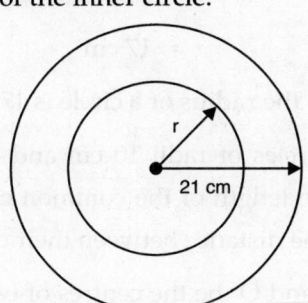

Sol. Let the radius of inner circle be *r*.

Area enclosed between two concentric circles

⇒ $\pi [(21)^2 - (r)^2] = 770$

⇒ $(21)^2 - (r)^2 = \dfrac{770}{\pi} = \dfrac{770 \times 7}{22}$

= 35 × 7

⇒ $(21)^2 - (r)^2 = 245$

⇒ $441 - r^2 = 245$

⇒ $441 - 245 = r^2$

⇒ $196 = r^2$

⇒ $14 = r$

The radius of inner circle = 14 cm.   **Ans.**

3. P and Q are the centre of circles of radius 9 cm and 2 cm respectively, PQ = 17 cm. R is the centre of circle of radius *x* cm, which touches the above circles externally, given that ∠PRQ = 90°. Write an equation in *x* and solve it.

Sol. Let the circle with centre R touch the given two circles at A and B. Then, P, A, R are collinear and Q, B, R are collinear.

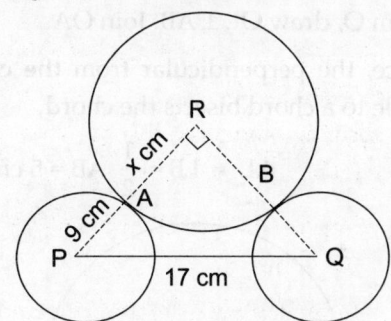

Since, ∠ PRQ = 90°, by Pythagoras theorem,

$$PQ^2 = PR^2 + QR^2$$

⇒ $17^2 = (9 + x)^2 + (2 + x)^2$

⇒ $x^2 + 11x - 102 = 0$

⇒ $(x + 17)(x - 6) = 0$

⇒ $x = 6$ cm

(*x* = − 17 is not possible).

Ans.

4. Find the length of a chord which is at a distance of 5 cm from the centre of a circle of radius 13 cm.

Sol. Let AB be a chord of a circle with centre O and radius 13 cm. Draw OL ⊥ AB.

Join OA. Clearly, OL = 5 cm and OA = 13 cm.

In the right triangle OLA, we have

$$OA^2 = OL^2 + AL^2$$

⇒ $13^2 = 5^2 + AL^2$

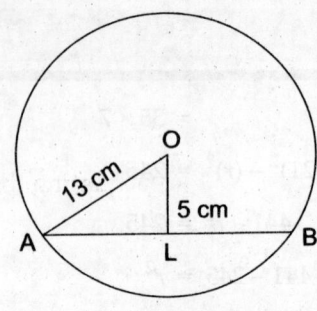

$$\Rightarrow \qquad AL^2 = 144 \text{ cm}^2$$

$$\Rightarrow \qquad AL = 12 \text{ cm}$$

Since, the perpendicular from the centre to the chord bisects the chord. Therefore,

$$AB = 2AL = (2 \times 12) \text{ cm}$$
$$= 24 \text{ cm}. \qquad \textbf{Ans.}$$

5. The radius of a circle is 13 cm and the length of one of its chord is 10 cm. Find the distance of the chord from the centre.

Sol. Let AB be a chord of a circle with centre O and radius 13 cm such that AB = 10 cm.

From O, draw OL ⊥ AB. Join OA.

Since, the perpendicular from the centre of a circle to a chord bisects the chord.

$$\therefore \qquad AL = LB = \frac{1}{2} AB = 5 \text{ cm}$$

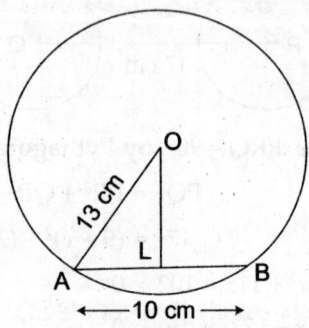

Now, in right triangle OLA, we have

$$OA^2 = OL^2 + AL^2$$

$$\Rightarrow \qquad 13^2 = OL^2 + 5^2$$

$$\Rightarrow \qquad 13^2 - 5^2 = OL^2$$

$$\Rightarrow \qquad OL^2 = 144$$

$$\Rightarrow \qquad OL = 12 \text{ cm}.$$

Hence, the distance of the chord from the centre is 12 cm. **Ans.**

6. Two chords AB, CD of lengths 16 cm and 30 cm, are parallel. If the distance between AB and CD is 23 cm, find the radius of the circle.

Sol. Let AB and CD be the two parallel chords of a circle with centre O and radius r cm.

OM ⊥ AB and ON ⊥ CD

$$AM = \frac{1}{2} AB = \frac{1}{2} \times 16 = 8 \text{ cm}$$

$$CN = \frac{1}{2} CD = \frac{1}{2} \times 30 \text{ cm} = 15 \text{ cm}$$

Let $\qquad OM = x \text{ cm}, MN = 23 \text{ cm}$

So , $\qquad ON = (23 - x) \text{ cm}$

$$OA = OC = r \text{ cm}$$

In △OAM, $OA^2 = AM^2 + OM^2$

$$\Rightarrow \qquad r^2 = (8)^2 + x^2 \qquad \text{...(i)}$$

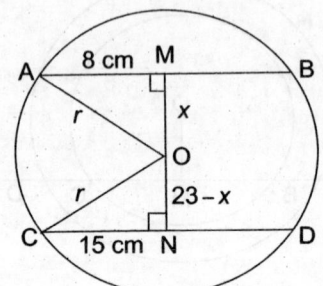

In △ OCN, $OC^2 = CN^2 + ON^2$

$$\Rightarrow \qquad r^2 = (15)^2 + (23 - x)^2 \qquad \text{...(ii)}$$

From (i) & (ii),

$$x^2 + 64 = 225 + (23 - x)^2$$

$$\Rightarrow \qquad x^2 + 64 = 225 + 529 - 46x + x^2$$

$$\Rightarrow \qquad 46x = 225 + 529 - 64$$

$$\Rightarrow \qquad 46x = 690$$

$$\Rightarrow \qquad x = 15 \text{ cm}$$

From (i), $\qquad r^2 = (8)^2 + (15)^2$

$$= 64 + 225 = 289$$

$$\Rightarrow \qquad r = 17 \text{ cm}$$

Hence, the radius of a circle is 17 cm. **Ans.**

7. Two circles of radii 10 cm and 8 cm intersect and the length of the common chord is 12 cm. Find the distance between their centres.

Sol. Let O and O′ be the centres of two circles with radii 10 cm and 8 cm, respectively.

So, $\qquad OP = 10 \text{ cm}, O'P = 8 \text{ cm}$

and $\qquad PQ = 12 \text{ cm}$

Then $\qquad PL = \frac{1}{2} PQ = \frac{1}{2} \times 12 = 6 \text{ cm}$

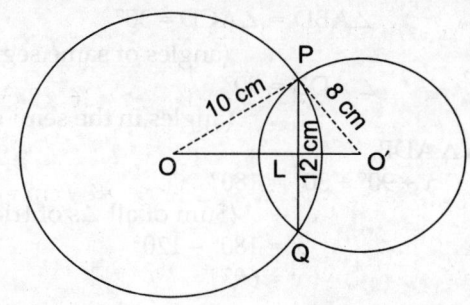

In ΔOLP, $\quad OP^2 = OL^2 + LP^2$

$\Rightarrow \qquad OL^2 = OP^2 - LP^2$

$\Rightarrow \qquad OL = \sqrt{(10)^2 - 6^2} = \sqrt{64} = 8$ cm

In $\Delta O'LP$,

$$O'L = \sqrt{O'P^2 - LP^2} = \sqrt{8^2 - 6^2}$$

$$= \sqrt{64 - 36}$$

$\Rightarrow \qquad O'L = \sqrt{28}$ cm

$$= 5.29 \text{ cm}$$

Distance between centres

$$OO' = OL + LO'$$

$$= (8 + 5.29) \text{ cm}$$

$$= 13.29 \text{ cm.} \qquad \textbf{Ans.}$$

8. AB and CD are two chords of a circle such that AB = 6 cm, CD = 12 cm and AB ∥ CD. If the distance between AB and CD is 3 cm, find the radius of the circle.

Sol. Let AB and CD be two parallel chords of a circle with centre O such that AB = 6 cm and CD = 12 cm. Let the radius of the circle be r cm. Draw OP ⊥ AB and OQ ⊥ CD. Since, AB ∥ CD and OP ⊥ AB, OQ ⊥ CD. Therefore, points O, Q and P are collinear. Clearly, PQ = 3 cm.

Let OQ = x cm. Then, OP = $(x + 3)$ cm.

In right triangles OAP and OCQ, we have

$$OA^2 = OP^2 + AP^2 \text{ and } OC^2 = OQ^2 + CQ^2$$

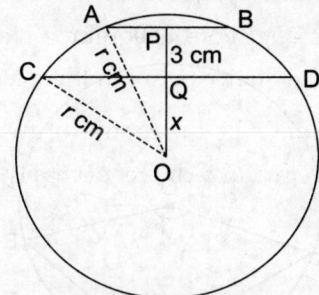

$\Rightarrow \qquad r^2 = (x + 3)^2 + 3^2$ and $r^2 = x^2 + 6^2$

$$\left[\because AP = \frac{1}{2} AB = 3 \text{ cm and } CQ = \frac{1}{2} CD = 6 \text{ cm} \right]$$

$\Rightarrow \qquad (x + 3)^2 + 3^2 = x^2 + 6^2$

(on equating the value of r^2)

$\Rightarrow \quad x^2 + 6x + 9 + 9 = x^2 + 36$

$\Rightarrow \qquad 6x = 18 \Rightarrow x = 3$ cm

Putting the value of x in $r^2 = x^2 + 6^2$, we get

$$r^2 = 3^2 + 6^2 = 45$$

$\Rightarrow \qquad r = \sqrt{45}$ cm $= 6.7$ cm

Hence, the radius of the circle is 6·7 cm. **Ans.**

9. In figure, O is the centre of the circle with radius 5 cm. OP ⊥ AB, OQ ⊥ CD, AB ∥ CD, AB = 6 cm and CD = 8 cm. Determine PQ.

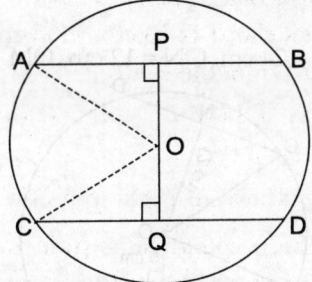

Sol. Join OA and OC.

Since, the perpendicular from the centre of the circle to a chord bisects the chord. Therefore, P and Q are midpoints of AB and CD respectively. Consequently,

$$AP = PB = \frac{1}{2} AB = 3 \text{ cm}$$

and $\qquad CQ = QD = \frac{1}{2} CD = 4$ cm

In right triangles OAP and OCQ, we have

$$OA^2 = OP^2 + AP^2$$

and $\qquad OC^2 = OQ^2 + CQ^2$

$\Rightarrow \qquad 5^2 = OP^2 + 3^2$

and $\qquad 5^2 = OQ^2 + 4^2$

$\Rightarrow \qquad OP^2 = 5^2 - 3^2$

and $\qquad OQ^2 = 5^2 - 4^2$

$\Rightarrow \qquad OP^2 = 16$

and $\qquad OQ^2 = 9$

$\Rightarrow \qquad OP = 4$

and $\qquad OQ = 3$

$\therefore \qquad PQ = OP + OQ$

$$= (4 + 3) \text{ cm} = 7 \text{ cm.} \qquad \textbf{Ans.}$$

10. In the figure given, O is the centre of the circle. AB and CD are two chords of the circle. OM is perpendicular to AB and ON is perpendicular to CD.

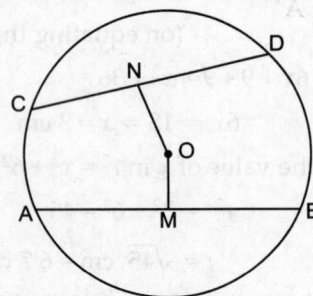

AB = 24 cm, OM = 5 cm, ON = 12 cm. Find the

(i) radius of the circle.

(ii) length of chord CD.

Sol. Given,

AB = 24 cm, ON = 12 cm, OM = 5 cm.

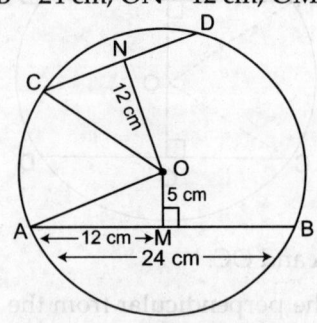

(i) In $\triangle$ AOM, $OA^2 = OM^2 + AM^2$

$$= (5)^2 + (12)^2$$
$$= 25 + 144 = 169$$

∴ OA = 13 cm

Thus, radius of the circle is 13 cm.

(ii) In $\triangle$ CON, $OC^2 = ON^2 + CN^2$

$$(13)^2 = (12)^2 + CN^2$$

[∵ OC = OA = 13 (Radius)]

⇒ $169 - 144 = CN^2$

⇒ $CN^2 = 25$

⇒ $CN = 5$

Thus, length of chord CD = 2 CN

$$= 2 \times 5$$
$$= 10 \text{ cm.}$$ **Ans.**

11. In the given circle with diameter AB, find the value of x.

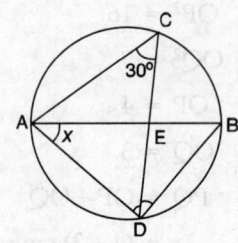

Sol.

$$\angle ABD = \angle ACD = 30°$$
(angles of same segment)

$$\angle ADB = 90°$$
(angles in the semi-circle)

In $\triangle$ ADB,

$$x + 90° + 30° = 180°$$
(Sum of all ∠s of triangle)

⇒ $x = 180° - 120°$

∴ $x = 60°$ **Ans.**

12. In the adjoining figure, AB is the diameter of the circle with centre O. If $\angle BCD = 120°$, calculate :

(i) $\angle BAD$ (ii) $\angle DBA$

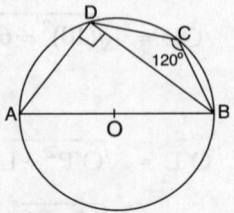

Sol. (i) Since AOB is a diameter

∴ $\angle ADB = 90°$ (C is a semicircle)

Also, ABCD is a cyclic quadrilateral.

∴ $\angle BCD + \angle BAD = 180°$

⇒ $\angle BAD = 180° - 120°$

⇒ $\angle BAD = 60°$

(ii) Now, in $\triangle$ BAD,

$$\angle BAD + \angle BDA + \angle DBA = 180°$$

⇒ $60° + 90° + \angle DBA = 180°$

⇒ $\angle DBA = 180° - 150°$

⇒ $\angle DBA = 30°$ **Ans.**

13. C is a point on the minor arc AB of the circle, with centre O. Given $\angle ACB = x°$ and $\angle AOB = y°$ express y in terms of x. Calculate x, if ACBO is a parallelogram.

Sol. Clearly, major arc AB subtends $x°$ at a point on the remaining part of the circle.

∴ reflex $\angle AOB = 2x°$

⇒ $360° - y° = 2x°$

⇒ $y° = 360° - 2x°$

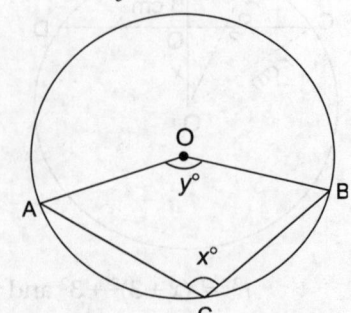

Thus, $y = 360° - 2x°$

If ACBO is a parallelogram, then

$$x° = y°$$

$$\Rightarrow \qquad x = 360° - 2x$$

$$\Rightarrow \qquad 3x = 360°$$

$$\Rightarrow \qquad x = 120°. \qquad \textbf{Ans.}$$

14. AB is a diameter of a circle with centre O and radius OD is perpendicular to AB. If C is any point on arc DB, find ∠ BAD and ∠ ACD.

Sol. Since, chord BD makes ∠ BOD at the centre and ∠ BAD at A.

$$\therefore \quad \angle BAD = \frac{1}{2} \angle BOD = \frac{1}{2} \times (90°) = 45°$$

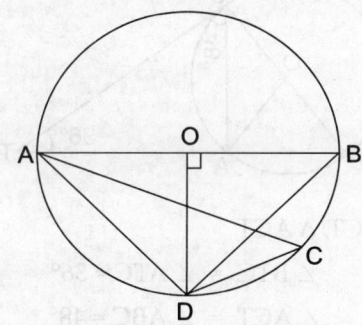

Similarly, chord AD makes ∠ AOD at the centre and ∠ ACD at C.

$$\therefore \qquad \angle ACD = \frac{1}{2} \angle AOD$$

$$= \frac{1}{2} \times (90°) = 45°$$

Thus, ∠ BAD = ∠ ACD = 45°. **Ans.**

15. In the given below figure,

$$\angle BAD = 65°$$
$$\angle ABD = 70°$$

and $\qquad \angle BDC = 45°$. Find :

(i) ∠ BCD, **(ii)** ∠ ADB.

Hence, show that AC is a diameter.

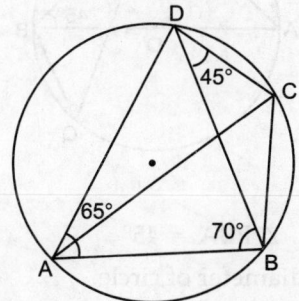

Sol. Given, $\qquad \angle BAD = 65°,$

$$\angle ABD = 70°$$

and $\qquad \angle BDC = 45°.$

(i) Quadrilateral ABCD is cyclic quadrilateral.

∴ ∠ DAB + ∠ BCD = 180°

⇒ 65° + ∠ BCD = 180°

∴ ∠ BCD = 180° − 65°

$$= 115° \qquad \textbf{Ans.}$$

(ii) In ∆ ADB,

∠ DAB + ∠ABD + ∠ ADB = 180°

⇒ 65° + 70° + ∠ ADB = 180°

⇒ ∠ ADB = 180° − 135°

⇒ ∠ ADB = 45° **Ans.**

16. If figure PT is a tangent to a circle. If m (∠BTA) = 45° and m (∠PTB) = 70°, find m ∠ (ABT).

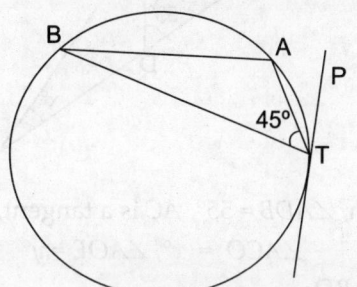

Sol. ∠ ATP = ∠ PTB − ∠ BTA

$$= 70° - 45° = 25°$$

∴ ∠ ABT = ∠ ATP

(Angles are in alternate segments)

⇒ ∠ ABT = 25°. **Ans.**

17. In the alongside figure, O is the centre of the circumcircle of triangle XYZ. Tangents at X and Y intersect at T. Given ∠XTY = 80° and ∠XOZ = 140°. Calculate the value of ∠ZXY.

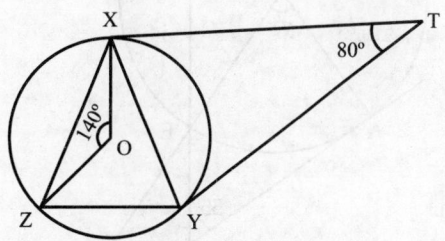

Sol. In the given circle,

∠ TXY = ∠ TYX = 50°(since XT = YT)

∠ OXZ = ∠ OZX = 20° (since OX = OZ)

[In ∆XOZ, 140° + ∠ OXZ + ∠ OZX = 180°]

⇒ ∠ OXZ = 20°

⇒ ∠ OXY = 40°, (since ∠ OXT = 90°)

∠ ZXY = ∠ OXZ + ∠ OXY

$$= 20° + 40° = 60°. \qquad \textbf{Ans.}$$

18. In the given figure AC is a tangent to the circle with centre O.

If $\angle ADB = 55°$, find x and y. Give reasons for your answer.*

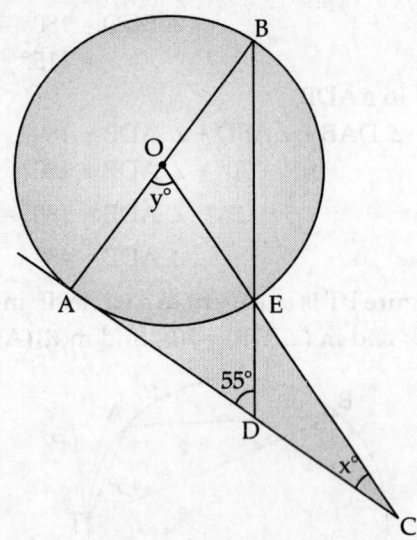

Sol. Given, $\angle ADB = 55°$, AC is a tangent,
$$\angle ACO = x°, \angle AOE = y°$$

In $\triangle ABD$,

∴ $\qquad \angle BAD = 90°$ $\qquad$ (∵ Radius OA is perpendicular to tangent AC)

∴ $\qquad \angle ABD + \angle BAD + \angle ADB = 180°$
$\qquad\qquad$ (Angle sum property)

⇒ $\qquad \angle ABD + 90° + 55° = 180°$

⇒ $\qquad \angle ABD = 180° - 145° = 35°$

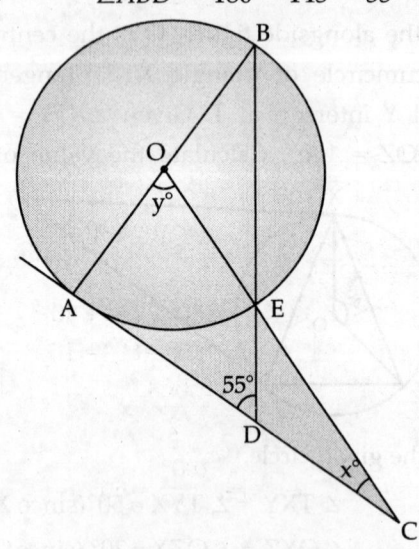

∴ $\qquad \angle AOE = 2 \times \angle ABD$
$\qquad$ (Angle at centre is twice the angle at circumference)

⇒ $\qquad y° = 2 \times 35°$

∴ $\qquad y° = 70°$

In $\triangle AOC$,
$$\angle ACO + \angle OAC + \angle AOC = 180°$$
$\qquad\qquad$ (Angle sum property)

⇒ $x° + 90° + 70° = 180°$ ($\angle OAC = 90°$, since radius is $\perp r$ to tangent)

⇒ $\qquad x° = 180° - 160°$
$\qquad\qquad = 20°$

Hence, $\qquad x = 20°$

and $\qquad y = 70°$ $\qquad\qquad$ **Ans.**

19. A, B and C are three points on a circle. The tangent at C meets BA produced at T. Given that $\angle ATC = 36°$ and $\angle ACT = 48°$, calculate the angle subtended by AB at the centre of the circle.

Sol. Join BC. Let O be the centre of the circle. Join OA and OB.

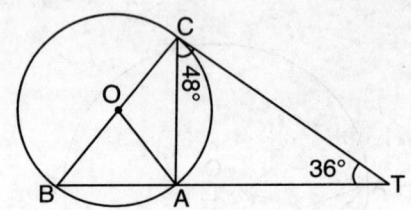

In $\triangle$ BCT, $\triangle$ ACT,
$$\angle BTC = \angle ATC = 36°$$
$$\angle ACT = \angle ABC = 48°$$
$$\angle BAC = \angle ACT + \angle ATC$$
$$= 48° + 36° = 84°$$

∴ $\qquad \angle BCA = 180° - (\angle ABC + \angle BAC)$
$$= 180° - (48° + 84°)$$
$$= 48°$$

∴ $\qquad \angle BOA = 2 \angle BCA$
$$= 2 \times 48° = 96°$$ $\qquad$ **Ans.**

20. In the given figure, O is the centre of the circle and $\angle PBA = 45°$. Calculate the value of $\angle PQB$.

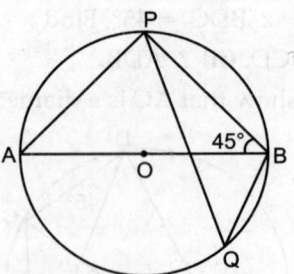

Sol. Given
$$\angle PBA = 45°$$

AOB is diameter of circle.

∴ $\qquad \angle APB = 90°$ $\quad$ (Angle in semi-circle)

So in $\triangle$ APB, $\angle PAB = 180° - (90° + 45°)$
$$= 45°$$

∠ PAB = ∠ PQB

(Angle in same segments)

∴   ∠ PQB = 45°.   **Ans.**

21. In the figure given below 'O' is the centre of the circle. If QR = OP and ∠ ORP = 20°. Find the value of '*x*' giving reasons.*

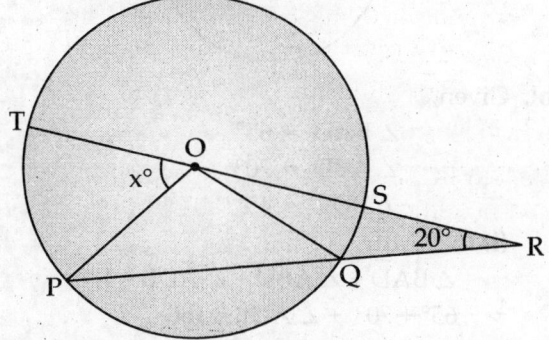

Sol. Given, QR = OP, ∠ ORP = 20°

But,   OP = OQ   (radius of circle)

⇒   OP = OQ = QR

∴   ∠ QOS = ∠ ORQ   (∵ QR = OQ)

          = 20°.

∴   ∠ OQP = ∠ QOR + ∠ ORQ

          (Exterior angle is equal to

          sum of interior opposite angles)

          = 20° + 20° = 40°

∴   ∠ OPQ = ∠ OQP   (∵ OP = OQ)

          = 40°

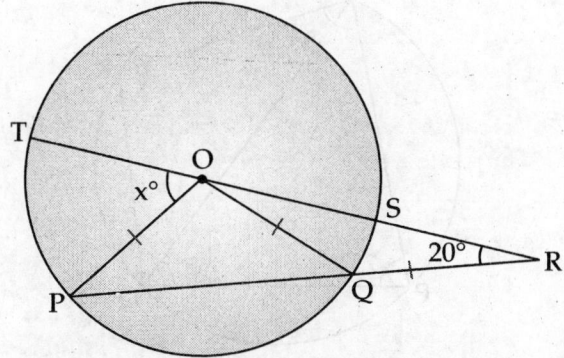

∴   ∠ POQ + ∠ OPQ + ∠ OQP = 180°

          (sum of angles in a triangle is180°)

⇒   ∠ POQ + 40° + 40° = 180°

⇒   ∠ POQ = 180° – 80° = 100°

∴ ∠ POT +∠ POQ + ∠ QOR = 180°

          (sum of angles on a straight line is 180°)

⇒   *x*° + 100° + 20° = 180°

⇒   *x*° = 180° – 120° = 60°.   **Ans.**

* Frequently asked previous years Board Exam Questions.

22. If O is the centre of the circle, find the value of *x* in each of the following figures :

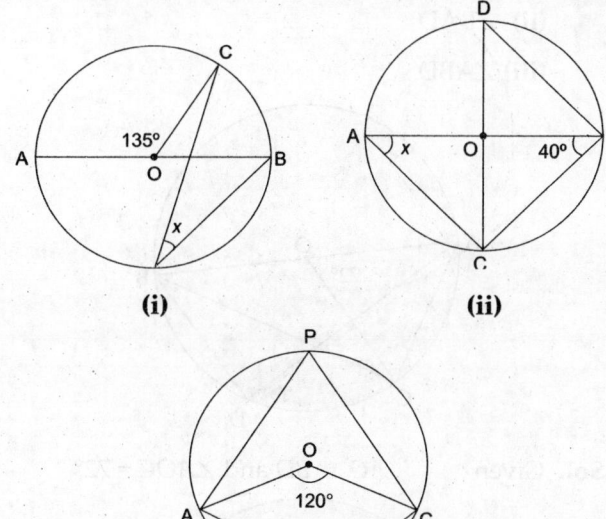

(i)   (ii)

(iii)

Sol. (i) We have ∠ AOC = 135°

then   ∠ COB = 180° – 135° = 45°

But $x = \dfrac{\angle COB}{2} = \left(\dfrac{45°}{2}\right)$

          $= 22\dfrac{1}{2}°$ **Ans.**

(ii) In ΔBOC,

          OB = OC   (radii)

So,   ∠ OCB = ∠ OBC = 40°

In Δ BOC,

          ∠ BOC = 180° – (40 + 40)°

          = 180° – 80° = 100°

So $x = \dfrac{\angle BOC}{2}$

          $= \dfrac{100°}{2} = 50°$ **Ans.**

(iii) $\angle APC = \dfrac{1}{2} \angle AOC$

          $= \dfrac{1}{2} \times 120° = 60°$

Since, ABCP is a cyclic quadrilateral.

So,   *x* = ∠ APC = 60°   **Ans.**

23. In the figure given below, O is the centre of the circle and AB is a diameter.*

If AC = BD and ∠AOC = 72°. Find :

(i) ∠ABC

(ii) ∠BAD

(iii) ∠ABD

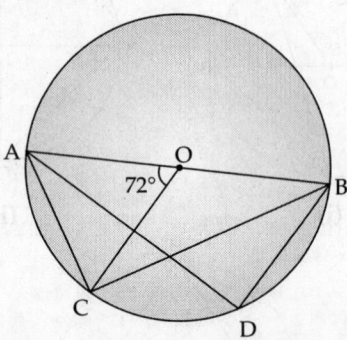

Sol. Given :   AC = BD and ∠AOC = 72°

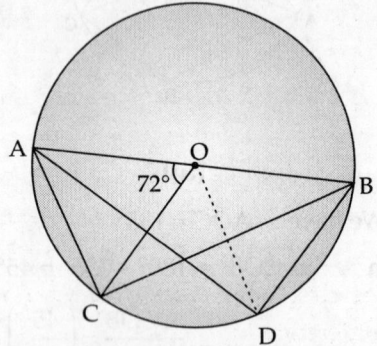

(i) ∵ Angle subtended by an arc at the centre is twice the angle subtended by the same arc at any point on the remaining part of the circle.

$$\therefore \qquad \angle AOC = 2\angle ABC$$

$$\Rightarrow \qquad \angle ABC = \frac{1}{2}\ \angle AOC$$

$$= \frac{1}{2} \times 72° = 36° \qquad \textbf{Ans.}$$

(ii) Since BD = AC and equal chords subtend equal angles at the centre.

So,   ∠BOD = ∠AOC = 72°

and, $\angle BAD = \dfrac{1}{2}\ \angle BOD$

$$= \frac{1}{2} \times 72° = 36° \qquad \textbf{Ans.}$$

(iii) In ΔABD,

$$\angle BAD + \angle ABD + \angle ADB = 180°$$

$$\Rightarrow \quad 36° + \angle ABD + 90° = 180°$$

[∵ ∠ADB is in semicircle and angles of a triangle adds upto 180°]

$$\Rightarrow \qquad \angle ABD = 180° - 126°$$

$$= 54° \qquad \textbf{Ans.}$$

24. In the given figure, ∠ BAD = 65°

∠ ABD = 70°, ∠ BDC = 45°

(i) Prove that AC is a diameter of the circle.

(ii) Find ∠ ACB.

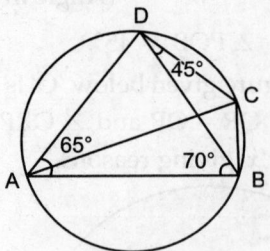

Sol. Given,

$$\angle BAD = 65°$$
$$\angle ABD = 70°$$
$$\angle BDC = 45°$$

(i) In Δ ABD,

$$\angle BAD + \angle ABD + \angle ADB = 180°$$

$$\Rightarrow \quad 65° + 70° + \angle ADB = 180°$$

{Sum of three angles of a Δ}

$$\therefore \qquad \angle ADB = 180° - (65° + 70°)$$

$$= 45°$$

$$\Rightarrow \qquad \angle ADC = \angle ADB + \angle BDC$$

$$= 45° + 45° = 90°$$

$$\Rightarrow \quad \text{AC is the diameter of the circle.}$$

[Angle in a semi circle is 90°]   **Hence Proved**

(ii)   ∠ ACB = ∠ ADB = 45°

{Angles in the same segment of a circle}

Ans.

25. PQRS is a cyclic quadrilateral. Given, ∠QPS = 73°, ∠PQS = 55° and ∠PSR = 82°, calculate :*

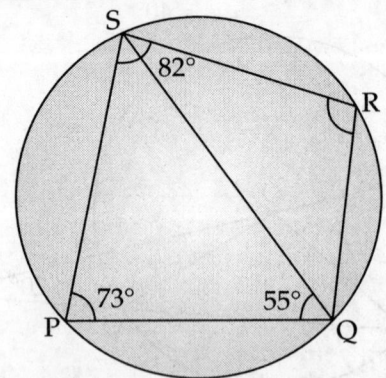

(i) ∠QRS

(ii) ∠RQS

(iii) ∠PRQ

Sol. Given, ∠QPS = 73°, ∠PQS = 55°, ∠PSR = 82°

(i)   ∠QRS + ∠QPS = 180°

(sum of opposite angles of a cyclic quadrilateral are supplementary)

$$\Rightarrow \qquad \angle QRS + 73° = 180°$$

$$\Rightarrow \qquad \angle QRS = 180° - 73° = 107°. \qquad \textbf{Ans.}$$

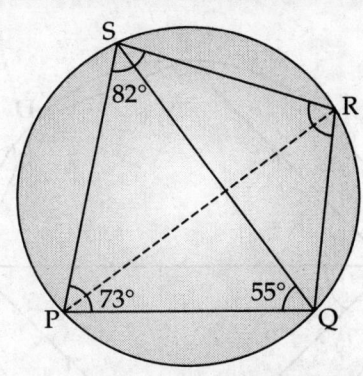

(ii)   ∠PQR + ∠PSR = 180°

         (sum of opposite angles of a cyclic
         quadrilateral are supplementary)

⇒   ∠PQR + 82° = 180°

⇒   ∠PQR = 180° – 82°

⇒   ∠PQR = 98°

⇒   ∠RQS + ∠PQS = 98°

⇒   ∠RQS + 55° = 98°

⇒   ∠RQS = 98° – 55° = 43°.   **Ans.**

(iii) ∠PSQ + ∠QPS + ∠PQS = 180°

         (sum of angles of a triangle is 180°)

⇒   ∠PSQ + 73° + 55° = 180°

⇒   ∠PSQ = 180° – 128° = 52°

∴   ∠PRQ = ∠PSQ

         (angles on same segment are equal)

⇒   ∠PRQ = 52°.   **Ans.**

26. In the given figure, AB is the diameter of a circle with centre O, ∠ BCD = 130°. Find :

(i)   ∠ DAB

(ii)   ∠ DBA

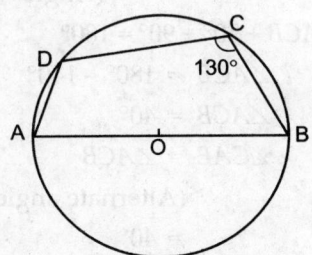

Sol. (i)   ∠ DAB + ∠ BCD = 180°

         [opp. angles of a cyclic quadrilateral]

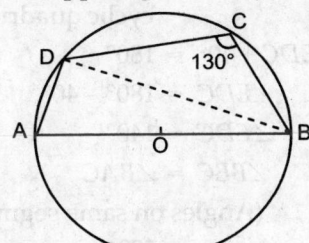

∴   ∠ DAB + 130° = 180°

⇒   ∠ DAB = 180° – 130°

⇒   ∠ DAB = 50°   **Ans.**

(ii)   ∠ ADB = 90° (angle in semi-circle)

     In △ ADB,

         ∠ DAB + ∠ ADB + ∠ DBA = 180°

                (angle sum property)

⇒   50° + 90° + ∠ DBA = 180°

⇒   ∠ DBA = 180° – 140°

⇒   ∠ DBA = 40°   **Ans.**

27. In figure, ABCD is a cyclic quadrilateral; O is the centre of the circle. If ∠ BOD = 160°, find the measure of ∠ BPD.

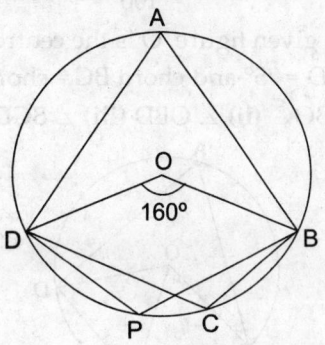

Sol. Consider the arc BCD of the circle. This arc makes angle ∠BOD = 160° at the centre of the circle and ∠ BAD at a point A on the circumference.

∴   ∠ BAD = $\frac{1}{2}$ ∠ BOD = 80°

Now, ABPD is a cyclic quadrilateral

∴   ∠ BAD + ∠ BPD = 180°

⇒   80° + ∠ BPD = 180°

⇒   ∠ BPD = 100°

⇒   ∠ BCD = 100°

       [∵ ∠ BPD and ∠ BCD are angles in

                the same segment

∴   ∠ BCD = ∠ BPD = 100°]   **Ans.**

28. In the given figure below, AB is parallel to DC, ∠ BCE = 80° and ∠ BAC = 25°. Find

(i) ∠ CAD, **(ii)** ∠ CBD, **(iii)** ∠ ADC

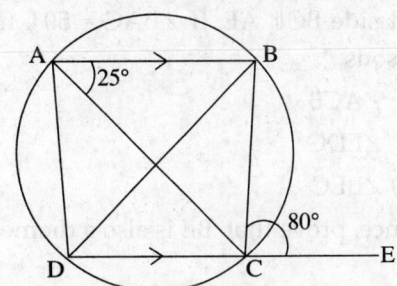

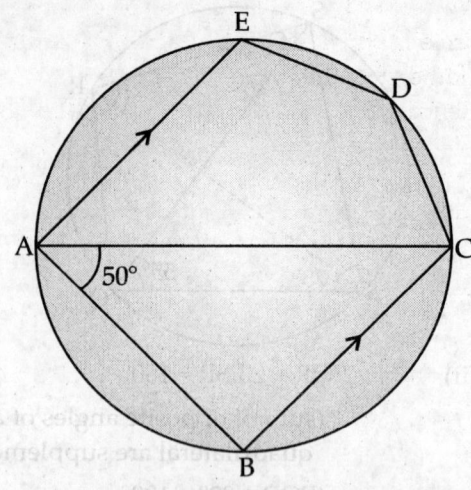

Sol. **(i)** ∵ Exterior angles of cyclic quadrilateral is equal to the sum of opposite interior angles.

∴ ∠ CAD = ∠ BCE – ∠ CAB

= 80° – 25°

= 55° **Ans.**

(ii) ∠ CBD = ∠ CAD

[Angles in the same segment]

= 55° **Ans.**

(iii) ∠ ADC = 180° – ∠ DAB

= 180° – 80°

= 100° **Ans.**

29. In the given figure, O is the centre of the circle, ∠ BAD = 75° and chord BC = chord CD. Find :

(i) ∠ BOC **(ii)** ∠ OBD **(iii)** ∠ BCD.

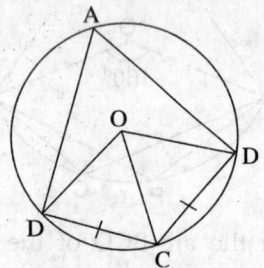

Sol. (i) ∠ BOD = 2 · ∠ BAD

= 2 × 75° = 150°

∠ BOC = ∠ COD

∵ BC = CD

∴ ∠ BOD = 2 ∠ BOC

∴ ∠ BOC = $\frac{1}{2}$ ∠ BOD = 75° **Ans.**

(ii) ∠ OBD = $\frac{1}{2}$ (180° – ∠ BOD)

= $\frac{1}{2}$ (180° – 150°) = 15° **Ans.**

(iii) ∠ BCD = 180° – ∠ BAD

(opp. ∠s of a cyclic quadrilateral is supplementary)

= 180° – 75°

= 105° **Ans.**

30. In the given figure, ABCDE is a pentagon inscribed in a circle such that AC is a diameter and side BC∥ AE. If ∠BAC = 50°, find giving reasons :*

(i) ∠ACB

(ii) ∠EDC

(iii) ∠BEC

Hence, prove that BE is also a diameter.

Sol. Given, *AC* is diameter, *BC* ∥ *AE*, and ∠BAC = 50°

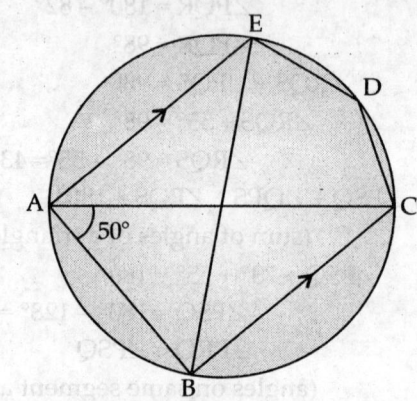

(i) ∠ABC = 90°

(∵ Angle at circumference of a semicircle)

In △*ABC*,

∴ ∠ACB + ∠BAC + ∠ABC = 180°

(Angles sum property)

⇒ ∠ACB + 50° + 90° = 180°

⇒ ∠ACB = 180° – 140°

∠ACB = 40° **Ans.**

(ii) ∠CAE = ∠ACB

(Alternate angles as BC ∥ AE)

= 40°

∴ ∠EDC + ∠CAE = 180°

(Sum of opposite angles of a cyclic quadrilateral is 180°)

⇒ ∠EDC + 40° = 180°

⇒ ∠EDC = 180° – 40°

∠EDC = 140° **Ans.**

(iii) ∠BEC = ∠BAC

(Angles on same segment are equal)

= 50° **Ans.**

Now, ∠BAE = ∠BAC + ∠CAE

= 50° + 40°

= 90°

We know that, if an angle of a triangle in a circle is 90°. Then, the hypotenuse must be the diameter of the circle.

Hence, BE is a diameter   (∵ ∠BAE = 90°)
                                            Hence Proved.

31. In figure, ΔPQR is an isosceles triangle with PQ = PR and ∠PQR = 35°. Find ∠QSR and ∠QTR.

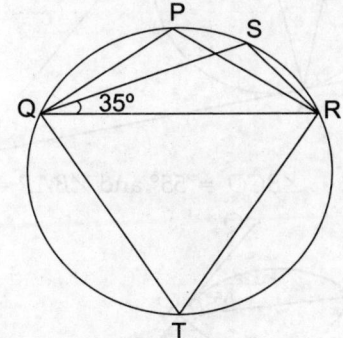

Sol. In ΔPQR, we have

$$PQ = PR$$
⇒   ∠PQR = ∠PRQ
⇒   ∠PRQ = 35°
∴   ∠QPR = 180° − (∠PQR + ∠PRQ)
        = 180° − (35° + 35°) = 110°.

Since, PQTR is a cyclic quadrilateral.

∴   ∠P + ∠T = 180°
⇒   ∠T = 180° − 110° = 70°   **Ans.**

In cyclic quadrilateral QSRT, we have

∠S + ∠T = 180°
⇒   ∠S = 180° − 70° = 110°.   **Ans.**

32. In fig., chord ED is parallel to the diameter AC of the circle. Given ∠CBE = 65°, calculate ∠DEC.

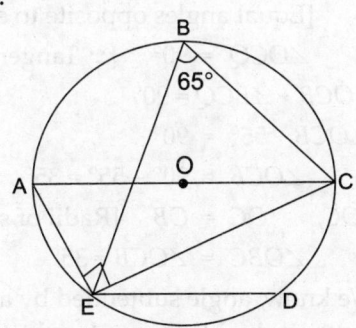

Sol. Consider the arc CDE. We find that ∠CBE and ∠CAE are the angles in the same segment of arc CDE.

∴   ∠CAE = ∠CBE
⇒   ∠CAE = 65°
        [∵ ∠CBE = 65°]

Since, AC is the diameter of the circle and the angle in a semi-circle is a right angle. Therefore, ∠AEC = 90°.

Now, in Δ ACE, we have

∠ACE + ∠AEC + ∠CAE = 180°
⇒   ∠ACE + 90° + 65° = 180°
⇒   ∠ACE = 25°

But ∠DEC and ∠ACE are alternate angles because AC ∥ DE.

∴   ∠DEC = ∠ACE = 25°. **Ans.**

33. In the figure, ∠DBC = 58°, BD is diameter of the circle. Calculate :
    (i) ∠ BDC,   **(ii)** ∠ BEC,   **(iii)** ∠ BAC.

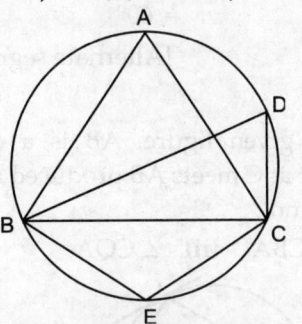

Sol. (i)   ∠ DBC = 58°   (given)
Now, BD is the diameter
        ∠ BCD = 90° (angle in a semicircle)
In Δ BDC,
    ∠ BDC + 90° + 58° = 180°
            (Sum of the angles of a triangle)
∴   ∠ BDC = 180° − (90° + 58°) = 32°

(ii) BECD is a cyclic quadrilateral
∵   ∠ BEC + ∠BDC = 180°
        (Opp. angles of a cyclic quadrilateral)
∴   ∠ BEC = 180° − ∠ BDC
            = 180° − 32° = 148°   **Ans.**

(iii)   ∠ BAC = ∠ BDC = 32°

        (angles in the same segment of a circle)
                                            Ans.

34. In the given circle with centre O, ∠ABC = 100°, ∠ACD = 40° and CT is a tangent to the circle at C. Find ∠ADC and ∠DCT.

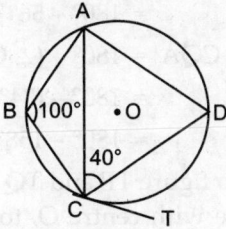

Sol. Given

    ∠ ABC = 100°
    ∠ ACD = 40°   (given)

∠ ABC + ∠ ADC = 180°

{opposite angles of a cyclic quadrilateral}

⇒ 100° + ∠ ADC = 180°

∴ ∠ ADC = 180° – 100° = 80°

Also

∠ ACD + ∠ ADC + ∠ CAD = 180°

{sum of angles of a Δ}

⇒ 40° + 80° + ∠ CAD = 180°

⇒ ∠ CAD = 180° – 120° = 60°

Now, ∠ DCT = ∠ CAD

= 60°

{Alternate segment theorem}

Ans.

35. In the given figure, AB is a diameter. The tangent at C meets AB produced at Q. If ∠ CAB = 34°, find :

(i) ∠ CBA, **(ii)** ∠ CQA.

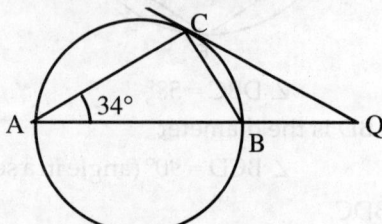

Sol. (i) AB is diameter.

∴ ∠ ACB = 90°

Angle in semi-circle is right angle.

∴ In Δ ACB,

∠ A + ∠ C + ∠ B = 180°

⇒ 34° + 90° + ∠ B = 180°

⇒ ∠ B = 180° – (90° + 34°)

⇒ ∠ B = 180° – 124°

∴ ∠ CBA = 56° **Ans.**

(ii) Now, CQ is tangent

∴ ∠ QCB = ∠ CAB

(Alternate segment angle)

= 34°

and ∠ CBQ = 180° – ∠ CBA

= 180° – 56° = 124°

∴ ∠ CQA = 180° – (∠ QCB + ∠ CBQ)

= 180° – (34° + 124°)

= 180° – 158° = 22° **Ans.**

36. In the given figure TP and TQ are two tangents to the circle with centre O, touching at A and C respectively. If ∠BCQ = 55° and ∠BAP = 60°, find :*

(i) ∠OBA and ∠OBC

---

* Frequently asked previous years Board Exam Questions.

(ii) ∠AOC **(iii)** ∠ATC

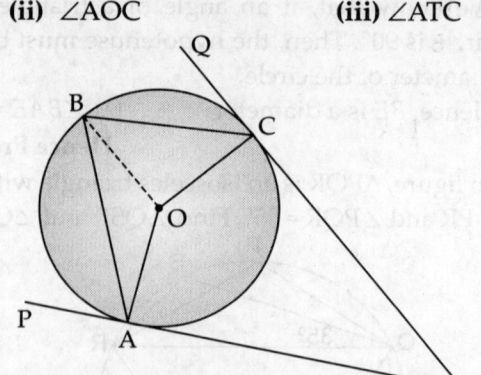

Sol. Given : ∠BCQ = 55° and ∠BAP = 60°

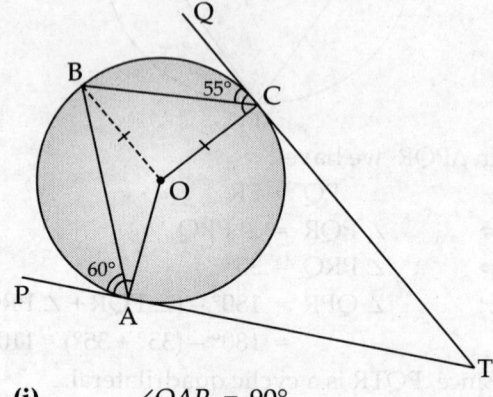

(i) ∠OAP = 90°

[∵ Tangent is ⊥ to radius]

⇒ ∠OAB + ∠PAB = 90°

⇒ ∠OAB + 60° = 90°

⇒ ∠OAB = 90° – 60° = 30°

Now, in ΔAOB

OA = OB [Radii of same circle]

∴ ∠OBA = ∠OAB = 30°

[Equal angles opposite to equal sides]

Now, ∠OCQ = 90° [∵ Tangent ⊥ radius]

⇒ ∠OCB + ∠BCQ = 90°

⇒ ∠OCB + 55° = 90°

⇒ ∠OCB = 90° – 55° = 35°

In ΔBOC, OC = OB [Radii of same circle]

⇒ ∠OBC = ∠OCB = 35° **Ans.**

(ii) We know, angle subtended by an arc at the centre is double the angle subtended on the remaining part of the circle.

∴ ∠AOC = 2∠ABC

= 2(∠OBA + ∠OBC)

= 2(30° + 35°)

= 2 × 65° = 130° **Ans.**

(iii) In quad. AOCT,

∠ATC + ∠OAT + ∠AOC + ∠OCT = 360°

⇒ ∠ATC + 90° + 130° + 90° = 360°

[∵ ∠OAT = ∠OCT = 90°]

⇒ ∠ATC = 360° – 310° = 50° **Ans.**

37. In the adjoining figure shown XAY is a tangent. If ∠BDA = 44°, ∠BXA = 36°, calculate :

(i) ∠BAX   (iii) ∠DAB

(ii) ∠DAY   (iv) ∠BCD.

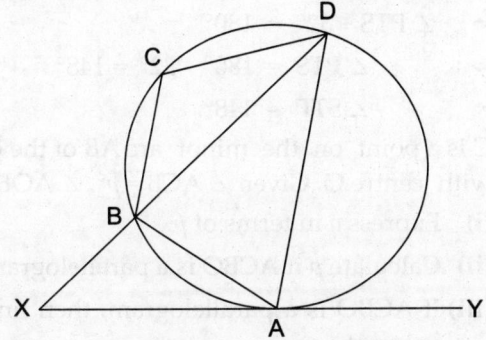

Sol. (i)   ∠BAX = ∠BDA = 44°

       [Angles in the alternate segment] **Ans.**

(ii)   ∠ABD = ∠BXA + ∠BAX

          = 36° + 44° = 80°

    [Ext. angles of a Δ = sum of int. opp. angles]

∴   ∠DAY = ∠ABD = 80°

       [Angles in alternate segment] **Ans.**

(iii)   ∠DAB = 180° – [∠BAX + DAY]

          = 180° – (44° + 80°)

          = 56°   **Ans.**

(iv)   ∠BCD = 180° – ∠DAB

          = 180° – 56° = 124°   **Ans.**

[Opp. angles of a cyclic quad. are supplementary]

38. In the given figure, if ∠ACE = 43° and ∠CAF = 62°, find the values of *a*, *b* and *c*.

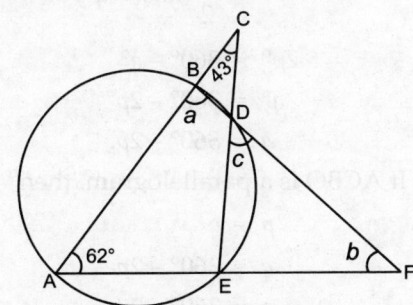

Sol. ABDE is a cyclic quadrilateral.

∴   ∠ABD + ∠AED = 180°

and   ∠EAB + ∠BDE = 180°

Now, in Δ ACE,

      ∠A + ∠C + ∠E = 180°

⇒   62° + 43° + ∠E = 180°

⇒   ∠E = 180° – 105° = 75°

So,   ∠ABD + ∠AED = 180°

∴   *a* + 75° = 180°

∴   *a* = 105°

       ∠ EDF = ∠ BAE

    (exterior angle of cyclic quadrilateral)

          62° = *c*

∴   *c* = 62°

In Δ ABF,

      ∠ ABF + ∠ BAF + ∠ BFA = 180°

⇒   105° + 62° + *b* = 180°

⇒   167° + *b* = 180°

⇒   *b* = 180° – 167°

⇒   *b* = 13°

∴   *a* = 105°, *b* = 13°

and   *c* = 62°   **Ans.**

39. In the following figure, O is the centre of the circle, ∠ PBA = 42°. Calculate :

(i) ∠ APB   (ii) ∠ PQB   (iii) ∠ AQB.

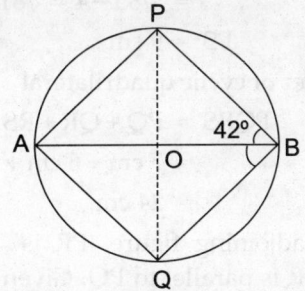

Sol. (i) In circle,

AB is the diameter.

So,   ∠ APB = 90°   (Angle in semi-circle)

(ii) Now, in ΔAPB,

      ∠ PAB = 180° – (∠ APB + ∠ ABP)

            = 180° – (90° + 42°)

            = 180° – 132° = 48°

    ∠ PQB = ∠ PAB = 48°

       (Angles of the same segment)

Hence,

      ∠ PQB = 48°.   **Ans.**

(iii) AQBP is a cyclic quadrilateral.

Therefore

∠ APB + ∠ AQB = 180°

⇒   90° + ∠ AQB = 180°

⇒   ∠ AQB = 180° – 90° = 90°.   **Ans.**

40. In the figure alongside PR is a diameter of the circle, PQ = 7 cm, QR = 6 cm and RS = 2 cm. Calculate the perimeter of the cyclic quadrilateral PQRS.

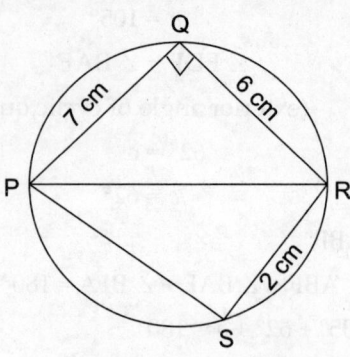

Sol. PR is the diameter of the circle

then ∠ PQR = 90° (Angle in semi-circle)

In Δ PQR, PR = $\sqrt{(7)^2 + (6)^2}$

= $\sqrt{49 + 36}$ = $\sqrt{85}$

Similarly, ∠ PSR = 90°

In ΔPSR, PS = $\sqrt{PR^2 - SR^2}$

= $\sqrt{85 - 4}$ = $\sqrt{81}$

⇒ PS = 9 cm

Perimeter of cyclic quadrilateral

PQRS = PQ + QR + RS + PS

= 7 cm + 6 cm + 2 cm + 9 cm

= 24 cm. **Ans.**

41. In the adjoining figure, PR is the diameter, chord SR is parallel to PQ. Given ∠PQR = 58°. Calculate :

(i) ∠ RPQ,

(ii) ∠ STP (T is a point on the minor arc).

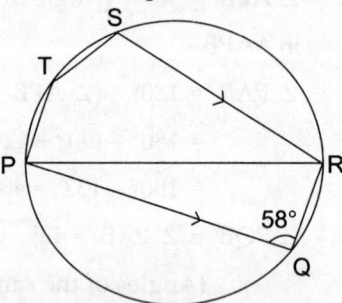

Sol. (i) ∠ PRQ = 90° (∠ in a semi-circle)

In Δ PQR,

∠ RPQ + ∠ PQR + ∠ PRQ = 180°

(∵ The sum of the three ∠s of a Δ is 180°)

⇒ ∠ RPQ + 58° + 90° = 180°

⇒ ∠ RPQ + 148° = 180°

⇒ ∠ RPQ = 180° – 148°

⇒ ∠ RPQ = 32° **Ans.**

(ii) ∵ PQ ‖ SR and RP intersects them

∠ PRS = ∠ RPQ (Alternate angles)

∴ ∠ PRS = 32°

∵ PTSR is a cyclic quadrilateral.

∴ ∠ PTS + ∠ PRS = 180°

(∵ Opposite ∠s of a cyclic quadrilateral are supplementary)

⇒ ∠ PTS + 32° = 180°

⇒ ∠ PTS = 180° – 32° = 148°

⇒ ∠ STP = 148°. **Ans.**

42. C is a point on the minor arc AB of the circle, with centre O. Given ∠ ACB = $p°$, ∠ AOB = $q°$.

(i) Express q in terms of p.

(ii) Calculate p if ACBO is a parallelogram.

(iii) If ACBO is a parallelogram, then find the value of $q + p$.

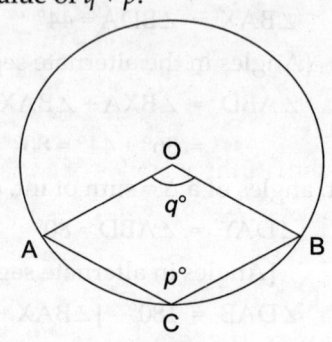

Sol. (i) Reflex

∠AOB = 360° – $q°$

∠ ACB = $\frac{1}{2}$ reflex ∠AOB

(angle at the centre property)

⇒ $p° = \frac{1}{2}(360° - q°)$

⇒ $2p° = 360° - q°$

⇒ $q° = 360° - 2p°$

⇒ $q = 360° - 2p$. **Ans.**

(ii) If ACBO is a parallelogram, then

$p = q$

∴ $q = 360° - 2p$

⇒ $p = 360° - 2p$

⇒ $p + 2p = 360°$

⇒ $3p = 360°$

⇒ $p = \frac{360°}{3} = 120°$. **Ans.**

(iii) If ACBO is a parallelogram, then

$p = q$

Also $p = 120°$ [From (ii)]

$p + q = p + p = 2p$

= 2 × 120° = 240°. **Ans.**

43. In the adjoining diagram, chords AB, BC and CD are equal. O is the centre of the circle. If ∠ABC = 120°, calculate :

    (i) ∠BAC (iii) ∠BED

    (ii) ∠BEC (iv) ∠COD.

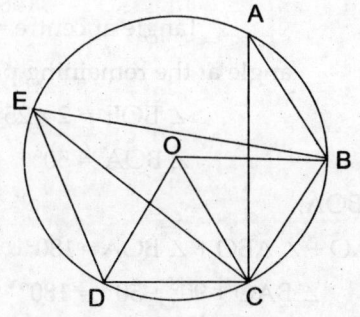

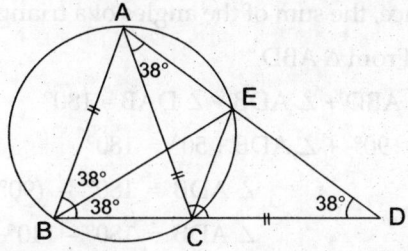

Sol. (i) In Δ ABC,

∠ ABC + ∠ BAC + ∠ BCA = 180°

(∵ The sum of three angles of a triangle is 180°)

⇒ 120° + ∠ BAC + ∠ BCA = 180°

[∵ ∠ ABC = 120° (given)]

⇒ ∠ BAC + ∠ BCA = 60°

But BA = BC

∴ ∠ BAC + ∠ BAC = 60°

⇒ 2∠ BAC = 60°

⇒ ∠ BAC = 30°. **Ans.**

(ii) ∠ BEC = ∠ BAC = 30°. **Ans.**

(iii) AB = BC = CD

∴ Arc AB = Arc BC = Arc CD

Now, ∠COB = 2 × ∠ CAB

= 2 × 30° = 60°

∴ ∠ DOC = ∠ COB = 60°

∴ ∠ DEC = $\frac{1}{2}$ × ∠DOC = $\frac{1}{2}$ × 60°

= 30°

∴ ∠ BED = ∠ BEC + ∠ DEC

= ∠ BAC + ∠ DEC

= 30° + 30° = 60°. **Ans.**

(iv) ∠ COD = 60°. **Ans.**

44. In the figure, AB = AC = CD, ∠ADC = 38°. Calculate :

    (i) ∠ ABC (ii) ∠ BEC.

Sol. Given,

AC = CD

∴ ∠ CAD = ∠ ADC = 38°

Now, in Δ ACD,

∠ ACD + ∠ CAD + ∠ ADC = 180°

⇒ ∠ ACD + 38° + 38° = 180°

⇒ ∠ ACD = 104°

Now, ∠ ACB + ∠ ACD = 180°

⇒ ∠ ACB + 104° = 180°

⇒ ∠ ACB = 76°

∵ AB = AC

∴ ∠ ABC = ∠ ACB = 76°. **Ans.**

(ii) In ΔABC,

∠ BAC + ∠ ABC + ∠ ACB = 180°

⇒ ∠ BAC + 76° + 76° = 180°

⇒ ∠ BAC = 28°

Now, ∠ BEC = ∠ BAC = 28°.

[Angles subtended by the same chord] **Ans.**

45. In the figure given alongside, AD is the diameter of the circle. If ∠BCD = 130°, calculate :

    (i) ∠ DAB (ii) ∠ ADB.

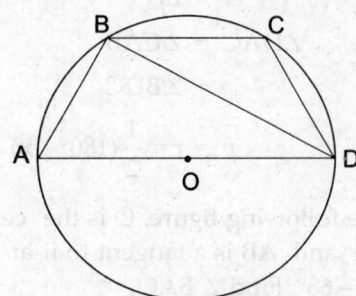

Sol. (i) Since ABCD is a cyclic quadrilateral.

∴ Its opposite angles are supplementary.

∴ ∠ DAB + ∠ BCD =180°

⇒ ∠ DAB = 180° − ∠ BCD

= 180° − 130°

= 50°. **Ans.**

(ii) Since, angle in the semi-circle is a right angle.

∴ In Δ ABD, ∠ABD = 90°

Since, the sum of the angles of a triangle is 180°.

∴ From Δ ABD,

∠ ABD + ∠ ADB + ∠ DAB = 180°

⇒ 90° + ∠ ADB + 50° = 180°

⇒ ∠ ADB = 180° – (90° – 50°)

⇒ ∠ ADB = 180° – 140°

∴ ∠ ADB = 40°   **Ans.**

46. In the figure, AC is the diameter of the circle, centre O. Chord BD is perpendicular to AC. Write down the angles *p, q, r* in term of *x*.

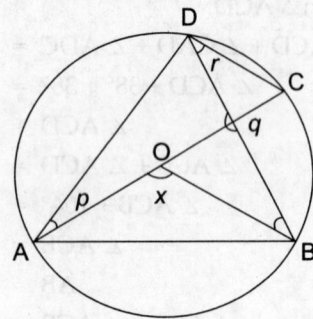

Sol. In the given circle,

⇒ $\angle ADB = \dfrac{1}{2}\angle AOB = \dfrac{x}{2}$

⇒ $\angle ADB = 90° - r$

⇒ $\angle ADB = \angle ACB = q$

Combining these, we get

$\dfrac{x}{2} = 90° - r = q$

⇒ $2r = 180° - x$

and $x = 2q$

$\angle DAC = \angle CAB$

$= \angle BDC$

⇒ $p = r = \dfrac{1}{2}(180° - x)$ **Ans.**

47. In the following figure, O is the centre of the circle and AB is a tangent to it at point B. ∠ BDC = 65°. Find ∠ BAO.

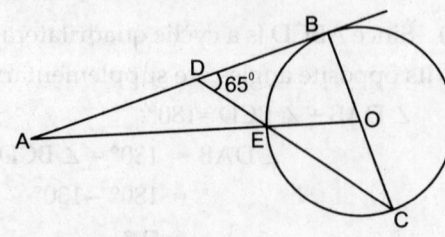

Sol. As AB is a tangent to the circle at B and OB is radius, ⇒ ∠ CBD = 90°

In Δ BCD,

∠ BCD + ∠ CBD + ∠ BDC = 180°

⇒ ∠ BCD + 90° + 65° = 180°

⇒ ∠ BCD + 155° = 180°

⇒ ∠ BCD = 180° – 155°

⇒ ∠ BCD = 25°

∴ ∠ BOE = 2 ∠ BCE

[angle at centre = double the angle at the remaining part of circle]

⇒ ∠ BOE = 2 × 25° = 50°

and ∠ BOA = 50°

In Δ BOA,

∠ BAO + ∠ ABO + ∠ BOA = 180°

⇒ ∠ BAO + 90° + 50° = 180°

⇒ ∠ BAO + 140° = 180°

⇒ ∠ BAO = 180° – 140°

⇒ ∠ BAO = 40°   **Ans.**

48. In the figure alongside O is the centre of circle ∠XOY = 40°, ∠TWX = 120° and XY is parallel to TZ.

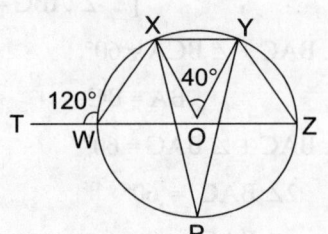

Find :

(i) ∠ XZY,   **(ii)** ∠ YXZ,   **(iii)** ∠ TZY.

Sol. (i) ∠ XOY = 2∠ XPY

(Angle subtended by an arc of a circle at the centre is twice the angle subtended by that arc at any point on the circumference of the circle)

⇒ 40° = 2∠ XPY

[∵ ∠ XOY = 40° (given)]

⇒ $\angle XPY = \dfrac{40Y}{2} = 20°$

∴ ∠ XZY = 20°   [∵ ∠ XPY = ∠ XZY]

Angles in a same segment of a circle are equal.

Ans.

(ii) ∠ XWT + ∠ XWZ = 180°

(Linear Pair Axiom)

⇒ 120° + ∠ XWZ = 180°

⇒ ∠ XWZ = 180° – 120° = 60°

So, ∠ XWZ + ∠ XYZ = 180°

(Opposite angles of a cyclic quadrilateral are supplementary)

⇒　　　　60° + ∠ XYZ = 180°

⇒　　　　∠ XYZ = 180° − 60° = 120°

In Δ XYZ,

　　∠ YXZ + ∠ XYZ + ∠ XZY = 180°

(The sum of the three angles of triangle is 180°)

⇒　　∠ YXZ + 120° + 20° = 180°

⇒　　　　∠ YXZ + 140° = 180°

⇒　　　　∠ YXZ = 180° − 140° = 40°. **Ans.**

(iii) ∵ XY ∥ TZ and transversal YZ intersects then

　　∠ XYZ + ∠ TZY = 180°

(Sum of the consecutive interior angles is 180°)

⇒　　120° + ∠ TZY = 180°

⇒　　　　∠ TZY = 180° − 120° = 60°. **Ans.**

49. In the diagram given alongside, AC is the diameter of the circle, with centre O. CD and BE are parallel. ∠ AOB = 80° and ∠ ACE = 10°. Calculate :

(i) ∠ BEC　　**(ii)** ∠ BCD　　**(iii)** ∠ CED.

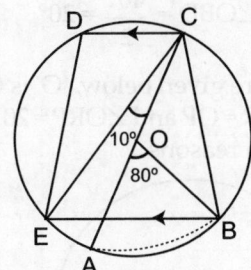

Sol. From the figure, we have

　　　　∠ AOB = 80°

　　　　∠ ACE = 10°

(i)　　　∠ BOC = 180° − ∠ AOB

　　　　　　= 180° − 80°

　　　　　　= 100°

　　　　∠ BEC = $\frac{1}{2}$ ∠ BOC

　　　　　[∵ ∠ subtended at the centre and

　　　　　∠ subtend by E by arc BC]

　　　　　　= $\frac{1}{2}$ × 100°

∴　　　　∠ BEC = 50°. **Ans.**

(ii)　　　∠ ACB = $\frac{1}{2}$ ∠AOB

[∵ angle subtended by arc AB at the centre and at C]

　　　　　　= $\frac{1}{2}$ × 80°

　　　　　　= 40°

　　　　∠ ECD = ∠ BEC

　　　　　[∵ Alternate angles as CD ∥ BE]

　　　　　　= 50°

　　　　∠ BCD = ∠ ACB + ∠ ECA + ∠ ECD

　　　　　　= 40° + 10° + 50°

　　　　　　= 100°. **Ans.**

(iii) BCDE is a cyclic quadrilateral,

　　[∵ Its opposite angles are supplementary]

⇒　　　　∠ BED = ∠ 180° − ∠ BCD

⇒　　　　∠ BED = 180° − 100°　　[From (ii)]

　　　　　　= 80°

　　∠ BEC + ∠ CED = 80°

⇒　　　　∠ CED = 80° − ∠ BEC

　　　　　　= 80° − 50°　　[From (i)]

∴　　　　∠ CED = 30°. **Ans.**

50. In the figure given below, AD is a diameter. O is the centre of the circle. AD is parallel to BC and ∠ CBD = 32°. Find :

(i)　∠ OBD

(ii)　∠ AOB

(iii)　∠ BED.

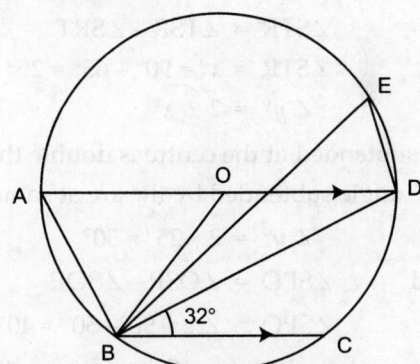

Sol. (i)　Since, AD is parallel to BC.

　　　　　∠ODB = ∠CBD

　　　　　(alternate interior angles)

Also,　　　　OB = OD　　(radii)

∴　　　　∠OBD = ∠ODB = 32°

Ans.

(ii) Now, AD is a diameter.

So,　　　　∠ABD = 90°

　　　　∠ABO = ∠ABD − ∠OBD

　　　　∠ABO = 90° − 32° = 58°

In Δ AOB,

　　∠OAB + ∠AOB + ∠OBA = 180°

$\Rightarrow$ $58° + \angle AOB + 58° = 180°$

($\because$ OA = OB and $\angle$ OAB = $\angle$OBA)

$\therefore$ $\angle AOB = 180° - 116°$

        $= 64°$ **Ans.**

(iii) $\angle BED = \angle BAD = 58°$

     (angles in same segment) **Ans.**

51. In the figure given below, O is the centre of the circle and SP is a tangent. If $\angle SRT = 65°$, find the values of x, y and z.

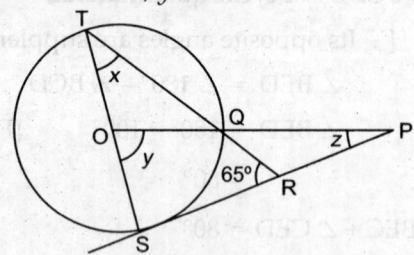

Sol. Given, $\angle SRT = 65°$ and SP is a tangent.

$\therefore$ $\angle TSR = 90°$

     (angle between the radius and tangent)

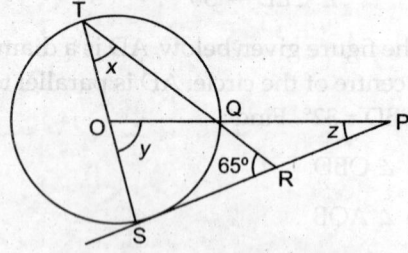

$\therefore$ $\angle SRT + \angle STR = \angle TSR = 90°$

$\Rightarrow$ $\angle STR = \angle TSR - \angle SRT$

$\therefore$ $\angle STR = x° = 90° - 65° = 25°$

       $\angle y° = 2 \angle x°$

(Angle subtended at the centre is double that of the angle subtended by the arc at same centre)

$\therefore$ $\angle y° = 2 × 25° = 50°$

and $\angle SPO = \angle OSP - \angle SOP$

$\therefore$ $\angle SPO = \angle z = 90° - 50° = 40°$

Hence, $\angle x = 25°$, $\angle y = 50°$ and $\angle z = 40°$ **Ans.**

52. In the figure given, O is the centre of the cricle. $\angle DAE = 70°$. Find, giving suitable reasons, the measure of :

(i) $\angle BCD$ **(ii)** $\angle BOD$ **(iii)** $\angle OBD$

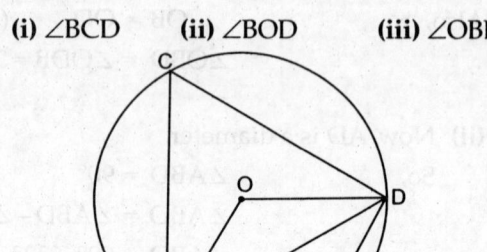

Sol. Given, $\angle DAE = 70°$

(i) $\angle BAD + \angle DAE = 180°$ (Linear pair)

$\Rightarrow$ $\angle BAD = 180° - 70° = 110°$

Now, $\angle BCD + \angle BAD = 180°$.

(Sum of opposite angles of cyclic quadrilateral is 180°)

$\Rightarrow$ $\angle BCD = 180° - 110°$

          $= 70°$ **Ans.**

(ii) $\angle BOD = 2 \angle BCD$

(Angle that an arc subtends at the centre is twice the angle at circumference of the circle)

        $= 2 × 70°$

        $= 140°$ **Ans.**

(iii) $\angle OBD = \angle ODB$ (OB = OD = radius)

$\therefore$ $\angle OBD + \angle OBD + 140° = 180°$

     (Sum of angles in a triangle is 180°).

$\Rightarrow$ $\angle OBD + \angle OBD + 140° = 180°$.

         ($\because \angle OBD = \angle ODB$)

$\Rightarrow$ $2 \angle OBD = 180° - 140°$

$\Rightarrow$ $\angle OBD = \dfrac{40°}{2} = 20°$ Ans.

53. In the figure given below, 'O' is the centre of the circle, if QR = OP and $\angle ORP = 20°$. Find the value of 'x' given reasons.

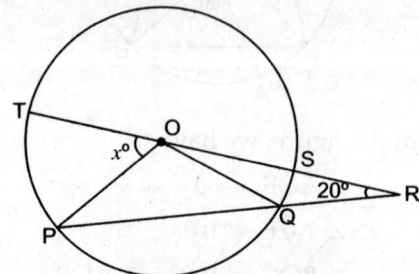

Sol. Given,   QR = OP, ORP = 20°

       OP = OQ   (radius of circle)

$\Rightarrow$ OP = OQ = QR

$\therefore$ $\angle QOS = \angle ORQ$ ($\because$ QR = OQ)

      $= 20°$.

$\therefore$ $\angle OQP = \angle QOR + \angle ORQ$

(Exterior angles is equal to sum of interior opposite angles)

      $= 20° + 20° = 40°$

$\therefore$ $\angle OPQ = \angle OQP$ ($\because$ OP = OQ)

      $= 40°$

$\therefore$ $\angle POQ + \angle OPQ + \angle OQP = 180°$

     (sum of angles in a triangle is 180°)

$\Rightarrow$ $\angle POQ + 40° + 40° = 180°$

$\Rightarrow$ $\angle POQ = 180° - 80° = 100°$

$\therefore$ $\angle POT + \angle POQ + \angle QOP = 180°$

(sum of angles on a straight line is 180°)

$\Rightarrow$ $x° + 100° + 20° = 180°$

$\Rightarrow$ $x° = 180° - 120°$

$= 60°$ **Ans.**

54. In the given figure, O is the centre of the circle and AB is a tangent at B. If AB = 15 cm and AC = 7·5 cm, calculate the radius of the circle.

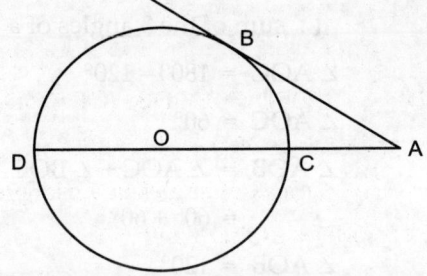

Sol. In the given circle,

$AB^2 = AC \times AD$ $(PT^2 = PA \times PB)$

$\Rightarrow$ $15^2 = 7.5 \times AD$

$\Rightarrow$ $AD = \dfrac{225}{7.5} = 30$

$\Rightarrow$ $CD = AD - AC$

$= 30 - 7.5 = 22.5$

$\therefore$ Radius $= \dfrac{1}{2} \times CD$

$\Rightarrow$ Radius $= \dfrac{1}{2} \times 22.5$

$\Rightarrow$ Radius $= 11.25$ cm. **Ans.**

55. In figure chords AB and CD of the circle intersect at O. AO = 5 cm, BO = 3 cm and CO = 2·5 cm. Determine the length of DO.

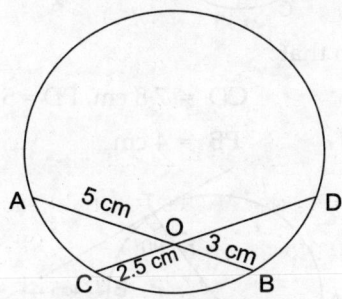

Sol. Clearly, chords AB and CD intersect at O.

$\therefore$ $OA \times OB = OC \times OD$

$\Rightarrow$ $5 \times 3 = 2.5 \times OD$

$\Rightarrow$ $OD = \left(\dfrac{5 \times 3}{2.5}\right) = 6$ cm. **Ans.**

56. In the figure given below, PT is a tangent to the circle. Find PT if AT = 16 cm and AB = 12 cm.

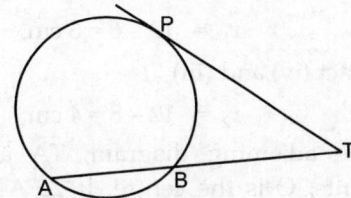

Sol. PT is tangent.

Hence by theorem,

$PT^2 = AT \times BT$

$= 16 \times (AT - AB)$

$= 16 \times (16 - 12)$

$= 16 \times 4 = 64$

$\therefore$ $PT = 8$ cm. **Ans.**

57. ABC is a triangle with AB = 10 cm, BC = 8 cm and AC = 6 cm (not drawn to scale). Three circles are drawn touching each other with the vertices as their centres. Find the radii of the three circles.

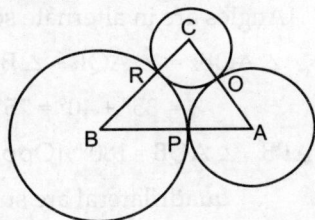

Sol. Given,

$AB = 10$ cm

$BC = 8$ cm

$AC = 6$ cm

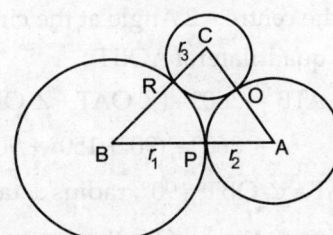

Let the radii of three circles be r_1, r_2 and r_3 (shown in fig.)

$r_1 + r_2 = 10 = AB$ ...(i)

$r_2 + r_3 = 6 = AC$ ...(ii)

$r_3 + r_1 = 8 = BC$ ...(iii)

Adding (i), (ii) and (iii), we get

$2(r_1 + r_2 + r_3) = 10 + 6 + 8 = 24$

$\Rightarrow$ $r_1 + r_2 + r_3 = 12$ ...(iv)

Subtract (iv) and (i)

$\Rightarrow \qquad r_3 = 12 - 10 = 2$ cm **Ans.**

Subtract (iv) and (ii)

$\Rightarrow \qquad r_1 = 12 - 6 = 6$ cm **Ans.**

Subtract (iv) and (iii)

$\Rightarrow \qquad r_2 = 12 - 8 = 4$ cm **Ans.**

58. In the adjoining diagram, TA and TB are tangents, O is the centre. If $\angle PAT = 35°$ and $\angle PBT = 40°$, calculate :

(i) $\angle$ AQP (iv) $\angle$ APB

(ii) $\angle$ BQP (v) $\angle$ AOB

(iii) $\angle$ AQB (vi) $\angle$ ATB.

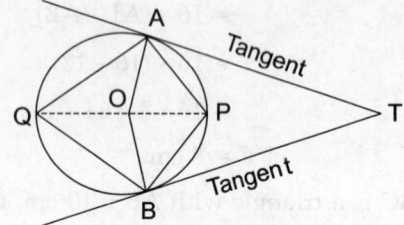

Sol. (i) $\qquad \angle AQP = \angle PAT = 35°$

[Angles are in alternate segment] **Ans.**

(ii) $\qquad \angle BQP = \angle PBT = 40°$

[Angles are in alternate segment] **Ans.**

(iii) $\qquad \angle AQB = \angle AQP + \angle BQP$

$\qquad = 35° + 40° = 75°.$ **Ans.**

(iv) $\angle APB + \angle AQB = 180°$ [Opp. $\angle$s of a cyclic

quadrilateral are supplementary]

$\therefore \quad \angle APB + 75° = 180°$

$\therefore \qquad \angle APB = 105°.$ **Ans.**

(v) $\qquad \angle AOB = 2\angle AQB$

$\qquad = 2(75°) = 150°.$ **Ans.**

[Angle at the centre = 2 Angle at the circumference]

(vi) In quadrilateral AOBT :

$\angle ATB = 360° - (\angle OAT + \angle OBT + \angle AOB)$

$= 360° - (90° + 150° + 90°) = 30°$

[$\angle$ OAT = $\angle$ OBT = 90°, radius $\perp$ tangent] **Ans.**

59. In the given figure, O is the centre of the circle. Tangents at A and B meet at C.

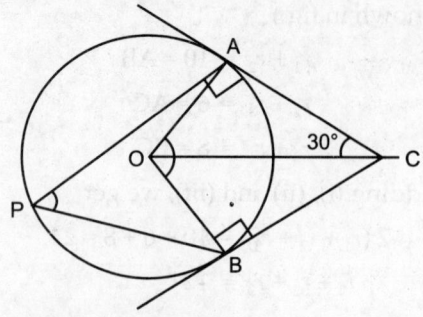

If $\angle ACO = 30°$, find :

(i) $\angle$ BCO, (ii) $\angle$ AOB, (iii) $\angle$ APB.

Sol. (i) $\qquad \angle BCO = \angle ACO = 30°$ **Ans.**

($\because$ C is the intersecting point of

tangents AC and BC)

(ii) $\qquad \angle OAC = \angle OBC = 90°$

$\qquad \angle ACO = 30°$ (Given)

$\therefore \qquad \angle AOC = \angle BOC$

$\qquad = 180° - (90° + 30°)$

($\because$ sum of the 3 angles of a Δ is 180°)

$\Rightarrow \qquad \angle AOC = 180° - 120°$

$\Rightarrow \qquad \angle AOC = 60°$

$\therefore \qquad \angle AOB = \angle AOC + \angle BOC$

$\qquad = 60° + 60°$

$\Rightarrow \qquad \angle AOB = 120°$ **Ans.**

(iii) $\qquad \angle APB = \dfrac{1}{2}\angle AOB = \dfrac{120°}{2} = 60°$

Ans.

($\because$ Angle substended at the remaining part of the circle is half the $\angle$ substended at the centre}

60. In the figure given below, diameter AB and chord CD of a circle meet at P. PT is a tangent to the circle at T. CD = 7·8 cm, PD = 5 cm, PB = 4 cm. Find :

(i) AB.

(ii) The length of tangent PT.

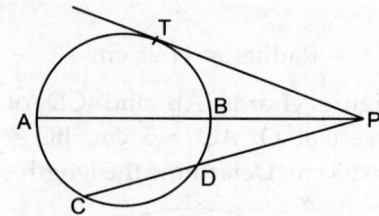

Sol. Given that

$\qquad CD = 7·8$ cm, $PD = 5$ cm,

$\qquad PB = 4$ cm

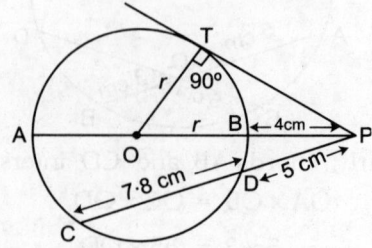

As we know,

$\qquad PT^2 = PD \times PC$

$\Rightarrow \qquad PT^2 = PD \times (PD + CD)$

$\Rightarrow \qquad PT^2 = 5 \times 12 \cdot 8$

$\Rightarrow \qquad PT^2 = 64$

$\Rightarrow \qquad PT = 8$ cm

Now in Δ POT

$PO^2 = OT^2 + PT^2$

$\Rightarrow \qquad (r + 4)^2 = r^2 + 64$

$\Rightarrow \qquad r^2 + 16 + 8r = r^2 + 64$

$\Rightarrow \qquad 8r = 48$

$\therefore \qquad r = 6$

(i) Thus, AB = $2r$ = 12 cm **Ans.**

(ii) Length of tangent PT = 8 cm. **Ans.**

61. In Δ PQR, PQ = 24 cm, QR = 7 cm and $\angle$ PQR = 90°. Find the radius of the inscribed circle.

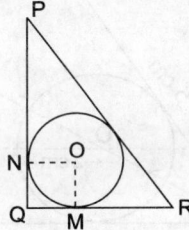

Sol. In the given diagram,

OM $\perp$ QR

ON $\perp$ PQ

$\begin{bmatrix} \text{Tangents and radius} \\ \text{perpendicular to each other} \end{bmatrix}$

OM = ON (r)

QM = QN

(Tangents from an external point)

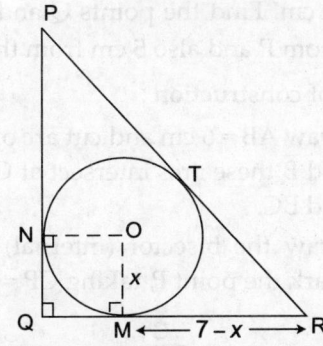

$\Rightarrow$ QMON is a square.

$\Rightarrow \qquad QM = OM = ON = QN = x$ cm.

So, $\qquad MR = (7 - x)$ cm

$PN = (24 - x)$ cm.

$PT = PN = 24 - x$

and $\qquad MR = RT = 7 - x$

[Tangents from an external point]

$\Rightarrow \qquad PR = PT + RT$

$= 24 - x + 7 - x = 31 - 2x$

Now, in Δ PQR,

$PR^2 = PQ^2 + QR^2$

$= 24^2 + 7^2$

$= 576 + 49 = 625$

$\therefore \qquad PR = 25$ cm

$\Rightarrow \qquad 31 - 2x = 25$

$\Rightarrow \qquad 2x = 31 - 25$

$\Rightarrow \qquad 2x = 6$

$\Rightarrow \qquad x = 3$ cm. **Ans.**

62. In figure AT is a tangent to the circle. If m$\angle$ABC = 50°, AC = BC, find $\angle$BAT.

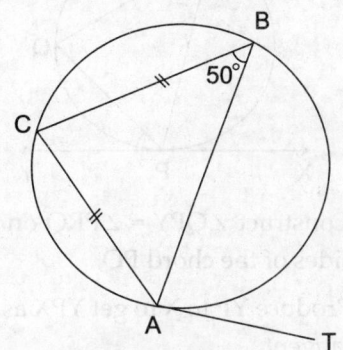

Sol. Given,

$AC = BC$

$\Rightarrow \qquad \angle CBA = \angle CAB$

$\Rightarrow \qquad \angle CAB = 50°$

$\therefore \qquad \angle ACB = 180° - (50° + 50°) = 80°$

Now, $\qquad \angle BAT = \angle BCA$

[Angles are in alternate segments]

$\Rightarrow \qquad \angle BAT = 80°.$ **Ans.**

Chapter 16. Constructions

1. Take a point O on the plane at the paper. With O as centre draw a circle of radius 3 cm. Take a point P on this circle and draw a tangent at P.

Sol. Steps of construction :

(i) Take a point O on the plane at the paper and draw a circle of radius 3 cm.

(ii) Take a point P on the circle and join OP.

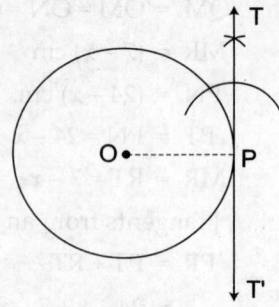

(iii) Construction ∠OPT = 90°.

(iv) Produce TP to T′ obtain the required tangent TPT′.

2. Draw a circle of radius 4 cm. Take a point on it. Without using the centre at the circle, draw a tangent to the circle at point P.

Sol. Steps of construction :

(i) Draw a chord PQ through the given point on the circle.

(ii) Take a point R on the circle and join P and Q to a point R.

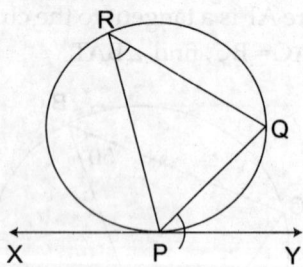

(iii) Construct ∠QPY = ∠PRQ on the opposite sides of the chord PQ.

(iv) Produce YP to X to get YPX as the required tangent.

3. Draw a circle of radius 3 cm. Take a point at 5·5 cm from the centre at the circle. From point P, draw two tangent to the circle.

Sol. Steps of construction :

(i) Take a point O in the plane paper and draw a circle of radius 3 cm.

(ii) Mark a point P at distance 5·5 cm from the centre O and join OP.

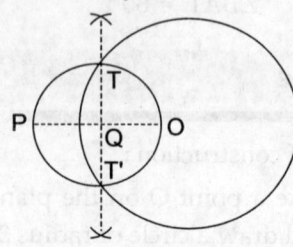

(iii) Draw the right bisector at OP, intersecting OP at Q.

(iv) Taking Q as centre and OQ = PQ as radius, draw a circle to intersect the given circle at T and T′.

(v) Join PT and PT′ to get the required tangent.

4. Use a ruler and a pair of compasses to construct ΔABC in which BC = 4·2 cm, ∠ ABC = 60° and AB = 5 cm. Construct a circle of radius 2 cm to touch both the arms of ∠ ABC of Δ ABC.

Sol. BC = 4·2 cm, ∠ ABC = 60° and AB = 5 cm.

Steps of construction :

(i) Draw BC of length 4·2 cm.

(ii) Draw an angle of 60° at B.

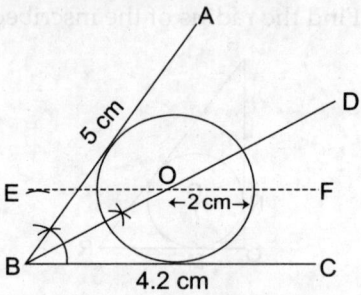

(iii) Cut BA = 5 cm and join A to B.

(iv) Draw angle bisector of ∠ ABC.

(v) Draw BD at 2 cm intersecting EF at O.

(vi) Taking O as centre and 2 cm as radius draw the required circle.

5. Construct an isosceles triangle ABC such that AB = 6 cm, BC = AC = 4 cm. Bisect ∠C internally and mark a point P on this bisector such that CP = 5 cm. Find the points Q and R which are 5 cm from P and also 5 cm from the line AB.

Sol. Steps of construction :

(i) Draw AB = 6 cm and cut arc of 4 cm from A and B these arcs intersect at C and join AC and BC.

(ii) Draw the bisector (internal) of ∠ C and mark the point P, taking CP = 5 cm.

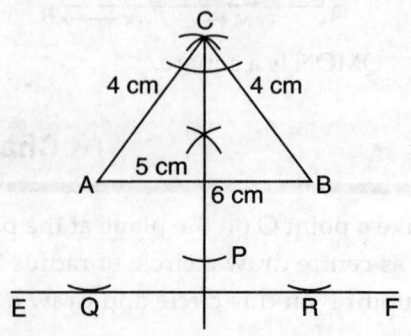

(iii) Draw a line EF parallel to AB at a distance of 5 cm.

(iv) Take P as centre cut two points on line EF as PQ and PR are each equal to 5 cm.

6. Draw two lines AB, AC so that ∠BAC = 40° :

    (i) Construct the locus of the centre of a circle that touches AB and has a radius of 3·5 cm.

    (ii) Construct a circle of radius 3·5 cm that touches both AB and AC, and whose centre lies within the ∠ BAC.

Sol. Steps of construction :

    (i) Draw a line AX perpendicular to AB.

    (ii) Mark off a point D on AX such that AD = 3·5 cm.

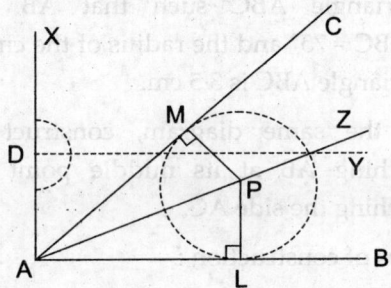

    (iii) At D, draw the line DY at right angles to AX.

    Then DY is the required locus of the centre of circle that touches AB and has a radius of 3·5 cm.

    (iv) Construct the bisector AZ of ∠ BAC intersecting DY at P.

    (v) Draw PL, PM perpendicular to AB and AC respectively.

    (vi) With P as centre and radius equal to 3·5, draw the circle which will pass through L and M.

    Then, this is the required circle that touches both AB and AC, and whose centre lies within the ∠ BAC.

7. Construct a triangle ABC, given that the radius of the circumcircle of triangle ABC is 3·5 cm, ∠ BCA = 45° and ∠ BAC = 60°.

Sol. Steps of construction :

    (i) Draw a circle with radius = 3·5 cm.

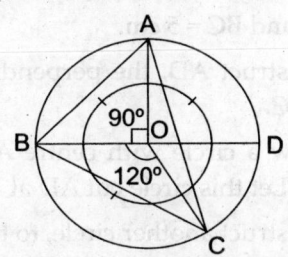

(ii) Draw diameter BOD and construct ∠ BOA = 90°.

(iii) Again make ∠ BOC = 120°.

(iv) Join AB, AC and BC. Then, ABC is the required triangle.

8. Construct an ∠PQR = 45°. Mark a point S on QR such that QS = 4·5 cm. Construct a circle to touch PQ at Q and also to pass through S.

Sol. Steps of construction :

    (i) Draw ∠ PQX = 90°.

    (ii) Bisect ∠ PQX and draw ∠ PQR = 45°.

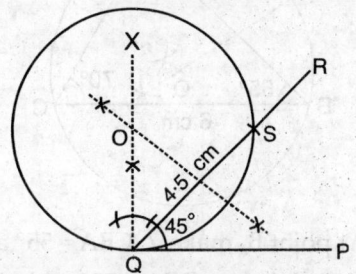

    (iii) Cut off QS = 4·5 cm from QR.

    (iv) Draw bisector of QS and it is intersect QX at O.

    (v) With O as centre and radius = OQ (or OS draw the required circle).

9. Using ruler and compass construct a triangle ABC where AB = 3 cm, BC = 4 cm and ∠ABC = 90°. Hence, construct a circle circumscribing the triangle ABC. Measure and write down the radius of the circle.*

Sol. Steps of construction:

    (i) Draw *BC* = 4 cm.

    (ii) Make an angle of 90° at *B* and cut an arc of radius 3 cm on it to get point *A*.

    (iii) Join *AC*. Thus, Δ*ABC* is obtained.

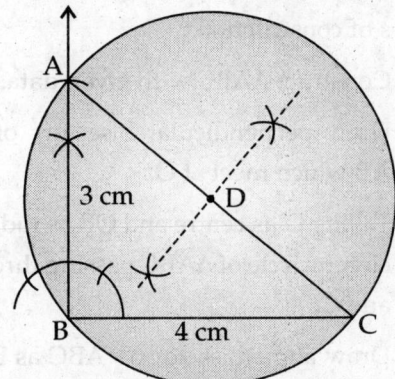

    (iv) Draw perpendicular bisector of *AC*, which meets *AC* at *D*.

---
* **Frequently asked previous years Board Exam Questions.**

(v) Taking D as centre and radius equal to AD or DC, draw a circle. Thus, it is a required circle.

Since, AC = 5 cm, so, AD = 2.5 cm.

10. Construct the circumcircle of the Δ ABC when BC = 6 cm, ∠ B = 55° and ∠ C = 70°.

Sol. Steps of construction :

(i) Draw a line segment BC = 6 cm.

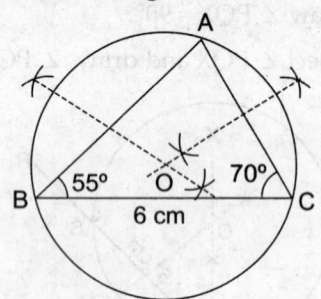

(ii) At point B, make ∠ CBA = 55° and at point C, make an ∠ BCA = 70° with the help of a protractor. Join AB and AC.

(iii) Draw the perpendicular bisectors of sides AB and AC. Let them intersect at O.

(iv) With O as centre and radius OA, draw a circle which passes through the point A, B and C.

This is the required circumcircle of Δ ABC.

11. Using ruler and compass only, construct a ΔABC such that BC = 5 cm and AB = 6.5 cm and ∠ABC = 120°.*

(i) Construct a circumcircle of ΔABC

(ii) Construct a cyclic quadrilateral ABCD, such that D is equidistant from AB and BC.

Sol. Given, BC = 5 cm, AB = 6.5 cm, ∠ABC = 120°

Steps of construction :

(i) Construct ΔABC with given data.

(ii) Draw perpendicular bisectors of BC and AB which meet at O.

(iii) Taking O as centre and OB as radius, draw circumcircle of ΔABC passing through A, B and C.

(iv) Draw angle bisector of ABC as BD which meets circle at D.

(v) Join AD and CD. ABCD is the required cyclic quadrilateral.

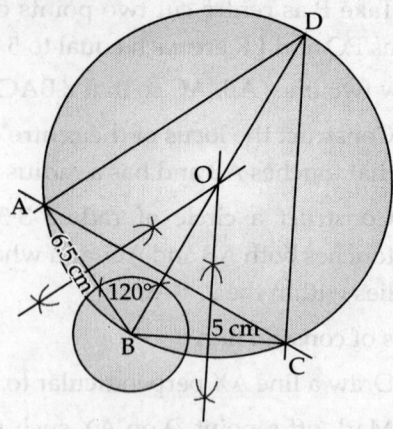

12. Using ruler and compass only, construct a triangle ABC such that AB = 5 cm, ∠ ABC = 75° and the radius of the circumcircle of triangle ABC is 3·5 cm.

On the same diagram, construct a circle, touching AB at its middle point and also touching the side AC.

Sol. Steps of construction :

(i) Draw a line segment AB = 5 cm long.

(ii) Make an angle of 75° at 'B' draw perpendicular bisector of AB and angular bisector of B.

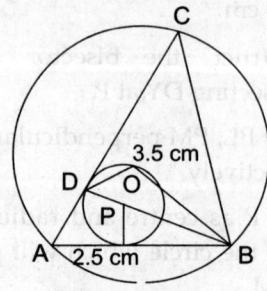

(iii) Mark 3·5 cm on the perpendicular bisector with O as centre and radius equal to OA or OB draw circumcircle.

(iv) Mark 2·5 cm on AC from A.

(v) Join BD, it will intersect at P, with P as centre and PD as radius draw another circle.

13. (i) Construct a Δ ABC, such that AB = AC = 7 cm and BC = 5 cm.

(ii) Construct AD, the perpendicular bisector of BC.

(iii) Draw a circle with centre A and radius 3 cm. Let this circle cut AD at P.

(iv) Construct another circle, to touch the circle with centre A, externally at P, and pass through B and C.

Sol. Steps of construction :

(i) 1. Draw BC = 5 cm.

2. With B and C as centres draw two arcs to length 7 cm cutting each other at A.

3. Join AB and AC.

4. Then, ABC is required triangle.

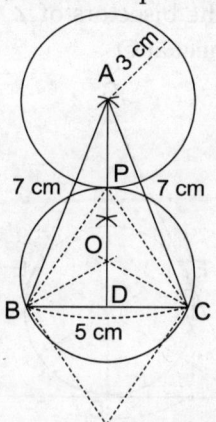

(ii) Draw AD, the right bisector of BC.

(iii) With A as centre and radius 3 cm draw a circle meeting AD at P.

(iv) 1. Join BP and CP.

2. Draw the right bisector of CP meeting AD at O.

3. With O as centre and radius equal to OP draw the required circle, passing through B and C.

14. Using ruler and compass construct a cyclic quadrilateral ABCD in which AC = 4 cm, ∠ ABC = 60 °, AB = 1·5 cm and AD = 2 cm. Also, write the steps of construction.

Sol. Steps of construction :

(i) Draw a line segment AC = 4 cm.

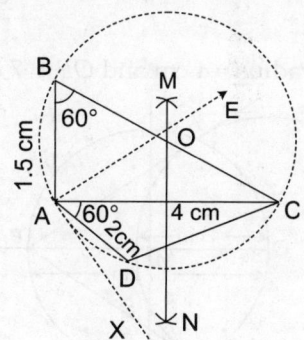

(ii) Draw ∠CAX = 60°.

(iii) Draw the perpendicular bisector MN of AC.

(iv) Draw EA ⊥ AX at the point A which intersects MN at O.

(v) With centre O and radius OA draw a circle.

(vi) Mark a point B on the circumference of the circle such that AB = 1·5 cm and mark a point D on the circumference so that AD = 2·0 cm.

(vii) Join BC and measure ∠ ABC = 60°.

Then, ABCD is the required cyclic quadrilateral.

15. Construct a triangle whose sides are 4·4 cm, 5·2 cm and 7·1 cm. Construct its circumcircle. Write also the steps of construction.

Sol. Steps of construction :

(i) Draw an line segment BC = 5·2 cm.

(ii) With centre B and radius BA = 4·4 cm, draw an arc.

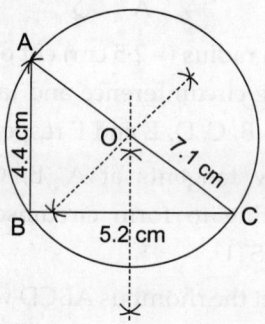

(iii) With C centre and radius CA = 7·1 cm, draw an arc intersecting the previous arc at A. Then, ABC is the given triangle.

(iv) Draw the perpendicular bisectors of any two sides, say BC and AC, intersecting at O. Then O is the circumcentre of Δ ABC.

16. Draw a circle of radius 3 cm. Construct a square about the circle.

Sol. Steps of construction :

(i) Draw a circle with centre O and radius equal to 3 cm.

(ii) Draw a diameter AC.

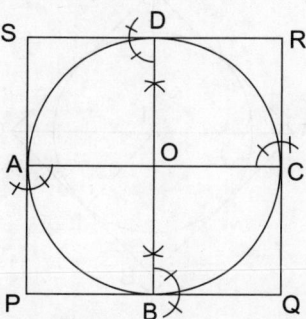

(iii) Draw another diameter BD which bisects AC at right angle.

(iv) Now, draw tangents to the given circle at the points A, B, C, D and let them meet at P,

Q, R, S. Then, PQRS is the required square about the given circle.

17. Draw a circle of radius 2·5 cm and circumscribe a regular hexagon about it.

Sol. Steps of construction :

(i) Draw a circle with centre O and radius = 2·5 cm.

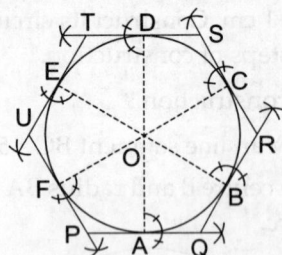

(ii) With radius (= 2·5 cm) cut off six equal arcs along circumference and take these points as A, B, C, D, E and F respectively.

(iii) Draw tangents at A, B, C, D, E and F meeting to form circumscribed hexagon PQRSTU.

18. Construct the rhombus ABCD whose diagonals AC and BD are of lengths 8 cm and 6 cm respectively. Construct the inscribed circle of the rhombus. Measure its radius.

Sol. Steps of construction :

(i) Draw AC = 8 cm.

(ii) Draw perpendicular bisector of AC = cut it at I.

(iii) Cut IB = $\frac{6}{2}$ = 3 cm and ID = 3 cm and join ABCD. Then, ABCD is the required rhombus.

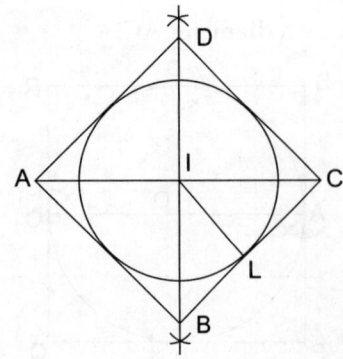

(iv) Now, from I draw a perpendicular to BC to meet it at L.

(v) With I as centre and IL as radius, draw a circle which is the required circle. Its radius = IL = 2·4 cm. **Ans.**

* Frequently asked previous years Board Exam Questions.

19. Draw an isosceles triangle with sides 6 cm, 4 cm and 6 cm. Construct the incircle of the triangle. Also, write the steps of construction.

Sol. Steps of construction :

(i) Construct a Δ ABC such that AB = 4 cm, AC = 6 cm, BC = 6 cm.

(ii) Draw the bisectors of ∠A and ∠B and let them meet at O.

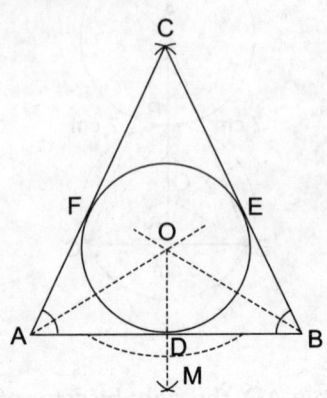

(iii) With O as centre draw OM the right bisector of AB meeting AB at D.

(iv) With O as centre and OD as radius draw a circle. The circle touches the sides of the Δ ABC at D, E and F.

Then, this is the required incircle of Δ ABC.

20. Use ruler and compass only for answering this question.

Draw a circle of radius 4 cm. Mark the centre as O. Mark a point P outside the circle at a distance of 7 cm from the centre. Construct two tangents to the circle from the external point P.

Measure and write down the length of any one tangent.*

Sol. Given, radius = 4 cm and *OP* = 7 cm

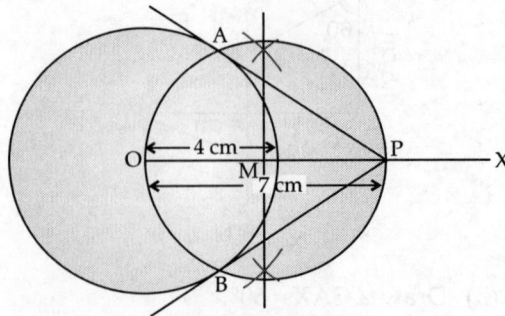

Steps of constructions :

(i) Draw a circle of radius 4 cm with centre at O.

(ii) Draw a line *OX* and cut-off *OP* = 7 cm.

(iii) Bisect *OP* at M.

(iv) With *M* as centre, draw a circle passing through the points *O* and *P* to cut the previous circle at *A* and *B*.

(v) Join *P* with *A* and *B*. Hence, *AP* and *BP* are the required tangents.

∴ The length of tangent, *AP* = 5.7 cm **Ans.**

21. Draw a circle of radius 4 cm. Take a point P out side the circle without using the centre at the circle. Draw two tangent to the circle from point P.

Sol. Steps of construction :

(i) Draw a circle of radius 4 cm.

(ii) Take a point P out side the circle and draw a secant PAB, intersecting the circle at A and B.

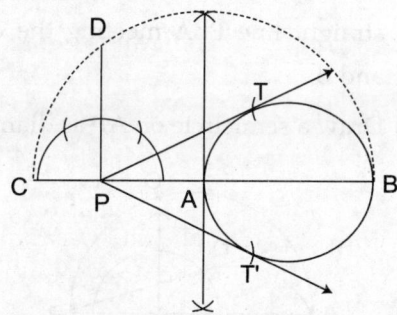

(iii) Produce AP to C such that AP = CP.

(iv) Draw a semi-circle with CB as diameter.

(v) Draw perpendicular from P to the circle intersecting the circle at D.

(vi) With P as centre and PD as radius draw arcs to intersect the given circle at T and T'.

(vii)Join PT and PT'. Then, PT and PT' are the required tangents.

22. Use ruler and compass only for this question construct the cyclic quadrilateral ABCD in which AB = 5 cm, BC = 8 cm, ∠ ABC = $67\frac{1}{2}^{\circ}$ and D is equidistant from B and C.

Sol.

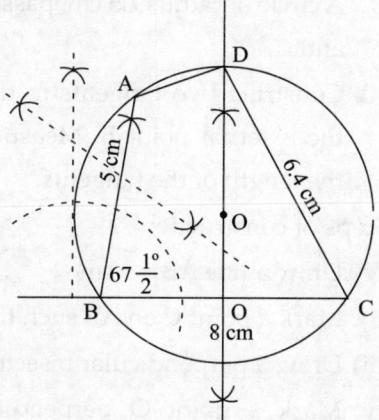

Steps of construction :

(i) Draw BC = 8 cm, construct ∠ B = $67\frac{1}{2}^{\circ}$ and cut off AB = 5 cm.

(ii) Draw ⊥ bisector of BC and AB and produce these to meet at O.

(iii) With O as centre, radius OA or OB or OC draw a circle to pass through ABC.

(iv) Produce the ⊥ bisector of BC to intersect the circumference of the circle. This intersection point is D.

(v) Join CD and AD.

(vi) ABCD is the required cyclic quadrilateral.

Length of CD = 6·4 cm. (By measurement) **Ans.**

23. Ruler and compasses in this question. All constructions lines and arcs must be clearly shown, and be sufficient length and clarity to permit assessment :

(i) Construct a triangle ABC, in which AB = 9 cm, BC = 10 cm and ∠ ABC = 45°.

(ii) Draw a circle, with centre A and radius 2·5 cm. Let it meet AB at D.

(iii) Construct a circle to touch the circle with centre A externally at D and also to touch the line BC.

Sol. Steps of construction :

(i) Take BC = 10 cm.

(ii) Make ∠ ABC = 45° and with centre B, cut the arc BA = 9 cm.

(iii) Join AC, so ABC is the required triangle.

(iv) With A as centre and radius = 2·5 cm, draw a circle. It will pass through D.

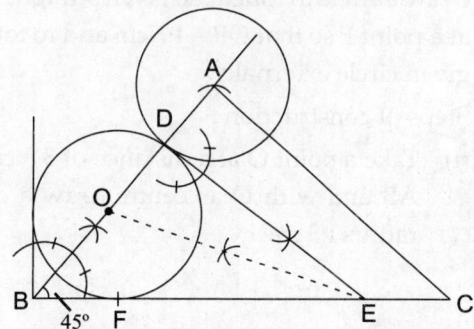

(v) Draw perpendicular from D which cuts BC at E.

(vi) Draw the angle bisector of BED which cut BD at O.

(vii)Taking radius = OD, draw a circle which touches the first circle at D and also touches the line BC at F.

(viii) This is the required circle. The radius OD = 2·7 cm.

24. (i) Construct a triangle ABC, in which AB = 5·0 cm, BC = 3·5 cm and ∠ ABC = $67\frac{1}{2}^\circ$

(Use a pair of compasses and ruler only).

(ii) Construct a circle to touch AB at B and it pass though C.

Sol. Steps of construction :

(i) Draw BC = 3·5 cm.

(ii) At B, draw BE such that ∠ EBC = $67\frac{1}{2}^\circ$. From BE cut off BA = 5 cm.

(iii) Join AC. Then, Δ ABC is the required triangle.

(iv) Produce EB to F.

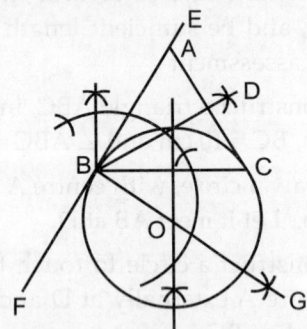

(v) At B, draw BG such that ∠ EBG = 90°.

(vi) Draw perpendicular bisector of BC to cut BG at O.

(vii) With O as centre and OB as radius draw a circle. This is the required circle to touch AB at B and pass through C.

25. The centre O of a circle of a radius 1·3 cm is at a distance of 3·8 cm from a given straight line AB. Draw a circle to touch the given straight line AB at a point P so that OP = 4·7 cm and to touch the given circle externally.

Sol. Steps of construction :

(i) Take a point O at a distance of 3·8 cm from AB and with O as centre draw a circle of radius 1·3 cm.

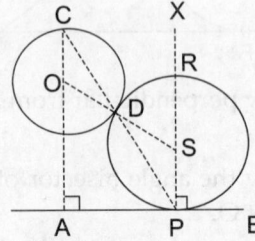

(ii) With O as centre and radius equal to 4·7 cm, draw an arc cut BA at P. Draw PX perpendicular to AB.

(iii) Produce AO to cut the circle at C and join CP cutting the circle at D.

(iv) Join OD and produce it to cut PX at S. With S as centre and radius = SD, draw the circle PDR. This is the required circle.

26. Draw a circle of radius 3 cm and construct a tangent to it from an external point without using the centre.

Sol. Steps of construction :

(i) With centre O and radius = 3 cm, draw a circle.

(ii) Take any point P outside the circle.

(iii) Through the external point P draw a straight line PBA meeting the circle at A and B.

(iv) Draw a semicircle on AP as diameter.

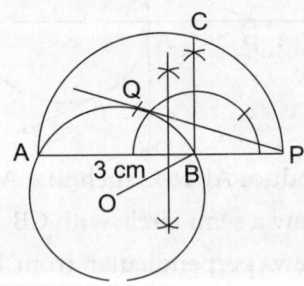

(v) Draw BC ⊥ AP, which intersects the semicircle at C.

(vi) With centre P and radius PC draw an arc cutting the circle at Q.

(vii) Join PQ. Then, PQ is the required tangent.

27. Draw a line AB = 5 cm. Mark a point C on AB such that AC = 3 cm. Using a ruler and a compass only, construct :

(i) A circle of radius 2.5 cm, passing through A and C.

(ii) Construct two tangents to the circle from the external point B. Measure and record the length of the tangents.

Sol. Steps of construction :

(i) Draw a line AB = 5 cm.

(ii) Mark a point C on AB such that AC = 3 cm.

(iii) Draw a perpendicular bisector of AC.

(iv) Mark a point O perpendicular bisector from A of length 2·5 cm.

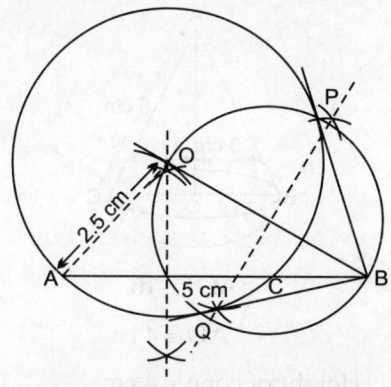

(v) Taking O as centre and OA as radius draw a circle, which is the required circle.

(vi) Join O and B.

(vii) Draw a circle with OB as diameter which cuts the given circle at points P and Q.

(viii) Join PB and QB, which are the required tangents. QB = PB = 3 cm.

Here, length of tangents is 3 cm.   **Ans.**

28. Construct a Δ ABC with BC = 6·5 cm, AB = 5·5 cm, AC = 5 cm. Construct the incircle of the triangle. Measure and record the radius of the incircle.

Sol. Steps of construction :

(i) Construct a ΔABC with the given data.

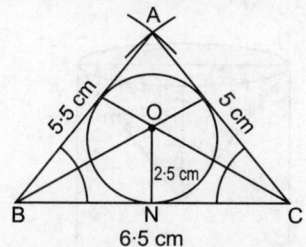

(ii) Draw the angle bisector of ∠B and ∠C. Let these bisctors cut at O.

(iii) Taking O as the centre. Draw a incircle which touches all the sides of the Δ ABC.

(iv) From O draw a perpendicular to side BC which cut at N.

(v) Measure ON which is the required radius of the incircle. ON = 1·5 cm.   **Ans.**

29. Construct a regular hexagon of side 5 cm. Construct a circle circumscribing the hexagon. All traces of construction must be clearly shown.

Sol. Steps of construction :

(i) Construct a regular hexagon ABCDEF with each side 5 cm.

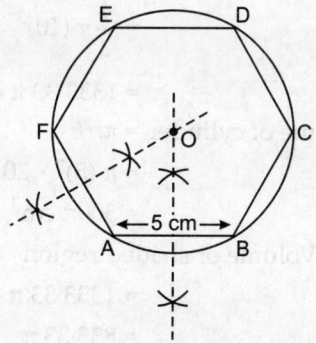

(ii) Draw the perpendicular bisectors of sides AB and AF which intersect each other at point O.

(iii) With O as centre and OA as radius draw a circle which will pass through all the vertices of the regular hexagon.

Chapter 17. Mensuration

1. Find the cost of digging a well 3 m in diameter and 24 m in depth at the rate of ₹ 10 per cu m.

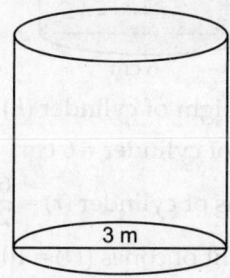

Sol. Given,

Diameter of well = 3 m

∴   Radius of well = 1·5 m

Depth of the well = 24 m

∴ Volume of the earth excavated

$$= \pi r^2 h$$

$$= \frac{22}{7} \times (1.5)^2 \times 24$$

$$= 169.646 \text{ cu m}$$

Now, cost per cu m = ₹ 10

∴   Total cost = 10 × 169·646

= ₹ 1696·46   **Ans.**

2. A right circular cylinder inscribed in a sphere of radius 10 cm. Find the volume of the shaded region. Give your answer in terms of π and rounded to the nearest tenth.

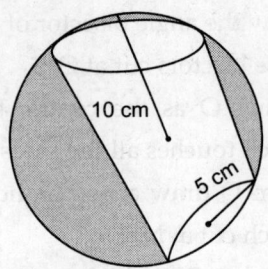

Sol. Given,

Radius of sphere = 10 cm = R

Radius of cylinder = 5 cm = r

∴ Height of cylinder = 10 cm = h

Volume of shaded region

$\qquad$ = Vol. of sphere

$\qquad\qquad$ – Vol. of cylinder

Vol. of sphere = $\frac{4}{3}\pi R^3$

$\qquad$ = $\frac{4}{3}\pi(10)^3$

$\qquad$ = 1333·33 π cm^3

Volume of cylinder = $\pi r^2 h$

$\qquad$ = $\pi(5)^2 \times 20$

$\qquad$ = 500π cm^3

Now, Volume of shaded region

$\qquad$ = 1333·33 π – 500 π

$\qquad$ = 833·33 π

∴ $\qquad$ Volume = 833·33 × 3·14

$\qquad$ = 2616·65 cm^3 $\qquad$ **Ans.**

Hence, the volume of the shaded region is 2616·65 cm^3. $\qquad\qquad$ **Ans.**

3. The given figure represents a hemisphere surmounted by a conical block of wood. The diameter of their bases is 6 cm each and the slant height of the cone is 5 cm. Calculate :

   (i) the height of the cone.

   (ii) the volume the solid.

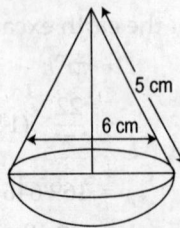

Sol. (i) In Δ ADC,

$\qquad$ $AC^2 = AO^2 + OC^2$

⇒ $\qquad$ $25 = AO^2 + 9$

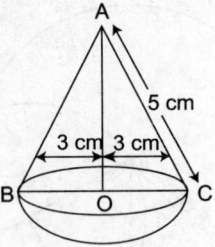

⇒ $\qquad\qquad$ $AO^2 = 16$

∴ $\qquad\qquad$ $AO = 4$ cm

∴ $\qquad$ Height of cone = 4 cm

(ii) Volume of solid = Volume of cone

$\qquad\qquad\qquad$ + Volume of hemisphere

$\qquad$ = $\frac{1}{3}\pi r^2 h + \frac{2}{3}\pi r^3$

$\qquad$ = $\frac{1}{3} \times \frac{22}{7} \times (3)^2 \times 4 + \frac{2}{3} \times \frac{22}{7} \times (3)^3$

$\qquad$ = 37·71 + 56·57

$\qquad$ = 94·28 cm^3 $\qquad\qquad$ **Ans.**

4. From a solid wooden cylinder of height 28 cm and diameter 6 cm, two conical cavities are hollowed out. The diameters of the cones are also of 6 cm and height 10.5 cm.*

   Taking $\pi = \frac{22}{7}$ find the volume of the remaining solid.

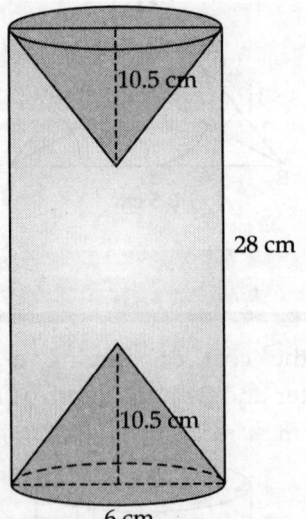

Sol. Given : Height of cylinder (h) = 28 cm

Diameter of cylinder = 6 cm

⇒ $\quad$ Radius of cylinder (r) = $\frac{6}{2}$ = 3 cm

Also, height of cones (H) = 10.5 cm

And, diameter of cones = 6 cm

⇒ Radius of cones (R) = $\frac{6}{2}$ = 3 cm

Now, volume of solid cylinder $= \pi r^2 h$

$$= \frac{22}{7} \times 3^2 \times 28$$

$$= \frac{22}{7} \times 9 \times 28$$

$$= 792 \text{ cm}^3$$

And, volume of two cones

$$= 2 \times \frac{1}{3} \pi R^2 H$$

$$= 2 \times \frac{1}{3} \times \frac{22}{7} \times 3^2 \times 10.5$$

$$= 198 \text{ cm}^3$$

So, volume of the remaining solid

$$= (792 - 198) \text{ cm}^3$$

$$= 594 \text{ cm}^3 \qquad \textbf{Ans.}$$

5. Given $\begin{bmatrix} 4 & 2 \\ -1 & 1 \end{bmatrix} M = 6\,I$, where M is a matrix and I is unit matrix of order 2×2.*

(i) State the order of matrix M.

(ii) Find the matrix M.

Sol. Given, $\begin{bmatrix} 4 & 2 \\ -1 & 1 \end{bmatrix} M = 6\,I$

$\Rightarrow \quad \begin{bmatrix} 4 & 2 \\ -1 & 1 \end{bmatrix} M = 6 \begin{bmatrix} 1 & 0 \\ 0 & 1 \end{bmatrix}$

$\Rightarrow \quad \begin{bmatrix} 4 & 2 \\ -1 & 1 \end{bmatrix} M = \begin{bmatrix} 6 & 0 \\ 0 & 6 \end{bmatrix} \qquad \ldots(i)$

(i) $(2 \times 2)\,(m \times n) = (2 \times 2) \to$ Order of matrix, $M = 2 \times 2$. **Ans.**

(ii) Let, $M = \begin{bmatrix} a & b \\ c & d \end{bmatrix}$

$\therefore \quad \begin{bmatrix} 4 & 2 \\ -1 & 1 \end{bmatrix}\begin{bmatrix} a & b \\ c & d \end{bmatrix} = \begin{bmatrix} 6 & 0 \\ 0 & 6 \end{bmatrix}$ [using (i)]

$\Rightarrow \quad \begin{bmatrix} 4a + 2c & 4b + 2d \\ -a + c & -b + d \end{bmatrix} = \begin{bmatrix} 6 & 0 \\ 0 & 6 \end{bmatrix}$

$\therefore \qquad 4a + 2c = 6 \qquad \ldots(ii)$

$\qquad -a + c = 0 \ldots(iii) \times 4$

Solving equations (ii) and (iii),

$\qquad 4a + 2c = 6$

$\qquad -4a + 4c = 0$

$\qquad \overline{\qquad 6c = 6 \qquad}$

$\Rightarrow \qquad c = 1$

From equation (iii),

$\qquad -a + 1 = 0$

$\Rightarrow \qquad a = 1$

and $\qquad 4b + 2d = 0 \qquad \ldots(iv)$

$\Rightarrow \qquad -b + d = 6 \qquad \ldots(v) \times 4$

Solving equations (iv) and (v),

$\qquad 4b + 2d = 0$

$\qquad -4b + 4d = 24$

$\qquad \overline{\qquad 6d = 24 \qquad}$

$\Rightarrow \qquad d = 4$

From equation (iv),

$\qquad -b + 4 = 6$

$\Rightarrow \qquad -b = 2$

$\Rightarrow \qquad b = -2$

$\therefore \qquad M = \begin{bmatrix} 1 & -2 \\ 1 & 4 \end{bmatrix} \qquad \textbf{Ans.}$

6. With reference to the figure given a alongside, a metal container in the form of a cylinder is surmounted by a hemisphere of the same radius. The internal height of the cylinder is 7 m and the internal radius is 3·5 m. Calculate :

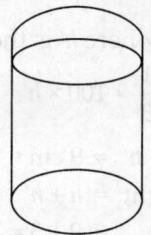

(i) The total area of the internal surface, excluding the base;

(ii) The internal volume of the container in m^3.

(Take $\pi = 22/7$)

Sol. **(i)** Total area of the internal surface, including base

$$= 2\pi r h + 2\pi r^2$$

$$= 2\pi r\,(h + r)$$

$$= 2 \times \frac{22}{7} \times 3.5 \times (7 + 3.5) \text{ m}^2$$

$$= \left(2 \times \frac{22}{7} \times 3.5 \times 10.5\right) \text{ m}^2$$

$$= 231 \text{ m}^2. \qquad \textbf{Ans.}$$

(ii) Internal volume of the container

$$= \pi r^2 h + \frac{2}{3}\pi r^3$$

$$= \frac{1}{3} \times \frac{22}{7} \times 3.5 \times 3.5 \times (21 + 7) \text{ m}^3$$

$$= \left(\frac{1}{3} \times \frac{22}{7} \times 3.5 \times 3.5 \times 28\right) \text{ m}^3$$

$$= 359.33 \text{ m}^3. \qquad \textbf{Ans.}$$

7. Given solid is made up of cone and the cylinder. The base area of the cylinder is 100 cm^2 and height of the cylinder is 3 cm. If the volume of the whole solid is 600 cubic cm. Find the height of the solid.

Sol. Given, base area of the cylinder

$$= 100$$
$$\pi r^2 = 100$$
$$r = 5.64 \text{ cm}$$

Height of the cylinder

$$= 3 \text{ cm}$$

Volume of the whole solid

$$= 600 \text{ cm}^3$$

Volume of the cylinder + volume of the cone

$$= 600 \text{ cm}^3$$
$$\pi r^2 h + \frac{1}{3} \pi r^2 h' = 600$$

[where h' is the height of the cone]

$$\Rightarrow \quad 100 \times 3 + \frac{1}{3} \times 100 \times h' = 600$$
$$\Rightarrow \quad h' = 9 \text{ cm}$$
$$\text{Total height} = h + h'$$
$$= 9 + 3 = 12 \text{ cm.} \qquad \textbf{Ans.}$$

8. Find what length of canvas $\frac{3}{4}$ m, wide is required to make a canonical tent 8 m in diameter and 3 m high.

Sol. Here, $d = 8 \text{ m}$
$$\Rightarrow \quad r = 4 \text{ m}$$
$$h = 3 \text{ m}$$

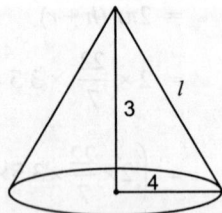

Lateral surface area of the canonical tent

$$= \pi r l$$
$$= \pi h \sqrt{h^2 + r^2}$$
$$= \pi (4) \sqrt{4^2 + 3^2}$$
$$= 20\pi$$
$$= 62.83 \text{ m}^2$$

Now, area of tent = 62.83

$$\text{width} = \frac{3}{4} \text{ m}$$
$$\text{length} = l = ?$$
$$\text{width} \times \text{length} = \text{area}$$

$$\Rightarrow \quad \frac{3}{4} \times l = 62.83$$
$$\Rightarrow \quad l = 83.78 \text{ m} \qquad \textbf{Ans.}$$

9. A hemispherical tank is made up of an iron sheet 1 cm thick. If the inner radius is 1 m then find the volume of the iron used to make the tank.

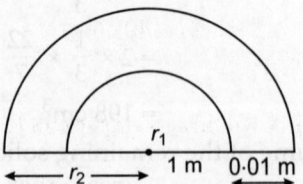

Sol. Thickness of tank

$$= 1 \text{ cm} = 0.01 \text{ m}$$

∴ Inner radius of hemispherical tank

$$= r_1 = 1 \text{ m}$$

and outer radius $r_2 = 1 \text{ m} + 0.01 \text{ m}$

$$= 1.01 \text{ m}$$

∴ Volume of tank $= \dfrac{2}{3} \pi (r_2{}^3 - r_1{}^3)$

$$= \frac{2}{3} \pi [(1.01)^3 - 1^3]$$
$$= \frac{2}{3} \times 3.14 \ [0.030301]$$
$$V = 0.06343 \text{ m}^3$$

∴ Volume of iron used is 0.06343 m³. **Ans.**

10. The volume of a metallic cylindrical pipe is 1408 cu. cm. Its length is 14 cm and its external radius is 9 cm. Find its thickness.

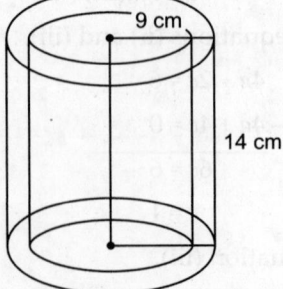

Sol. Let
$$R = \text{external radius}$$
$$= 9 \text{ cm}$$
$$h = \text{length of pipe}$$
$$= 14 \text{ cm}$$
$$r = \text{internal radius}$$

V = Volume of pipe

= 1408 cu. cm.

Now, $V = \pi h (R^2 - r^2)$

$1408 = 3.14 \times 14 (9^2 - r^2)$

$\Rightarrow \quad 1408 = 43.96 (81 - r^2)$

$\Rightarrow \quad 32 = 81 - r^2$

$\Rightarrow \quad r^2 = 49$

$\Rightarrow \quad r = 7$ cm

Therefore, thickness of pipe is R – r

= 9 – 7 = 2 cm   **Ans.**

11. A right circular cylinder having diameter 12 cm and height 15 cm is full with icecream. The icecream is to be filled in cones of height 12 cm and diameter 6 cm having a hemispherical shape on the top. Find the number of such cones which can be filled with icecream.

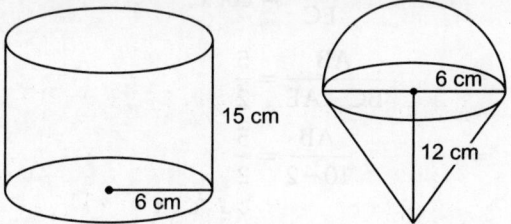

Sol. Radius of cylinder

= r = 6 cm

height of cylinder = h = 15 cm

∴ Volume of cyinder

= $\pi r^2 h$

= $\pi (6)^2 \times 5$

= 540π cm^3

Now, radius of cone

= radius of hemisphere

= 3 cm

∴ Volume of cone = $\frac{1}{3} \pi r^2 h$

= $\frac{1}{3} \pi (3)^2 \times 12$

= 36π cm^3

and volume of hemisphere

= $\frac{2}{3} \pi r^3$

= $\frac{2}{3} \pi (3)^3$

= 18π

∴ Total volume of one cone

= Volume of cone

+ Volume of hemisphere

= $36\pi + 18\pi$

= 54π

∴ No. of cones = $\dfrac{\text{Volume of cylinder}}{\text{Total Volume of cone}}$

= $\dfrac{540\pi}{54\pi} = 10$.   **Ans.**

Chapter 18. Trigonometry

1. The angle of elevation from a point P of the top of a tower QR, 50 m high is 60° and that of the tower PT from a point Q is 30°. Find the height of the tower PT, correct to the nearest metre.*

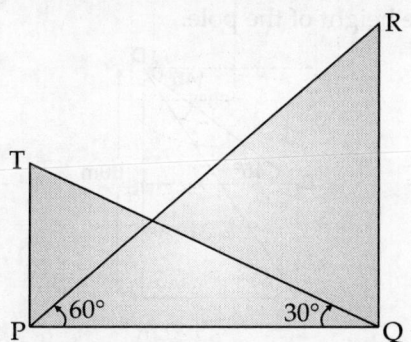

Sol. Given, QR = 50 m, ∠ RPQ = 60°, ∠ PQT = 30°.

Let PT = x m, PQ = y m

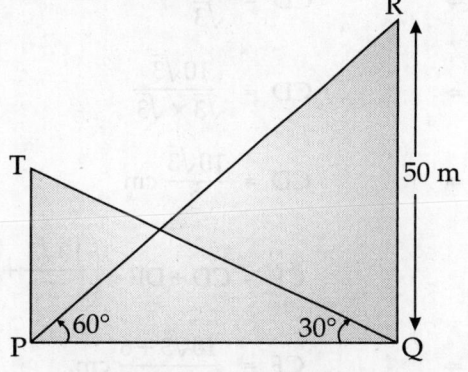

∴ In ΔPQR, tan 60° = $\dfrac{QR}{PQ}$

---

* Frequently asked previous years Board Exam Questions.

$$\Rightarrow \qquad \sqrt{3} = \frac{50}{y}$$

$$\Rightarrow \qquad y = \frac{50}{\sqrt{3}} \qquad \text{...(i)}$$

In $\triangle PQT$, $\tan 30° = \dfrac{PT}{PQ}$

$$\Rightarrow \qquad \frac{1}{\sqrt{3}} = \frac{x}{y}$$

$$\Rightarrow \qquad x = \frac{y}{\sqrt{3}} \qquad \text{...(ii)}$$

$$= \frac{\dfrac{50}{\sqrt{3}}}{\sqrt{3}} \qquad \text{[using eqn. (i)]}$$

$$= \frac{50}{\sqrt{3} \times \sqrt{3}} = \frac{50}{3}$$

$$= 16.6$$

$$= 17 \text{ m} \qquad \textbf{Ans.}$$

(correct to the nearest metre)

2. In the given figure, find the length CF.

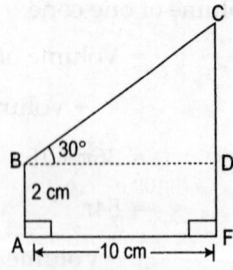

Sol. In the given figure,

$$BD = AF$$

$$\therefore \qquad BD = 10 \text{ cm}$$

In $\triangle BCD$, we have

$$\tan 30° = \frac{CD}{BD}$$

$$\Rightarrow \qquad \frac{1}{\sqrt{3}} = \frac{CD}{10}$$

$$\Rightarrow \qquad CD = \frac{10}{\sqrt{3}}$$

$$\Rightarrow \qquad CD = \frac{10\sqrt{3}}{\sqrt{3} \times \sqrt{3}}$$

$$\Rightarrow \qquad CD = \frac{10\sqrt{3}}{3} \text{ cm}$$

$$CF = CD + DF = \left(\frac{10\sqrt{3}}{3} + 2\right) \text{ cm}$$

$$\Rightarrow \qquad CF = \frac{10\sqrt{3} + 6}{3} \text{ cm.} \qquad \textbf{Ans.}$$

3. With reference to the figure given alongside, a man stands on the ground at a point A, which is on the same horizontal plane as B, the foot of a vertical pole BC. The height of the pole is 10 m. The man's eye is 2 m above the ground. He observes the angle of elevation at C, the top of the pole as $x°$, where $\tan x° = 2/5$. Calculate :

(i) The distance AB in m;

(ii) The angle of elevation of the top when he is standing 15 m from the pole.

Give your answer to the nearest degree. See the figure alongside.

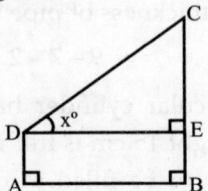

Sol. (i) In right angled $\triangle CDE$, we have

$$\frac{DE}{EC} = \cot x°$$

$$\Rightarrow \qquad \frac{AB}{BC - AE} = \frac{5}{2}$$

$$\Rightarrow \qquad \frac{AB}{10 - 2} = \frac{5}{2}$$

$$\Rightarrow \qquad AB = \left(\frac{5}{2} \times 8\right) \text{ m} = 20 \text{ m.} \qquad \textbf{Ans.}$$

(ii) When AB = 15 m, then DE = 15 m.

In right angled $\triangle CDE$, we have

$$\tan \angle EDC = \frac{EC}{DE} = \frac{8}{15} = 0.5333$$

From tables of natural tangents, we have

$$\angle EDC = 28°2' \text{ nearest}$$

$$\approx 28° \text{ (nearest degree)} \qquad \textbf{Ans.}$$

4. From the top of a tower 60 m high, the angles of depression of the top and bottom of pole are observed to be 45° and 60° respectively. Find the height of the pole.

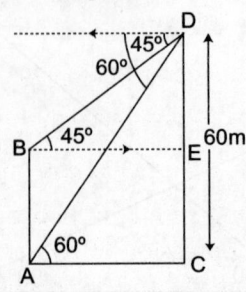

Sol. From the adjoining figure, in right angled $\triangle$ BED,

$$\frac{DE}{BE} = \tan 45°$$

⇒   DE = BE   ... (i)

In right angled Δ ACD,

$$\frac{CD}{AC} = \tan 60°$$

⇒ $\frac{60}{AC} = \sqrt{3}$

⇒   AC $= \frac{60\sqrt{3}}{\sqrt{3} \times \sqrt{3}}$

⇒   AC $= 20\sqrt{3}$

⇒ From (i),

     DE = BE = AC = $20\sqrt{3}$

Now,   AB = CD – DE

         $= (60 - 20\sqrt{3})$ m

         $= 20(30 - \sqrt{3})$ m.   **Ans.**

5. In triangle ABC, AB = 12 cm, ∠B = 58°, the perpendicular from A to BC meets it at D. The bisector of angle ABC meets AD at E. Calculate :

(i) The length of BD;

(ii) The length of ED.

Give your answers correct to one decimal place.

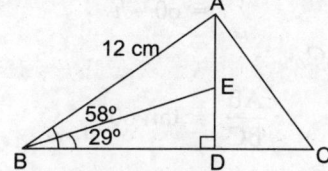

Sol. (i) In right angled Δ ABD,

⇒ $\frac{BD}{BA} = \cos 58°$

⇒   BD = BA cos 58°

         = 12 × (0·5299) cm

         = 6·3588 cm   **Ans.**

(ii) In right angled Δ EBD,

$$\frac{ED}{BD} = \tan 29°$$

⇒   ED = BD tan 29°

         = (6·3588) (0·5543) cm

         = 3·52 cm. (approx.)   **Ans.**

6. From the top of a light house 100 m high the angles of depression of two ships on opposite sides of it are 48° and 36° respectively. Find the distance between the two ships to the nearest metre.

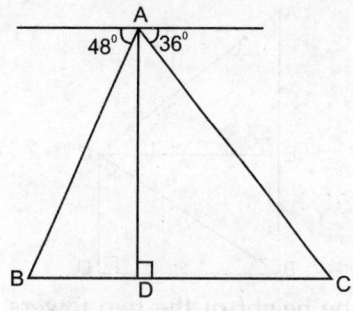

Sol. From right angle Δ ADC,

$$\frac{AD}{CD} = \tan 36°$$

⇒ $\frac{100}{y} = \tan 36°$

⇒ $y = \frac{100}{\tan 36Y}$

         $= \frac{100}{0·7265}$

⇒   y = 137·646 m

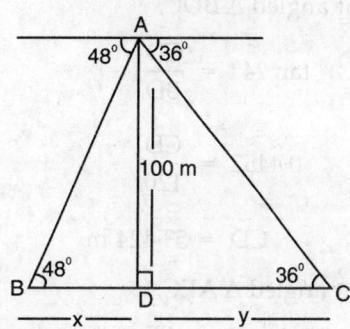

From right angle Δ ADB,

$$\frac{100}{x} = \tan 48°$$

⇒ $x = \frac{100}{1·1106}$

         = 90·04 m.

∴   Distance between the ships

         = x + y

         = 137·638 + 90·04

         = 227·678 m

         = 228 m. (approx.)   **Ans.**

7. The horizontal distance between two towers is 120 m. The angle of elevation of the top and angle of depression of the bottom of the first tower as observed from the second tower is 30° and 24° respectively.

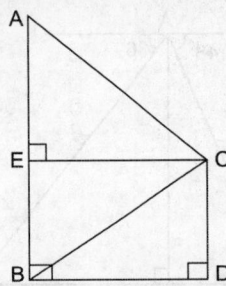

Find the height of the two towers. Give your answer correct to 3 significant figures.

Sol. Clearly, BD = 120 m, and AB and CD be towers.

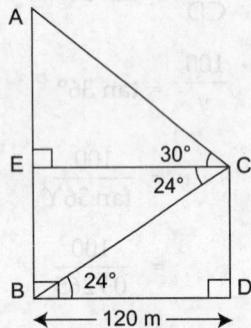

In right angled $\triangle$ BDC,

$$\tan 24° = \frac{CD}{BD}$$

$$\Rightarrow \quad 0.4452 = \frac{CD}{120}$$

$$\Rightarrow \quad CD = 53.424 \text{ m}$$

In right angled $\triangle$ AEC,

$$\tan 30° = \frac{AE}{EC} = \frac{AE}{BD} \qquad (\because EC = BD)$$

$$\Rightarrow \quad \frac{1}{\sqrt{3}} = \frac{AE}{120}$$

$$\Rightarrow \quad AE = \frac{120}{\sqrt{3}}$$

$$\Rightarrow \quad AE = 69.284 \text{ m}$$

$$\therefore \quad AB = AE + EB$$

$$= 69.284 + 53.424$$

$$= 122.708 \text{ m}$$

Hence, the height of the towers are 53.424 m and 122.708 m. **Ans.**

8. In the figure given, from the top of a building AB = 60 m high, the angles of depression of the top and bottom of a vertical lamp post CD are observed to be 30° and 60° respectively. Find :

(i) the horizontal distance between AB and CD.

(ii) the height of the lamp post.

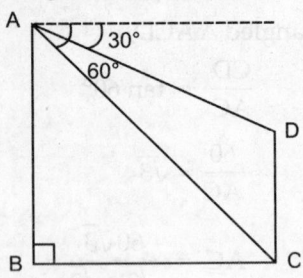

Sol. We draw DE $\perp$ AB

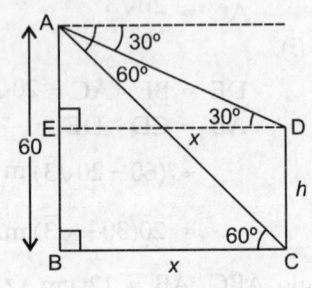

Let
$$BC = x = ED$$
$$AB = 60 \text{ (given)}$$
$$DC = h$$
$$\Rightarrow \quad BE = CD = h$$
$$\therefore \quad AE = AB - BE$$
$$= 60 - h$$

In $\triangle$ ABC,

$$\frac{AB}{BC} = \tan 60°$$

$$\Rightarrow \quad \frac{60}{x} = \sqrt{3}$$

$$\Rightarrow \quad x = \frac{60}{\sqrt{3}} \times \frac{\sqrt{3}}{\sqrt{3}}$$

$$= \frac{60\sqrt{3}}{3} = 20\sqrt{3} \qquad \textbf{Ans.}$$

In $\triangle$ AED,

$$\frac{AE}{ED} = \tan 30°$$

$$\Rightarrow \quad \frac{60-h}{x} = \frac{1}{\sqrt{3}}$$

$$\Rightarrow \quad \frac{60-h}{20\sqrt{3}} = \frac{1}{\sqrt{3}}$$

$$\Rightarrow \quad 60 - h = 20$$

$$\Rightarrow \quad h = 60 - 20 = 40 \text{ m} \qquad \textbf{Ans.}$$

❑❑

Graphical Depiction

Chapter 11. Co-ordinate Geometry

1. Given a line segment AB joining the points A $(-4, 6)$ and B $(8, -3)$. Find :

(i) the ratio in which AB is divided by the Y-axis.

(ii) find the coordinates of the point of intersection.

Sol.

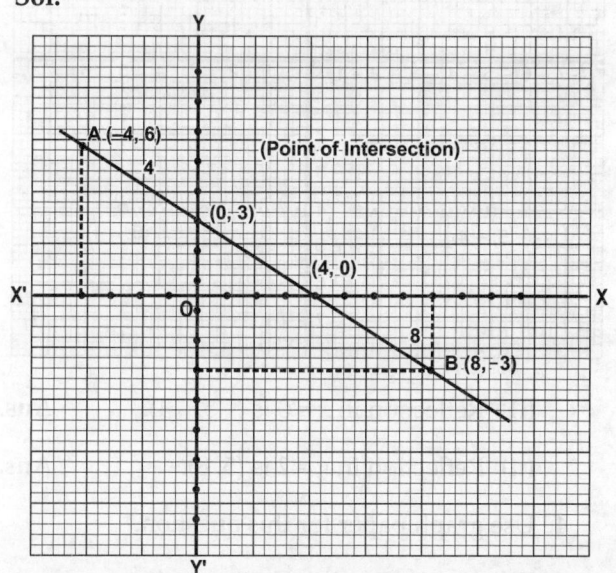

A $(-4, 6)$, B $(8, -3)$

Let ratio be $k : 1$.

(i) Where the Y-axis divide AB, $x = 0$

$$\therefore \qquad x = \frac{m_1 x_2 + m_2 x_1}{m_1 + m_2}$$

$$\therefore \qquad 0 = \frac{k \times 8 + 1 \times (-4)}{k + 1}$$

$$\Rightarrow \qquad 8k - 4 = 0$$

$$\Rightarrow \qquad 8k = 4$$

$$\Rightarrow \qquad k = \frac{4}{8}$$

$$= \frac{1}{2}$$

So, ratio is $1 : 2$. **Ans.**

(ii) Now, $\qquad y = \dfrac{1 \times (-3) + 2 \times 6}{1 + 2}$

$$= \frac{-3 + 12}{3}$$

$$= 3$$

So, point of intersection $(0, 3)$. **Ans.**

Chapter 12. Reflection

1. Find the co-ordinates of the images of the following under reflection in the origin :

(i) $(3, -7)$ **(ii)** $\left(\dfrac{-5}{2}, \dfrac{-1}{2} \right)$ **(iii)** $(0, 0)$.

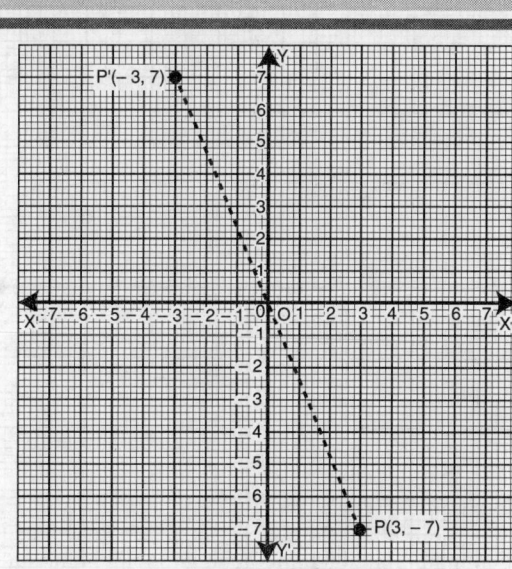

Sol. (i) The reflection (image) of the point P$(3, -7)$ at the origin is the point P$'(-3, 7)$.

Note : To find the reflection of a point in the origin change : (a) The sign of abscissa; *i.e.,* X co-ordinate.

(b) The sign of ordinate; *i.e.,* Y co-ordinate.

(ii) The reflection of the point P $\left(\dfrac{-5}{2}, \dfrac{-1}{2}\right)$ at the origin is the point P' $\left(\dfrac{5}{2}, \dfrac{1}{2}\right)$.

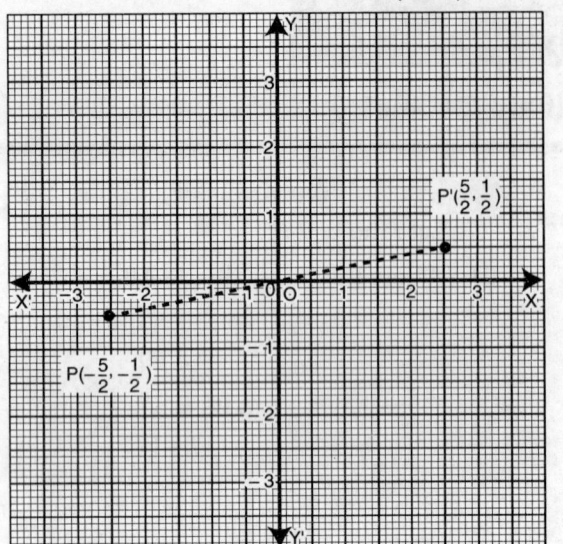

(iii) The reflection (image) of the point (0, 0) at the origin is the point (0, 0) itself.

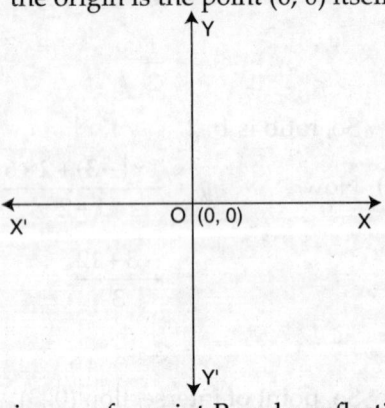

2. The image of a point P under reflection on the X-axis is (5, – 2). Write down the co-ordinates of P.*

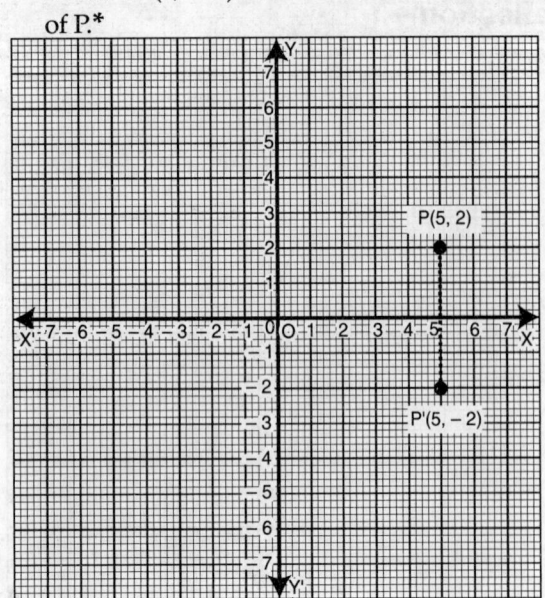

Sol. The image of a point P under reflection on the X-axis is P'(5, – 2).

So, co-ordinates of P = (5, 2).

3. Write down the co-ordinates of the image of (5, – 4).

(i) Reflection in $x = 0$

(ii) Reflection in $y = 2$.

Sol.

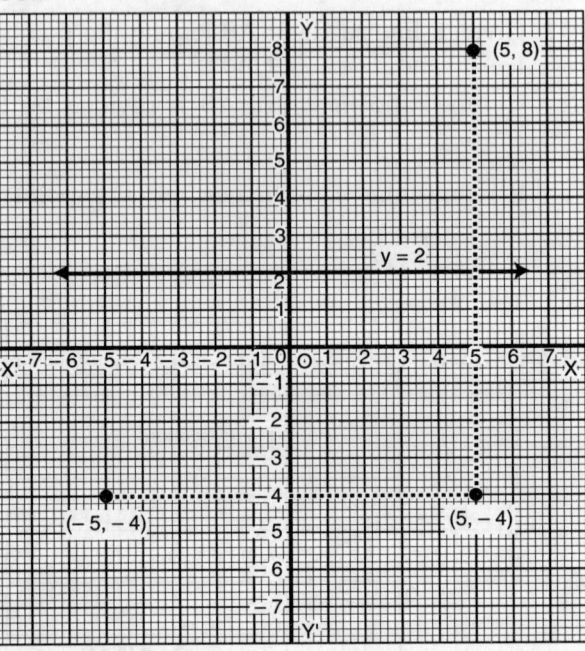

(i) Reflection in $x = 0$ is (– 5, – 4). **Ans.**

(ii) Reflection in $y = 2$ is (5, 8). **Ans.**

4. Use graph paper for this question.*

Take 1 cm = 1 unit on both x and y axes.

(i) Plot the following points on your graph sheets :

A (– 4, 0), B (–3, 2), C (0, 4), D (4, 1) and E (7, 3)

(ii) Reflect the points B, C, D and E on the x-axis and name them as B', C', D' and E' respectively.

(iii) Join the points A, B, C, D, E, E', D', C', B' and A in order.

(iv) Name the closed figure formed.

* Frequently asked previous years Board Exam Questions.

Graphical Depiction

Sol.

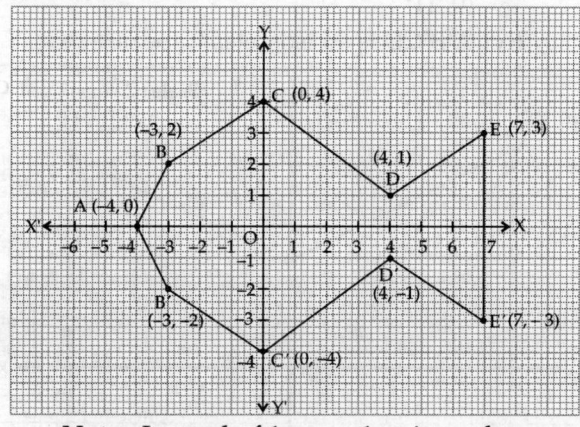

Note : Instead of 1 cm = 1 unit, we have used 0.5 cm = 1 unit on both axes.

(i), (ii) and **(iii)** see graph.

(iv) Nonagon (irregular), polygon fish

5. Use a graph sheet for this questions.

Take 1 cm = 1 unit along both X- and Y-axis.*

(i) Plot the following points :

A(0, 5), B(3, 0), C(1, 0) and D(1, – 5)

(ii) Reflect the points B, C and D on the Y axis and name them as B', C' and D' respectively.

(iii) Write down the coordinates of B', C' and D'.

(iv) Join the points A, B, C, D, D', C', B', A in order and give a name to the closed figure ABCDD'C'B'.

Sol. (i) The given points A (0, 5), B (3, 0), C (1, 0) and D (1, – 5) are plotted on the graph.

(ii) The points B, C and D are reflected on the Y-axis as B', C' and D' respectively.

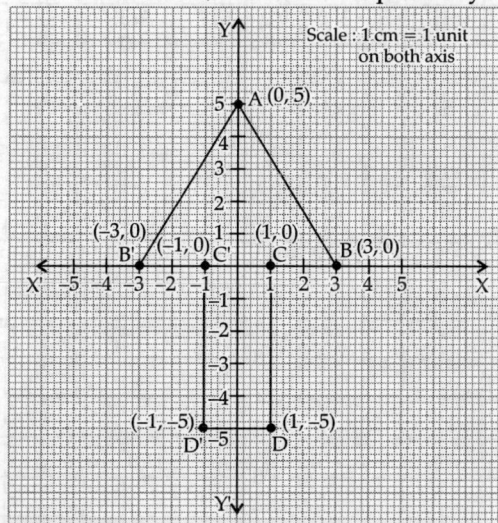

(iii) The coordinates of

$$B' = (-3, 0), \quad C' = (-1, 0),$$
$$\text{and} \qquad D' = (-1, -5) \qquad \textbf{Ans.}$$

(iv) The name of the closed figure ABCDD'C'B' is arrow or heptagon. **Ans.**

6. Use a graph paper for this question.

(i) The point P(2, – 4) is reflected about the line x = 0 to get the image Q. Find the co-ordinates of Q.

(ii) Point Q is reflected about the line y = 0 to get the image R. Find the co-ordinates of R.

(iii) Name the figure PQR.

(iv) Find the area of figure PQR.

Sol. (i) P (2, – 4) is reflected in (x = 0) Y-axis and Q-image.

$$P(2, -4) \xrightarrow{\ M_y\ } Q(-2, -4) \qquad \textbf{Ans.}$$

(ii) Q (– 2, – 4) is reflected in (y = 0) X-axis to get R.

$$Q(-2, -4) \xrightarrow{\ M_x\ } R(-2, 4) \qquad \textbf{Ans.}$$

(iii) The figure PQR is right angle triangle as shown ahead : **Ans.**

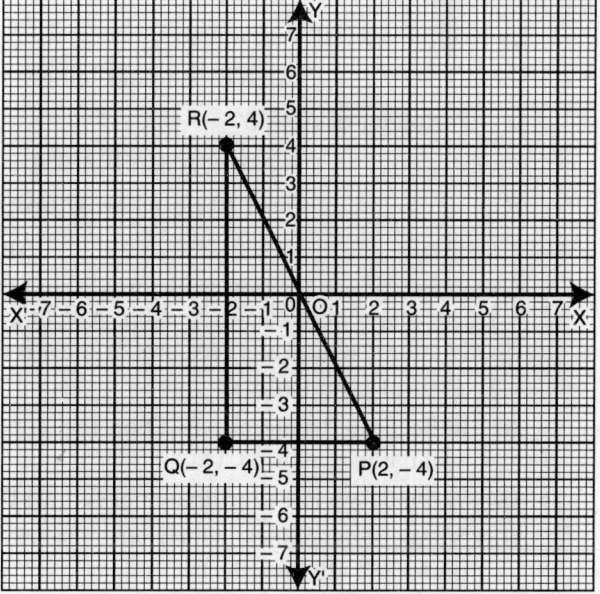

(iv) Area of $\Delta PQR = \dfrac{1}{2} \times PQ \times QR$

$$= \dfrac{1}{2} \times 4 \times 8 = 16 \text{ sq. units.}$$

Ans.

Graphical Depiction

---

* Frequently asked previous years Board Exam Questions.

7. Using a graph paper, plot the points A (6, 4) and B (0, 4).

   (i) Reflect A and B in the origin to get the images A' and B'.

   (ii) Write the co-ordinates of A' and B'.

   (iii) State the geometrical name for the figure ABA'B'.

   (iv) Find its perimeter.

Sol. (i)

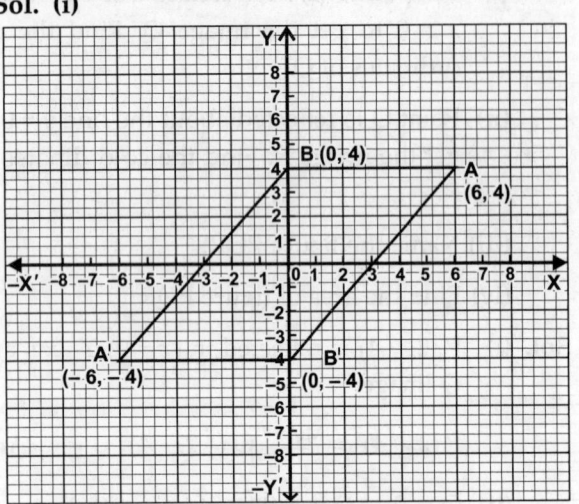

(ii) A' (– 6, – 4) and B' (0, – 4)   **Ans.**

(iii) ABA'B' is a parallelogram.   **Ans.**

(iv) From the figure AB = 6, BB' = 8, A'B' = 6

   In ΔABB',

   $$(AB')^2 = (AB)^2 + (BB')^2$$
   $$= 6^2 + 8^2 = 100$$

   ∴   AB' = 10 = A'B

   {ABA'B' is a parallelogram}

   ∴   Perimeter of ABA'B'

   $$= AB + BA' + A'B' + B'A$$
   $$= 6 + 10 + 6 + 10 = 32 \text{ units}$$

                                          Ans.

8. Use graph paper for this question (Take 2 cm = 1 unit along both X and Y axis). ABCD is a quadrilateral whose vertices are A(2, 2), B (2, – 2), C(0, – 1) and D(0, 1).*

   (i) Reflect quadrilateral ABCD on the Y-axis and name it as A'B'CD.

   (ii) Write down the coordinates of A' and B'.

   (iii) Name two points which are invariant under the above reflection.

   (iv) Name the polygon A'B'CD.

Sol. (i) Reflected quadrilateral A'B'CD is shown in graph.

   (ii) Coordinates of A' = (– 2, 2)

   Coordinates of B' = (– 2, – 2)

(iii) Two invariant points are C(0, – 1) and D (0, 1)

(iv) A'B'CD is an isosceles trapezium.

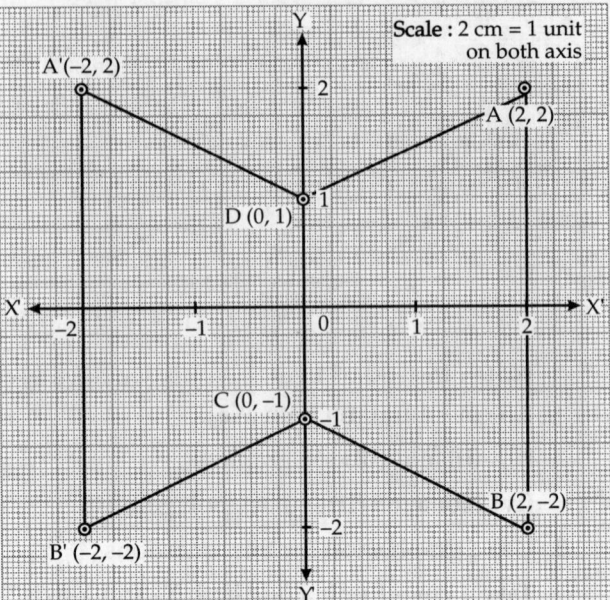

9. (i) Find the reflection of the point (3, 5) on X-axis.

   (ii) Find the reflection of the point (– 3, 5) on X-axis.

   (iii) Find the reflection of the point (– 3, – 5) on X-axis.

   (iv) Find the reflection of the point (3, – 5) on X-axis.

Sol. (i) A (3, 5) $\xrightarrow{Mx}$ D (3, – 5)

   (ii) B (– 3, 5) $\xrightarrow{Mx}$ C (– 3, – 5)

   (iii) C (– 3, – 5) $\xrightarrow{Mx}$ B (– 3, 5)

   (iv) D (3, – 5) $\xrightarrow{Mx}$ A (3, 5)

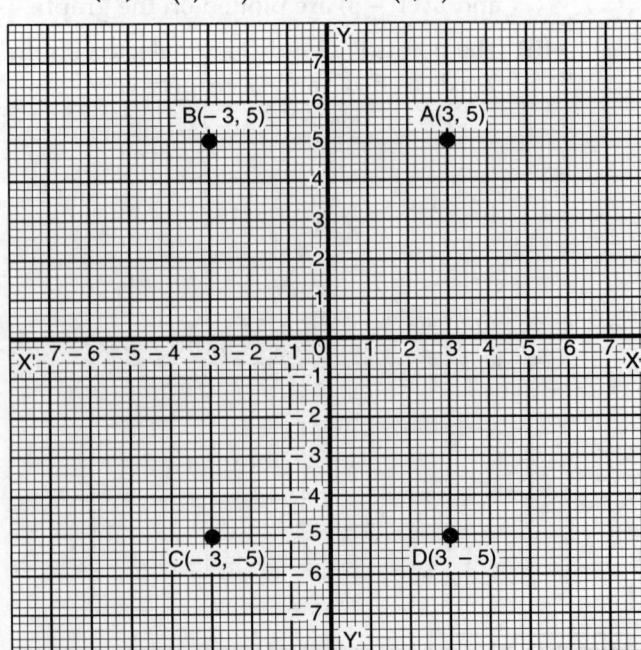

---

* **Frequently asked previous years Board Exam Questions.**

10. P, Q have co-ordinates (– 1, 2) and (6, 3) respectively. Reflect P on the X-axis to P′. Find :

(i) The coordinate of P′

(ii) Length of P′Q.

(iii) Length of PQ.

(iv) Is P′Q = PQ ?

Sol.

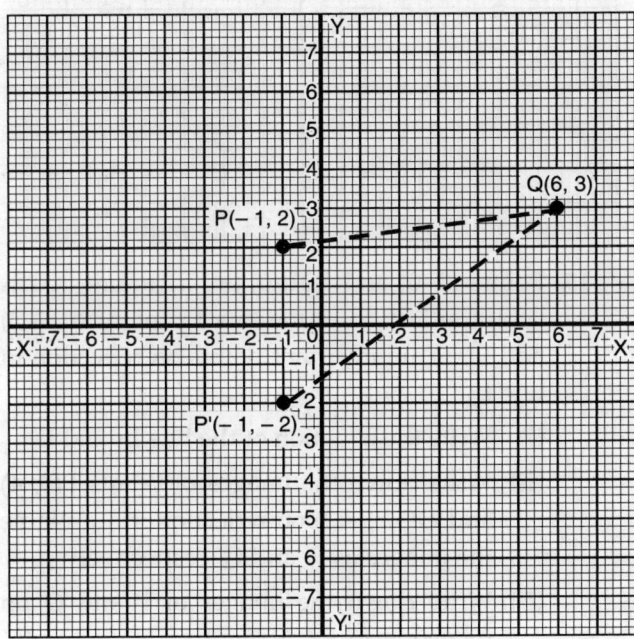

(i) Coordinate of P′ are (– 1, – 2). **Ans.**

(ii) $$P′Q = \sqrt{(6+1)^2 + (3+2)^2}$$
$$= \sqrt{49+25} = \sqrt{74}.$$ **Ans.**

(iii) $$PQ = \sqrt{(6+1)^2 + (3-2)^2}$$
$$= \sqrt{49+1} = \sqrt{50}.$$ **Ans.**

(iv) No, (P′Q ≠ PQ) **Ans.**

11. A point P(4, – 1) is reflected to P′ in the line $y = 2$ followed by the reflection to P″ in the line $x = -1$. Find :

(i) The coordinates of P′.

(ii) The coordinates of P″.

(iii) The length of PP′.

(iv) The length of P′P″.

Sol.

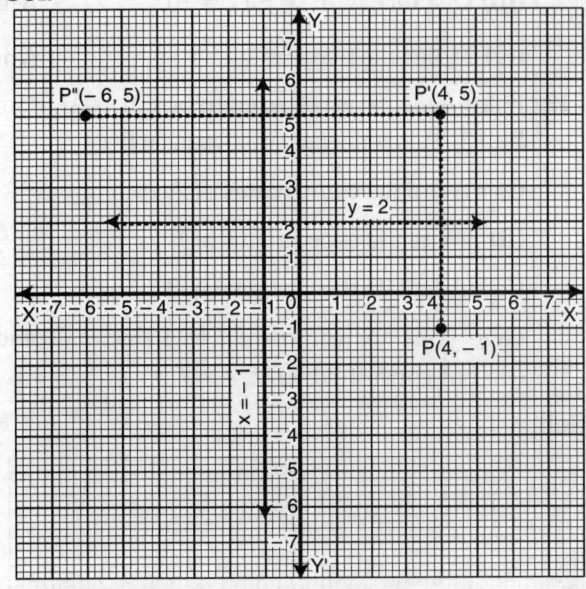

(i) The coordinates of P′ are (4, 5). **Ans.**

(ii) The coordinates of P″ are (– 6, 5). **Ans.**

(iii) PP′ = 6 units **Ans.**

(iv) P′P″ = 10 units **Ans.**

12. Point A (5, 1) on reflection on X-axis is mapped as A′. Also A′ on reflection on Y-axis is mapped as A″.

(i) Write the coordinates of A′.

(ii) Write the coordinates of A″.

(iii) Calculate the distance A′A″.

(iv) On which coordinate axis does the middle point M of A″A′ lie ?

Sol. See graph,

(i) The coordinates of A′ are (5, – 1). **Ans.**

(ii) The coordinates of A″ are (– 5, – 1). **Ans.**

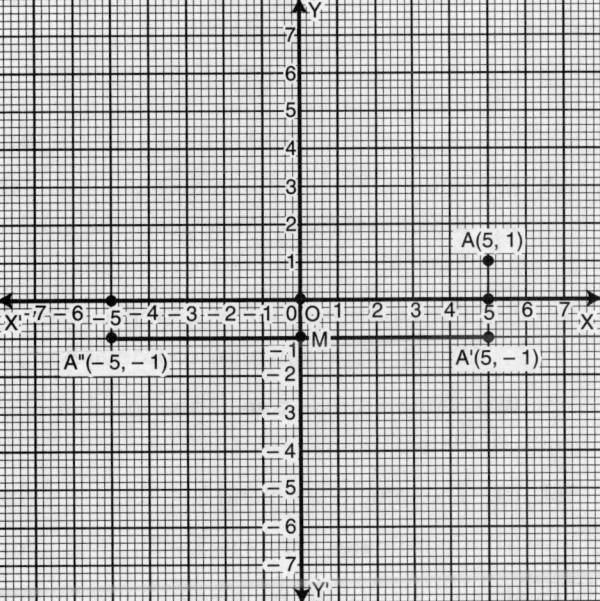

(iii) Distance A′A″ = 5 + 5 = 10. **Ans.**

(iv) M lies on *Y*-axis. **Ans.**

13. Point A (2, – 4) is reflected in origin as A′. Point B (– 3, 2) is reflected on X-axis as B′.

   (i) Write the coordinates of A′.

   (ii) Write the coordinates of B′.

   (iii) Calculate the distance A′B′.

   Give your answer correct to 1 decimal place (do not consult tables).

Sol.

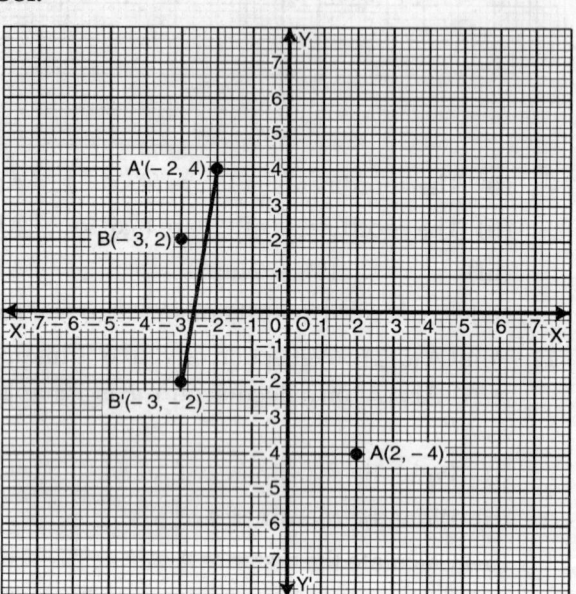

(i) Coordinates of A′ are (– 2, 4). **Ans.**

(ii) Coordinates of B′ are (– 3, – 2). **Ans.**

(iii) Distance A′B′ = $\sqrt{(-3+2)^2 + (-2-4)^2}$

$$= \sqrt{1 + 36}$$

$$= \sqrt{37}$$

$$= 6·1$$ **Ans.**

14. **(i)** Point P(*a*, *b*) reflected on the X-axis to P′(5, 2). Write down the value of *a* and *b*.

   (ii) P″ is the image of P when reflected on the Y-axis. Write down the coordinates of P″.

   (iii) Name a single transformation that maps P′ to P″.

Sol. (i) The value of *a* = 5 and *b* = – 2. **Ans.**

   (ii) Coordinates of P″ = (– 5, – 2). **Ans.**

   (iii) $(x, y) \rightarrow (-x, -y)$. **Ans.**

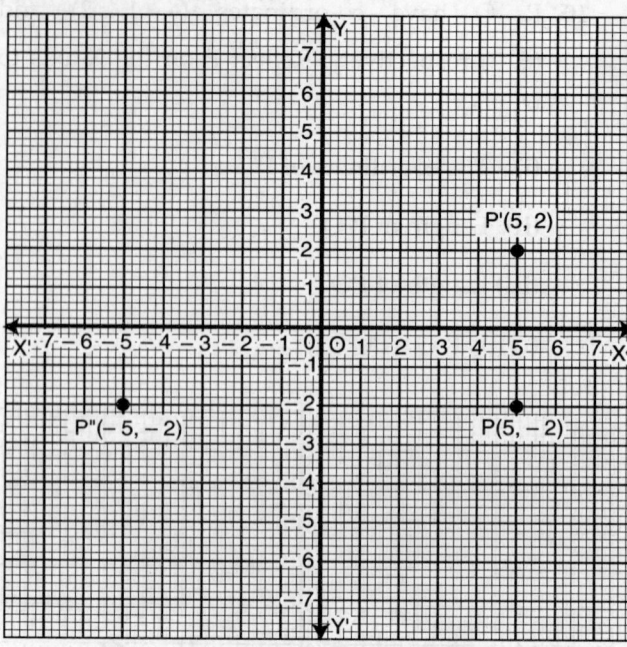

15. Points (3, 0) and (– 1, 0) are invariant points under reflection in the line L_1; point (0, – 3) and (0, 1) are invariant points on reflection in line L_2.

   (i) Write the equation of the line L_1 and L_2.

   (ii) Write down the images of points P(3, 4) and Q(– 5, – 2) on reflection in L_1. Name the images as P′ and Q′ respectively.

   (iii) Write down the images of P and Q on reflection in L_2. Name the images as P″ and Q″ respectively.

Sol. (i) (3, 0) and (– 1, 0) lies on X-axis, so these are invariant under reflection on the X-axis. Hence, L_1 lies on X-axis. So, equation of line L_1, is $y = 0$.

   (0, – 3) and (0, 1) lies on Y-axis, so these are invariant under reflection on the Y-axis. So, equation of line L_2 is $x = 0$. **Ans.**

   (ii) Coordinates of P′ are (3, – 4).

   Coordinates of Q′ are (– 5, 2). **Ans.**

   (iii) Coordinates of P″ are (– 3, 4).

   Coordinates of Q″ are (5, – 2). **Ans.**

16. A point P(*a*, *b*) is reflected in the X-axis to P′ (2, – 3). Write down the value of *a* and *b*. P″ is the image of P, when reflected on the Y-axis. Write down the coordinates of P″ when P is reflected in the line parallel to the Y-axis, such that $x = 4$.

Sol. Reflection of P (*a*, *b*) on the X-axis P′ (*a*, – *b*)

   (i) ∴ P′ (*a*, – *b*) = P′ (2, – 3)

$+a = +2, \therefore a = 2$

$-b = -3, \therefore b = 3$

P (2, 3)   **Ans.**

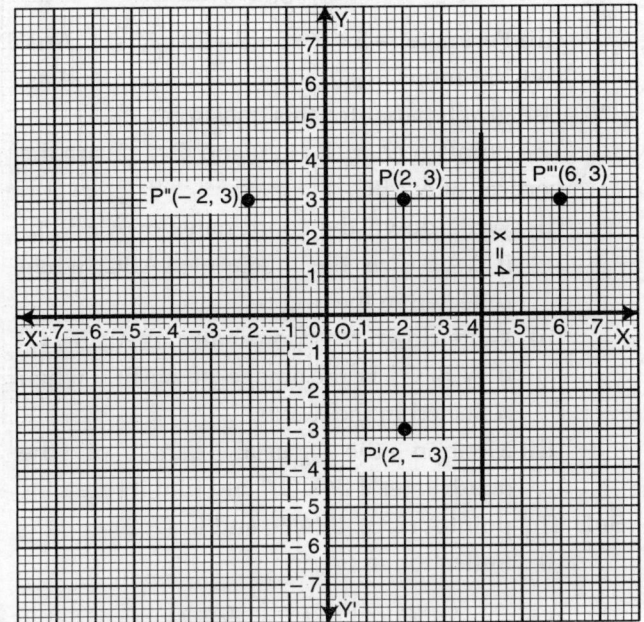

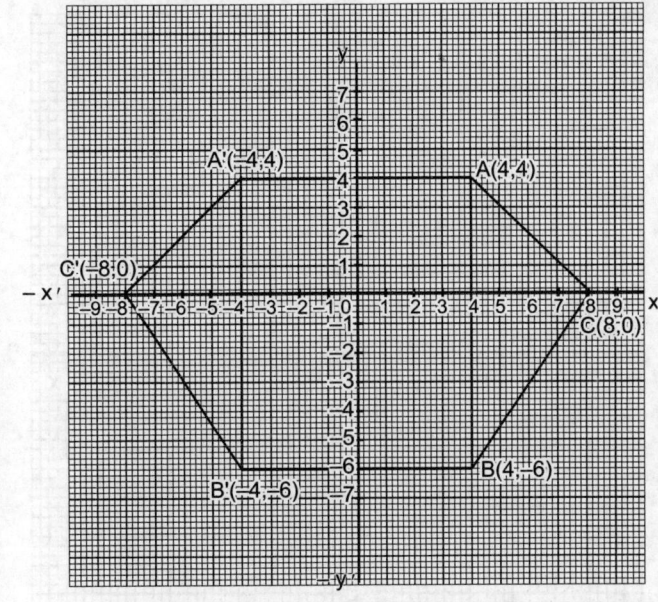

(ii) P″ is the image of P(2, 3) under reflection

Y-axis = P″(– 2, 3).   **Ans.**

(iii) P‴ is the image of P (2, 3) under reflection

$x = 4 \Rightarrow$ P‴(6, 3).   **Ans.**

17. Use a graph paper to answer the following questions (Take 1 cm = 1 unit on both axis) :

(i) Plot A (4, 4), B (4, – 6) and C (8, 0), the vertices of a triangle ABC.

(ii) Reflect ABC on the Y-axis and name it as A′B′C′.

(iii) Write the coordinates of the images A′, B′ and C′.

(iv) Give a geometrical name for the figure AA′C′B′BC.

(v) Identify the line of symmetry of AA′ C′ B′ BC.

Sol. (i) and **(ii)** see the given graph.

(iii) A′ (– 4, 4), B′ (– 4, – 6), C′ (– 8, 0)   **Ans.**

(iv) AA′ C′ B′ BC is a Hexagon.   **Ans.**

(v) Y-axis is the line of symmetry.   **Ans.**

18. Use a graph paper for this question. (Take 10 small divisions = 1 unit on both axis). P and Q have coordinates (0, 5) and (– 2, 4).

(i) P is invariant when reflected in an axis. Name the axis.

(ii) Find the image of Q on reflection in the axis found in (i).

(iii) (0, k) on reflection in the origin is invariant. Write the value of k.

(iv) Write the coordinates of the image of Q, obtained by reflecting it in the origin following by reflection in X-axis.

Sol. (i) The axis is Y-axis or $x = 0$.

(ii) Image of 'Q'

$Q' = M_{x=0} (-2, 4)$

$= (2, 4)$ **Ans.**

(iii) $M_0 (a, b) = (-a, -b)$

$\therefore$ $M_0 (0, k) = (0, -k)$

$k = -k$

$\therefore$ $2k = 0$

$\therefore$ $k = 0$ **Ans.**

(iv) $Q'' = M_x M_0 Q$

$= M_x M_0 (-2, 4)$

$= M_x (2, -4)$

$= (-2, -4)$ **Ans.**

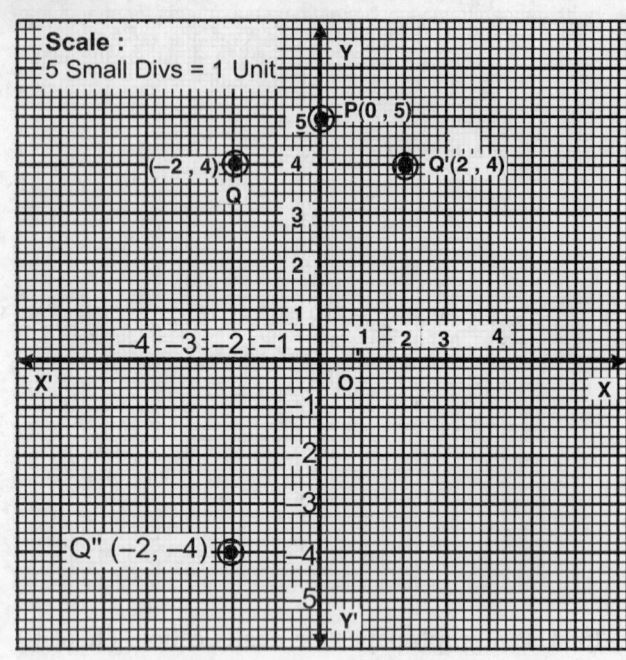

19. The point P(3, 4) is reflected to P′ in the X-axis and O′ is the image of O (the origin) in the line PP′. Find :

    (i)   The coordinates of P′ and O′.

    (ii) The length of segment PP′ and OO′.

    (iii) The perimeter of the quadrilateral POP′O′.

    (iv) What is the special name of the quadrilateral POP′O′.

Sol. (i) P′ (3, – 4), O′(6, 0)   **Ans.**

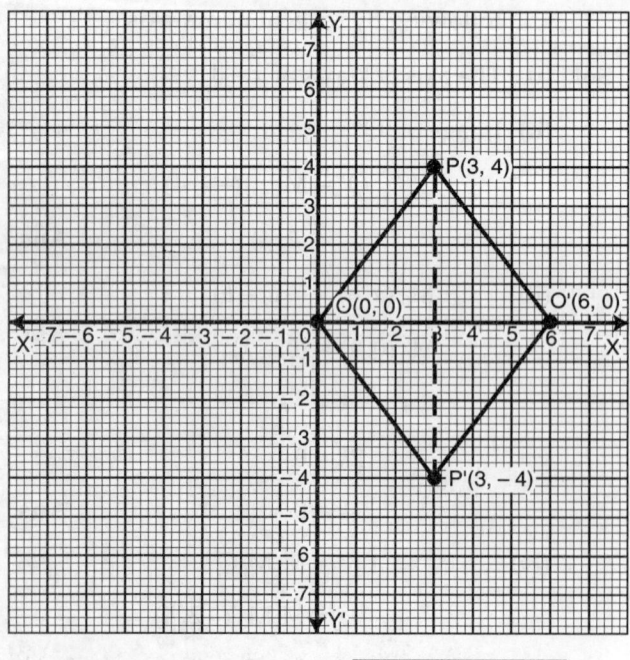

(ii) $PP' = \sqrt{(3-3)^2 + (-4-4)^2}$

$= \sqrt{64} = 8$ units.

$$OO' = \sqrt{(0-6)^2 + (0-0)^2}$$

$$= \sqrt{36} = 6 \text{ units.} \qquad \textbf{Ans.}$$

(iii) Perimeter = 5 + 5 + 5 + 5 = 20 units.   **Ans.**

(iv) Rhombus.   **Ans.**

20. Use graph paper for this question :

    The points A (2, 3), B (4, 5) and C (7, 2) are the vertices of Δ ABC.

    (i)   Write down the coordinates of A′, B′, C′ if ΔA′B′C′ is the image of ΔABC, when reflected in the origin.

    (ii) Write down the coordinates of A″, B″, C″ if A″B″C″ is the image of ΔABC, when reflected in the X-axis.

    (iii) Mention the special name of the quadrilateral BCC″B″ and find its area.

Sol. The point A (2, 3), B (4, 5) and C (7, 2).

(i) Reflection in origin

$$(x, y) \xrightarrow{\ \text{M}_0\ } = (-x, -y)$$

$$\therefore \ A (2, 3) \xrightarrow{\ \text{M}_0\ } = A' (-2, -3)$$

$$B (4, 5) \xrightarrow{\ \text{M}_0\ } = B' (-4, -5)$$

$$C (7, 2) \xrightarrow{\ \text{M}_0\ } = C' (-7, -2)$$

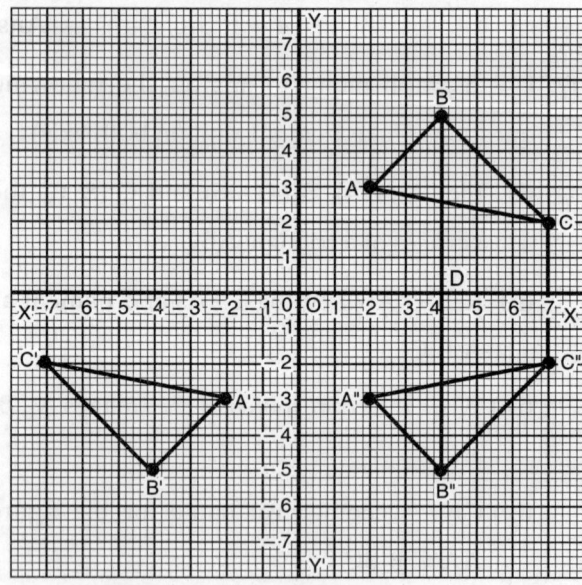

(ii) Now A, B, C is reflected in X-axis.

Reflection in X-axis

$$(x, y) \xrightarrow{\ \text{M}_x\ } = (x, -y)$$

$$\therefore \ A (2, 3) \xrightarrow{\ \text{M}_x\ } = A'' (2, -3)$$

$$B (4, 5) \xrightarrow{\ \text{M}_x\ } = B'' (4, -5)$$

$$C (7, 2) \xrightarrow{\ \text{M}_x\ } = C'' (7, -2) \qquad \textbf{Ans.}$$

(iii) BCC"B" is an isosceles trapezium.

Distance between its parallel sides

$$= 7 - 4 = 3$$

$$CC'' = 2 + 2 = 4$$

and $$BB'' = 5 + 5 = 10$$

Area of trapezium = $\frac{1}{2}$ (CC" + BB") × CD

$$= \frac{1}{2} (4 + 10) \times 3$$

$$= \frac{1}{2} \times 14 \times 3 = 21 \text{ sq. units}$$

Ans.

21. Use a graph paper for this question (take 10 small divisions = 1 unit on both axis).

Plot the points P (3, 2) and Q (–3, –2), from P and Q draw perpendicular PM and QN on the X-axis.

(i) Name the image of P on reflection at the origin.

(ii) Assign, the special name to the geometrical figure. PMQN and find its area.

(iii) Write the coordinates of the point to which M is mapped on reflection in (a) X-axis, (b) Y-axis, (c) origin.

Sol.

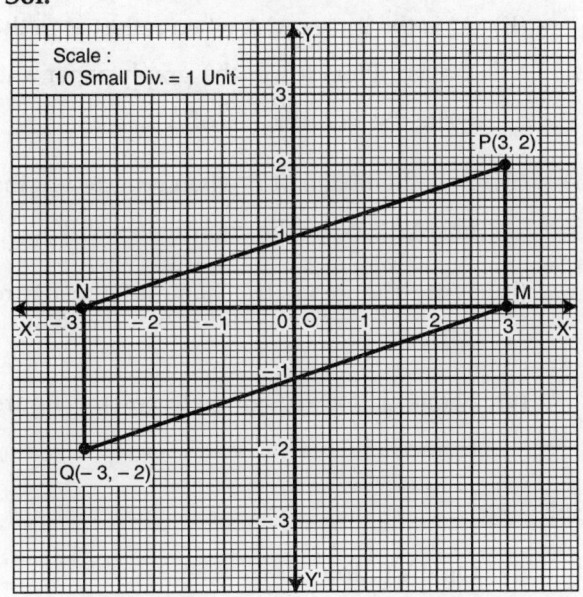

In the graph paper

(i) Q (– 3, – 2)   **Ans.**

(ii) Parallelogram.

Area of Δ PMN= $\frac{1}{2}$ PM × MN

$$= \frac{1}{2} \times 2 \times 6 = 6 \text{ sq. unit}$$

∴   Area of PMQN = 2 × Δ PMN

$$= 2 \times 6$$

$$= 12 \text{ sq. units} \qquad \textbf{Ans.}$$

(iii) Co-ordinates of M (3, 0)

(a) (3, 0), (b) (–3, 0), (c) (–3, 0)   **Ans.**

22. Using graph paper and taking 1 cm = 1 unit along both X-axis and Y-axis.

(i) Plot the points A (– 4, 4) and B (2, 2).

(ii) Reflect A and B in the origin to get the images A′ and B′ respectively.

(iii) Write down the coordinates of A ′ and B′.

(iv) Give the geometrical name for the figure ABA′B′.

(v) Draw and name its lines of symmetry.

Sol. (i), (ii) (In the graph paper)

(iii) A′ (4, – 4) and B′ (– 2, – 2)

(iv) Rhombus

(v) AA′ and BB′.

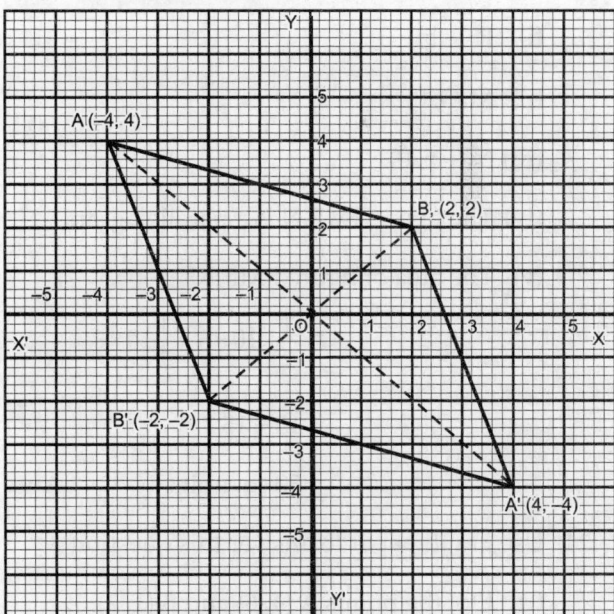

23. Use graph paper for this question.

The point P (5, 3) was reflected in the origin to get the image P′.

(i) Write down the coordinates of P′.

(ii) If M is the foot of the perpendicular form of P to the X-axis, find the coordinates of M.

(iii) If N is the foot of the perpendicular form of P′ to the X-axis, find the coordinates of N.

(iv) Name the figure PMP′N.

(v) Find the area of the figure PMP′N.

Sol.

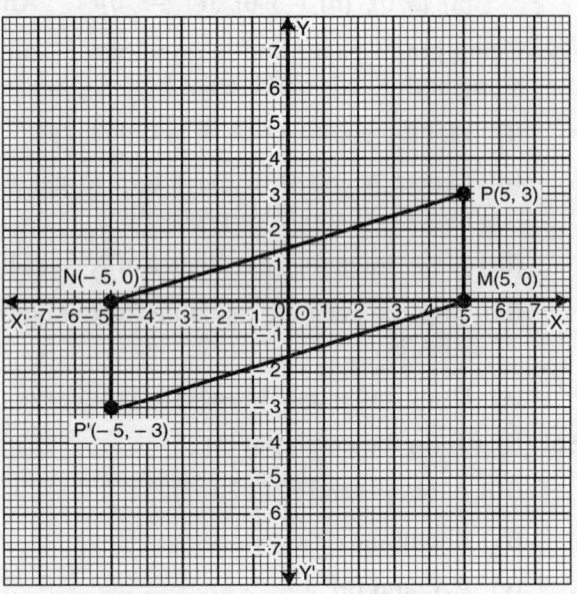

(i) P′ (– 5, – 3).

(ii) M (5, 0).

(iii) N (– 5, 0).

(iv) The figure PMP′N is a parallelogram.

(v) The area of figure PMP′N

$$= \frac{1}{2} \times 10 \times 3 + \frac{1}{2} 10 \times 3$$

$$= 15 + 15$$

$$= 30 \text{ sq. units.} \qquad \textbf{Ans.}$$

24. Use graph paper to answer this question :

(i) Plot the points A (4, 6) and B (1, 2).

(ii) A′ is the image of A when reflected in X-axis.

(iii) B′ is the image of B when B is reflected in the line AA′.

(iv) Give the geometrical name for the figure AB A′B′.

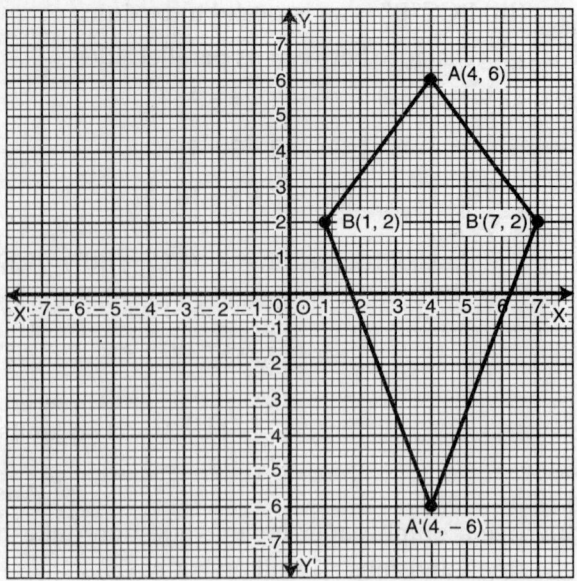

Sol. (i) In the graph paper.

(ii) A (4, 6) → A′ (4, – 6)

(iii) B (1, 2) → B′ (7, 2)

(iv) ABA′B′ is a kite.   **Ans.**

25. Use graph paper to answer the following questions. (Take 2 cm = 1 unit on both axis).

(i) Plot the points A (– 4, 2) and B (2, 4).

(ii) A′ is the image of A when reflected in the Y-axis. Plot it on the graph paper and write the coordinates of A′.

(iii) B′ is the image of B when reflected in the line AA′. Write the coordinates of B′.

(iv) Write the geometric name of the figure ABA′B′.

(v) Name a line of symmetry of the figure formed.

Sol.

(i) On the graph.

(ii) Coordinates of A′ = (4, 2).

(iii) Coordinates of B′ = (2, 0).

(iv) Geometric name of figure ABA′B′ is Kite.

(v) Line of symmetry = AA′.

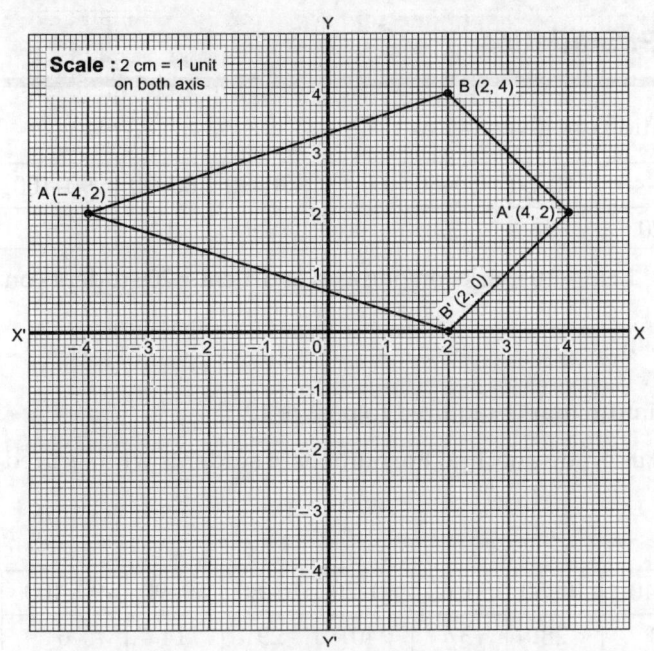

26. Use graph paper for this question.

(Take 1 cm = 1 unit along both X and Y axis).

Plot the points O (0, 0), A (– 4, 4), B (–3, 0) and C (0, – 3).

(i) Reflect points A and B on the Y-axis and name them A′ and B′ respectively. Write down their coordinates.

(ii) Name the figure OABCB′A′.

(iii) State the line of symmetry of this figure.

Sol. (i) Coordinates of A′ = (4, 4)

Coordinates of B′ = (3, 0)

(ii) Hexagon

(iii) The line of symmetry of this figure is Y-axis.

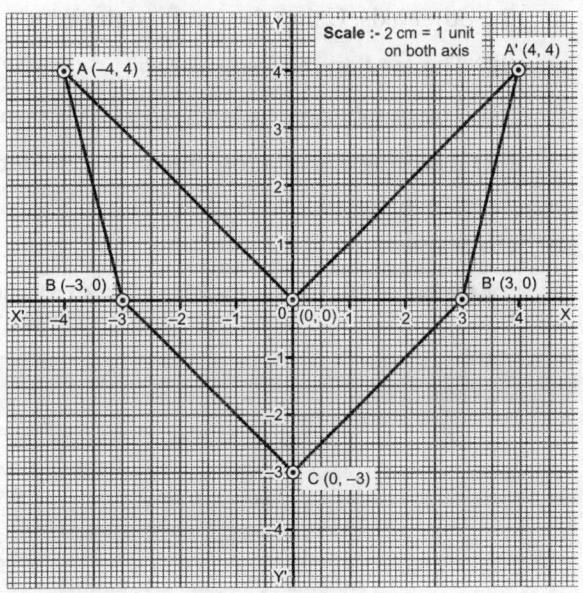

Chapter 14. Loci

1. Use graph paper for this question. Take 2 cm = 1 unit on both axes.

(i) Plot the points A (1, 1), B (5, 3) and C (2, 7);

(ii) Construct the locus of points equidistant from A and B;

(iii) Construct the locus of points equidistant from AB and AC;

(iv) Locate the point P such that PA = PB and P is equidistant from AB and AC;

(v) Measure and record the length PA in cm.

Sol. (i) Plot the points A (1, 1), B (5, 3) and C (2, 7) as shown.

(ii) Join AB. Draw right bisector *l* of AB. Then, *l* is the locus of points equidistant from A and B.

(iii) Join AC. Draw bisector *m* of ∠CAB. Then, *m* is the locus of the points equidistant from AB and AC.

(iv) The point of intersection P of right bisector of AB and angle bisector of ∠CAB is the point such that PA = PB and P is equidistant from AB and AC.

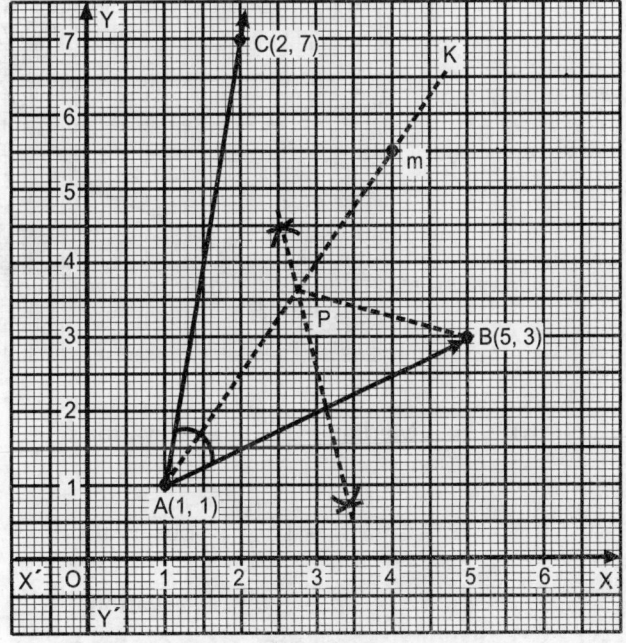

(v) On measuring PA = 2·5 cm. **Ans.**

Chapter 19. Statistics

1. Marks obtained by 200 students in an examination are given below :

Marks	0–10	10–20	20–30	30–40	40–50	50–60	60–70	70–80	80–90	90–100
Frequency	5	11	10	20	28	37	40	29	14	6

Draw an ogive for the given distribution taking 1 cm = 10 marks on one axis and 1 cm = 20 students on the other axis. Using the graph, determine :

(i) The median marks.

(ii) The number of students who failed if minimum marks required to pass is 40.

(iii) If scoring 85 and more marks is considered as grade one, find the number of students who secured grade one in the examination.

Sol. On graph

Marks	0–10	10–20	20–30	30–40	40–50	50–60	60–70	70–80	80–90	90–100
f	5	11	10	20	28	37	40	29	14	6
$c.f.$	5	16	26	46	74	111	151	180	194	200

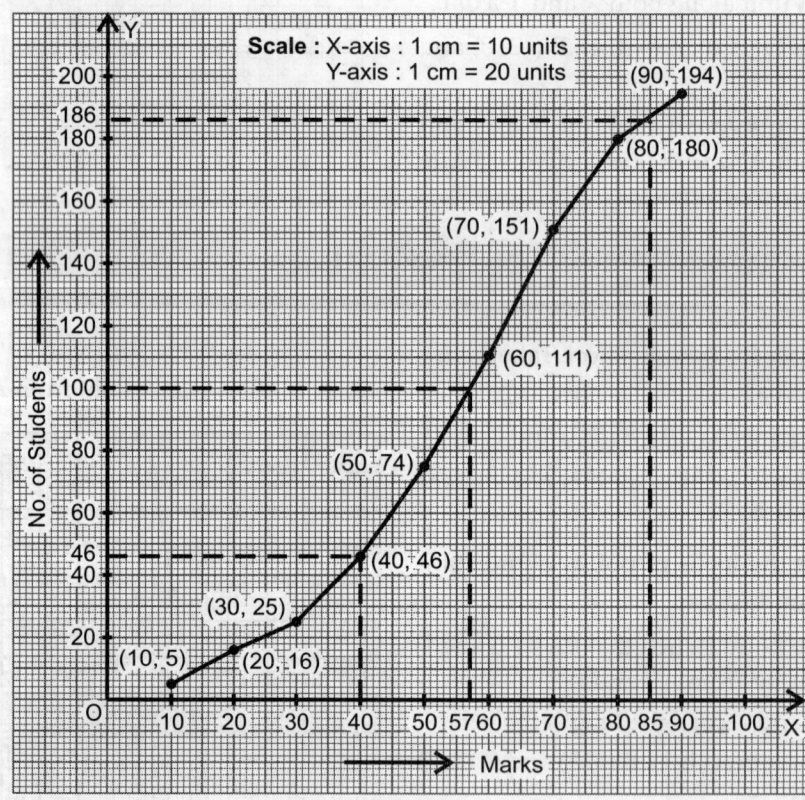

(i)

$$\text{Median} = \left(\frac{n}{2}\right)^{th} \text{observation}$$

$$= \left(\frac{200}{2}\right)^{th} \text{observation}$$

$$= 100^{th} \text{ observation}$$

$$= 57 \qquad \textbf{Ans.}$$

(ii) No. of students who failed = 46   **Ans.**

(iii) No. of students who secured grade one =
200 – 186 = 14 **Ans.**

2. Draw a histogram from the following frequency distribution and find the mode from the graph :

Class	Frequency
0 – 5	2
5 – 10	5
10 – 15	18
15 – 20	14
20 – 25	8
25 – 30	5

Sol.

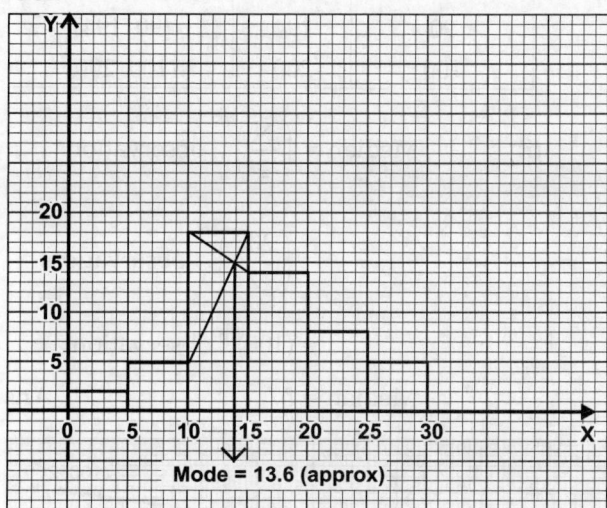

Mode = 13·6 **Ans.**

3. Use Graph paper for this question.*

A survey regarding height (in cm) of 60 boys belonging to Class 10 of a school was conducted. The following data was recorded :

Height in cm	No. of boys
135 – 140	4
140 – 145	8
145 – 150	20
150 – 155	14
155 – 160	7
160 – 165	6
165 – 170	1

Taking 2 cm = height of 10 cm along one axis and 2 cm =10 boys along the other axis draw an ogive of the above distribution. Use the graph to estimate the following :

(i) the median

(ii) lower quartile

(iii) if above 158 cm is considered as the tall boys of the class. Find the number of boys in the class who are tall.

Sol.

Height in cm	No. of Boys	c.f.
135 – 140	4	4
140 – 145	8	12
145 – 150	20	32
150 – 155	14	46
155 – 160	7	53
160 – 165	6	59
165 – 170	1	60
	n = 60	

(i) Median = $\frac{n}{2}$ th observation

$= \frac{60}{2}$ th observation

= 30th observation

= 150 cm (from ogive) **Ans.**

(ii) Lower quartile = $\frac{n}{4}$ th observation

$= \frac{60}{4}$ th observation

= 15th observation

= 146 cm (from ogive) **Ans.**

(iii) No. of boys whose height is less than 158 cm = 51. (from ogive)

∴ No. of tall boys = 60 – 51 = 9. **Ans.**

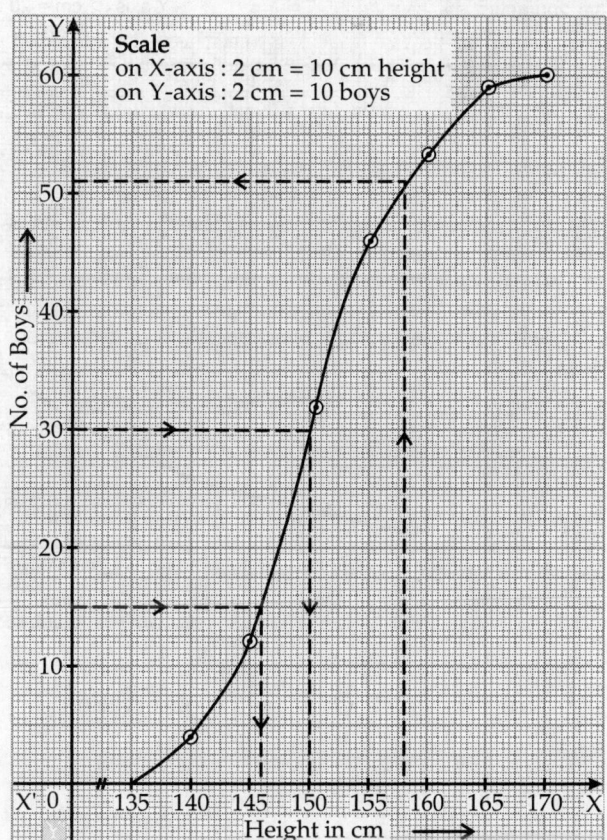

Scale
on X-axis : 2 cm = 10 cm height
on Y-axis : 2 cm = 10 boys

No. of Boys

Height in cm

---

* **Frequently asked previous years Board Exam Questions.**

4. The marks obtained by 200 students in an examination are given below :

Marks	Number of students
0–10	5
10–20	10
20–30	11
30–40	20
40–50	27
50–60	38
60–70	40
70–80	29
80–90	14
90–100	6

Using a graph paper, draw an ogive for the above distribution. Use your ogive to estimate :

(i) the median;

(ii) the lower quartile;

(iii) the number of students who obtained more than 80% marks in the examination and

(iv) the number of students who did not pass, if the pass percentage was 35.

Use the scale as 2 cm = 10 marks on one axis and 2 cm = 20 students on the other axis.

Sol.

Less than	c. f.	Points
10	5	(10, 5)
20	15	(20, 15)
30	26	(30, 26)
40	46	(40, 46)
50	73	(50, 73)
60	111	(60, 111)
70	151	(70, 151)
80	180	(80, 180)
90	194	(90, 194)
100	200	(100, 200)

(i)
$$\text{Median} = \left(\frac{N}{2}\right)^{th} \text{ observation}$$

$$= \left(\frac{200}{2}\right)^{th} \text{ observation}$$

$$= (100)^{th} \text{ observation}$$

Median = 57 **Ans.**

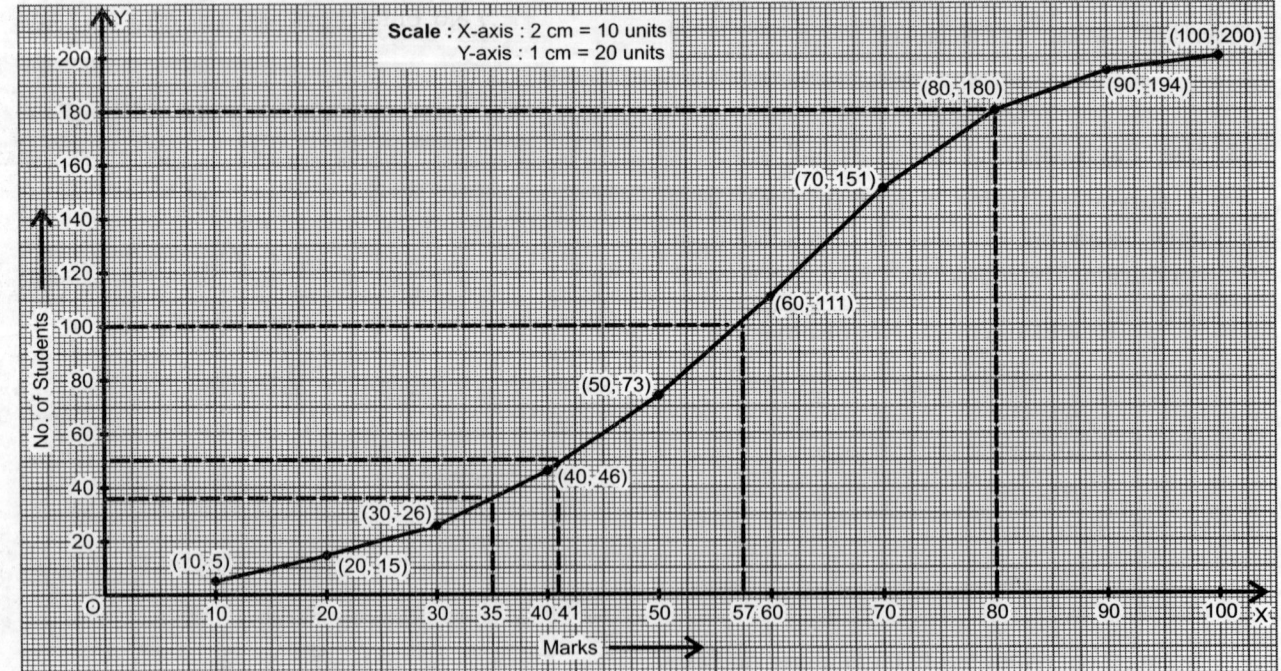

Scale : X-axis : 2 cm = 10 units
Y-axis : 1 cm = 20 units

(ii)
$$Q_1 = \left(\frac{N}{4}\right)^{th} \text{ observation}$$

$$= \left(\frac{200}{4}\right)^{th} \text{ observation}$$

$$= (50)^{th} \text{ observation}$$

$$= 41 \qquad \textbf{Ans.}$$

(iii) 200 – 180 = 20 students **Ans.**

(iv) 35 students did not pass. **Ans.**

5. The monthly income of a group of 320 employees in a company is given below :

Monthly	No. of Employees
6000–7000	20
7000–8000	45
8000–9000	65
9000–10000	95
10000–11000	60
11000–12000	30
12000–13000	5

Draw an ogive of the given distribution on a graph sheet taking 2 cm = ₹ 1000 on one axis and 2 cm = 50 employees on the other axis. From the graph determine :

(i) the median wage

(ii) the number of employees whose income is below ₹ 8,500.

(iii) If the salary of a senior employee is above ₹ 11,500, find the number of senior employees in the company.

(iv) the upper quartile.

Sol.

Monthly	No. of Employees	c.f.
6000–7000	20	20
7000–8000	45	65
8000–9000	65	130
9000–10000	95	225
10000–11000	60	285
11000–12000	30	315
12000–13000	5	320

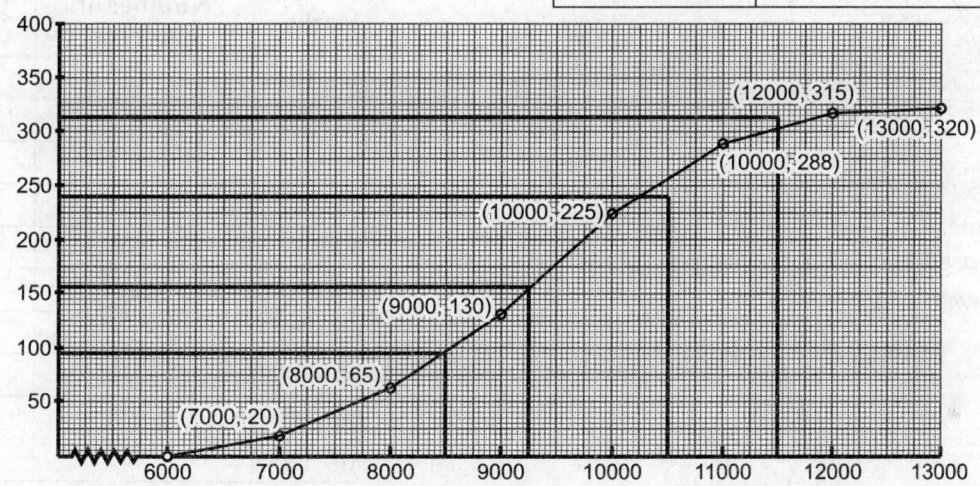

(i) From the graph, the median wage = 160·5 (approx.) **Ans.**

(ii) The number of employees whose income is below ₹ 8,500 = 90 (approx.) **Ans.**

(iii) The number of senior employees whose salary is above ₹ 11,500 = 20 (approx.) **Ans.**

(iv) The upper quartile Q_3 = 240 (approx.) **Ans.**

6. 40 students enter for a game of shot-put competition. The distance thrown (in metres) is recorded below :*

Distance in m	Number of Students
12 – 13	3
13 – 14	9
14 – 15	12
15 – 16	9
16 – 17	4

17 – 18	2
18 – 19	1

Use a graph paper to draw an ogive for the above distribution.

Use a scale of 2 cm = 1 m on one axis and 2 cm = 5 students on the other axis.

Hence using your graph find :

(i) the median

(ii) Upper Quartile

(iii) Number of students who cover a distance which is above $16\frac{1}{2}$ m.

Sol.

Distance in m	Frequency (f)	c.f.
12 – 13	3	3
13 – 14	9	12
14 – 15	12	24

15 – 16	9	33
16 – 17	4	37
17 – 18	2	39
18 – 19	1	40

20 – 30	16
30 – 40	22
40 – 50	26
50 – 60	18
60 – 70	11
70 – 80	6
80 – 90	4
90 – 100	3

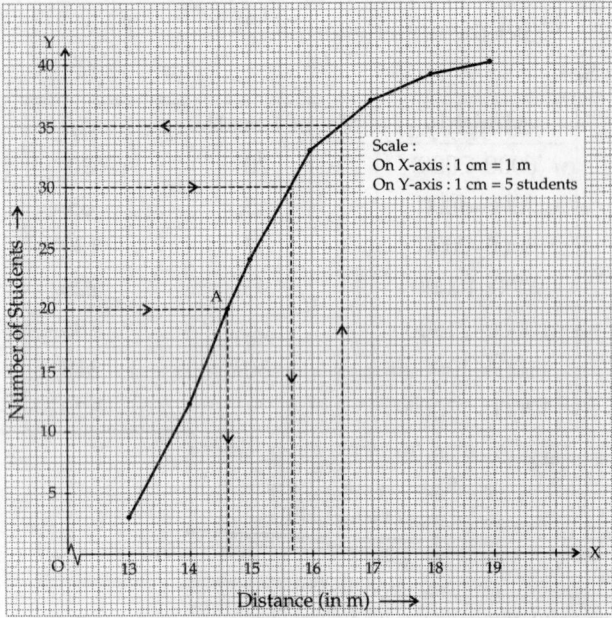

Scale :
On X-axis : 1 cm = 1 m
On Y-axis : 1 cm = 5 students

Note : Instead of 2 cm = 1 m and 2 cm = 5 students, we have used 1 cm = 1 m and 1 cm = 5 students on X and Y axes, respectively.

(i) $\quad$ Median $= \left(\dfrac{N}{2}\right)^{th}$ term

$\quad\quad\quad\quad\quad = \left(\dfrac{40}{2}\right)^{th}$ term

$\quad\quad\quad\quad\quad =$ 20th term

On the graph, through a point 20 on y-axis, draw a horizontal line which meets the ogive at point A. Through A, draw a vertical line which meets the x-axis at 14.7.

∴ $\quad\quad\quad$ Median = 14.7 $\quad\quad\quad\quad$ **Ans.**

(ii) Upper quartile $(Q_3) = \left(\dfrac{3N}{4}\right)^{th}$ term

$\quad\quad\quad\quad\quad = \left(\dfrac{3 \times 40}{4}\right)^{th}$ term

$\quad\quad\quad\quad\quad =$ 30th term

$\quad\quad\quad\quad\quad =$ 15.7 $\quad\quad\quad\quad$ **Ans.**

(iii) Number of students who cover more than $16\dfrac{1}{2}$ m $= 40 - 35 = 5$ $\quad\quad$ **Ans.**

7. Use graph paper for this question.

The marks obtained by 120 students in an English test are given below :*

Marks	Number of students
0 – 10	5
10 – 20	9

Draw the ogive and hence, estimate :
(i) the median marks.
(ii) the number of students who did not pass test if the pass percentage was 50.
(iii) the upper quartile marks.

Sol.

Marks	Number of students	Cumulative frequency
0 – 10	5	5
10 – 20	9	14
20 – 30	16	30
30 – 40	22	52
40 – 50	26	78
50 – 60	18	96
60 – 70	11	107
70 – 80	6	113
80 – 90	4	117
90 – 100	3	120

$\Rightarrow \quad\quad\quad\quad N = 120$

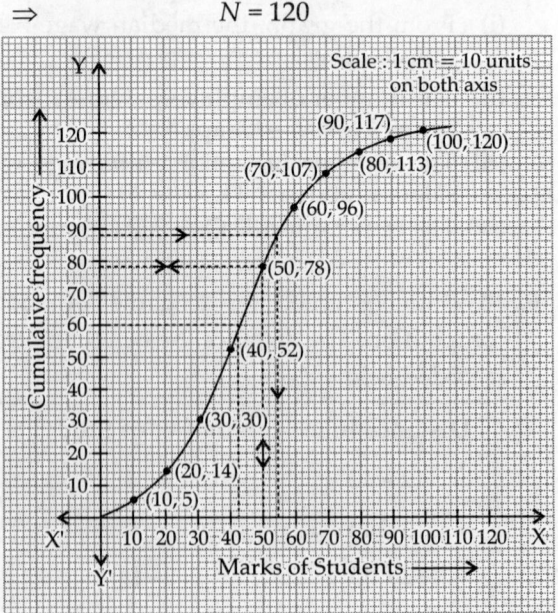

Scale : 1 cm = 10 units on both axis

(i) $\quad$ Median marks $= \dfrac{N}{2}$ th observation

$\quad\quad\quad\quad\quad = \dfrac{120}{2}$ th observation

= 60th observation

= 43 (from ogive)   **Ans.**

(ii) Number of students who did not pass

= 78 (from ogive)   **Ans.**

(iii) Upper quartile = $\dfrac{3N}{4}$ th observation

= $\dfrac{3 \times 120}{4}$ th observation

= 90th observation

= 56 (from ogive)   **Ans.**

8. Attempt this question on graph paper. Marks obtained by 200 students in examination are given below:

Marks	0–10	10–20	20–30	30–40	40–50	50–60	60–70	70–80	80–90	90–100
No. of students	5	10	14	21	25	34	36	27	16	12

Draw an ogive for the given distribution taking 1 cm = 10 marks on one axis and 1 cm = 20 students on the other axis.

From the graph find :

(i) the median

(ii) the upper quartile

(iii) number of student scoring above 65 marks.

Sol.

Marks	No. of Students	c.f.	Points
0–10	5	5	(10, 5)
10–20	10	15	(20, 15)
20–30	14	29	(30, 29)
30–40	21	50	(40, 50)
40–50	25	75	(50, 75)
50–60	34	109	(60, 109)
60–70	36	145	(70, 145)
70–80	27	172	(80, 172)
80–90	16	188	(90, 188)
90–100	12	200	(100, 200)
	n = 200		

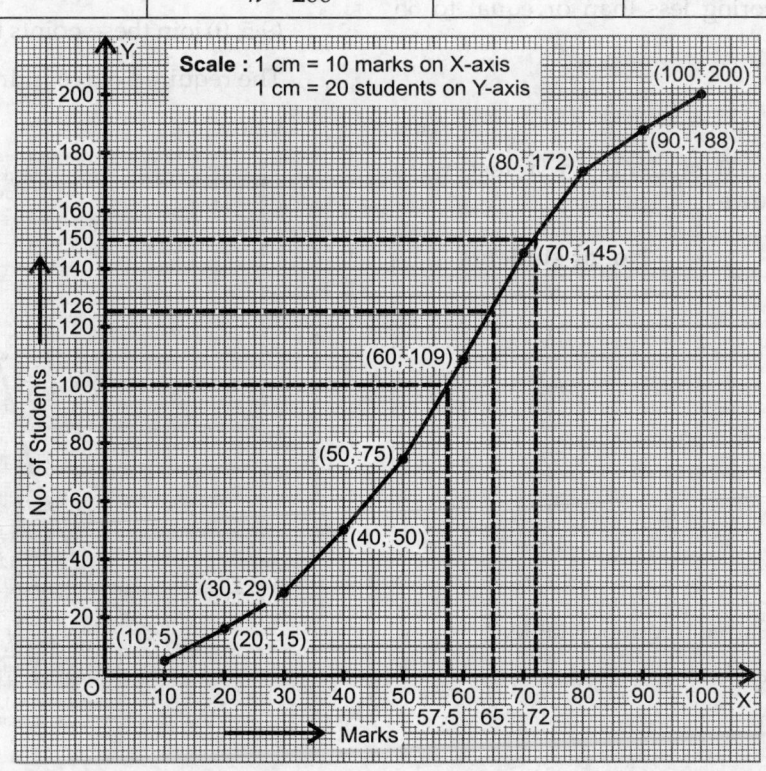

(i) Let A be the point on Y-axis representing frequency.

Here, n (no. of students) = 200 (even)

$$\text{Median} = \left(\frac{n}{2}\right)^{th} \text{term}$$

$$\therefore \quad \text{Median} = \left(\frac{200}{2}\right)^{th} \text{term}$$

$$= 100^{th} \text{term}$$

From the graph 100th term = 57·5

$$\therefore \quad \text{Median} = 57\cdot5 \qquad \textbf{Ans.}$$

(ii) Upper quartile $= \left(\frac{3n}{4}\right)^{th}$ term

$$= \left(\frac{3 \times 200}{4}\right)^{th} \text{term}$$

$$= \left(\frac{600}{4}\right)^{th} \text{term}$$

$$= 150^{th} \text{term}$$

From graph 150th term = 72

Upper quartile= 72   **Ans.**

(iii) No. of students scoring above 65 marks = Total number of students – Number of students scoring less than or equal to 65 marks

$$= 200 - 126$$

$$= 74 \text{ (approx.)} \qquad \textbf{Ans.}$$

9. The marks of 200 students in a test were recorded as follows :

Marks %	No. of students
10–19	7
20–29	11
30–39	20
40–49	46
50–59	57
60–69	37
70–79	15
80–89	7

Draw the cumulative frequency table.

Draw an ogive and use it to find :

(i) The median

(ii) The number of students who scored more than 35% marks.

Sol. The given frequency distribution is discontinuous, to convert it into continuous distribution.

Adjustment factor $= \dfrac{20-19}{2} = 0\cdot5.$

Cumulative (continuous) frequency table for the given data is :

Marks % (Classes before adjustment)	Marks % (Classes after adjustment)	Frequency	Cumulative frequency
10–19	9·5–19·5	7	7
20–29	19·5–29·5	11	18
30–39	29·5–39·5	20	38
40–49	39·5–49·5	46	84
50–59	49·5–59·5	57	141
60–69	59·5–69·5	37	178
70–79	69·5–79·5	15	193
80–89	79·5–89·5	7	200

Take 1 cm along X-axis = 10% marks and 1 cm along Y-axis = 25 students.

Plot the points (19·5, 7), (29·5, 18), (39·5, 38), (49·5, 84), (59·5, 141), (69·5, 178), (79·5, 193), (89·5, 200) and (9·5, 0) join these points by a free hand drawing.

The required ogive is drawn in the figure given below :

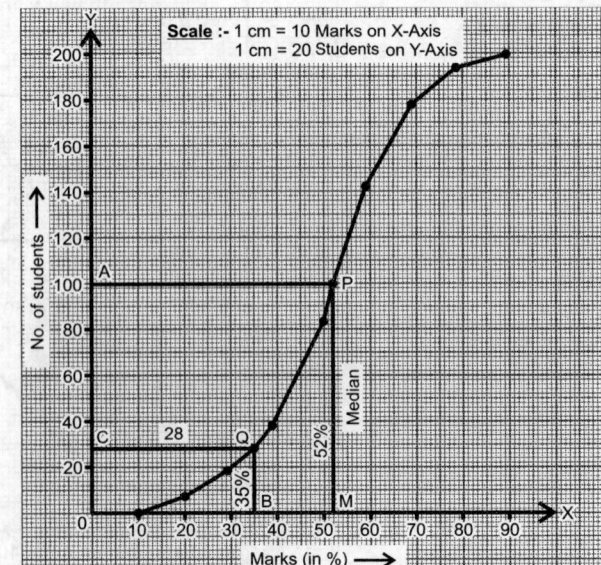

(i) To find the median : Let A be a point on Y-axis representing frequency

$$= \left(\frac{n}{2}\right)^{th} \text{ term}$$

$$= \left(\frac{200}{2}\right)^{th} \text{ term}$$

$$= 100^{th} \text{ term}$$

Through A draw a horizontal line to meet the ogive at P. Through P draw a vertical line to meet X-axis at M. The abscissae of point M represents 52%.

∴ The required median = 52%.   **Ans.**

(ii) Let the point B on X-axis represent 35% marks. Through B draw a vertical line to meet the ogive at Q. Through Q draw a horizontal line to meet Y-axis at C. The ordinate of the point C represents 28 students on Y-axis.

∴ The number of students who scored more than 35% marks = total no. of students – no. of students who scored less than or equal to 35%

$$= 200 - 28$$
$$= 172. \qquad \textbf{Ans.}$$

10. Following table present educational level (middle stage) of females in Arunachal Pradesh according to 1981 census :

Age group	Number of females (to the nearest ten)
10–14	300
15–19	980
20–24	800
25–29	380
30–34	290

Draw a histogram to represent the above data.

Sol. Let us convert the given class intervals into continuous class intervals. Then the given frequency distribution takes the form :

Age group	Number of females (to the nearest ten)
9·5–14·5	300
14·5–19·5	980
19·5–24·5	800
24·5–29·5	380
29·5–34·5	290

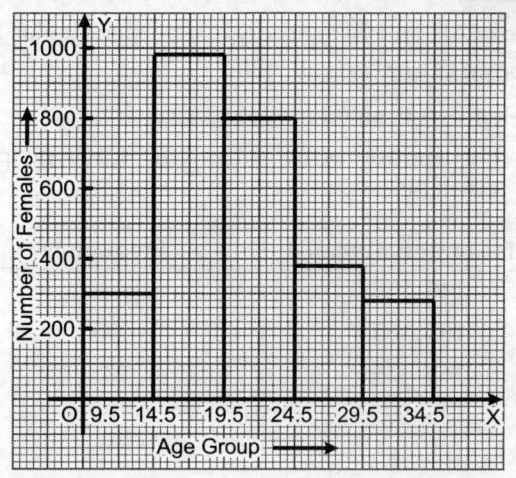

Ans.

11. Draw a histogram for the given data, using a graph paper :*

Weekly Wages (in ₹)	No. of People
3000–4000	4
4000–5000	9
5000–6000	18
6000–7000	6
7000–8000	7
8000–9000	2
9000–10000	4

Estimate the mode from the graph.

Sol.

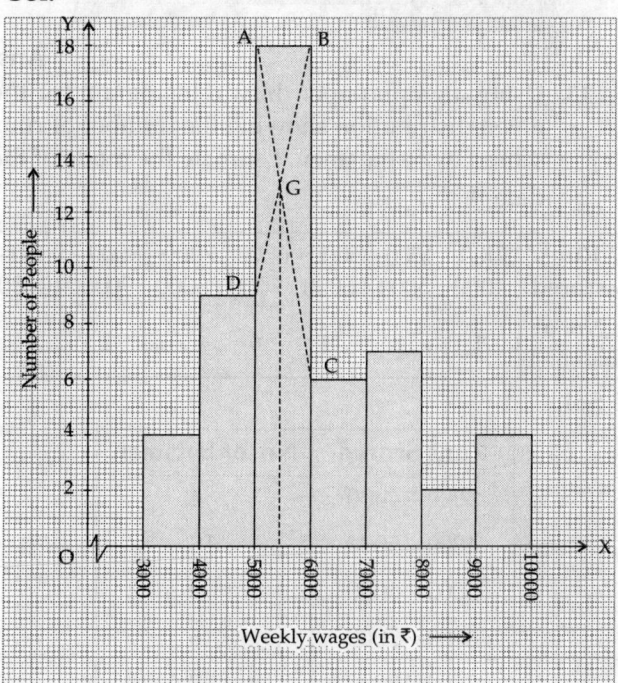

We have, maximum frequency = 18

∴   Modal class = 5000 – 6000

---

* Frequently asked previous years Board Exam Questions.

Join AC and BD and draw a perpendicular from point G to X-axis at 5450.

Hence, estimated mode is 5450. **Ans.**

12. Distribution of height in cm of 100 people is given below :

Class interval (cm)	Frequency
145–155	3
155–165	35
165–175	25
175–185	15
185–195	20
195–205	2

Draw a histogram to represent the above data.

Sol.

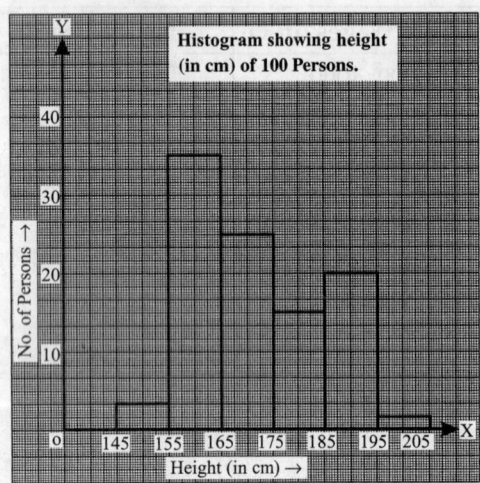

Histogram showing height (in cm) of 100 Persons.

Ans.

13. Using a graph paper draw a histogram for the given distribution showing the number of runs scored by 50 batsmen. Estimate the mode of the data :*

Runs scored	3000–4000	4000–5000	5000–6000	6000–7000	7000–8000	8000–9000	9000–10000
No. of batsmen	4	18	9	6	7	2	4

Sol.

Runs Scored	No. of batsmen
3000 – 4000	4
4000 – 5000	18
5000 – 6000	9
6000 – 7000	6
7000 – 8000	7
8000 – 9000	2
9000 – 10000	4

Frequently asked previous years Board Exam Questions.

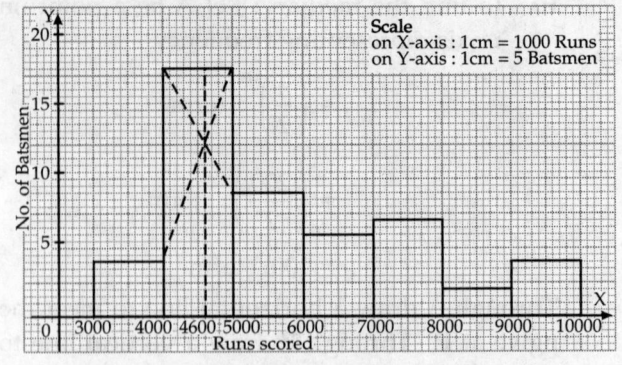

Scale
on X-axis : 1cm = 1000 Runs
on Y-axis : 1cm = 5 Batsmen

∴ Mode = 4600 **Ans.**

14. The time taken, in seconds, to solve a problem for each of 25 persons is as follows :

16	20	26	27	28
30	33	37	38	40
42	43	46	46	47
48	49	50	53	58
59	60	64	52	20

(i) Construct a frequency distribution for these data using a class internal of 10 seconds.

(ii) In a school the weekly pocket money of 50 students is as follows :

Weekly pocket money (₹)	No. of student
40–50	2
50–60	8
60–70	12
70–80	14
80–90	8
90–100	6

Draw a histogram and a frequency polygon on the same graph. Find mode from the graph.

Sol. (i) Frequency table

Time (in second)	Tally marks	Frequency
10–20	I	1
20–30	ꜰꜰꜰ	5
30–40	IIII	4
40–50	ꜰꜰꜰ III	8
50–60	ꜰꜰꜰ	5
60–70	II	2

Histogram representing the time taken in second, to solve. A problem for each of 25 persons.

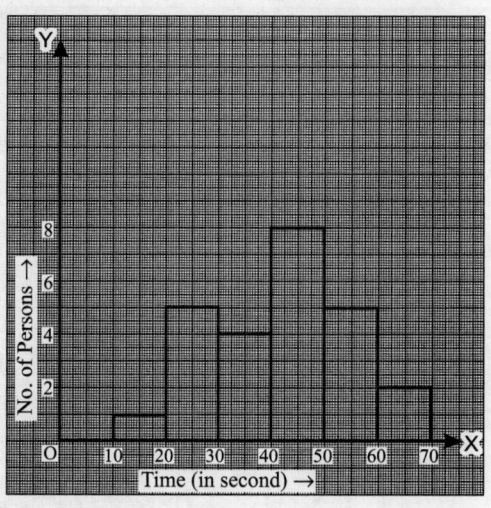

Ans.

(ii) Frequency distribution table is

Weekly pocket money (in ₹)	Class Marks	No. of Students
40–50	45	2
50–60	55	8
60–70	65	12
70–80	75	14
80–90	85	8
90–100	95	6

Draw the histogram and frequency polygon on the graph.

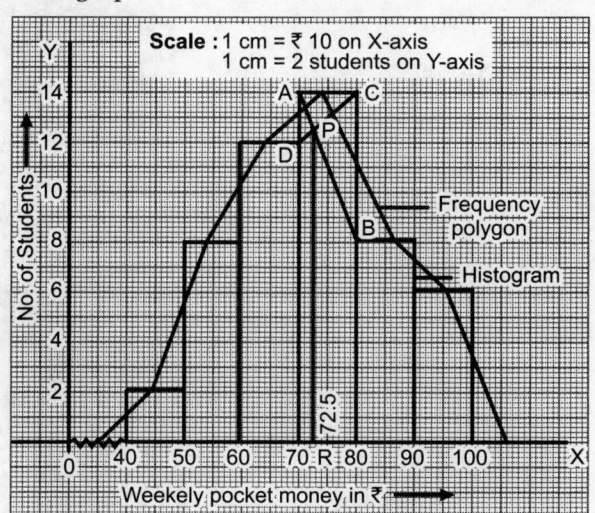

Now, in the highest rectangle, draw two straight line AB and CD from the corners of the rectangle on either sides of the highest rectangle to opposite corners of the highest rectangle. They intersect at P. Draw PR perpendicular to X-axis, then abscissa of the point prepresents ₹ 72·5.

Hence, the required mode is ₹ 72·5. **Ans.**

15. Using a graph paper, drawn an ogive for the following distribution which shows a record of the weight in kilograms of 200 students.

Weight	Frequency
40–45	5
45–50	17
50–55	22
55–60	45
60–65	51
65–70	31
70–75	20
75–80	9

Use your ogive to estimate the following :

(i) The percentage of students weighing 55 kg or more.

(ii) The weight above which the heaviest 30% of the students fall.

(iii) The number of students who are :

(1) under-weight and

(2) over-weight, if 55·70 kg is considered as standard weight.

Sol.

Weight	Frequency	c.f.
40–45	5	5
45–50	17	22
50–55	22	44
55–60	45	89
60–65	51	140
65–70	31	171
70–75	20	191
75–80	9	200

(i) Number of student weighing 55 kg or more

$$= 200 - 44 = 156$$

$$\therefore \quad \text{Percentage} = \frac{156 \times 100}{200}$$

$$= 78\% \qquad \textbf{Ans.}$$

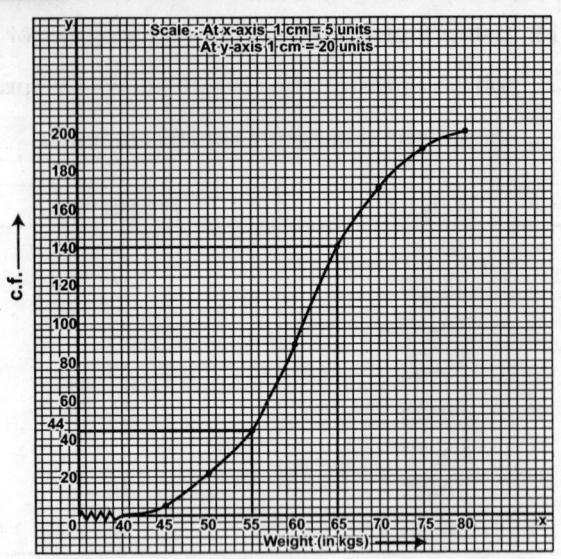

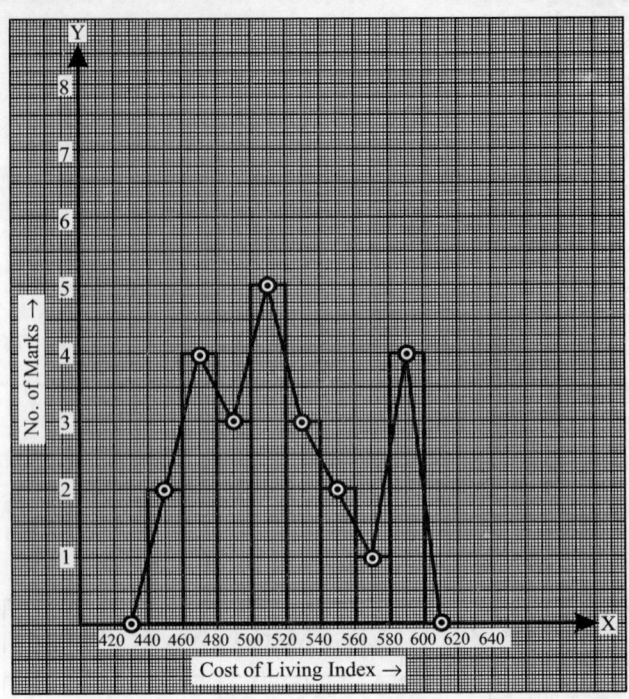

(ii) 30% of 200 = 60

∴   Heaviest wt. (least)

$$= (200 - 60)^{th} \text{ student}$$

$$= 140^{th} \text{ student}$$

$$= 65 \text{ kg or more} \qquad \textbf{Ans.}$$

(iii)   From ogive *c.f* against 55·70 kg = 45

∴   **(1)** number of under weight students = 44

Ans.

(2) number of over-weight students

$$= 200 - 44$$

$$= 156 \qquad \textbf{Ans.}$$

16. Draw a histogram and frequency polygon to represent the following data (on the same scale) which shows the monthly cost of living index of a city in a period of 2 years :

Cost of living index	Number of months
440–460	2
460–480	4
480–500	3
500–520	5
520–540	3
540–560	2
560–580	1
580–600	4
Total	24

Sol. Histogram and frequency polygon representing the cost of living index of city in a period of 2 years :

Ans.

17. Draw the histogram for the following frequency distribution and hence estimate the mode for the distribution :

Class	Frequency
0–5	2
5–10	7
10–15	18
15–20	10
20–25	8
25–30	5
Total	24

Sol.

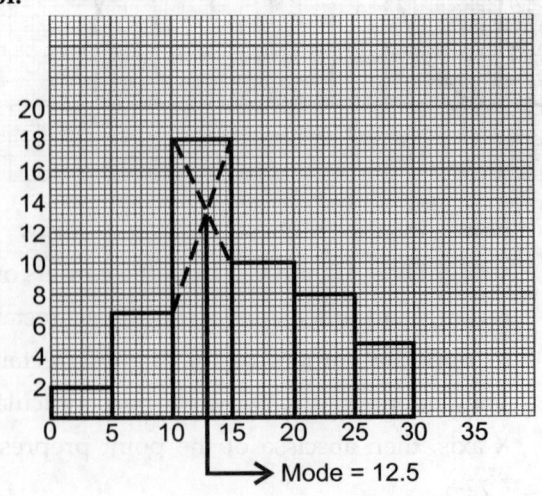

Mode = 12.5

Ans.

Graphical Depiction

18. The frequency distribution of scores obtained by 230 candidates in a medical entrance test is as ahead :

Cost of living index	Number of months
400–450	20
450–500	35
500–550	40
550–600	32
600–650	24
650–700	27
700–750	18
750–800	34
Total	230

Draw a cumulative polygon (ogive) to represent the above data.

Sol. The cumulative frequency table for the given frequency table as given below :

Interval	Frequency	Cumulative
400–450	20	20
450–500	35	55
500–550	40	95
550–600	32	127
600–650	24	151
650–700	27	178
700–750	18	196
750–800	34	230

Ogive representing the scores obtained by 230 candidates in a medical entrance test.

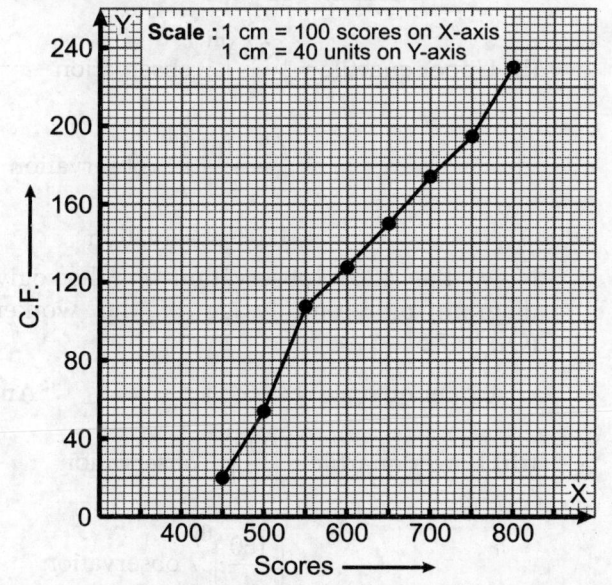

Ans.

19. Attempt this question on a graph paper. The table shows the distribution of marks gained by a group of 400 students in an examination :

Marks less than	No. of students
10	5
20	10
30	30
40	60
50	105
60	180
70	270
80	355
90	390
100	400

Using a scale of 2 cm to represents 10 marks and 2 cm to represent 50 students, plot these values and draw a smooth curve through the points.

Estimate for the graph **(i)** the median mark, **(ii)** the quartile marks.

Sol. By plotting the points (10, 5), (20, 10), (30, 30), (40, 60), (50, 105), (60, 180), (70, 270), (80, 355), (90, 390) and (100, 400), we get the ogive for the given frequency table, as shown in the figure.

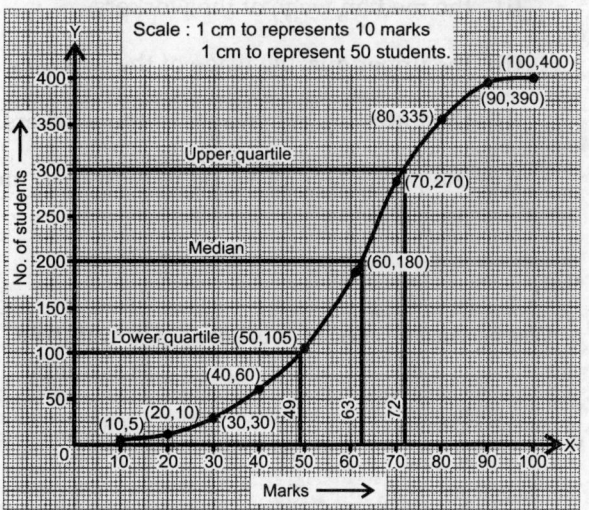

(i) To find the median, we shall draw horizontal line at *c.f.* : $\dfrac{N}{2} = \dfrac{400}{2} = 200$.

Intersecting the ogive at the point (200, 63).

Hence the median is 63. **Ans.**

(ii) To find the lower quartile, we shall construct a horizontal line at c.f. $\frac{N}{4} = \frac{400}{4}$

= 100, intersecting the ogive at the point (49, 100). Hence, 49 is the lower line at c.f. :

$\frac{3N}{4} = \frac{3 \times 400}{4} = 300$. Intersecting the ogive at the point (300, 72). Hence, the upper quartile mark is 72. **Ans.**

20. The daily wages of 160 workers in a building project are given below :

Wages (in ₹)	No. of workers
0–10	12
10–20	20
20–30	30
30–40	38
40–50	24
50–60	16
60–70	12
70–80	8

Using a graph paper, draw an ogive for the above distribution.

Use your ogive to estimate :

(i) the median wage of the workers.

(ii) the upper quartile wage of the workers.

(iii) the lower quartile wages of the workers.

(iv) the percentage of workers who earn more than ₹ 45 a day.

Sol.

Wages (in ₹)	No. of workers	Cumulative Frequency
0–10	12	12
10–20	20	32
20–30	30	62
30–40	38	100
40–50	24	124
50–60	16	140
60–70	12	152
70–80	8	160

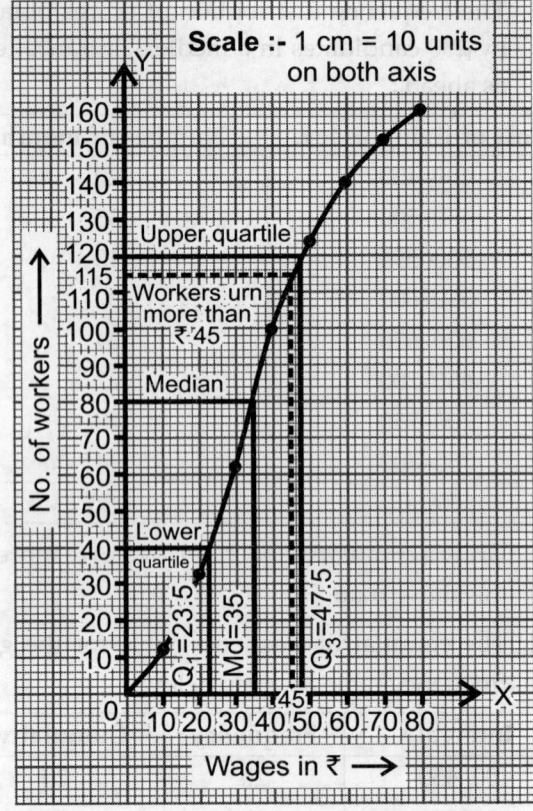

Scale :- 1 cm = 10 units on both axis

(i) Median $= \left(\frac{n}{2}\right)^{th}$ observation

$= \left(\frac{160}{2}\right)^{th}$ observation

$= 80^{th}$ observation

Now, the 80th position in the ogive diagram represent the median wage of workers by the graph = 35.

∴ Median = 35 **Ans.**

(ii) Upper quartile $= \left(\frac{3n}{4}\right)^{th}$ observation

$= \left(\frac{3 \times 160}{4}\right)^{th}$ observation

$= 120^{th}$ observation

Now, the 120th observation in the ogive diagram represents wage of the workers (Q_3) = 47·5

Upper quartile = 47·5. **Ans.**

(iii) Lower quartile $= \left(\frac{n}{4}\right)^{th}$ observation

$= \left(\frac{160}{4}\right)^{th}$ observation

$= 40^{th}$ observation

The 40th observation in the ogive diagram represents wage of the workers $Q_1 = 23.5$

   Lower quartile = 23.5   **Ans.**

(iv) The percentage of workers earn more than ₹ 45

$$= \frac{160 - 115}{160} \times 100$$

$$= \frac{45 \times 10}{16}$$

$$= 28 \cdot 125\%$$ **Ans.**

21. The marks obtained by 120 students in a test are given below :

Marks	0–10	10–20	20–30	30–40	40–50	50–60	60–70	70–80	80–90	90–100
No. of Students	5	9	16	22	26	18	11	6	4	3

Draw an ogive for the given distribution on a graph sheet.

Use suitable scale for ogive to estimate the following :

(i) The median.

(ii) The number of students who obtained more than 75% marks in the test.

(iii) The number of students who did not pass the test if minimum marks required to pass is 40.

Sol.

Marks C. I.	No. of Students f	c. f.
0–10	5	5
10–20	9	14
20–30	16	30
30–40	22	52
40–50	26	78
50–60	18	96
60–70	11	107
70–80	6	113
80–90	4	117
90–100	3	120

(i) Here $n = 120$, even

∴   Median $= \left(\dfrac{120}{2}\right)^{\text{th}}$ observation

$= 60^{\text{th}}$ observation

$= 42 \cdot 5$ (approx.)   **Ans.**

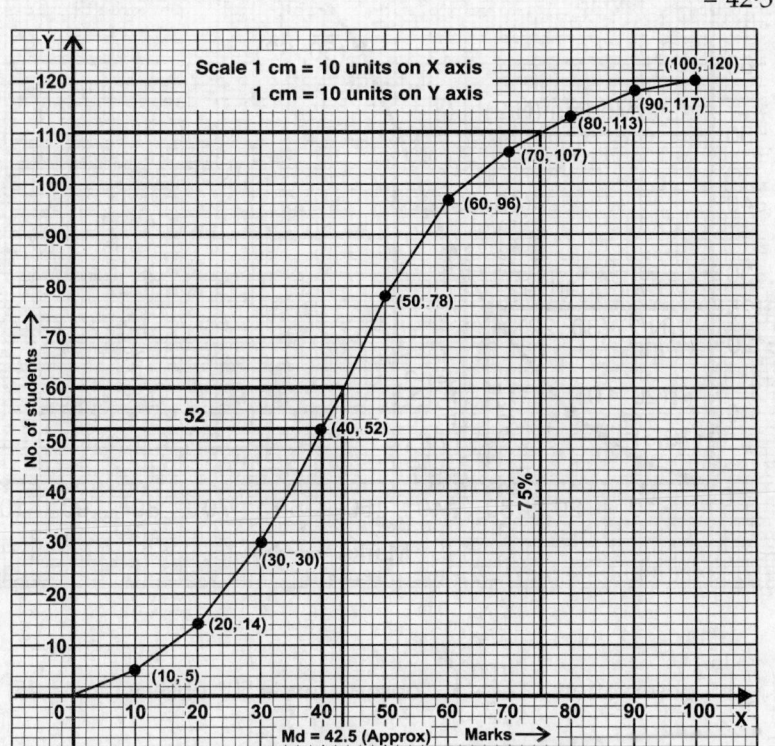

(ii) Number of students who obtained more than 75% marks in the test

$$= 120 - 110 = 10 \quad \textbf{Ans.}$$

(iii) Number of students who did not pass the test if minimum marks required to pass is 40

$$= 52. \quad \textbf{Ans.}$$

22. The marks obtained by 100 students in a Mathematics test are given below :

Marks	0–10	10–20	20–30	30–40	40–50	50–60	60–70	70–80	80–90	90–100
No. of Students	3	7	12	17	23	14	9	6	5	4

Draw an ogive for the given distribution on a graph sheet.

(Use a scale of 2 cm = 10 units on both axis).

use the ogive to estimate the :

(i) Median.

(ii) Lower quartile.

(iii) Number of students who obtained more than 85% marks in the test.

(iv) Number of students who did not pass in the test if the pass percentage was 35.

Sol.

Marks	c.f.	Points
0–10	3	(10, 3)
10–20	10	(20, 10)
20–30	22	(30, 22)
30–40	39	(40, 39)
40–50	62	(50, 62)
50–60	76	(60, 76)
60–70	85	(70, 85)
70–80	91	(80, 91)
80–90	96	(90, 96)
90–100	100	(100, 100)

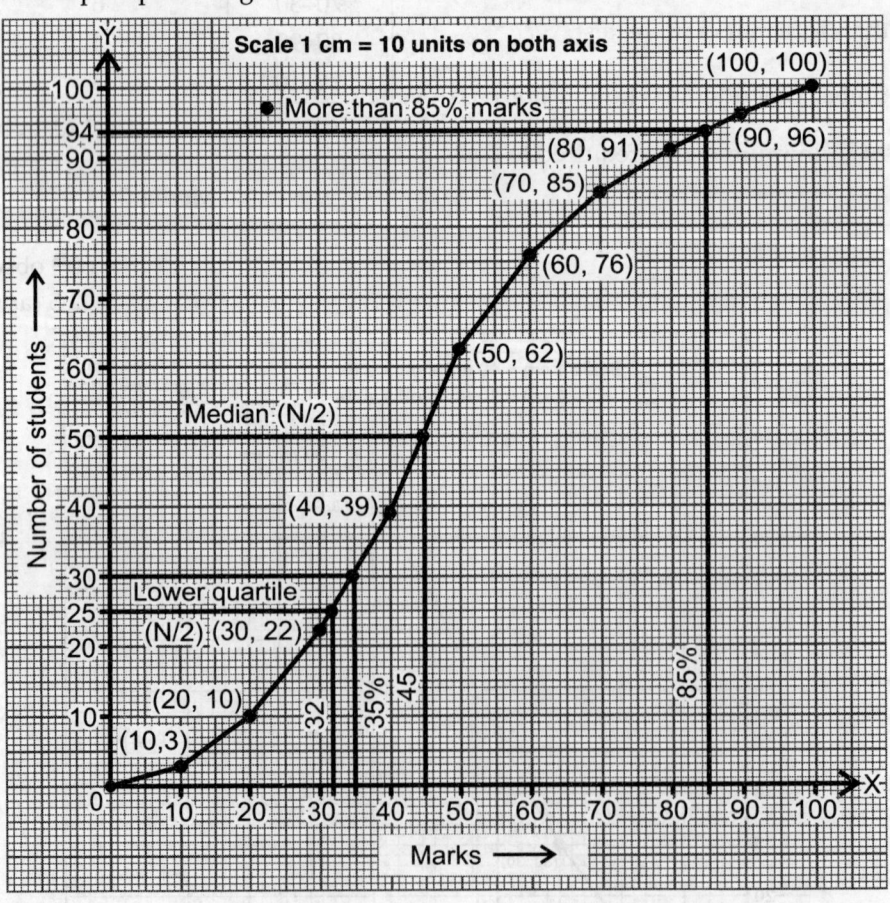

(i) Median $= \left(\dfrac{n}{2}\right)^{th}$ observation $= \left(\dfrac{100}{2}\right)^{th}$ observation $= 50^{th}$ observation $= 45$ **Ans.**

(ii) Lower Quartile $(Q_1) = \left(\dfrac{N}{4}\right)^{th}$ observation

$= \left(\dfrac{100}{4}\right)^{th}$ observation $= 25^{th}$ observation

$= 32$ **Ans.**

(iii) Number of students who obtained more than 85% marks $= (100 - 94) = 6.$ **Ans.**

(iv) Number of students who did not pass if passing % of marks is 35 $= 30.$ **Ans.**

□□

Concept Based Questions | Set 8 |

Chapter 1. Goods and Service Tax (G.S.T.)

1. During a financial year, a shopkeeper purchased goods worth ₹ 4,15,000 and paid a total tax of ₹ 38,000. During the same financial year, he sold all the goods purchased as below :

(i) goods worth ₹ 50,000 at 5% tax,

(ii) goods worth ₹ 3,20,000 at 12% tax and

(iii) goods worth ₹ 45,000 which are exempted from tax.

Calculate the tax liability (under GST) for the financial year under consideration.

Sol. $\because$ Turnover of goods taxable at 5%

$$= ₹ 50,000$$

$\therefore$ Tax charged = 5% of ₹ 50,000

$$= \frac{5}{100} \times ₹ 50,000$$

$$= ₹ 2,500$$

$\because$ Turnover of goods taxable at 12%

$$= ₹ 3,20,000$$

$\therefore$ Tax charged = 12% of ₹ 3,20,000

$$= \frac{12}{100} \times ₹ 3,20,000$$

$$= ₹ 38,400$$

Tax exempted sales = Sale which is not liable for tax under GST

$$= ₹ 45,000$$

Total tax charged = ₹ 2,500 + ₹ 38,400

$$= ₹ 40,900$$

Tax paid = ₹ 38,000

$\therefore$ Tax liability (under GST)

= Total tax charged – Tax paid

= ₹ 40,900 – ₹ 38,000

= ₹ 2,900   **Ans.**

2. An article was bought by a distributor for ₹ 15,000 (excluding tax). He sold it to a trader for ₹ 20,000. The trader sold the article to a retailer for ₹ 22,000 (excluding tax). Find the GST paid by the distributor and by the trader if the tax rate was 10 percent.

Sol. (i) For the distributor :

Cost of the article = ₹ 15,000

Tax paid = 10% of 15,000

$$= \frac{10 \times 15,000}{100} = ₹ 1,500$$

Selling price of the article

$$= ₹ 20,000$$

Tax charged = 10% of 20,000

$$= \frac{10 \times 20,000}{100} = ₹ 2,000$$

$\therefore$ GST paid by distributor = Tax recovered on sale – Tax paid on purchase

$$= ₹ 2,000 – ₹ 1,500$$

$$= ₹ 500 \qquad \textbf{Ans.}$$

GST paid by distributor

= Tax on (S.P. – C.P.)

= 10% of (₹ 20,000 – ₹ 15,000)

$$= \frac{10}{100} \times 5,000$$

$$= ₹ 500. \qquad \textbf{Ans.}$$

(ii) For the trader :

Cost of the article = ₹ 20,000

[$\because$ S.P. of distributor = C.P. of trader]

Tax paid = 10% of 20,000

$$= ₹ 2,000$$

Selling price of the article = ₹ 22,000

Tax charged = 10% of 22,000

$$= \frac{10 \times 22,000}{100}$$

$$= ₹ 2,200$$

∴ GST paid by the trader = Tax recovered on sale
− Tax paid on purchase

$$= ₹ 2,200 − ₹ 2,000$$

$$= ₹ 200 \qquad \textbf{Ans.}$$

3. A shopkeeper sells an article at the listed price of ₹ 1,500 and the rate of GST is 12% at each stage of sale. If the shopkeeper pays a GST of ₹ 36 to the Government, what was the price, inclusive of Tax, at which the shopkeeper purchased the article from the wholesaler ?

Sol. Let the profit of the shopkeeper = ₹ x.

GST by shopkeeper = ₹ 36

$$12\% \text{ of } x = 36$$

$$\Rightarrow \qquad \frac{12}{100} \circ x = 36$$

$$\Rightarrow \qquad x = \frac{36 \times 100}{12} = ₹ 300$$

∴ The price at which the shopkeeper bought the article

$$= ₹ 1,500 − ₹ 300 = ₹ 1,200$$

∴ The price at which the shopkeeper purchased the article inclusive of GST

$$= 1,200 + \frac{12}{100} \times 1,200$$

$$= ₹ (1,200 + 144)$$

$$= ₹ 1,344 \qquad \textbf{Ans.}$$

4. A manufacturer sells a washing machine to a wholesaler for ₹ 15,000. The wholesaler sells it to a trader at a profit of ₹ 1,200 and the trader in turn sells it to a consumer at a profit of ₹ 1,800. If the rate of GST is 8%, find :

(i) The amount of GST received by the State Government on the sale of this machine from the manufacturer and the wholesaler.

(ii) The amount that the consumer pays for the machine.

Sol. (i) GST paid by the manufacturer

$$= 8\% \text{ of } 15,000$$

$$= \frac{8}{100} \times 15,000 = ₹ 1,200$$

GST paid by the wholesaler

$$= 8\% \text{ of } 1,200$$

$$= \frac{8}{100} \times 1,200 = ₹ 96$$

Total GST received by the state government on the sale of machine from the manufacturer and the wholesaler

$$= ₹ (1,200 + 96)$$

$$= ₹ 1,296 \qquad \textbf{Ans.}$$

(ii) Amount paid by the consumer

$$= ₹ (15,000 + 1,200 + 1,800)$$

$$+ \text{GST @ 8\%}$$

$$= ₹ \left(18,000 + \frac{8}{100} \times 18,000 \right)$$

$$= ₹ (18,000 + 1,440)$$

$$= ₹ 19,440 \qquad \textbf{Ans.}$$

Chapter 5. Quadratic Equations

1. The hypotenuse of a right angled triangle is $3\sqrt{5}$. If the smaller side is tripled and the larger side is doubled, the new hypotenuse will be 15 cm. Find the length of each side.

Sol. Let the smaller side of the right triangle be x cm and the longer side by y cm.

Using Pythagoras theorem, we have

$$x^2 + y^2 = (3\sqrt{5})^2$$

$$\Rightarrow \qquad x^2 + y^2 = 45 \qquad \text{...(i)}$$

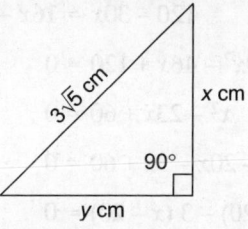

If the smaller side is tripled and larger side is doubled, then

The smaller side = $3x$ cm

Larger side = $2y$ cm

New hypotenuse = 15 cm

Then, by Pythagoras theorem, we have

$$(3x)^2 + (2y)^2 = (15)^2$$

$$\Rightarrow \qquad 9x^2 + 4y^2 = 225 \qquad \qquad ...(ii)$$

From (i), $y^2 = 45 - x^2$ and putting in (ii), we get

$$9x^2 + 4(45 - x^2) = 225$$

$$\Rightarrow \quad 9x^2 + 180 - 4x^2 = 225$$

$$\Rightarrow \qquad 5x^2 = 225 - 180 = 45$$

$$\Rightarrow \qquad x^2 = 9$$

$$\Rightarrow \qquad x = \pm 3.$$

But $x = -3$ is not possible as length can't be – ve.

Then, $x = 3$ cm.

From (i), we have

$$x^2 + y^2 = 45$$

$$\Rightarrow \qquad 9 + y^2 = 45$$

$$\Rightarrow \qquad y^2 = 36$$

$$\Rightarrow \qquad y = \pm 6$$

Rejecting – ve sign then $y = 6$

Hence, the length of the smaller side = 3 cm.

The length of the longer side = 6 cm. **Ans.**

2. Sum of two natural numbers is 8 and the difference of their reciprocal is $\dfrac{2}{15}$. Find the numbers.

Sol. Let, the two natural numbers be x and $8 - x$.

$\therefore$ From question,

$$\frac{1}{x} - \frac{1}{8-x} = \frac{2}{15}$$

$$\Rightarrow \qquad \frac{8-x-x}{x(8-x)} = \frac{2}{15}$$

$$\Rightarrow \qquad (8-2x)\,15 = 16x - 2x^2$$

$$\Rightarrow \qquad 120 - 30x = 16x - 2x^2$$

$$\Rightarrow \qquad 2x^2 - 46x + 120 = 0$$

$$\Rightarrow \qquad x^2 - 23x + 60 = 0$$

$$\Rightarrow \qquad x^2 - 20x - 3x + 60 = 0$$

$$\Rightarrow \quad x(x-20) - 3(x-20) = 0$$

$$\Rightarrow \qquad (x-3)(x-20) = 0$$

$$\Rightarrow \qquad x = 3$$

or $\qquad \qquad x = 20$ (neglect it)

($\because$ Sum of two natural numbers is 8)

Thus, one number = 3 and other number
= 8 – 3 = 5

$\therefore$ The natural numbers are 3 and 5. **Ans.**

3. A two digit positive number is such that the product of its digits is 6. If 9 is added to the number, the digits interchange their places. Find the number.

Sol. Let the unit digit be x, then tens digit will be $\dfrac{6}{x}$,

then two digit number is $\dfrac{6}{x} + x$.

From question,

$$\frac{60}{x} + x + 9 = 10x + \frac{6}{x}$$

$$\Rightarrow \qquad 60 + x^2 + 9x = 10x^2 + 6$$

$$\Rightarrow \qquad 9x^2 - 9x - 54 = 0$$

$$\Rightarrow \qquad x^2 - x - 6 = 0$$

$$\Rightarrow \qquad x^2 - 3x + 2x - 6 = 0$$

$$\Rightarrow \quad x(x-3) + 2(x-3) = 0$$

$$\Rightarrow \qquad (x-3)(x+2) = 0$$

$$\Rightarrow \qquad x = -2 \text{ or } 3$$

As x can't be – ve.

So, required two digit number

$$= \frac{60}{3} + 3 = 23. \qquad \textbf{Ans.}$$

4. ₹ 7,500 were divided equally among a certain number of children. Had there been 20 less children, each would have received ₹ 100 more. Find the original number of children.

Sol. Let the original number of children be x.

Total amount to be distributed = ₹ 7,500

$\therefore$ Each will receive = $\dfrac{7,500}{x}$

If the number of children are $x - 20$,

Then, each will receive = $\dfrac{7,500}{x-20}$

According to question,

$$\frac{7,500}{x-20} - \frac{7,500}{x} = 100$$

$$\Rightarrow \quad 7,500\left(\frac{1}{x-20} - \frac{1}{x}\right) = 100$$

$$\Rightarrow \qquad \frac{x-x+20}{x(x-20)} = \frac{100}{7,500}$$

$$\Rightarrow \qquad \frac{20}{x^2-20x} = \frac{1}{75}$$

$$\Rightarrow \qquad x^2 - 20x = 1,500$$

$$\Rightarrow \qquad x^2 - 20x - 1,500 = 0$$

$$\Rightarrow \qquad x^2 - 50x + 30x - 1,500 = 0$$

$$\Rightarrow \qquad x(x-50) + 30(x-50) = 0$$

$$\Rightarrow \qquad (x-50)(x+30) = 0$$

$$\Rightarrow \qquad x - 50 = 0 \text{ or } x + 30 = 0$$

$$\Rightarrow \qquad x = 50 \text{ or } x = -30$$

$$\therefore \qquad x = 50 \ (\because x \text{ cannot be negative})$$

$\therefore$ The original number of children = 50. **Ans.**

Chapter 9. Arithmetic Progression

1. Find x and the common difference if the following numbers form an A.P. 14, x, 32, ...

Sol. Since sequence is in A.P. therefore

$$x - 14 = 32 - x$$

$$\Rightarrow \qquad 2x = 46$$

$$\Rightarrow \qquad x = 23$$

and $\qquad d = x - 14 = 23 - 14 = 9$ **Ans.**

2. If $(k-3)$, $(2k+1)$ and $(4k+3)$ are three consecutive terms of an A.P., find the value of k.

Sol. Given, $(k-3)$, $(2k+1)$, $(4k+3)$ are 3 consecutive terms of an A.P.

As the difference between the consecutive terms in A.P. are same, i.e., $a_2 - a_1 = a_3 - a_2 = a_4 - a_3 = ... = d$.

$$\therefore \quad (2k+1) - (k-3) = (4k+3) - (2k+1)$$

$$\Rightarrow \quad 2k + 1 - k + 3 = 4k + 3 - 2k - 1$$

$$\Rightarrow \qquad k + 4 = 2k + 2$$

$$\Rightarrow \qquad k - 2k = 2 - 4$$

$$\Rightarrow \qquad -k = -2$$

$$\Rightarrow \qquad k = 2 \qquad \textbf{Ans.}$$

3. The 10th term of an A.P. is -15 and 31st term is -57, find the 15th term.

Sol. Let a be the first term and d be the common difference of the A.P. Then from the formula :

$$t_n = a + (n-1)d,$$

we have $\qquad t_{10} = a + (10-1)d = a + 9d$

$$t_{31} = a + (31-1)d = a + 30d$$

we have, $\quad a + 9d = -15$ \qquad ...(i)

$$a + 30d = -57 \qquad ...(ii)$$

Solve equations (i) and (ii) to get the values of a and d.

Subtracting (i) from (ii), we have

$$21d = -57 + 15 = -42$$

$$\therefore \qquad d = \frac{-42}{21} = -2$$

Again from (i), $a = -15 - 9d$

$$= -15 - 9(-2)$$

$$= -15 + 18 = 3$$

Now, $\qquad t_{15} = a + (15-1)d$

$$= 3 + 14(-2) = -25 \qquad \textbf{Ans.}$$

4. The 4th term of an A.P. is 22 and 15th term is 66. Find the first term and the common difference. Hence, find the sum of the series to 8 terms.*

Sol. Let a be the first term and d be the common difference of given A.P.

$$\therefore \qquad a_4 = 22 \text{ and } a_{15} = 66 \qquad \text{(Given)}$$

$$\Rightarrow \qquad a + 3d = 22 \qquad ...(i)$$

and $\qquad a + 14d = 66 \qquad ...(ii)$

Subtracting equation (i) from equation (ii), we get

$$a + 14d = 66$$
$$a + 3d = 22$$
$$\overline{}$$
$$11d = 44$$

$$\Rightarrow \qquad d = 4$$

From equation (i),

$$a + 3 \times 4 = 22$$

$$\Rightarrow \qquad a = 22 - 12 = 10$$

$$\therefore \qquad a = 10, d = 4.$$

Sum of series to 8 terms,

$$S_8 = \frac{n}{2}[2a + (n-1)d]$$

$$= \frac{8}{2}[2 \times 10 + (8-1)4]$$

$$= 4(20 + 28)$$

$$= 4 \times 48 = 192 \qquad \textbf{Ans.}$$

---

* Frequently asked previous years Board Exam Questions.

5. Is 184 a term of the sequence 3, 7, 11, ... ?

Sol. Since, we have $a = 3$ and $d = 4$.

Let the nth term of the given sequence be 184.

Then $\qquad a_n = a + (n-1)\,d = 184$

$\Rightarrow \qquad 3 + (n-1) \times 4 = 184$

$\Rightarrow \qquad\qquad 4n = 185$

$\Rightarrow \qquad\qquad n = \dfrac{185}{4}$

which is not a natural number.

So, 184 is not a term of the given sequence. **Ans.**

6. The sum of the first ten terms of an A.P. is zero, and the sum of the first and second term is 24. Find the first three terms.

Sol. Given,

$\qquad\qquad S_{10} = 0$

$\Rightarrow \qquad 5\,(2a + 9d) = 0$

$\Rightarrow \qquad\quad 2a + 9d = 0 \qquad\qquad ...(i)$

Also, $\quad a + (a + d) = 24$

$\Rightarrow \qquad\quad 2a + d = 24 \qquad\qquad ...(ii)$

From (i) and (ii), we get

$\qquad\qquad d = -3$

and $\qquad\qquad a = 13\dfrac{1}{2}.$

Hence, the A.P. is

$\qquad 13\dfrac{1}{2}, 10\dfrac{1}{2}, 7\dfrac{1}{2}, ... \qquad$ **Ans.**

7. Find the sum of terms of the A.P. $a_1, a_2, a_3, ...$ if it is known that

$\qquad a_1 + a_5 + a_{10} + a_{15} + a_{20} + a_{24} = 225.$

Sol. In an A.P., the sum of the terms equidistant from the beginning and end is always same and is equal to the sum of first and last term *i.e.*,

$$a_1 + a_n = a_2 + a_{n-1}$$
$$= a_3 + a_{n-2} = ...,$$

So, if an A.P. consists of 24 terms, then

$$a_1 + a_{24} = a_5 + a_{20} = a_{10} + a_{15}.$$

Now,

$\qquad a_1 + a_5 + a_{10} + a_{15} + a_{20} + a_{24} = 225$

$\Rightarrow \; (a_1 + a_{24}) + (a_5 + a_{20}) + (a_{10} + a_{15}) = 225$

$\Rightarrow \qquad\quad 3\,(a_1 + a_{24}) = 225$

$\Rightarrow \qquad\qquad a_1 + a_{24} = 75$

$\therefore \qquad\qquad S_{24} = \dfrac{24}{2}\,[a_1 + a_{24}]$

$\qquad\qquad = \dfrac{24}{2} \times 75 = 900$

$\therefore \qquad\qquad S_{24} = 900. \qquad$ **Ans.**

8. The first term of an A.P. is 10, the last term is 50. If the sum of all the terms is 480, find the common difference and the number of terms.

Sol. We have

$\qquad a = 10,\; l = t_n = 50,\; S_n = 480.$

By substituting the values of a, t_n and S_n in the formulae

$$S_n = \dfrac{n}{2}\,[2a + (n-1)\,d]$$

$\Rightarrow \qquad 480 = \dfrac{n}{2}\,[20 + (n-1)\,d] \qquad ...(i)$

and $\qquad t_n = a + (n-1)\,d$, we get

$\Rightarrow \qquad 50 = 10 + (n-1)\,d \qquad\qquad ...(ii)$

From (ii),

$\qquad\qquad (n-1)\,d = 50 - 10 = 40 \qquad ...(iii)$

From (i), we have

$\qquad\qquad 480 = \dfrac{n}{2}\,(20 + 40)$

$\Rightarrow \qquad\quad 60n = 2 \times 480$

$\Rightarrow \qquad\qquad n = \dfrac{2 \times 480}{60} = 16$

From (iii),

$\qquad\qquad d = \dfrac{40}{15} = \dfrac{8}{3} \qquad\qquad$ **Ans.**

9. Find the sum of the sequence 2, 3, 5, 9, 8, 15, 11, ... to $(2n + 1)$ terms.

Sol. Let S denote the sum. Then,

$S = 2 + 3 + 5 + 9 + 8 + 15 + 11 + ... (2n + 1)$ terms

$= [2 + 5 + 8 + 11 + ... (n + 1)$ terms$]$

$\qquad\qquad + [3 + 9 + 15 + 21 + ... n$ terms$]$

$= \dfrac{n+1}{2}\,[2 \times 2 + (n + 1 - 1)\,3]$

$\qquad\qquad + \dfrac{n}{2}\,[2 \times 3 + (n-1)\,6]$

$= \dfrac{n+1}{2}\,[4 + 3n] + \dfrac{n}{2}\,[6 + 6n - 6]$

$= \dfrac{1}{2}\,[4n + 4 + 3n^2 + 3n] + \dfrac{1}{2}\,[6n^2]$

$= \dfrac{1}{2}\,[4n + 4 + 3n^2 + 3n + 6n^2]$

$= \dfrac{1}{2}\,[9n^2 + 7n + 4] \qquad\qquad$ **Ans.**

10. If the first term of an A.P. is 2 and the sum of first five terms is equal to one-fourth of the sum of the next five terms, find the sum of first 30 terms.

Sol Let $a_1, a_2, a_3, \ldots$ be given A.P. with common difference d. It is given that

$$a_1 = 2$$

and $a_1 + a_2 + a_3 + a_4 + a_5 = \dfrac{1}{4}(a_6 + a_7 + a_8 + a_9 + a_{10})$

$\Rightarrow \quad 4(a_1 + a_2 + a_3 + a_4 + a_5) = (a_6 + a_7 + a_8 + a_9 + a_{10})$

$\Rightarrow \quad 5(a_1 + a_2 + \ldots + a_5) = a_1 + a_2 \ldots + a_{10}$

$\Rightarrow \quad 5 S_5 = S_{10}$

$\Rightarrow 5\left\{\dfrac{5}{2}(2 \cdot 2 + (5-1)d)\right\} = \dfrac{10}{2}[2 \times 2 + (10-1)d]$

$\Rightarrow \quad 50(1+d) = 20 + 45d$

$\Rightarrow \quad d = -6$

$\therefore \quad S_{30} = \dfrac{30}{2}[2 \times 2 + (30-1)(-6)]$

$S_{30} = -2550.$ **Ans.**

11. The sum of the first three terms of an Arithmetic Progression (A.P.) is 42 and the product of the first and third term is 52. Find the first term and the common difference.*

Sol. Let a and d be the first term and common difference respectively.

By first condition,

$$a_1 + a_2 + a_3 = 42$$

$\Rightarrow a + a + d + a + 2d = 42$

$\Rightarrow \quad 3a + 3d = 42$

$\Rightarrow \quad 3(a+d) = 42$

$\Rightarrow \quad a + d = \dfrac{42}{3} = 14$

$\Rightarrow \quad d = 14 - a$ ...(i)

By second condition,

$$a_1 \times a_3 = 52$$

$\Rightarrow \quad a \times (a + 2d) = 52$

$\Rightarrow \quad a^2 + 2ad = 52$ ...(ii)

From equations (i) and (ii), we have

$$a^2 + 2a(14 - a) = 52$$

$\Rightarrow \quad a^2 + 28a - 2a^2 = 52$

$\Rightarrow \quad -a^2 + 28a = 52$

$\Rightarrow \quad a^2 - 28a + 52 = 0$

$\Rightarrow \quad a^2 - 26a - 2a + 52 = 0$

$\Rightarrow \quad a(a-26) - 2(a-26) = 0$

$\Rightarrow \quad (a-26)(a-2) = 0$

$\Rightarrow \quad a - 26 = 0 \text{ or } a - 2 = 0$

$\Rightarrow \quad a = 26 \text{ or } a = 2$

$\therefore \quad a = 26 \text{ or } 2$

From equation (i),

when $a = 26$, $d = 14 - 26 = -12$

and when $a = 2$, $d = 14 - 2 = 12$ **Ans.**

Then, $d = 12$ or -12

12. Use the fact that the positive multiples of 7 form an A.P. to find how many multiples of 7 lie between 1,000 and 10,000.

Sol. The positive multiples of 7 form an A.P. 7, 14, 21, ...

So, $a = 7$ and $d = 7$

The nth term of the A.P. is

$$a_n = a + (n-1)d$$

$$= 7 + 7(n-1)$$

$$= 7n$$

To find the multiples of 7 between 1,000 and 10,000, put

$$1000 < a_n < 10,000$$

$\Rightarrow \quad 1000 < 7n < 10,000$

$\Rightarrow \quad 142\dfrac{6}{7} < n < 1428\dfrac{4}{7}$

So, there are 1428 multiples of 7 less than 10,000 and 142 less than 1,000, leaving 1428 − 142 = 1286 multiples of 7 between 1,000 and 10,000. **Ans.**

13. **(a)** Find how many negative terms there are in the sequence $a_n = 12n - 100$, and find the first positive term (its number and its value).

(b) How many positive terms are less than 200?

Sol. (a) Let nth term will be less than 0 (*i.e.*, negative)

Put $\qquad a_n < 0$

then $12n - 100 < 0$

$\Rightarrow \qquad n < 8\dfrac{1}{3}$

So, there are eight negative terms and the first positive term is

$$a_9 = 12 \times 9 - 100$$

$\qquad\qquad\qquad = 108 - 100$

$\qquad\qquad\qquad = 8$ **Ans.**

(b) Put $\qquad 0 < a_n < 200,$

$\Rightarrow \qquad 0 < 12n - 100 < 200$

$\Rightarrow \qquad 8\dfrac{1}{3} < n < 25,$

So, the 16 terms from a_9 to a_{24} inclusive are positive and less than 200. **Ans.**

Chapter 10. Geometric Progression

1. Find the value of x such that 3, $x + 4$, and $x + 10$ form a geometric sequence.

Sol. Put $\qquad \dfrac{x+10}{x+4} = \dfrac{x+4}{3}$

$\Rightarrow \qquad 3(x + 10) = (x + 4)^2$

$\Rightarrow \qquad x^2 + 5x - 14 = 0$

$\Rightarrow \quad x^2 + 7x - 2x - 14 = 0$

$\Rightarrow \qquad (x + 7)(x - 2) = 0$

So, $x = 2$, gives geometric sequence 3, 6 and 12.

or $x = -7$, gives geometric sequence 3, -3 and 3.

Ans.

2. Find the first term a and the common ratio r of a G.P. in which the fourth term is 30 and the sixth term is 480.

Sol. Since $\qquad a_4 = 30$

$\Rightarrow \qquad ar^3 = 30 \qquad$ ...(i)

and $\qquad a_6 = 480$

$\Rightarrow \qquad ar^5 = 480 \qquad$ ...(ii)

Dividing (ii) by (i), we get

$\qquad\qquad r^2 = 16$

So, $\qquad r = 4$ and $a = \dfrac{15}{32}$

or $\qquad r = -4$ and $a = \dfrac{-15}{32}.$ **Ans.**

3. The 4th term of a G.P. is 16 and the 7th term is 128. Find the first term and common ratio of the series.*

Sol. Let a be the first term and r be the common ratio of the given G.P.

$\therefore \qquad T_4 = 16$ and $T_7 = 128$

$\Rightarrow \qquad ar^3 = 16 \qquad$ ...(i)

and $\qquad ar^6 = 128 \qquad$ ...(ii)

Dividing equation (ii) by equation (i), we get

$$\dfrac{ar^6}{ar^3} = \dfrac{128}{16}$$

$\Rightarrow \qquad r^3 = 8$

$\Rightarrow \qquad r = 2$

$\therefore$ From equation (i), $a \times 2^3 = 16$

$\Rightarrow \qquad a = \dfrac{16}{8} = 2$

$\therefore \qquad a = 2, r = 2.$ **Ans.**

4. Which term of the G.P. 5, -10, 20, -40, ... is 320 ?

Sol. In this case

$$a = 5, r = \dfrac{-10}{5} = -2.$$

Suppose that 320 is the nth term of the G.P. By the formula, $t_n = ar^{n-1}$

we get $\qquad t_n = 5.(-2)^{n-1}$

$\therefore \qquad 5.(-2)^{n-1} = 320 \qquad$ (Given)

$\Rightarrow \qquad (-2)^{n-1} = 64 = (-2)^6$

$\Rightarrow \qquad n - 1 = 6$

$\therefore \qquad n = 7$

Hence, 320 is the 7th term of the G.P. **Ans.**

5. For the G.P. 1,000, 400, 160, ... find the first term less than $\dfrac{1}{1000}.$

Sol. Put $\qquad a_n < \dfrac{1}{1000}.$

$\Rightarrow \quad 1000 \times \left(\dfrac{2}{5}\right)^{n-1} < \dfrac{1}{1000}$

$\Rightarrow \qquad \left(\dfrac{2}{5}\right)^{n-1} < \dfrac{1}{(1000)^2}$

$\Rightarrow \qquad \left(\dfrac{5}{2}\right)^{n-1} > (1000)^2$

$\Rightarrow \qquad n - 1 > \log_{5/2} 1000000$

* Frequently asked previous years Board Exam Questions.

$\Rightarrow \qquad n - 1 > 15 \cdot 07 \ldots \quad$ (using log table)

$\Rightarrow \qquad n > 16 \cdot 07 \ldots$

Hence, the first term less than $\dfrac{1}{1000}$ is

$$a_{17} = 1000 \times \left(\dfrac{2}{5}\right)^{16}$$

$$= 0 \cdot 000429. \qquad \textbf{Ans.}$$

6. Find the sum of the G.P. :

$$\dfrac{1}{\sqrt{3}}, 1, \sqrt{3} \ldots, 81$$

Sol. Here, $a = \dfrac{1}{\sqrt{3}}, r = \sqrt{3}$ and $t_n = l = 81$

Now, $\qquad t_n = 81$

$$= \dfrac{1}{\sqrt{3}}(\sqrt{3})^{n-1}$$

$$= (\sqrt{3})^{n-2}$$

$\therefore \qquad (\sqrt{3})^{n-2} = 3^4 = (\sqrt{3})^8$

$\Rightarrow \qquad n - 2 = 8$

or $\qquad n = 10$

$\therefore \qquad S_n = \dfrac{\dfrac{1}{\sqrt{3}}[(\sqrt{3})^{10} - 1]}{\sqrt{3} - 1}$

$$= \dfrac{(\sqrt{3})^{10} - 1}{3 - \sqrt{3}} \qquad \textbf{Ans.}$$

7. How many terms of the following G.P. 64, 32, 16, ... has the sum $127\dfrac{1}{2}$?

Sol. Here, $\qquad a = 64, r = \dfrac{32}{64} = \dfrac{1}{2} \ (< 1)$

and $\qquad S_n = 127\dfrac{1}{2} = \dfrac{255}{2}.$

$$S_n = \dfrac{a(1 - r^n)}{1 - r}$$

we get $\qquad S_n = \dfrac{64\left\{1 - \left(\dfrac{1}{2}\right)^n\right\}}{1 - \dfrac{1}{2}}$

$\Rightarrow \qquad \dfrac{64\left\{1 - \left(\dfrac{1}{2}\right)^n\right\}}{1 - \dfrac{1}{2}} = \dfrac{255}{2} \qquad$ (Given)

or $\qquad 128\left[1 - \left(\dfrac{1}{2}\right)^n\right] = \dfrac{255}{2}$

$\Rightarrow \qquad 1 - \left(\dfrac{1}{2}\right)^n = \dfrac{255}{256}$

$\Rightarrow \qquad \left(\dfrac{1}{2}\right)^n = 1 - \dfrac{255}{256} = \dfrac{1}{256} = \left(\dfrac{1}{2}\right)^8$

$\therefore \qquad n = 8$

Thus, the required number of terms is 8. **Ans.**

8. Find the sum of the following sequence : 2, 22, 222, ... to n terms.

Sol. Let S denote the sum. Then

$$S = 2 + 22 + 222 + \ldots \text{ to } n \text{ terms}$$

$$= 2 (1 + 11 + 111 + \ldots \text{ to } n \text{ terms})$$

$$= \dfrac{2}{9} (9 + 99 + 999 + \ldots \text{ to } n \text{ terms})$$

$$= \dfrac{2}{9} \{(10 - 1) + (10^2 - 1) + (10^3 - 1)$$

$$+ \ldots \text{ to } n \text{ terms}\}$$

$$= \dfrac{2}{9} \{(10 - 10^2 + 10^3 + \ldots \text{ to } n \text{ terms})$$

$$- (1 + 1 + 1 + \ldots \text{ to } n \text{ terms})\}$$

$$= \dfrac{2}{9}\left(\dfrac{(10^n - 1)}{10 - 1} - n\right)$$

$[\because 10 - 10^2 + 10^3 - \ldots$ is a G.P. with $r = -10 < 1]$

$$= \dfrac{2}{9}\left(\dfrac{(10^n - 1 - 9n)}{9}\right)$$

$$= \dfrac{2}{81} (10^n - 1 - 9n) \qquad \textbf{Ans.}$$

9. Find the sum of the G.P. : 0·6, 0·06, 0·006, 0·0006, ... to n terms.

Sol. Here, $\qquad a = 0 \cdot 6 = \dfrac{6}{10}$

and $\qquad r = \dfrac{0 \cdot 06}{0 \cdot 6} = \dfrac{1}{10}$

We know

$$S_n = \dfrac{a(1 - r^n)}{1 - r}$$

we have $\qquad S_n = \dfrac{\dfrac{6}{10}\left\{1 - \left(\dfrac{1}{10}\right)^n\right\}}{1 - \dfrac{1}{10}} \qquad [\because r < 1]$

$$= \frac{6}{9}\left(1 - \frac{1}{10^n}\right)$$

$$= \frac{2}{3}\left(1 - \frac{1}{10^n}\right)$$

Hence, the required sum is $\frac{2}{3}\left(1 - \frac{1}{10^n}\right)$. **Ans.**

10. Find the sum up to n terms of the sequence : 0·7, 0·77, 0·777, ...

Sol. Let S denote the sum, then

$$S = 0·7 + 0·77 + 0·777 + ... \text{ to } n \text{ terms}$$

$$= 7\,(0·1 + 0·11 + 0·111 + ... \text{ to } n \text{ terms})$$

$$= \frac{7}{9}\,(0·9 + 0·99 + 0·999 + ... \text{ to } n \text{ terms})$$

$$= \frac{7}{9}\,\{(1 - 0·1)\, + (1 - 0·01) + (1 - 0·001)$$

$$+ ... \text{ to } n \text{ terms}\}$$

$$= \frac{7}{9}\,\{(1 + 1 + 1 + ... \, n \text{ terms})$$

$$- (0·1 + 0·01 + 0·001 + ... \text{ to } n \text{ terms})\}$$

$$= \frac{7}{9}\left[n - \left(\frac{1}{10} + \frac{1}{10^2} + \frac{1}{10^3} + ... \text{ to } n \text{ terms}\right)\right]$$

$$= \frac{7}{9}\left\{n - \frac{\frac{1}{10}\left(1 - \frac{1}{10^n}\right)}{1 - \frac{1}{10}}\right\} \qquad (\text{Since } r < 1)$$

$$= \frac{7}{9}\left\{n - \frac{1}{9}\left(1 - \frac{1}{10^n}\right)\right\}$$

$$= \frac{7}{9}\left(\frac{9n - 1 + 10^{-n}}{9}\right)$$

$$= \frac{7}{81}\,(9n - 1 + 10^{-n}) \qquad \textbf{Ans.}$$

11. Find the sum to n terms of the series : $0·4 + 0·94 + 0·994 + ...$

Sol. Let

$$S = 0·4 + 0·94 + 0·994 + ... \text{to } n \text{ terms}$$

$$= (1 - 0·6) + (1 - 0·06)$$

$$+ (1 - 0·006) + ... \text{ to } n \text{ terms}$$

$$S = (1 + 1 + 1 \, ... \, n \text{ terms})$$

$$- [0·6 + 0·06 + 0·006 \, ... \text{ to } n \text{ terms}]$$

$$= n - \left[0·6\left(\frac{1 - (0·1)^n}{1 - 0·1}\right)\right]$$

$$= n - \left[\frac{0·6}{0·9}(1 - (0·1)^n)\right]$$

$$= n - \frac{6}{9}\,[1 - (0·1)^n] \qquad \textbf{Ans.}$$

12. Find the least value of n for which the sum $1 + 3 + 3^2 + ...$ to n terms is greater than 7,000.

Sol. Let

$$S_n = 1 + 3 + 3^2 + ... + 3^{n-1}$$

$$= \frac{1\,(3^n - 1)}{3 - 1}$$

$$= \frac{3^n - 1}{2}$$

$$\Rightarrow \qquad \frac{3^n - 1}{2} > 7,000$$

$$\Rightarrow \qquad 3^n - 1 > 14,000$$

$$\Rightarrow \qquad 3^n > 14,001$$

But $\qquad\qquad 3^8 = 6561$

and $\qquad\qquad 3^9 = 19683$

$\therefore \quad n$ lies between 8 and 9.

$\therefore \quad$ Least value of n is 9. $\qquad\qquad\qquad$ **Ans.**

13. Find all the sequences which are simultaneously A.P. and G.P.

Sol. Let $< a_n >$ be a sequence which is both an A.P. and a G.P.

Let a_n, a_{n+1}, a_{n+2} be three consecutive terms of the A.P., then

$$2a_{n+1} = a_n + a_{n+2},\, n \geq 1 \qquad ...(i)$$

Let r be the common ratio of the sequence when it is considered a G.P.

Then, $\qquad\qquad a_n = a_1 r^{n-1},$

$$a_{n+1} = a_1 r^n,$$

and $\qquad\qquad a_{n+2} = a_1 r^{n+1}$

Putting these values in (i), we get

$$2a_1 r^n = a_1 r^{n-1} + a_1 r^{n+1}$$

$$\Rightarrow \qquad\qquad 2r = 1 + r^2$$

$$\Rightarrow \qquad\qquad (r - 1)^2 = 0$$

$$\Rightarrow \qquad\qquad r = 1$$

So, $\qquad\qquad a_1 = a_2 = a_3 = ...$

i.e., the constant sequence is the only sequence which is both an A.P. and a G.P. **Ans.**

14. Express the recurring decimal $0·\overline{3}$ as an infinite G.P. and find its value in rational form.

Sol. $\qquad\qquad 0·\overline{3} = 0·3333333 ...$

$$= 0·3 + 0·03 + 0·003 + 0·0003 + ...$$

$$= \frac{3}{10} + \frac{3}{10^2} + \frac{3}{10^3} + \frac{3}{10^4} + \ldots$$

The above is an infinite G.P. with the first term

$$a = \frac{3}{10} \text{ and } r = \frac{\frac{3}{10^2}}{\frac{3}{10}} = \frac{1}{10} < 1$$

Hence, by using the formula

$$S = \frac{a}{1-r}, \text{ we get}$$

$$0.\overline{3} = \frac{\frac{3}{10}}{1 - \frac{1}{10}} = \frac{\frac{3}{10}}{\frac{9}{10}}$$

$$= \frac{3}{9} = \frac{1}{3}$$

Hence, the recurring decimal $0.\overline{3} = \frac{1}{3}$. **Ans.**

15. Three numbers whose sum is 15 are in A.P. if 1, 4, 19 be added to them respectively, then they are in G.P. Find the numbers.

Sol. Let the three numbers are $a - d$, a, $a + d$.

Then   sum = 15

⇒ $a - d + a + a + d = 15$

⇒ $3a = 15$

⇒ $a = 5$.

So, the numbers are $5 - d$, 5, $5 + d$.

Adding 1, 4, 19 respectively to these numbers, we get

$$6 - d, 9, 24 + d.$$

These numbers are in G.P.

∴ $9^2 = (6 - d)(24 + d)$

⇒ $d^2 + 18d - 63 = 0$

⇒ $(d + 21)(d - 3) = 0$

⇒ $d = -21 \text{ or } d = 3$

Hence, the numbers are

$$26, 5, -16 \text{ or } 2, 5, 8.$$ **Ans.**

Chapter 17. Mensuration

1. The radius of two right circular cylinder are in the ratio of 2 : 3 and their heights are in the ratio of 5 : 4, calculate the ratio of their curved surface areas and also the ratio of their volumes.

Sol. Let the radii of two cylinders be $2r$ and $3r$ respectively and their heights be $5h$ and $4h$ respectively. Let S_1 and S_2 be curved surface area of the two cylinders and V_1 and V_2 be their volumes.

Then, S_1 = Curved surface area of the cylinders of height $5h$ and radius $2r$.

$$= 2\pi \times 2r \times 5h = 20\,\pi rh \text{ sq. units}$$

S_2 = Curved surface area of cylinder of height $4h$ and radius $3r$

$$= 2\pi \times 3r \times 4h = 24\pi rh \text{ sq. units}$$

$$\frac{S_1}{S_2} = \frac{20\pi rh}{24\pi rh} = \frac{5}{6}$$

⇒ $S_1 : S_2 = 5 : 6$

V_1 = Volume of cylinder of height $5h$ and radius $2r$

$$= \pi \times (2r)^2 \times 5h = 20\,\pi r^2 h \text{ cubic units}$$

V_2 = Volume of cylinder of height $4h$ and radius $3r$

$$= \pi \times (3r)^2 \times 4h = 36\,\pi r^2 h \text{ cubic units}$$

∴ $\frac{V_1}{V_2} = \frac{20\pi r^2 h}{36\pi r^2 h} = \frac{5}{9} \Rightarrow V_1 : V_2 = 5 : 9$. **Ans.**

2. A vessel in the form of an inverted cone is filled with water to the brim. Its height is 20 cm and diameter is 16.8 cm. Two equal solid cones are dropped in it so that they are fully submerged. As a result, one-third of the water in the original cone overflows. What is the volume of each of the solid cones submerged ?

Sol. Given, for the cone, height = 20 cm,

diameter = 16.8 cm or radius = $\frac{16.8}{2}$ = 8.4 cm.

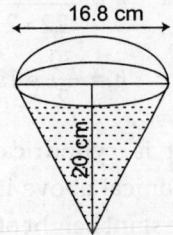

Volume of water in bigger cone

$$= \frac{1}{3}\pi r^2 h$$

$$= \frac{1}{3} \times \frac{22}{7} \times 8.4 \times 8.4 \times 20$$

$$= 1478.4 \text{ cm}^3$$

Volume of water overflows when two equal cone is submerged

$$= \frac{1}{3} \times 1478 \cdot 4$$

$$= 492 \cdot 8 \text{ cm}^3$$

∴ Volume of two equal cones

$$= 492 \cdot 8$$

So, Volume of each cone

$$= \frac{1}{2} \times 492 \cdot 8$$

$$= 246 \cdot 4 \text{ cm}^3 \qquad \textbf{Ans.}$$

3. A conical tent is accommodate to 11 persons each person must have 4 sq. metre of the space on the ground and 20 cubic metre of air to breadth. Find the height of the cone.

Sol. Area of the base

$$= 11 \times 4 = 44 \text{ m}^2$$

and Volume of the cone

$$= 11 \times 20 = 220 \text{ m}^3$$

$$\frac{1}{3} \times \pi R^2 h = 220 \text{ m}^3 \qquad \text{...(i)}$$

Area of the base $= \pi R^2$

$$\pi R^2 = 44$$

$$\Rightarrow \qquad R^2 = \frac{44}{22} \times 7$$

$$\Rightarrow \qquad R^2 = 14$$

$$\Rightarrow \qquad R = \sqrt{14} \qquad \text{...(ii)}$$

By equations (i) and (ii), we get

$$\frac{1}{3} \times \frac{22}{7} \times \sqrt{14} \times \sqrt{14} \times h = 220$$

$$\Rightarrow \qquad h = \frac{220 \times 3}{22 \times 2}$$

$$\therefore \qquad h = \frac{30}{2} = 15 \text{ cm.} \qquad \textbf{Ans.}$$

4. A circus tent is cylindrical to a height of 3 metres and conical above it. If its diameter is 105 m and the slant height of the conical portion is 53 m, calculate the length of the canvas which is 5 m wide to make the required tent.

Sol. Cylindrical area $= 2\pi rh$

$$= 2 \times \frac{22}{7} \times \frac{105}{2} \times 3 \text{ m}^2$$

and conical area $= \pi r l$

$$= \frac{22}{7} \times \frac{105}{2} \times 53 \text{ m}^2$$

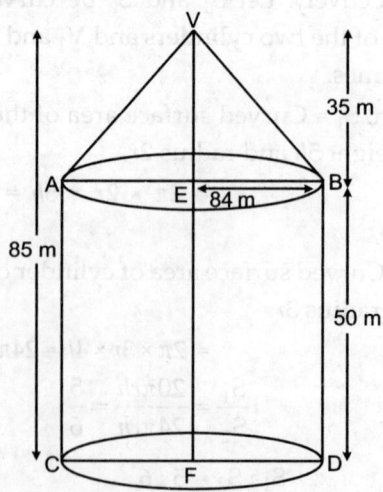

Area of canvas

$$= 2 \times \frac{22}{7} \times \frac{105}{2} \times 3 + \frac{22}{7} \times \frac{105}{2} \times 53$$

$$= 15 \times 11(2 \times 3 + 53)$$

$$= 15 \times 11 \times 59$$

$$= 165 \times 59 \text{ m}^2$$

Length of canvas $= \dfrac{165 \times 59}{5} \text{ m}$

$$= 33 \times 59 \text{ m}$$

$$= 1947 \text{ m.} \qquad \textbf{Ans.}$$

5. An exhibition tent is in the form of a cylinder surmounted by a cone. The height of the tent above the ground is 85 m and the height of the cylindrical part is 50 m. If the diameter of the base is 168 m, find the quantity of canvas required to make the tent. Allow 20% extra for folds and for stitching. Give your answer to the nearest m².

Sol. Radius of box $= \dfrac{168}{2} = 84 \text{ m}$

Height of the cone = 35 m

Height of cylinder = 50 m

Curved surface of the tent

$$= 2\pi rh + \pi r l$$

$$= 2 \times \frac{22}{7} \times 84 \times 50 + \frac{22}{7} \times 84 \times 91$$

$$[l^2 = (35)^2 + (84)^2 \text{ i.e., } l = 91]$$

$$= 44 \times 12 \times 50 + 22 \times 12 \times 91$$

$$= 26,400 + 24,024$$

$$= 50,424 \text{ sq. m.}$$

Area of the canvas required with (20% extra)

$$= \frac{120}{100} \times 50,424$$

$$= 60,508 \cdot 8 \text{ sq. m}$$

$$= 60,509 \text{ m}^2 \qquad \textbf{Ans.}$$

6. The radius of a sphere is 10 cm. If we increase the radius 5% then, how many percentage will increase in volume ?

Sol. Volume of sphere $= \frac{4}{3} \pi r^3$

Given, radius $r = 10$ cm

$\therefore$ Volume of sphere $= \frac{4}{3} \pi \times 10 \times 10 \times 10$

$$= \frac{4000\pi}{3} \text{ cm}^3$$

Now, increase in the radius is 5%.

Radius of new sphere $= \frac{10 \times 105}{100}$

$$= \frac{21}{2} \text{ cm}$$

Volume of new sphere $= \frac{4}{3} \pi \times \frac{21}{2} \times \frac{21}{2} \times \frac{21}{2}$

$$= \frac{9261\pi}{6} \text{ cm}^3$$

Increase volume = Volume of new sphere
$$\qquad\qquad - \text{ Volume of sphere}$$

$$= \frac{9261\pi}{6} - \frac{4000\pi}{3}$$

$$= \frac{9261\pi - 8000\pi}{6}$$

$$= \frac{1261\pi}{6} \text{ cm}$$

Percentage of increase in volume

$$= \frac{\dfrac{1261\pi}{6} \times 100}{\dfrac{4000\pi}{3}}$$

$$= \frac{1261 \, \pi \times 100 \times 3}{4000 \, \pi \times 6} = \frac{1261}{80} \%$$

$$= 15\frac{61}{80}\%. \qquad \textbf{Ans.}$$

7. The cylinder of radius 12 cm have filled the 20 cm with water. One piece of iron drop in the stands of water goes up 6·75 cm. Find the radius of sphere piece.

Sol. Given, radius of cylinder
$$= 12 \text{ cm}$$

Height of cylinder = 6·75 cm

Volume of water $= \pi r^2 h$

$$= \pi \times 12 \times 12 \times 6 \cdot 75 \text{ cm}^3$$

Let the radius of iron sphere piece = R cm

$\therefore$ Volume of sphere = Volume of water

$$\frac{4}{3}\pi R^3 = \pi \times 12 \times 12 \times 6 \cdot 75$$

$$\Rightarrow \qquad R^3 = \frac{\pi \times 12 \times 12 \times 6 \cdot 75 \times 3}{4\pi}$$

$$\Rightarrow \qquad R^3 = 729$$

$$\therefore \qquad R = \sqrt[3]{729} = 9 \text{ cm}$$

Hence, the radius of sphere piece = 9 cm. **Ans.**

8. The radius of the internal and external surfaces of a hollow spherical shell are 3 cm and 5 cm respectively. If it is melted and recast into a solid cylinder of height $\frac{8}{3}$ cm, find the diameter of the cylinder.

Sol. Internal radius of hollow spherical shell,
$$(r_1) = 3 \text{ cm}$$

External radius of hollow spherical,
$$(r_2) = 5 \text{ cm}$$

Volume of hollow spherical

$$= \frac{4}{3} \pi (r_1^3 - r_2^3)$$

$$= \frac{4}{3} \pi [(5)^3 - (3)^3]$$

$$= \frac{4}{3} \pi (125 - 27)$$

$$= \frac{4\pi \times 98}{3} = \frac{392\pi}{3} \text{ cm}^3$$

Volume of cylinder $= \pi r^2 h$

$$= \pi r^2 \times \frac{8}{3}$$

$$= \frac{8\pi r^2}{3} \text{ cm}^3$$

Volume of cylinder = Volume of hollow sphere

$$\frac{8\pi r^2}{3} = \frac{392\pi}{3}$$

$$\Rightarrow \qquad r^2 = \frac{392\pi \times 3}{8\pi \times 3}$$

$$\Rightarrow \qquad r^2 = 49$$

$$\Rightarrow \qquad r = \sqrt{49}$$

$$\therefore \qquad r = 7 \text{ cm}$$

The diameter of cylinder = $2r = 2 \times 7 = 14$ cm.

Ans.

9. The surface area of a solid metallic sphere is 616 cm². It is melted and recast into smaller spheres of diameter 3·5 cm. How many such spheres can be obtained ?

Sol. The surface area of sphere = $4\pi r^2$

$$4\pi r^2 = 616$$

$$\Rightarrow \qquad r^2 = \frac{616 \times 7}{4 \times 22} = 49$$

$$\Rightarrow \qquad r = \sqrt{49}$$

$$\therefore \qquad r = 7 \text{ cm}$$

Volume of big sphere = $\frac{4}{3}\pi r^3 = \frac{4}{3} \times \frac{22}{7} \times (7)^3$

Volume of small sphere = $\frac{4}{3}\pi\left(\frac{3·5}{2}\right)^3$

$\therefore$ Number of smaller sphere

$$= \frac{\text{Vol. of big sphere}}{\text{Vol. of small sphere}}$$

$$= \frac{\frac{4}{3}\pi(7)^3}{\frac{4}{3}\pi\left(\frac{3·5}{2}\right)^3} = 64 \quad \textbf{Ans.}$$

10. A metallic cylinder has radius 3 cm and height 5 cm. It is made of metal A. To reduce its weight, a conical hole is drilled in the cylinder, as shown and it is completely filled with a lighter metal B. The conical hole has a radius of $\frac{3}{2}$ cm and its depth is $\frac{8}{9}$ cm. Calculate the ratio of the volume of the metal A to the volume of the metal B in the solid.

Sol. Volume of metal A

= Volume of the cylinder – Volume of the cone

$$= \pi(3)^2 \times 5 - \frac{1}{3}\pi\left(\frac{3}{2}\right)^2 \times \frac{8}{9}$$

$$= \pi\left(45 - \frac{2}{3}\right)$$

$$= \frac{133}{3}\pi \text{ cm}^3$$

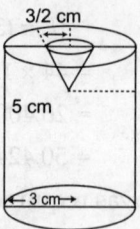

Volume of metal B

= Volume of the conical cavity

$$= \frac{1}{3}\pi\left(\frac{3}{2}\right)^2 \frac{8}{9} = \frac{2}{3}\pi$$

Hence, ratio of the volume of the metal A to the volume of the metal B

$$= \frac{\frac{133}{2}\pi}{\frac{2\pi}{3}} = \frac{133}{2}$$

$$= 66·5 : 1. \qquad \textbf{Ans.}$$

11. An iron pillar has some part in the form of a right circular cylinder and remaining in the form of a right circular cone. The radius of the base of each of cone and cylinder is 8 cm. The cylindrical part is 240 cm high and the conical part is 36 cm high. Find the weight of the pillar if one cubic cm of iron weight is 7·8 grams.

Sol. Let r_1 cm and r_2 cm denote the radii of the base of the cylinder and cone respectively. Then,

$$r_1 = r_2 = 8 \text{ cm}$$

Let h_1 and h_2 cm be the height of the cylinder and the cone respectively. Then,

$$h_1 = 240 \text{ cm and } h_2 = 36 \text{ cm}$$

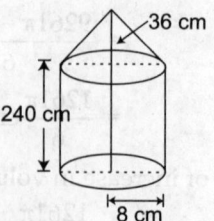

Now, Volume of the cylinder

$$= \pi r_1^2 h_1 \text{ cm}^3$$

$$= (\pi \times 8 \times 8 \times 240) \text{ cm}^3$$

$$= (\pi \times 64 \times 240) \text{ cm}^3$$

Volume of the cone = $\frac{1}{3}\pi r_2^2 h_2 \text{ cm}^3$

$$= \left(\frac{1}{3}\pi \times 8 \times 8 \times 36\right) \text{cm}^3$$

$$= \left(\frac{1}{3}\pi \times 64 \times 36\right) \text{cm}^3$$

∴ Total volume of iron

= Volume of the cylinder

+ Volume of the cone

$$= \left(\pi \times 64 \times 240 + \frac{1}{3}\pi \times 64 \times 36\right) \text{cm}^3$$

$$= \pi \times 64 \times (240 + 12) \text{cm}^3$$

$$= \frac{22}{7} \times 64 \times 252 \text{ cm}^3$$

$$= 22 \times 64 \times 36 \text{ cm}^3$$

Hence, total weight of the pillar

= Volume × Weight per cm³

= (22 × 64 × 36) × 7·8 gm

= 395366·4 gm

= 395·3664 kg **Ans.**

12. A spherical ball of radius 3 cm is melted and recast into three spherical balls. The radii of two of the balls are 1·5 cm and 2 cm. Find the diameter of the third ball.

Sol. The radius of spherical ball = 3 cm

Volume of spherical ball $= \frac{4}{3}\pi r^3$

$$= \frac{4}{3}\pi \times 3 \times 3 \times 3$$

$$= 36\pi \text{ cm}^3$$

Given, the radii of the balls are 1·5 cm and 2 cm.

Let the radius of third ball = r

∴ Volume of spherical ball

= Total volume of three small spherical balls

$$\Rightarrow 36\pi = \frac{4}{3}\pi\left(\frac{3}{2}\right)^3 + \frac{4}{3}\pi(2)^3 + \frac{4}{3}\pi r^3$$

$$\Rightarrow 36\pi = \frac{4}{3}\pi \times \frac{27}{8} + \frac{4}{3}\pi \times 8 + \frac{4}{3}\pi r^3$$

$$\Rightarrow 36\pi = \frac{4}{3}\pi\left(\frac{27}{8} + 8 + r^3\right)$$

$$\Rightarrow \frac{36\pi + 3}{4\pi} = \frac{27}{8} + 8 + r^3$$

$$\Rightarrow 27 = \frac{27 + 64}{8} + r^3$$

$$\Rightarrow 27 = \frac{91}{8} + r^3$$

$$\Rightarrow 27 - \frac{91}{8} = r^3$$

$$\Rightarrow \frac{216 - 91}{8} = r^3$$

$$\Rightarrow \frac{125}{8} = r^3$$

$$\Rightarrow r = \sqrt[3]{\frac{125}{8}}$$

$$\therefore r = \frac{5}{2} \text{ cm}$$

The diameter of the third ball = $2r = 2 \times \frac{5}{2}$ = 5 cm.

Ans.

13. A buoy is made in the form of a hemisphere surmounted by a right cone whose circular base coincides with the plane surface of hemisphere. The radius of the base of the cone is 3.5 metres and its volume is two-thirds of the hemisphere. Calculate the height of the cone and the surface area of buoy carrect to two places of decimal.

Sol. According to question,

$\frac{2}{3}$ (Volume of hemisphere) = Volume of cone

$$\frac{2}{3}\left(\frac{2}{3}\pi r^3\right) = \frac{1}{3}\pi r^2 h$$

$$\Rightarrow \frac{4}{9}(3.5)^3 = \frac{1}{3}(3.5)^2 \cdot h$$

$$h = \frac{4 \times 3.5 \times 3.5 \times 3.5 \times 3}{3.5 \times 3.5 \times 9}$$

$$= \frac{42.0}{9} = \frac{14}{3} \text{ m} = 4.67 \text{ m}$$

$$l = \sqrt{r^2 + h^2}$$

$$= \sqrt{(3.5)^2 + (4.67)^2}$$

$$= \frac{35}{6} \text{ m}$$

Now, Surface area of buoy

= Surface area of right cone

+ Surface area of hemisphere

$$= \pi r l + 2\pi r^2$$

$$= \pi r \, (l + 2r)$$

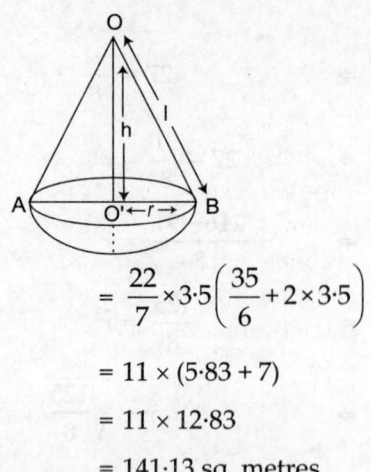

$$= \frac{22}{7} \times 3 \cdot 5 \left(\frac{35}{6} + 2 \times 3 \cdot 5 \right)$$

$$= 11 \times (5 \cdot 83 + 7)$$

$$= 11 \times 12 \cdot 83$$

$$= 141 \cdot 13 \text{ sq. metres} \qquad \textbf{Ans.}$$

14. The following figure represents a solid consisting of right circular cylinder with a hemisphere at one end and a cone at the other. Their common radius is 7 cm. The height of the cylinder and cone are each of 4 cm. Find the volume of the solid.*

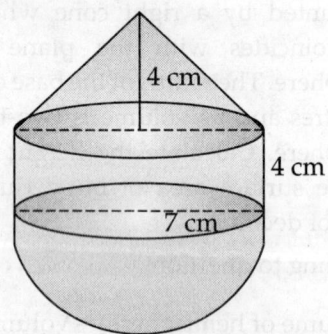

Sol. Given, common radius (r) = 7 cm.

Height of cylinder=Height of cone

$$= h = 4 \text{ cm.}$$

∴ Volume of solid = Volume of cone

+ Volume of cylinder

+ Volume of hemisphere

$$= \frac{1}{3}\pi r^2 h + \pi r^2 h + \frac{2}{3}\pi r^3$$

$$= \pi r^2 \left(\frac{1}{3}h + h + \frac{2}{3}r \right)$$

$$= \frac{22}{7} \times 7^2 \left(\frac{1}{3} \times 4 + 4 + \frac{2}{3} \times 7 \right)$$

$$= 22 \times 7 \left(\frac{4}{3} + 4 + \frac{14}{3} \right)$$

$$= 154 \left(\frac{4 + 12 + 14}{3} \right)$$

$$= 154 \left(\frac{30}{3} \right)$$

$$= 154 \times 10 = 1540 \text{ cm}^3. \textbf{ Ans.}$$

Frequently asked previous years Board Exam Questions.

15. Water flows at the rate of 10 m per minute through a cylindrical pipe 5 mm of diameter. How much time would it take to fill a conical vessel whose diameter at the surface is 40 cm and depth is 24 cm ?

Sol. Volume that flows in 1 min

$$= [\pi \times (0 \cdot 25)^2 \times 1000] \text{ cm}^3$$

Volume of the conical vessel

$$= \frac{1}{3} \pi \times (20)^2 \times 24 \text{ cm}^3$$

$$\text{Required time} = \frac{\frac{1}{3}\pi \times (20)^2 \times 24}{\pi \times (2 \cdot 5)^2 \times 1000}$$

$$= 51 \text{ min } 12 \text{ sec.} \qquad \textbf{Ans.}$$

16. The diameter of the cross-section of a water pipe is 5 cm. Water flows through it at 10 km/hr into a cistern in the form of a cylinder. If the radius of the base of the cistern is 2·5 m, find the height to which the water will rise in the cistern in 24 minutes. (Take $\pi = 3 \cdot 142$)

Sol. Area of the cross-section of the water pipe = πr^2

$$= 3 \cdot 142 \times \frac{5}{2} \times \frac{5}{2}$$

Speed of the water = 10 km/hr

$$= \frac{10 \times 1000 \times 100}{60} \text{ cm/minute}$$

∴ Quantity of water supplied in 24 minutes

$$= 3 \cdot 142 \times \frac{5}{2} \times \frac{5}{2} \times \frac{100000}{6} \times 24$$

$$= 78,55,000 \text{ cm}^3.$$

Let the height of water in the cistern be h cm. The quantity of water collected in the cistern

$$= 3 \cdot 142 \times 250 \times 250 \times h \text{ cm}^3$$

Both the above quantities must be equal

$$3 \cdot 142 \times 250 \times 250 \times h = 78,55,000$$

∴

$$h = 78,55,000 \times \frac{1}{3 \cdot 142 \times 250 \times 250}$$

$$= 40 \text{ cm.} \qquad \textbf{Ans.}$$

17. Water flows through a cylindrical pipe of internal diameter 7 cm at 36 km/hr. Calculate

Concept Based Questions

the time in minutes it would take to fill cylindrical tank, the radius of whose base is 35 cm and height is 1 m.

Sol. Radius of pipe $= \dfrac{7}{2}$ cm

Rate of water flow = 36 km/h

$$= 36 \times \dfrac{5}{18} \text{ m/s}$$

$$= 10 \text{ m/s}$$

$$= 10 \times 100 \text{ cm/s}$$

$$= 1000 \text{ cm/s}$$

∴ Volume of water flowing in 1 second $= \pi r^2 h$

$$= \pi \times \dfrac{7}{2} \times \dfrac{7}{2} \times 1000$$

$$= \pi \times 7 \times 7 \times 250 \text{ cm}^3 \quad …(i)$$

Radius of tank (R) = 35 cm

Height of tank (H) = 1 m

$$= 100 \text{ cm}$$

∴ Volume of tank $= \pi r^2 H$

$$= \pi \times 35 \times 35 \times 100 \text{ cm}^3 …(ii)$$

∴ Time taken to fill the tank

$$= \dfrac{\text{Volume of tank}}{\text{Volume of water flowing in 1 second}}$$

$$= \dfrac{\pi \times 35 \times 35 \times 100}{\pi \times 7 \times 7 \times 250}$$

$$= 10 \text{ seconds}$$

$$= \dfrac{10}{60} \text{ minute}$$

$$= \dfrac{1}{6} \text{ minute.} \qquad \textbf{Ans.}$$

18. A bucket is raised from a well by means of a rope which is wound round a wheel of diameter 77 cm. Given that the ascends in 1 minute 28 seconds with a uniform speed of 1·1 m/sec, calculate the number of complete revolutions the wheel makes in raising the bucket.

(Take $\pi = 22/7$)

Sol. Time of ascent = 1 minute 28 seconds

$$= 88 \text{ seconds}$$

Distance moved by the bucket

$$= \text{Speed} \times \text{Time}$$

$$= [1·1 \times 88] \text{ metre}$$

$$= 96·8 \text{ metres}$$

Circumference of wheel $= 2\pi r$

$$= 2 \times \dfrac{22}{7} \times \dfrac{77}{2} \text{ cm}$$

$$\left(\because r = \dfrac{d}{2} = \dfrac{77}{2} \text{ cm} \right)$$

$$= 242 \text{ cm} = 2·42 \text{ metres}$$

∴ Number of complete revolutions the wheel makes in raising the bucket

$$= \dfrac{\text{Distance}}{\text{Circumference}}$$

$$= \left(\dfrac{96·8}{2·42} \right) = 40 \qquad \textbf{Ans.}$$

Chapter 18. Trigonometry

1. From the top of a cliff, the angle of depression of the top and bottom of a tower are observed to be 45° and 60° respectively. If the height of the tower is 20 m.*

Find :

(i) the height of the cliff

(ii) the distance between the cliff and the tower.

Sol. Let *AB* be the cliff and *CD* be the tower.

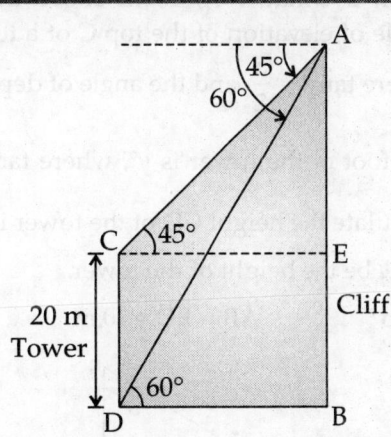

Also, let *DB*= *CE* = *x* m and *AB* = *h* m

(i) In △ABD,

$$\tan 60° = \frac{AB}{DB}$$

$$\sqrt{3} = \frac{h}{x}$$

$$h = x\sqrt{3} \qquad \text{...(i)}$$

And, in ΔACE,

$$\tan 45° = \frac{AE}{CE}$$

$$\Rightarrow \qquad 1 = \frac{AB - BE}{x}$$

$$\Rightarrow \qquad 1 = \frac{h - 20}{x}$$

$$x = h - 20 \qquad \text{...(ii)}$$

Putting the value of x in equation (i), we get

$$h = (h - 20)\sqrt{3}$$

$$\Rightarrow \qquad h = \sqrt{3}h - 20\sqrt{3}$$

$$\Rightarrow \qquad \sqrt{3}h - h = 20\sqrt{3}$$

$$\Rightarrow \qquad h(\sqrt{3} - 1) = 20\sqrt{3}$$

$$\Rightarrow \qquad h = \frac{20\sqrt{3}}{\sqrt{3} - 1} \times \frac{\sqrt{3} + 1}{\sqrt{3} + 1}$$

$$= \frac{20\sqrt{3}(\sqrt{3} + 1)}{3 - 1}$$

$$= 10(3 + \sqrt{3}) = 10(3 + 1.732)$$

$$= 10 \times 4.732$$

$$= 47.32 \text{ m}$$

Hence, the height of cliff is 47.32 m. **Ans.**

(ii) Putting the value of h in equation (ii), we get

$$x = h - 20 = 47.32 - 20$$

$$= 27.32$$

Hence, the distance between the cliff and the tower is 27.32 m. **Ans.**

2. From a window A, 10 m above the ground angle of elevation of the top C of a tower is $x°$, where $\tan x = \frac{5}{2}$ and the angle of depression of the foot of the tower is $y°$, where $\tan y° = \frac{1}{4}$, calculate the height CD of the tower in metres.

Sol. Let h be the height of the tower.

Also $\qquad AB = ED = 10 \text{ m}$

In Δ DAE,

$$\tan y° = \frac{DE}{AE}$$

$$\Rightarrow \qquad \frac{1}{4} = \frac{10}{AE}$$

$$\Rightarrow \qquad AE = 40 \text{ m}$$

Now, in Δ CAE,

$$\tan x° = \frac{CE}{AE}$$

$$\Rightarrow \qquad \frac{5}{2} = \frac{CE}{40}$$

$$\Rightarrow \qquad CE = \frac{40 \times 5}{2}$$

$$= 100 \text{ m}$$

Height of the tower, $h = CE + ED$

$$= 100 + 10 = 110 \text{ m}. \qquad \textbf{Ans.}$$

3. A man on the deck of a ship is 10 m above water level. He observes that the angle of elevation of the top of a cliff is 42° and the angle of depression of the base is 20°. Calculate the distance of the cliff from the ship and the height of the cliff.

Sol. Let the height of the cliff be h metres and the distance of the cliff from the ship be x metres.

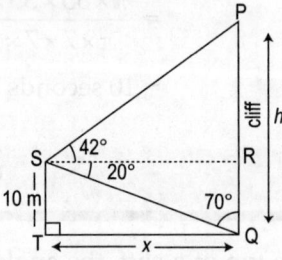

In right angled Δ QRS,

$$QR = ST = 10 \text{ m}, \quad TQ = RS = x \text{ m}$$

$$\therefore \qquad \tan 70° = \frac{RS}{QR}$$

$$\Rightarrow \qquad 2·747 = \frac{x}{10 \text{ m}}$$

$$\therefore \qquad x = 27·47 \text{ m}$$

Hence, the distance of the cliff from the ship

$$= 27·47 \text{ m.} \qquad \textbf{Ans.}$$

Again in right angled Δ PRS,

$$\tan 42° = \frac{PR}{RS}$$

$$\Rightarrow \qquad 0.9004 = \frac{PR}{27.47}$$

$$\Rightarrow \qquad PR = [0.9004 \times 27.47] \text{ m}$$

$$= 24.73 \text{ m}$$

$$\therefore \qquad PQ = PR + RQ$$

$$= [24.73 + 10] \text{ m}$$

$$= 34.73 \text{ m}.$$

Hence, the height of the cliff

$$= 34.73 \text{ m}. \qquad \textbf{Ans.}$$

4. Vertical tower is 20 m high. A man standing at some distance from the tower knows that the cosine of the angle of elevation of the top of the tower is 0.53. How far is he standing from the foot of the tower ?

Sol. Given, $\cos \theta = 0.53$

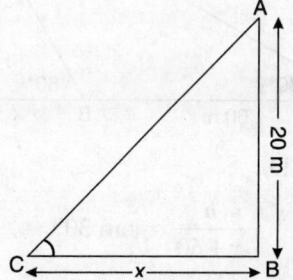

Let the man is standing at a distance of 'x' m from the foot of the tower

$$\cos \theta = \frac{BC}{AC} = \frac{x}{\sqrt{x^2 + 400}}$$

$$0.53 = \frac{x}{\sqrt{x^2 + 400}}$$

$$\Rightarrow \qquad (0.53)^2 = \frac{x^2}{x^2 + 400}$$

$$\Rightarrow \quad 0.2809 \, x^2 + 112.36 = x^2$$

$$\Rightarrow \quad x^2 - 0.2809 \, x^2 = 112.36$$

$$\Rightarrow \qquad x^2 = \frac{112.36}{0.7191}$$

$$\Rightarrow \qquad x^2 = 156.25$$

$$x = 12.5$$

∴ The man is standing from the foot of the tower is 12·5 metres. **Ans.**

5. From a light house, the angles of depression of two ships on opposite sides of the light house were observed to be 30° and 45°. If the height of the light house is 90 metres and the line joining the two ships passes through the foot of the light house, find the distance between the two ships, correct to two decimal places.

Sol. Let AB is the light house, C and D are the position of two ships.

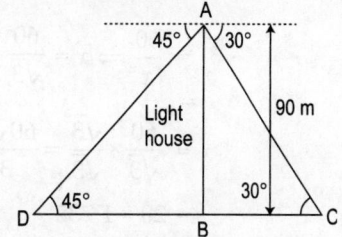

From right angled Δ ABC,

$$\tan 30° = \frac{AC}{BC}$$

$$\Rightarrow \qquad \frac{1}{\sqrt{3}} = \frac{90 \text{ m}}{BC}$$

$$\Rightarrow \qquad BC = [90 \times \sqrt{3}] \text{ m}$$

$$\therefore \qquad BC = 155.88 \text{ m}$$

Again, from right angled Δ ABD,

$$\tan 45° = \frac{AB}{BD}$$

$$\Rightarrow \qquad 1 = \frac{90 \text{ m}}{BD}$$

$$\Rightarrow \qquad BD = 90 \text{ m}$$

Hence, the distance between the two ships

$$= BC + BD$$

$$= (155.88 + 90) \text{ m}$$

$$= 245.88 \text{ m}. \qquad \textbf{Ans.}$$

6. The angles of depression of two ships A and B as observed from the top of a lighthouse 60 m high are 60° and 45° respectively. If the two ships are on the opposite sides of the lighthouse, find the distance between the two ships. Give your answer correct to the nearest whole number.

Sol. Let CD be the light house

$$\therefore \qquad CD = 60 \text{ m}$$

Let $\qquad AD = x \text{ m}, BD = y \text{ m}.$

In ΔACD,

$$\tan 60° = \frac{CD}{AD}$$

$$\Rightarrow \quad \sqrt{3} = \frac{60}{x} \Rightarrow x = \frac{60}{\sqrt{3}}$$

$$\Rightarrow \quad x = \frac{60}{\sqrt{3}} \times \frac{\sqrt{3}}{\sqrt{3}} = \frac{60\sqrt{3}}{3}$$

$$= 20 \times 1·732$$

$$= 34·64 \text{ m}$$

In $\triangle BCD$,

$$\tan 45° = \frac{CD}{BD}$$

$$\Rightarrow \quad 1 = \frac{60}{y} \Rightarrow y = 60 \text{ m}$$

$\therefore$ Distance between two ships = $x + y$

$$= 34·64 + 60$$

$$= 94·64 \text{ m}$$

$$= 95 \text{ m}$$

(correct to nearest whole number) **Ans.**

7. An aeroplane at an altitude of 250 m observes the angle of depression of two boats on the opposite banks of a river to be 45° and 60° respectively. Find the width of the river. Write the answer correct to the nearest whole number.

Sol. Let aeroplane be at position A and BC be the river. Drop a perpendicular from A on BC let it intersect BC at D.

In $\triangle ADB$,

$$\tan 60° = \frac{AD}{BD}$$

$$\Rightarrow \quad \sqrt{3} = \frac{250}{x}$$

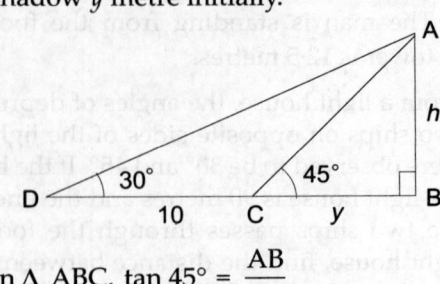

$$\Rightarrow \quad x = \frac{250}{\sqrt{3}} \text{ m} \qquad \dots(i)$$

In $\triangle ADC$,

$$\tan 45° = \frac{AD}{DC}$$

$$\Rightarrow \quad 1 = \frac{250}{y}$$

$$\Rightarrow \quad y = 250 \text{ m}$$

Thus, width of the river

$$= 250 \times \frac{250}{\sqrt{3}} = 394 \text{ m} \quad \textbf{Ans.}$$

8. A man observes the angle of elevation of the top of a building to be 30°. He walks towards it in a horizontal line through its base. On covering 60 m the angle of elevation changes to 60°. Find the height of the building correct to the nearest metre.

Sol. Let the height be h

In $\triangle BCD$, $\dfrac{h}{x} = \tan 60°$

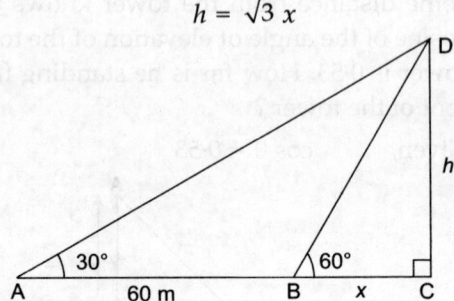

$$\Rightarrow \quad \frac{h}{x} = \sqrt{3}$$

$$h = \sqrt{3}\, x$$

In $\triangle ACD$,

$$\Rightarrow \quad \frac{h}{x+60} = \tan 30°$$

$$\Rightarrow \quad \frac{h}{x+60} = \frac{1}{\sqrt{3}}$$

$$\Rightarrow \quad h\sqrt{3} = x + 60$$

$$\Rightarrow \quad 3x - x = 60$$

$$\Rightarrow \quad 2x = 60$$

$$\Rightarrow \quad x = 30$$

Now, $h = \sqrt{3}\, x$

$$\Rightarrow \quad h = 30 \times \sqrt{3}$$

$$= 30 \times 1·732$$

$\therefore$ Height = $51·96$ m **Ans.**

9. The shadow of a vertical tower on a level ground increases by 10 m when the altitude of the sun changes from 45° to 30°. Find the height of the tower, correct to two decimal places.

Sol. Let the height of tower be h metre and length of shadow y metre initially.

In $\triangle ABC$, $\tan 45° = \dfrac{AB}{BC}$

Concept Based Questions

$$\Rightarrow \qquad 1 = \frac{h}{y}$$

$$\Rightarrow \qquad y = h \qquad \qquad \dots \text{(i)}$$

In $\triangle$ ABD,

$$\tan 30° = \frac{AB}{DB}$$

$$\Rightarrow \qquad \frac{1}{\sqrt{3}} = \frac{h}{y+10}$$

$$\Rightarrow \qquad y + 10 = h\sqrt{3} \qquad \dots \text{(ii)}$$

Put $y = h$ in equation (ii),

$$h + 10 = h\sqrt{3}$$

$$\Rightarrow \qquad h(\sqrt{3}-1) = 10$$

$$\Rightarrow \qquad h = \frac{10(\sqrt{3}+1)}{(\sqrt{3}-1)(\sqrt{3}+1)}$$

$$= \frac{10}{(3-1)}(\sqrt{3}+1)$$

$$= \frac{10}{2}(\sqrt{3}+1)$$

$$= 5(1·732+1)$$

$$= 5 \times 2·732$$

$$= 13·66 \text{ metre} \qquad \textbf{Ans.}$$

10. A man on the top of vertical observation tower observes a car moving at a uniform speed coming directly towards it. If it takes 12 minutes for the angle of depression to change from 30° to 45°, how soon after this will the car reach the observation tower ? (Give your answer correct to nearest seconds).

Sol. Here, $\angle$ACB = 30° and $\angle$ADB = 45°. Let C denote the initial position of the car and D be its position after 12 minutes. Let the speed of the car be x metre/minute, then

$$CD = 12x \text{ metres}$$

$$(\because \text{ Distance} = \text{Speed} \times \text{Time})$$

Let the car take t minutes to reach the tower from D. Then,

$$DB = tx \text{ metres}$$

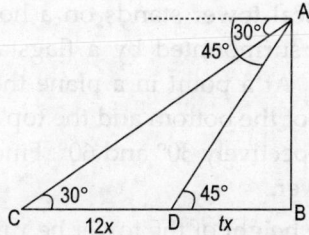

Now, in the right angled triangle ACB,

$$\tan 30° = \frac{AB}{CB}$$

$$\Rightarrow \qquad \frac{1}{\sqrt{3}} = \frac{AB}{CD+DB}$$

$$\Rightarrow \qquad \frac{1}{\sqrt{3}} = \frac{AB}{12x+tx}$$

$$\Rightarrow \qquad AB = \frac{12x+tx}{\sqrt{3}} \qquad \dots \text{(i)}$$

Also, in the right angled triangle ADB,

$$\tan 45° = \frac{AB}{DB}$$

$$\Rightarrow \qquad 1 = \frac{AB}{DB}$$

$$\Rightarrow \qquad AB = DB = tx \qquad \dots \text{(ii)}$$

From (i) and (ii), we have

$$t = \frac{12}{\sqrt{3}-1} = \frac{12(\sqrt{3}+1)}{2}$$

$$= 6(\sqrt{3}+1)$$

$$= 16.39$$

$$\therefore \qquad \text{Time} = 16.39 \text{ minutes}$$

$$= 16 \text{ minutes } 23 \text{ seconds.}$$

$$\textbf{Ans.}$$

11. Two men on either side of a temple 75 m high observed the angle of elevation of the top of the temple to be 30° and 60° respectively. Find the distance between the two men.

Sol. Given, height of the temple AB = 75 m

Now, in right angled $\triangle$ ABC,

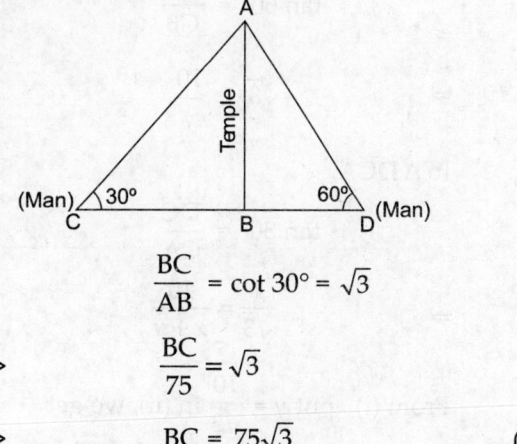

$$\frac{BC}{AB} = \cot 30° = \sqrt{3}$$

$$\Rightarrow \qquad \frac{BC}{75} = \sqrt{3}$$

$$\Rightarrow \qquad BC = 75\sqrt{3} \qquad \dots \text{(i)}$$

Also, in right angled $\triangle$ ABD,

$$\frac{BD}{AB} = \cot 60°$$

$$\Rightarrow \qquad \frac{BD}{75} = \frac{1}{\sqrt{3}}$$

$$\Rightarrow \qquad BD = \frac{75}{\sqrt{3}} \times \frac{\sqrt{3}}{\sqrt{3}}$$

$$= 25\sqrt{3} \qquad \text{...(ii)}$$

Now, the distance between the two men = CD

$$= BC + BD$$

$$= 75\sqrt{3} + 25\sqrt{3}$$

$$= 100\sqrt{3}$$

Hence, the distance between two men

$$= 100\sqrt{3} \text{ m.}$$

$$= 173 \cdot 2 \text{ m} \qquad \textbf{Ans.}$$

12. From two points A and B on the same side of a building, the angles of elevation of the top of the building are 30° and 60° respectively. If the height of the building is 10 m, find the distance between A and B correct to two decimal places.

Sol. Let CD is the building, A and B are two given points using horizontally on the same side of building.

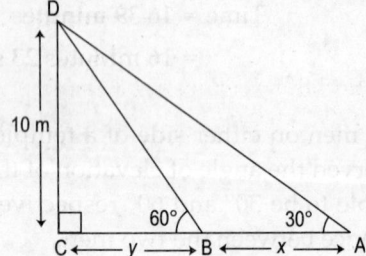

In Δ DBC,

$$\tan 60° = \frac{DC}{CB}$$

$$\Rightarrow \qquad \sqrt{3} = \frac{10}{y} \qquad \text{...(i)}$$

In Δ DCA,

$$\tan 30° = \frac{DC}{CA}$$

$$\Rightarrow \qquad \frac{1}{\sqrt{3}} = \frac{10}{x+y} \qquad \text{...(ii)}$$

From (i), put $y = \dfrac{10}{\sqrt{3}}$ in (ii), we get

$$\frac{1}{\sqrt{3}} = \frac{10}{x + \dfrac{10}{\sqrt{3}}}$$

$$\Rightarrow \qquad \frac{1}{\sqrt{3}} = \frac{10\sqrt{3}}{\sqrt{3}x + 10}$$

$$\Rightarrow \qquad 30 = \sqrt{3}x + 10$$

$$\Rightarrow \qquad x = \frac{20}{\sqrt{3}}$$

$$\Rightarrow \qquad x = 11 \cdot 55 \text{ m.}$$

Hence, distance between two points A and B is 11·55 m. **Ans.**

13. An aeroplane when 3,000 metres high passes vertically above another aeroplane at an instance when their angles of elevation at the some observation points are 60° and 45° respectively. How many metres higher is the one than the other?

Sol. Let P_1 and P_2 denote the positions of the two planes.

Then, in right angled Δ P_1AB,

$$\frac{P_1B}{AB} = \tan 45° \Rightarrow P_1B = AB$$

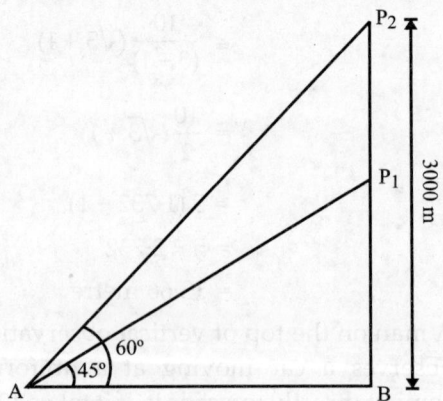

In right angled Δ P_2AB,

$$\frac{P_2B}{AB} = \tan 60° = \sqrt{3}$$

$$\Rightarrow \qquad AB = \frac{P_2B}{\sqrt{3}}$$

$$= \frac{3,000}{\sqrt{3}}$$

$$= 1,000\sqrt{3}$$

∴ Vertical distance between the two planes is

$$P_1P_2 = P_2B - P_1B = 3,000 - 1,000\sqrt{3}$$

$$= 1,000(3 - \sqrt{3}) \text{ m.} \qquad \textbf{Ans.}$$

14. A vertical tower stands on a horizontal plane and is surmounted by a flagstaff of height 7 metres. At a point in a plane the angle of elevation of the bottom and the top of the flagstaff are respectively 30° and 60°. Find the height of the tower.

Sol. Let the height of the tower be x m and distance DC = y m

∴   AB = Height of flagstaff = 7 m

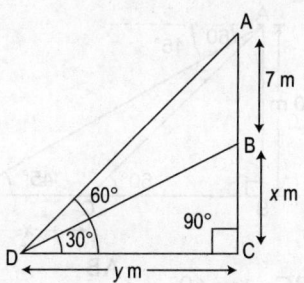

Now, in right angled △ BCD,

$$\frac{BC}{CD} = \tan 30°$$

∴ $\frac{x}{y} = \frac{1}{\sqrt{3}}$

⇒ $y = \sqrt{3}\, x$ ...(i)

Also, in right angled △ ACD,

$$\frac{AC}{CD} = \tan 60°$$

⇒ $\frac{x+7}{y} = \sqrt{3}$

⇒ $x + 7 = \sqrt{3}y$

⇒ $x + 7 = \sqrt{3}(\sqrt{3}x)$ [from (i)]

⇒ $x + 7 = 3x$

⇒ $2x = 7$

⇒ $x = \dfrac{7}{2} = 3.5$ m.

Hence, the height of the tower

       = 7 + 3·5

       = 10·5 m   **Ans.**

15. A pole being broken by the wind the top struck the ground at an angle of 30° and at a distance of 8 m from the foot of the pole. Find the whole height of the pole.

Sol. Let ABC be the pole. When broken at B by the wind, let its top A strike the ground such that

       ∠ CAB = 30°

       AC = 8 m

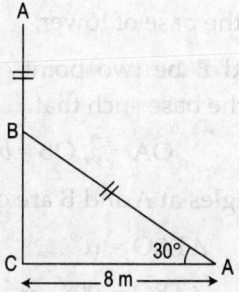

In △ ACB,

$$\tan 30° = \frac{BC}{AC}$$

⇒ $\frac{1}{\sqrt{3}} = \frac{BC}{8}$

⇒ $BC = \frac{8}{\sqrt{3}}$

Again in △ ACB,

$$\cos 30° = \frac{AC}{AB}$$

⇒ $\frac{\sqrt{3}}{2} = \frac{8}{AB}$

⇒ $AB = \frac{16}{\sqrt{3}}$

Height of the pole = AC = AB + BC

       $= \frac{16}{\sqrt{3}} + \frac{8}{\sqrt{3}}$

       $= 8\sqrt{3}$ m or 13·86 m.   **Ans.**

16. Two persons standing on the same side of a tower in a straight line with it measure the angle of elevation of the top of the tower as 25° and 50° respectively. If the height of the tower is 70 m find the distance between the two persons.

Sol. Let CD be the distance between the two persons.

In △ ABC,

$$\cot 50° = \frac{BC}{AB}$$

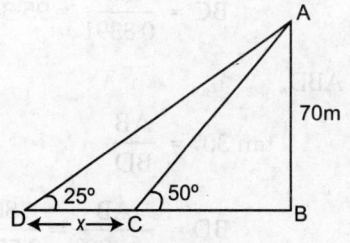

⇒ $\cot 50° = \frac{BC}{70}$

⇒ $BC = 70 \cot 50°$

       $= 70 \times 0.8391 = 58.74$ m

In △ ABD,

$$\cot 25° = \frac{BD}{AB}$$

⇒ $\cot 25° = \frac{BD}{70}$

⇒ $BD = 70 \cot 25°$

       $= 70 \times 2.14451$

= 150·12 m

CD = 150·12 – 58·74

= 91·38 m

∴ The distance between the two persons be 91·38 m. **Ans.**

17. As observed from the top of a 80 m tall lighthouse, the angles of depression of two ships on the same side of the lighthouse in horizontal line with its base are 30° and 40° respectively. Find the distance between the two ships. Give your answer correct to the nearest metre.

Sol. In fig. AB is 80 m tall lighthouse, the two ships are C and D.

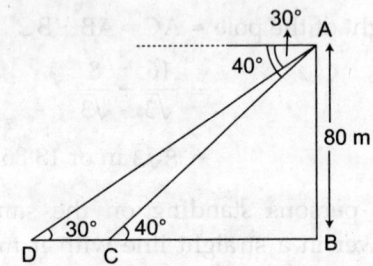

In Δ ABC,

$$\tan 40° = \frac{AB}{BC}$$

⇒ $$BC = \frac{AB}{\tan 40°}$$

⇒ $$BC = \frac{80}{0·8391} = 95·34 \text{ m}$$

In Δ ABD,

$$\tan 30° = \frac{AB}{BD}$$

⇒ $$BD = \frac{AB}{\tan 30°} = \frac{80}{0·5774}$$

= 138·55 m

Distance between two ships

DC = BD – BC

= 138·55 – 95·34

= 43·21 m ≈ 43 m. **Ans.**

18. An aeroplane at an altitude of 250 m observes the angle of depression of two boats on the opposite banks of a river to be 45° and 60° respectively. Find the width of the river. Write the answer correct to the nearest whole number.

Sol. Let the width of the river CD be x.

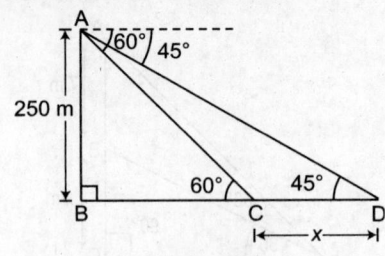

In Δ ABC, $$\tan 60° = \frac{AB}{BC}$$

⇒ $$\sqrt{3} = \frac{250}{BC}$$

⇒ $$BC = \frac{250}{\sqrt{3}} \times \frac{\sqrt{3}}{\sqrt{3}}$$

⇒ $$= \left(\frac{250}{3}\right)\sqrt{3} \qquad ...(i)$$

In Δ ABD, $$\tan 45° = \frac{AB}{BD}$$

⇒ $$AB = BD = 250 \qquad ...(ii)$$

∴ BD = BC + CD

⇒ $$250 = \left(\frac{250}{3}\right)\sqrt{3} + x$$

[using (i) and (ii)]

∴ $$x = 250 - \left(\frac{250}{3}\right) \times 1·732$$

= 250 – 83·33 × 1·732

= 250 – 144·33

= 105·67 m

= 106 m

(Correct to the nearest whole numbers)

Thus, width of the river is 106 m. **Ans.**

19. The angles of elevation of the top of a tower from two points A and B at distance of *a* and *b* respectively from the base and in the same straight line with it are complementary. Prove that the height of the tower is $\sqrt{ab}$.

Sol. Let the height of the tower, 'OT' = h

Let O be the base of tower.

Let A and B be two points on the same line through the base such that

OA = *a*, OB = *b*

∵ The angles at A and B are complementary

∴ ∠TAO = α

then ∠TBO = 90° – α

In right angled $\triangle$ OAT,

$$\tan \alpha = \frac{OT}{OA} = \frac{h}{a} \qquad \ldots(i)$$

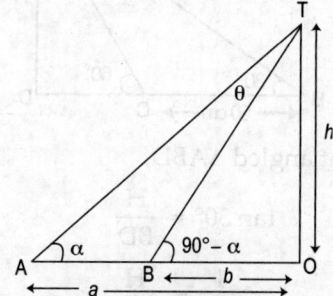

In right angled $\triangle$ OBT,

$$\tan (90° - \alpha) = \frac{OT}{OB} = \frac{h}{b}$$

$\Rightarrow \qquad \cot \alpha = \dfrac{h}{b} \qquad \ldots(ii)$

Multiplying equations (i) and (ii), we have

$$\tan \alpha \cot \alpha = \frac{h}{a} \times \frac{h}{b} = \frac{h^2}{ab}$$

$\Rightarrow \qquad 1 = \dfrac{h^2}{ab}$

$\Rightarrow \qquad h^2 = ab$

$\Rightarrow \qquad h = \sqrt{ab}$

Hence, the height of the tower = $\sqrt{ab}$. **Ans.**

20. From the top of a hill, the angles of depression of two consecutive kilometre stones, due east are found to be 30° and 45° respectively. Find the distance of the two stones from the foot of the hill.

Sol. Let AB be hill of which B is foot of hill and D and C are two consecutive kilometre stones.

$\therefore \qquad DC = 1 \text{ km}$

$\qquad\qquad = 1000 \text{ m}$

In right angled $\triangle$ ABC,

$$\tan 45° = \frac{AB}{BC}$$

$\Rightarrow \qquad 1 = \dfrac{h}{x}$

$\Rightarrow \qquad x = h \qquad \ldots(i)$

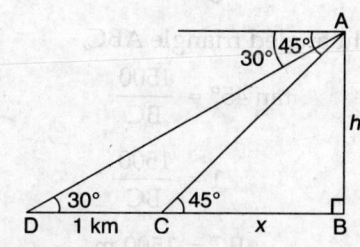

In right angled $\triangle$ ABD,

$$\tan 30° = \frac{AB}{BD}$$

$\Rightarrow \qquad \dfrac{1}{\sqrt{3}} = \dfrac{h}{x+1000}$

$\Rightarrow \qquad x + 1000 = h\sqrt{3} \qquad \ldots(ii)$

But from equation (i), $x = h$,

$\therefore \qquad x + 1000 = x\sqrt{3}$

$\Rightarrow \qquad x(\sqrt{3} - 1) = 1000$

$\Rightarrow \qquad x = \dfrac{1000}{\sqrt{3} - 1} \times \dfrac{\sqrt{3} + 1}{\sqrt{3} + 1}$

$\qquad\qquad = \dfrac{1000(\sqrt{3} + 1)}{2}$

$\qquad\qquad = 500(\sqrt{3} + 1)$

$\qquad\qquad = 500 \times 2 \cdot 732$

$\qquad\qquad = 1366 \text{ metre}$

$\qquad\qquad = 1 \cdot 366 \text{ km}$

$\therefore$ First stone is 1·366 km and second stone is 2·366 km from foot of hill. **Ans.**

21. A man observes the angle of elevation of the top of the tower to be 45°. He walks towards it in a horizontal line through its base. On covering 20 m the angle of elevation changes to 60°. Find the height of the tower correct to 2 significant figures.*

Sol. Let $AB = x$ be the height of the tower and $CD = 20$ m be the distance he walked towards the tower

Let $\qquad\qquad BD = y$

In $\triangle ABD$,

$$\tan 60° = \frac{x}{y}$$

$\Rightarrow \qquad \sqrt{3} = \dfrac{x}{y}$

$\Rightarrow \qquad y = \dfrac{x}{\sqrt{3}} \qquad \ldots(i)$

In $\triangle ABC$,

$$\tan 45° = \frac{x}{y + 20}$$

$\Rightarrow \qquad 1 = \dfrac{x}{y + 20}$

$\Rightarrow \qquad x = y + 20 \qquad \qquad …(ii)$

From equations (i) and (ii), we get

$$x = \frac{x}{\sqrt{3}} + 20$$

$\Rightarrow \qquad \sqrt{3}\,x = x + 20\sqrt{3}$

$\Rightarrow \qquad \sqrt{3}\,x - x = 20\sqrt{3}$

$\Rightarrow \qquad (\sqrt{3} - 1)\,x = 20\sqrt{3}$

$\Rightarrow \qquad x = \dfrac{20\sqrt{3}}{\sqrt{3} - 1}$

$\Rightarrow \qquad x = \dfrac{20\sqrt{3}\,(\sqrt{3} + 1)}{(\sqrt{3} - 1)(\sqrt{3} + 1)}$

$\Rightarrow \qquad x = \dfrac{20\sqrt{3}\,(\sqrt{3} + 1)}{(\sqrt{3})^2 - (1)^2}$

$\qquad \qquad = \dfrac{20\sqrt{3}\,(\sqrt{3} + 1)}{3 - 1}$

$\qquad \qquad = \dfrac{20\sqrt{3}\,(\sqrt{3} + 1)}{2}$

$\qquad \qquad = 10\sqrt{3}\,(\sqrt{3} + 1)$

$\qquad \qquad = 10\sqrt{3} \times \sqrt{3} + 10\sqrt{3}$

$\qquad \qquad = 30 + 10 \times 1.732$

$\qquad \qquad = 30 + 17.32$

$\qquad \qquad = 47.32$ m

(Correct to 2 significant figures)

$\therefore$ Height of tower is 47.32 m. **Ans.**

22. A man standing on the bank of a river observes that the angle of elevation of a tree on the opposite bank is 60°. When he moves 50 m away from the bank, he finds the angle of elevation to be 30°. Calculate :

(i) The width of the river and

(ii) The height of the tree.

Sol. Let height of the tree be H metre.

In right angled $\triangle$ ACD,

$$\tan 60° = \frac{H}{CD}$$

$\Rightarrow \qquad \sqrt{3} = \dfrac{H}{CD}$

$\therefore \qquad CD = \dfrac{H}{\sqrt{3}} \qquad \qquad …(i)$

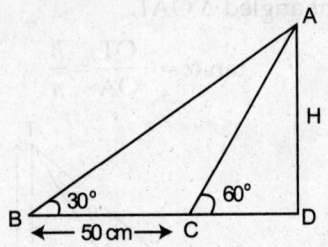

In right angled $\triangle ABD$,

$$\tan 30° = \frac{H}{BD}$$

$\Rightarrow \qquad \dfrac{1}{\sqrt{3}} = \dfrac{H}{BD}$

$\therefore \qquad BD = \sqrt{3}\,H \qquad \qquad …(ii)$

$\qquad \qquad BD - CD = 50$

$\Rightarrow \qquad \dfrac{\sqrt{3}\,H}{1} - \dfrac{H}{\sqrt{3}} = 50 \qquad$ [Using (i) and (ii)]

$\therefore \qquad \dfrac{3H - H}{\sqrt{3}} = 50$

$\Rightarrow \qquad 2H = 50\sqrt{3}$

or $\qquad H = \dfrac{50\sqrt{3}}{2} = 25\sqrt{3}$

$\Rightarrow \qquad H = 43\cdot3$ m

(i) The width of the river $CD = \dfrac{25\sqrt{3}}{\sqrt{3}} = 25$ m

Ans.

(ii) The height of the tree H = 43·3 m. **Ans.**

23. An aeroplane at an altitude of 1500 metres finds that two ships are sailing towards it in the same direction. The angles of depression as observed from the aeroplane are 45° and 30° respectively. Find the distance between the two ships.

Sol. Let AB be the altitude and C and D are the positions of two ships.

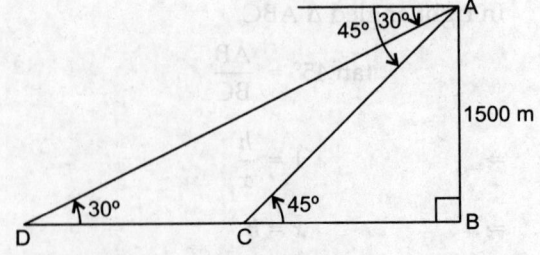

In right angled triangle ABC,

$$\tan 45° = \frac{1500}{BC}$$

$\Rightarrow \qquad 1 = \dfrac{1500}{BC}$

$\Rightarrow \qquad BC = 1500$ m

In right angled triangle ABD,

$$\tan 30° = \frac{1500}{BD}$$

$$\Rightarrow \qquad \frac{1}{\sqrt{3}} = \frac{1500}{BD}$$

$$\Rightarrow \quad BD = 1500\sqrt{3} = 1500 \times 1\cdot732 = 2598 \text{ m}$$

∴ Distance between the two ships

$$= CD$$
$$= BD - BC$$
$$= 2598 - 1500$$
$$= 1098 \text{ m} \qquad \textbf{Ans.}$$

24. A man is standing on the deck of a ship, which is 10 m above water level. He observes the angle of elevation of the top of a hill as 60° and the angle of depression of the base of the hill as 30°. Calculate the distance of the hill from the ship and the height of hill.

Sol. Let AB be the height of the hill.

In right angled △ BCD,

$$\frac{CD}{DB} = \tan 30°$$

$$\Rightarrow \qquad DB = 10\sqrt{3} \text{ m}$$

Distance of the hill from the ship

$$= 10\sqrt{3} \text{ m} \qquad \textbf{Ans.}$$

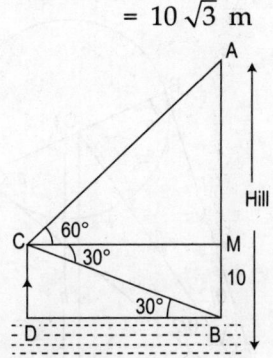

In right angled △ AMC,

$$\frac{AM}{CM} = \tan 60°$$

$$\Rightarrow \qquad AM = \sqrt{3}\ CM$$
$$\Rightarrow \qquad AM = \sqrt{3}\ DB$$
$$= \sqrt{3} \times 10\sqrt{3} = 30 \text{ m}$$

Thus, $\qquad AB = AM + MB$
$$= (30 + 10) \text{ m} = 40 \text{ m}.$$

∴ Height of the hill is 40 m. **Ans.**

25. (i) The angle of elevation of a cloud from a point 200 metres above a lake is 30° and the angle of depression of its reflection in the lake is 60°. Find the height of the cloud.

(ii) If the angle of elevation of a cloud from a point h metres above a lake is α and the

angle of depression of its reflection in the lake is β. Prove that the height of the cloud is

$$\frac{h\,(\tan\beta + \tan\alpha)}{\tan\beta - \tan\alpha}$$

Sol. (i) Let P be the point of observation and C, the position of cloud. CN perpendicular from C on the surface of the lake and C′ be the reflection of the cloud in the lake so that

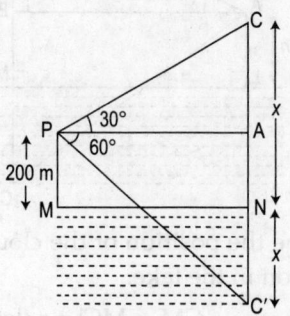

$$CN = NC′ = x \text{ (say)}$$

Then, $\qquad PM = 200 \text{ m}$

∴ $\qquad AN = MP = 200 \text{ m}$
$$CA = CN - AN$$
$$= (x - 200) \text{ m}$$
$$C′A = NC′ + AN$$
$$= (x + 200) \text{ m}$$

Let $\qquad PA = y \text{ m}$

Then, in right angled △ PAC,

$$\frac{CA}{PA} = \tan 30°$$

$$\Rightarrow \qquad \frac{x - 200}{y} = \frac{1}{\sqrt{3}}$$

$$\Rightarrow \qquad y = \sqrt{3}\,(x - 200) \qquad \text{...(i)}$$

Also, in right angled △ C′AP,

$$\frac{C′A}{PA} = \tan 60°$$

$$\Rightarrow \qquad \frac{x + 200}{y} = \sqrt{3}$$

$$\Rightarrow \qquad x + 200 = \sqrt{3}y$$

$$\Rightarrow \qquad y = \frac{x + 200}{\sqrt{3}} \qquad \text{...(ii)}$$

From equations (i) and (ii),

$$\frac{x + 200}{\sqrt{3}} = \sqrt{3}\,(x - 200)$$

$$\Rightarrow \qquad x + 200 = 3(x - 200)$$

$$\Rightarrow \qquad x + 200 = 3x - 600$$

$$\Rightarrow \qquad 2x = 800$$

$$\Rightarrow \qquad x = 400 \text{ m}$$

Hence, the height of the cloud = 400 m. **Ans.**

(ii) Let LM be the upper surface of the lake and A be a point such that AL = h.

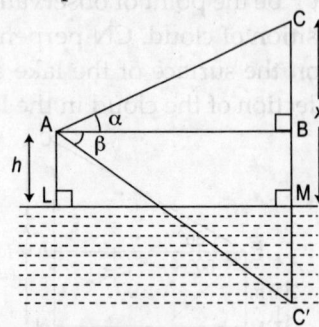

Let C be the position of the cloud and C' be its reflection in the lake.

$$CM = MC' = x \text{ (let)}$$

$$\angle BAC = \alpha \text{ and } \angle BAC' = \beta$$

Now, in $\triangle$ CBA,

$$\tan \alpha = \frac{CB}{AB}$$

$$\Rightarrow \qquad \tan \alpha = \frac{x-h}{AB}$$

$$\Rightarrow \qquad AB = \frac{x-h}{\tan \alpha} \qquad \qquad …(i)$$

In $\triangle$ C'BA,

$$\tan \beta = \frac{C'B}{AB}$$

$$\Rightarrow \qquad \tan \beta = \frac{x+h}{AB}$$

$$\Rightarrow \qquad AB = \frac{x+h}{\tan \beta} \qquad \qquad …(ii)$$

From equations (i) and (ii),

$$\frac{x-h}{\tan \alpha} = \frac{x+h}{\tan \beta}$$

or $$\frac{x+h}{x-h} = \frac{\tan \beta}{\tan \alpha}$$

Applying componendo and dividendo, we get

$$\frac{x+h+x-h}{x+h-x+h} = \frac{\tan \beta + \tan \alpha}{\tan \beta - \tan \alpha}$$

$$\Rightarrow \qquad \frac{2x}{2h} = \frac{\tan \beta + \tan \alpha}{\tan \beta - \tan \alpha}$$

$$\Rightarrow \qquad x = \frac{h(\tan \beta + \tan \alpha)}{\tan \beta - \tan \alpha}$$

$\therefore$ Height of the cloud is

$$x = \frac{h(\tan \beta + \tan \alpha)}{\tan \beta - \tan \alpha}.$$

Hence Proved.

26. A round balloon of radius '*a*' subtends an angle θ at the eye of the observer while the angle of elevation of its centre is ϕ. Prove that the height of the centre of the balloon is $a \sin \phi \, \text{cosec} \, \dfrac{\theta}{2}$.

Sol. Let C be the centre of the balloon, O be the position of man's eye.

Let *h* be the height of the centre of the balloon

then $$\angle AOB = \theta$$

So, $$\angle BOC = \angle COA$$

$$= \theta/2$$

In $\triangle$ OAC,

$$\sin \frac{\theta}{2} = \frac{a}{OC}$$

$$\Rightarrow \qquad OC = a \, \text{cosec} \, \frac{\theta}{2}$$

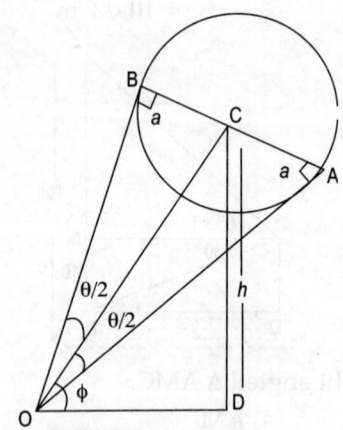

In $\triangle$ COD,

$$\sin \phi = \frac{h}{OC}$$

$$\Rightarrow \qquad h = OC \sin \phi$$

$$\Rightarrow \qquad h = a \, \text{cosec} \, \frac{\theta}{2} \cdot \sin \phi.$$

$$\Rightarrow \qquad h = a \sin \phi \, \text{cosec} \, \frac{\theta}{2}.$$

Hence Proved.

Chapter 19. Statistics

1. The median of the following observations 11, 12, 14, $(x-2)$, $(x+4)$, $(x+9)$, 32, 38, 47 arranged in ascending order is 24. Find the value of x and hence find the mean.

Sol. Given observations are 11, 12, 14, $(x-2)$, $(x+4)$, $(x+9)$, 32, 38, 47

$$n = 9 \text{ (odd)}$$

$\therefore \qquad$ Median $= \left(\dfrac{9+1}{2}\right)^{th}$

$\Rightarrow \qquad 24 = 5^{th}$ observation $= (x+4)$

$\Rightarrow \qquad 24 = x + 4 \qquad$ (as Median = 24)

$\Rightarrow \qquad 24 - 4 = x$

$\Rightarrow \qquad x = 20$

$\therefore \quad$ Observations are 11, 12, 14, $(20-2)$,

$$(20+4), (20+9), 32, 38, 47$$

or $\qquad$ 11, 12, 14, 18, 24, 29, 32, 38, 47

$$\text{Mean} = \overline{X}$$

$$= \frac{11+12+14+18+24+29+32+38+47}{9}$$

$$= \frac{225}{9} = 25 \qquad \textbf{Ans.}$$

2. The mean of 16 numbers is 8. If 2 is added to every number, what will be the new mean?

Sol. Let $x_1, x_2, x_3, \ldots, x_{16}$ be 16 numbers with their mean equal to 8. Then

$$\overline{X} = \frac{1}{n}\left(\sum_{i=1}^{16} x_i\right)$$

$\Rightarrow \qquad 8 = \dfrac{x_1 + x_2 + \ldots + x_{16}}{16}$

$\Rightarrow \quad x_1 + x_2 + \ldots + x_{16} = 16 \times 8 = 128 \qquad \ldots(i)$

New numbers are $x_1 + 2, x_2 + 2, x_3 + 2, \ldots, x_{16} + 2$.

Let $\overline{X}$ be the mean of new numbers. Then,

$$\overline{X} = \frac{(x_1+2)+(x_2+2)+\ldots+(x_{16}+2)}{16}$$

$$= \frac{(x_1+x_2+\ldots+x_{16})+2\times16}{16}$$

$$= \frac{128+32}{16}, \qquad \text{[Using (i)]}$$

$$= \frac{160}{16} = 10. \qquad \textbf{Ans.}$$

3. The mean monthly salary of 10 members of a group is ₹ 1,445, one more member whose monthly salary is ₹ 1,500 has joined the group. Find the mean monthly salary of 11 members of the group.

Sol. Here, $\qquad n = 10$, $\overline{X} = 1445$.

So, $\qquad\qquad \overline{X} = \dfrac{1}{n}\,(\Sigma x_i)$

$\Rightarrow \qquad\qquad n\,\overline{X} = \Sigma x_i$

$\Rightarrow \qquad 10 \times 1445 = \Sigma x_i$

$\Rightarrow \qquad\qquad \Sigma x_i = 14450$.

So, total monthly salary of 10 persons is ₹ 14,450.

Monthly salary of one more person who joined the group is ₹ 1,500.

$\therefore \quad$ Total monthly salary of 11 persons

$$= ₹\ 14{,}450 + ₹\ 1{,}500$$

$$= ₹\ 15{,}950$$

So, average monthly salary of 11 persons

$$= \frac{\text{Total monthly salary}}{11}$$

$$= \frac{15{,}950}{11} = ₹\ 1{,}450. \qquad \textbf{Ans.}$$

4. The mean of 40 observations was 160. It was detected on rechecking that the value of 165 was wrongly copied as 125 for computation of mean. Find the correct mean.

Sol. Here, $n = 40$, $\overline{X} = 160$.

So, $\qquad\qquad \overline{X} = \dfrac{1}{n}\,(\Sigma x_i)$

$\Rightarrow \qquad 160 = \dfrac{1}{40}\,(\Sigma x_i)$

$\Rightarrow \qquad \Sigma x_i = 160 \times 40 = 6400$

$\therefore \quad$ Incorrect value of $\Sigma x_i = 6400$.

Now, correct value of

$$\Sigma x_i = \text{Incorrect value of } \Sigma x_i$$

$$- \text{Incorrect value} + \text{Correct value}$$

$$= 6400 - 125 + 165 = 6440$$

$\therefore \quad$ Correct mean

$$= \frac{\text{Correct value of } \Sigma x_i}{n}$$

$$= \frac{6440}{40} = 161. \qquad \textbf{Ans.}$$

5. The mean of 100 items was found to be 30. If at the time of calculation two items were wrongly taken as 32 and 12 instead of 23 and 11, find the correct mean.

Sol. Here, $n = 100$, $\overline{X} = 30$.

So, $\overline{X} = \dfrac{1}{n}(\Sigma x_i)$

$\Rightarrow \qquad \Sigma x_i = n\overline{X}$

$\Rightarrow \qquad \Sigma x_i = 100 \times 30 = 3000$

$\therefore$ Incorrect value of $\Sigma x_i = 3000$

Now, correct value of Σx_i

$\qquad$ = Incorrect value of Σx_i
$\qquad$ – (Sum of incorrect values)
$\qquad$ + (Sum of correct values)
$\qquad$ = $3000 - (32 + 12) + (23 + 11)$
$\qquad$ = 2990.

$\therefore$ Correct mean

$\qquad = \dfrac{\text{Correct value of } \Sigma x_i}{n}$

$\qquad = \dfrac{2990}{100} = 29.9$. **Ans.**

6. If $\overline{X}$ is the mean of n observations $x_1, x_2, x_3, \ldots,$ x_n then the mean of $\dfrac{x_1}{a}, \dfrac{x_2}{a}, \dfrac{x_3}{a}, \ldots, \dfrac{x_n}{a}$ is $\dfrac{\overline{X}}{a}$, where a is an non-zero number.

i.e., if each observation is divided by a non-zero number, then the mean is also divided by it.

Sol. We have

$\qquad \overline{X} = \dfrac{1}{n}\left(\displaystyle\sum_{i=1}^{n} x_i\right)$ $\qquad$ ...(i)

So, let $\overline{Y}$ be the mean of $\dfrac{x_1}{a}, \dfrac{x_2}{a}, \ldots, \dfrac{x_n}{a}$.

Then, $\qquad \overline{Y} = \dfrac{1}{n}\left(\dfrac{x_1}{a} + \dfrac{x_2}{a} + \ldots + \dfrac{x_n}{a}\right)$

$\qquad = \dfrac{1}{n}\left(\dfrac{x_1 + x_2 + \ldots + x_n}{a}\right)$

$\qquad = \dfrac{1}{a}\left(\dfrac{x_1 + x_2 + \ldots + x_n}{n}\right)$

$\qquad = \dfrac{1}{a}\left[\dfrac{1}{n}\left(\displaystyle\sum_{i=1}^{n} x_i\right)\right]$

$\qquad = \dfrac{1}{a}(\overline{X})$ $\qquad$ [Using (i)]

$\qquad = \dfrac{\overline{X}}{a}$. **Ans.**

7. The average score of girls in class X examination in school is 67 and that of boys is 63. The average score for the whole class is 64·5. Find the percentage of girls and boys in the class.

Sol. Let the number of girls and boys be n_1 and n_2 respectively.

We have

$\qquad \overline{X}_1$ = Average score of girls = 67

$\qquad \overline{X}_2$ = Average score of boys = 63

$\qquad \overline{X}$ = Average score of the whole class = 64·5

$\therefore \qquad \overline{X} = \dfrac{n_1\overline{X}_1 + n_2\overline{X}_2}{n_1 + n_2}$

$\Rightarrow \qquad 64.5 = \dfrac{67n_1 + 63n_2}{n_1 + n_2}$

$\Rightarrow \qquad 64.5n_1 + 64.5n_2 = 67n_1 + 63n_2$

$\Rightarrow \qquad 2.5n_1 = 1.5n_2$

$\Rightarrow \qquad 25n_1 = 15n_2$

$\Rightarrow \qquad 5n_1 = 3n_2$

Total number of students in the class = $n_1 + n_2$.

$\therefore$ Percentage of girls = $\dfrac{n_1}{n_1 + n_2} \times 100$

$\qquad = \dfrac{n_1}{n_1 + \dfrac{5n_1}{3}} \times 100$

$\qquad\qquad\qquad [\because\ 5n_1 = 3n_2]$

$\qquad = \dfrac{3n_1}{3n_1 + 5n_1} \times 100$

$\qquad = \dfrac{3}{8} \times 100 = 37.5\%$

and Percentage of boys = $\dfrac{n_2}{n_1 + n_2} \times 100$

$\qquad = \dfrac{n_2}{\dfrac{3n_2}{5} + n_2} \times 100$

$\qquad = \dfrac{5n_2}{3n_2 + 5n_2} \times 100$

$\qquad = 62.5\%$

Hence, there are 37·5% girls and 62·5% boys in the class. **Ans.**

8. The mean weight of 150 students in a certain class is 60 kg. The mean weight of boys in the class is 70 kg and that of girls is 55 kg. Find the number of boys and the number of girls in the class.

Sol. Let the number of boys and girls in the class be n_1 and n_2 respectively. Then

$$n_1 + n_2 = 150 \qquad \dots(i)$$

We have

$\overline{X}_1$ = Mean weight of boys = 70 kg

$\overline{X}_2$ = Mean weight of girls = 55 kg

$\overline{X}$ = Mean weight of all students = 60 kg

$$\therefore \qquad \overline{X} = \frac{n_1\overline{X}_1 + n_2\overline{X}_2}{n_1 + n_2}$$

$$\Rightarrow \qquad 60 = \frac{n_1 \times 70 + n_2 \times 55}{n_1 + n_2}$$

$$\Rightarrow \qquad 60(n_1 + n_2) = 70n_1 + 55n_2$$

$$\Rightarrow \qquad 60n_1 + 60n_2 = 70n_1 + 55n_2$$

$$\Rightarrow \qquad 10n_1 = 5n_2$$

$$\Rightarrow \qquad 2n_1 = n_2 \qquad \dots(ii)$$

Putting $n_2 = 2n_1$ from (ii) in (i), we get

$$n_1 + 2n_1 = 150$$

$$\Rightarrow \qquad 3n_1 = 150$$

$$\Rightarrow \qquad n_1 = 50.$$

Putting $n_1 = 50$ in $n_2 = 2n_1$, we get

$$n_2 = 100.$$

Hence, there are 50 boys and 100 girls in the class. **Ans.**

9. The numbers 6, 8, 10, 12, 13, and x are arranged in an ascending order. If the mean of the observations is equal to the median, find the value of x.

Sol. The numbers are 6, 8, 10, 12, 13 and x.

$$n = 6$$

$$\text{Mean} = \frac{6 + 8 + 10 + 12 + 13 + x}{6}$$

$$= \frac{49 + x}{6} \qquad \dots(i)$$

For Median, $n = 6$ (even)

$$\text{Median} = \frac{\left(\frac{n}{2}\right)^{th} \text{term} + \left(\frac{n}{2}+1\right)^{th} \text{term}}{2}$$

$$= \frac{3^{rd} \text{term} + 4^{th} \text{term}}{2}$$

$$= \frac{10 + 12}{2}$$

$$= \frac{22}{2} = 11 \qquad \dots(ii)$$

Using (i) and (ii) (From question),

$$\text{Median} = \text{Mean}$$

$$\Rightarrow \qquad 11 = \frac{49 + x}{6}$$

$$\Rightarrow \qquad x = 66 - 49$$

$$\Rightarrow \qquad x = 17. \qquad \textbf{Ans.}$$

Chapter 20. Probability

1. An unbiased dice is thrown. What is the probability of getting a number other than 4.

Sol. Sample space (S)= {1, 2, 3, 4, 5, 6}

$$\Rightarrow \qquad n(S) = 6$$

Event (E) = {other than 4}

$$= \{1, 2, 3, 5, 6\}$$

$$\Rightarrow \qquad n(E) = 5$$

$$\therefore \qquad P(E) = \frac{n(E)}{n(S)} = \frac{5}{6}. \qquad \textbf{Ans.}$$

2. Two dice are thrown simultaneously. Find the probability of getting six as the product.

Sol. $$n(S) = 36$$

Event (E) = {getting 6 as a product}

$$= \{(1, 6), (2, 3), (3, 2), (6, 1)\}$$

$$\Rightarrow \qquad n(E) = 4$$

$$\therefore \qquad P(E) = \frac{n(E)}{n(S)}$$

$$= \frac{4}{36} = \frac{1}{9} \qquad \textbf{Ans.}$$

3. If the probability of winning a game is $\frac{5}{11}$. What is the probability of losing?

Sol. Given, $$P(E) = \frac{5}{11}$$

$\therefore$ Probability of losing,

$$P(\overline{E}) = 1 - P(E)$$

$$= 1 - \frac{5}{11}$$

$$= \frac{6}{11} \qquad \textbf{Ans.}$$

4. Find the probability of getting a tail in a throw of a coin.

Sol. Sample space $(S) = \{H, T\}$

$\Rightarrow \quad n(S) = 2$

Event $(E) = \{T\}$

$\Rightarrow \quad n(E) = 1$

$\therefore \quad P(E) = \dfrac{n(E)}{n(S)}$

$= \dfrac{1}{2}$ **Ans.**

5. In a cricket match a batsman hits a boundary 6 times out of 30 balls he plays. Find the probability that he did not hit the boundary ?

Sol. $n(S) = 30$

$E = \{\text{not hitting the boundary}\}$

$\Rightarrow \quad n(E) = 30 - 6 = 24$

Probability of not hitting boundary,

$\therefore \quad P(E) = \dfrac{n(E)}{n(S)}$

$= \dfrac{24}{30} = \dfrac{4}{5}.$ **Ans.**

6. It is known that a box of 600 electric bulbs contain 12 defective bulbs. One bulb is taken out at random from this box. What is the probability that it is a non-defective bulb ?

Sol. Number of non-defective bulbs

$= 600 - 12 = 588$

$n(E) = 588$

$n(S) = 600$

$P(E) = ?$

$\therefore \quad P(E) = \dfrac{n(E)}{n(S)} = \dfrac{588}{600} = 0.98$ **Ans.**

7. 1000 tickets of a lottery were sold and there are 5 prizes on these tickets. If Namita has purchased one lottery ticket, what is the probability of winning a prize ?

Sol. $n(S) = 1000$

$n(E) = 5$

$P(E) = ?$

$\therefore \quad P(E) = \dfrac{n(E)}{n(S)}$

$= \dfrac{5}{1000} = 0.005$ **Ans.**

8. A coin is tossed 100 times with the following frequencies :

Head = 55, Tail = 45

find the probability for each event **(i)** head, **(ii)** tail.

Sol. (i) Event $= \{\text{Head}\}$

$n(E) = 55$

$\therefore$ Probability of event $= \dfrac{n(E)}{n(S)}$

$= \dfrac{55}{100} = \dfrac{11}{20}$ **Ans.**

(ii) Event $= \{\text{Tail}\}$

$\Rightarrow \quad n(E) = 45$

$\therefore$ Probability of event $= \dfrac{n(E)}{n(S)}$

$= \dfrac{45}{100} = \dfrac{9}{20}$ **Ans.**

9. Namita tossed a coin once. What is the probability of getting **(i)** Head, **(ii)** Tail ?

Sol. (i) Sample space,

$S = \{H, T\}$

$n(S) = 2$

Event $= \{\text{Head}\}$

$n(E) = 1$

$\therefore \quad P(E) = \dfrac{n(E)}{n(S)}$

$\Rightarrow \quad P(E) = \dfrac{1}{2}$ **Ans.**

(ii) Sample space $S = \{H, T\}$

$\Rightarrow \quad n(S) = 2$

Event $= \{\text{Tail}\}$

$\Rightarrow \quad n(E) = 1$

$\therefore \quad P(E) = \dfrac{n(E)}{n(S)} = \dfrac{1}{2}$ **Ans.**

10. Two coins are tossed once. Find the probability of getting :

(i) 2 heads, **(ii)** at least 1 tail.

Sol. If two coins are tossed once, then

$S = \{HH, HT, TH, TT\}$

$\Rightarrow \quad n(S) = 4$

(i) E : getting two heads

$\therefore \quad n(E) = 1$

$\therefore \quad P(E) = \dfrac{n(E)}{n(S)}$

$= \dfrac{1}{4}$ **Ans.**

(ii) At least one tail

$\therefore$ Favourable outcome $= 3$

Required probability $= \dfrac{3}{4}.$ **Ans.**

11. A die has 6 faces marked by the given numbers as shown below :

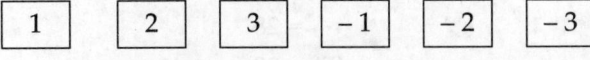

The die is thrown once. What is the probability of getting :

(i) a positive integer,

(ii) an integer greater than – 3,

(iii) the smallest integer ?

Sol. Given, die has faces that are

| 1 | 2 | 3 | – 1 | – 2 | – 3 |

Total number of outcomes = 6

(i) P (a positive integer) = $\dfrac{3}{6} = \dfrac{1}{2}$ **Ans.**

(ii) P (an integer greater than – 3) = $\dfrac{5}{6}$ **Ans.**

(iii) P (the smallest integer) = $\dfrac{1}{6}$ **Ans.**

12. 1800 families with 2 children were selected randomly and the following data were recorded:

No. of girls in a family	2	1	0
No. of families	700	850	250

Compute the probability of a family chosen at random having :

(i) 2 girls   **(ii)** 1 girl   **(iii)** No girl.

Sol. **(i)** Total no. of families, n (S) = 1800

Event (E) = {2 girls}

n (E) = 700

P (E) = ?

∴   P (E) = $\dfrac{n(E)}{n(S)} = \dfrac{700}{1800} = \dfrac{7}{18}$.   **Ans.**

(ii)   Event (E) = {1 girl}

n (E) = 850

P (E) = ?

∴   P (E) = $\dfrac{n(E)}{n(S)}$

= $\dfrac{850}{1800} = \dfrac{17}{36}$.   **Ans.**

(iii)   Event (E) = {No girl}

n (E) = 250

P (E) = ?

∴   P (E) = $\dfrac{n(E)}{n(S)} = \dfrac{250}{1800} = \dfrac{5}{36}$ **Ans.**

13. A card is drawn at random from a well shuffled pack of 52 cards. Find the probability that at the card drawn is neither a red card nor a queen.

Sol. n (S) = 52

Event = {getting neither a red card nor a queen}

∴ There are 26 red cards and 2 more queens are there.

Number of cards each one of which is either a red card or a queen = 28.

The event that the card drawn is neither a red card nor a queen = 52 – 28 = 24.

n (E) = 24

n (S) = 52

P (E) = ?

∴   P (E) = $\dfrac{n(E)}{n(S)} = \dfrac{24}{52} = \dfrac{6}{13}$.   **Ans.**

14. A dice is thrown once. What is the probability that the

(i) number is even,

(ii) number is greater than 2 ?

Sol. **(i)** n (S) = 6

Event (E) = {Even number}

= {2, 4, 6}

⇒ n (E) = 3

P (E) = ?

∴   P (E) = $\dfrac{n(E)}{n(S)} = \dfrac{3}{6} = \dfrac{1}{2}$.   **Ans.**

(ii)   Event (E) = {Number is greater than 2}

= {3, 4, 5, 6}

⇒ n (E) = 4

P (E) = ?

∴   P (E) = $\dfrac{n(E)}{n(S)}$

= $\dfrac{4}{6} = \dfrac{2}{3}$.   **Ans.**

15. A box contains some black balls and 30 white balls. If the probability of drawing a black ball is two-fifths of a white ball, find the number of black balls in the box.

Sol. Let the number of black balls = x

Number of white balls = 30

Total balls = $x + 30$

P (Black ball) = $\dfrac{x}{x + 30}$

P (White ball) = $\dfrac{30}{x + 30}$

According to question,

$$P \text{ (Black ball)} = \frac{2}{5} P \qquad \text{(White ball)}$$

$$\Rightarrow \qquad \frac{x}{x+30} = \frac{2}{5} \times \frac{30}{x+30}$$

or $\qquad x = \frac{2}{5} \times 30$

$\Rightarrow \qquad x = 12$

∴ Number of black balls = 12. **Ans.**

16. From a pack of 52 playing cards all cards whose numbers are multiples of 3 are removed. A card is now drawn at random.

What is the probability that the card drawn is :

(i) a face card (King, Jack or Queen)

(ii) an even numbered red card ?

Sol. The numbers which are multiple of 3 in 52 playing cards are 3, 6 and 9 *i.e.* 3 cards of each denomination

∴ All cards whose numbers are multiples of 3 are (in 4 sets)

$\qquad = 4 \times 3 = 12$ cards

Remaining cards = 52 – 12 = 40

Now, Number of face cards = 12

(i) $\quad P \text{ (face card)} = \frac{12}{40} = \frac{3}{10}$ **Ans.**

(ii) Again, even numbered cards are 2, 4, 6, 8 and 10 each of heart (red) and Diamond (red).

But 6 is removed.

∴ Total even numbered red card = 4 × 2 = 8

P (even numbered red card)

$$= \frac{8}{40} = \frac{1}{5} \qquad \textbf{Ans.}$$

17. One card is drawn from a pack of 52 cards, each of the 52 cards being equally likely to be drawn. Find the probability that the card drawn is (i) an ace, (ii) red, (iii) either red or king, (iv) red and a king, (v) a face card, (vi) a red face card, (vii) '2' of spade, (viii) '10' of a blacksuit.

Sol. $\qquad n \text{ (S)} = 52$

(i) $\qquad$ Event (E) = {an ace}

$\qquad\qquad n \text{ (E)} = 4$

$\qquad\qquad P \text{ (E)} = ?$

∴ $\qquad P \text{ (E)} = \frac{n \text{ (E)}}{n \text{ (S)}} = \frac{4}{52} = \frac{1}{13}.$ **Ans.**

(ii) $\qquad$ Event (E) = {red cards}

$\qquad\qquad n \text{ (E)} = 26$

$\qquad\qquad P \text{ (E)} = ?$

∴ $\qquad P \text{ (E)} = \frac{n \text{ (E)}}{n \text{ (S)}} = \frac{26}{52} = \frac{1}{2}.$ **Ans.**

(iii) $\qquad$ Event (E) = {either red or king}

$\qquad\qquad = \{26 \text{ red cards} + 2 \text{ kings}\}$

$\qquad\qquad = 28$

$\qquad\qquad n \text{ (E)} = 28$

$\qquad\qquad P \text{ (E)} = ?$

∴ $\qquad P \text{ (E)} = \frac{n \text{ (E)}}{n \text{ (S)}} = \frac{28}{52} = \frac{7}{13}.$ **Ans.**

(iv) $\qquad$ Event (E) = {red and a king}

$\qquad\qquad = \text{(there are 2 red kings in}$
$\qquad\qquad\qquad \text{a pack of 52 cards}\}$

$\Rightarrow \qquad n \text{ (E)} = 2$

$\qquad\qquad P \text{ (E)} = ?$

∴ $\qquad P \text{ (E)} = \frac{n \text{ (E)}}{n \text{ (S)}} = \frac{2}{52} = \frac{1}{26}.$ **Ans.**

(v) $\qquad$ Event (E) = {face cards}

$\Rightarrow \qquad n \text{ (E)} = 12$

$\qquad\qquad P \text{ (E)} = ?$

∴ $\qquad P \text{ (E)} = \frac{n \text{ (E)}}{n \text{ (S)}} = \frac{12}{52} = \frac{3}{13}.$ **Ans.**

(vi) $\qquad$ Event (E) = {red face cards}

There are 3 types of face cards (King, Queen and Jack) each of four types.

Hence, total number of face cards

$\qquad\qquad = 4 \times 3 = 12$

Total number of red face cards

$$= \frac{12}{2} = 6$$

$\Rightarrow \qquad n \text{ (E)} = 6$

$\qquad\qquad P \text{ (E)} = \frac{n \text{ (E)}}{n \text{ (S)}}$

$$= \frac{6}{52}$$

$$= \frac{3}{26} \qquad \textbf{Ans.}$$

(vii) $\qquad$ Event (E) = {'2' of spade}

$\Rightarrow \qquad n \text{ (E)} = 1$

$\qquad\qquad P \text{ (E)} = ?$

$$\therefore \qquad P(E) = \frac{n(E)}{n(S)} = \frac{1}{52}. \qquad \textbf{Ans.}$$

(viii) Event (E) = {'10' of blacksuit}

$$\Rightarrow \qquad n(E) = 2$$

$$P(E) = ?$$

$$\therefore \qquad P(E) = \frac{n(E)}{n(S)} = \frac{2}{52} = \frac{1}{26}. \qquad \textbf{Ans.}$$

18. Two dice are thrown simultaneously. Find the probability of getting :

(i) an even number as the sum, **(ii)** the sum as a prime number, **(iii)** a total of at least 10, **(iv)** a doublet of even number, **(v)** a multiple of 3 as the sum.

Sol. $\qquad n(S) = 36$

Such as

(1, 1), (1, 2), (1, 3), (1, 4), (1, 5), (1, 6), (2, 1), (2, 2), (2, 3), (2, 4), (2, 5), (2, 6), (3, 1), (3, 2), (3, 3), (3, 4), (3, 5), (3, 6), (4, 1), (4, 2), (4, 3), (4, 4), (4, 5), (4, 6), (5, 1), (5, 2), (5, 3), (5, 4), (5, 5), (5, 6), (6, 1), (6, 2), (6, 3), (6, 4), (6, 5), (6, 6)

(i) Event = {even number as the sum}

i.e., = {(1, 1), (1, 3), (3, 1), (2, 2), (1, 5), (5, 1), (2, 4), (4, 2), (3, 3), (2, 6), (6, 2), (4, 4), (5, 3), (3, 5), (5, 5), (6, 4), (4, 6) and (6, 6)}

$$\Rightarrow \qquad n(E) = 18$$

$$P(E) = ?$$

$$\therefore \qquad P(E) = \frac{n(E)}{n(S)} = \frac{18}{36} = \frac{1}{2}. \qquad \textbf{Ans.}$$

(ii) Event = {the sum as a prime number}

i.e., = {(1, 1), (1, 2), (2, 1), (1, 4), (4, 1), (2, 3), (3, 2), (1, 6), (6, 1), (2, 5), (5, 2), (3, 4), (4, 3), (6, 5) and (5, 6)}

$$\Rightarrow \qquad n(E) = 15$$

$$P(E) = ?$$

$$\therefore \qquad P(E) = \frac{n(E)}{n(S)} = \frac{15}{36} = \frac{5}{12}. \qquad \textbf{Ans.}$$

(iii) Event = {getting a total of at least 10}

$$= \{(6, 4), (4, 6), (5, 5), (6, 5),$$
$$(5, 6), (6, 6)\}$$

$$\Rightarrow \qquad n(E) = 6$$

$$P(E) = ?$$

$$\therefore \qquad P(E) = \frac{n(E)}{n(S)} = \frac{6}{36} = \frac{1}{6}. \qquad \textbf{Ans.}$$

(iv) Event = {getting a doublet of even number}

$$= \{(2, 2), (4, 4), (6, 6)\}$$

$$\Rightarrow \qquad n(E) = 3$$

$$P(E) = ?$$

$$\therefore \qquad P(E) = \frac{n(E)}{n(S)} = \frac{3}{36} = \frac{1}{12}. \qquad \textbf{Ans.}$$

(v) Event = {multiple of 3 as a sum}

$$= \{(1, 2), (2, 1), (1, 5), (5, 1), (2, 4), (4, 2),$$
$$(3, 3), (3, 6), (6, 3), (5, 4), (4, 5), (6, 6)\}$$

$$\Rightarrow \qquad n(E) = 12$$

$$P(E) = ?$$

$$\therefore \qquad P(E) = \frac{n(E)}{n(S)} = \frac{12}{36} = \frac{1}{3}. \qquad \textbf{Ans.}$$

19. Find the probability that leap year selected at random, will contain 53 sundays.

Sol. In a leap year there are 366 days. In 366 days, we have 52 weeks and 2 days. Thus, we can say that leap year has always 52 sundays.

The remaining two days can be :

(i)   Sunday and Monday

(ii) Monday and Tuesday

(iii) Tuesday and Wednesday

(iv) Wednesday and Thursday

(v)   Thursday and Friday

(vi) Friday and Saturday

(vii) Saturday and Sunday.

From above it is clear that there are 7 elementary events associated with this random experiment.

Clearly the event A will happen if the last two days of the leap year are either Sunday and Monday or Saturday and Sunday.

$$\therefore \qquad n(E) = 2 \text{ and } n(S) = 7$$

$$P(E) = ?$$

$$\therefore \qquad P(E) = \frac{n(E)}{n(S)} = \frac{2}{7}. \qquad \textbf{Ans.}$$

❑❑

Practice Exercises

Chapter 1. Goods and Service Tax (G.S.T.)

1. The cost of an article is ₹ 6,000 to a distributor. He sells it to a trader for ₹ 7,500 and the trader sells it to a customer for ₹ 8,000. If the GST rate is 12·5%, find the GST paid by the : (i) distributor, (ii) trader.

2. A shopkeeper purchases an article for ₹ 6,200 and sells it to a customer for ₹ 8,500. If the GST is 8%, find the GST paid by the shopkeeper.

3. The printed price of an article is ₹ 2,500. A wholesaler sells it to a retailer at 20% discount and charges GST at the rate of 10%. Now, the retailer, in turn, sells the article to a customer at its list price and charges the GST at the same rate. Find :
   (i) the amount that retailer pays to the wholesaler.
   (ii) the GST paid by the retailer.

4. A shopkeeper buys an article at a discount of 30% and pays GST at the rate of 8%. The shopkeeper, in turn, sells the article to a customer at the printed price and charges GST at the same rate. If the printed price of the article is ₹ 2,500; find :
   (i) the price paid by the shopkeeper.
   (ii) the price paid by the customer.
   The GST paid by the shopkeeper.

5. A manufacturer marks an article for ₹ 10,000. He sells it to a wholesaler at 40% discount. The wholesaler sells this article to a retailer at 20% discount on the marked price of the article. If retailer sells the article to a customer at 10% discount and the rate of GST is 12% at each stage, find the amount of GST paid by the :
   (i) wholesaler   (ii) retailer.

6. A manufacturer marks an article at ₹ 5,000. He sells this article to a wholesaler at a discount of 25% on the marked price and the wholesaler sells it to a retailer at a discount of 15% on its marked price. If the retailer sells the article without any discount and at each stage the GST

is 8%, calculate the amount of GST paid by :
   (i) the wholesaler
   (ii) the retailer.

7. A shopkeeper buys 15 identical articles for ₹ 840 and pays GST at the rate of 8%. He sells 6 of these articles at ₹ 65 each and charges GST at the same rate. Calculate the GST paid by the shopkeeper against the sale of these six articles.

8. An article is marked ₹ 500. The wholesaler sells it to a retailer at 20% discount and charges GST on the remaining price at 12·5%. The retailer, in turn, sells the article to a customer at its marked price and charges GST at the same rate. Calculate :
   (i) the price paid by the customer.
   (ii) the amount of GST paid by the retailer.

9. A company sells an article to a dealer for ₹ 40,500 including GST. The dealer sells it to some other dealer for ₹ 42,500 plus GST. The second dealer sells it to a customer at a profit of ₹ 3,000. If the rate of GST is 8%, find :
   (i) the cost of the article (excluding tax) to the first dealer.
   (ii) the total tax (under GST) received by the Government.
   (iii) the amount that a customer pays for the article.

10. A shopkeeper buys a camera at a discount of 20% from the wholesaler, the printed price of the camera being ₹ 1,600 and the rate of GST is 6%. The shopkeeper sells it to the buyer at the printed price and charges tax at the same rate. Find :
    (i) the price at which the camera can be bought from the shopkeeper.
    (ii) the GST paid by the shopkeeper.

11. An article is marked at ₹ 4,500 and the rate of GST on it is 6%. A trader buys this article at some discount and sells it to a customer at the

Practice Exercises

marked price. If the trader pays ₹ 81 as GST, find :

(i) how much percent discount does the trader get ?

(ii) the total money paid by the trader, including tax, to buy the article.

12. A shopkeeper bought a washing machine at a discount of 20% from a wholesaler, the printed price of the washing machine being ₹ 18,000. The shopkeeper sells it to a consumer at a discount of 10% on the printed price. If the rate of GST is 8%, find :

(i) the GST paid by the shopkeeper.

(ii) the total amount that the consumer pays for the washing machine.

13. A wholesaler buys a TV from the manufacturer for ₹ 25,000. He marks the price of the TV 20% above his cost price and sells it to a retailer at 10% discount on the marked price. If the rate of GST is 8%, find the :

(i) marked price.

(ii) retailer's cost price inclusive of tax.

(iii) GST paid by the wholesaler.

14. Mohit, a dealer in electronic goods, buys a high class TV set for ₹ 61,200. He sells this TV set to Geeta, Geeta to Rohan and Rohan sells it to Manoj. If the profit at each stage is ₹ 2,000 and the rate of GST at each stage is 12·5%, find :

(i) total amount of tax (under GST) paid to the Government.

(ii) money paid by Manoj to buy the TV set.

15. Producer 'P' sells a T.V. to a trader 'Q' for ₹ 12,500. Trader 'Q' sells it to a trader 'R' at a profit of ₹ 800 and trader 'R' sells it to a customer at a profit of ₹ 1,300. If rate of GST is 8%, find :

(i) the amount of tax received by State Government on the sale of this T.V.

(ii) the amount that the customer pays for the T.V.

16. From the following chart, calculate :

(i) the GST charged at each stage at 10%.

(ii) the C.P. for the customer.

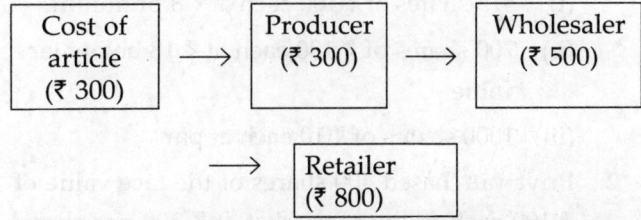

Chapter 2. Banking (Recurring Deposit Account)

1. Mr. Bajaj need ₹ 30,000 after 2 years. What least money (in multiple of ₹ 5) must he deposit every month in a recurring deposit account to get required money at the end of the 2 years, the rate of interest being 8% p.a. ?

2. Pallavi opened a recurring deposit account with a Nationalised Bank for a period of 2 years. If the bank pays interest at the rate of 6% per annum and the monthly instalment is ₹ 1,000, find the :

(i) interest earning in 2 years.

(ii) maturity value.

3. Mr. Mayank deposits a certain sum of money each month in a Recurring Deposit Account of a bank. If the rate of interest is of 8% per annum and Mr. Mayank gets ₹ 8,088 from the bank after 3 years, find the value of his monthly instalment.

4. Gopal has a cumulative deposit account and deposits ₹ 900 per month for a period of 4 years.

If he gets ₹ 52,020 at the time of maturity, find the rate of interest.

5. (i) Prakash has a Recurring Deposit Account in the Bank of India and deposits ₹ 140 per month for 4 years. If he gets ₹ 8,092 on maturity, find the rate of interest given by the bank.

(ii) David opened a Recurring Deposit Account in a bank and deposited ₹ 300 per month for two years. If he received ₹ 7,725 at the time of maturity, find the rate of interest per annum.

6. Each of P and Q opened a recurring deposit account in a bank. If P deposited ₹ 1,200 per month for 3 years and Q deposited ₹ 1,500 per month for $2\frac{1}{2}$ years; find, on maturity, who will get more amount and by how much ? The rate of interest paid by the bank is 10% per annum.

7. A man has a Recurring Deposit Account in a bank for $3\frac{1}{2}$ years. If the rate of interest is 12% per annum and the man gets ₹ 10,206 on maturity, find the value of monthly instalments.

8. Amit deposited ₹ 150 per month in a bank for 8 months under the Recurring Deposit scheme. What will be the maturity value of his deposits, if the rate of interest is 8% per annum and interest is calculated at the end of every month ?

9. A recurring deposit account of ₹ 1,200 per month has a maturity value of ₹ 12,440. If the rate of interest is 3% and the interest is calculated at the end of every month; find the time (in months) of this Recurring Deposit Account.

10. Mohan deposits ₹ 80 per month in a cumulative deposit account for six years. Find the amount payable to him on maturity, if the rate of interest is 6% per annum.

11. Without using table calculate the maturity value of a R.D. account of ₹ 50 per month for one year at the rate of 12% p.a.

12. Amol needs ₹ 4,000 after 72 months. What least amount per month must he save and put in a recurring deposit scheme to get the required amount at rate of interest 12·78%.

Chapter 3. Shares and Dividends

1. Find the investment in buying :
   (i) 475 shares of ₹ 100 each at ₹ 8 premium.
   (ii) 700 shares of ₹ 100 each at ₹ 18 below face value.
   (iii) 1000 shares of ₹ 10 each at par.

2. Priya purchased 400 shares of the face value of ₹ 100 each from the market at ₹ 300 per share. If the company paid a dividend of 30%, what percentage does Priya get on her investment ?

3. Which share is more profitable : 4% share at ₹ 80 or $4\frac{1}{2}$ % share at ₹ 88 ?

4. How much should a man invest in ₹ 25 shares selling at ₹ 30 to obtain an income of ₹ 450, if the dividend declared is 15% ?

5. A man bought 1,000 shares each of face value ₹ 5 at ₹ 7 per share. At the end of the year, the company from which he bought the shares declared a dividend of 8%. Calculate :
   (i) The amount of money invested
   (ii) The percentage return on his outlay (correct to one decimal place).

6. A man invests ₹ 16,800 in buying shares of nominal value ₹ 24 and selling at 12% premium. The dividend on the shares is 15% per annum.
   (i) Calculate the number of shares he buys.
   (ii) Calculate the dividend he receives annually.

7. Which is the better investment : 10% shares at ₹ 140 or 6% shares at ₹ 132, if the investment is ₹ 26,400 ?

8. A dividend of 9% was declared on ₹ 100 shares selling at a certain price, if the rate of return is $7\frac{1}{2}$ %. Calculate the market value of the share.

9. A man sold 500 shares of ₹ 20 each, paying 8% at ₹ 18 and invested the proceeds in ₹ 10 shares paying 12% at ₹ 15. How many ₹ 10 shares did he buy and what was the change in his annual income ?

10. ₹ 8,000 and ₹ 10,000 were invested in shares giving dividends 12% and 8% respectively. The dividends are collected and all the shares are sold at a loss of 2% and 3% respectively on the investment. Find :
    (i) The dividend collected
    (ii) The total sale proceeds
    (iii) Gain % on whole.

11. Mukul invests ₹ 9,000 in a company paying a dividend of 6% per annum when a share of face value 100 stands at ₹ 150. What is the annual income ? He sells 50% of his shares when the price rises to ₹ 200. What is his gain on this transaction ?

Practice Exercises

12. A man invests a sum of money in ₹ 100 shares, paying 15% dividend, quoted at 20% premium. If his annual dividend is ₹ 540, calculate :

    (i) his total investment

    (ii) the rate of return on his investment.

13. ₹ 50 shares of company are quoted at a discount of 10%. Find the rate of dividend given by the company, the return on the investment on these shares being 20%.

14. Mrs. Namita Gaur bought a ₹ 20 share of a company at such a price as to drive an income of 12% on her investment. If the company pay 9% dividend, for how much did she buy share ?

Chapter 4. Linear Inequations

1. Solve the inequation and represent the solution set on number line :
$$-\frac{2}{3} < -\frac{x}{3} + 1 \le \frac{2}{3}, x \in R$$

2. Find the range of the value of x, which satisfies
$$-2 \le \frac{x}{2} + 3 < 6, x \in N.$$
Represent the solution set on the number line.

3. Solve : $|\, 2x + 3 \,| \ge -6$, $x \in R$ and represent the solution on the number line.

4. Given :
$$L = \{x : 5 < 3x - 1 \le 11, x \in R\},$$
$$M = \{x : -2 \le 3 + 5x < 25, x \in I\}.$$
where R = real number, I = integers, represent L and M on number lines. Write down the elements of LAM.

5. Solve for x over real numbers. Graph the solution set on the number line :
$$-\frac{2x}{5} < x + 6, x \in R.$$

6. List the element of the solution set of the inequation :
$$-3 < x - 2 \le 9 - 2x, x \in N$$
Graph the set of solution on number line.

7. P is the solution set of $7x - 2 > 4x + 1$ and Q is the solution set of $9x - 45 \ge 5(x - 5); x \in R$. Represent

    (i) P ∩ Q, (ii) P ∩ Q′ on number line.

8. If $x \in$ {Real number} and $-1 < 3 - 2x \le 7$, evaluate x and represent it on a number line.

9. If $x \in$ {Real number}, find the range of values of x which $-1 < 2x + 1 \le 7$. Represent the range of a number line.

Chapter 5. Quadratic Equations

Solve for x (from Q. 1 to 7)

1. $a(x^2 + 1) = x(a^2 + 1)$, where $a \in R$.

2. $\dfrac{x+3}{x+2} = \dfrac{3x-7}{2x-3}$

3. $\dfrac{x+3}{x-2} - \dfrac{1-x}{x} = \dfrac{17}{4}$

4. $\dfrac{x-3}{x+3} - \dfrac{x+3}{x-3} = 6\dfrac{6}{7}$, $x \ne 3$ and $x \ne -3$.

5. $\dfrac{2x}{x-4} + \dfrac{2x-5}{x-3} = \dfrac{25}{3}$

6. $ad^2 x \left(\dfrac{ax}{b} + \dfrac{2c}{d} \right) + c^2 b = 0$

7. $a^2x^2 - 3abx + 2b^2 = 0$, $a, b \in R$

8. Solve for x :
$$\frac{x-1}{x-2} - \frac{x-2}{x-3} = \frac{x-5}{x-6} - \frac{x-6}{x-7}.$$

9. From the quadratic equation whose roots are :

    (i) $\sqrt{3}, 2\sqrt{3}$

    (ii) $3 + 2\sqrt{3}, 3 - 2\sqrt{3}$

    (iii) $\dfrac{4+\sqrt{3}}{2}, \dfrac{4-\sqrt{3}}{2}$

    (iv) $-3, -5$

10. Find the sum and product of the roots of each of the following equations :

    (i) $7x^2 - 50x + 7 = 0$

(ii) $16x^2 - 9x + 1 = 0$

(iii) $2x^2 - 7x + 4 = 0$

(iv) $4\sqrt{2}x^2 - 3\sqrt{2}x - \sqrt{2} = 0$

11. Find the value of k so that the sum of the roots of the quadratic equation $(k-1)x^2 + (2k+1)x - 9 = 0$ is equal to the product of the roots.

12. Find the value of k such that the quadratic equation $x^2 - (2k+1)x + (3k+7) = 0$ has the sum of the roots as one-third of their product.

Solve the following equation (Q. 13 to 26) :

13. $x + \dfrac{1}{x} = \dfrac{26}{5}$.

14. $\dfrac{2x-1}{x+2} + \dfrac{x+2}{2x-1} = \dfrac{10}{3}$, $x \ne -2$, $x \ne \dfrac{1}{2}$.

15. $\sqrt{\dfrac{x}{x+10}} + \sqrt{\dfrac{x+10}{x}} = 2\dfrac{1}{12}$, $x \ne 0$, $x \ne -10$.

16. $6\left(\dfrac{x-4}{x-1}\right)^2 + 13\left(\dfrac{x-4}{x-1}\right) + 5$, $x \ne 1$

17. $\left(\dfrac{x-1}{x+1}\right)^4 - 13\left(\dfrac{x-1}{x+1}\right)^2 + 36 = 0$

18. $\sqrt{x^2 - 16} - \sqrt{x^2 - 8x + 16} = \sqrt{x^2 - 5x + 4}$

19. $6\left(x^2 + \dfrac{1}{x^2}\right) - 25\left(x - \dfrac{1}{x}\right) + 12 = 0$

20. $4^{x+1} + 4^{1-x} = 10$

21. $2^{2x+3} = 65(2x-1) + 57$

22. $(x-5)(x-7)(x+6)(x+4) = 504$

23. $2x^4 - x^4 - 11x^2 - x + z = 0$

24. $x^4 + 2x^3 - 13x^2 + 2x + 1 = 0$

25. $2^{2x+3} + 2^{x+3} = 1 + 2^x$

26. $2^{2x} - 3 \cdot 2^{x+2} + 32 = 0$.

27. A father is three times as old as his son. After twelve years his age will be twice as that of the age of his son. Find their present ages.

28. The sum of the ages of a father and his son is 45 years. Five years ago, the product of their ages was four times the father's age at that time. Find their present ages.

Chapter 6. Ratio and Proportion

1. Find the duplicate ratio of :

   (i) $5x : 3y$ (ii) $\sqrt{3} : \sqrt{5}$

2. Find the triplicate ratio of :

   (i) $(a+b)^{2/3} : (a-b)^{2/3}$ (ii) $xy^{2/3} : x^{2/3}y$.

3. Find the sub-duplicate ratio of :

   (i) $4a^2x^2 : 9b^4y^2$ (ii) $\sqrt{a} : \sqrt{b}$

4. Find the sub-triplicate ratio of :

   (i) $64x^3 : 27y^6$ (ii) $a : b$.

5. Find the reciprocal ratio of :

   (i) $2 : 5$ (ii) $2a : 3b$.

6. Find the compound ratio of :

   (i) $(x-y) : (x+y)$ and $(y^2 + xy) : (x^2 - xy)$

   (ii) $(x^2 - 25) : (x^2 + 3x - 10)$, $(x^2 - 4) : (x^2 + 3x + 2)$ and $(x+1) : (x^2 + 2x)$

7. (i) If $a > b > 0$, show that $(a^2 - b^2) : (a^2 + b^2)$ is greater than $(a-b) : (a+b)$.

   (ii) If a and $b > 0$, show that $(a^3 + b^3) : (a^2 + b^2)$ is greater than $(a^2 + b^2) : (a+b)$.

8. (i) If $(2a - x) : (b - 2x)$ be the sub-duplicate ratio of $a : b$, show that $x^2 = ab$.

   (ii) If $(3x + 3) : (9x + 7)$ is duplicate ratio of $3 : 5$, find x.

9. Find the ratio of $a : b$ if $12a^2 + 35b^2 - 43ab = 0$.

10. If $(7p + 3q) : (3p - 2q) = 43 : 2$, show that $p : q = 4 : 5$.

11. If $(3x - 7) : (4x + 3)$ is the sub-triplicate ratio of $8 : 27$, find x.

12. In the ratio of $7 : 8$, if the consequent is 40, what is the antecedent ?

13. What should be added to each term of the ratio $7 : 13$, so that the ratio becomes $2 : 3$.

14. If two numbers are in the ratio of $2 : 3$ and their L.C.M. is 108, find the numbers.

15. What number should be subtracted from each of the numbers 23, 30, 57 and 78 so that the remainder are in proportion.

16. A and B has ₹ 40 and ₹ 450 respectively. A spends ₹ 18 and B spends ₹ 21. Who is more extravagent ?

17. Two men's ages are in the ratio of 3 : 4. In 10 years time they will be in the ratio of 5 : 6. Find their ages.

18. If one-fourth of A, one-fifth of B and one-sixth of C are equal, find A : B : C.

19. The ages of two girls are in the ratio of 5 : 7, 8 years ago their ages were in the ratio of 7 : 13. Find their present ages.

20. A mixture of 25 litre of milk and water in the ratio of 4 : 1. How much milk should be added so that the new ratio of milk and water becomes 2 : 1 ?

21. A bag contains ₹ 200 in the form of 1 rupee, 50 paise and 25 paise coins in the ratio of 4 : 5 : 6. Find the number of each type of coins.

22. Find the value of x in each of the following cases :

    (i) $6 : 4 = 45 : x$ (ii) $2 : 5 = x : 9$

    (iii) $2^3 : 3^3 = 3 : x$ (iv) $x : 5 = 6 : 7$.

23. Find the third proportional between :

    (i) $5 + 2\sqrt{3}$ and $37 + 20\sqrt{3}$

    (ii) ab, ab^2

    (iii) $a^2 - \dfrac{1}{a^2}$ and $a + \dfrac{1}{a}$.

24. If y is the mean proportional between x and z, prove that $(xy + yz)$ is the mean proportional between $(x^2 + y^2)$ and $(y^2 + z^2)$.

25. Find the mean proportional to :

    (i) $\sqrt{27} - \sqrt{18}$ and $\sqrt{27} + \sqrt{18}$

    (ii) $\dfrac{a-b}{a+b}$ and $\dfrac{a^2 b^2}{a^2 - b^2}$

26. Find two numbers such that their mean proportional is 9 and their third proportional is 243.

27. Find the mean proportional between $\dfrac{x^2}{4ab}$ and $\dfrac{a}{by^2}$.

28. Find the mean proportional between $6 + \sqrt{27}$ and $6 - \sqrt{27}$.

29. If b is the mean proportional between a and c, show that $b(b + c)$ is the mean proportional between $(a^2 + b^2)$ and $(b^2 + c^2)$.

30. If a, b, c, d are in continues proportion, prove that

$$\frac{a}{d} = \frac{a^3 + b^3 + c^3}{b^3 + c^3 + d^3}$$

31. If $(4a + 9b)(4c - 9d) = (4a - 9b)(4c + 9d)$, prove that

$$\frac{a}{b} = \frac{c}{d}.$$

32. If $p : q :: r : s$, show that

$$mp + nq : q :: mr + ns : s.$$

33. If $\dfrac{a}{b} = \dfrac{c}{d}$, prove that

$$(5a + 7b)(2c - 3d) = (5c + 7d)(2a - 3b).$$

34. If $a : b = c : d$, prove that

$$(a + b) : (c + d) = \sqrt{a^2 + 5b^2} = \sqrt{c^2 + d^2}.$$

35. If $\dfrac{x^3 + 3xy^2}{3x^2 y + y^3} = \dfrac{p^3 + 3pq^2}{3p^2 q + q^3}$, prove that $\dfrac{x}{y} = \dfrac{p}{q}$.

36. If $p = \dfrac{\sqrt{x^2 + xy} + \sqrt{x^2 - xy}}{\sqrt{x^2 + xy} - \sqrt{x^2 - xy}}$, then show that

$$py^2 - 2px + y = 0.$$

37. If $\dfrac{x+y}{ax+by} = \dfrac{y+z}{ay+bz} = \dfrac{z+x}{az+bx}$, prove that each of these ratio is equal to $\dfrac{2}{a+b}$ unless

$$x + y + z = 0.$$

Chapter 7. Factorization

1. Show that $(x - 3)$ is a factor of the polynomial $x^3 - 3x^2 + 4x - 12$.

2. Find whether $(x + 1)$ and $(2x - 3)$ are the factors of $2x^3 - 9x^2 - x + 12$.

3. Find the value of k, if $x + 3$ is a factor of $3x^2 + kx + 6$.

4. Determine the value of a for which the polynomial $2x^4 - ax^3 + 4x^2 + 2x + 1$ is divisible by $1 - 2x$.

5. Find the value of a and b so that the polynomial $x^3 + 10x^2 - ax + b$ is exactly divisible by $(x - 1)$ as well as with $(x - 2)$.

6. If both $(x - 2)$ and $x - \dfrac{1}{2}$ are factors of $px^2 + 5x + r$, show that $p = r$.

7. Use factor theorem to verify that $x + a$ is a factor of $x^n + a^n$ for any odd positive integer.

8. Find the values of a and b when $x - 2$ and $x + 3$ both are the factors of expression
$$x^3 + ax^2 + bx - 12.$$

9. If $x^3 + ax^2 + bx + 6$ has $x - 2$ as a factor and leave a remainder 3 when divided by $x - 3$. Find the values of a and b.

10. Using remainder theorem factorize the expression $3x^3 + 10x^2 + x - 6$.

11. Find the remainder when $3x^3 + 5x^2 + 7x - 7$ is divided by $(3x - 1)$.

12. If $ax^3 + 3x^2 + bx - 2$ has a factor $(2x + 3)$ and leave remainder 7 when divided by $(x + 2)$, find the values of a and b with these values of a and b, factorize the given expression.

Chapter 8. Matrices

1. Construct a 2×2 matrix whose elements are given by :

   (i) $a_{ij} = \dfrac{(i - j)^2}{2}$ (ii) $\dfrac{(2i - j)^2}{2}$

   (iii) $a_{ij} = \dfrac{|2i - 3j|}{2}$ (iv) $a_{ij} = \dfrac{|-3i + j|}{2}$

2. If matrix $\begin{bmatrix} a+b & 2 \\ 5 & ab \end{bmatrix} = \begin{bmatrix} 6 & 2 \\ 5 & 8 \end{bmatrix}$, find the values of a and b.

3. Given $3 \begin{bmatrix} x & y \\ z & w \end{bmatrix} = \begin{bmatrix} x & 6 \\ -1 & 2w \end{bmatrix} + \begin{bmatrix} 4 & x+y \\ z+w & 3 \end{bmatrix}$, find the values of x, y, z and w.

4. Find X and Y if
$$X + Y = \begin{bmatrix} 7 & 0 \\ 2 & 5 \end{bmatrix} \text{ and } X - Y = \begin{bmatrix} 3 & 0 \\ 0 & 3 \end{bmatrix}.$$

5. If $A = \begin{bmatrix} 2 & -1 \\ 4 & 2 \end{bmatrix}$, $B = \begin{bmatrix} 4 & 3 \\ -2 & 1 \end{bmatrix}$

   and $C = \begin{bmatrix} -2 & -3 \\ -1 & -2 \end{bmatrix}$

   find (i) $A + B + C$, (ii) $2B + 3C$.

6. Find a matrix X such that $2A - B + X = 0$, where
$$A = \begin{bmatrix} -1 & 2 \\ 3 & 4 \end{bmatrix}, \ B = \begin{bmatrix} 3 & -2 \\ 1 & 5 \end{bmatrix}.$$

7. Find the values of x and y from the following equation :
$$2 \begin{bmatrix} x & 5 \\ 7 & y-3 \end{bmatrix} + \begin{bmatrix} 3 & -4 \\ 1 & 2 \end{bmatrix} = \begin{bmatrix} 7 & 6 \\ 15 & 14 \end{bmatrix}.$$

8. Find x, y, z, t if
$$2 \begin{bmatrix} x & z \\ y & t \end{bmatrix} + 3 \begin{bmatrix} 1 & -1 \\ 0 & 2 \end{bmatrix} = 3 \begin{bmatrix} 4 & 5 \\ 4 & 6 \end{bmatrix}.$$

9. If $A = \begin{bmatrix} 3 & 4 \\ 1 & -6 \end{bmatrix}$, $B = \begin{bmatrix} -2 & 5 \\ 6 & 1 \end{bmatrix}$, find a matrix X satisfying the equation $A + 2X = B$.

10. Find X if $Y = \begin{bmatrix} 3 & 2 \\ 1 & 4 \end{bmatrix}$ and $2X + Y = \begin{bmatrix} 1 & 0 \\ -3 & 2 \end{bmatrix}$.

11. Find $f(A)$:
    If $A = \begin{bmatrix} 4 & 2 \\ -1 & 1 \end{bmatrix}$, find $(A - 2I)(A - 3I)$.

12. If $A = \begin{bmatrix} 1 & 4 \\ 1 & 0 \end{bmatrix}$, $B = \begin{bmatrix} 2 & 1 \\ 3 & -1 \end{bmatrix}$ and $C = \begin{bmatrix} 2 & 3 \\ 0 & 5 \end{bmatrix}$, compute $(AB)C$ and $(CB)A$. Is $(AB)C = (CB)A$?

Practice Exercises

13. Given the matrices

$$A = \begin{bmatrix} 2 & 1 \\ 4 & 2 \end{bmatrix}, B = \begin{bmatrix} 3 & 4 \\ -1 & -2 \end{bmatrix} \text{ and } C = \begin{bmatrix} -3 & +1 \\ 0 & -2 \end{bmatrix}$$

Find the products of (i) ABC, (ii) ACB and state whether they are equal.

14. If $A = \begin{bmatrix} 1 & -2 & 1 \\ 2 & 1 & 3 \end{bmatrix}$, $B = \begin{bmatrix} 2 & 1 \\ 3 & 2 \\ 1 & 1 \end{bmatrix}$

(i) Write down the product matrix AB.

(ii) Would it be possible to form the product matrix BA ? If so compute BA. If not, give reason, why it is not possible ?

15. (i) Solve the matrix equation

$$\begin{bmatrix} 2 & 1 \\ 5 & 0 \end{bmatrix} - 3X = \begin{bmatrix} -7 & 4 \\ 2 & 6 \end{bmatrix}$$

(ii) If $A = \begin{bmatrix} 1 & 2 \\ 2 & 1 \end{bmatrix}$ and $B = \begin{bmatrix} 2 & 1 \\ 1 & 2 \end{bmatrix}$, find A(BA).

16. $A = \begin{bmatrix} 1 & 2 \\ 3 & 4 \end{bmatrix}, B = \begin{bmatrix} 2 & 1 \\ 4 & 2 \end{bmatrix}, C = \begin{bmatrix} 5 & 1 \\ 7 & 4 \end{bmatrix}$,

compute A(B + C) and (B + C)A.

17. (i) If $\begin{bmatrix} x-2 & 5 \\ 3 & 3 \end{bmatrix} = \begin{bmatrix} 4 & 2 \\ y & 5 \end{bmatrix} + \begin{bmatrix} -4 & 3 \\ -1 & -2 \end{bmatrix}$, find the

values of x and y.

(ii) If $A = \begin{bmatrix} 1 & 2 \\ 2 & 3 \end{bmatrix}$, $B = \begin{bmatrix} 2 & 1 \\ 3 & 2 \end{bmatrix}$, $C = \begin{bmatrix} 1 & 3 \\ 3 & 1 \end{bmatrix}$,

find the matrix C(B − A).

18. If $A = \begin{bmatrix} 1 & 4 \\ 2 & 3 \end{bmatrix}$ and $B = \begin{bmatrix} 1 & 2 \\ -3 & -1 \end{bmatrix}$, compute

3A + 4B.

19. (a) State with reason, whether the following are true or false, A, B, C are matrices of order 2 × 2 :

(i) A·B = B·A

(ii) A·(B C) = (AB)·C

(iii) $(A + B)^2 = A^2 + 2A·B + B^2$

(iv) A·(B + C) = A·B + A·C

(b) Given $\begin{bmatrix} 8 & -2 \\ 1 & 4 \end{bmatrix} \cdot X = \begin{bmatrix} 12 \\ 10 \end{bmatrix}$ write down

(i) The order of the matrix X,

(ii) The matrix X.

20. Evaluate x, y if

$$\left(3\begin{bmatrix} 4 & 1 & 3 \\ 0 & -1 & -3 \end{bmatrix} - 2\begin{bmatrix} 3 & 2 & 4 \\ -6 & 1 & -3 \end{bmatrix} \right) \begin{bmatrix} 1 \\ 3 \\ -2 \end{bmatrix} = \begin{bmatrix} x \\ y \end{bmatrix}$$

21. Evaluate without using trigonometric table

$$\begin{bmatrix} 2\cos 60° & -2\sin 30° \\ -\tan 45° & \cos 0° \end{bmatrix} \begin{bmatrix} \cot 45° & \operatorname{cosec} 30° \\ \sec 60° & \sin 90° \end{bmatrix}$$

Chapter 9. Arithmetic Progression

1. Find the 31st term of an A.P. whose 11th term is 38 and the 16th term is 73.

2. An A.P. consists of 50 terms of which 3rd term is 12 and the last term is 106. Find the 29th term.

3. If the 3rd and the 9th terms of an A.P. are 4 and − 8 respectively. Which term of this A.P. is zero ?

4. If 17th term of an A.P. exceeds its 10th term by 7. Find the common difference.

5. Which term of the A.P.

3, 15, 27, 39,…will be 132

more than its 54th term ?

6. How many 3 digit numbers are divisible by 7 ?

7. How many multiple of 4 lie between 10 and 250 ?

8. For what value of n, are the nth terms of two APs 63, 65, 67 and 3, 10, 17, … , equal.

9. Two A.P.s have the same common difference. The difference between their 100th terms is 100, what is the difference between their 100th terms ?

10. The sum of 4th and 8th terms of an A.P. is 24 and the sum of the 6th and 10th term is 44. Find the first three terms of the A.P.

11. In an A.P. :

(i) Given $a = 5$, $d = 3$, $a_n = 50$, find n and S_n.

(ii) Given $a = 7$, $a_{13} = 35$, find d and S_{13}.

(iii) Given $a_n = 4$, $d = 2$, $S_n = -14$, find n and a.

(iv) Given $a = 3$, $n = 8$, $S = 192$, find d.

(v) Given $l = 28$, $S = 144$ and there are total 9 terms. Find a.

12. If the sum of first 7 terms of an A.P. is 49 and that of 17 terms is 289, find the sum of first n terms.

13. Find the sum of the odd numbers between 0 and 50.

14. The 15th term of an A.P. exceeds its 8th terms by 7. Find its common difference.

15. Find a and b, if 12, $a + b$, $2a$ and b are in A.P.

16. If the mth term of an A.P. is $\dfrac{1}{n}$ and the nth term of it is $\dfrac{1}{m}$.

Show that : (mn)th term of this A.P. is 1.

17. Find the 31st term of an A.P. whose 11th term is 38 and the 16th term is 73.

18. The sum of first 15 terms of an A.P. is 0. If its 4th term is 12, find its 12th term.

19. The sum of first n, $2n$ and $3n$ terms of an A.P. are S_1, S_2 and S_3 respectively.

Prove that : $S_3 = 3 (S_2 - S_1)$.

20. In an A.P., show that :

$(m + n)$th term + $(m - n)$th term = $2 \times m$th term

Chapter 10. Geometric Progression

1. Find the 8th term of G.P. 4, 12, 36, ...

2. Which term is 729 in the G.P. $\dfrac{-1}{27}, \dfrac{1}{9}, \dfrac{-1}{3}$ ...

3. Find the third term from last in the G.P. $\dfrac{2}{27}, \dfrac{2}{9}, \dfrac{2}{3}, \ ......$

4. If sixth term and common ratio of G.P. be $\dfrac{-64}{9}$ and $\dfrac{-2}{3}$ then find the first term.

5. If fifth term in nine times the third term in a G.P. and second term of progression is 6, find G.P.

6. Find the sum of n terms of the series
$$a - ar + ar^2 - ar^3 + \ ......$$

7. If $(p + q)$th term be m and $(p - q)$th term be n then find the pth and qth terms of the G.P.

8. The mth term of G.P. is $(-b)^m$. Find the sum of m terms.

9. If sum of infinite terms of geometrical progression is 8 and the second term is 2, then find the first term and common ratio.

10. Find the sum of 10 terms of the series 128 + 64 + 32 + ...

11. Find the sum of first n terms of the series 5 + 55 + 555 + ...

12. Find how many terms of G.P. $\dfrac{2}{9} - \dfrac{1}{3} + \dfrac{1}{2} - ...$ must be added to get the sum equal to $\dfrac{55}{72}$.

13. If the sum of $1 + 2 + 2^2 + ... + 2^{n-1}$ is 255, find the value of n.

14. Find the sum of G.P.
$$\dfrac{x+y}{x-y} + 1 + \dfrac{x-y}{x+y} + ... \text{ upto } n \text{ terms.}$$

15. Find the sum of G.P.
$$\sqrt{3} + \dfrac{1}{\sqrt{3}} + \dfrac{1}{3\sqrt{3}} + ... \text{ to } n \text{ terms.}$$

16. Find the sum of infinite series
$$\dfrac{1}{3} + \dfrac{1}{3^2} + \dfrac{1}{3^3} + ...$$

17. Find the geometric mean between :
(i) $2a$ and $8a^3$ (ii) $\dfrac{4}{9}$ and $\dfrac{9}{4}$.

18. A G.P. has first term $a = 3$, last term $l = 96$ and sum of n terms $S = 189$. Find the number of terms in it.

Chapter 11. Co-ordinate Geometry

1. In what ratio is the line joining (2, – 3) and (5, 6) divided by the X-axis ?

2. If A = (– 4, 3) and B = (8, – 6)
(i) find the length of AB.

(ii) in what ratio is the line joining A and B, divided by the X-axis ?

3. In what ratio is the join of (4, 3) and (2, – 6) divided by the X-axis ? Also, find the coordinates of the point of intersection.

4. The line joining the points A (– 3, – 10) and B (– 2, 6) is divided by the point P such that $\dfrac{PB}{AB} = \dfrac{1}{5}$. Find the coordinates of P.

5. The line segment joining A (4, 7) and B (– 6, – 2) is intercepted by the Y-axis at the point K. Write down the abscissa of the point K. Hence, find the ratio in which K divides AB. Also find the coordinates of the point K.

6. Calculate the ratio in which the line joining A (6, 5) and B (4, – 3) is divided by the line $y = 2$.

7. A (2, 5), B (– 1, 2) and C (5, 8) are the coordinates of the vertices of the triangle ABC.

   Points P and Q lie on AB and AC respectively, such that AP : PB = AQ : QC = 1 : 2.

   (i) Calculate the coordinates of P and Q.

   (ii) Show that $PQ = \dfrac{1}{3} BC$.

8. Points A, B, C and D divide the line segment joining the point (5, – 10) and the origin in five equal parts. Find the coordinates of B and D.

9. In what ratio does the point (a, 6) divide the join of (– 4, 3) and (2, 8) ?

   Also, find the value of a.

10. Show that A (3, – 2) is a point of trisection of the line segment joining the points (2, 1) and (5, – 8). Also find the coordinates of the other point of trisection.

11. The line segment joining the points M (5, 7) and N (– 3, 2) is intersected by the Y-axis at point L. Write down the abscissa of L. Hence, find the ratio in which L divides MN.

    Also, find the coordinates of L.

12. Show that the line segment joining the points (– 5, 8) and (10, – 4) is trisected by the coordinate axes.

13. P is a point on the line joining A (4, 3) and B (– 2, 6) such that 5AP = 2BP. Find the coordinates of P.

14. The line segment joining A (2, 3) and B (6, – 5) is intercepted by X-axis at the point K. Write down the ordinate of the point K. Hence, find the ratio in which K divides AB.

    Also, find the coordinates of the point K.

15. The line joining P (– 4, 5) and Q (3, 2) intersects the Y-axis at point R. PM and QN are perpendiculars from P and Q on the X-axis. Find :

    (i) the ratio PR : RQ.

    (ii) the coordinates of R.

    (iii) the area of the quadrilateral PMNQ.

16. A (– 3, 4), B (3, – 1) and C (– 2, 4) are the vertices of a triangle ABC. Find the length of the line segment AP, where point P lies inside BC, such that BP : PC = 2 : 3.

17. In what ratio does the point (1, a) divide the join of (– 1, 4) and (4, –1) ?

    Also, find the value of a.

18. A (20, 0) and B (10, – 20) are two fixed points. Find the coordinates of the point P in AB such that : 3PB = AB. Also, find the coordinates of some other point Q in AB such that : AB = 6AQ.

19. (i) Write down the coordinates of the point P that divides the line joining A (– 4, 1) and B (17, 10) in the ratio 1 : 2.

    (ii) Calculate the distance OP, where O is the origin.

    (iii) In what ratio does the Y-axis divide the line AB ?

20. A line segment joining A $\left(-1, \dfrac{5}{3}\right)$ and B (a, 5) is divided in the ratio 1 : 3 at P, the point where the line segment AB intersects the Y-axis.

    (i) Calculate the value of 'a'.

    (ii) Calculate the coordinates of 'P'.

21. Find the coordinates of the centroid of a triangle ABC whose vertices are :

    A (– 1, 3), B (1, – 1) and C (5, 1).

22. In what ratio is the line joining A (0, 3) and B (4, – 1) divided by the X-axis ?

23. Prove that the points A (– 5, 4), B (– 1, – 2) and C (5, 2) are the vertices of an isosceles right angled triangle. Find the coordinates of D so that ABCD is a square.

24. Calculate the ratio in which the line joining A (– 4, 2) and B (3, 6) is divided by point P (x, 3). Also, find (i) x, (ii) length of AP.

25. M is the mid-point of the line segment joining the points A (– 3, 7) and B (9, – 1). Find the coordinates of point M. Further, if R (2, 2) divides the line segment joining M and the origin in the ratio $p : q$, find the ratio $p : q$.

26. A (– 8, 0), B (0, 16) and C (0, 0) are the vertices of a triangle ABC. Point P lies on AB and Q lies on AC such that AP : PB = 3 : 5 and AQ : QC = 3 : 5.

    Show that : PQ = $\frac{3}{8}$ BC.

27. Points A (– 5, x), B (y, 7) and C (1, – 3) are collinear (*i.e.*, lie on the same straight line) such that AB = BC. Calculate the values of x and y.

28. Calculate the coordinates of the centroid of the triangle ABC, if A = (7, – 2), B = (0, 1) and C (– 1, 4).

29. The mid-point of the line segment joining (2a, 4) and (– 2, 2b) is (1, 2a + 1). Find the values of a and b.

30. The mid-point of the line segment joining (4a, 2b – 3) and (– 4, 3b) is (2, – 2a). Find the values of a and b.

Chapter 12. Reflection

1. Point (3, 0) and (– 1, 0) are invariants under reflection in the line L_1; Points (0, – 3) and (0, 1) are invariant points under reflection in the line L_2. State single transformation that marks P'' onto P''.

2. Find the reflection in Y-axis of the point :
   (i) A(1, 3),   (ii) B(– 1, 2),
   (iii) C(– 3, – 3),   (iv) D(2, – 4).

3. The triangle ABC, when A(1, 2), B(4, 8), C(6, 8) is reflected in the X-axis to triangle A'B'C'. Triangle A'B'C' is then reflected in the origin to triangle A''B''C''.
   (i)   Write down the coordinates of A''.
   (ii) Write down the coordinates of B''.
   (iii) Write down the coordinates of C''.
   (iv) Write down the single transformation that maps ABC into A''B''C''.

4. (i)   Point P (a, b) is reflected in the X-axis to P'(5, – 2). Write down the values of a and b.
   (ii) P'' is the image of P when reflected in the Y-axis. Write down the values of a and b.
   (iii) Name a single transformation that maps P' to P''.

5. A point P is reflected on the X-axis. Coordinates of its image are (8, – 6).
   (i)   Find the coordinates of P.
   (ii) Find the coordinates of the image of P under reflection in the Y-axis.
   (iii) Find the coordinates of the image of P under reflection on the origin.

6. Write down the coordinates of the image of the point (– 2, 4) under :

(i)   Reflection at the origin.
(ii) Reflection on the Y-axis.
(iii) Reflection on the X-axis.

7. A point C(3, 4) is reflected on the X-axis. If C' is the image, write down :
   (i)   The coordinates of C',
   (ii) The length of the segment CC',
   (iii) If O' is the image of C, with respect to origin O, calculate the perimeter of the figure COC'O'.

8. B, C have the coordinates (3, 2) and (0, 3). Find :
   (i)   The image B' of B under reflection on the X-axis.
   (ii) The image C' of C under reflection in the line BB'.
   (iii) Calculate the length of BC'.

9. On a graph paper draw a triangle ABC with A(3, 1), B(5, 0) and C(7, 4). Draw the image of the triangle ABC under reflection in the line $x = 2$. What are their coordinates ?

10. The point P(a, b) is first reflected in the origin and then reflected on the Y-axis to P'. If P' has coordinates (7, – 5), calculate a, b.

11. The point P(– 3, – 2) on reflection on X-axis is mapped on P'. Then P' on reflection in the origin is mapped as P''. Find the coordinates of P' and P''.

    Write down a single transformation that maps P onto P''.

12. A point P is reflected to P' on the X-axis. The coordinates of its image are (2, – 3). Find :
    (i)   The coordinates of P.

(ii) The coordinates of the image P'' of P under reflection on the Y-axis.

(iii) The coordinates of the image Q' of the point Q(1, 2) in the line PP'.

13. Points (3, 0) and (– 1, 0) are invariant points under reflection in the line L_1; points (0, – 3) and (0, 1) are invariant points on reflection in line L_2.

   (i) Name the lines L_1 and L_2.

   (ii) Write down the images of points P(3, 4) and Q(– 5, – 2) on reflection in L_1. Name the images of P' and Q' respectively.

   (iii) Write down the images of P and Q on reflection L_2. Name the images as P'' and Q'' respectively.

   (iv) State or describe a single transformation that maps P' onto P''.

14. The points A(2, 1), B(0, 3) and C(– 2, – 2) are the vertices of a triangle.

   (i) Plot the points on the graph paper.

   (ii) Draw the triangle formed by reflecting these points on the X-axis.

   (iii) Are the two triangles congruent ?

15. Points (5, 0) and (– 2, 0) are invariant points under reflection in the line L_1 points (0, – 5) and (0, 2) are invariant points on reflection in L_2.

   (i) Name the lines L_1 and L_2.

   (ii) Write down the images of point P(5, 8) and Q(– 3, – 4) on reflection L_1. Name the images of P' and Q' respectively.

(iii) Write down the images of P and Q on reflection in L_2. Name the images P'' and Q'' respectively.

(iv) State or describe a single transformation that maps P' on to P''.

16. Use graph paper for this question :

   (i) Plot the points A(3, 5) and B(– 2, – 4). Use 1 cm = 1 unit on both axes.

   (ii) A' is the image of A when reflected on the X-axis. Write down the coordinates of A' and plot it on the graph paper.

   (iii) B' is the images of B when reflected on the X-axis, followed by reflection in the origin. Write down the coordinates of B' and plot it on the graph paper.

   (iv) Write down the geometrical name of the figure AA'BB'.

   (v) Name two invariant points under reflection on the X-axis.

17. The point P (3, 4) is reflected to P' in the X-axis and O' is the image of O (origin) when reflected in the line PP'. Using graph paper, give :

   (i) The co-ordinates of P' and O''

   (ii) The length of the segments PP' and OO''.

   (iii) The perimeter of the quadrilateral POP'O'.

   (iv) The geometrical name of the figure POP'O'.

Chapter 13. Similarity

1. In two similar triangles ABC and PQR, if their corresponding altitudes AD and PS are in the ratio of 4 : 9, find the ratio of the areas of ∆ABC and ∆PQR.

2. If ∆ABC is similar to ∆DEF such that BC = 3 cm, EF = 4 cm and area of ∆ABC = 54 cm². Determine the area of ∆DEF.

3. If ∆ABC ~ ∆DEF such that area of ∆ABC is 9 cm² and area of ∆DEF is 16 cm² and BC = 2.1 cm, find the length of EF.

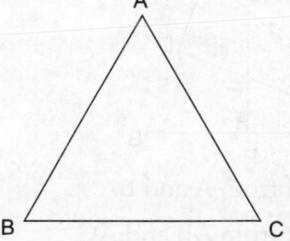 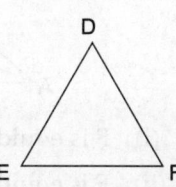

4. If PB and QA are perpendiculars to segment AB. If PO = 5 cm, QO = 7 cm and area ∆POB = 150 cm², find the area of ∆QOA.

5. In the following figure (not drawn to scale LM is parallel to BC. AB = 6 cm, AL = 2 cm and AC = 9 cm. Calculate :

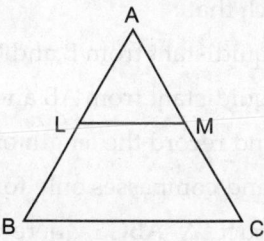

   (i) The length of CM

   (ii) The value of the ratio

$$= \frac{\text{Area } (\Delta ALM)}{\text{Area of trapezium BCML}}.$$

6. Two isosceles triangles have equal vertical angles and their areas are in the ratio of 16 : 25. Find the ratio between their corresponding heights.

7. ABC is a triangle and AN ⊥ BC, BC = 12 cm and AC = 5 cm. Find the ratio between the areas of ΔANC and ΔABC, where ∠A = 90°.

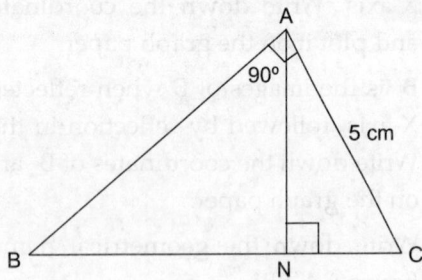

8. In figure, DE ∥ BC.

   (i) If DE = 4 cm, BC = 6 cm and area (ΔADE) = 16 cm², find the area of ΔABC.

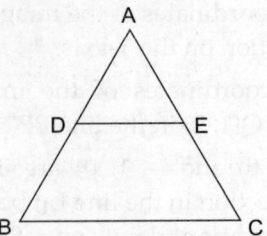

(ii) If DE = 4 cm, BC = 8 cm and area (ΔADE) = 25 cm², find the area of ΔABC.

(iii) If DE : BC = 3 : 5, calculate the ratio between the area of ΔADE and the trapezium BCED.

9. The areas of two similar triangles are 169 cm² and 121 cm² respectively. If the longest side of the larger triangle is 26 cm, find the longest side of the smaller triangle.

10. In a ΔABC, P divides the side AB such that AP : PB = 1 : 2, Q is a point in AC such that PQ ∥ BC. Find the ratio of the areas of ΔAPQ and trapezium BPQC.

Chapter 14. Loci

1. Construct a triangle ABC in which AB = 6 cm, BC = 7 cm and CA = 6·5 cm. Find a point P equidistant from B and C and also equidistant from AB and BC.

2. Find a point on the base of a scalene triangle equidistant from its sides.

3. In the figure given below, find a point P on CD equidistant from point A and B.

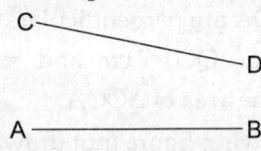

4. Construct a triangle ABC, with AB = 7 cm, BC = 8 cm and ∠ABC = 60°. Locate by construction the point P such that :

   (i) P is equidistant from B and C.

   (ii) P is equidistant from AB and BC.

   Measure and record the length of PB.

5. Use ruler and compasses only for this question :

   (i) Construct Δ ABC, where AB = 3·5 cm, BC = 6 cm and ∠ABC = 60°.

   (ii) Construct the locus of points inside the triangle which are equidistant from BA and BC.

(iii) Construct the locus of points inside the triangle which are equidistant from B and C.

(iv) Mark the point P which is equidistant from AB, BC and also equidistant from B and C. Measure and record the length of PB.

6. In triangle LMN, bisectors of interior angles at L and N intersect each other at point A. prove that :

   (i) point A is equidistant from all the three sides of the triangles.

   (ii) AM bisects angle LMN.

7. The given figure shows a triangle ABC in which AD bisects angle BAC. EG is perpendicular bisector of side AB which intersects AD at point F. Prove that :

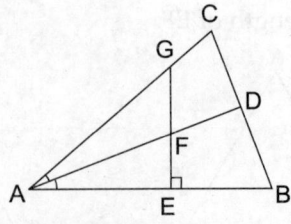

   (i) F is equidistant from A and B.

   (ii) F is equidistant from AB and AC.

8. Draw an angle ABC = 75°. Draw the locus of all the points equidistant from AB and BC.

9. Construct an isosceles triangle ABC such that AB = 6 cm, BC = AC = 4 cm. Bisect ∠C internally and mark a point P on this bisector such that CP = 5 cm. Find the points Q and R which are 5 cm from P and also 5 cm from the line AB.

10. Construct a triangle BCP given BC = 5 cm, BP = 4 cm and ∠PBC = 45°.

(i) Complete the rectangle ABCD such that :

(a) P is equidistant from AB and BC.

(b) P is equidistant from C and D.

(ii) Measure and record the length of AB.

Chapter 15. Circles

1. If O is the centre of the circle. Find the value of x in each of the following figures :

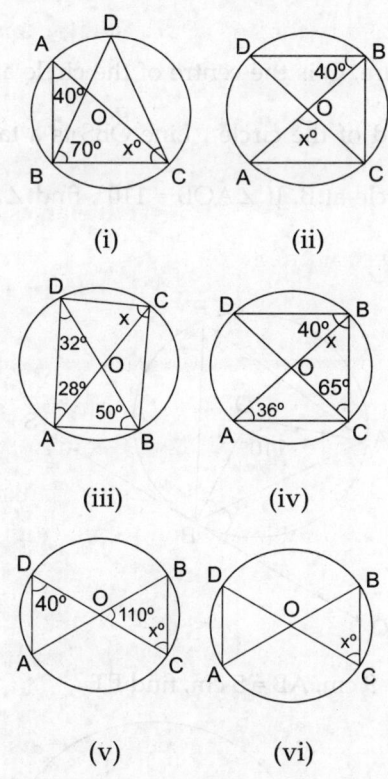

(i)   (ii)

(iii)   (iv)

(v)   (vi)

2. In Figure ∆ABC is equilateral triangle. Find m ∠BDC.

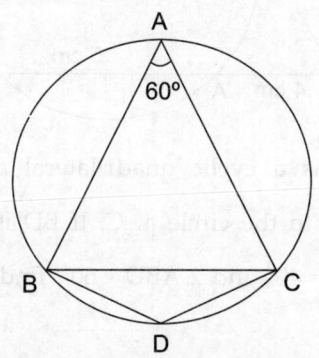

3. In Fig. O is the centre of the circle. If ∠BOD = 160°, find the values of $x°$ and $y°$.

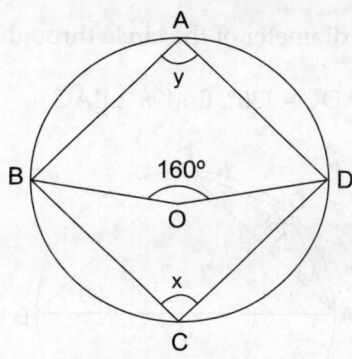

4. ABCD is a cyclic quadrilateral. If ∠BCD = 100° and ∠ABD = 70°, find ∠ADB.

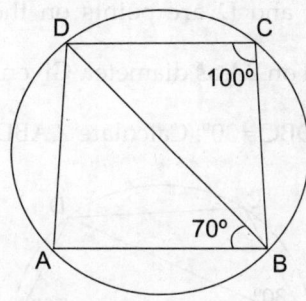

5. In Fig., calculate the measurement of ∠AOC.

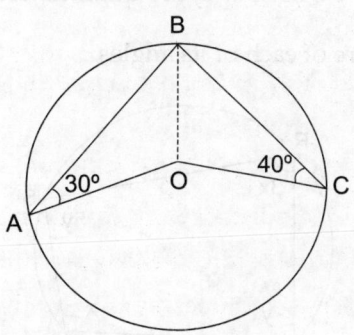

6. In Fig. ∆ABC is an isosceles triangle with AB = AC and ∠ABC = 50°. Find ∠BDC and ∠BEC.

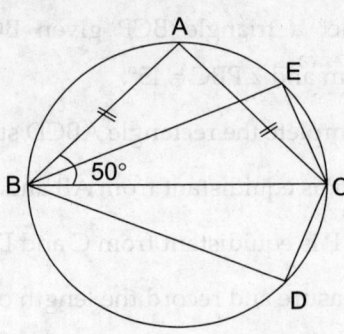

7. In Fig. ABCD is a cyclic quadrilateral whose side

AB is a diameter of the circle through A, B, C, D.

If $m \angle ADC = 130°$, find $m \angle BAC$.

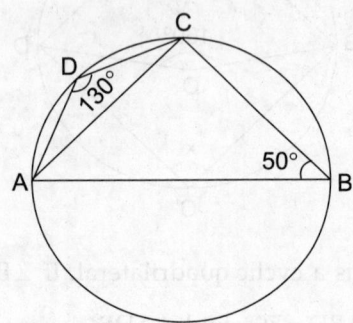

8. In Fig. C and D are points on the semi-circle

described on BA as diameter. Given $\angle BAD = 70°$

and $m \angle DBC = 30°$. Calculate $\angle ABD$ and $\angle BDC$.

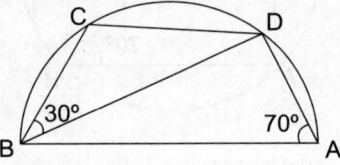

9. In Fig. PQRS is a cyclic quadrilateral. Find the

measure of each of its angles.

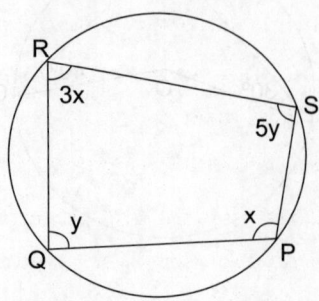

10. In the given figure $\angle A = 60°$ and $\angle ABC = 80°$.

Find $\angle DPC$ and $\angle BQC$.

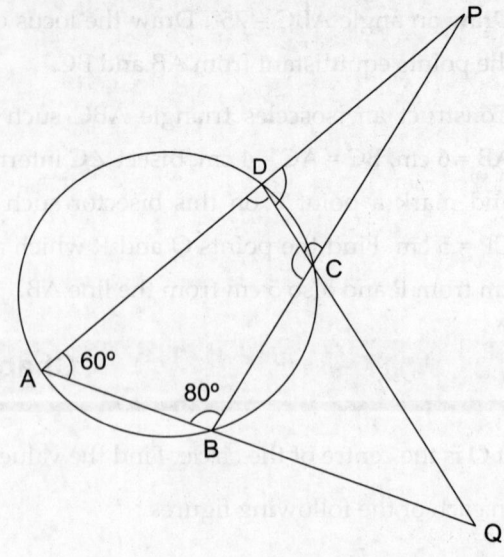

11. In figure, O is the centre of the circle and AB is

a chord of the circle . Line QBS is a tangent to

the circle at B. If $\angle AOB = 110°$, find $\angle APB$ and

$\angle ABQ$.

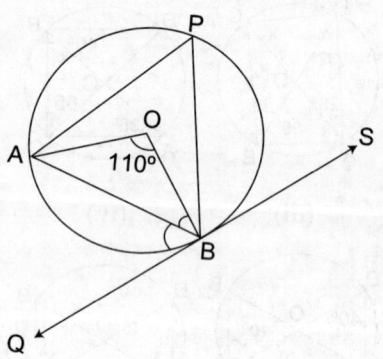

12. If PB = 9 cm, AB = 5 cm, find PT.

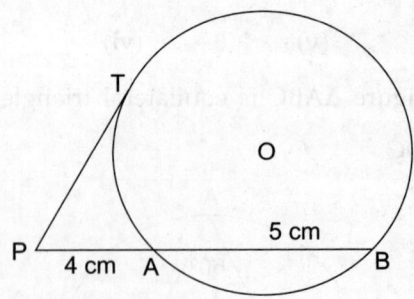

13. ABCD is a cyclic quadrilateral and PQ is a

tangent to the circle at C. If BD is a diameter,

$\angle DCQ = 40°$ and $\angle ABD = 60°$, find the measure

of :

(i) $\angle DBC$ (ii) $\angle BCP$

(iii) $\angle BDC$ (iv) $\angle ADB$.

Practice Exercises

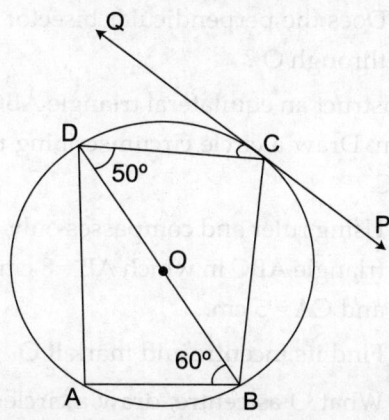

14. The radii of two concentric circles are 17 cm and 10 cm; a line PQRS cuts the larger circle at P and S and the smaller circle at Q and R. If QR = 12 cm, calculate PQ.

15. In the given figure PQRS is a cyclic quadrilateral in which PQ = QR and RS is produced to T. If angle QPR = 52°, calculate angle PST.

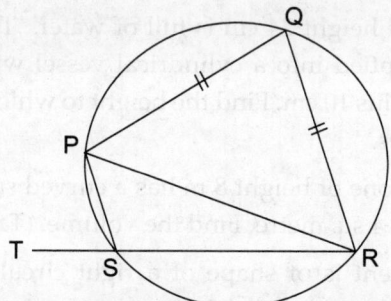

16. The length of the direct common tangent to two circles of radii 12 cm and 4 cm is 15 cm. Calculate the distance between their centres.

17. In Fig. AB is a diameter and AC is a chord of a circle such that ∠BAC = 30°. The tangent at C intersects AB produced in D. Prove that BC = BD.

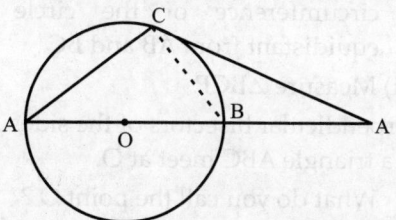

18. In the following figure, ABCD is cyclic quadrilateral, ∠ADC = 80° and ∠ACD = 52°. Find the value of ∠CBD and ∠ABC.

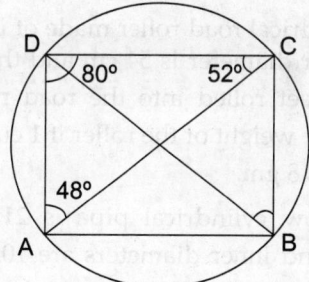

Chapter 16. Constructions

1. Using ruler and compasses only :

   (i) Construct a triangle ABC with the following data :

   Base AB = 6 cm, BC = 6·2 cm and ∠CAB = 60°.

   (ii) In the same diagram, draw a circle which passes through the points A, B and C and mark its centre O.

   (iii) Draw a perpendicular from O to AB which meets AB in D.

   (iv) Prove that : AD = BD.

2. Construct a regular hexagon of side 4 cm. Construct a circle circumscribing the hexagon.

3. Construct a triangle ABC in which base BC = 5·5 cm, AB = 6 cm and ∠ABC = 120°.

   (i) Construct a circle circumscribing the triangle ABC.

   (ii) Draw a cyclic quadrilateral ABCD so that D is equidistant from B and C.

4. Draw a circle of radius 3·5 cm. Mark a point P outside the circle at a distance of 6 cm from the centre. Construct two tangents from P to the given circle. Measure and write down the length of one tangent.

5. Using ruler and compasses only construct a triangle ABC in which BC = 4 cm, ∠ACB = 45° and perpendicular from A on BC is 2·5 cm. Draw a circle circumscribing the triangle ABC.

6. The bisectors of angles A and B of a scalene triangle ABC meet at O.

   (i) What is the point O called ?

   (ii) OR and OQ are drawn perpendiculars to AB and CA respectively. What is the relation between OR and OQ ?

   (iii) What is the relation between angle ACO and angle BCO ?

7. Using a ruler and compasses only :
   (i) Construct a triangle ABC with the following data :
       AB = 3·5 cm, BC = 6 cm and ∠ABC = 120°.
   (ii) In the same diagram, draw a circle with BC as diameter. Find a point P on the circumference of the circle which is equidistant from AB and BC.
   (iii) Measure ∠BCP.

8. Perpendicular bisectors of the sides AB and AC of a triangle ABC meet at O.
   (i) What do you call the point O ?
   (ii) What is the relation between the distances OA, OB and OC ?
   (iii) Does the perpendicular bisector of BC pass through O ?

9. Construct an equilateral triangle ABC with side 6 cm. Draw a circle circumscribing the triangle ABC.

10. (i) Using ruler and compasses only, construct a triangle ABC in which AB = 8 cm, BC = 6 cm and CA = 5 cm.
    (ii) Find its incentre and mark it O.
    (iii) What O as centre, draw a circle which will cut off 2 cm chords from each side of the triangle.

Chapter 17. Mensuration

Practice Exercises

1. A cylindrical road roller made of iron 1 m wide. Its inner diameter is 54 cm and thickness of the iron sheet rolled into the road roller is 9 cm. Find the weight of the roller if 1 cubic cm of iron weights 8 gm.

2. A hollow cylindrical pipe is 21 cm long. Its outer and inner diameters are 10 cm and 6 cm respectively. Find the volume of the copper used in making the pipe.

3. Find the volume of a right circular cylinder which has a height of 21 cm and the base radius 5 cm. Find also the curved surface area of the cylinder.

4. Water is flowing at the rate of 7 metre per second through a circular pipe whose internal diameter is 2 cm into a cylindrical tank the radius of whose base is 40 cm. Determine the increase in the water level in 1/2 hour.

5. Water is flowing at the rate of 3 km/hr through a circular pipe of 20 cm internal diameter into a circular cistern of diameter 10 m and depth 2 m. In how much time will the cistern be filled ?

6. The interior of a building is in the form of right circular cylinder of diameter 4·2 m and height 4 m surmounted by a cone. The vertical height of cone is 2·1 m. Find the outer surface area and volume of the building. (Take π = 22/7)

7. The interior of a building is in the form of cylinder of diameter 4·3 m and height 3·8 cm, surmounted by a cone whose vertical angle is a right angle. Find the area of the surface and the volume of the building. (Take π = 3·14).

8. A conical vessel whose internal radius is 5 cm and height 24 cm is full of water. The water is emptied into a cylindrical vessel with internal radius 10 cm. Find the height to which the water rises.

9. A cone of height 8 m has a curved surface are a 188·4 sq. metre. Find the volume. (Take π = 3·14)

10. A tent is of shape of a right circular cylinder upto a height of 3 metre and then becomes a right circular cone with a maximum height of 13·5 metre above the ground. Calculate the cost of painting the inner side of the tent at the rate of ₹ 2 per square metre, if the radius of the base is 14 metre.

11. A solid sphere of radius 3 cm is melted and then casted into small spherical balls each of diameter 0·6 cm. Find the number of balls thus obtained.

12. Find the volume and surface area of a sphere of radius 4·2 cm. (Take π = 22/7)

13. Find the volume and the total surface area of a hemisphere of radius 3·5 cm. (Take π = 22/7)

14. The surface area of a solid metallic sphere is 1256 cm². It is melted and recasted into a solid cone height 8 cm and radius 2·5 cm, calculated :
    (i) The radius of solid sphere.
    (ii) The number of cones recast.

15. A hemisphere bowl of internal diameter 36 cm contains a liquid. This liquid is to be filled in cylindrical bottles of radius 3 cm and height

Practice Exercises

6 cm. How many bottles are required to empty the bowl ?

16. A solid wooden toy is in the shape of a right circular cone mounted on a hemisphere. If the radius of the hemisphere is 4·2 cm and the total height of the toy is 10·2 cm, find the volume of the wooden toy.

17. A solid metallic cylinder of radius 14 cm and height 21 cm is melted down and recasted into a sphere of radius 3·5 cm. Calculate the number of spheres that can be made.

18. A solid is in the form of a right circular cone mounted on a hemisphere. The radius of the hemisphere is 3·5 cm and the height of the cone is 4 cm. The solid is placed in a cylindrical tub, full of water in such a way that the whole solid is submerged in water. If the radius of the cylinder is 5 cm and its height is 10·5 cm, find the volume of water left in the cylindrical tub. (Take $\pi = 22/7$)

19. The diameter of sphere is 42 cm. The sphere is melted and is drawn into a cylinder. If the diameter of cylinder is 28 cm. Find its height.

20. How many spherical lead shots each 4·2 cm in diameter can be obtained from a rectangular solid of lead with dimensions 66 cm, 42 cm, 21 cm. (Take $\pi = 22/7$)

21. A sphere of diameter 6 cm is dropped in a right circular cylindrical vessel partly filled with water. The diameter of the cylindrical vessel is 12 cm. If the sphere is completely submerged in water, how much will the level of water rise in the cylindrical vessel ?

22. A cylindrical container of radius 6 cm and height 15 cm is filled with icecream. The whole icecream has to be distributed to 10 children in equal cones with hemisphere tops. If the height of the conical portion is four times the radius of its base, find the radius of icecream cone.

23. A solid is composed of a cylinder with hemisphere ends. If the whole length of the solid is 108 cm and the diameter of the hemisphere ends is 36 cm, find the cost of polishing the surface of the solid at the rate of 7 paise per sq. cm. (Take $\pi = 22/7$)

24. The internal and external diameters of a hollow hemispherical vessel are 24 cm and 25 cm respectively. The cost to paint one sq. cm of the surface is 7 paise. Find the total cost to paint the vessel all over. (Ignore the area of edge)

25. A toy is in the shape of a right circular cylinder with a hemisphere on one end and a cone on the other. The height and radius of the cylindrical part are 13 cm and 5 cm respectively. The radii of the hemispherical and conical parts are the same as that of the cylindrical part. Calculate the surface area of the toy if height of the conical part is 12 cm.

26. A spherical canon ball, 28 cm in diameter is melted and cast into a right circular conical mould, the base of which is 35 cm diameter. Find the height of the cone, correct to one place of decimal.

27. The volumes of two spheres are in the ratio 64 : 27. Find their radii if the sum of their radii is 21 cm.

28. The internal and external diameters of a hollow hemispherical vessel are 24 cm and 25 cm respectively. The cost to paint 1 cm² the surface is ₹ 0·05. Find the total cost to paint the vessel all over. (Take $\pi = 22/7$)

29. The largest sphere is curved out of a cube of a side 7 cm. Find the volume of the sphere.

30. A vessel is in the form of a hemispherical bowl mounted by a hollow cylinder. The diameter of the sphere is 14 cm and the total height of the vessel is 13 cm. Find its capacity. (Take $\pi = 22/7$)

31. A lead bar of length 12 cm, width 6 cm and thickness 3 cm is melted down and made in four equal spherical bullets. Find the radius of each bullet.

32. A solid cylinder of brass is 10 cm in diameter and 3 m long. How many spherical balls each 2 cm in radius, can be made from it.

33. Prove that the relation between the volumes and the surface areas of the cylinder, sphere and cone is 3 : 2 : 1 and 1 : 1 : $\dfrac{\sqrt{5}}{4}$ when their heights and diameters are equal.

34. How many square metre of copper will be required to cover a hemispherical dome 30 cm in diameter.

35. The radii of the internal and external surface of a hollow spherical shell are 3 m and 5 m respectively. If the same amount of material were formed into cube what would be the length of the edge of the cube ?

36. A spherical canon ball, 6 cm in diameter is melted and cast into a conical mould the base of which is 12 cm in diameter. Find the height of the cone.

37. A storage tank, in the form of a cylinder with hemispherical ends, 15 m long overall and 2 m in diameter. Calculate the weight of water, in litre, contained when the tank is one-third full.

38. A circular disc of leads 3 cm in thickness and 12 cm diameter, is wholly converted into shots of radius 5 cm. Determine the number of shots.

39. A right angled triangle of which the sides are 65 cm, 60 cm and 25 cm in length is made to turn its hypotenuse. Determine the volume of the double cone thus formed.

40. The generating line of a right circular cone is inclined at an angle 60° to horizontal if the height of the cone is 15 cm. Determine its volume and lateral surface area.

41. Find the volume of the largest right circular cone that can be cut out of a cube whose edge is 2·8 m.

Chapter 18. Trigonometry

1. A pole 5 m high is fixed on the top of a tower. The angle of elevation of the pole observed from a point A on the ground is 60° and the angle of depression of the point A from the top of the tower is 45°. Find the height of the tower.

2. The angle of elevation of a Jet plane from a point P on the ground is 60°. After a flight of 15 second, the angle of elevation changes to 30°. If the Jet plane is flying at a constant height of $1500\sqrt{3}$ m, find the speed of the Jet plane.

3. From the top of a tower, the angles of depression of two objects on the same side of the tower are found to be α and β ($\alpha > \beta$). If the distance between objects is 'p' metre, show that the height 'h' of the tower is given by

$$h = \frac{p - \tan\alpha\,\tan\beta}{\tan\alpha - \tan\beta}$$

Also determine the height of tower if $p = 50$ metre, $\alpha = 60°$ and $\beta = 30°$.

4. The angle of elevation of the top of a tower from a point on the same level as the foot of the tower is α. On advancing 'p' metre towards the foot of the tower, the angle of elevation becomes β. Show that the height of tower is given by

$$h = \frac{p - \tan\alpha\,\tan\beta}{\tan\beta - \tan\alpha}$$

Also determine the height of the tower if $p = 150$ metre, $\alpha = 30°$ and $\beta = 60°$.

5. A man on the deck of a ship is 16 m above water level. He observes that the angle of elevation of the top of a cliff 45° and the angle of depression of the base is 30°. Calculate the distance of the cliff from the ship and the height of the cliff.

6. A man in a boat rowing away from a lighthouse 100 m high takes 2 minute to change the angle of elevation of the top of lighthouse from 60° to 45°. Find the speed of the boat.

7. From a point P on level ground, the angle of elevation of the top of tower is 30°. If the tower is 100 m high, how far is P from the foot of the tower.

8. A kite is flawn with a thread 250 metre long. If the thread is assumed stretched straight and makes an angle of 60° with the horizontal, find the height of the kite above the ground.

9. The angle of elevation of the top of a tower from a point 50 m towards the tower the angle of elevation A (on the level ground) is 30°. On walking close towards the tower is found to be 60°. Calculate :

   (i) the height of the tower (correct to one decimal place),

   (ii) the distance of the tower form A.

10. Two men on either side of a cliff 80 m high observe the angle of elevation of the top of the cliff to be 30° and 60° respectively. Find the distance between two men.

11. The horizontal distance between two trees of different heights is 60 m. The angle of depression of the first tree when seen from the top of second tree is 45°. If the height of the second tree is 80 m, find the height of the first tree.

12. The horizontal distance between two towers is 70 m. The angle of depression of the top of the first tower when seen from the top of second tower is 30°. If the height of the second tower is 120 m, find the height of the first tower.

13. A vertically straight tree, 15 m high, is broken by the wind in such a way that its top just touches the ground and makes an angle of 60° with the ground. At what height from the ground did the tree break ?

14. A vertical tower stands on a horizontal plane and is surmounted by a vertical flagstaff of height 5 metre. At a point on the plane, the angle of elevation of the bottom and the top of the flagstaff are respectively 30° and 60°. Find the height of the tower.

15. Two men on either side of a tower 60 m high observes the angle of elevation of the top of the tower to be 45° and 60° respectively. Find the distance between the two men.

16. An aeroplane flying horizontally 1 km above the ground is observed at an elevation of 60°.

After 10 second its elevation is observed to be 30°. Find the speed of the aeroplane in km/hr.

17. From the top of a hill, the angle of depression of two consecutive kilometre stands due east are found to be 30° and 45°. Find the height of the hill.

18. A person observed the angle of elevation of the top of a tower as 30°. He walked 50 m towards the foot of the tower along level ground and found the angle of elevation of the·top of the tower as 60°. Find the height of the tower.

19. A balloon moving in a straight line passes vertically above two points A and B on a horizontal plane 1000 m apart. When above A it has an altitude of 60° as seen from B and when above B it has an altitude of 45° as seen from A. Find the distance from A of the point at which it will touch the plane.

20. In the following figure, the angle of elevation of top P of the vertical tower from a point X is 60°, at a point Y, 40 m vertically above X, the angle of elevation is 45°, find :

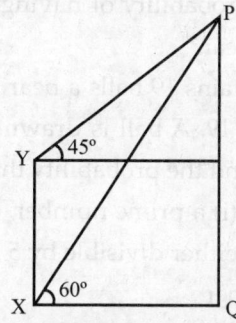

(i) the height of the tower PQ.
(ii) the distance XQ.

Chapter 19. Statistics

1. Vijay secored 36 marks in English, 44 marks in Physics, 75 makrs in Mathematics and x marks in Chemistry. If he has scored an average of 50 marks, find x.

2. There are 50 students in a class in which 40 are boys and the rest girls. The average weight of the students in the class is 44 kg and the average weight of the girls is 40 kg. Find the average weight of boys.

3. The mean of 7 variates is 12. If six of them are 5, 13, 9, 17, 14 and 10. Find the seventh variate.

4. The mean of 20 numbers is 18. If 3 is added to each of the first ten numbers, find the mean of new set of 20 numbers.

5. Find the value of x, if the mean of the following distribution is 18 :

x	13	15	17	19	20 + x	23
f	8	2	3	4	5x	6

6. The table below shows, a distribution of a scores obtained by 120 shooters, in a shooting competition. Using a graph sheet, draw an ogive for the distribution :

Scores obtained	Number of shooters
0–10	5
10–20	9
20–30	16
30–40	22
40–50	26
50–60	18
60–70	11
70–80	6
80–90	4
90–100	3

Use your ogive to estimate :
(i) The median
(ii) The interquartile range
(iii) The number of shooters who obtained more than 75% score.

7. Find the mean of the following distribution :

C.I.	Frequency
20–30	10
30–40	6
40–50	8
50–60	12
60–70	5
70–80	9

Chapter 20. Probability

1. A dice is thrown once. What is the probability of getting a number greater than 4 ?

2. Find the probability of having 53 sundays in a non leap year.

3. A box contains 19 balls a bearing numbers 1, 2, 3, 4, ……, 19. A ball is drawn at random from the box. Find the probability that the number on the ball is (i) a prime number, (ii) divisible by 3 or 5, (iii) neither divisible by 5 nor by 10, (iv) an even number.

4. Three unbiased coins are tossed simultaneously. Find the probability of getting exactly 2 heads.

5. 1000 families with 2 children were selected randomly and the following data were recorded :

Number of boys in a family	Number of families
0	140
1	560
2	300

If a family is chosen at random, find the probability that it has (i) no boy, (ii) one boy, (iii) 2 boys, (iv) at least one boy, (v) at most one boy.

6. Find the probability of drawing a red king or red queen from a well shuffled pack of 52 cards.

7. A die is tossed once. Find the probability of getting :

(i) number 4
(ii) a number greater than 4
(iii) a number less than 4
(iv) an even number
(v) a number greater than 6
(vi) a number less than 7.

8. A bag contains 6 red balls, 8 white balls, 5 green balls and 3 black balls. One ball is drawn at random from the bag. Find the probability that the ball is (i) white, (ii) red or black, (iii) not green.

□□

Answers of Practice Exercises

Chapter 1. Goods and Service Tax (G.S.T.)

1. (i) ₹ 187·50   (ii) ₹ 62·50
2. ₹ 184
3. (i) ₹ 2,200   (ii) ₹ 50
4. (i) ₹ 1,890   (ii) ₹ 2,700
5. (i) ₹ 240   (ii) ₹ 120
6. (i) ₹ 40   (ii) ₹ 60
7. ₹ 4·32
8. (i) ₹ 562·50   (ii) ₹ 12·50
9. (i) ₹ 37,500   (ii) ₹ 3,640
   (iii) ₹ 49,140

10. (i) ₹ 1,696   (ii) ₹ 19·20
11. (i) 30%   (ii) ₹ 3,339
12. (i) ₹ 144   (ii) ₹ 17,496
13. (i) ₹ 30,000   (ii) ₹ 29,160
    (iii) ₹ 160
14. (i) ₹ 8,400   (ii) ₹ 75,600
15. (i) ₹ 1,168   (ii) ₹ 15,768
16. (i) Producers GST ₹ 10
    Wholesaler GST ₹ 20
    Retailer GST ₹ 30
    (ii) ₹ 880.

Chapter 2. Banking (Recurring Deposit Account)

1. ₹ 1,155
2. (i) ₹ 1,500   (ii) ₹ 25,500
3. ₹ 200
4. ₹ 10%
5. (i) 10%   (ii) 7%
6. Q, ₹ 952·50

7. ₹ 200
8. ₹ 1,236
9. 9 months
10. ₹ 6,811·20
11. ₹ 640
12. ₹ 40·00

Chapter 3. Shares and Dividends

1. (i) ₹ 51,300   (ii) ₹ 57,400
   (iii) ₹ 10,000.
2. 10%
3. Second is more profitable
4. ₹ 3,600
5. (i) ₹ 7,000   (ii) 5·7%
6. (i) 625,   (ii) ₹ 2,250
7. 10% shares at ₹ 140 is better.

8. 70 shares
9. There is a loss of ₹ 80.
10. (i) ₹ 1,760   (ii) ₹ 17,540
    (iii) Gain $7\frac{2}{9}$%
11. ₹ 360, ₹ 1,500
12. (i) ₹ 4,320   (ii) 12·5%.
13. 18%
14. ₹ 15.

Chapter 4. Linear Inequations

1. $1 \leq x < 5$

2. $-10 \leq x < 6$

3. $-4 \cdot 5 \leq x \leq 1 \cdot 5$

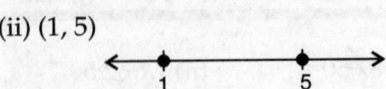

4. $L = \{ x : 2 < x \leq 4 \}$

$M = \{-1, 0, 1, 2, 3, 4\}$

5. $\dfrac{-30}{7} < x$

6. $\{1, 2, 3\}$

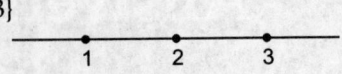

7. (i) $[5, \infty)$

(ii) $(1, 5)$

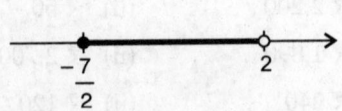

8. $\dfrac{-7}{2} \leq x < 2$

9. $-2 \leq x < 2$

Chapter 5. Quadratic Equations

1. $x = a, -\dfrac{1}{a}$

2. $x = -1, 5$

3. $x = 4, \dfrac{-2}{9}$

4. $x = -4, \dfrac{9}{4}$

5. $x = 6, \dfrac{40}{13}$

6. $x = \dfrac{-bc}{ad}$

7. $x = \dfrac{b}{a}, \dfrac{2b}{a},$

8. $x = \dfrac{9}{2}$

9. (i) $x^2 - 3\sqrt{3}x + 6 = 0$

(ii) $x^2 - 6x - 3 = 0$

(iii) $4x^2 - 16x + 13 = 0$

(iv) $x^2 + 8x + 15$

10. (i) $\dfrac{50}{7}, 1$

(ii) $\dfrac{9}{16}, \dfrac{1}{16}$

(iii) $\dfrac{7}{2}, 2$

(iv) $\dfrac{3}{4}, -\dfrac{1}{4}$

11. $k = 4$

12. $k = \dfrac{4}{3}$.

13. $5, \dfrac{1}{5}$

14. $1, -7$

15. $\dfrac{90}{7}, \dfrac{-160}{7}$

16. $\dfrac{11}{2}, \dfrac{13}{7}$

17. $-3, -\dfrac{1}{3}, -2, -\dfrac{1}{2}$

18. $4, 5, \dfrac{-13}{3}$

19. $-\dfrac{1}{2}, 2, -\dfrac{1}{3}, 3$

20. $\dfrac{1}{2}, -\dfrac{1}{2}$

21. $-3, 3$

22. $-7, -2, 3, 8$

23. $\dfrac{3 + \sqrt{5}}{2}, -2, -\dfrac{1}{2}$

24. $\dfrac{-5 \pm \sqrt{21}}{2}, \dfrac{3 \pm \sqrt{5}}{2}$

25. -3

26. $2, 3$

27. 12 years, 36 years

28. 9 years, 36 years

Chapter 6. Ratio and Proportion

1. (i) $25x^2 : 9y^2$

(ii) $3 : 5$

2. (i) $(a + b)^2 : (a - b)^2$

(ii) $x^3 y^2 : x^2 y^3$ or $x : y$

3. (i) $2ax : 3b^2 y$

(ii) $a^{1/4} : b^{1/4}$

4. (i) $4x : 3y^2$

(ii) $a^{1/3} : b^{1/3}$

5. (i) $5 : 2$

(ii) $3b : 2a$

6. (i) $y : x$

(ii) $(x - 5) : x(x + 2)$

8. (ii) $x = 2$

9. $\dfrac{a}{b} = \dfrac{7}{3}$ or $\dfrac{a}{b} = \dfrac{5}{4}$

11. 27

12. 35

13. 5

14. 36, 54

15. 6

16. B is more extravagant.

17. 15 yrs, 20 yrs.

18. $4 : 5 : 6$

19. 15 yrs, 21 yrs

20. 10 litre

21. 100, 125 and 150.

22. (i) 30   (ii) $\dfrac{18}{5}$

(iii) $\dfrac{81}{8}$ (iv) $\dfrac{30}{7}$.

23. (i) $305 + 774\sqrt{3}$ (ii) ab^3

(iii) $\dfrac{a^2+1}{a^2-1}$.

25. (i) 3   (ii) $\dfrac{ab}{a+b}$.

26. (a) $x^2 + 6x + 8$ (b) $a^2 - b^2$.

27. 3, 27   **28.** $\dfrac{x}{2by}$

29. 3

Chapter 7. Factorization

2. $(x + 1)$ and $(2x - 3)$ are not factors of given polynomial.

3. $k = -11$,   **4.** $a = 25$

5. $a = 37, b = 26$ **8.** $a = 3, b = -4$

9. $a = -\dfrac{11}{2}, b = \dfrac{22}{7}$ **10.** $(x + 1)(x + 3)(3x - 2)$

11. -4 **12.** $a = -\dfrac{22}{7}, b = \dfrac{39}{7}$

Chapter 8. Matrices

1. (i) $\begin{bmatrix} 0 & 1/2 \\ 1/2 & 0 \end{bmatrix}$ (ii) $\begin{bmatrix} 9/2 & 8 \\ 25/2 & 18 \end{bmatrix}$

(iii) $\begin{bmatrix} 1/2 & 1 \\ 1/2 & 1 \end{bmatrix}$ (iv) $\begin{bmatrix} 1 & 1/2 \\ 5/2 & 2 \end{bmatrix}$

2. $a = 2, b = 4$ or $a = 4, b = 2$

3. $x = 2, y = 4, z = 1$ and $w = 3$

4. $X = \begin{bmatrix} 5 & 0 \\ 1 & 4 \end{bmatrix}$ and $Y = \begin{bmatrix} 2 & 0 \\ 1 & 1 \end{bmatrix}$

5. (i) $\begin{bmatrix} 4 & -1 \\ 1 & 1 \end{bmatrix}$ (ii) $\begin{bmatrix} 2 & -3 \\ -7 & -4 \end{bmatrix}$

6. $\begin{bmatrix} -5 & -6 \\ -5 & -3 \end{bmatrix}$

7. $x = 2, y = 9$

8. $x = \dfrac{9}{2}, y = 6, z = 9, t = 6$

9. $\begin{bmatrix} -5/2 & 1/2 \\ 5/2 & 7/2 \end{bmatrix}$

10. $\begin{bmatrix} -1 & -1 \\ -2 & -1 \end{bmatrix}$.

11. 0

12. $(AB)C = \begin{bmatrix} 28 & 27 \\ 4 & 11 \end{bmatrix}$

$(CB)A = \begin{bmatrix} 12 & 52 \\ 10 & 60 \end{bmatrix}$

$(AB)C \neq (CB)A$.

13. (i) $ABC = \begin{bmatrix} -15 & -7 \\ -30 & -14 \end{bmatrix}$

(ii) $ACB = \begin{bmatrix} -18 & -24 \\ -36 & -48 \end{bmatrix}$

$ABC \neq ACB$

14. (i) $\begin{bmatrix} -3 & -2 \\ 10 & 7 \end{bmatrix}$ (ii) $\begin{bmatrix} 4 & -3 & 5 \\ 7 & -4 & 9 \\ 3 & -1 & 4 \end{bmatrix}$

15. (i) $X = \begin{bmatrix} 3 & -1 \\ 1 & -2 \end{bmatrix}$ (ii) $\begin{bmatrix} 14 & 13 \\ 13 & 14 \end{bmatrix}$

16. $A(B + C) = \begin{bmatrix} 29 & 14 \\ 65 & 30 \end{bmatrix}$, $(B + C)A = \begin{bmatrix} 13 & 22 \\ 29 & 46 \end{bmatrix}$

17. (i) $x = 2, y = 4$ (ii) $\begin{bmatrix} 4 & -4 \\ 4 & -4 \end{bmatrix}$

18. $\begin{bmatrix} 7 & 20 \\ 18 & 5 \end{bmatrix}$

19. (a) (i) Not always true   (ii) True   (iii) True   (iv) True

(b) (i) 2×1 (ii) $X = \begin{bmatrix} 2 \\ 2 \end{bmatrix}$

20. $x = 1, y = 3$

21. $\begin{bmatrix} -1 & 1 \\ 1 & -1 \end{bmatrix}$

Chapter 9. Arithmetic Progression

1. 178
2. 64
3. 5th term
4. 1
5. 65th term
6. 128
7. 60
8. 13
9. 100
10. $-3, -8$ and -3
11. (i) 16, 440   (ii) $\dfrac{7}{3}, 273$

(iii) $7, -8$ (iv) 6

(v) 4

12. n^2
13. 625
14. 1
15. $a = 4, b = 6$
17. 178
18. 12

Chapter 10. Geometric Progression

1. 8748
2. 10th term
3. 18
4. 54
5. 2, 6, 18, 54
6. $a\left[\dfrac{1+(-1)^{n+1} \, r^n}{1+r}\right]$
7. $\sqrt{mn}$ and $\left[m\dfrac{2q-p}{2q}\right], \left[n\dfrac{p}{2q}\right]$
8. $\dfrac{-b[1-(-b)^m]}{1+b}$
9. 4 and $\dfrac{1}{2}$
10. $255\dfrac{3}{4}$

11. $\dfrac{50}{81}(10^n - 1) - \dfrac{5}{9}n$
12. 5
13. 8
14. $\dfrac{(x+y)^2}{2y(x-y)}\left[10\left(\dfrac{x-y}{x+y}\right)^n\right]$
15. $\dfrac{3\sqrt{3}}{2}\left(1-\dfrac{1}{3^n}\right)$
16. $\dfrac{1}{2}$
17. (i) $4a^2$ (ii) 1
18. 6.

Chapter 11. Co-ordinate Geometry

1. $1:2$
2. (i) 15 unit   (ii) $1:2$
3. $1:2$ and $\left(\dfrac{10}{3}, 0\right)$
4. $\left(\dfrac{-11}{5}, \dfrac{14}{5}\right)$
5. Abscissa $= 0$, Ratio $= 2:3$, $K = \left(0, \dfrac{17}{5}\right)$
6. $3:5$ 7. (i) P (1, 4), Q (3, 6)
8. B $(3, -6)$ and D $(1, -2)$
9. $3:2$ and $a = -\dfrac{2}{5}$ 10. $(4, -5)$
11. Abscissa L $= 0$, Ratio $= 5:3$, L $= \left(0, \dfrac{31}{8}\right)$
13. $\left(\dfrac{16}{7}, \dfrac{27}{7}\right)$
14. Ordinate $= 0$, Ratio $= 3:5$, $K = \left(3\dfrac{1}{2}, 0\right)$
15. (i) $4:3$ (ii) $\left(0, \dfrac{23}{7}\right)$

(iii) 24·5 sq. unit

16. 5 units
17. $2:3$ and $a = 2$
18. $P = \left(\dfrac{40}{3}, \dfrac{-40}{3}\right), Q = \left(\dfrac{55}{3}, \dfrac{-10}{3}\right)$
19. (i) (3, 4)   (ii) 5 unit

(iii) $4:17$
20. (i) $a = 3$ (ii) $P = \left(0, \dfrac{5}{2}\right)$
21. $\left(\dfrac{5}{3}, 1\right)$
22. Ratio $= 3:1$, Point $= (3, 0)$
23. (1, 8)
24. (i) $-\dfrac{9}{4}$ (ii) $\dfrac{\sqrt{65}}{4}$
25. (3, 3) and $1:2$
27. $x = 17$ and $y = -2$
28. (2, 1)
29. $a = 2$ and $b = 3$
30. $a = 2$ and $b = -1$

Chapter 12. Reflection

1. Reflection in the origin.
2. (i) (– 1, 3), (ii) (1, 2), (iii) (3, – 3), (iv) (– 2, – 4).
3. (i) A˝ → (– 1, 2), (ii) B˝ → (– 4, 8),
   (iii) C˝ → (– 6, 8), (iv) Reflection in Y-axis.
4. (i) $a = 5$, $b = 2$, (ii) (–5, 2), (iii) Reflection in the origin.
5. (i) P(8, 6), (ii) (– 8, 6), (iii) (– 8, – 6).
6. (i) (2, – 4), (ii) (2, 4), (iii) (– 2, – 4).
7. (i) (3, – 4), (ii) 8, (iii) 20.
8. (i) (3, – 2), (ii) (6, 3), (iii) $\sqrt{10}$
9. (1, 1), (– 1, 0) and (– 3, 4).
10. $a = 7$, $b = 5$.
11. (– 3, 2), (3, – 2). The reflection on Y-axis
12. (i) (2, 3),
    (ii) (– 2, 3),
    (iii) (3, 2).
13. (i) X-axis, Y-axis.

(ii) (3, – 4) and(– 5, 2)
(iii) (– 3, 4) and (5, – 2)
(iv) Reflection through the origin.
14. (iii) Yes
15. (i) X-axis and Y-axis.
    (ii) (5, – 8), (– 3, 4).
    (iii) (– 5, 8), (3, – 4).
    (iv) P˝ is reflection of P′ in the origin.
16. (i) (3, – 5)
    (ii) (– 2, 4)
    (iv) Isosceles trapezium.
    (v) Two invariant points under reflection on the X-axis are (3, 0) and (– 2, 0).
17. (i) P′ (3, – 4), O′ (6, 0)
    (ii) OO′ = 6 units, PP′ = 8 units
    (iii) 20 units
    (iv) rhombus.

Chapter 13. Similarity

1. 16 : 81
2. 96 cm²
3. 2·8 cm
4. 294 cm²
5. (i) 6 cm (ii) 1 : 8
6. 4 : 5
7. 25 : 144
8. (i) 36 cm² (ii) 100 cm² (iii) 9/16
9. 22 cm
10. 1 : 8.

Chapter 15. Circles

1. (i) 80°, (ii) 100°,
   (iii) 82° (iv) 80°,
   (v) 52°, (vi) 100°.
2. 120°
3. $x = 80, y = 100$
4. 30°
5. 140°
6. ∠ BDC = 80°, ∠ BEC = 100°
7. 40°
8. 20°, 40°
9. 45°, 135°, 30°, 150°
10. 40°, 20°
11. 55°, 55°
12. 2 $\sqrt{5}$ cm
13. (i) 40°, (ii) 50°, (iii) 50°, (iv) 30°
14. 7 cm
15. 76°
16. 17 cm
18. ∠CBD = 48°, ∠ABC = 100°

Chapter 17. Mensuration

1. 1424·304 kg
2. 1056 cm³
3. 1650 cm³, 660 cm²

4. 787·5 cm
5. 1 hr 40 min
6. 72·40 m², 65·142 cm³
7. 71·83 m², 65·55 m³
8. 2 cm.
9. 301·44 cm³
10. ₹ 2,068
11. 1000 balls
12. 310·464 cm³, 221·76 cm²
13. 115·5 cm², 89·83 cm³
14. 9.99 cm, 79
15. 72 bottles
16. 226·11 cm³
17. 72
18. 883·83 cm³
19. 63 cm
20. 1500 lead shots

21. 1 cm
22. 3 cm
23. ₹ 855·36
24. ₹ 132·11
25. 770 cm²
26. 35·84 cm
27. 12 cm and 9 cm
28. ₹ 96·28
29. 179·66 cm³
30. 1642·66 cm³
31. 2·34 cm
32. 703 balls
34. 1413·72 sq. m
35. 7·43 m
36. 3 cm
37. 17104·23 litre
38. 648 cm
39. 36283·97
40. 1178.03 cu cm, 471·2 sq. cm.
41. 5·747 cu m.

Chapter 18. Trigonometry

1. 6·83 m
2. 720 km/h
3. 43·3 m
4. 129·9 m
5. 27·712 m, 43·712 m
6. 1·269 km/h
7. $100\sqrt{3}$ m
8. 216.5 m
9. (i) 43·3 m, (ii) 75 m
10. 184·5 m

11. 20 m
12. 79·6 m
13. 6·96 m
14. 2·5 m
15. 94·64 m
16. 415·66 km/h
17. 1·37 km
18. 43·3 m
19. $500\sqrt{3}\,(\sqrt{3}+1)$
20. (i) 95 m, (ii) 55 m.

Chapter 19. Statistics

1. 45
2. 45 kg
3. 16
4. 19·5

5. $x = 1$
6. (i) 43, (ii) 27, (iii) 10
7. 49·6

Chapter 20. Probability

1. $\dfrac{1}{3}$
2. $\dfrac{1}{7}$
3. $\dfrac{8}{19}, \dfrac{8}{19}, \dfrac{16}{19}, \dfrac{9}{19}$
4. $\dfrac{3}{8}$

5. (i) 0·14, (ii) 0·56, (iii) 0·3, (iv) 0·86 (v) 0·7
6. $\dfrac{1}{13}$
7. (i) $\dfrac{1}{6}$, (ii) $\dfrac{1}{3}$, (iii) $\dfrac{1}{2}$, (iv) $\dfrac{1}{2}$, (v) 0, (vi) 1
8. (i) $\dfrac{4}{11}$, (ii) $\dfrac{9}{22}$, (iii) $\dfrac{17}{22}$.

ICSE Solved Paper 2020

(Two Hours and a half)

Answers to this Paper must be written on the paper provided separately.

You will **not** be allowed to write during the first **15** minutes.

This time is to be spent in reading the question paper.

The time given at the head of this Paper is the time allowed for writing the answers.

Attempt **all** questions from **Section A** and **any four** questions from **Section B**.

All working, including rough work, must be clearly shown and must be done on the same sheet as the rest of the answer.

Omission of essential working will result in loss of marks.

The intended marks for questions or parts of questions are given in brackets [].

Mathematical tables are provided.

SECTION—A (40 Marks)

(Attempt **all** questions from this Section)

Question 1.

(a) Solve the following quadratic equation : **[3]**
$$x^2 - 7x + 3 = 0$$
Give your answer correct to two decimal places.

(b) Given $A = \begin{bmatrix} x & 3 \\ y & 3 \end{bmatrix}$ **[3]**

If $A^2 = 3I$, where I is the identity matrix of order 2, find x and y.

(c) Using ruler and compass, construct a triangle ABC where $AB = 3$ cm, $BC = 4$ cm and $\angle ABC = 90°$. Hence, construct a circle circumscribing the triangle ABC. Measure and write down the radius of the circle. **[4]**

Solution 1.

(a) Given : $x^2 - 7x + 3 = 0$

Here, $a = 1, b = -7$ and $c = 3$

$\therefore \quad x = \dfrac{-b \pm \sqrt{b^2 - 4ac}}{2a}$

$= \dfrac{-(-7) \pm \sqrt{(-7)^2 - 4 \times 1 \times 3}}{2 \times 1}$

$= \dfrac{7 \pm \sqrt{49 - 12}}{2}$

$= \dfrac{7 \pm \sqrt{37}}{2} = \dfrac{7 \pm 6.08}{2}$

Taking positive sign,
$$x = \frac{7 + 6.08}{2} = 6.541$$

Taking negative sign,
$$x = \frac{7 - 6.08}{2} = 0.458$$

Hence, $x = 6.54$ and 0.46 **Ans.**

(b) Given : $A = \begin{bmatrix} x & 3 \\ y & 3 \end{bmatrix}$

Also, $A^2 = 3I$

$\Rightarrow \begin{bmatrix} x & 3 \\ y & 3 \end{bmatrix}\begin{bmatrix} x & 3 \\ y & 3 \end{bmatrix} = 3\begin{bmatrix} 1 & 0 \\ 0 & 1 \end{bmatrix}$

$\Rightarrow \begin{bmatrix} x^2 + 3y & 3x + 9 \\ xy + 3y & 3y + 9 \end{bmatrix} = \begin{bmatrix} 3 & 0 \\ 0 & 3 \end{bmatrix}$

Comparing both sides, we get
$$3x + 9 = 0$$

$\Rightarrow \quad x = -\dfrac{9}{3} = -3$

and $\quad 3y + 9 = 3$

$\Rightarrow \quad 3y = 3 - 9 = -6$

$\Rightarrow \quad y = -\dfrac{6}{3} = -2$

$\therefore \quad x = -3$ and $y = -2$ **Ans.**

(c) Steps of construction:

(i) Draw $BC = 4$ cm.

(ii) Make an angle of 90° at B and cut an arc of radius 3 cm on it to get point A.

(iii) Join AC. Thus, $\triangle ABC$ is obtained.

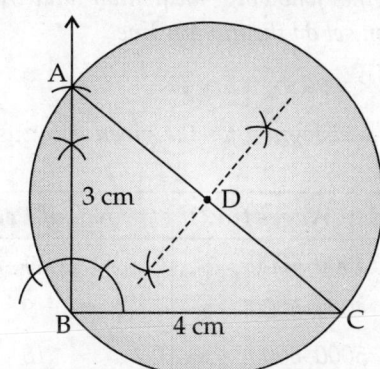

(iv) Draw perpendicular bisector of AC, which meets AC at D.

(v) Taking D as centre and radius equal to AD or DC, draw a circle. Thus, it is a required circle.

Since, $AC = 5$ cm, so, $AD = 2.5$ cm.

🌶 Comments of Examiners

1. (a) Some of the common errors made by candidates in this question were:

   (i) Using incorrect formula for finding roots of the quadratic equation.

   (ii) Using correct formula but substituting incorrectly, e.g. - 7 was taken as +7

   (iii) For finding square root of 37, a number of candidates used division method instead of using Mathematical tables and thereby made calculation errors; some did not go up to the required number of decimal places. Hence, the final answer was incorrect. Many candidates found the square root of 37 only up to two decimal places, even while using tables.

   (iv) Calculation error such as: 7 - 6.083 = 1.083 instead of 0.917.

   (v) Error in rounding off, such as 0.4584 rounded to two decimal places was written as 0.45 instead of 0.46

   (b) In finding A^2 many candidates squared each of the elements instead of finding the product A × A. Some candidates made mistakes in identifying the 2 × 2 identity matrix.

   Some candidates did incorrect calculation e.g. x.x was taken as $2x$ instead of x^2; $3.x + 9 = 0$ was solved and written as $x = -2$

   (c) Many candidates constructed 900 with a protractor. The most common error was that for perpendicular bisector, candidates drew arcs only on one side of the line to be bisected. Many others did not measure and record the radius of the circle. Some candidates bisected the angles instead of sides to draw the circumcircle.

Answering Tips

➢ Students should be aware of the mathematical tables and their use in finding square roots of numbers to help them to get the correct answer and also to save time.

➢ Give sufficient practice to reduce the errors, such as using incorrect formulae and basic calculation errors.

➢ The importance of rounding off the numbers should be well known.

➢ In matrix multiplication the student should be aware of the fact that the meaning of A2 means 'A' multiplied by 'A' and not the square of the corresponding elements of 'A', and in an identity matrix, the leading diagonal elements are 1 and all other elements are zero.

➢ Give adequate practice on locus, geometrical properties and construction of triangles.

➢ Practice construction of geometrical figures, showing all traces of construction, using the ruler and compass only, unless otherwise specified in the question.

➢ Stress upon maintaining the accuracy of measurements.

Question 2.

(a) Use factor theorem to factorise $6x^3 + 17x^2 + 4x - 12$ completely. [3]

(b) Solve the following inequation and represent the solution set on the number line.

$$\frac{3x}{5} + 2 < x + 4 \le \frac{x}{2} + 5, x \in R \quad [3]$$

(c) Draw a histogram for the given data, using a graph paper : [4]

Weekly Wages (in ₹)	No. of People
3000–4000	4
4000–5000	9
5000–6000	18
6000–7000	6
7000–8000	7
8000–9000	2
9000–10000	4

Estimate the mode from the graph.

Solution 2.

(a) Let $p(x) = 6x^3 + 17x^2 + 4x - 12$

∵ $p(-2) = 6 \times (-2)^3 + 17 \times (-2)^2 + 4(-2) - 12$

$= 6 \times (-8) + 17 \times 4 - 8 - 12$

$= -48 + 68 - 20$

$= -68 + 68 = 0$

∴ $(x + 2)$ is a factor of $p(x)$

Dividing $p(x)$ by $(x + 2)$, see get

$$
\begin{array}{r}
6x^2 + 5x - 6 \\
x + 2 \overline{)\ 6x^3 + 17x^2 + 4x - 12} \\
6x^3 + 12x^2 \\
\hline
5x^2 + 4x \\
5x^2 + 10x \\
\hline
-6x - 12 \\
-6x - 12 \\
\hline
0
\end{array}
$$

ICSE Solved Paper 2020

Now for the quotient

$$\because \quad 6x^2 + 5x - 6 = 6x^2 + 9x - 4x - 6$$
$$= 3x(2x + 3) - 2(2x + 3)$$
$$= (3x - 2)(2x + 3)$$

Therefore,

$$6x^3 + 17x^2 + 4x - 12 = (x + 2)(6x^2 + 5x - 6)$$
$$= (x + 2)(2x + 3)(3x - 2) \textbf{ Ans.}$$

(b) Given : $\dfrac{3x}{5} + 2 < x + 4 \leq \dfrac{x}{2} + 5$

Now, $\dfrac{3x}{5} + 2 < x + 4$

$\Rightarrow \qquad \dfrac{3x}{5} - x < 4 - 2$

$\Rightarrow \qquad \dfrac{3x - 5x}{5} < 2$

$\Rightarrow \qquad -2x < 10$

$\Rightarrow \qquad x > -\dfrac{10}{2}$

$\Rightarrow \qquad x > -5$

And, $\qquad x + 4 \leq \dfrac{x}{2} + 5$

$\Rightarrow \qquad x - \dfrac{x}{2} \leq 5 - 4$

$\Rightarrow \qquad \dfrac{x}{2} \leq 1$

$\Rightarrow \qquad x \leq 2$

Hence, $\qquad -5 < x \leq 2$

Solution $\{x : -5 < x \leq 2, \in x\ \text{R}\}$

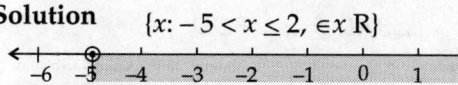

(c)

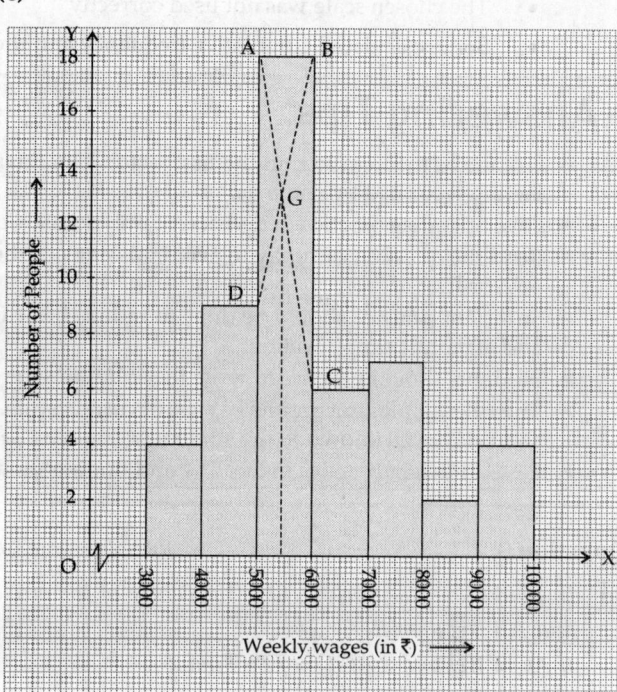

We have, maximum frequency = 18

$\therefore \qquad$ Modal class = 5000 – 6000

Join AC and BD and draw a perpendicular from point G to X-axis at 5450.

Hence, estimated mode is 5450. **Ans.**

💡 Comments of Examiners

2. **(a)** Many candidates did not use factor theorem to identify the first factor as specified in the question. Some made mistakes in finding out the quotient while dividing the given polynomial by the factor found. Many candidates did not write the answer in the product form, e.g. $(x + 2)(3x - 2)(2x + 3)$.

Some candidates were unable to factorize the quadratic quotient obtained by dividing the polynomial.

(b) Many candidates made errors in transposing like terms on the same side. e.g. $\dfrac{3x}{5} - x < 2 - 4$

Some candidates made various types of errors in simplification. e.g. $x + 4 \leq \dfrac{x}{2} + 5$ was written as $2x + 4 \leq x + 5$.

$-2x < 10$ on solving was written as $x < -5$ instead of $x \geq 5$

The solution set was not represented in set builder form. Some candidates did not write the solution set. A large number of candidates made errors in representation of solution set on the number line. e.g., Real number solution was represented incorrectly by using dots. Some candidates failed to put extra numbers on each side of the solution for indicating the continuity of the number line.

(c) Numerous errors made by the candidates while plotting the histogram:
- Many candidates did not show the kink.
- The three guidelines to locate mode were not drawn correctly.
- Class interval was represented below each bar as 3000 – 4000, 4000 – 5000, etc.
- A few candidates did not join the end points of highest bar with corresponding end points of preceding and succeeding bars to locate mode.

- The chosen scale was not used correctly.
- Some calculated cumulative frequency and then plotted the bars of increasing heights.

Answering Tips

➤ Use factor theorem to find the first factor. The final answer should be expressed in the product form and not factors separated by commas.
➤ Give adequate practice in division of polynomials by binomials.
➤ Read the question carefully to avoid missing out the conditions given in the question e.g., *x* belongs to N or W or Z or R.
➤ Sufficient practice should be done to reduce basic mistakes of solving inequations, such as, transposing sides and algebraic simplification.
➤ Students should practice to write the solution set.
➤ The rules of plotting graphs i.e., use of correct scale, when kink is put on the axis, reading of values from graph should be well known to the student.
➤ Give sufficient practice in locating and finding mode from the graph.

Question 3.

(a) *In the figure given below, O is the centre of the circle and AB is a diameter.* **[3]**

If AC = BD and ∠AOC = 72°. Find :

(i) ∠ABC

(ii) ∠BAD

(iii) ∠ABD

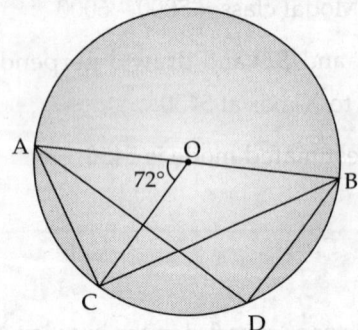

(b) *Prove that :* **[3]**

$$\frac{\sin A}{1 + \cot A} - \frac{\cos A}{1 + \tan A} = \sin A - \cos A$$

(c) *In what ratio is the line joining P (5, 3) and Q (– 5, 3) divided by the y-axis ? Also find the coordinates of the point of intersection.* **[4]**

Solution 3.

(a) Given : $AC = BD$ and $\angle AOC = 72°$

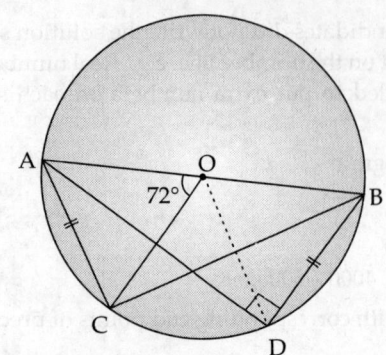

(i) ∵ Angle subtended by an arc at the centre is twice the angle subtended by the same arc at any point on the remaining part of the circle.

∴ $\angle AOC = 2\angle ABC$

⇒ $\angle ABC = \dfrac{1}{2} \angle AOC$

$= \dfrac{1}{2} \times 72° = 36°$ **Ans.**

(ii) Since $BD = AC$ and equal chords subtend equal angles at the centre.

So, $\angle BOD = \angle AOC = 72°$

and, $\angle BAD = \dfrac{1}{2} \angle BOD$

$= \dfrac{1}{2} \times 72° = 36°$ **Ans.**

(iii) In $\triangle ABD$,

$\angle BAD + \angle ABD + \angle ADB = 180°$

⇒ $36° + \angle ABD + 90° = 180°$

[∵ ∠ADB is in semicircle and angles of a triangle adds upto 180°]

⇒ $\angle ABD = 180° - 126°$

$= 54°$ **Ans.**

(b) To prove :

$$\frac{\sin A}{1 + \cot A} - \frac{\cos A}{1 + \tan A} = \sin A - \cos A$$

Taking, L.H.S. $= \dfrac{\sin A}{1 + \cot A} - \dfrac{\cos A}{1 + \tan A}$

$= \dfrac{\sin A \times \sin A}{\sin A + \cos A} - \dfrac{\cos A \times \cos A}{\cos A + \sin A}$

$= \dfrac{\sin^2 A - \cos^2 A}{\sin A + \cos A}$

$= \dfrac{(\sin A - \cos A)(\sin A + \cos A)}{(\sin A + \cos A)}$

[∵ $a^2 - b^2 = (a - b)(a + b)$]

$= \sin A - \cos A$ = R.H.S. **Ans.**

(c) Given points are $P(5, 3)$ and $Q(-5, 3)$

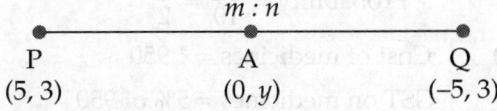

$$
\begin{array}{ccc}
\bullet & \bullet & \bullet \\
\text{P} & \text{A} & \text{Q} \\
(5, 3) & (0, y) & (-5, 3)
\end{array}
$$

Let the coordinates of the point where this line meets y-axis be $A(0, y)$ and the ratio be $m : n$. Using section formula, we have

$$(x, y) = \left(\frac{mx_2 + nx_1}{m + n}, \frac{my_2 + ny_1}{m + n} \right)$$

$\Rightarrow \qquad 0 = \dfrac{-5m + 5n}{m + n}$

$\Rightarrow \qquad 0 = -5m + 5n$

$\Rightarrow \qquad 5m = 5n$

or $\qquad m : n = 5 : 5 = 1 : 1$

Now, $\qquad y = \dfrac{m \times 3 + 3 \times n}{m + n}$

$\qquad\qquad = \dfrac{1 \times 3 + 1 \times 3}{1 + 1}$

$\qquad\qquad = \dfrac{3 + 3}{2}$

$\qquad\qquad = \dfrac{6}{2} = 3$

Hence, the required ratio is $1 : 1$ and the point of intersection is $(0, 3)$. **Ans.**

💡 Comments of Examiners

3. **(a)** Only a few candidates could solve this question correctly giving suitable reasons.

   (i) Many candidates were able to find $\angle ABC$ but could not find the other two angles.

   (ii) Properties of circles like, angle in a semicircle, equal arc subtends equal angle at circumference, etc. were not applied correctly.

   (iii) A few candidates could not use the properties of isosceles triangle and congruency of triangles correctly.

      Some candidates made calculation mistakes. Appropriate reasons supporting the answers were also missing in many scripts.

(b) Some candidates failed to express tan A and cot A in terms of sin A and cos A correctly. Errors were also made in writing the numerator and denominator of resulting trigonometric expressions.

   e.g., $\{\sin^2 A / (1 + \cos A)\} - \{\cos^2 A / (1 + \sin A)\}$

   Some took the LCM correctly but went wrong in simplifying the expression. A few candidates could not express $\sin^2 A - \cos^2 A = (\sin A + \cos A)(\sin A - \cos A)$

(c) Several candidates did not take the point on y - axis as $(0, y)$. Some candidates could not apply the section formula correctly. Many applied mid-point formula to get the coordinates of the required point. Others found the ratio correctly but did not write it in ratio form. Simple calculation errors were common. Some candidates obtained the coordinates but did not write them within the brackets. Multiplication of $(m + n)$ by 0 was taken as $(m + n)$ instead of '0'.

Answering Tips

➤ Emphasise on giving reasons supporting each answer while solving geometry problems.
➤ Give adequate practice in properties of circles to enable to solve problems based on circles.
➤ Naming of the angles should be done correctly.
➤ The students should apply theorems and properties correctly in problems.
➤ The students should understand the application of a specific theorem to a given question, correctly.
➤ The student should be aware to solve trigonometry identities by different methods. While solving an identity, never work with both sides taken together. Proof must be from left hand side to right hand side or the reverse.
➤ The students should be aware of the fact that at a point on the x-axis has its ordinate = 0 and a point on y-axis has its abscissa = 0. Give sufficient practice on problems involving section formula.

Question 4.

(a) *A solid spherical ball of radius 6 cm is melted and recast into 64 identical spherical marbles. Find the radius of each marble.* **[3]**

(b) *Each of the letters of the word 'AUTHORIZES' is written on identical circular discs and put in a bag. They are well shuffled. If a disc is drawn at random from the bag, what is the probability that the letter is :* **[3]**

   (i) *a vowel*

   (ii) *one of the first 9 letters of the English alphabet which appears in the given word.*

   (iii) *one of the last 9 letters of the English alphabet which appears in the given word ?*

(c) *Mr. Bedi visits the market and buys the following articles :* **[4]**

Medicines costing ₹ 950, GST @ 5%

A pair of shoes costing ₹ 3000, GST @ 18%

A laptop bag costing ₹ 1000 with a discount of 30%, GST @ 18%.

(i) *Calculate the total amount of GST paid.*

(ii) *The total bill amount including GST paid by Mr. Bedi.*

Solution 4.

(a) Let the radius of each spherical marble be r cm.

Then, volume of 64 spherical marbles

= volume of solid spherical ball

$$\Rightarrow \quad 64 \times \frac{4}{3}\pi r^3 = \frac{4}{3} \times \pi \times 6^3$$

$$\Rightarrow \quad r^3 = \frac{6 \times 6 \times 6}{64}$$

$$\Rightarrow \quad r^3 = \left(\frac{6}{4}\right)^3$$

or $\qquad r = \frac{6}{4} = 1.5$

Hence, the radius of each marble is 1.5 cm. **Ans.**

(b) Letters are $A, U, T, H, O, R, I, Z, E, S$.

$\Rightarrow$ Total number of letters in the given word

= 10.

(i) Here, vowels are A, U, O, I, E.

$\Rightarrow$ Number of vowels = 5

So, probability (a vowel) = $\frac{5}{10} = \frac{1}{2}$ **Ans.**

(ii) Letters in the given word which are in first 9 letters of english alphabets are A, I, E and H.

$\Rightarrow$ Number of such letters = 4

$\therefore \qquad$ Probability = $\frac{4}{10} = \frac{2}{5}$ **Ans.**

(iii) Letters in the given word which are in last 9 letters of english alphabets are U, T, R, Z and S.

$\Rightarrow$ Number of such letters = 5

$\therefore \qquad$ Probability = $\frac{5}{10} = \frac{1}{2}$ **Ans.**

(c) (i) Cost of medicines = ₹ 950

GST on medicines = 5% of 950

$$= \frac{5}{100} \times 950$$

= ₹ 47.50

Cost of a pair of shoes = ₹ 3000

GST on shoes = 18% of ₹ 3000

$$= \frac{18}{100} \times 3000$$

= ₹ 540

Cost of laptop bag = ₹ 1000

Discount on bag = 30% of 1000

$$= \frac{30}{100} \times 1000$$

= ₹ 300

$\therefore$ Cost of laptop bag after discount

= ₹ (1000 – 300)

= ₹ 700

GST on laptop bag = 18% of ₹ 700

$$= \frac{18}{100} \times 700$$

= ₹ 126

$\therefore$ Total GST on all items

= ₹ (47.50 + 540 + 126)

= ₹ 713.50 **Ans.**

(ii) Total bill including GST = cost of (medicines + shoes + laptop bag) + Total GST on all items.

= ₹ (950 + 3000 + 700)

+ ₹ 713.50

= ₹ (4650 + 713.50)

= ₹ 5363.50 **Ans.**

🖢 Comments of Examiners

4. **(a)** A number of candidates used incorrect formulae to calculate volume of a sphere e.g. $4/3 \pi r^2$ or $2/3 \pi r^3$. Some candidates made calculation errors. Several candidates simplified and came to the result $r^3 = \{216\}/\{64\}$ but could not find the value of r by taking cube root. Some used a longer calculation method and calculated the radius as cube root of 3.375 but could not calculate further.

(b) (i) Some candidates wrote the number of vowels as '4' instead of '5'. Most candidates did not write the answer in the simplest form.

(ii) A few candidates used incorrect form for finding probability (total outcomes / number of favourable outcomes). Most candidates did not write the answer in the simplest form.

(iii) Total outcome of event was incorrect, or favourable outcomes were incorrect.

(c) The concept of finding GST as simple percentage was not clear to some candidates.

ICSE Solved Paper 2020

(i) Several candidates missed out the discount of 30% on the laptop bag and directly calculated the tax. Hence, they got incorrect value of GST.

(ii) Many candidates calculated the total amount of tax and total bill amount correctly, but the answer was not expressed correctly to two places of decimal, for example: Rs 713.50 and Rs 5363.50 were expressed as Rs 713.5 and Rs 5363.5.

Some candidates made errors in calculation.

Answering Tips

➢ Give sufficient practice in problems based on volume and surface area of the three different solids, cylinder, cone, and sphere.
➢ Drill on the concepts of square root and cube root of numbers by factor method.
➢ Give practice in calculation of combination of solids by taking pi and other terms common and then cancelling/simplifying to save time and to minimise calculation errors.
➢ List all the outcomes as well as the outcomes favourable for the events.
➢ Read the questions carefully to find the number of favourable outcomes and the total number of outcomes. In probability, emphasis must be given to express the answers in the simplest form.
➢ Identify vowels and consonants in the given word, its analysis and procedure to find out the favourable outcome/s of the probability sum.
➢ Drill extensively on the concept of G.S.T and its calculation under given conditions.
➢ Always express the bill amount in rupees correct to two decimal places.
➢ Give adequate practice to students in finding discounted price.

SECTION—B (40 Marks)

(*Attempt any four questions from this Section*)

Question 5.

(a) *A company with 500 shares of nominal value ₹ 120 declares an annual dividend of 15%. Calculate :* **[3]**

   (i) *the total amount of dividend paid by the company.*

   (ii) *annual income of Mr. Sharma who holds 80 shares of the company.*

If the return percent of Mr. Sharma from his shares is 10%, find the market value of each share.

(b) *The mean of the following data is 16. Calculate the value of f.* **[3]**

Marks	5	10	15	20	25
No. of Students	3	7	f	9	6

(c) *The 4th, 6th and the last term of a geometric progression are 10, 40 and 640 respectively. If the common ratio is positive, find the first term, common ratio and the number of terms of the series.* **[4]**

Solution 5.

(a) (i) Total number of shares = 500

Nominal value of each share = ₹ 120

And, Dividend = 15%

Total value of shares = ₹ (500 × 120)

= ₹ 60,000

So, Total dividend = 15% of ₹ 60,000

= $\frac{15}{100}$ × 60,000

= ₹ 9,000   **Ans.**

(ii) Annual income of 80 shares

= 15% of (80 × 120)

= $\frac{15}{100}$ × 9600

= ₹ 1,440   **Ans.**

Let the market value of each share be ₹ x.

So, 10% of 80x = 1440

⇒ $\frac{10}{100}$ × 80x = 1440

⇒ $x = \frac{1440 \times 10}{80}$

x = 180

So, the market value of each share is ₹ 180.   **Ans.**

(b)

Marks x_i	No. of students f_i	$f_i x_i$
5	3	15
10	7	70
15	f	15f
20	9	180
25	6	150
	$\sum f_i = 25 + f$	$\sum f_i x_i = 415 + 15f$

We know, mean = $\frac{\sum f_i x_i}{\sum f_i}$

⇒ $16 = \frac{415 + 15f}{25 + f}$

⇒ $400 + 16f = 415 + 15f$

$$\Rightarrow \qquad 16f - 15f = 415 - 400$$
$$\Rightarrow \qquad f = 15 \qquad \textbf{Ans.}$$

(c) Given : $\qquad a_4 = 10, a_6 = 40, a_n = 640$

$\therefore \qquad ar^3 = 10 \qquad \qquad ...(i)$

and $\qquad ar^5 = 40 \qquad \qquad ...(ii)$

On dividing (ii) by (i),

$$\frac{ar^5}{ar^3} = \frac{40}{10}$$

$$\Rightarrow \qquad r^2 = 4$$

$$\Rightarrow \qquad r = 2 \qquad [\because r \text{ is positive}]$$

Putting $r = 2$ in equation (i), we get

$$a \times 2^3 = 10$$

$$\Rightarrow \qquad a = \frac{10}{8} = \frac{5}{4}$$

Now, $\qquad a_n = 640$

$$\Rightarrow \qquad ar^{n-1} = 640$$

$$\Rightarrow \qquad \frac{5}{4} \times (2)^{n-1} = 640$$

$$\Rightarrow \qquad 2^{n-1} = \frac{640 \times 4}{5} = 128 \times 4$$

$$\Rightarrow \qquad 2^{n-1} = 2^9$$

$$\therefore \qquad n - 1 = 9$$

$$\therefore \qquad n = 9 + 1 = 10$$

Hence, $a = \dfrac{5}{4}, r = 2$ and $n = 10$ \qquad **Ans.**

📖 Comments of Examiners

5. **(a)** Common errors made by many candidates were in finding annual income and the market value of each share.

   (i) Some candidates found the dividend on only one share instead of finding the total amount of dividend paid by the company.

   (ii) Several candidates made mistakes in finding the dividend on 80 shares of Mr. Sharma. The concept of return percent being not very clear. Many candidates could not find the market value of each share of the company. A few candidates used incorrect formulae to find market value of each share. Some made errors in calculation.

   (b) The question was on calculation of mean of ungrouped frequency distribution. Some candidates converted it to grouped frequency distribution which did not tally with the given data and hence went wrong with the sum.

   Many candidates wrote incorrect Class mark of the given distribution which led to incorrect value of Σfx. A few candidates wrote Σff as $25f$ instead of $25 + f$ and Σfx as $430f$ instead of $415 + 15f$. Several candidates made errors in multiplying $(25 + f)$ by 16 and hence got the incorrect answers. Some made mistakes in applying the formula for mean and solving the equation to find 'f'.

   (c) Simple calculation errors were observed. Some candidates took the terms as of A. P. instead of G. P. The values of 'a' and 'r' were correctly found by many candidates, but they could not find the value of 'n' correctly.

Answering Tips

➢ Lay stress on problems based on commercial mathematics.
➢ Understand the terms like NV, MV, dividend, etc.
➢ Give adequate practice on sums based on Shares and Dividend, for conceptual clarity.
➢ Understand the concept of return percent / yield percent thoroughly and give sufficient drill on sums based on return percent.
➢ Do not change the data from the given form to some other form understand all types of distribution.
➢ Repeatedly practice the problems to prevent in making the basic conceptual errors.
➢ Read the question carefully and analyse the given conditions before solving the problem.
➢ Understand the concepts of common difference and common ratio thoroughly.
➢ Give repeated practice in finding the nth term and sum of n terms of both A.P., and G.P.

Question 6.

(a) If $A = \begin{bmatrix} 3 & 0 \\ 5 & 1 \end{bmatrix}$ and $B = \begin{bmatrix} -4 & 2 \\ 1 & 0 \end{bmatrix}$ \qquad **[3]**

Find $A^2 - 2AB + B^2$

(b) In the given figure AB = 9 cm, PA = 7.5 cm and PC = 5 cm. Chords AD and BC intersect at P. **[3]**

   (i) Prove that $\triangle PAB \sim \triangle PCD$

   (ii) Find the length of CD.

   (iii) Find area of $\triangle PAB$: area of $\triangle PCD$

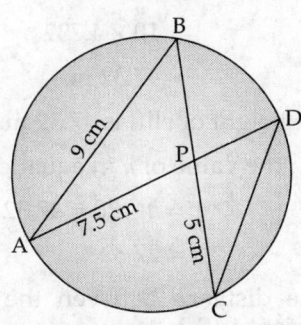

(c) *From the top of a cliff, the angle of depression of the top and bottom of a tower are observed to be 45° and 60° respectively. If the height of the tower is 20 m.* **[4]**
Find :
(i) *the height of the cliff*
(ii) *the distance between the cliff and the tower.*

Solution 6.

(a) Given : $A = \begin{bmatrix} 3 & 0 \\ 5 & 1 \end{bmatrix}$ and $B = \begin{bmatrix} -4 & 2 \\ 1 & 0 \end{bmatrix}$

Now, $A^2 - 2AB + B^2 = \begin{bmatrix} 3 & 0 \\ 5 & 1 \end{bmatrix}\begin{bmatrix} 3 & 0 \\ 5 & 1 \end{bmatrix}$

$\qquad -2\begin{bmatrix} 3 & 0 \\ 5 & 1 \end{bmatrix}\begin{bmatrix} -4 & 2 \\ 1 & 0 \end{bmatrix} + \begin{bmatrix} -4 & 2 \\ 1 & 0 \end{bmatrix}\begin{bmatrix} -4 & 2 \\ 1 & 0 \end{bmatrix}$

$= \begin{bmatrix} 9+0 & 0+0 \\ 15+5 & 0+1 \end{bmatrix} - 2\begin{bmatrix} -12+0 & 6+0 \\ -20+1 & 10+0 \end{bmatrix}$

$\qquad + \begin{bmatrix} 16+2 & -8+0 \\ -4+0 & 2+0 \end{bmatrix}$

$= \begin{bmatrix} 9 & 0 \\ 20 & 1 \end{bmatrix} - 2\begin{bmatrix} -12 & 6 \\ -19 & 10 \end{bmatrix} + \begin{bmatrix} 18 & -8 \\ -4 & 2 \end{bmatrix}$

$= \begin{bmatrix} 9 & 0 \\ 20 & 1 \end{bmatrix} + \begin{bmatrix} 24 & -12 \\ 38 & -20 \end{bmatrix} + \begin{bmatrix} 18 & -8 \\ -4 & 2 \end{bmatrix}$

$= \begin{bmatrix} 9+24+18 & 0-12-8 \\ 20+38-4 & 1-20+2 \end{bmatrix}$

$= \begin{bmatrix} 51 & -20 \\ 54 & -17 \end{bmatrix}$ **Ans.**

(b) Given : $AB = 9$ cm, $PA = 7.5$ cm and $PC = 5$ cm

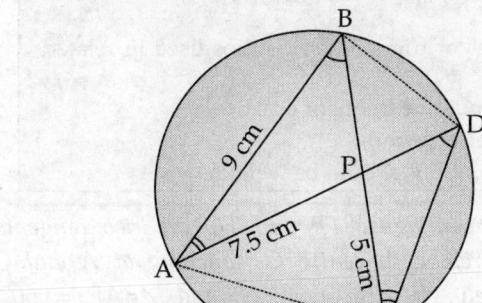

(i) In $\triangle PAB$ and $\triangle PCD$,
$\qquad \angle ABC = \angle ADC$
[Angles made by same arc AC or angles in the same segment are equal]

$\qquad \angle BAD = \angle BCD$
[Angles made by same arc BD]
$\therefore \qquad \triangle PAB \sim \triangle PCD$
[By AA similarity axiom]
Hence Proved.

(ii) $\because$ Ratio of corresponding sides of similar triangles is equal.

$\therefore \qquad \dfrac{AB}{CD} = \dfrac{PA}{PC} = \dfrac{PB}{PD}$

$\Rightarrow \qquad \dfrac{9}{CD} = \dfrac{7.5}{5} = \dfrac{PB}{PD}$

$\Rightarrow \qquad CD = \dfrac{9 \times 5}{7.5} = 6$ cm   **Ans**

(iii) $\qquad \dfrac{ar(\triangle PAB)}{ar(\triangle PCD)} = \dfrac{AB^2}{CD^2}$

$\qquad\qquad = \dfrac{9^2}{6^2} = \dfrac{81}{36} = \dfrac{9}{4}$ **Ans.**

(c) Let AB be the cliff and CD be the tower.

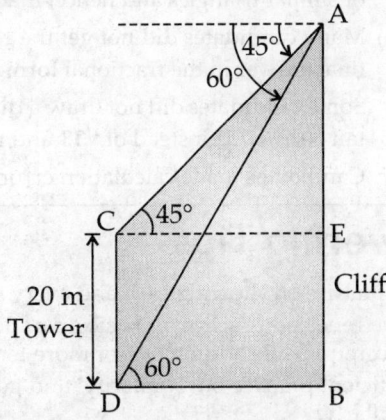

Also, let $DB = CE = x$ m and $AB = h$ m

(i) In $\triangle ABD$,

$\qquad \tan 60° = \dfrac{AB}{DB}$

$\qquad \sqrt{3} = \dfrac{h}{x}$

$\qquad h = x\sqrt{3}$ ...(i)

And, in $\triangle ACE$,

$\qquad \tan 45° = \dfrac{AE}{CE}$

$\Rightarrow \qquad 1 = \dfrac{AB - BE}{x}$

$\Rightarrow \qquad 1 = \dfrac{h - 20}{x}$

$\qquad x = h - 20$ ...(ii)

Putting the value of x in equation (i), we get

$\qquad h = (h - 20)\sqrt{3}$

$$\Rightarrow \qquad h = \sqrt{3}\,h - 20\sqrt{3}$$

$$\Rightarrow \qquad \sqrt{3}\,h - h = 20\sqrt{3}$$

$$\Rightarrow \qquad h(\sqrt{3} - 1) = 20\sqrt{3}$$

$$\Rightarrow \qquad h = \frac{20\sqrt{3}}{\sqrt{3} - 1} \times \frac{\sqrt{3} + 1}{\sqrt{3} + 1}$$

$$= \frac{20\sqrt{3}\,(\sqrt{3} + 1)}{3 - 1}$$

$$= 10(3 + \sqrt{3}) = 10(3 + 1.732)$$

$$= 10 \times 4.732$$

$$= 47.32 \text{ m}$$

Hence, the height of cliff is 47.32 m. **Ans.**

(ii) Putting the value of h in equation (ii), we get

$$x = h - 20 = 47.32 - 20$$

$$= 27.32$$

Hence, the distance between the cliff and the tower is 27.32 m. **Ans.**

💡 Comments of Examiners

6. **(a)** Matrix multiplication was a very common area of error, e.g. for finding square of 'A' and square of 'B', candidates found the square of each corresponding element instead of finding A × A and B × B. Many candidates found the product A x B by multiplying the corresponding elements of each Matrix. Some candidates made mistakes in simplifying the expression $A^2 - 2AB + B^2$.

(b) **(i)** Many candidates assumed that AB is parallel to CD, hence they could not identify the correct pairs of equal angles to prove $\triangle$ PAB ~ $\triangle$ PCD

    (ii) Some candidates calculated the length of CD correctly. A few could not write the corresponding ratio of sides of similar triangles and hence, made mistakes in finding the length of CD.

    (iii) Many candidates did not get the ratio of area of $\triangle$PAB: area of $\triangle$PCD correctly. Some candidates wrote the final answer in the fractional form 9/4 instead of writing it in the ratio form 9 : 4 as asked in the question.

(c) **(i)** Some candidates did not draw a diagram for this question or drew an incorrect diagram. Some used value of tan 60 as 1.732 instead of $\sqrt{33}$ and made mistakes in dividing 20 by 0. 732.

    (ii) Candidates made calculation errors and did not arrive at the final answers as 47.32 and 27.32.

Answering Tips

➤ Emphasise on showing each and every step of product of matrices. Stress upon finding square of a matrix.

➤ Give repeated practice on basic operations with matrix addition, subtraction, and multiplication of matrices. Be careful while adding two or more terms with +/- sign.

➤ Sufficient practice on 'similarity' and getting the proportionality of corresponding sides, etc. should be given regularly.

➤ Give practice on properties of circle with emphasis on writing correct reasons for the working.

➤ Always express answers to sums in the simplest form.

➤ Give practice on sums based on proving similarity of triangles.

➤ Always express the ratio of the area of the triangles correctly. Also do not leave the answer in the fractional form.

➤ Draw diagrams for all problems in geometry and trigonometry. In problems of heights and distances, it is necessary to draw diagrams.

➤ Give adequate practice to students on the values of standard angles of trigonometric ratios used in related sums.

➤ Clearly understand the angle of elevation, and angle of depression and give frequent practice.

➤ Rationalize the denominator, wherever it is possible, to avoid calculation errors.

➤ Methods of simplifying the problem to avoid long complicated calculations should be well known.

Question 7.

(a) *Find the value of 'p' if the lines, 5x – 3y + 2 = 0 and 6x – py + 7 = 0 are perpendicular to each other. Hence, find the equation of a line passing through (– 2, – 1) and parallel to 6x – py + 7 = 0.* **[3]**

(b) *Using properties of proportion find x : y, given :*

$$\frac{x^2 + 2x}{2x + 4} = \frac{y^2 + 3y}{3y + 9}$$ **[3]**

(c) *In the given figure TP and TQ are two tangents to the circle with centre O, touching at A and C respectively. If $\angle BCQ = 55°$ and $\angle BAP = 60°$, find :* **[4]**

(i) $\angle OBA$ and $\angle OBC$

(ii) $\angle AOC$

(iii) $\angle ATC$

ICSE Solved Paper 2020

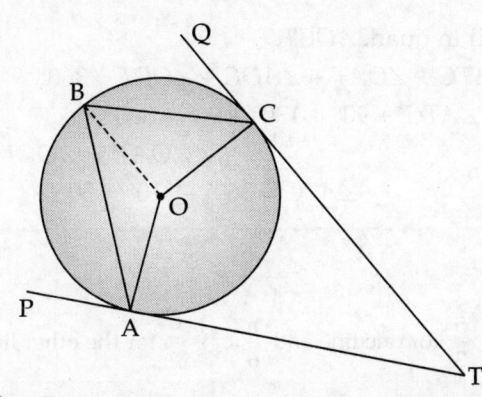

Solution 7.

(a) Given lines are,

$$5x - 3y + 2 = 0$$
and $$6x - py + 7 = 0$$

Now, $5x - 3y + 2 = 0$

$\Rightarrow \qquad 3y = 5x + 2$

$\Rightarrow \qquad y = \dfrac{5}{3}x + \dfrac{2}{3}$

$\therefore \qquad$ Slope (m_1) = $\dfrac{5}{3}$

and $\qquad 6x - py + 7 = 0$

$\Rightarrow \qquad py = 6x + 7$

$\Rightarrow \qquad y = \dfrac{6}{p}x + \dfrac{7}{p}$

$\therefore \qquad$ Slope (m_2) = $\dfrac{6}{p}$

Since, given lines are perpendicular to each other,

So, $\qquad m_1 \times m_2 = -1$

$$\dfrac{5}{3} \times \dfrac{6}{p} = -1$$

$\Rightarrow \qquad p = -10$

Now, slope (m_2) = $\dfrac{6}{p} = \dfrac{6}{-10} = -\dfrac{3}{5}$

$\because$ Slopes of parallel lines are equal.

So, slope of required line is $\left(-\dfrac{3}{5}\right)$.

Now, equation of required line is

$$\dfrac{y - y_1}{x - x_1} = m$$

$\Rightarrow \qquad \dfrac{y + 1}{x + 2} = -\dfrac{3}{5}$

$\Rightarrow \qquad 5y + 5 = -3x - 6$

$\Rightarrow \quad 3x + 5y + 5 + 6 = 0$

$\Rightarrow \qquad 3x + 5y + 11 = 0$ **Ans.**

(b) Given : $\dfrac{x^2 + 2x}{2x + 4} = \dfrac{y^2 + 3y}{3y + 9}$

Using componendo and dividendo,

$$\dfrac{x^2 + 2x + 2x + 4}{x^2 + 2x - 2x - 4} = \dfrac{y^2 + 3y + 3y + 9}{y^2 + 3y - 3y - 9}$$

$\Rightarrow \qquad \dfrac{x^2 + 4x + 4}{x^2 - 4} = \dfrac{y^2 + 6y + 9}{y^2 - 9}$

$\Rightarrow \qquad \dfrac{(x + 2)^2}{(x - 2)(x + 2)} = \dfrac{(y + 3)^2}{(y - 3)(y + 3)}$

$\Rightarrow \qquad \dfrac{x + 2}{x - 2} = \dfrac{y + 3}{y - 3}$

Again, using componendo and dividendo

$$\dfrac{x + 2 + x - 2}{x + 2 - x + 2} = \dfrac{y + 3 + y - 3}{y + 3 - y + 3}$$

$\Rightarrow \qquad \dfrac{2x}{4} = \dfrac{2y}{6}$

$\Rightarrow \qquad \dfrac{x}{y} = \dfrac{4}{6} = \dfrac{2}{3}$

Hence, $x : y = 2 : 3$ **Ans.**

(c) Given : $\angle BCQ = 55°$ and $\angle BAP = 60°$

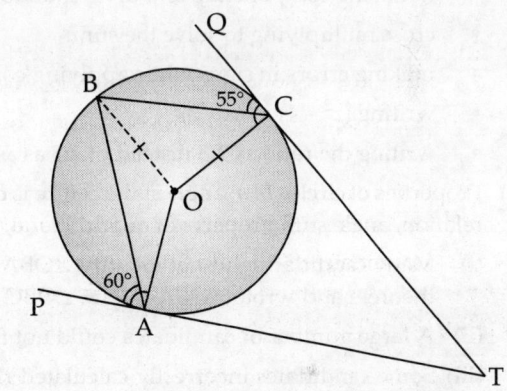

(i) $\qquad \angle OAP = 90°$ [$\because$ Tangent is $\perp$ to radius]

$\Rightarrow \angle OAB + \angle PAB = 90°$

$\Rightarrow \qquad \angle OAB + 60° = 90°$

$\Rightarrow \qquad \angle OAB = 90° - 60° = 30°$

Now, in $\triangle AOB$

$$OA = OB$$
[Radii of same circle]

$\therefore \qquad \angle OBA = \angle OAB = 30°$

[Equal angles opposite to equal sides]

Now, $\qquad \angle OCQ = 90°$ [$\because$ Tangent $\perp$ radius]

$\Rightarrow \angle OCB + \angle BCQ = 90°$

$\Rightarrow \qquad \angle OCB + 55° = 90°$

$\Rightarrow \qquad \angle OCB = 90° - 55° = 35°$

In $\triangle BOC$,

$$OC = OB \text{ [Radii of same circle]}$$

$\Rightarrow \qquad \angle OBC = \angle OCB = 35°$ **Ans.**

(ii) We know, angle subtended by an arc at the centre is double the angle subtended on the remaining part of the circle.

∴   ∠AOC = 2∠ABC

= 2(∠OBA + ∠OBC)

= 2(30° + 35°)

= 2 × 65° = 130°   **Ans.**

(iii) In quad. *AOCT*,

∠ATC + ∠OAT + ∠AOC + ∠OCT = 360°

⇒ ∠ATC + 90° + 130° + 90° = 360°

[∵ ∠OAT = ∠OCT = 90°]

⇒   ∠ATC = 360° − 310° = 50°   **Ans.**

🏅 Comments of Examiners

7. **(a)** Many candidates found the slopes of the two lines as $\frac{3}{5}$ or $-\frac{5}{3}$ for one line and $\frac{p}{6}$ or $-\frac{6}{p}$ for the other line.

Some candidates found the slopes correctly but made mistakes in applying the condition that for two lines to be perpendicular the product of slopes is -1.

Many candidates got incorrect equations of the line parallel to $6x - py + 7 = 0$. Some candidates found the equation correctly but did not give the answer in the simplest form.

(b) Some common errors observed in candidates answers to the question were:

* not reading the instructions given in the question carefully.
* not using componendo and dividendo to work out the sum.
* cross multiplying to solve the sum.
* making errors in signs while applying componendo and dividendo.
* writing $(x^2 - 4)$ as $(x - 2)^2$
* writing the ratio as 2/3 instead of 2:3 as asked for in the question.

(c) Properties of circles like, angle at the centre is double the angle at the circumference, radius tangent perpendicular relation, angle sum property of quadrilateral, tangent secant relation, etc. were not applied correctly.

(i) Many candidates did not identify ∠OBA = 30° or ∠OBC = 35° Some used the property of alternate segment theorem and wrote ∠OBA= 60° & ∠OBC = 55°.

(ii) A large number of candidates could not find the value of ∠AOC.

(iii) Some candidates incorrectly calculated the value of ∠OBA. A few candidates solved the question without giving proper reasoning. In some scripts, simple calculation errors were observed.

Answering Tips

➢ The concept of slopes for parallel and perpendicular lines should be known to the students.

➢ Understand the method to find the slope of a line by writing the given equation in the form $y = mx + c$.

➢ Solve the sums based on Ratio and Proportion using properties of proportion like, Componendo and Dividendo to minimise the calculation work.

➢ Read the question carefully and to answer as per the specifications given in the question.

➢ Insist upon answering the geometry-based problems with logical reasons.

➢ Exhaustive drill of properties of circle theorems and application-based sums is a must and should be given a through practice for the same.

➢ Name the angles with three letters, specifically, when there are two or more angles at the same point.

➢ Theorems and their applications should be known in detail and revise them frequently.

Question 8.

(a) What must be added to the polynomial $2x^3 - 3x^2 - 8x$, so that it leaves a remainder 10 when divided by $2x + 1$?   **[3]**

(b) Mr. Sonu has a recurring deposit account and deposits ₹ 750 per month for 2 years. If he gets ₹ 19125 at the time of maturity, find the rate of interest.   **[3]**

(c) Use graph paper for this question.   **[4]**

Take 1 cm = 1 unit on both x and y axes.

(i) Plot the following points on your graph sheets :

A (− 4, 0), B (−3, 2), C (0, 4), D (4, 1) and E (7, 3)

(ii) Reflect the points B, C, D and E on the x-axis and name them as B', C', D' and E' respectively.

(iii) Join the points A, B, C, D, E, E', D', C', B' and A in order.

(iv) Name the closed figure formed.

ICSE Solved Paper 2020

Solution 8.

(a) Let k be the required term to be added.

So, $p(x) = 2x^3 - 3x^2 - 8x + k$

$\because$ $p(x)$ leaves remainder 10 when divided by $2x + 1$,

$\therefore$ $\quad p\left(-\dfrac{1}{2}\right) = 10$

$\Rightarrow 2 \times \left(-\dfrac{1}{2}\right)^3 - 3 \times \left(-\dfrac{1}{2}\right)^2 - 8 \times \left(-\dfrac{1}{2}\right) + k = 10$

$\Rightarrow 2 \times \left(-\dfrac{1}{8}\right) - 3 \times \dfrac{1}{4} + 4 + k = 10$

$\Rightarrow -\dfrac{1}{4} - \dfrac{3}{4} + 4 + k = 10$

$\Rightarrow \quad k = 10 - 4 + \dfrac{1+3}{4}$

$\Rightarrow \quad k = 6 + 1 = 7$

$\therefore \quad k = 7$ **Ans.**

(b) Here, $P = ₹\,750$, $n = 2$ years $= 24$ months and M.V. $= ₹\,19125$

We know, $\quad$ M.V. $= P \times n + \dfrac{P \times n(n+1)}{2 \times 12} \times \dfrac{r}{100}$

$\Rightarrow \quad 19125 = 750 \times 24$

$\qquad + \dfrac{750 \times 24\,(24+1)}{2 \times 12} \times \dfrac{r}{100}$

$\Rightarrow \quad 19125 = 18000 + 750 \times 25 \times \dfrac{r}{100}$

$\Rightarrow \quad 19125 - 18000 = \dfrac{750 \times r}{4}$

$\Rightarrow \quad 1125 = \dfrac{750 \times r}{4}$

$\Rightarrow \quad r = \dfrac{1125 \times 4}{750} = 6$

Hence, the rate of interest is 6% p.a. **Ans.**

(c)

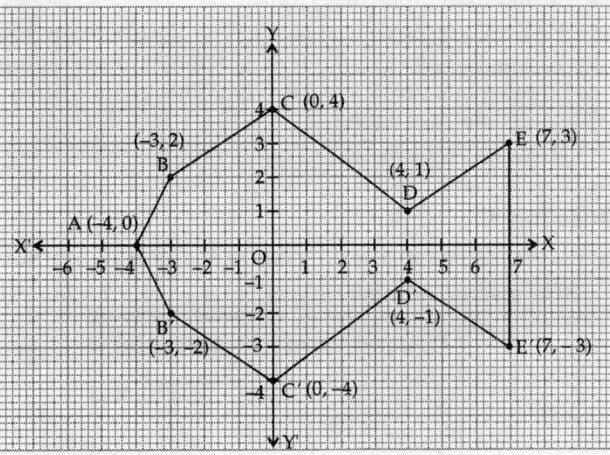

Note : Instead of 1 cm = 1 unit, we have used 0.5 cm = 1 unit on both axes.

(i), (ii) and **(iii)** see graph.

(iv) Nonagon (irregular), polygon fish

🏛 Comments of Examiners

8. **(a)** A very common error made by candidates in this question was the incorrect substitution of the value of x, which was substituted as ½ instead of – ½. Another common conceptual error made by candidates was of writing $(-1/2)^3$ as equal to 1/8 instead of – 1/8 and $(1/2)^2$ as –1/4 instead of ¼. This error was mostly caused due to not using the bracket.

   Some candidates substituted correctly but were unable to come to the correct answer $k = 7$

   (b) Simple calculation errors were found, such as, the product of 750 and 24 being expressed as 1800, instead of 18000.

   Some candidates took 'n' as 2 years instead of 24 months.

   Mistakes were made in applying the formula for interest. Candidates found it difficult to express interest in terms of 'r'. Hence, many candidates were unable to find rate of interest, r.

   (c) Most candidates dealt well with this question.

   Common errors were observed in taking the scale and plotting the points.

   (i) A few candidates plotted the points incorrectly. Most mistakes were made in plotting the points (0, 4) and (–4, 0).

   (ii) Some candidates made mistakes in marking the X-axis and the Y-axis. Positive and negative points of the two axes were incorrectly marked.

   (iii) Some candidates marked the points B', C', D' and E' incorrectly or did not join the points in order.

   (iv) A few candidates did not name the figure or named it as 'octagon' or 'trapezium', etc.

Answering Tips

➤ Give enough practice in problem solving involving algebraic expressions with the use of remainder/factor theorem.

➤ The term to be added or subtracted must be taken as any constant '*k*' or '*a*', etc. Enough problems involving such cases must be done.

➤ The changes taking place if the brackets are not used in the correct place.

➤ Read a recurring deposit sum carefully, analyse it and note down what is given and what is required to be found.

➤ Understand the basic concepts such as, monthly installment, qualifying principal, to find interest, time in months and maturity value.

➤ Read the question asking to plot the graph carefully. Use the scale given in the question.

➤ Practice plotting numerous points on the graph paper and their reflection on the *x*-axis, *y*-axis, origin. Give adequate practice to identify points on the *x* and *y* axis. Complete the figure formed. Revise the names of basic geometrical figures.

➤ Read the question carefully and answer all parts.

Question 9.

(a) *40 students enter for a game of shot-put competition. The distance thrown (in metres) is recorded below :* **[6]**

Distance in m	Number of Students
12 – 13	3
13 – 14	9
14 – 15	12
15 – 16	9
16 – 17	4
17 – 18	2
18 – 19	1
15 – 16	9	33
16 – 17	4	37
17 – 18	2	39
18 – 19	1	40

Use a graph paper to draw an ogive for the above distribution.

Use a scale of 2 cm = 1 m on one axis and 2 cm = 5 students on the other axis.

Hence using your graph find :

(i) *the median*

(ii) *Upper Quartile*

(iii) *Number of students who cover a distance which is above $16\frac{1}{2}$ m.*

(b) *If $x = \dfrac{\sqrt{2a+1} + \sqrt{2a-1}}{\sqrt{2a+1} - \sqrt{2a-1}}$, prove that $x^2 - 4ax + 1 = 0$*
[4]

Solution 9.

(a)

Distance in m	Frequency (f)	c.f.
12 – 13	3	3
13 – 14	9	12
14 – 15	12	24

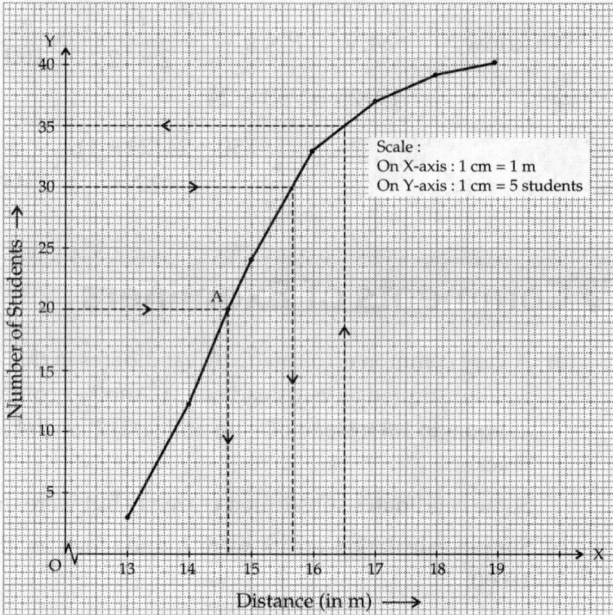

Scale :
On X-axis : 1 cm = 1 m
On Y-axis : 1 cm = 5 students

Note : Instead of 2 cm = 1 m and 2 cm = 5 students, we have used 1 cm = 1 m and 1 cm = 5 students on X and Y axes, respectively.

(i)   Median $= \left(\dfrac{N}{2}\right)^{\text{th}}$ term

$= \left(\dfrac{40}{2}\right)^{\text{th}}$ term

= 20th term

On the graph, through a point 20 on *y*-axis, draw a horizontal line which meets the ogive at point *A*. Through *A*, draw a vertical line which meets the *x*-axis at 14.7.

∴   Median = 14.7   **Ans.**

(ii) Upper quartile $(Q_3) = \left(\dfrac{3N}{4}\right)^{th}$ term

$= \left(\dfrac{3 \times 40}{4}\right)^{th}$ term

$= $ 30th term

$= 15.7$ **Ans.**

(iii) Number of students who cover more than $16\dfrac{1}{2}$ m $= 40 - 35 = 5$ **Ans.**

(b) Given : $x = \dfrac{\sqrt{2a+1} + \sqrt{2a-1}}{\sqrt{2a+1} - \sqrt{2a-1}}$

Using componendo and dividendo,

$\dfrac{x+1}{x-1} = \dfrac{+\sqrt{2a+1} - \sqrt{2a-1}}{\sqrt{2a+1} + \sqrt{2a-1}} \begin{array}{c} \sqrt{2a+1} + \sqrt{2a-1} \\ \\ -\sqrt{2a+1} + \sqrt{2a-1} \end{array}$

$\Rightarrow \qquad \dfrac{x+1}{x-1} = \dfrac{2\sqrt{2a+1}}{2\sqrt{2a-1}}$

$\Rightarrow \qquad \left(\dfrac{x+1}{x-1}\right)^2 = \left(\dfrac{\sqrt{2a+1}}{\sqrt{2a-1}}\right)^2$

[Squaring on both sides]

$\Rightarrow \qquad \dfrac{x^2+1+2x}{x^2+1-2x} = \dfrac{2a+1}{2a-1}$

Again, using componendo and dividendo,

$\dfrac{x^2+1+2x+x^2+1-2x}{x^2+1+2x-x^2-1+2x} = \dfrac{2a+1+2a-1}{2a+1-2a+1}$

$\Rightarrow \qquad \dfrac{2(x^2+1)}{4x} = \dfrac{4a}{2}$

$\Rightarrow \qquad \dfrac{x^2+1}{2x} = 2a$

$\Rightarrow \qquad x^2+1 = 4ax$

$\Rightarrow \qquad x^2 - 4ax + 1 = 0$ **Hence Proved.**

💡 Comments of Examiners

9. **(a)** The following errors were observed in this question:
   - Some candidates made mistakes in finding the cumulative frequency. In many cases, the last cumulative frequency did not tally with the total of the given distribution which was given as 40.
   - A number of candidates did not follow the scale given in the question.
   - Some plotted the ogive with respect to the lower boundaries instead of upper boundaries.
   - A few candidates used a ruler to draw the graph instead of a freehand curve.
   - Kink was not shown on the graph sheet between 0 and 12 to keep uniform gaps between each interval, by some candidates.
   - In a few cases, perpendicular lines were not dropped to find the values from the ogive.
   - The values of median, upper quartiles were read incorrectly from the graph, by a number of candidates.

   (b) Many candidates made errors while applying Componendo and Dividendo, especially in the denominator. Mistakes were made while squaring both the sides. Calculation errors were also common. The final expression was not worked out following all the steps of correct working. Being a proof, some candidates wrote the correct answer from incorrect working.

Answering Tips

➤ Cross-check the cumulative frequency found.
➤ Be cautious in selecting correct axis and scale.
➤ Mark the kink when it is required. Draw Ogive, a cumulative frequency curve as a free hand curve. The points must not be joined with a ruler.
➤ Practice needs to be given of drawing the ogive. The graph needs to be plotted with respect to upper boundaries and corresponding cumulative frequency.
➤ Sufficient practice is required of reading values from the graph.
➤ Practice in problems on properties of ratio and proportion, especially Componendo and Dividendo and squaring / expansion / transformation of algebraic expression must be done frequently.
➤ Emphasise on the importance of brackets in algebraic expressions.

Question 10.

(a) *If the 6th term of an A.P. is equal to four times its first term and the sum of first six terms is 75, find the first term and the common difference.* **[3]**

(b) *The difference of two natural numbers is 7 and their product is 450. Find the numbers.* **[3]**

(c) *Use ruler and compass for this question. Construct a circle of radius 4.5 cm. Draw a chord AB = 6 cm.* **[4]**

(i) *Find the locus of points equidistant from A and B. Mark the point where it meets the circle as D.*

(ii) *Join AD and find the locus of points which are equidistant from AD and AB. Mark the point where it meets the circle as C.*

(iii) *Join BC and CD. Measure and write down the length of side CD of the quadrilateral ABCD.*

Solution 10.

(a) Let the first term of an A.P. be a and the common difference be d.

$$\because \qquad a_6 = 4a \qquad \text{[Given]}$$
$$\Rightarrow \qquad a + 5d = 4a$$
$$\Rightarrow \qquad 5d = 3a$$
$$\therefore \qquad a = \frac{5d}{3} \qquad \text{...(i)}$$

Also, $\qquad S_6 = 75 \qquad$ [Given]

$$\Rightarrow \quad \frac{6}{2}[2a + (6-1)d] = 75$$
$$\Rightarrow \quad 3\left[2 \times \frac{5d}{3} + 5d\right] = 75 \qquad \text{[Using (i)]}$$
$$\Rightarrow \quad 3\left[\frac{10d + 15d}{3}\right] = 75$$
$$\Rightarrow \qquad 25d = 75$$
$$\therefore \qquad d = \frac{75}{25} = 3$$
$$\therefore \qquad a = \frac{5d}{3} = \frac{5 \times 3}{3} = 5$$

Hence, $\qquad a = 5$ and $d = 3$ **Ans.**

(b) Let the two natural numbers be x and y such that $x > y$.

Then, $\qquad x - y = 7$
$$\Rightarrow \qquad x = 7 + y \qquad \text{...(i)}$$
and $\qquad xy = 450$
$$\Rightarrow \qquad (7 + y)y = 450 \qquad \text{[Using (i)]}$$
$$\Rightarrow \qquad y^2 + 7y - 450 = 0$$
$$\Rightarrow \quad y^2 + 25y - 18y - 450 = 0 \quad \text{(on factorisation)}$$

$$\Rightarrow \quad y(y + 25) - 18(y + 25) = 0$$
$$\Rightarrow \qquad (y + 25)(y - 18) = 0$$
$$\Rightarrow \qquad y = -25 \qquad \text{[Neglected]}$$
or $\qquad y = 18$
$$\therefore \qquad y = 18$$
$$\therefore \qquad x = 7 + 18 = 25$$

Hence, the numbers are 25 and 18. **Ans.**

(c) Steps of construction :

1. Draw a circle of radius 4.5 cm.

2. Take a point A on the circle. Taking A as centre, draw an arc of radius 6 cm, which cuts circle at B.

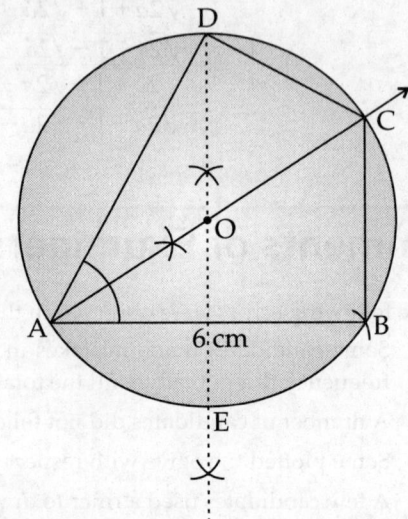

3. Join AB.

(i) Draw perpendicular bisector of AB which meets the circle at D and E.

Thus, DE is the required locus.

(ii) Join AD and draw angle bisector of $\angle DAB$ which meets the circle at C.

Thus, AC is the required locus.

(iii) Length of side $CD = 5$ cm.

💡 Comments of Examiners

10. **(a)** Some candidates used incorrect formula for finding the 6th term of an arithmetic progression and summation of six terms of an A.P. As per the given condition in the question i.e., 6th term of an A.P.is equal to four times its first term was written as: $a + 5d = 4a + d$ instead of $a + 5d = 4a$. Some candidates wrote the equations correctly but made mistakes in solving the two equations: $a + 5d = 4a$ and $3(2a + 5d) = 75$

(b) Some candidates made mistake in taking the two natural numbers according to given condition as x and $7 - x$ instead of x and $x - 7$ or x and $x + 7$.

Few candidates made mistakes in forming the quadratic equation. Some candidates after solving found the two values of x as -25 and 18.

According to the question the two numbers are natural numbers. Hence neglecting negative number, the two numbers should have been 25 and 18.

(c) All the necessary arcs for side bisectors and angle bisectors were not constructed. Concepts of locus theorems were not clear to some candidates.

    (i) Some candidates constructed the circle with radius = 6 cm. Bisector of AB was drawn but point D was not located.

    (ii) All the necessary arcs for bisector angle BAD were not shown. Point 'C' was not located on the circumference of the circle.

    (iii) Many candidates forgot to measure and record the length of CD and wrote = 5cm

Answering Tips

➢ The concepts of the two series: Arithmetic Progression (AP) and Geometric Progression (GP) and their differences with different examples should be known essentially. Revise formulae for finding a term, common difference and summation of certain number of terms in Arithmetic Progression frequently.

➢ Ensure that adequate practice of different kinds of word problems is done frequently.

➢ Read construction-based questions with the conditions, carefully.

➢ Adequate practice in identifying the locus of points under different geometrical conditions should be done essentially.

➢ Show all traces of construction clearly while working with Geometry Constructions.

➢ Clarify the concept of loci theorem in detail.

➢ Give enough practice in drawing perpendicular bisectors of straight lines.

Question 11.

(a) *A model of a high rise building is made to a scale of 1 : 50.* **[3]**

    (i) *If the height of the model is 0.8 m, find the height of the actual building.*

    (ii) *If the floor area of a flat in the building is 20 m², find the floor area of that in the model.*

(b) *From a solid wooden cylinder of height 28 cm and diameter 6 cm, two conical cavities are hollowed out. The diameters of the cones are also of 6 cm and height 10.5 cm.* **[3]**

Taking $\pi = \dfrac{22}{7}$ find the volume of the remaining solid.

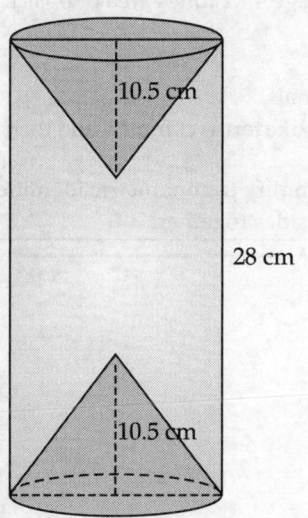

(c) *Prove the identity* **[4]**
$$\left(\frac{1 - \tan \theta}{1 - \cot \theta}\right)^2 = \tan^2\theta$$

Solution 11.

(a) Given :   Scale = 1 : 50

    (i) Let the actual height of the building be h m.

$$\therefore \qquad \frac{0.8}{h} = \frac{1}{50}$$

$$\Rightarrow \qquad h = 50 \times 0.8 = 40 \text{ m} \qquad \textbf{Ans.}$$

    (ii) Let the floor area of the model be x m².

$$\therefore \qquad \frac{x}{20} = \left(\frac{1}{50}\right)^2$$

$$\Rightarrow \qquad \frac{x}{20} = \frac{1}{2500}$$

$$\Rightarrow \qquad x = \frac{20}{2500} \text{ m}^2$$

$$= 0.008 \text{ m}^2 \text{ or } 80 \text{ cm}^2 \qquad \textbf{Ans.}$$

(b) Given : Height of cylinder (h) = 28 cm

    Diameter of cylinder = 6 cm

$$\Rightarrow \text{ Radius of cylinder } (r) = \frac{6}{2} = 3 \text{ cm}$$

    Also, height of cones (H) = 10.5 cm

    And, diameter of cones = 6 cm

$$\Rightarrow \text{ Radius of cones } (R) = \frac{6}{2} = 3 \text{ cm}$$

    Now, volume of solid cylinder = $\pi r^2 h$

$$= \frac{22}{7} \times 3^2 \times 28$$

$$= \frac{22}{7} \times 9 \times 28$$

$$= 792 \text{ cm}^3$$

    And, volume of two cones

$$= 2 \times \frac{1}{3} \pi R^2 H$$

$$= 2 \times \frac{1}{3} \times \frac{22}{7} \times 3^2 \times 10.5$$

$$= 198 \text{ cm}^3$$

So, volume of the remaining solid

$$= (792 - 198) \text{ cm}^3$$

$$= 594 \text{ cm}^3 \qquad \textbf{Ans.}$$

(c) To prove :

$$\left(\frac{1-\tan\theta}{1-\cot\theta}\right)^2 = \tan^2\theta$$

Taking　　L.H.S. $= \left(\dfrac{1-\tan\theta}{1-\cot\theta}\right)^2$

$$= \left(\frac{1-\tan\theta}{1-\dfrac{1}{\tan\theta}}\right)^2$$

$$= \left(\frac{1-\tan\theta}{\dfrac{\tan\theta-1}{\tan\theta}}\right)^2$$

$$= \left(\frac{-\tan\theta(1-\tan\theta)}{1-\tan\theta}\right)^2$$

$$= (-\tan\theta)^2$$

$$= \tan^2\theta$$

$$= \text{R.H.S.} \qquad \textbf{Hence Proved.}$$

🏛 Comments of Examiners

11. (a) (i) Many candidates made mistakes in applying the scale factor to find the height of the actual building.

(ii) Some candidates made mistakes in applying the scale factor to find the ratio of area as square of the scale factor. Several candidates made errors in calculation and conversion of units.

Some left the answer of the second part in fractional form as (1/ 125).

(b) Some candidates used incorrect formulae for volume of cone and cylinder. The diameter of the cone and cylinder was given in the sum as 6 cm, but some took the radius as '6'. The volume of cone was not multiplied by '2'. Simple calculation errors were very common. The value for π was given as $\dfrac{22}{7}$ but some took it as 3.14.

(c) Some candidates wrote the given trigonometric expression as $1 - \tan^2\theta/1 - \cot^2\theta$

Some candidates failed to express tan A and cot A in terms of sin A and cos A correctly.

Others made errors in writing the numerator and denominator of resulting trigonometric expressions correctly. A few candidates were unable to identify $(\cos\theta - \sin\theta) = -(\sin\theta - \cos\theta)$, hence, could not obtain the correct answer.

Answering Tips

➢ Clarify the concept of scale factor. Understand the concept of area being proportional to square of sides and volume proportional to cube of sides.

➢ Focus on conversions from one system of units to another, like cm to m, m to km, mm to m, cm^2 to m^2, etc.

➢ Do not to leave the final answer in a fractional form.

➢ If each side of the image is k times each side of object then Area of image = k2 times area of object.

➢ Give regular practice with emphasis on manual calculations.

➢ Use the value given in the question.

➢ Give sufficient practice in multiplication and division involving decimals.

➢ Calculate the volume of a combination of solids by taking $\pi\pi$ and other like terms common and then simplifying to save time and to avoid calculation errors.

➢ Give ample practice on basic algebraic operations and identities to simplify trigonometric identities.

➢ Prove identities with one side at a time instead of working with both sides together.

NOTES

NOTES